Pelican Books
My Life: An Attempt at an Autobiography

Leon Trotsky was born Lev Davidovich Bronstein to a Ukrainian Jewish family in 1879. Arrested as a revolutionary in 1898, he was exiled to Siberia, but escaped and joined Lenin in London in 1902. In the split in the Russian Social-democratic party he occupied an independent position, trying to reconcile the Bolshevik and Menshevik function. He returned to Russia in 1905 and became the leader of the first Soviet in the capital. He was again exiled to Siberia and again escaped. When the February Revolution broke out in 1917 he was in New York, but arrived back in Petrograd in May, and by October was Chairman of the Petrograd Soviet. He became Commissar for Foreign Affairs and delayed the signing of the Treaty of Brest-Litovsk by his brilliant debating tactics. When the Civil War began he was appointed Commissar for War and created the Red Army. After Lenin's death he was pushed out of office by Stalin, expelled from the party in 1927 and deported in 1929 to Turkey. There he wrote the epic *History of the Russian Revolution*. The remaining years of his last exile were spent in France, Norway, and finally Mexico, where he was murdered by a Stalinist agent in August 1940.

The Young Lenin; 1905; My Life and *The Struggle Against Fascism in Germany* are all available in Penguins.

D1352564

Leon Trotsky

My Life

An Attempt at an
Autobiography

with an introduction by
Joseph Hansen

Penguin Books

Penguin Books Ltd, Harmondsworth,
Middlesex, England
Penguin Books Australia Ltd, Ringwood,
Victoria, Australia
Penguin Books (N.Z.) Ltd,
182-190 Wairau Road, Auckland 10, New Zealand

First published by Pathfinder Press 1971
Published in Penguin Books 1975
Copyright © Pathfinder Press Inc. 1970

Made and printed in Great Britain by
Hazell Watson & Viney Ltd
Aylesbury, Bucks
Set in Monotype Plantin

Contents

Introduction

With Trotsky in Coyoacán
by Joseph Hansen

Several times I have heard of plans to make a film of the life of Trotsky or at least of his final years in Mexico. One attempt was made at a television show on the assassination. It was a miserable business, more slanderous than truthful. A Hollywood entrepreneur that I know of even spent time in Mexico studying the locale and gathering material. In three cases, I have been asked to provide information to help lend verisimilitude to productions that were planned. Two of them fell through and the third may suffer the same fate – which, perhaps, is not altogether to be deplored. The producers began with their own preconceived notions as to what constitutes dramatic material and how Trotsky might be bent into these notions. None of them had much interest in portraying Trotsky's real inner drives or his central commitment and goal in life. The audience they had in mind might not accept this as a good evening's entertainment.

To make a truthful film of Trotsky requires taking him as a political figure, but not the kind characteristic of the bourgeois world of today. He was of a different kind – committed, like a great artist, to presenting a faithful reflection of his times, or, more accurately, a scientist who has become convinced that the main problem facing mankind is to change the framework of our times, to end the long agonized epoch of warring classes and to replace it with a society built on the foundation of a rationally planned economy. He could also be pictured truthfully as a tribune and fighter preoccupied with constructing the organization required to win socialism on a world scale.

To make a film of Trotsky in which all this is cast aside is like presenting Pierre and Marie Curie without their drive to discover the secret of radioactivity or the drudgery of fractionating huge amounts of pitchblende in order to isolate the mysterious substances, polonium and radium; or a 'drama' of Louis Pasteur without his passionate interest in bacteriology and the painstaking laboratory work he engaged in against the advice of well-meaning friends who sought to persuade him not to waste his valuable time on chimerical and insoluble problems.

Isn't this rather obvious? Yet a person as perspicacious as Isaac Deutscher did not see it. Even Deutscher viewed Trotsky's engagement in building a world party of socialist revolution as a 'foible'.

Trotsky, who was well acquainted with Freud's work, understood himself very well. In many places he has made perfectly clear how thoroughly he was guided by fully conscious aims; and he has specified what they were.

In the foreword to *My Life* he tells us that 'except for the years of the civil war', the 'main content of my life . . . has been party and literary activity'. Almost 'a third of a century of my conscious life was entirely filled with revolutionary struggle. And if I had to live it over again, I would unhesitatingly take the same path.'

For the eleven years remaining to him after he wrote *My Life*, Trotsky continued to do what he had done in the previous three decades. His order of priorities was not the same as that of so many intellectuals who came to admire his genius. They put in first place his best-known books, *Literature and Revolution*, *The History of the Russian Revolution*, *The Revolution Betrayed*, *Stalin – An Appraisal of the Man and His Influence*. They rated as next in the list the mass of articles, pamphlets, booklets – on German fascism, on the Spanish revolution, on the deepening crisis in France, on the whole turbulent course of events as the world moved towards its second global war.

Few of them were attracted by the contributions Trotsky made in the internal discussions of the Fourth International. This is understandable, for these writings can be fully appreciated only by cadres with a considerable Marxist background. As for Trotsky's 'party' activities, particularly in the final eleven-year period, the intellectuals at best have simply not been interested.

Trotsky himself, however, took a different attitude. In the journal which he kept for a time in France and Norway, he jotted the following very revealing thoughts in his 25 March 1933 entry:*

> For a long time now I have not been able to satisfy my need to exchange ideas and discuss problems with someone else. I am reduced to carrying on a dialogue with the newspapers, or rather through the newspapers with facts and opinions.
>
> And still I think that the work in which I am engaged now, despite its extremely insufficient and fragmentary nature, is the most important work of my life – more important than 1917, more important than the period of the Civil War or any other.
>
> For the sake of clarity I would put it this way. Had I not been present in 1917 in Petersburg, the October Revolution would still have taken place – *on the condition that Lenin was present and in command.* If neither Lenin nor I had been present in Petersburg, there would have been no October Revolution: the leadership of the Bolshevik Party would have prevented it from occurring – of this I have not the slightest doubt! If Lenin had not been in Petersburg, I doubt whether I could have managed to overcome the resistance of the Bolshevik leaders. The struggle with 'Trotskyism' (i.e., with the proletarian revolution) would have commenced in May, 1917, and the outcome of the revolution would have been in question. But I repeat, granted the presence of Lenin the October Revolution would have been victorious anyway. The same could by and large be said of the Civil War, although in its first period, especially at the time of the fall of Simbirsk and Kazan, Lenin wavered and was beset by doubts. But this was undoubtedly a passing mood which he probably never even admitted to anyone but me. [*Trotsky adds a footnote here:* I must tell about this in greater detail.]
>
> Thus I cannot speak of the 'indispensability' of my work, even about the period from 1917 to 1921. But now my work is 'indispensable' in the full sense of the word. There is no arrogance in this claim at all. The collapse of the two Internationals has posed a problem which none of the leaders of these Internationals is at all equipped to solve. The vicissitudes of my personal fate have confronted me with this problem and armed me with important experience in dealing with it. There is now no one except me to carry out the mission of arming a new generation with the revolutionary method over the heads of the leaders of the Second and Third Internationals. And I am in a com-

*Reprinted by permission of the publishers from Leon Trotsky, *Trotsky's Diary in Exile, 1935*, Cambridge, Mass: Harvard University Press, Copyright, 1958, by the President and Fellows of Harvard College.

plete agreement with Lenin (or rather Turgenev) that the worst vice is to be more than 55 years old! I need at least about five more years of uninterrupted work to ensure the succession.

Trotsky had just five more years to live, but it was not uninterrupted. During those five years he lived in constant insecurity, the target of reaction ranging from the Norwegian Fascists to the implacable killers of Stalin's G P U. Nevertheless Trotsky did what he could to pass on as much as possible of his experience.

Among the youngest of us who came to live with him and Natalia in the final years of their exile, L. D. did not speak directly of this problem. We felt it, however. Day in and day out, the life of the household was an engagement in building the Fourth International. The importance of continuity in programme, in method, in succession of cadres, became part of our elementary thinking. All of us were committed, dedicated even, to this work as essential preparation for the coming revolutionary opportunities that history was certain to provide. Everything Trotsky himself did was directed towards this goal.

If a certain romanticism may be thought to attach to this, the impression is mistaken. In practice it amounted to hard work, learning how to handle details, following through efficiently without ever losing sight of the great ultimate objective. What separates this kind of party-building from any other sustained and difficult enterprise is its purpose and goal which is to assure the survival of mankind and to make possible the expansion of civilization on a truly human basis.

In a short article on Rosa Luxemburg and the Fourth International, written in June 1935, Trotsky, arguing against the theory of the spontaneity of the masses and for the necessity of a Leninist party, put it like this: 'Without the slightest exaggeration it may be said: The whole world situation is determined by the crisis of the proletarian leadership.'

This crisis, he continued,

cannot, of course, be overcome by means of an abstract formula. It is a question of an extremely humdrum process. But not of a purely 'historical' process, that is, of the objective premises of conscious activity, but of an uninterrupted chain of ideological, political and organizational measures for the purpose of fusing together the best, most conscious elements of the world proletariat beneath a spotless banner, elements whose number and self-confidence must be constantly strengthened, whose connections with wider sections of the proletariat must be developed and deepened – in a word: to restore to the proletariat, under new and highly difficult and onerous conditions, its historical leadership.

When Trotsky agreed in the mid-summer of 1937 to the proposal made by the leadership of the American movement that I join his small staff of secretaries and guards, the first assignment I got was to bring a new Dodge sedan from Ohio, where it had been purchased, to Mexico. Max Sterling, the husband of Rae Spiegel, Trotsky's Russian secretary at the time, came along. We reached Mexico City well after dark and I was for waiting until the next morning to go out to Coyoacán. Max, however, had been there before, knew the streets, and was anxious to find Rae, who might be at the house.

Avenida Londres was very dark. The high walls, some of them capped with broken glass that glittered in our headlights, and the shuttered windows barred with iron in the Spanish tradition hardly looked hospitable. Dogs barked as we passed. Others picked up the cry from a distance. We had to wait a long time in the deserted street before our ring was answered. Max's voice was recognized and the small door set in the huge double one swung open sufficiently for the person on duty to slip out. It was Jean van Heijenoort who had been with Trotsky for a number of years. Rae, it turned out, was staying in an apartment in the city. Jean suggested we come back in the morning.

I felt rather relieved, for to tell the truth I felt diffident about meeting Trotsky.

Trotsky's name had come into my consciousness when I was eight or nine years old. It was after the First World War in the Utah farming town of some 3,000 people where my father worked as a tailor. Even here the Russian revolution, which had ended Tsarism, was regarded favourably and was much discussed, at least among the immigrant families, who were mostly from Scandinavia. The politics of the town was a reactionary mixture of Republicanism and Mormonism; and the weekly paper, the *Richfield Reaper*, was decidedly anti-Bolshevik even though the editor was something of a pariah, being a Democrat. I can still remember his headlines about Trotsky and the Red Army on the verge of defeat. It was a headline that was repeated a number of times. For a child turned early in the direction of rebellion, it was natural to favour Trotsky and the Red Army.

I began to take an interest in politics, and the campaigns and debates associated with it, when I was ten, the year Cox ran against Harding, an election I remember well, since I happened to read a pamphlet in the public library probably slipped among the books by a migrant 'Wobbly'. It was an exposure by Daniel De Leon of the tariff, a key issue in Utah with its sugar-beet industry. De Leon used the case of low-cost Cuban sugar to drive home his socialist arguments against the tariff. I repeated these in the school yard. The lesson of how easy it is to gain notoriety and how hard it is to overcome it has served me ever since.

While I thus became known as a 'socialist' and 'bomb thrower' at a tender age, it was not until I was at the University of Utah during the catastrophe of the Great Depression that I began to study Marxism and the different currents in the radical movement in a serious way. After two years of this I passed up all the other tendencies to join the Trotskyists, organized at that time in the Communist League of America. I had some reservations, particularly concerning what appeared to me to be the obscure way many things were presented in the Trotskyist press, but its honesty and above all the clarity and searching nature of its reasoning on the big issues were absolutely convincing. The way in which the Stalinists broke up a meeting where Max Shachtman, a speaker from New York on a national tour, was explaining the German events and Stalin's role in paving the way for Hitler also played a role in bringing me into the Trotskyist movement.

That was in Salt Lake City in 1934. Trotsky was then in France where he had succeeded in winning temporary asylum and somewhat greater security than in Prinkipo, which lay in the shadow of the Soviet Union and Stalin's GPU. Soon the French government, responding to Soviet pressure and its own fears of Trotsky's possible influence in the crisis-ridden domestic political scene, made the conditions of his asylum intolerable and finally revoked his asylum altogether.

Trotsky's situation was desperate. For us, the rebel youth of that time, who had joined his cause and were eager for action, it was anguishing not to be able to do much.

Then Norway granted asylum to the man on the planet without a visa. This likewise proved to be but a temporary haven, as Stalin put pressure on the Norwegian shipping industries and exporters of fish products. Trotsky was placed under virtual house arrest as the first 'great' Moscow show trial was staged in 1936, with him and his son Leon Sedov named *in absentia* as the main defendants. For a time it appeared that Trotsky might even be deported from Norway, that is, turned over to Stalin's executioners.

The decision of the Mexican government to grant asylum to Trotsky came just in time. President Lázaro Cárdenas made the decision to admit Trotsky because he really believed in bourgeois democracy, and because Diego Rivera, Mexico's leading artist and a follower of Trotsky, came to him personally. The decision also showed that the tradition of the 1910 Mexican Revolution was still alive.

Now Trotsky was in Coyoacán. How long would this last before Stalin's killers sought to close in again?

All this was in my mind. That and my measure of the stature of Trotsky. In my eyes Trotsky was one of the giants of history, looming so large that he seemed like a remote figure, belonging to another age. Besides that I had been forewarned, by people in position to know, that Trotsky could be very difficult to get along with.

In the morning in the bright sun Coyoacán looked much different from the night before. Tall eucalyptus trees soared above walls draped with purple bougainvillea. In the patios one caught glimpses of geraniums. The smell of burning charcoal coming from the adobe huts of the poor had a pleasant fragrance. Coyoacán was even picturesque, not having changed much since the time of Cortés, who lived there. The blue walls of Frida Kahlo's house on Avenida Londres which had been turned over to the Trotskys might enclose a garden, secluding it from the dust of the unpaved street.

This proved to be a correct impression. In the patio were rose bushes and an orange tree, still fresh and sparkling from being watered. We went up the four steps or so leading to the walk with its balustrade connecting the rooms laid out on three sides of the patio.

This was where I first saw Trotsky. He came out of the secretary's room that connected with the bedroom used by him and Natalia. Trotsky was not as tall as I had expected. His walk was very energetic as he came towards us. He was pleased, as could be seen from his face, and he threw his arms around us.

He wanted to know about our trip and how the comrades were in New York. I relaxed immediately, feeling astonished that he must have anticipated we might be uncertain or nervous and that he had welcomed us in this way to help ease things.

The main source of information today about Trotsky's life in Coyoacán is the last volume of Isaac Deutscher's biography, *The Prophet Outcast*. Deutscher relied almost exclusively on what he could find in the archives at Harvard. Natalia made it possible for him to examine the closed sections and he was thus able to read material not yet available to the general public. Some of this is brought into the final volume, providing us with valuable new facts of a personal nature. However, Deutscher could only guess at the meaning of some of it. There are other reasons, too, for indicating some reservations about the chapter.

Deutscher chose not to seek material from certain of Trotsky's close collaborators in that period who were still living. He did not visit Mexico. Although he came to the United States, he did not get in touch with the Socialist Workers Party, whose leaders played a special role in the last years of Trotsky's life.

Later, in London, Deutscher showed me the final chapter of his biography only in the page proofs. On the whole I found it excellent but it contained various inaccuracies. It was not easy to rectify these at this point. And of course Deutscher could not do much with any new information. A clear example of the difficulty of making alterations in the page proofs can be found in the caption for the photograph facing page 480: 'Two views of the "little fortress" at Coyoacán.' Actually they are photographs not of *one* house but of two *different* houses Trotsky lived in, one after the other. Deutscher did not know about this.

On other, more important, items involving Deutscher's interpretation of this period in Trotsky's life it was pointless to engage in much argument. I debated with Deutscher briefly and let the items go as things on which 'we have a difference'.

Deutscher's picture of the years in Coyoacán is of virtually unrelieved gloom, life in Trotsky's home as he interpreted it being overcast by a hopeless battle against the Kremlin's executioners. This was not the way it was.

The struggle remained in the background – a part of the daily life, but not continuously intruding into immediate attention. As a matter of fact, one of the problems was to maintain alertness. This held true for everyone. Even Natalia grew impatient at times with the security measures to the point of not adhering to them completely. Stalin's decision to murder Trotsky was understood by everyone in the household, but none of us could know by what means the GPU would seek to carry it out. No matter how the rules and schedules were made to conform to defence needs, the 'inmates', as we sometimes called ourselves, became inured to it as part of the way of life, a routine that dropped out of the centre of attention. Periodically we tried to break this up by vigorous measures of one kind or another. Sometimes this was met by considerable resistance. Inertia is a problem even for a small, highly devoted, self-sacrificing group – even a group of revolutionists.

The truth is that Trotsky's major interest was not in this particular armed combat, although he was the central figure involved. He participated in it as a disciplined Bolshevik and army man, but it did not preoccupy him. Trotsky's central interest lay in the Fourth International; there was no question whatever about this. Absorbed by it, he gave it his liveliest attention.

Articles for the general press were undertaken reluctantly.

When finances were low – and sometimes they were very low – he wrote something almost as if it were a pot-boiler, regretting the time lost. A cheque from a publisher gave him another reprieve. His attitude towards writing books of the kind likely to interest publishing houses was much the same as towards articles. He agreed to do a biography of Stalin only after considerable resistance and only after his collaborators overcame his objections with the contention that he could include material of special interest to the Fourth International. I argued with him, for instance, that he could use Stalin as a foil for putting the record straight about the history of the Bolshevik party and that this was very important for the generation I belonged to.

He continually deferred work on his biography of Lenin because of his absorption in internal developments in the Fourth International.

Deutscher viewed Trotsky's preoccupation with the Fourth International as a deplorable weakness in this otherwise preeminent genius. We who were living with Trotsky considered it evidence of his singleness of purpose and capacity to put the proper priority on his projects.

For the guards and secretaries Coyoacán was a school of the Fourth International. All of us followed personal studies which Trotsky, we were aware, noted without intervening – he would unexpectedly drop in on us in our rooms, or ask about a book we happened to be reading in the patio. Also we held classes where we took up various subjects, including Spanish for the American guards. In a more encompassing way Trotsky utilized the entire situation, including the organization of our defence, diplomatic relations with the outside, arriving at political decisions, answering the heavy correspondence, even the articles he wrote, to pass on as much as he could to us from the tradition of the past. There appeared to be no deliberate pedagogy about this; it was just the pattern in which everything was discussed, decided, and carried out.

He could be a severe taskmaster. Life quickly became miserable for anyone around Trotsky who found it difficult to break with bohemian habits or who found it insurmountably difficult to learn preciseness, thoroughness, workmanship.

The best days were those that brought news of encouraging developments in one section or another of the Fourth International, successes however modest. The biggest occasions were visits of members of the Fourth International from other countries. This meant conferences, discussions, sometimes very lively debates – for with Trotsky, none of his followers, none who had absorbed his spirit, hesitated to express differences. If they did not express differences, they could expect to be pressed for their opinions just the same.

For weeks after, a visit of this kind still echoed in the household, one of the indications being a surge of production on Trotsky's broad writing-desk.

It was following just such a visit by James P. Cannon and other leaders of the Socialist Workers Party that L. D. wrote the key document for the forthcoming founding congress of the Fourth International in 1938, 'The Death Agony of Capitalism and the Tasks of the Fourth International', a document that came, under the name of 'The Transitional Programme', to play an increasingly central role in the programmatic concepts of the world Trotskyist movement.

The discussions that inspired Trotsky to write this document were not recorded – the tape machine still lay in the future. However, the highlights of part of the discussions were jotted down in shorthand by one of Trotsky's secretaries and the transcription of these notes is now available in English, the language in which the conversations were conducted. [See *Writings of Leon Trotsky, 1938–39*, Merit Publishers, New York, 1969.] They provide a good indication of the nature of a conference with Trotsky in the Coyoacán period.

The exchange of opinion was actually more extended than the transcript might lead one to guess. In this instance ten days or more, if I recall correctly. It included a number of purely personal 'get-togethers'. These really provided for the freest kind of discussion on all kinds of problems current in the Fourth International, since no matter how the informal conversations started they always ended with politics, especially the politics of the Fourth International.

There were festive times, too, in Coyoacán. Whenever a secretary or guard returned home, a farewell party was organized for a proper send-off. Each year 7 November was a holiday, all of us wearing a red carnation or red rose.

In 1937 when we celebrated the October revolution, Diego Rivera and Frida Kahlo came to the house long before dawn. They brought a huge bunch of red carnations to decorate the long table around which the entire household, except those on guard duty, sat together for meals.

Diego and Frida snipped off the heads of the carnations and worked several hours to arrange them on the white cloth at the head of the table where L. D. and Natalia had their places. At first Frida worked at it while Diego looked on, his round face beaming in its customary way. Frida was very picturesque in her Tehuantepec costume, bright yarns woven into the thick black braids coiled on her head. She started over again. They discussed it. Diego became more and more involved in the project. Presently his hands were occupied with the carnations while Frida watched. Diego tried a large number '4'. Then '4' plus the word '*Internacional*'. Then all over again in a different proportion. Eventually he ended up with '*La Cuarta*'. It was an excellent lettering job.

At dawn the marimba band the Riveras had hired began serenading L. D. and Natalia outside their bedroom window. I don't know what they made of it at first, since it was a surprise. In any case, it was a pleasant way to wake up in Mexico on the anniversary of the October revolution, which was also L. D.'s birthday.

During the day the patio and house filled with people coming for the fiesta. They were mostly very poor people, members of the unions in which Trotsky's Mexican followers were active. They brought food as gifts, including a few live chickens, their feet tied. Several five-gallon cans, converted into household utensils, were brought in filled with *atole*, a thin chocolate-flavoured gruel which we sipped out of cups. The men wore white cotton trousers and shirts, the women the long loose dark skirts that were universal in Mexico at the time. In their *huaraches*, with the dazzling sun coming down on their heads, the crowd looked very typical of the working class. The students, and some of the others who came, were better dressed.

Trotsky, of course, was called on to make a speech. I noticed that he seemed hesitant. No doubt he would have preferred to avoid it. After all, he had arrived in Mexico only the previous January and the speech had to be given in Spanish. Despite his reluctance, there was no escape.

He appeared to brace himself, as if he were taking a deep breath. He stepped forward to the balustrade; and he was transformed. He took complete possession and spoke out as if this were completely natural and something he did every day. He pitched his voice so that it soared somewhat and could be heard with complete ease.

It was a simple speech of thanks and appreciation. A few words about the October revolution and its meaning. An expression of gratitude for the hospitality of Mexico and the warmth of the Mexican people.

Trotsky spoke only a few minutes but it gave me a glimpse of him as a speaker. It was quite clear that he had studied the art and had practised it until it had become virtually effortless for him. He was decidedly not of the school that speaks at an audience or reads it a lecture, glass of water in one hand, hanging onto the podium with the other.

The audience responded with emotion and acclaim.

From his post of observation in Coyoacán Trotsky became more and more fascinated by the American political scene. A steady stream of visitors of all kinds widened his knowledge of various facets.

A young schoolteacher showed up one time. He had been in or around the Socialist Party and knew a little about Trotskyism. Like other footloose persons who showed up occasionally, he had decided he wanted to talk with Trotsky. It turned out that he was a farm boy and rather at loose ends. He had about made up his mind to give up schoolteaching. Trotsky took me aside after a few days. 'Wouldn't he make a good guard?'

I was surprised. I had discovered that actually he was a pacifist.

'Couldn't you persuade him to become a guard?'

I demurred. He was from somewhere in the Middle West but that was hardly a guarantee as to his reliability.

'He is a real American peasant.'

It became clear why Trotsky wanted us to bring him in. He had never had the opportunity to study the American peasant at close range. Here was a live one within reach!

It turned out that the peasant was a crack shot with a rifle. The only trouble was that he didn't want to kill anything, above all a human being. In this special instance, however, he agreed that if we were attacked he would shoot to kill.

In addition, he knew how to work. A specialist with cement, his imagination had been caught with the possibilities of adobe construction. One of his reasons for coming to Mexico was to study this. The end of it was that he became a guard and we recruited him to the party.

In the United States at that time the threat of fascism had become very real. A wing of the American fascist movement was tied in with Hitlerism; but the most important sector was the completely indigenous, red-blooded, flag-waving ultrapatriotic variety. Some of the fascist demagogues, such as Father Coughlin, had gained nationwide notoriety. Trotsky called attention to an even more sinister figure, less easily identifiable as a fascist, Jersey City's Mayor Hague, a political boss of the Democratic Party.

In their visits to Coyoacán, members of the Socialist Workers Party brought the latest information about the struggle against fascism in the United States. Trotsky became quite involved in this, offering any number of specific suggestions on how to meet the threat most effectively. This is reflected in some of his writings of the time, particularly the Transitional Programme, but the degree to which he entered into some of the aspects of this work was, it appears certain, unknown to Isaac Deutscher.

On the question of building defence guards, for instance, the Socialist Workers Party gained a great deal directly from Trotsky although it had already assembled a valuable store of experience in the decades of strike struggles in which its cadres had been involved.

In the battle against fascism, Trotsky saw opportunities for building a mass revolutionary socialist party at an 'American pace'. With characteristic energy, he pressed for maximum utilization of the openings.

Trotsky understood to perfection that a party is built through the accumulation and education of cadres. Leaving aside the official visitors, his interest in younger visitors – and some not so young – invariably ran along two lines: What are the possibilities of recruiting them or, if not recruiting, of getting a financial contribution for the movement from them? I can bear testimony for the Americans on the staff as to how closely we functioned with Trotsky in this kind of work in relation to some of his visitors. When a person was recruited or made a substantial contribution, or combined the two, Trotsky never hid his pleasure.

For those of us on the inside it was therefore the most natural thing in the world for Trotsky to give top priority to the 1939 factional struggle in the Socialist Workers Party. This struggle involved not only key political and theoretical questions of the utmost importance to the fate of the Russian revolution and the first workers' state as a whole; the well-being of one of the largest sections of the Fourth International at the time was involved and along with it all the cadres on a worldwide scale. Not one of us had the slightest cause to wonder that Trotsky put everything else aside to pay full attention to this development.

True, what he wrote was designed for a restricted audience. This audience, however, was the one bearing the Bolshevik tradition, the one in which the living continuity of the revolutionary Marxist movement resided.

In writing for this audience in the very last year of his life, Trotsky did not waste his time. He was working in a very direct way on his primary objective of ensuring 'the succession'. For the sake of giving everything in his power to the Fourth International, he did not permit even the machine-gun assault on his home in May 1940 to divert him. For the cadres, these last contributions made by Trotsky are among the most valuable he ever wrote. [They are collected in *In Defense of Marxism*, Merit Publishers, New York, 1965.]

The Mexican Trotskyists regularly supplied one or two

guards, who most often participated in the night watches or on weekends. Among the most faithful were the Fernándezes – the father, a schoolteacher in his fifties, and three of his boys, Octavio, Carlos and Mario. This family, too, was very close to the household. At times in taking a drive we would pay them a surprise visit at their very modest home in the Tacuba district. This was always immediately converted into a festive party. Mama Fernández brought out fresh *pulque* which she had prepared with fruit flavouring. The youngest children were sent out for more, and for beer. The young girls, Graciela and Ofelia, exceptionally lithe and beautiful, and like the rest of the family superb dancers, pressed the guards, who were inclined to awkwardness, to join them in Mexican folk dancing. If the guards did not know how, it was easy to learn! Trotsky took the side of the girls in putting on the pressure, although neither he nor Natalia attempted to join in. Dancing was for the young ones. As was the *pulque*. And the beer.

Among the Mexican guards some were very poor. They came in their *huaraches*, sandals made of discarded automobile tyres, and the grey *serapes* to be seen everywhere in the most poverty-stricken areas of Mexico. Trotsky was very appreciative of their participation. Some had to make long trips after a hard day's work. Also it gave him an opportunity to talk directly with representatives of this layer of the population. He enjoyed in particular talking with one comrade who was illiterate. Sometimes they talked for an hour or more, barely discernible in the dimly lighted patio. His arms clasped under his *serape*, this Mexican worker made no gestures, appearing stolid. Actually he was surprisingly well informed and did not hesitate to express his opinions.

Mexico drew Trotsky's interest in a strong way. Seeing a Latin American country first hand was an educational experience, he told us. I recall two observations he made on what he had learned. One was the capacity of the indigenous bourgeoisie to assume at times a relatively independent role in relation to imperialism. The Mexican bourgeoisie, under the leadership of Cárdenas, proved capable of going so far as to mobilize the workers as a supporting force in seeking concessions from imperialism. Upon expropriating the oil industry, the government placed the management in the hands of the workers. In noting how the Mexican bourgeoisie mobilized the workers, Trotsky did not thereby assign any universal 'independent' role to the indigenous bourgeoisie in the colonial revolution; for, as he noted, the moment the workers and peasants began seriously to press their own demands this same bourgeoisie at once reversed its attitude, joining with imperialism to suppress the incipient movement towards socialist revolution.

The second observation was the importance of the labour aristocracy in a country like Mexico. This layer was exceptionally thin, and in its standard of living stood well below the labour aristocracy in the industrially developed countries. In Mexico, however, the position of this layer in comparison to the rest of the work force made it relatively more privileged than the labour aristocracy in the advanced countries. It constituted an extremely conservative force, representing a major obstacle and problem for the socialist revolution.

Trotsky took an interest in the Mexican section of the Fourth International but could not participate in its activities because of the conditions of his asylum. As with most other young sections, the Mexican movement was faced with growth problems that were complicated by lack of experience. Consequently the Mexican comrades sought Trotsky's advice. This created a standing difficulty since their eagerness coincided with Trotsky's own inclinations.

Occasionally the organization took actions that could not but affect Trotsky. Thus, under the influence of some of the émigrés from the defeated Spanish revolution, Grandizo Munis in particular, the Mexican section on one occasion printed a huge poster to be pasted on walls, the aim of which was to influence a strike from the outside. The poster carried in enormous letters a one-word slogan: 'Sabotaje!'

It is dubious that the call for sabotage had much effect on the course of the strike. In Coyoacán, however, the effect of this ultraleftist action was considerable. The Old Man was outraged at the obvious lack of political thought.

Munis, it should be made clear, was a very loyal Trotskyist, who had fought in the Spanish civil war. After Trotsky's death, he played a role for several years in helping to sustain Natalia. This had one unfortunate consequence in the influence it had in some of Natalia's political decisions. Later Munis went to France and from there into the underground in Spain when an upsurge appeared imminent. He was captured by Franco's political police and spent many years in prison.

Trotsky's influence in the Mexican section was shown in a different way in his literary collaboration in the magazine *Clave* (*Key*), which began publication in October 1938 as a monthly magazine of Marxist opinion. The editorial board consisted of Adolfo Zamora, José Ferrel, and Diego Rivera. The managing editor was Octavio Fernández. So attracted was Trotsky by this project that he tended to become involved in the smallest details. When the first issue came off the press and a copy was placed on his desk, he reached for an editorial pencil. A pair of quotation marks had been printed around the name 'Clave' on the cover. Trotsky put a delete sign on each of them. In the next issue, the name appeared without the offending marks.

Among the friends of the household in 1937, the closest were probably the Riveras. Both Diego and Frida came to the house frequently, and the Trotskys reciprocated, visiting the Riveras in their home in San Angél, which was not far from Coyoacán. This close relationship extended to the secretaries and guards, with whom Frida and her sister Cristina were particularly close, since they belonged to the same younger generation. Diego, who had just entered his fifties, came closer to the generation to which L. D. and Natalia belonged.

Joint excursions into the countryside were organized as relaxation, for Diego was continually on the go and liked to show the Mexico he knew to his friends. These trips sometimes involved four or five automobiles for long distances over some very rough mountain roads.

L.D. was strongly attracted to Diego, to the imagination, charm, transparency, and geniality of the great artist. For Diego and Frida, of course, the household was absorbing because of the intellectual stimulation to be found talking with L. D. and

Natalia, and not only them but the secretaries and guards and the visitors from other countries.

Eventually, as is well known, this relationship was broken off. On the personal level Natalia was not without fault in this. The extreme tension under which she lived, the barbaric blows she had suffered, the expectation of fresh ones, sometimes showed up in the form of irritability. Natalia was well aware of this and sought to keep it under control, as she told me one time on a trip the two of us took together from Mexico City to Nuevo Laredo where I crossed the border to re-register the Dodge. She could not always manage it, however, and there would be a flare-up. Various persons in the household ran into this. If they appreciated what was involved, they did not blame Natalia. Yet they sometimes permitted themselves to make an angry retort despite their better judgement. It seemed particularly hard for some of the women comrades, who were rebels and revolutionists, not to respond in kind in defence of their dignity. After the harsh words, Natalia, deeply remorseful, would try to make up in an almost excessive way. In some instances, those caught in such a situation felt even more repelled by this turn than by the previous aggressiveness that had seemed on the surface so unjustified and uncalled for.

This happened with Frida. Bewildered and outraged, she drew away. In a very unhappy frame of mind in the following weeks, Frida told me what the situation was, how she felt. Unfortunately, not much could be done to restore this relationship to what it had been.

More important than this, however, was the way Diego became involved in supporting a bourgeois candidate in an election. Under the circumstances the stand Diego took could easily be twisted by the Stalinists to make it appear that Trotsky was Diego Rivera's mentor in the move and that it was aimed against Cárdenas. Trotsky had to make a public disavowal in order to show that he had nothing to do with an action that for him would have been in violation of the condition of his asylum – not to intervene in Mexican politics – and in violation of his basic principles. In short, Trotsky had to break with Diego Rivera politically.

I don't think that Trotsky's personal regard for Diego was changed in the least. His admiration and appreciation remained and he still talked about him as if their friendship had not been affected. Trotsky didn't really consider Diego to be wholly responsible in politics; his imagination tended to run away with him.

In February 1938 the relations between the Riveras and the Trotskys were still close. It was Diego who called us one afternoon to ask if we had heard that Leon Sedov had died in a Paris hospital. We did not even know that he was in a hospital. Diego said the news still remained to be confirmed and he would do everything to find out as soon as possible if it were really true, if necessary putting a call through to Paris.

Natalia was in her room. Trotsky was not in the house at all. During the previous weeks the Stalinists had stepped up their press campaign against Trotsky. We had taken this, along with other indications, as proof that they were preparing a new attempt against Trotsky's life. Consequently, we had increased our precautions. In fact, we had become so convinced that another effort to assassinate Trotsky was being prepared that we had resorted to a special measure. We had smuggled him out of the house and taken him to the villa of a sympathizer where he could remain in hiding for a time. In case an attack were carried out on the house, the assailants would not find Trotsky there.

Under the circumstances we decided not to tell Natalia about the report that had been relayed to Diego. Early in the evening, he came to the house himself to tell us the bitter news. It was true.

Diego was very close to all of us. He was as deeply affected as we were and as troubled about how to tell Natalia and L. D.

The best course, we thought, was still not to tell Natalia, but to break it first to L. D. As to which one of us should undertake this task, opinion at first leaned in my direction. After thinking about it, it appeared to me that it would be best to sound out Diego. Diego was of the same generation as Trotsky and was probably closer to the inner man than we who were in our late twenties. Diego considered it and agreed. 'If you think it best . . .'

I drove to the villa, which was some distance away. Diego

lifted his huge bulk out of the car and moved towards the gate. We could hear the bell when he pushed the button. The electric light came on, converting him into a broad silhouette at the gate. A servant let him in.

It was a half hour or more before Diego returned. Trotsky was with him. Without a word, Trotsky climbed into the back seat.

Quietly, clearing his throat a little, Diego said in English, 'We drive back to the house.' He got in beside Trotsky and closed the door. During the whole trip back no one spoke a word.

At the house the guards were on the alert, and as we came they swung open the double doors in accordance with our routine so that we could drive in rapidly without stopping, thereby giving a possible sniper a more difficult shot. Trotsky immediately got out of the car, strode through the guard's patio to the main patio and went to Natalia.

The suffering of the couple in the following days could be seen especially in Natalia's face, swollen from weeping, when she emerged occasionally from their darkened bedroom. We did not see Trotsky for several days.

I became very worried over them. The thought came to me of the impact the suicide of Paul and Laura Lafargue (Marx's daughter) had had on the revolutionary socialist movement in 1911 when the couple, at the age of seventy, decided that their usefulness had ended. Lenin spoke at their funeral in Paris. Krupskaya said that Lenin told her, 'If one cannot work for the Party any longer, one must be able to look truth in the face and die like the Lafargues.'

Perhaps it would have been wiser for the young generation of revolutionists to have questioned themselves as to what role they had sought to make for the Lafargues. In any case that suicide pact deeply stirred the socialist movement at the time and echoes of it were still to be heard when I joined the movement.

I pushed back the thought, telling myself that it most likely arose from some obscure reaction of my own; or that the idea reflected the convictions I had heard others express. Then Rae, who was very close to Natalia, and who was making sure that meals were brought to them and that anything they might want was attended to, confessed the same fear to me. Especially worrisome was the small automatic pistol which L. D. generally left lying on his desk like a paper-weight. We decided to remove it. After all, it probably needed cleaning and oiling.

Several days later, coming into the patio on an inspection tour, I saw that the folding doors of the bedroom had been opened. L. D. had moved a small table there for the light. He was seated at the table writing. In the evening he was still there, working under a lamp he had set up. I watched him for a while, his high forehead illuminated by the light in the otherwise dark patio. There could be no doubt about it; he was working on a manuscript. He worked very late.

The feeling that a new catastrophe was impending suddenly left me. They were safely out of the abyss. What the Old Man was writing, in fact, was his farewell to his son, *Leon Sedov – Son, Friend, Fighter*.

The wound of Leon's death remained very raw for a while. Even small things could touch off an explosive reaction. The translation of the farewell, for example, brought a dressing down from L. D. Half of the translation was done in Coyoacán and half in New York because of his insistence on speed. Neither text measured up to his expectations. No doubt he was right – the English did not, could not, meet the nuances of the Russian in the way he wanted.

Other small changes were to be noted. Before Leon's death, the Old Man and Natalia had often sát in the dining-room, reading with the Telefunken radio turned to a local station that broadcast classical music. They now gave this up. I do not know why. Of the two, Natalia was the one who most appreciated music.

After a time I noticed a rather marked change in the Old Man. It was hard to state what this was precisely. The word that occurred to me then was mellowness; yet that was not quite right. He did not seem to drive others as hard as he had before. He had more consideration, I felt, for weaknesses in his collaborators. It was subtle but definitely there so that it became a new element in the relationships within the household. Perhaps it is even detectable in the tone in the parts of the biography of Stalin that were completed before he was finally struck down by the assassin.

The household was still in agony over the death of Leon Sedov when Stalin made another move. On 23 February the Mexican trade-union confederation, which was controlled by the Mexican Communist Party through Lombardo Toledano, passed a slanderous resolution against Trotsky. The aim of the resolution was to put pressure on the Cárdenas government to cancel Trotsky's asylum and deport him.

There was no alternative but to answer immediately. Trotsky did this the following day.

Unknown to us or the public in general, on precisely the same day that Laborde and Lombardo Toledano had their resolution passed by the CTM, Andrei Vyshinsky, the procurator of the USSR, signed an indictment against twenty-one members of a 'Bloc of Rights and Trotskyites'. This was announced in Moscow on 27 February. The trial was to open on 2 March.

Among the defendants were some internationally famous names, including Nikolai I. Bukharin and Alexei I. Rykov. As part of the 'amalgam', Stalin included one of his own faithful lieutenants, Yagoda, the former head of the secret political police and organizer of the first 'great' show trial in 1936 that doomed Zinoviev and Kamenev and others. A poignant figure for L. D. and Natalia was Christian Rakovsky, a long-time friend of the family.

As in the previous trials the main defendant, of course, was Trotsky, named by the prosecutor as the chief conspirator and arch-plotter.

Although Stalin had taken a year to prepare the script, he had no intention whatever of prolonging the show. This was indicated by the suddenness of the announcement and the short time permitted the defendants before the trial opened. Stalin's purpose in carrying the affair through at such a fast pace was to block efforts in other countries to mount pressure for a fair trial. It could be expected that the courtroom drama would be brief and that the defendants, or at least most of them, would be immediately executed. Perhaps Stalin counted on the whole thing being completed and the victims buried before Trotsky could expose the frame-up. Then, as interest died, let the exiled revolutionary leader and his handful of followers try to overcome the weight of the world-wide propaganda machine of the Comintern backed by the mighty resources of the Soviet state . . .

We held our first consultation in the late afternoon, or perhaps it was early evening, of the day the news was received. In Coyoacán, in addition to our meetings of an educational nature or of discussion on current political topics, the secretaries and guards regularly held staff meetings – sometimes separated by as much as a month – in which the agenda was usually confined to organizational questions involving the household or the guard routine. L. D. often attended but hardly ever took the lead in these sessions. In cases where sharp differences of opinion arose, he even sought to avoid the role of arbitrator. In this meeting, however, Trotsky took over from the beginning.

He outlined the problem. We had no way of knowing how long the trial would last; it could well be for only a few days. During this period, the trial would be the centre of international attention. Whatever we had to say had to be said quickly. Timing was absolutely crucial for us. Even hours could make a difference. Consequently we had to prepare for an extraordinary effort.

The Old Man did not talk in a dramatic way. He was merely intense. We were moved all the more because of what we felt it took for him to turn from the death of his son to this new attack from the treacherous and murderous-minded foe.

All of us had anticipated what we would have to do, and so we could say, 'Already done', to some of the next points.

Our first problem was to get the text of the indictment or as much of it as possible. Here we had to rely on the *New York Times*. This could be obtained from a bookstore in downtown Mexico City which received a daily bundle by airmail. Our comrades in New York also arranged to send us clippings by airmail. I forget from which source we first got the required document; but my memory of the next item is very vivid.

At seven in the morning, when the sun was still slanting at a low angle through the trees, brightening the blue wall inside the patio, there was L. D. on the walk connecting the rooms around the patio, moving slowly as he went over the indictment. He had on his jacket and beret, for the air was still cool and fresh at this time of year and this elevation. When he paused to make a notation, the picture was unforgettable as his glasses and goatee came close to the newspaper.

I was later able to see the evidence of the thoroughness with which he performed this distasteful chore. Here and there in red or blue an 'NB' – *nota bene* – occasional marks in the margin, a word or two in some sections in Russian.

Then the work really began. Calls came in continually from the newspapers, from the wire services, from independent journalists. Whatever L. D. had to say in reply to the frame-up artists in Moscow was front-page, if not headline, news in every country free of authoritarian rule.

The Old Man scarcely left his desk, eating in snatches, not bothering to shave. He was of the generation of writers antedating the typewriter. He wrote entirely with a pencil or pen and was such a steady writer that he suffered from an occupational hazard that is scarcely known today. His finger grew tender and he had to wear a bandage while he worked.

He was excellent at dictation, pacing himself according to the speed of the stenographer, whose strokes, hooks and curves he occasionally paused to admire; but dictation offered only some relief since he proceeded by successive approximations, going over his manuscripts repeatedly. 'Sometimes,' he told me once, 'the most obvious thought comes only after the last draft is finished.' The 'last draft' was then reworked.

L. D.'s handwritten manuscripts were typed up and returned to his desk for correction. When they became difficult to follow because of the many changes, they were retyped. The clean copy went through the process again.

Under the pressure of an emergency such as this one, with deadlines set by circumstances over which he had no control, the Old Man curtailed his emendations and rewriting considerably.

From the final Russian draft the secretariat made English, French, and Spanish versions, helping each other with translation difficulties. Occasionally one of our problems would lead L. D. to change the Russian original. There were few translations made in Coyoacán that L. D. did not finally check himself, sometimes arguing for a different word or turn of phrase. His choices in English were not always felicitous. It was not that he considered himself a master of English; it was part of his general tendency to follow through on details. He could not bear sloppiness or imprecision in anything.

As the Moscow trial proceeded L. D. followed the press closely. Each day he wrote a long statement which was then translated, typed up in a number of copies, taken to the wire services and daily papers in Mexico City, and air-mailed to our co-thinkers in various areas. We did not use a mimeograph, partly because it would have meant another step in a process where speed was at a premium.

Trotsky worked relentlessly – something like eighteen hours a day during the opening phase of the trial. Some of us who were younger worked still longer. We did not miss a single deadline.

Thus we functioned as a quite efficient and rather smooth, if small, team. This was in the tradition of Trotsky's earlier staffs, a tradition handed down from one group of secretaries to another. In Russia Trotsky's secretariat was famed. Stalin had good reason to strike special blows at its members in hope of reducing and crippling Trotsky's effectiveness. I never had the privilege of meeting the Russians. They perished in the concentration camps or from a shot in the head from a GPU pistol. But I know what they were like. They were the kind that enjoy work, do not mind working under high pressure, are independent minded, and not without skills in several fields. With such co-workers, Trotsky collaborated on an equal basis, all working together for the great common goal. And this inspired them to reach a bit beyond themselves.

The impact of Trotsky's statements on the third 'great' Moscow trial was devastating. The swift response to the indictment, exposing the frame-up before the show even opened, turned the trial against Stalin in the eyes of world opinion from the first day, and each day became worse. Trotsky, the chief defendant, succeeded in turning the tables on Stalin, becoming the chief accuser. From then on, among knowledgeable people, it was definitive. Stalin, already branded by the findings of the John Dewey Commission in 1937, which had shown Trotsky and Leon Sedov to be innocent of the charges levelled in the previous frame-up trials, was now burdened with a 'credibility gap' from which he could never escape.

Working with Trotsky was a serious matter – he was no dabbler in politics and he found dabbling intolerable in others; qut it was also an extraordinary school for the young comrades on his staff. The way he responded to the March 1938 Moscow trial served as a model demonstration of the importance of timing in meeting a deadly challenge and converting it into an opportunity. It meant pushing everything else aside with the utmost decisiveness, rising above personal problems, concentrating on the work at hand with maximum energy and every resource available. It was a rare opportunity for those of us then in our twenties to see Trotsky in action as a political fighter in a very acute battle.

October 1969

Foreword

Our times again are rich in memoirs, perhaps richer than ever before. It is because there is much to tell. The more dramatic and rich in change the epoch the more intense the interest in current history. The art of landscape-painting could never have been born in the Sahara. The 'crossing' of two epochs, as at present, gives rise to a desire to look back at yesterday, already far away, through the eyes of its active participants. That is the reason for the enormous growth in the literature of reminiscence since the days of the last war. Perhaps it will justify the present volume as well.

The very fact of its coming into the world is due to the pause in the author's active political life. One of the unforeseen, though not accidental, stops in my life has proved to be Constantinople. Here I am camping – but not for the first time – and patiently waiting for what is to follow. The life of a revolutionary would be quite impossible without a certain amount of 'fatalism'. In one way or another the Constantinople interval has proved the most appropriate moment for me to look back before circumstances allow me to move forward.

At first I wrote cursory autobiographical sketches for the newspapers, and thought I would let it go at that. And here I would like to say that, from my refuge, I was unable to watch the form in which those sketches reached the public. But every work has its own logic. I did not get into my stride until I had nearly finished those articles. Then I decided to write a book. I applied a different and infinitely broader scale, and carried out the whole work anew. The only point in common between the original newspaper articles and this book is that both discuss the same subject. In everything else they are two different products.

I have dealt in especial detail with the second period of the

Soviet revolution, the beginning of which coincided with Lenin's illness and the opening of the campaign against 'Trotskyism'. The struggle of the epigones for power, as I shall try to prove, was not merely a struggle of personalities; it represented a new political chapter – the reaction against October and the preparation of the Thermidor. From this the answer to the question that I have so often been asked – 'How did you lose power?' – follows naturally.

An autobiography of a revolutionary politician must inevitably touch on a whole series of theoretical questions connected with the social development of Russia, and in part with humanity as a whole, but especially with those critical periods that are called revolutions. Of course I have not been able in these pages to examine complicated theoretical problems critically in their essence. The so-called theory of permanent revolution, which played so large a rôle in my personal life, and, what is more important, is acquiring such poignant reality in the countries of the East, runs through this book as a remote leitmotive. If this does not satisfy the reader, I can say that the consideration of the problem of revolution in its essence will constitute a separate book, in which I shall attempt to give form to the principal theoretical conclusions of the experiences of the last decades.

As many people pass through the pages of my book, portrayed not always in the light that they would have chosen for themselves or for their parties, many of them will find my account lacking the necessary detachment. Even extracts that have been published in the newspapers have elicted certain denials. That is inevitable. One has no doubt that even if I had succeeded in making my autobiography a mere daguerreotype of my life – which I never intended it to be – it would nevertheless have called forth echoes of the discussion started at the time by the collisions described in the book. This book is not a dispassionate photograph of my life, however, but a component part of it. In these pages I continue the struggle to which my whole life is devoted. Describing, I also characterize and evaluate; narrating, I also defend myself, and more often attack. It seems to me that this is the only method of making an autobiography objective in a higher sense, that is, of making it the most adequate expression of personality, conditions, and epoch.

Objectivity is not the pretended indifference with which confirmed hypocrisy, in speaking of friends and enemies, suggests indirectly to the reader what it finds inconvenient to state directly. Objectivity of this sort is nothing but a conventional trick. I do not need it. Since I have submitted to the necessity of writing about myself – nobody has as yet succeeded in writing an autobiography without writing about himself – I can have no reason to hide my sympathies or antipathies, my loves or my hates.

This is a book of polemics. It reflects the dynamics of that social life which is built entirely on contradictions. The impertinence of the schoolboy towards his master; the pin-pricks of envy in the drawing-room, veiled by courtesies, the constant competition of commerce; the frenzied rivalry in all branches of pure and applied science, of art, and sport; the parliamentary clashes that reveal the deep opposition of interests; the furious struggle that goes on every day in the newspapers; the strikes of the workers; the shooting down of participants in demonstrations; the packages of explosives that civilized neighbours send each other through the air; the fiery tongues of civil war, almost never extinguished on our planet – all these are the forms of social 'polemics', ranging from those that are usual, constant and normal, almost unnoticed despite their intensity, to those of war and revolution that are extraordinary, explosive and volcanic. Such is our epoch. We have all grown up with it. We breathe it and live by it. How can we help being polemical if we want to be true to our period in the mode of the day?

But there is another and more elementary criterion, one that relates to plain conscientiousness in stating facts. Just as the most bitter revolutionary struggle must take account of time and place, the most polemical work must observe the proportions that exist between objects and men. I hope that I have observed this demand, not only in its entirety, but also in its particulars.

In certain cases – although these are not very numerous – I relate long-ago conversations in dialogue form. No one will demand a verbatim report of conversations repeated many years after. Nor do I claim such accuracy. Some of these dialogues have rather a symbolic character. Everyone, however, has had moments in his life when some particular conversation has impressed itself indelibly on his memory. One usually repeats that sort of conversation to one's personal or political friends; thanks to this, they become fixed in one's memory. I am thinking primarily, of course, of all conversations of a political nature.

I may state here that I am accustomed to trust to my memory. Its testimony has been subjected to verification by fact more than once, and it has stood the test perfectly. But a reservation is necessary. If my topographic memory, not to mention my musical one, is very weak, and my visual memory and my linguistic memory fairly mediocre, still my memory of ideas is considerably above the average. And, moreover, in this book ideas, their evolution, and the struggle of men for these ideas, have the most important place.

It is true that memory is not an automatic reckoner. Above all, it is never disinterested. Not infrequently it expels or drives into a dark corner episodes not convenient to the vital instinct that controls it – usually ambition. But this is a matter for 'psychoanalytic' criticism, which is sometimes very ingenious and instructive, but more often capricious and arbitrary.

Needless to say, I have persistently checked my memory by documentary evidence. Difficult as the conditions of my work have been, in the business of making inquiries in libraries or searching out archives I have been able to verify all the more important facts and dates that were needed.

Beginning with 1897, I have waged the fight chiefly with a pen in my hand. Thus the events of my life have left an almost uninterrupted trail in print over a period of thirty-two years. The factional struggle in the party, which began in 1903, has been rich in personal episodes. My opponents, like myself, have not withheld blows. All of them have left their scars in print. Since the October revolution, the history of the revolutionary movement has held an important place in the research work of young Soviet scholars and of entire institutions. Everything of interest is sought out in the archives of the revolution and of the

Tsarist police department and published with detailed factual commentaries. In the first years, when there was as yet no need of disguising anything, this work was carried on most conscientiously. The 'works' of Lenin and some of mine were issued by the State Publishing House, with notes that took up dozens of pages in each volume and contained invaluable factual material concerning both the activities of the authors and the events of the corresponding period. All this of course facilitated my work, helping me to fix the correct chronological pattern and to avoid errors of fact, at least the most serious ones.

I cannot deny that my life has not followed quite the ordinary course. The reasons for that are inherent in the conditions of the time, rather than in me. Of course certain personal traits were also necessary for the work, good or bad, that I performed. But under other historical conditions these personal peculiarities might have remained completely dormant, as is true of so many propensities and passions on which the social environment makes no demands. On the other hand other qualities, today crowded out or suppressed, might have come to the fore. Above the subjective there rises the objective, and in the final reckoning it is the objective that decides.

My intellectual and active life, which began when I was about seventeen or eighteen years old, has been one of constant struggle for definite ideas. In my personal life there were no events deserving public attention in themselves. All the more or less unusual episodes in my life are bound up with the revolutionary struggle and derive their significance from it. This alone justifies the appearance of my autobiography. But from this same source flow many difficulties for the author. The facts of my personal life have proved to be so closely interwoven with the texture of historical events that is has been difficult to separate them. This book, moreover, is not altogether an historical work. Events are treated here not according to their objective significance, but according to the way in which they are connected with the facts of my personal life. It is quite natural, then, that the accounts of specific events and of entire periods lack the proportion that would be demanded of them if this book were an historical work.

I had to grope for the dividing line between autobiography and the history of the revolution. Without allowing the story of my life to become lost in an historical treatise, it was necessary at the same time to give the reader a base of the facts of the social development. In doing this, I assumed that the main outlines of the great events were known to him, and that all his memory needed was a brief reminder of historical facts and their sequence.

By the time this book is published, I shall have reached my fiftieth birthday. The date coincides with that of the October revolution. Mystics and Pythagoreans may draw from this whatever conclusions they like. I myself noticed this odd coincidence only three years after the October uprising. Until I was nine years old I lived in a remote little village. For eight years I studied at school. I was arrested for the first time a year after I left school. For universities, like many others of my time, I had prison, Siberia, and foreign exile. In the Tsar's prisons I served four years in two periods. In the Tsarist exile I spent about two years the first time, a few weeks the second. I escaped from Siberia twice. As a foreign émigré I lived for about twelve years altogether in various European countries and in America – two years before the revolution of 1905, and nearly ten years after its defeat. In 1915 during the war I was sentenced in my absence to imprisonment in Hohenzollern Germany; the next year I was expelled from France and Spain, and after a brief stay in the Madrid prison, and a month in Cadiz under the surveillance of the police, I was deported to America. I was there when the February Revolution broke out. On my way from New York I was arrested by the British in March 1917 and detained for a month in a concentration camp in Canada. I took part in the revolutions of 1905 and 1917, and I was the chairman of the St Petersburg Soviet of delegates in 1905, and again in 1917. I took an intimate part in the October Revolution, and was a member of the Soviet government. As the People's Commissary for foreign affairs, I conducted peace negotiations at Brest-Litovsk with the delegates of Germany, Austria-Hungary, Turkey and Bulgaria. As People's Commissary for military and naval affairs, I devoted about five years to organizing the Red army and restoring the Red navy. During the year 1920 I added to that the direction of the country's disorganized railway system.

The main content of my life, however, except for the years of the civil war, has been party and literary activity. In 1923 the State Publishing House began the publication of my collected works. It succeeded in bringing out thirteen volumes, not counting the previously published five volumes on military subjects. Publication was discontinued in 1927, when the persecution of 'Trotskyism' became especially intense.

In January 1928 I was sent into exile by the present Soviet government; I spent a year on the Chinese frontier; in February 1929 I was deported to Turkey, and I am now writing these lines from Constantinople.

Even in this condensed synopsis the outward course of my life could hardly be called monotonous. On the contrary, counting the number of turns, surprises, sharp conflicts, ups and downs, one might say that my life was rather full of 'adventure'. But I must say that, by natural inclination, I have nothing in common with seekers after adventure. I am rather pedantic and conservative in my habits. I like and appreciate discipline and system. Not to provide a paradox, but because it is a fact, I must add that I cannot endure disorder or destruction. I was always an accurate and diligent schoolboy, and I have preserved these two qualities all my life. In the years of the civil war, when I covered by train a distance equal to several times round the earth, I was greatly pleased to see each new fence constructed of freshly cut pine boards. Lenin, who knew this passion of mine, often twitted me about it in a friendly way. A well-written book in which one can find new ideas, and a good pen with which to communicate one's own ideas to others, for me have always been and are today the most valuable and intimate products of culture. The desire for study has never left me, and many times in my life I felt that the revolution was interfering with my systematic work. Yet almost a third of a century of my conscious life was entirely filled with revolutionary struggle. And if I had to live it over again, I would unhesitatingly take the same path.

I am obliged to write these lines as an émigré – for the third time – while my closest friends are filling the places of exile and the prisons of that Soviet republic in whose creating they took so decisive a part. Some of them are vacillating, withdrawing, bowing before the enemy. Some are doing it because they are morally exhausted; others because they can find no other way out of the maze of circumstances; and still others because of the pressure of material reprisals. I had already lived through two instances of such mass desertion of the banner: after the collapse of the revolution of 1905, and at the beginning of the World War. Thus I know well enough, from my own experience, the historical ebb and flow. They are governed by their own laws. Mere impatience will not expedite their change. I have grown accustomed to viewing the historical perspective not from the standpoint of my personal fate. To understand the causal sequence of events and to find somewhere in the sequence one's own place – that is the first duty of a revolutionary. And at the same time it is the greatest personal satisfaction possible for a man who does not limit his tasks to the present day.

L. TROTSKY

Prinkipo, 1929

I
Yanovka

Childhood is looked upon as the happiest time of life. Is that always true? No, only a few have a happy childhood. The idealization of childhood originated in the old literature of the privileged. A secure, affluent, and unclouded childhood, spent in a home of inherited wealth and culture, a childhood of affection and play, brings back to one memories of a sunny meadow at the beginning of the road of life. The grandees of literature, or the plebeians who glorify the grandees, have canonized this purely aristocratic view of childhood. But the majority of the people, if it looks back at all, sees, on the contrary, a childhood of darkness, hunger and dependence. Life strikes the weak – and who is weaker than a child?

My childhood was not one of hunger and cold. My family had already achieved a competence at the time of my birth. But it was the stern competence of people still rising from poverty and having no desire to stop half-way. Every muscle was strained, every thought set on work and savings. Such a domestic routine left but a modest place for the children. We knew no need, but neither did we know the generosities of life – its caresses. My childhood does not appear to me like a sunny meadow, as it does to the small minority; neither does it appear like a dark cave of hunger, violence and misery, as it does to the majority. Mine was the greyish childhood of a lower-middle-class family, spent in a village in an obscure corner where nature is wide, and manners, views and interests are pinched and narrow.

The spiritual atmosphere which surrounded my early years and that in which I passed my later, conscious life are two different worlds, divided not only in time and space by decades and by far countries, but by the mountain chains of great events and by those inner landslides which are less obvious but are fully as important to one's individuality. When I first began to draft these memoirs, it often seemed to me as if I were not writing of my own childhood but of a long-past journey into a distant land. I even attempted to write my story in the third person, but this conventional form all too easily smacks of fiction, which is something that I should want to avoid at all costs.

In spite of the contradiction between these two worlds the unity of the personality passes through hidden channels from one world into the other. This, generally speaking, accounts for the interest that people take in the biographies and autobiographies of those who, for one reason or another, have occupied a somewhat more spacious place in the life of society. I shall therefore try to tell the story of my childhood in some detail – without anticipating and predetermining the future, that is, without selecting the facts to suit preconceived generalities – simply narrating what occurred as it is preserved in my memory.

At times it has seemed to me that I can remember suckling at my mother's breast; probably I apply to myself only what I have seen in the younger children. I have a dim recollection of a scene under an apple-tree in the garden which took place when I was a year and a half old, but that memory too is doubtful. More securely do I remember another event: I am with my mother in Bobrinetz, visiting the Z. family, where there is a little girl of two or three. I am the bridegroom, the little girl is the bride. The children are playing on the painted floor of the parlour; the little girl fades away; the little boy is standing dazed and petrified beside a chest of drawers. His mother and the hostess come in. His mother looks at the boy, then at the puddle beside him, and then at the boy again, shakes her head reproachfully and says: 'Aren't you ashamed of yourself?' The boy looks at his mother, at himself, and at the puddle, as if it all had nothing whatever to do with him.

'Never mind,' the hostess says, 'the children have played too long.'

The little boy feels neither shame nor repentance. How old was he then? About two years, possibly three.

It was about this time that I ran into a poisonous snake while walking in the garden with my nurse. 'Look, Lyova!'* she cried, pointing to a bright object in the grass. 'Here is a snuff-box buried in the ground!' My nurse took a stick and began to dig it out. She herself was not more than sixteen years old. The snuff-box uncoiled itself, stretched into a snake, and, hissing, began to crawl in the grass. 'Ai! Ai!' screamed my nurse, and, catching me by the hand, ran quickly. It was hard for me to move my legs fast enough. Choking with excitement, I told afterwards of our finding in the grass a snuff-box which turned into a snake.

I remember another early scene that took place in our main kitchen. Neither my father nor my mother is at home. The cook and the maid and their guests are there. My older brother, Alexander, who is at home for the holidays, is also buzzing about, standing on a wooden shovel, as if on a pair of stilts, and dancing on it across the earthen floor. I beg my brother to let me have the shovel, and try to climb up on it, but I fall down and cry. My brother picks me up, kisses me, and carries me out of the kitchen in his arms.

I must have been about four years old when someone put me on the back of a big grey mare as gentle as a sheep, with neither bridle nor saddle, only a rope halter. I spread my legs wide apart and held on to the mane with both hands. The mare quietly took me to a pear-tree and walked under a branch, which caught me across the middle. Not realizing what the matter was, I slid over the mare's rump, and hit the grass. I was not hurt, only puzzled.

I had almost no ready-made toys in my childhood. Once, however, my mother brought me a cardboard horse and a ball from Kharkoff. My younger sister and I played with dolls which we made ourselves. Once Aunt Fenya and Aunt Raisa, my father's sisters, made some rag dolls for us and Aunt Fenya

---

*Trotsky's full and original name was Lev Davydovich Bronstein, his father's name being Davyd Leontiyevich Bronstein. 'Lyova' is one of the many similar diminutives of Lev, which literally means 'Lion'. In English and French usage, Trotsky has become known as Leon, in German as Leo. In ensuing pages the reader will frequently find him referred to as Lev Davydovich, and often in quotations from his wife's journal simply as L.D. – *Translator.*

marked their eyes, noses and mouths with a pencil. The dolls seemed remarkable to me; I can remember them to this day. One winter evening our mechanic, Ivan Vasilyevich, cut a little railway-car with wheels and windows out of cardboard and pasted it together. My older brother, at home for Christmas, instantly announced that he could make a car too, in no time. He began by pulling my car to pieces; then he armed himself with a ruler, pencil and scissors, and drew for a long time. But when he cut out what he had drawn there was no railway-car.

Our relatives and friends, when going to town, would sometimes ask what I wanted from Elizavetgrad or Nikolayev. My eyes would shine. What should I ask for? They would come to my help. One would suggest a toy horse, another books, another coloured crayons, another a pair of skates. 'I want half-Halifax skates!' I would cry, having heard this expression from my brother. But they would forget their promises as soon as they had crossed the threshold. I lived in hope for several weeks, and then suffered a long disappointment.

A bee sits on a sunflower in the garden. Because bees sting and must be handled with care, I pick up a burdock leaf and with it seize the bee between two fingers. I am suddenly pierced by an unendurable pain. I run screaming across the yard to the machine-shop, where Ivan Vasilyevich pulls out the sting and smears a healing liquid on my finger.

Ivan Vasilyevich had a jar full of sunflower-oil in which tarantulas were floating. This was considered the best cure for stings. Victor Ghertopanov and I together used to catch these tarantulas. To do this, we would fasten a piece of wax to a thread and drop it into one of their burrows. The tarantula would seize the wax in its claws and stick tight. We then had only to draw it out and catch it in an empty match-box. These tarantula hunts, however, must have belonged to a later period.

I remember a conversation on a long winter evening during which my elders discussed over their tea when it was that Yanovka had been bought, how old such and such a child was at the time, and when Ivan Vasilyevich had come to work for us. My mother speaks, glancing slyly at me: 'We brought Lyova here from the farm all ready made.' I try to reason that out for myself, and finally say aloud: 'Then I was born on the farm?' 'No,' they answer me, 'you were born here at Yanovka.'

'Then why did Mother say that you brought me here ready made?'

'Mother was just joking!'

But I am not satisfied, and I think it is a queer joke. I hold my peace, however, for I notice that particular smile that I never can bear on the faces of the older initiates. It is from these recollections exchanged at leisure over our winter tea that a certain chronology emerges: I was born on 26 October. My parents must have moved from the little farm to Yanovka either in the spring or summer of 1879.

The year of my birth was the year of the first dynamite assaults against Tsarism. The recently formed terrorist party, the 'People's Will', had on 26 August 1879, two months before my appearance in the world, pronounced the death sentence on Alexander II. And on 19 November an attempt was made to dynamite the Tsar's train. The ominous struggle which led to the assassination of Alexander II on 1 March 1881, and at the same time resulted in the annihilation of the 'People's Will', was just beginning.

The Russo–Turkish War had ended the year before. In August 1879 Bismarck laid the foundations of the Austro–Germanic Alliance. In this year Zola brought out his novel, *Nana*, in which the future originator of the Entente, then only the Prince of Wales, was introduced as a refined connoisseur of musical-comedy stars. The wind of reaction which had risen after the Franco–Prussian War and the fall of the Paris Commune was still blowing strongly through the politics of Europe. Social Democracy in Germany had already fallen under Bismarck's discriminatory legislation. In 1879 Victor Hugo and Louis Blanc demanded in the French Chamber of Deputies an amnesty for the Communards.

But neither the echoes of parliamentary debates nor those of diplomatic events, not even those of the explosions of dynamite, could be heard in the village of Yanovka where I first saw the light, and where I spent the first nine years of my life. On the boundless steppes of Kherson and of all South Russia was a kingdom of wheat and sheep, living by laws all its own. It was firmly guarded against the invasion of politics by its great open spaces and the absence of roads. Only the numerous barrows on the steppes remained as landmarks of the great migration of nations.

My father was a farmer, first on a small scale and later on a larger one. As a little boy he had left with his parents the Jewish town in the Province of Poltava, where he had been born, when they went to seek their fortune on the free steppes of the South. There were at that time about forty Jewish agricultural colonies in the provinces of Kherson and Ekaterinoslav, with a total population of about 25,000 souls. The Jewish farmers were on an equal footing with the other peasants not only as regards their legal rights (until 1881), but also as regards their property. By indefatigable, cruel toil that spared neither himself nor others, and by hoarding every penny, my father rose in the world.

The registration book was not kept very accurately in the colony of Gromokley, and many entries were made after the date of the events recorded. When the time came for me to enter high school, it appeared that I was still too young for admission. The year of my birth was then changed in the birth certificate from 1879 to 1878; so I always had two records, my official age and the one observed by my family.

For the first nine years of my life I hardly stuck my nose outside my native village. Its name, Yanovka, came from the name of the landlord Yanovsky, from whom the estate had been bought. The old proprietor, Yanovsky, had risen from the ranks to a Colonelcy, had won the favour of the powers that be in the reign of Alexander II, and had been given the choice of one thousand acres of land on the uninhabited steppes of the province of Kherson. He built himself a mud hut thatched with straw, and equally crude farm-buildings. But his farming did not prosper, and after the Colonel's death his family moved to Poltava. My father bought over two hundred and fifty acres of land from Yanovsky and leased about four hundred more. I remember the Colonel's widow well. She was a dried-up little old woman who came once or twice a year to collect her rent from us and to see that everything was in order. We would send our spring wagon to meet her at the station and bring a chair to the front steps to make it easier for her to alight. The phaeton made its appearance at my father's later, after he had acquired driving stallions. The Colonel's widow would be served chicken bouillon and soft-boiled eggs. Walking with my sister in the garden, she would scratch the resin from the fence-posts with her shrivelled fingers and assure her that it was the most delicate sweetmeat in the world.

My father's crops increased, as did the herds of cattle and horses. There was even an attempt to keep Merino sheep, but the venture was unsuccessful; on the other hand there were plenty of pigs. They wandered freely all over the place, rooted everywhere, and completely destroyed the garden. The estate was managed with care, but in an old-fashioned way. One measured profit or loss with the eye. For that very reason it would have been difficult to fix the extent of father's fortune. All of his substance was always either in the ground, or in the crop above, or in the stocks on hand, which were either in bins or on their way to a port. Sometimes in the midst of tea or supper my father would suddenly exclaim: 'Come, write this down! I have received thirteen hundred roubles from the commission merchant. I gave the Colonel's widow six hundred, and four hundred to Dembovsky. Put down, too, that I gave Theodosia Antonovna one hundred roubles when I was in Elizavetgrad last spring.' That is about the way he kept his books. Nevertheless, my father slowly but obstinately kept climbing upwards.

We lived in the little mud house that the Colonel had built. The straw roof harboured countless sparrows' nests under the eaves. The walls on the outside were seamed with deep cracks which were a breeding-place for adders. Sometimes these adders were mistaken for poisonous snakes, and boiling water from the samovar went into the cracks, but to no avail. The low ceilings leaked during a heavy rain, especially in the hall, and pots and basins would be placed on the dirt floor to catch the water. The rooms were small, the windows dim; the floors in the two bedrooms and the nursery were of clay, and bred fleas. The dining-room boasted a wooden floor which was rubbed once a week with yellow sand. But the floor in the main room, which was solemnly named the parlour, though only about eight paces long, was painted. The Colonel's widow stayed here.

Yellow acacias, red and white roses, and in summer a climbing vine, grew around the house. The courtyard was not fenced in at all. A big mud house with a tile roof, which my father had built, contained the machine-shop, the main kitchen, and the servants' quarters. Next to it stood the 'little' wooden barn and beyond that the 'big' barn. Beyond that again came the 'new' barn. All were thatched with reeds. The barns were raised upon stones so that water trickling under them would not mould the grain. In hot or cold weather the dogs, pigs and chickens would take refuge under the barns. There the hens found a quiet place to lay their eggs. I used to fetch out the eggs, crawling in among the stones on my stomach; the space was too small for a grown person to squeeze into. Storks would nest every year on the roof of the 'big' barn. They would raise their red bills to heaven as they swallowed adders and frogs – a terrible sight! Their bodies would wriggle from their bills downward, and it looked as if the snake were eating the stork from the inside.

The barns, divided into bins, held fresh-smelling wheat, rough-prickly barley, smooth, almost liquid flaxseed, the blue-black beads of the winter rape, and light, slender oats. When the children played at hide-and-seek, they were allowed, on occasions when there were special guests, to hide in the barns. Crawling over one of the partitions into a bin, I would scramble up the mound of wheat and slip down on the other side. My arms would be buried to the elbows and my legs to the knees in the sliding mass of wheat, and my shirt and shoes, too often torn, would be filled with grain; the door of the barn would be shut, and someone, for the sake of appearances, would hang a padlock on the outside without snapping it, according to the rules of the game. I would be lying in the cool barn, buried in grain, breathing its dust, and listening to Senya V. or Senya J. or Senya S. or my sister Liza or someone else running about the courtyard, finding the others but not finding me, submerged in the winter-wheat.

The stable, the cowshed, the pigsty, and the chicken-house all stood on the other side of our dwelling. These were all made of mud and straw and twigs, somehow stuck together with clay. The tall well-sweep rose towards heaven about a hundred yards from the house. Beyond the well lay the pond that watered the gardens of the peasants. The spring freshets carried the dam away every year, and it had to be rebuilt with earth and manure and straw. On the hill above the pond stood the mill – a wooden shed which sheltered a ten-horse-power steam-engine and two millstones. Here, during the first years of my childhood, my mother spent the greater part of her working hours. The mill worked not only for our own estate but for the whole neighbourhood as well. The peasants brought their grain in from ten and fifteen miles around and paid a tenth measure for the grinding. In hot weather, on the eve of the threshing season, the mill worked day and night, and when I had learned to count and write I used to weigh the peasants' grain and calculate the price of the grinding. When the harvest was over the mill was closed and the engine went out to thresh. Later a stationary engine was installed in a new stone and tile building. Our old mud house, too, was replaced by a large brick one with a tin roof. But all this happened when I had already reached my seventeenth year. During my last summer holidays I used to calculate the distance between the windows, and the sizes of the doors for our new house, but I never could make the lines meet. On my next visit to the country I saw the stone foundation being built. I never lived in the house itself. It is now used as a Soviet school.

The peasants often used to wait at the mill for weeks to have their grain ground. Those who lived near by would leave their sacks in line and go home. Those who came from far away lived in their wagons, and in rainy weather slept in the mill. One of these peasants once lost a bridle. Someone had seen a boy roving about near a certain horse. The peasants rushed to his father's wagon and looked under the straw; there lay the bridle! The boy's father, a gloomy, bearded peasant, faced the East and crossed himself, swearing that the damned little rascal, the scoundrelly jailbird, had taken it unknown to himself, and that he would take the hide off him for it. But no one believed the father. So the peasant caught his son and began beating him with the stolen bridle. I watched this scene from behind the backs of the grown-ups. The boy screamed and swore he would never steal again. The peasants stood about, gloomily looking on, entirely indifferent to the cries of the boy. They smoked their cigarettes and muttered in their beards that the father was speciously beating his son only for appearances' sake, and that he himself should be flogged too.

Beyond the barns and the sheds for animals extended two enormous sheds hundreds of feet long, one of reeds and the other of straw, built in the shape of a gabled roof resting directly on the ground, without walls. The fresh grain was piled under these sheds, and here the men worked with winnowers and sieves in rainy or windy weather. Beyond the sheds lay the threshing-floor. Across a ravine lay the cow pen, its walls built entirely of dry manure.

All my childish life is connected with the Colonel's mud house and the old sofa in the dining-room there. This sofa was veneered to look like red wood, and on it I sat for tea, for dinner and for supper. Here I played dolls with my sister, and here I would later read. The cover was torn in two places. The smaller hole was near the chair where Ivan Vasilyevich sat, the larger where I sat, next to my father. 'This sofa should have a new cover,' Ivan Vasilyevich used to say.

'It should have had one long ago,' my mother would reply. 'We haven't covered it since the year the Tsar was killed.'

'But you know,' my father would justify himself, 'when one gets to that damned city, one runs here and there, the cab costs money, one is thinking all the time about how to get back quickly to the farm, and forgets all about what one came to buy.'

A rough, unpainted rafter stretched across the low ceiling of the dining-room, and on this the most varied objects found their resting-place: plates of provisions for safekeeping from the cat, nails, string, books, ink-bottles stoppered with paper, a penholder with an old rusty pen. There was no superfluity of pens at Yanovka. There were times when I made a pen for myself out of wood with the help of a table-knife, for copying horses out of old numbers of the illustrated magazine, *Field*. Up under the ceiling, where the chimney went out, lived the cat. There she raised her kittens, bravely jumping down with them in her teeth when it grew too hot up there. If a guest were tall he always hit the rafter with his head when he rose from the table, so that we had acquired the habit of pointing upwards and saying: 'Mind your head!'

The most striking object in the parlour was an old spinet that occupied at least a quarter of the room. I can remember when it appeared. The wife of a bankrupt landowner, who lived some fifteen miles away, moved into town and sold her household goods. From her we bought the sofa, three bent-wood chairs, and the old tumble-down spinet with broken strings that had been standing in an outhouse for years. My father paid sixteen roubles for it and brought it to Yanovka on a cart. A pair of dead mice were found in it when it was overhauled in the machine-shop. The shop was occupied by the spinet for several winter weeks. Ivan Vasilyevich cleaned it, glued it, polished it, found new strings, and put them in and tuned them. All the keys were replaced, and the voice of the spinet resounded in the parlour. It was feeble, but irresistible. Ivan Vasilyevich transferred his magic fingers from the stops of his accordion to the keys of the spinet, and played the Kamarinskaya, polkas, and 'Mein Lieber Augustine'. My oldest sister began to take music lessons. My oldest brother had taken violin lessons for several months in Elizavetgrad, and he would strum occasionally. And at last I too would play, with one finger, from my brother's violin music. I had no ear, and my love of music always remained helpless and unexpressed.

In the springtime the courtyard changed into a sea of mud. Ivan Vasilyevich would make a pair of wooden galoshes, or rather buskins, for himself, and I used to watch him with delight, stridling along a foot above his usual height. In time the old saddler appears upon the scene. No one, it seems, knows his name. He is more than eighty years old and has served twenty-five years in the army of Nicholas I. Huge and broad-shouldered, with white beard and hair, he scarcely moves his heavy feet as he shuffles across to the barn, where his itinerant work-shop has been installed. 'My legs are getting weak,' he has been complaining for the past ten years. On the contrary, his hands, which smell of leather, are stronger than pincers. His nails resemble the ivory keys of the spinet, and are very sharp at the ends.

'Would you like me to show you Moscow?' asks the saddler. Of course I should! The old man puts his thumbs under my ears and raises me up. His dreadful nails press into me, and I am offended and hurt. I kick my heels and try to get down. 'If you don't want to see Moscow, you needn't!' In spite of being offended I do not run away. 'Hello!' says the old man, climbing the barn stairs. 'Look what's here in the loft!' I suspect a trick and hesitate to go in. It turns out that Constantine, the youngest miller, is in the loft with Katy, the cook. Both are handsome, jolly, and hardworking. 'When are you and Katy going to get married?' asks their mistress. 'Why, we are getting on very well as we are,' answers Constantine. 'It costs ten roubles to get married, and I should rather buy Katy a pair of boots.'

After the hot, tense summer of the steppe is over, and its toilsome climax of reaping and harvesting has passed, comes the early autumn to take stock of a year's penal labour. The threshing is now in full swing. The centre of activity has moved to the threshing-floor beyond the sheds, a quarter of a mile from the house. A cloud of dust floats over the threshing-floor. The drum of the thresher is whining. Philip the miller, wearing glasses, is standing beside it. His black beard is covered with grey dust. The men are carrying in sheaves from the wagon. He takes them without looking at them, unties them, shakes them apart, and throws them into the thresher. At each armful the thresher growls like a dog with a bone. The straw-shaker throws out the straw, playing with it as it goes. The chaff pours out of a pipe at the side and is carried to the straw stack on a drag, with me standing on its wooden tailboard and holding on by the rope reins. 'Mind you don't fall!' cries my father. And down I go for the tenth time. I fall now into the straw, now into the chaff. The grey dust cloud thickens over the threshing-floor, the engine groans, the hulls get into one's shirt and nose and make one sneeze. 'Hey, Philip! not so fast!' warns my father from below, as the thresher growls too fiercely. I lift the drag. It slips out of my hands and falls with its whole weight on my finger. The pain is so intense that my head swims. I slip to one side so that the men shall not see me crying, and then run home. My mother pours cold water on my hand and bandages my finger, but the pain does not diminish. The wound festers during several days of torture.

Sacks of wheat now fill the barns and the sheds and are piled in heaps under tarpaulins in the courtyard. The master himself often stands at the sieve and shows the men how to turn the hoop, so as to blow away the chaff, and how, with one sharp push, to empty the clean grain into a pile without leaving any behind. In the sheds and barns, where there is shelter from the wind, the winnower and the tare-separators are working. The grain is cleaned there and made ready for the market.

And now merchants come with copper vessels and scales in neatly painted boxes. They test the grain and name a price, pressing earnest-money on my father. We treat them with respect and give them tea and cakes, but we do not sell them the grain. They are but small fry; the master has outgrown these channels of trade. He has his own commission merchant in Nikolayev. 'Let it be awhile, grain doesn't ask to be fed!' he says.

A week later a letter comes from Nikolayev, or sometimes a telegram, offering five kopecks a pood more. 'So we have found a thousand roubles!' says the master. 'And they don't grow on every bush!' But sometimes the reverse happens; sometimes the price falls. The secret power of the world market makes itself felt even in Yanovka. Then my father says gloomily, returning from Nikolayev: 'It seems that – what is the name? – the Argentine, sent out too much wheat this year.'

Winter was a peaceful time in the country. Only the machine-shop and the mill were still really active. For fuel we burned straw which the servants brought in huge armfuls, scattering it along the way and sweeping it up after themselves. It was jolly to stuff this straw into the stoves and watch it blaze up. Once Uncle Gregory found my younger sister and me alone in the dining-room, which was filled with blue charcoal fumes. I was turning round and round in the middle of the room, not knowing where I was, and at my uncle's cry I fell in a dead faint. We often found ourselves alone in the house on winter days, especially during my father's absences, when all the work of the place fell on my mother. In the dusk my little sister and I used to sit side by side on the sofa, pressed close together, wide-eyed and afraid to move.

A giant would come out of the cold outside into the dark dining-room, shuffling his huge boots, and wrapped in an enormous greatcoat with a huge collar, and wearing a huge hat. His hands were encased in huge mittens. Large icicles hung from his beard and moustache, and his great voice would boom out in the darkness: 'Good evening!' Squeezed together in a corner of the sofa, we would be afraid to answer him. Then the monster would light a match and see us in our corner. The giant would turn out to be one of our neighbours. Sometimes the loneliness in the dining-room became absolutely unbearable, and then I ran out into the outer hall in spite of the cold, opened the front door, stepped out onto the big stone that lay on the threshold, and screamed into the darkness: 'Mashka! Mashka! Come into the dining-room!' over and over again. Maska was busy with her own affairs in the kitchen, in the servants' room, or somewhere else. My mother would come in at last, perhaps from the mill, light a lamp, and the samovar would be brought in.

We usually sat in the dining-room in the evening until we fell asleep. People came and went in the dining-room, taking or returning keys, making arrangements of various kinds, and planning the work for the following day. My younger sister Olya, my older sister Liza, the chambermaid and myself then lived a life of our own, which was dependent on the life of the grown-ups, and subdued by theirs. Sometimes a chance word of one of the elders would waken some special reminiscence in us.

Then I would wink at my little sister, she would give a low giggle, and the grown-ups would look absent-mindedly at her. I would wink again, and she would try to stifle her laughter under the oilcloth and would hit her head against the table. This would infect me and sometimes my older sister too, who, with thirteen-year-old dignity, vacillated between the grown-ups and the children. If our laughter became too uncontrollable,

I was obliged to slip under the table and crawl among the feet of the grown-ups, and, stepping on the cat's tail, rush out into the next room, which was the nursery. Once back in the dining-room, it all would begin over again. My fingers would grow so weak from laughing that I could not hold a glass. My head, my lips, my hands, my feet, every inch of me would be shaking with laughter. 'Whatever is the matter with you?' my mother would ask. The two circles of life, the upper and the lower, would touch for a moment. The grown-ups would look at the children with a question in their eyes that was sometimes friendly but more often full of irritation. Then our laughter, taken unawares, would break out tempestuously into the open. Olya's head would go under the table again, I would throw my-self on the sofa, Liza would bite her upper lip, and the chamber-maid would slip out of the door.

'Go to bed!' the grown-ups would cry.

But we would not go. We would hide in corners, afraid to look at one another. My little sister would be carried away, but I usually went to sleep on the sofa. Someone would pick me up in his arms and take me out. Then I would perhaps give a loud yell, imagining, half-asleep, that I was being attacked by dogs, that snakes were hissing below me, or that robbers were carrying me away into the woods. The child's nightmare would break into the life of the grown-ups. I would be quieted on the way to bed; they would pat and kiss me. So I would go from laughter into sleep, from nightmares into wakefulness, and back into sleep again in a feather-bed in the warm bedroom.

Winter was the family time of year. There came days when my mother and father hardly left the house. My older brother and sister came home for Christmas from their schools. On Sundays, Ivan Vasilyevich, all washed and shaved, and armed with a comb and scissors, would cut first my father's hair, then Sasha's, and then mine. Sasha asks:

'Can you cut hair *à la Capoul*, Ivan Vasilyevich?' Every one looks at Sasha, and he explains that in Elizavetgrad the barber once cut his hair beautifully *à la Capoul*, but that next day the supervisor gave him a severe reprimand.

After the hair-cutting is over we sit down to dinner, my father and Ivan Vasilyevich in armchairs at each end of the table, the children on the sofa, and my mother opposite them. Ivan Vasilyevich took his meals with us until he was married. In winter we ate slowly and sat talking afterwards. Ivan Vasilyevich would smoke and blow ingenious rings. Sometimes Sasha or Liza was made to read aloud. My father would doze in the recess of the stove. Once in a while in the evening we played old-maid, from which a great deal of noise and laughter resulted, and sometimes a little quarrelling. We thought it particularly amusing to cheat my father, who played carelessly, and laughed when he lost. My mother, on the other hand, played better, and would grow excited and watch my oldest brother sharply to see that he was not cheating her.

It was twenty-three kilometres from Yanovka to the nearest post-office, and more than thirty-five to the railroad. From there it was a long way again to the Government offices, to the stores and to a civic centre, and still farther to the world with its great events. Life at Yanovka was regulated entirely by the rhythm of the toil on the farm. Nothing else mattered, nothing but the price of grain in the world market. We never saw any magazines or newspapers in the country in those days. That followed later, when I had become a high-school boy. We got letters only on special occasions. Sometimes a neighbour would find a letter for us at Bobrinetz and carry it in his pocket for a week or two. A letter was an event; a telegram was a catastrophe. Someone explained to me that telegrams came on wires, but with my own eyes I saw a man on horseback bring a telegram from Bobrinetz for which my father had to pay two roubles and fifty kopecks. A telegram was a piece of paper, like a letter. There were words written on it in pencil. Did the wind blow it along a wire? I was told that it came by electricity. That was still worse. Uncle Abram once carefully explained to me: 'The current comes over the wire and makes marks on a ribbon. Repeat what I have said.' I repeated: 'Current over the wire and marks on a ribbon.'

'Do you understand?'

'Yes, I understand, but how do they make a letter out of it?' I asked, thinking of the telegraph blank which had come from Bobrinetz.

'The letter comes separately,' my uncle answered. I puzzled for a moment and then asked: 'And why do they need the current if the letter comes by a man on horseback?' But here my uncle lost patience. 'Oh, let that letter alone!' he cried. 'I try to explain to you about telegrams and you begin on letters!' So the question remained unanswered.

Paulina Petrovna, a lady from Bobrinetz, came to stay with us. She had long ear-rings and a curl on her forehead. Later my mother took her back to Bobrinetz and I went with them. When we had passed the mound that marks the eleventh verst, a row of telegraph poles appeared, and the wires were humming.

'How do telegrams come?' I asked my mother.

'Ask Paulina Petrovna,' my mother answered, at a loss. 'She will explain it to you.'

Paulina Petrovna explained:

'The marks on the ribbon stand for letters. The operator copies them on paper, and the paper is sent by a man on horseback.' I could understand that.

'But how can the current go without any one seeing it?' I asked, looking at the wire.

'The current goes inside,' answered Paulina Petrovna. 'All those wires are made like little tubes and the current runs along inside.'

I could understand that too, and was satisfied for a long time afterwards. The electro-magnetic fluid which my teacher of physics told me about four years later seemed a much less reasonable explanation to me.

My father and mother lived out their hard-working lives with some friction, but very happily on the whole. My mother came from a family of townspeople who looked down upon farmers, with their rough hands. But my father had been handsome and graceful in his youth, with a manly, energetic face. He succeeded in getting together the means that later enabled him to buy Yanovka. The young woman who had been taken from the city and flung out onto the lonely steppes found it difficult at first to adjust herself to the stern conditions of life on a farm. But she succeeded at last in adapting herself perfectly, and once in the

traces, she did not relinquish her toil for forty-five years. Of the
eight children born of this marriage, four survived. I was the
fifth in order of birth. Four died in infancy, of diphtheria and of
scarlet fever, deaths almost as unnoticed as was the life of those
who survived. The land, the cattle, the poultry, the mill, took all
my parents' time; there was none left for us. The seasons succeeded one another, and waves of farm work swept over domestic
affection. There was no display of tenderness in our family,
especially during my early years, but there was a strong comrade-
ship of labour between my father and mother.

'Give your mother a chair!' my father would cry as soon as
my mother crossed the threshold, white with dust from the
mill.

'Mashka! Light the samovar quick,' my mother would command even before she had reached the house. 'Your master will
soon be in from the fields.' Both knew what it was to have
reached the limit of physical exhaustion.

My father was undoubtedly superior to my mother, both in
intellect and character. He was deeper, more reserved, and more
tactful. He had an unusually good eye both for things and people.
My father and mother bought very little, especially during our
early years; they both knew how to save every penny. My father
never made a mistake in what he bought: cloth, hats, shoes,
horses or machinery, he always got his money's worth. 'I don't
like money,' he once said to me later, as if apologizing for being
so mean, 'but I like it less when there is none of it. It is bad to
need money and not have any.' He spoke a broken mixture of
the Russian and Ukrainian tongues, with a preponderance of
the Ukrainian. He judged people by their manners, their faces
and their habits, and he always judged them correctly.

'I don't like that student of yours,' he would sometimes say
of one of our guests. 'Confess it, don't you yourself think he is
an idiot?' Our feelings would be hurt for our guest's sake, but
we knew in our hearts that our father was right. After visiting
once in a family, he summed up the domestic situation there
very correctly.

After bearing many children and after much hard work, my
mother once fell ill, and went to see a doctor in Kharkoff. Such

a journey was a great event, and many preparations were made for it. My mother went well supplied with money, jars of butter, bags of sweet biscuits, fried chicken and so forth. She had great expenses ahead of her. The doctor's fee was three roubles a visit. My mother and father always spoke of this to each other and to their guests with uplifted hands and an expression on their faces that signified their respect for the benefits of science, their regret that they cost so dear, and their pride that they were able to pay such an unheard-of price for them. We awaited my mother's return with great excitement. She came back in a new dress that looked incredibly grand in our dining-room at Yanovka.

When we children were young, my father was quieter and gentler with us than my mother. My mother would often lose her temper with us, sometimes without reason, and would vent on us her fatigue or her chagrin over some domestic failure. We always found it more remunerative to ask our father for favours than our mother. But as time went on my father grew sterner. The cause of this lay in the hardships of his life, in the cares which grew as his business increased, and more especially in the conditions growing out of the agrarian crisis of the eighties, as well as in the disappointment which his children gave him.

My mother loved to read during the long winters, when Yanovka was swept by the snow drifting from all the corners of the steppe and rising over the windows. She would sit on a small three-cornered seat in the dining-room with her feet on a chair before her, or, when the early winter twilight fell, she would move into my father's armchair near the small, frosty window, and read in a loud whisper from some worn novel out of the library at Bobrinetz, following the words with her toil-worn finger. She often grew confused, and faltered over some especially long sentence. Sometimes an explanation from any one of the children would throw an entirely new light for her on the story she had been reading. But she continued to read persever-ingly and untiringly, and on quiet winter days we could hear her monotonous whisper as far as the front hall.

My father learned to spell out words even when he was quite

an old man, in order to be able to read at least the titles of my books. I followed him with excitement in Berlin in 1910, when he perseveringly tried to understand my book on German Social Democracy.

The October revolution found my father a very prosperous man. My mother had died in 1910, but my father lived to see the rule of the Soviets. At the height of the civil war, which raged with especial fury in the South and was accompanied by constant changes of government, the old man of seventy was obliged to walk hundreds of miles to find shelter in Odessa. The Reds were a menace to him because he was rich; the Whites persecuted him because he was my father. After the South had been freed of White soldiers by the Soviet troops, he was enabled to come to Moscow. He had lost all his savings in the revolution. For more than a year he ran a small state mill near Moscow. The Commissar of Food at that time, Tzyurupa, used to enjoy chatting with him on agricultural subjects. My father died of typhus in the spring of 1922, at the very moment when I was reading my report at the Fourth Congress of the Communist International.

A very important, in fact the most important, place at Ya-novka was the machine-shop, where Ivan Vasilyevich Gryeben worked. He came to work there when he was twenty, the year that I was born. He addressed all the children, even the older ones, as 'thou', while we spoke to him respectfully as 'you'. When he had to report for military service my father went with him. They gave someone a bribe, and Gryeben stayed at Yanovka. This Ivan Vasilyevich was handsome and gifted. He wore a dark reddish moustache and a beard cut in the French fashion. His technical knowledge was comprehensive. He could rebuild an engine, repair a boiler, turn a metal or a wooden ball, cast a brass bearing, make a spring carriage, mend a clock, tune a piano, upholster furniture, or make a bicycle minus the tyres. It was on a bicycle of his manufacture that I learned to ride in the year when I was between the primary and first grades. The neighbouring German settlers would bring in their seed-drills and binders to be repaired by him, and would invite him to go with them to buy a threshing-machine or a steam-engine. People came to my father for advice about farming, and to Ivan Vasilyevich for advice about machinery. There were assistants as well as apprentices employed in the machine-shop. In many ways I was the pupil of these apprentices.

I was sometimes allowed to cut the threads of nuts and screws in the machine-shop. I liked this work because I could see the direct result in my hands. I sometimes tried to grind the material for paint on a round, smooth stone, but I soon tired, and would ask more and more frequently whether the work was nearly finished. Stirring the thick mixture with his finger, Ivan Vasilyevich would shake his head, and I would hand over the stone to one of the apprentices.

Ivan Vasilyevich would sometimes sit down on a chest in the corner behind the work-bench, a tool in hand. He would smoke and gaze into the distance, perhaps pondering something or remembering something or simply resting without thinking at all. At such times I used to sit down beside him and gently curl his thick, auburn moustache around my finger, or examine his hands, those unmistakable hands of the artisan. Their skin was all covered with little black spots that he had got from cutting millstones. His fingers were as tenacious as roots, but not hard. They were broad at the tips but very supple, and his thumb turned far backwards, forming an arch. Each finger was self-conscious, and lived and acted by itself, but together they formed a very effective labour-union. I was still quite young, but already I could feel that that hand did not hold a hammer or a pair of pliers as other hands did. A deep scar encircled his left thumb. Ivan Vasilyevich had very nearly cut it off with a hatchet the day I was born. It was hanging almost by the skin alone. My father had happened to see the young mechanic lay his hand on a board, about to chop his thumb off altogether. 'Stop a moment!' he had cried. 'Your finger will grow on again!'

'It will grow on again, you think?' the mechanic had asked, and laid the hatchet aside. And the thumb had grown on, and again worked well, except that it did not turn back as far as the other.

Ivan Vasilyevich once made a shotgun out of an old Berdan

rifle and tried his skill at marksmanship. Everyone in turn tried at a distance of several paces to put out a candle by striking the primer. Not everyone succeeded. My father chanced to pass by. When he raised the gun to his shoulder, his hands trembled and he held it without assurance. But he put the candle out at the first trial. He had a good eye for everything, and Ivan Vasilyevich knew this. There were never any altercations between them, though my father would scold the other workmen and find fault with their work.

I never lacked occupation in the machine-shop. I would tug the handle of the blower which Ivan Vasilyevich had made according to a plan of his own. The ventilator was out of sight in the loft, and this excited surprise in everyone who saw it. I would turn the lathe till I was exhausted, especially when croquet-balls of acacia wood were being made. The conversations that took place in the machine-shop seemed each more interesting than the last. Propriety did not always rule there – or rather I might say that it never ruled there. My horizon was widened there hourly. Foma told stories about the estate where he used to work, and about the adventures of the ladies and gentlemen there. I must say that he was not very complimentary to them. Philip, the miller, would follow with stories of army life. Ivan Vasilyevich would ask questions, restrain the others, or supplement what they said.

The fireman Yashka was a surly, red-haired man of thirty who never kept any position for long. Something would come over him, and he would disappear either in the spring or in the autumn, and return six months later. He did not drink often, but periodically. He passionately loved hunting, but nevertheless he sold his gun for drink. Foma told how Yashka had come into a store in Bobrinetz barefooted, his feet plastered with black mud, and had asked for a box of caps. He purposely spilled the caps on the floor, and stooped to pick them up. In doing so, he stepped on some of them with his muddy feet, and went out taking them with him.

'Is Foma lying?' asked Ivan Vasilyevich.

'Why do you think he is lying?' asked Yashka. 'I hadn't a penny to pay for them.'

This seemed to me a good way of getting something you wanted, and one worthy of imitation.

'Our Ignat has come,' Mashka, the housemaid, came in to tell us. 'But Dunka isn't here, she has gone home for the holiday.'

We called the fireman Ignat 'our' Ignat, to distinguish him from humpbacked Ignat, who had been an Elder before Taras came. 'Our' Ignat had gone to be drafted for military service – Ivan Vasilyevich himself had measured his chest and had said, 'They wouldn't take him for anything!' The examination board put Ignat into the hospital for a month, on trial. There he made the acquaintance of some workmen from the city, and resolved to try his luck in a factory. When he came back he was wearing city boots and a sheepskin coat with a front embroidered in colours. Ignat spent the whole day after his return in the machine-shop, telling the men about the city and about the work, conditions, machinery and wages he had found there.

'Of course, it's a factory,' began Foma meditatively.

'A factory isn't a machine-shop!' observed Philip. And they all looked thoughtful, as if seeing beyond the machine-shop.

'Is there much machinery in the city?' asked Victor eagerly.

'A whole forest of it!'

I listened with all my ears, and saw in my mind's eye a factory with machines in it as thick as trees in a forest; machines to the right, to the left, before, behind; machines everywhere. And in the midst of it all I pictured Ignat standing with a tight leather belt round his waist. Ignat had also acquired a watch, which was passed from hand to hand. In the evening Ignat walked up and down the courtyard with my father, followed by the steward. I was there too, running now beside my father and now beside Ignat.

'Well, and how do you live?' asked my father, 'Do you buy your bread and milk? Do you rent a room?'

'To be sure, you have to pay for absolutely everything,' Ignat assented, 'but the wages aren't the same as they are here.'

'I know they aren't the same, but they all go for food.'

'No,' answered Ignat stoutly. 'I have been able to save enough in six months to buy some clothes and a watch. Here it is in my pocket.' And he pulled out his watch again. The argument was unanswerable, and my father said nothing. Then he asked again:

'Have you been drinking, Ignat? With so many teachers around you it should not be hard to learn!'

'Why, I never even think of vodka.'

'And are you going to take Dunka back with you, Ignat?' my mother asked him.

Ignat smiled a little guiltily and did not answer.

'Oh, I see, I see,' said my mother. 'So you have already found some city slut! Confess to it, you scoundrel!'

So Ignat went away again from Yanovka.

We children were forbidden to go into the servants' room, but who could prevent our doing so? There was always much that was new there. Our cook for a long time was a woman with high cheek-bones and a sunken nose. Her husband, who was an old man and was paralysed down one side of his face, was our shepherd. We called them Muscovites because they came from one of the governments of the interior. This couple had a pretty little daughter eight years old, with blue eyes and blonde hair. She was used to seeing her father and mother forever quarrelling.

On Sundays the girls used to hunt for lice in the boys' hair or in their own. On a pile of straw in the servants' room the two Tatyanas would be lying side by side, Big Tatyana and Little Tatyana. Afanasy, the stable boy, son of Pud the steward and brother to Paraska, the cook, would sit down between them, throwing his leg over Little Tatyana and leaning against Big Tatyana.

'What a Mohammedan you are!' the young steward would cry enviously. 'Isn't it time to water the horses?'

This red-haired Afanasy and the black-haired Mutuzok were my persecutors. If I chanced to come in while the pudding or the porridge was being handed around, they would cry laughingly: 'Come on, Lyova, and have dinner with us!' or, 'Why don't you ask your mother for a bit of chicken for us, Lyova?' I would feel embarrassed and go out without answering. At Easter my mother was wont to bake cakes for the workmen and colour eggs for them. Aunt Raisa was an artist at painting eggs. She once brought some gaily painted eggs with her from Gromokley and gave me two. We used to roll our eggs down the slides behind the cellar to see which was the strongest. Once I was left to the end; only Afanasy and I remained.

'Aren't these pretty?' I asked, showing him my painted eggs.

'Yes, they are pretty enough,' answered Afanasy, with an air of indifference. 'Let me see which is the strongest.'

I did not dare to refuse the challenge. Afanasy struck my egg and it cracked on top.

'So that one is mine!' said Afanasy. 'Now let's try the other.' I obediently offered him my second painted egg.

Afanasy struck again.

'That one is mine too!'

Afanasy picked up both eggs in a businesslike way and went off without looking back. I watched him go in astonishment, and felt very much like crying, but there was nothing to be done about it.

There were very few permanent labourers who worked all the year round on the estate. Most of them – and there were hundreds of these on the estate in years of large crops – were temporary only, and comprised men from Kiev, Chernigov, and Poltava, who were hired until the first of October. In the years when the harvest was good, the Province of Kherson alone would require two or three hundred thousand of these labourers. The reapers received forty to fifty roubles for the four summer months and their board. The women received from twenty to thirty roubles. The open field was their home in fine weather, in bad weather they took shelter under the haystacks. For dinner they had vegetable soup and porridge, for supper millet soup. They never had any meat. Vegetable fat was all they ever got, and that in small quantities. This diet was sometimes a ground for complaint. The labourers would leave the fields and collect in the courtyard. They would lie face downward in the shade of the barns, brandishing their bare, cracked straw-pricked feet in the air, and wait to see what would happen. Then my father would give them some clabber, or water-melons, or half a sack of dried fish, and they would go back to work again, often singing. These were the conditions on all the farms. We had wiry old reapers who had been coming to work for us ten years on end, knowing that work was always assured them. These received a few roubles more than the others and a glass of vodka from time to time, as they set the standard of efficiency for the others. Some of them appeared at the head of a long family procession. They walked from their own provinces on foot, taking a whole month to make the journey, living on crusts of bread, and spending the nights in the market-places. One summer all the labourers fell ill in an epidemic of night-blindness. They moved about in the twilight with their hands stretched out before them. My mother's nephew, who was visiting us, wrote an article to the newspapers about it. It was spoken of in the Zemstvo*, and an inspector was sent to Yanovka. My father and mother were vexed with the newspaper correspondent, who was much liked, and he himself was sorry that he had begun it. Nothing unpleasant came of it all, however. The inspector decided that the sickness was due to a lack of fat in the diet, and that it was common all over the province as the labourers were fed in the same manner everywhere and sometimes even worse.

In the machine-shop, the kitchen, and the backyard a life stretched before me which was different from and more spacious than the one I led in my own family. The film of life has no end, and I was only at the beginning. No one took any notice of my presence when I was little. Tongues wagged freely, especially when Ivan Vasilyevich and the steward were absent, for they half belonged to the ruling class. By the light of the blacksmith's forge or the kitchen fire, I often saw my parents, my relatives and our neighbours in quite a new light. Many of the conversations I overheard when I was young will remain in my memory as long as I live. Many of them, perhaps, laid the foundation of my attitude towards society today.

*An elective rural organization in charge of the administration of country districts. – *Translator*.

2

Our Neighbours and My First School

A verst or less from Yanovka lay the property of the Dembovskys. My father leased land from them and was connected with
them by many business ties. Theodosia Antonovna, the owner,
was an old Polish woman who had once been a governess. After
the death of her first rich husband she married her manager,
Kasimir Antonovich, who was twenty years younger than herself. Theodosia Antonovna had not lived with her second husband for years, though he still managed the property. Kasimir
Antonovich was a tall, bearded, noisy and jolly Pole. He often
had tea with us at the big oval table, and would uproariously tell
the same silly story over and over again, repeating individual
words and emphasizing them by snapping his fingers.

Kasimir Antonovich kept some hives of bees at a distance
from the stable and cowsheds, since bees cannot bear the smell
of horses. The bees made honey from the fruit trees, the white
acacias, the winter rape, and the buckwheat – in a word, they
were in the midst of abundance. From time to time Kasimir
Antonovich would bring us two plates covered with a napkin,
between which lay a piece of honeycomb full of clear, golden
honey.

One day Ivan Vasilyevich and I went together to get some
pigeons for breeding purposes from Kasimir Antonovich. In a
corner room of the great empty house, Kasimir Antonovich gave
us tea, butter, honey, and curds on large plates that smelled
damp. I sat drinking tea out of my saucer and listening to the
lagging conversation. 'Shan't we be late?' I whispered to Ivan
Vasilyevich. 'No, wait a little longer. We must give them time
to settle down in their loft. You can see them up there still.' I
grew weary. At last we climbed up into the loft over the barn,
carrying a lantern. 'Look out now!' cried Kasimir Antonovich

to me. The loft was long and dark, with rafters in all directions. It had a strong smell of mice, bees, cobwebs and birds. Someone put out the lantern. 'There they are! Grab them!' Kasimir Antonovich whispered. An infernal uproar broke loose; the loft was filled with a whirlwind of wings. It seemed to me for a moment that the end of the world had come, and that we were all lost. Gradually I came to, and heard an anxious voice saying: 'Here's another! This way, this way – that's right, put him in the sack.' Ivan Vasilyevich had brought a sack along, and all the way back we had behind us a continuation of the scene in the loft. We made a pigeon-loft over the machine-shop. I climbed up there ten times a day after that, taking water, wheat, millet and crumbs to the pigeons. A week later I found two eggs in a nest. But before we were able fully to appreciate this important event, the pigeons began to return to their old home, one pair at a time. Only three pairs who had had their wings cut were left behind, and these flew away too when their wings had grown out, leaving the beautiful loft we had made for them, with its nests and its system of halls. Thus ended our venture in raising pigeons.

My father leased some land near Elizavetgrad from Mrs T., who was a widow of forty with a strong character. In constant attendance on her was a priest, also widowed, who was a lover of cards and of music and of many other things besides. Mrs T., accompanied by the priest, once came to Yanovka to see about the terms of our contract with her. We assigned the sitting-room and the room adjoining it to them, and gave them fried chicken, cherry wine and cherry dumplings for dinner. After the meal was over I stayed in the parlour and saw the priest sit down beside her and laughingly whisper something into her ear. Turning back the front of his coat, he took a silver cigarette-case with a monogram out of the pocket of his striped trousers and lit a cigarette, lightly blowing rings of smoke. He then told us, while his mistress was out of the room, that she read only the dialogue in novels. Everyone smiled politely, but refrained from criticism, for we knew that he would not only repeat it to her, but add to it something of his own invention.

My father began to lease land from Mrs T. in partnership

with Kasimir Antonovich. The latter's wife died at about this time, and a sudden change occurred in him. The grey hairs disappeared from his beard; he wore a starched collar, and a tie with a tie-pin, and carried a lady's photograph in his pocket. Although, like everyone else, Kasimir Antonovich laughed at my Uncle Gregory, it was to him that he turned in all affairs of the heart. He took the photograph out of its envelope and showed it to him.

'Look!' he cried to Uncle Gregory, almost fainting with ecstasy. 'I said to this beautiful being: "Lady, your lips are made for kisses!"' Kasimir Antonovich married the beautiful being, but he died suddenly after a year and a half of married life. A bull caught him on his horns in the courtyard of the T. estate and gored him to death.

The brothers F. owned a property of thousands of acres about eight versts from ours. Their house resembled a palace and was richly furnished, with many guest-rooms, a billiard-room and much besides. The two F. brothers, Lev and Ivan, had inherited all this from their father Timothy and were gradually going through their inheritance. The administration of the property was in the hands of a steward, and the books showed a deficit, in spite of double-entry bookkeeping.

'Davyd Leontiyevich is richer than I am, if he does live in a mud house!' the elder brother would say of my father, and when we repeated this to my father, he was obviously pleased. The younger brother, Ivan, once rode through Yanovka with two of his huntsmen, their guns on their backs, and a pack of white wolfhounds at their heels. This had never been seen before at Yanovka.

'They will soon go through their money at that rate!' said my father disapprovingly.

The seal of doom was on these families of the Province of Kherson. They were all progressing with extraordinary rapidity, and all in the same direction: towards downfall. And this was true in spite of the many differences between them, for some belonged to the hereditary nobility, some were Government officials endowed with land for their services, some were Poles, some were Germans, and some were Jews who had been able to buy land before 1881. The founders of many of these steppe dynasties were men prominent in their way, successful, and robbers by nature.

I had never known any of them, however, as they had all died during the early eighties. Many of them had begun life with a broken penny but with the knack of cleverness, even if it was sometimes that of a criminal, and they had acquired tremendous possessions. The second generation of these people grew up as a new-made aristocracy, with a knowledge of French, with billiard-rooms in their houses, with all sorts of bad ways to their credit. The agricultural crisis of the eighties, brought on by trans-Atlantic competition, hit them unmercifully. They fell like dead leaves. The third generation produced a lot of half-rotten scoundrels, worthless fellows, unbalanced, premature invalids.

The highest peak of aristocratic ruin was reached in the Ghertopanov family. A large village and a whole county were called by their name. The whole countryside had once belonged to them. The old heir to it all had now only one thousand acres left, and these were mortgaged over and over again. My father leased this land, and the rents went into the bank. Ghertopanov lived by writing petitions, complaints and letters for the peasants. When he came to see us he used to hide tobacco and lumps of sugar up his sleeve, and his wife did the same. With drivelling lips she would tell us stories of her youth with its serfs, its grand pianos, its silks and its perfumery. Their two sons grew up almost illiterate. The younger, Victor, was an apprentice in our machine-shop.

A family of Jewish landowners lived about six versts from Yanovka. Their name was M—sky. They were a queer, mad lot. Their father, Moissey Kharitonovich, was sixty years old, and was distinguished by having received an education of the aristocratic variety. He spoke French fluently, played the piano, and knew something about literature. His left hand was weak, but his right hand was fit, he said, to play in a concert. His neglected finger-nails, striking the keys of our old spinet, made a noise like castanets. Beginning with a Polonaise by Oginsky, he would pass imperceptibly into a Rhapsody by Liszt and suddenly slip into the 'Maiden's Prayer'; his conversation was equally erratic. He would often stop in the midst of his playing and get up and go to the mirror. Then, if no one was by, he would singe his beard on all sides with his burning cigarette, with the idea of keeping it tidy. He smoked incessantly, and sighed as he did so, as if he disliked it. He had not spoken to his heavy, old wife for fifteen years. His son David was thirty-five years old. He invariably wore a white bandage over one side of his face, showing above it a red, twitching eye. David was an unsuccessful suicide. When he was in military service, he had insulted an officer on duty. His officer had struck him. David gave the officer a slap in the face, ran into the barracks, and tried to shoot himself with his rifle. The bullet went through his cheek, and for that reason he now wore that inevitable white bandage. The guilty soldier was threatened with a stern court martial, but the patriarch of the house of M—sky was still alive at that time – old Khariton, rich, powerful, illiterate, despotic. He roused the whole countryside and had his grandson declared irresponsible. Perhaps, after all, it was not far from the truth! From that time on, David lived with a pierced cheek and the passport of a lunatic.

The M—sky family were still on the downward path at the time I first knew them. During my earliest years, Moissey Kharitonovich used to come to see us in a phaeton drawn by fine carriage horses. When I was tiny, perhaps four or five years old, I visited the M—sky family with my oldest brother. They had a large, well-kept garden, with – actually! – peacocks walking about in it. I saw these marvellous creatures there for the first time in my life, with crowns on their capricious heads, lovely little mirrors in their tails, and spurs on their legs. The peacocks vanished in after years, and much more went with them; the garden fence fell to pieces, the cattle broke down the fruit-trees and the flowers. Moissey Kharitonovich now came to Yanovka in a wagon drawn by farm horses. The sons made an effort to bring the property up, but as farmers, not as gentlemen. 'We shall buy some old nags and drive them in the morning, as Bronstein does!'

'They won't succeed!' said my father. David was sent to the Fair at Elizavetgrad to buy the 'old nags'. He walked about the

Fair, appraising the horses with the eye of a cavalryman, and chose a troika. He came home late in the evening. The house was full of guests in their light summer clothes. Abram went out onto the porch with a lamp in his hand to look at the horses. A crowd of ladies, students and young people followed him. David suddenly felt that he was in his element and extolled the good points of each horse, especially of the one which he said resembled a young lady. Abram scratched his beard and said: 'The horses are all right.' It ended in a picnic. David took the slippers off a pretty young lady, filled them with beer, and held them to his lips.

'You aren't going to drink it?' cried the girl, blushing either with alarm or with delight.

'If I wasn't afraid to shoot myself –' answered our hero, pouring the contents of the slipper down his throat.

'Don't always be boasting of that exploit of yours!' unexpectedly retorted his usually silent mother. She was a big, flabby woman on whom fell all the burden of the household.

'Is that winter wheat?' Abram M—sky once inquired of my father, to show how shrewd he was.

'Not spring wheat, certainly.'

'Is it Nikopol wheat?'

'I tell you it is winter wheat.'

'I know it is winter wheat, but what variety is it? Nikopol or Girka?'

'Somehow or other I have never heard of Nikopol winter wheat. Perhaps somebody has it, but I haven't got it. Mine is Sandomir wheat,' my father answered.

Nothing came of the sons' efforts. A year later my father was leasing their land from them again.

The German settlers constituted a group apart. There were some really rich men among them. They stood more firmly on their feet than the others. Their domestic relations were stricter, their sons were seldom sent to be educated in town, their daughters habitually worked in the fields. Their houses were built of brick with iron roofs painted green or red, their horses were well bred, their harness was strong, their spring carts were called 'German wagons'. Our nearest neighbour among the

Germans was Ivan Ivanovich Dorn, a fat, active man with low shoes on his bare feet, with a tanned and bristling face, and grey hair. He always drove about in a fine, bright-painted wagon drawn by black stallions whose hoofs thundered over the ground. And there were many of these Dorns.

Above them all towered the figure of Falz-Fein the Sheep King, a 'Kannitverstan' of the steppes.

In driving through the country, one would pass a huge flock of sheep. 'Whom do these belong to?' one would ask. 'To Falz-Fein.' You met a hay-wagon on the road. 'Whom was that hay for?' 'For Falz-Fein.' A pyramid of fur dashes by in a sleigh. It is Falz-Fein's manager. A string of camels suddenly startles you with its bellowing. Only Falz-Fein owns camels. Falz-Fein had imported stallions from America and bulls from Switzerland.

The founder of this family, who was called only Falz in those days, without the Fein, had been a shepherd on the estate of the Duke of Oldenburg. Oldenburg had been granted a large sum of money by the government for the breeding of Merino sheep. The duke made about a million of debts and did nothing. Falz bought the property and managed it like a shepherd and not like a duke. His flocks increased as well as his pastures and his business. His daughter married a sheep-breeder called Fein, and the two pastoral dynasties were thus united. The name of Falz-Fein rang like the sound of the feet of ten thousand sheep in motion, like the bleating of countless sheep voices, like the sound of the whistle of a shepherd of the steppes with his long crook on his back, like the barking of many sheep-dogs. The very steppe breathed this name both in summer heat and winter cold.

The first five years of my life are behind me. I am gaining experience. Life is full of invention, and is just as industrious at working out its combinations in an obscure little corner as it is on the world arena. Events crowd upon me, one after another.

A working girl is brought in bitten by a snake in the field. The girl is weeping piteously. They bandage her swollen leg tightly above the knee and bathe it in a barrel of sour milk. The girl is taken away to Bobrinetz, to the hospital. She returns and is at work again. On her bitten leg is a stocking, dirty and tattered, and the workingmen will call her nothing but 'lady'.

The boar-pig gnawed at the forehead, shoulders and arms of the man who was feeding him. It was a new, huge boar-pig that had been brought in to improve the entire herd of pigs. The fellow was frightened to death and sobbed like a boy. He too was taken to the hospital.

Two young workmen standing on wagon-loads of sheaves of grain tossed pitchforks to each other. I fairly devoured this scene. One of them fell down moaning with a pitchfork in his side.

All this happened in the course of one summer. And no summer passed without its events.

One autumn night the entire wooden superstructure of the mill was swept into the pond. The piles had long since rotted, and the board walls were carried away like sails by the hurricane. The engine, the millstones, the coarse-grain grinder, the tare-separator stood out starkly in the ruins. From under the boards enormous mill-rats would dash out now and then.

Stealthily I would follow the water-carrier into the field to hunt marmots. With precision, not too rapidly and not too slowly, one would pour water into the burrow and await, with stick in hand, the appearance at the opening of the rat-like snout with its matted wet hair. An old marmot would resist a long time, stopping up the burrow with his rump, but a second bucket of water would make him surrender and jump out to meet his death. One had to cut off the paws of the dead animal and string them on a thread – the Zemstvo would pay one kopeck for each marmot. They used to demand to be shown the tail, but clever fellows learned to make a dozen tails out of the skin of one animal; so the Zemstvo now required the paws. I would return all wet and dirty. At home such adventures were not encouraged. They preferred me to sit on the divan in the dining-room and draw the blind Oedipus and Antigone.

One day my mother and I were returning on a sleigh from Bobrinetz, the nearest town. Blinded by the snow, lulled by the ride, I was drowsy. The sleigh overturned on a curve and I fell face downwards. The rug and the hay smothered me. I heard the alarmed cries of my mother but was unable to answer. The driver, a large, red-headed young fellow who was new, lifted the rug and found me. We resumed our seats and continued on our way. But I began to complain that chills were running up and down my spine. 'Chills?' asked the red-bearded driver, turning his face to me and showing his firm white teeth. Looking at his mouth I answered: 'Yes, you know, chills.' The driver laughed. 'It's nothing,' he added, 'we'll be there soon!' and he urged on the light-bay horse. The following night that very driver vanished, together with the bay horse. There was a great to-do on the estate. A posse headed by my elder brother was quickly organized. He saddled Mutz, promising to mete out cruel punishment to the thief. 'You better catch him first!' my father suggested gloomily. Two days passed before the posse returned. My brother blamed the fog for his not catching the horse-thief. A handsome jolly fellow with white teeth – such is a horse-thief!

I suffered from fever and tossed about. My arms, legs and head were in the way; they seemed inflated, pressing against the wall and the ceiling, and there was no escape from all these impediments because they sprang from within. I was all aflame; my throat pained. My mother looked into it, then my father did the same; they exchanged alarmed glances and decided to apply some salve to the throat. 'I am afraid,' Mother said, 'that Lyova has diphtheria.'

'If it had been diphtheria,' replied Ivan Vasilyevich, 'he would have been on the stretcher long ago.'

Vaguely I surmised that lying on the stretcher meant being dead, as had been the case with my younger sister Rozochka. But I could not believe that they were speaking of me, and listened calmly to their talk. In the end it was decided to take me to Bobrinetz. My mother was not very orthodox, but on the Sabbath day she would not travel to town. Ivan Vasilyevich accompanied me. We put up at the house of Little Tatyana, our former servant, who had married in Bobrinetz. She had no children, and therefore there was no danger of contagion. Dr Shatunovsky examined my throat, took my temperature, and as usual asserted that it was too early to know anything. Tatyana gave me a beer-bottle in the interior of which a complete little church had been constructed out of tiny sticks and boards. My legs and arms ceased to bother me. I recovered. When did this occur? Not long before the beginning of the new era in my life.

That came about in this way. Uncle Abram, an old egotist, who would neglect the children for weeks, called me over in a bright moment and asked: 'Now tell me, without mincing words, what year is it? Ah, you don't know? It's 1885! Repeat that and remember it, for I'll ask you again.' I could not comprehend the meaning of the question. 'Yes, it's 1885 now,' said my first cousin, the quiet Olga, 'and then it will be 1886.' This I could not believe. If one admitted that time had a name, then 1885 should exist forever, that is, very, very long, like that large stone at the threshold of the house, like the mill, or in fact like myself. Betya, the younger sister of Olga, did not know whom to believe. The three of us all felt disturbed at the thought of entering a new realm, as if someone had suddenly thrown open a door leading into a dark, empty room where voices echoed loudly. At last I had to yield. Everybody sided with Olga. And so 1885 became the first numbered year in my consciousness. It put an end to the formless, prehistoric, chaotic epoch of my earlier life: from now on I knew a chronology. I was six years old at the time. It was a year of crop failures, of crises, and of the first large labour disturbances in Russia. But it was the incomprehensible name of the year that had struck me. Apprehensively I endeavoured to divine the hidden relation between time and numbers. There followed a series of years which moved slowly at first and then faster and faster. But 1885 stood out amongst them as an elder does, as the head of the clan. It marked an era.

The following incident stands out. I once climbed into the driver's seat of our baggage-wagon and, while waiting for my father, picked up the reins. The young horses raced off and made for the estate of the Dembovskys, flying past the house, the barn, the garden, and across the roadless field. There were cries behind and a ditch ahead. The horses tore on. Only on the very edge of the ditch, with a swerve which almost upset the wagon, did they stop as if rooted to the spot. After us came running the driver, followed by two or three labourers and my father. My mother was screaming, my elder sister was wringing her hands. My mother went on screaming even while I was dashing over to her. It should also be recorded that my father, deathly pale, treated me to a couple of slaps. I was not even offended, so extraordinary did it all seem.

It must have been in the same year that I accompanied my father on a trip to Elizavetgrad. We started at dawn, and went slowly. In Bobrinetz the horses were fed. We reached Vshivaya* in the evening. We called it Shvivaya out of delicacy. There we stayed until daybreak, as robbers were reported on the outskirts. Not a single capital in the world, neither Paris nor New York, made in after years such an impression on me as Elizavetgrad with its sidewalks, green roofs, balconies, shops, policemen and red balloons. For several hours, with my eyes wide open, I gaped at the face of civilization.

A year later I began to study. One morning, after getting up and washing hastily – one always washed hastily in Yanovka – I entered the dining-room, looking forward to the new day and, above all, to the breakfast of tea with milk and buttered cake. I found my mother there in the company of a stranger, a lean, wanly smiling, obsequious man. My mother and the stranger looked at me in a way that made it clear that I had been the subject of their conversation.

'Shake hands, Lyova,' said my mother. 'Meet your teacher.' I looked at the teacher with some fear, but not without interest. The teacher greeted me with that mildness with which every teacher greets his future pupil in the presence of parents. Mother completed the business arrangements right before me: for so many roubles and so many sacks of flour the teacher undertook to instruct me at his school in the colony, in Russian, arithmetic, and the Old Testament in the original Hebrew. The extent of the instruction, however, was left rather vague, as my mother was none too competent in such matters. Sipping my tea with milk, I seemed to taste the coming change in my destiny.

The following Sunday my father took me to the colony and

*In the Russian this means 'lousy'. – *Translator.*

placed me with Aunt Rachel. At the same time we brought her a load of produce, including wheat flour, barley flour, buckwheat, and millet.

The distance from Gromokley to Yanovka was four versts. Through the colony ran a ravine: on the one side was the Jewish settlement, on the other, the German. The two parts stood out in sharp contrast. In the German section the houses were neat, partly roofed with tile and partly with reeds, the horses large, the cows sleek. In the Jewish section the cabins were dilapidated, the roofs tattered, the cattle scrawny.

It is strange that my first school left very few impressions: a slate blackboard on which I first traced the letters of the Russian alphabet; the skinny index-finger of the teacher holding a pen; the reading of the Bible in unison; the punishment of some boy for stealing – all vague fragments, misty bits, not a single vivid picture. Perhaps the exception was the wife of the teacher, a tall, portly woman who from time to time took a part in our school life, always unexpectedly. Once during a session she complained to her husband that the new flour had a peculiar odour, and when he put his sharp nose to her handful of flour, she threw it in his face. That was her idea of a joke. The boys and girls laughed. Only the teacher looked downcast. I pitied him, standing in the midst of his class with a powdered face.

I lived with my good Aunt Rachel without being aware of her. On the same courtyard, in the main house, Uncle Abram ruled. He treated his nephews and nieces with complete indifference. Once in a while he would single me out, invite me in and treat me to a bone with marrow, adding: 'I wouldn't take ten roubles for this bone.'

My uncle's house was almost at the entrance to the colony. At the opposite end lived a tall, dark, thin Jew who had the name of being a horse-thief and of carrying on unsavoury deals. He had a daughter – she too had a dubious reputation. Not far from the horse-thief lived the cap-maker, stitching away on his machine – a young Jew with a fiery red beard. The wife of the cap-maker would come to the official inspector of the colony, who always stayed at the house of Uncle Abram, to complain against the daughter of the horse-thief for stealing her husband.

Apparently the inspector offered no aid. Returning from school one day, I saw a mob dragging a young woman, the daughter of the horse-thief, through the street. The mob was shouting, screaming, and spitting at her. This biblical scene was engraved on my memory forever. Several years later Uncle Abram married this very woman. By that time her father, by action of the colonies, had been exiled to Siberia as an undesirable member of the community.

My former nurse Masha was a servant in the home of Uncle Abram. I frequently ran to her in the kitchen; she symbolized my bond with Yanovka. Masha had visitors, sometimes rather impatient ones, and then I would be gently ushered out. One bright morning I learned, together with the rest of the children in the colony, that Masha had given birth to a baby. With great relish we whispered about it secretly. A few days later my mother arrived from Yanovka and went to the kitchen to see Masha and the child. I sneaked in behind my mother. Masha was wearing a kerchief which came down to her eyes. On a wide bench was the tiny creature, lying on its side. My mother looked at Masha, then at the child, and then shook her head reproachfully, saying nothing. Masha continued silent, with eyes downcast; then she looked at the infant and said: 'Look how he puts his little hand under his cheek like a grown-up.'

'Don't you pity him?' my mother asked.

'No,' replied Masha deceitfully, 'he is so sweet.'

'It's a lie, you are sorry,' retorted my mother in a conciliatory tone. The tiny infant died a week later as mysteriously as it had come into the world.

I often left school and returned to my village, remaining there almost a week at a time. I had no intimate friends among my schoolmates, as I did not speak Yiddish. The school season lasted only a few months. All of which may explain the paucity of my recollections of this period. And yet Shufer – that was the name of the Gromokley teacher – had taught me to read and write, both of which stood me in good stead in my later life, and for that reason I remember my first teacher with gratitude.

I began to make my way through lines of print. I copied verse. I even wrote verse myself. Later on I started a magazine, together with my cousin, Senya Z. And yet the new path was a thorny one. Scarcely had I mastered the art of writing when it seduced me. Once, while alone in the dining-room, I began to put down in printed script such special words as I had heard in the shop and in the kitchen and which I had never heard from my family. I realized that I was doing something which I should not be doing, but the words lured me just because they were forbidden. I had decided to hide the little paper in an empty match-box and then to bury it behind the barn. I was far from completing the list when my elder sister entered the room, and became interested. I seized the paper. My mother came in after my sister. They demanded that I show them the writing. Burning with shame, I threw the paper behind the divan. My sister tried to reach for it, but I cried out hysterically: 'I'll get it myself.' I crawled under the divan and there tore the paper into bits. There were no bounds to my despair, nor to my tears.

It must have been during Christmas week of 1886, because I already knew how to write at the time, that a troop of mummers tumbled into the dining-room one evening while we were at tea. It was so sudden that I fell on the divan from fright. I was quieted, and listened avidly to 'Tsar Maximilian'. For the first time a fantastic world was revealed to me, a world transformed into a theatrical reality. I was amazed when I learned that the main rôle was being played by the working man Prokhor, a former soldier. Next day, with pencil and paper in hand, I penetrated into the servants' quarters after dinner, and besought Tsar Maximilian to dictate his monologues to me. Prokhor was none too willing, but I clung to him, begged, demanded, implored, gave him no peace. Finally we made ourselves comfortable at the window, and I began to record, using the scratched window-sill as a table, the rhymed speech of Tsar Maximilian. Five minutes had scarcely passed when my father appeared at the door, took in the scene at the window and sternly said: 'Lyova, to your room!' Inconsolable, I cried on the divan all afternoon.

I composed verses, feeble lines which perhaps showed my early love for words but certainly forecast no poetical future. My elder sister knew of my verses, through her my mother knew, and through my mother, my father. They would ask me to read my verses aloud before guests. It was painfully embarrassing. I would refuse. They would urge me, at first gently, then with irritation, finally with threats. Sometimes I would run away, but my elders knew how to get what they wanted. With a pounding heart, with tears in my eyes, I would read my verses, ashamed of my borrowed lines and limping rhymes.

Be that as it may, I had tasted of the tree of knowledge. Life was unfolding, not merely daily but even hourly. From the torn divan in the dining-room threads stretched to other worlds. Reading opened a new era in my life.

3
Odessa: My Family and My School

In 1888 great events began to take place in my life: I was sent off to Odessa to study. It happened this way: My mother's nephew, Moissey Filippovich Schpentzer, a man of about twenty-eight, spent a summer in our village. He was a fine and intelligent person who for a minor political offence had been barred from the university on his graduation from high school. He was a bit of a journalist and a bit of a statistician. He came out to the country to fight off tuberculosis. Monya, as he was called, was the pride of his mother and of his several sisters, both because of his abilities and because of his fine character. My family inherited this respect for him. Everybody was pleased at the prospect of his arrival. Quietly I shared this feeling. When Monya entered the dining-room I was at the threshold of the so-called 'nursery' – a tiny corner room – and did not have enough courage to come forward because my shoes had two gaping holes. This was not due to poverty – the family at the time was already well-to-do – but to the indifference of country folk, to overburdening toil, to the low level of our home standards.

'Hello, boy,' said Moissey Filippovich, 'come here.'

'Hello,' the boy answered, but did not budge from his place. They explained to the guest, with a guilty laugh, why I did not stir. He gaily relieved me of my embarrassment by lifting me across the threshold and embracing me heartily.

Monya was the centre of attention at dinner. Mother served him the best cuts, asking how he enjoyed his food and what his favourite dishes were. In the evening, after the herd had been driven into the cow pen, Monya said to me: 'Come on, let's get some fresh milk. Take along some glasses . . . Now darling, you should hold the glasses with your fingers on the outside, not on the inside.'

From Monya I learned many things I did not know: how to hold a glass, how to wash, how to pronounce certain words, and why milk fresh from the cow is good for the chest. He walked a lot, he wrote, he played ninepins, he taught me arithmetic and Russian grammar, preparing me for the first class of the *gymnasium*. He enraptured me but at the same time disquieted me. One sensed in him the element of a more exacting discipline in life – the element of city civilization.

Monya was friendly to his country relatives. He jested a lot and sometimes hummed in a soft tenor voice. At times he seemed gloomy and at the dinner-table would sit silent, sunk in meditation. He would get anxious glances and would be asked if something ailed him. His answers were brief and evasive. Only towards the end of his stay in the village, and then only vaguely, did I begin to surmise the cause of his moody spells. Monya was upset by the rude manners of the village or by some injustice. It was not that his uncle or aunt were especially stern masters – that cannot be said under any circumstances. The nature of the prevailing relations with the labourers and peasants was in no sense worse than on other estates. But it was not much better – and this means that it was oppressive. When the overseer once struck a shepherd with a long knout because he had kept the horses out late, Monya grew pale and hissed between his teeth, 'How shameful!' And I felt that it was shameful. I do not know if I would have felt the same way if he had not made his remark – I am inclined to think I would. But in any event he helped me to feel that way, and this alone was enough to instil in me a lifelong sense of gratitude.

Schpentzer was about to marry the principal of the State School for Jewish Girls. No one in Yanovka knew her, but everybody assumed that she must be out of the ordinary, because she was a school principal and Monya's bride. It was decided to send me to Odessa the following spring; there I would live with the Schpentzers and attend the *gymnasium*. The tailor of the colony somehow fitted me out. A large trunk was packed with vessels containing butter, jars full of jam and other gifts for the city relatives. The farewell was a long one. I wept copiously, so did my mother, and so did my sisters, and for the first time I felt how dear to me was Yanovka, with all it held. We drove to the station across the steppe, and I wept until we came out on the main road.

From Novy Bug we took the train to Nikolayev, where we transferred to a steamboat. The siren sent shivers down my spine; it sounded like the call to a new life. The sea was ahead of us, for we were still on the River Bug. A great deal indeed was ahead. There was the pier, the cabman, the Pokrovsky Alley, and a big old house where the School for Girls and its principal were lodged. I was scrutinized from every angle. First a young woman, then an older one – her mother – kissed me on the forehead and both cheeks. Moissey Filippovich jested in his usual manner, inquiring about Yanovka, its inhabitants, and even the familiar cows. To me the cows seemed such insignificant beings that I was embarrassed to discuss them in such select company. The apartment was none too large. I was assigned a corner in the dining-room, behind a curtain. And it was here that I spent the first four years of my school life.

All at once I found myself in the grip of that alluring but exacting discipline which Moissey Filippovich radiated when he was with us in the country. The régime was not stern but it was regular; it was on that account that it seemed severe in the beginning. I had to go to bed at nine. This hour gradually receded as I advanced in the school. I was reminded at every turn not to fail to say good-morning, to keep my hands and fingernails tidy, not to eat with a knife, not to be tardy, always to thank the servants, and not to speak ill of people behind their backs. I learned that scores of words which seemed beyond question at home were not Russian but Ukrainian jargon. Every day there was revealed to me some aspect of a cultural environment greater than that in which I had passed the first nine years of my life. Even the shop at home began to dim and to lose its magic as compared with the spell of classical literature and the charm of the theatre. I was becoming a little urbanite. Occasionally, however, the village would flare up in my consciousness and draw me on like a lost paradise. Then I would pine, wander about, and trace with my finger on the window-pane messages to my mother, or I would cry into my pillow.

Life in the home of Moissey Filippovich was modest. He had barely means enough to make ends meet. The head of the family had no steady work. He did translations of the Greek tragedies with commentaries, he wrote tales for children, he studied Schloesser and other historians, planning to compile graphic chronological tables, and he helped his wife to conduct the school. It was later that he formed a small publishing house which grew with difficulty in the first years but rose to a high position subsequently. In about ten or twelve years he became the outstanding publisher in southern Russia, the owner of a large printing establishment and of a private residence. I lived for six years with this family, during the first period of the publishing concern. I became very familiar with type, make-up, layout, printing, paging, and binding. Proof-reading was my favourite pastime. My love for the freshly printed page has its origin in those far-away years as a schoolboy.

As would be the case in bourgeois, especially petty-bourgeois, homes, the servant occupied not a small although not a noticeable rôle in my life. The first maid, Dasha, made me her secret confidant, entrusting her various secrets to me. After dinner, when everybody was resting, I would stealthily make for the kitchen. There Dasha would give me fragrants of her life and tell me of her first love. Dasha was followed by a divorced Jewess from Jitomir. 'What a rascal he was,' she would complain of her former husband. I began to teach her how to read. Every day she would spend not less than half an hour at my desk, trying to penetrate into the mystery of the alphabet and the formation of words. By this time there was an infant in the family, and a wet-nurse was taken in. I wrote letters for her. She complained of her troubles to her husband, who was in America. At her request I painted them in the darkest colours, adding that 'our baby is the only bright star on the dark skyline of my life'. The nurse was in ecstasy. I myself reread the letter aloud with some satisfaction, although the closing part, where there was something about sending dollars, embarrassed me. Then she added:

'And now, one more letter.'

'To whom?' I asked, preparing for the creative task.

'To my cousin,' replied the nurse somewhat uncertainly. This letter also spoke of her dark life, but said nothing about the star, and ended with a suggestion that she visit him if he so desired. Hardly had the nurse left with the letters when my pupil, the maid, who had apparently been eavesdropping, appeared. 'But he isn't at all a cousin of hers,' she whispered to me indignantly. 'What is he then?' I asked. 'Just somebody,' she replied. And I had occasion to contemplate the complexity of human relations.

At dinner Fanny Solomonovna* said to me, smiling strangely: 'How about some more soup, author?'

'What?' I asked, alarmed.

'Oh nothing, you composed a letter for the wet-nurse, so you are an author. How did you put it: a star on the dark skyline? – an author, indeed!' And no longer able to restrain herself, she burst out laughing.

'It's well written,' said Moissey Filippovich soothingly, 'but you know, you shouldn't write letters for her any more; let Fanny herself write them.'

The bewildering wrong side of life, recognized neither at home nor at school, did not however cease to exist because of that, and proved sufficiently powerful and all-pervading to command attention even from a ten-year-old boy. Barred from the schoolroom as well as from the front door of the home, it found its way in through the kitchen.

The law limiting the admission of Jews to the state schools to ten per cent of the entire number was first introduced in 1887. It was an almost hopeless effort to gain entrance into a *gymnasium*, requiring 'pull' or bribery. The *realschule* differed from the *gymnasium* in the absence from its curriculum of ancient languages and in its broader course in mathematics, natural sciences and modern languages. The ten-per-cent statute applied also to the *realschule*. In the case of the latter the stream of applicants was smaller and the chances for admission were therefore greater. For a long time a debate raged in the newspapers and magazines as to the merits of a classical *vs* a *realschule* education.

* The wife of Moissey Filippovich.

The conservatives held that classicism fosters discipline – it was more likely a hope that the citizen who had endured Greek in his childhood would be able to endure the Tsarist régime the rest of his life. The liberals, on the other hand, without repudiating classicism, which is a sort of a foster-brother to liberalism, since both trace their origin to the Renaissance, still favoured the *realschule*. When I was about to start my high-school education, these debates had died down, the result of a special order prohibiting discussion as to which was the more desirable type of education.

In the fall I took my examinations for the first class of the St Paul *realschule*. I passed the entrance examination with average marks: a '3' in Russian, a '4' in arithmetic.* This was not enough, as the ten-per-cent statute meant the most rigid selection – complicated, of course, by bribery. It was decided to put me in the preparatory class, attached to the school as a private institution. Jews were transferred from there to the first class according to the statute, it is true, but with preference over outsiders.

The St Paul School had originally been a German institution. It had been founded by the Lutheran parish to serve the numerous German residents of Odessa and of the southern district in general. Although the St Paul School was endowed with all state rights, it was necessary, because it had only six grades, to take the seventh year at another *realschule* in order to be admitted to a university. Apparently the assumption was that in the last grade the remnants of the German spirit would be wiped out. This spirit, by the way, waned in the St Paul School year by year. Germans formed less than half of the student body. The Germans on the staff were persistently being forced out.

The first days of study at school were days of sorrow; then they became days of joy. I started for school in a brand-new uniform, wearing a new cap with a yellow border and a remarkable metal badge which contained, between two trefoils, the

---

*In the Russian system of grading, '5' was the highest and '1' the lowest mark. – *Translator*.

complicated monogram of the school. On my back was a brand-new leather school-bag, holding new text-books in bright bindings and a handsome pencil-case stuffed with freshly sharpened pencils, a new penholder, and an eraser. In transports, I carried this entire, magnificent load through the long Uspensky Street, happy that the distance to the school was great. It seemed to me that the passers-by looked with amazement and sometimes even with envy at my astonishing equipment. Trustingly and with interest I surveyed everybody I met. Then, quite suddenly, a tall skinny boy of about thirteen, evidently a shop-apprentice, for he carried some tin object, stopped in front of this superb schoolboy and coming within a step or two, threw his head back, made a loud noise and spat amply at the shoulder of my new jacket. Looking contemptuously at me, he passed on without a word. What made him do it? I know the reason now. The impoverished boy, dressed in a tattered shirt, with broken boots on bare feet, the boy whose job it was to carry out the dirty errands of his masters while their pampered sons flaunted school uniforms, vented upon me his sense of social protest. But at the time I was not interested in generalities. I wiped my shoulder for a long time with some leaves, boiling within from the helpless insult, and completed the last part of my journey in a gloomy mood.

The second blow awaited me in the courtyard of the school. 'Peter Pavlovich,' the boys cried, 'here is another from the preparatory class in uniform!' What did that mean? It appeared that the preparatory school was a private affair, and its members were strictly forbidden to don the St Paul uniform. Peter Pavlovich, the black-bearded monitor, explained to me that I must remove the badge, the braid and the belt-buckle, and must replace the buttons, which had an eagle stamped on them, with ordinary ones. This was my second misfortune.

That day there were no classes at school. The German pupils and many others were all gathered in the Lutheran church whose name the school bore. I found myself under the guidance of a thick-set boy who had been left in the preparatory class for a second year and who knew the system. He put me next to him on a bench at the church. For the first time I heard an organ, and its sounds filled me with quivers. Then appeared a tall, shaven man, the facing of his coat all white; his voice reverberated through the church like a series of waves. The strangeness of his speech accentuated tenfold the grandeur of his sermon. 'Who is that speaking?' I asked, all agitated. 'It's Pastor Binneman himself,' explained my new friend, Carlson. 'He's a terribly wise man, the wisest in Odessa.'

'And what is he saying?'

'Well, you know, the regular things,' said Carlson with much less enthusiasm. 'That one should be a good pupil, study hard, get along well with the boys.' This heavy-jawed admirer of Binneman turned out to be a most obstinate sluggard and a terrible scrapper who, during recesses, distributed black eyes right and left.

The second day brought its comforts. I promptly distinguished myself in arithmetic, and copied the lesson from the blackboard well. The teacher, Rudyenko, praised me before the entire class and gave me two 'fives'. This reconciled me to the plain buttons on my jacket. The director himself, Christian Christianovich Schwannebach, taught German to the junior classes. He was a sleek official who had attained his high position only because he was the brother-in-law of Binneman himself. Christian Christianovich began by examining the hands of all the pupils. He found that mine were clean. Then, when I had copied his lesson from the blackboard accurately, the director voiced his approval and gave me a '5'. Thus it came about that after the first actual day of school I was returning with a load of three 'excellent' marks. I carried them in my leather kit like a treasure, and ran rather than walked into the Pokrovsky Alley, driven by the thirst for home glory.

So I became a schoolboy. I would rise early, drink my morning tea in a hurry, thrust a package containing my lunch into my overcoat pocket, and run to school in order to reach there in time for the morning prayer. I was not tardy. I was quiet at my desk. I listened attentively and copied carefully. I worked diligently at home over my lessons. I went to bed at the prescribed hour, in order to hurry through my tea the following morning and run to school for fear of being late for the prayer. I passed from grade to grade without difficulty. Whenever I met one of my teachers in the street, I bowed with all possible deference.

The percentage of freaks among people in general is very considerable, but it is especially high among teachers. In the St Paul *realschule* the level of the teachers was perhaps above the average. The standing of the school was high, and not without reason. The régime was stern and exacting; the reins were drawn tighter and tighter every year, especially after the director's power had passed from the hands of Schwannebach into those of Nikolay Antonovich Kaminsky. He was a physicist by profession, a humanity-hater by temperament. He never looked at the person with whom he talked; he moved about the corridors and the classrooms noiselessly on rubber heels. He spoke in a small, hoarse, falsetto voice which, without being raised, could be terrifying. Outwardly Kaminsky seemed even in temper, but inwardly he was always in a state of habitual irritation. His attitude towards even the best students was one of armed neutrality. That, incidentally, was his attitude towards me.

In his capacity of physicist Kaminsky invented a special apparatus to demonstrate the Boyle–Mariotte law of the resistance of gases. After each demonstration there were always two or three boys who in a studied whisper would exchange the words, 'Well done!' Someone would rise and in a doubtful tone inquire: 'And who is the inventor of this apparatus?' Kaminsky would answer casually in his frozen falsetto: 'I built it.' Everybody would exchange glances, and the two-mark boys would emit as loud a sigh of rapture as possible.

After Schwannebach had been replaced by Kaminsky as a measure for Russification, the teacher of literature, Anton Vasilyevich Krizhanovsky, became the inspector of the school. He was a red-bearded, crafty fellow, an ex-theologian, a great lover of gifts – a man with a slightly liberal tendency, very clever at disguising his designs under an assumed kindliness. As soon as he was appointed inspector he became more rigorous and conservative. Krizhanovsky taught Russian from the first grade upwards. He singled me out for my grammar and love of the language. He made it a fixed rule to read my written works aloud to the class, giving me a mark of '5 plus'.

The mathematician, Yurchenko, was a stubby, phlegmatic, shrewd person, who was known as the 'bindyuzhnik', which in Odessa slang meant a 'heavy truck-driver'. Yurchenko addressed everybody, from the first grade to the last, by the familiar 'thou', and was not finicky about his expressions. With his consistent gruffness he inspired a certain amount of respect which melted away, however, in the course of time, for the boys learned that Yurchenko took bribes. The other teachers were also susceptible to bribery in one form or another. A backward pupil, if he was from out of town, would be lodged with that teacher whom he needed most. If the pupil happened to be a local resident, he would employ the threatening pedagogue as a private tutor at a high price.

The second mathematician, Zlotchansky, was the opposite of Yurchenko. He was thin, with a prickly moustache on a greenish-yellow face; his eyeballs were muddy, his movements as sluggish as if he had just awakened. He coughed noisily and spat in the classroom. It was known that he had had an unhappy love-affair, that he was dissipating and drinking. Although not a bad mathematician, Zlotchansky would stare beyond his pupils, beyond his studies, and even beyond his mathematics. Several years later he cut his throat with a razor.

My relations with the two mathematicians were smooth and pleasant, since I was strong in the subject. When I was in the last grades of the *realschule*, I planned to go in for higher mathematics.

The teacher of history was Lyubimov, a large and imposing man with gold-rimmed glasses on a small nose, and with a manly young beard around his full face. Only when he smiled did it suddenly appear, clearly even to us boys, that the impressiveness of the man was superficial, that he was weak-willed, timid, torn within himself, and fearful lest people find out something about him.

I plunged into history with an increasing though diffused interest. Gradually I widened the circle of my studies, abandoning the poor official text-books for the university courses or the solid tomes of Schloesser. There was undoubtedly some element of sport in my fascination for history. I learned by heart many unnecessary names and details, burdensome to the memory, in order to give occasional embarrassment to the teacher. Lyubimov was unable to cope with his class. Sometimes he would suddenly flare up during the lesson and look angrily about, catching a whisper that he imagined to be an insulting remark concerning himself. The class would prick up its ears in astonishment. Lyubimov also taught at a *gymnasium* for girls, and there, too, it was observed that he was acting strangely. The end was an attack of insanity, as a result of which Lyubimov hanged himself from a window-frame.

The geography teacher, Zhukovsky, was feared more than fire. He mowed the boys down like an automatic meat-axe. Zhukovsky demanded an entirely impossible silence in his classroom. Not infrequently stopping a student in the midst of his recitation, he would look up sharply like a bird of prey listening to the sound of distant danger. Everybody knew what it meant: not to stir and if possible not to breathe. I recall only one occasion when Zhukovsky loosed his reins somewhat. I think it was on his birthday. One of the students said something to him that was semi-private, that is, with no bearing on the lesson. Zhukovsky tolerated it. This in itself was an event. Immediately Vakker, the fawner, arose and, with a smirk, remarked: 'It's common talk that Lyubimov can't hold a candle to Zhukovsky.' Zhukovsky suddenly grew tense. 'What's that? Sit down!' At once there descended that special silence known only in the geography class. Vakker sat down as if crushed by a blow. Glances full of reproach and disgust were turned upon him from all sides. 'I swear, it's the truth,' Vakker replied in a whisper, hoping to touch the heart of the geographer, with whom his standing was low.

The full-fledged teacher of German at the school was Struve, a huge German with a large head and a beard which reached to his waistline. This man carried his heavy body, which seemed a vessel of kindliness, on almost childlike limbs. Struve was a most honest person; he suffered over the failures of his pupils, he shared their agitation, he coaxed them, and was pained over every '2'. He never descended as low as a '1'; he tried never to leave a pupil behind for another year. It was he who had obtained admission to the school for the nephew of his cook, the Vakker boy, who turned out, however, to be ungifted and unattractive. Struve was a bit droll, but on the whole a sympathetic figure.

The teacher of French was Gustave Samoylovich Burnande, a Swiss – a lean person with a profile so flat that it seemed to have just been squeezed in a press. He had a small bald spot, thin, blue, unkindly lips, a sharp nose, and a mysterious large scar in the form of the letter X on his forehead. Burnande was disliked unanimously, and with reason. A sufferer from indigestion, he kept swallowing tablets during the classroom hours, and regarded every pupil as a personal enemy. The scar on his forehead was a constant source of conjecture and theory. It was said that Gustave in his youth had fought a duel, and that his opponent succeeded in tracing a twisted cross on his forehead with a rapier. This was denied several months later. It was then asserted that there had been no duel but instead a surgical operation, in the course of which part of his forehead was employed to repair his nose. The boys carefully scrutinized his nose, and the more venturesome ones affirmed that they could see the stitches. Then there were more judicial minds who sought to explain the scar as an accident of his early childhood – a fall down stairs. But this explanation was repudiated as too prosaic. Moreover, it was altogether impossible to imagine Burnande as a child.

The chief janitor, who played a not unimportant rôle in our life, was the imperturbable German Anton, with imposing and greying side-whiskers. When it came to tardiness, being kept after school, incarceration, Anton's authority was merely a routine affair, but actually it was great, and it was necessary to keep on friendly terms with him. My attitude towards him was one of indifference, as was his towards me, for I was not among his clients. I came to school on time, my kit was in order, my card was always in the left pocket of my jacket. But scores of pupils were daily at the mercy of Anton and courted his benevolence in every way. In any event he was for all of us one of the pillars of the St Paul *realschule*. Imagine our amazement when, on our return from the summer vacation, we learned that old man Anton had shot the eighteen-year-old daughter of another janitor in a fit of passion and jealousy, and was lodged in jail.

In this way the regulated life of the school and the suppressed, crushed public life of the period would be punctured by individual personal calamities which always made an exaggerated impression, like a sob in an empty vault.

There was an orphanage attached to the church of St Paul. It occupied a corner of our courtyard. Dressed in blue, wash-worn denim, the inmates appeared in the yard with unhappy faces, wandering dejectedly in their corner and droopingly climbing the stairs. In spite of the fact that the courtyard was common ground and the orphanage not segregated, the schoolboys and the inmates represented two completely separate worlds. Once or twice I tried to converse with the boys in blue denim, but they answered gruffly, unwillingly, hurrying to their own section. They were under strict orders not to interfere in the affairs of the students. For seven years I played in this courtyard and never knew the name of a single orphan. One must suppose that Pastor Binneman blessed them at the beginning of the year, according to the abbreviated mass-book.

In the part of the courtyard which adjoined the orphanage was the complicated apparatus for gymnastics: rings, poles, ladders – both vertical and inclined – trapezes, parallel bars, et cetera. Soon after I entered school I wanted to repeat a stunt performed before me by one of the orphanage boys. Climbing the vertical ladder and suspending myself by my shoe-tips from the upper bar, head downwards, I caught the lowest rung within reach and, releasing my feet, let myself go, expecting to make a loop of 180 degrees and land on the ground in one bound. But I failed to let go my hands in time and, after describing the loop, struck the ladder with my body. My chest was crushed, my breath stifled; I wriggled on the ground like a worm, grasping at the legs of the boys around me, and then losing consciousness. From then on I was more careful with my gymnastics.

My life was not of the street, of the market-place, of sports and outdoor exercises. I made up for these deficiencies when on vacation in the village. The city seemed to me created for study and reading. The boys' street brawls seemed to me disgraceful. Yet there was never any lack of cause for a fight.

The *gymnasium* students, on account of their silver buttons and badges, were dubbed 'herrings', while the brass-buttoned *realschule* boys were called 'kippers'. Returning home along the Yamskaya, I was accosted once by a long-bodied *gymnasium* student who kept asking: 'What do you charge for kippers?' Getting no answer to his question, he shoved me along with his shoulder. 'What do you want of me?' I asked in a tone of extreme courtesy. The student was taken aback.

He hesitated for a moment and then asked:

'Have you got a sling-shot?'

'A sling-shot,' I asked in turn, 'what's that?'

The long-bodied student silently pulled out of his pocket a small apparatus consisting of a rubber band on a pronged stick, and a piece of lead. 'From the window I kill pigeons on the roof, and then fry them,' he said. I looked at my new acquaintance with surprise. Such an occupation was not uninviting, but it seemed nevertheless somewhat out of place and almost indecent in city surroundings.

Many of the boys went boating on the sea, many fished from the breakwater. These pleasures I did not know. Strangely enough, the sea had no part in my life in that period, although I spent seven years on its shores. During all that time I never was in a boat at sea, never fished, and generally encountered the sea only during my trips to the village and back. When Carlson showed up on Monday with a sunburned nose from which the skin was peeling, and boasted of catching chubs from a boat, his joys seemed remote and did not touch me at all. The passionate hunter and fisherman in me had not yet awakened in those days.

While in the preparatory class I became very chummy with Kostya R., the son of a physician. Kostya was one year younger than I, smaller in size, quiet in appearance, but actually a scapegrace and a rogue, with keen little eyes. He knew the town well and in this respect had a great advantage over me. He did not excel in his studies, whereas I had from the beginning maintained a record of the highest marks. At home Kostya did nothing but talk of his new friend. The result was that his mother, a little, dried-up woman, came to Fanny Solomonovna with the request that the two boys study together. After the conference, in which I participated, permission was granted. For two or three years we occupied the same bench. Then Kostya was left a grade behind, and we parted. Our relations, however, continued in later years.

Kostya had a sister in the *gymnasium* about two years his senior. The sister had girl friends. These friends had brothers. The girls studied music. The boys hung around their sisters' friends. On birthdays the parents invited guests. There was a little world of sympathies, jealousies, dancing, games, envies, and animosities. The centre of this little world was the family of the wealthy merchant A., who occupied an apartment in the same house and on the same floor where Kostya lived. The corridors of the apartments all faced the same balcony in the courtyard. It was on the balcony that all sorts of meetings took place, casual and otherwise. In the home of A. there was an atmosphere altogether different from the one to which I had grown accustomed at the Schpentzers'. Here were many schoolboys and schoolgirls practising the art of flirtation under the patronizing smile of the mistress of the house. In the course of conversation it would crop out who was interested in whom. For such matters I always displayed the greatest contempt, which was, however, a bit hypocritical. 'When you fall in love with any one,' the fourteen-year-old daughter of A. would instruct me, 'you must tell me.'

'I can promise you that, since I am in no danger of doing it,' I would answer with the assumed pride of a man who knows his value – I was then already in the second grade. A couple of weeks later the girls gave an exhibition of *tableaux vivants*. The younger daughter, with her hands raised, represented Night, against the background of a large black shawl sprinkled with stars made from silver paper.

'Look how pretty she is,' remarked the older sister, nudging me. I looked, agreed in my heart, and right there and then made a decision: the hour had come to fulfil the promise. Soon the older sister began to question me. 'Have you nothing to tell me?' Dropping my eyes, I replied: 'I have.'

'Who is she, then?'

But my tongue would not move. She proposed that I give the first letter of her name. This made it easier. The name of the older girl was Anna. The younger sister was named Bertha. I gave the second letter of the alphabet, and not the first.

'B?' she repeated, obviously disappointed, and there the conversation ended.

The following day I was on my way to Kostya to study, walking as usual through the long corridor of the third floor. From the staircase I had already observed that the two sisters were sitting on the balcony with their mother. When I was within a few feet of the group, I felt myself pierced by their needle-like glances of irony. The younger girl did not smile, but on the contrary looked away from me, her face wearing an expression of terrifying indifference. This convinced me at once that I had been betrayed. The mother and the older girl shook hands with me in a manner which clearly said: 'Fine gosling, now we know what is underneath your seriousness.' The younger sister stretched out her hand, flat as a little board, without looking at me and without answering my handclasp. I still had quite a walk along the balcony to negotiate, in full sight of my tormentors. All the time I felt their murderous arrows in my back. After that unheard-of treachery I decided to sever my relations completely with this perfidious clan, not to call on them, to forget them, tear them out of my heart forever. I was helped by the vacation period, which came soon afterwards.

Unexpectedly for me, it appeared that I was near-sighted. I was taken to an eye-specialist, who supplied me with glasses. This did not hurt my pride at all, for the glasses gave me a sense of added importance. Not without some satisfaction did I anticipate my appearance in Yanovka wearing glasses. For my father, however, the glasses were a great blow. He held that it was affectation and swank on my part, and peremptorily demanded that I remove them. In vain did I protest that I could not read the writing on the blackboard and the signs on the streets. In Yanovka I wore the glasses only secretly.

And yet in the country I was much more courageous and enterprising, and showed more abandon. I shook off the discipline of the city. I would go to Bobrinetz on horseback all alone, and return the same day towards evening. This was a journey of fifty kilometres. In Bobrinetz I displayed my glasses publicly and had no doubt as to the impression they made. There was but one municipal boys' school in Bobrinetz. The nearest *gymnasium* was in Elizavetgrad, fifty kilometres away. There was a junior girls' high school in Bobrinetz, and during the school season the girls recruited their friends from among the students of the municipal school. In the summer things were different. The high-school boys would return from Elizavetgrad, and the magnificence of their uniforms and the finesse of their manners would push the municipal pupils into the background. The antagonism was bitter. The offended Bobrinetz schoolboys would form fighting groups and on occasion would resort not only to sticks and stones but to knives as well. As I was sitting nonchalantly eating berries on the branch of a mulberry tree in the garden of some friends, someone threw a stone at me from behind a fence, hitting me on the head. This was but one small incident in a long and not entirely bloodless warfare, interrupted only by the departure of the privileged class from Bobrinetz. Things were different in Elizavetgrad. There the high-school students dominated both streets and hearts. In the summer, however, the university students would arrive from Kharkoff, Odessa and more distant cities, and shove the high-school boys into their backyards. Here the struggle was likewise fierce, and the perfidy of the girls was indescribable. But the fight, as a rule, was waged only with spiritual or moral weapons.

In the country I played croquet and ninepins, led in forfeits, and was insolent to the girls. It was there that I learned to ride a bicycle made entirely by Ivan Vasilyevich. Because of that, I dared later to exercise on the Odessa track. In the village, moreover, I managed all alone a blooded stallion in a two-wheeled gig. By this time there were already fine driving-horses in Yanovka. I offered to take my uncle Brodsky, the brewer, for a ride. 'I won't be thrown out?' asked my uncle, who was not inclined to daring enterprise. 'How can you, uncle?' I replied, so indignantly that with a meek sigh he sat down behind me. I made for the ravine and passed the mill, going along a road fresh from a summer rain. The bay stallion was seeking the open spaces, and, irritated by the necessity of going uphill, suddenly tore ahead. I pulled on the reins, pushing against the foot-bar, and raised myself high enough so that my uncle could not see that I was hanging onto the reins. But the stallion had his mind made up. He was three times younger than I – only four years old. Annoyed, he pulled the gig up the hill like a cat trying to run away from a tin can tied to its tail. I began to sense that my uncle had stopped smoking behind me, that he was breathing faster and was about to issue an ultimatum. I settled down more solidly, loosening the reins on the bay stallion and, to appear fully confident, I clicked my tongue in time with the spleen, which was pounding beautifully in the bay. 'Now don't you play, boy,' I admonished him patronizingly when he tried to gallop. I spread my arms more at ease and felt that my uncle had calmed down and had taken up his cigarette again. The game was won, although my heart was beating like the spleen of the horse.

Returning to town, I again bent my neck to the yoke of discipline. It was no great effort. Exercises and sports gave way to books and occasionally the theatre. I surrendered to the city, but hardly came in contact with it. Its life almost passed by me. And not by me alone – even the grown-ups dared not stick their heads too far out of the windows. Odessa was perhaps the most police-ridden city in police-ridden Russia. The main personage in town was the governor, the former Admiral Zelenoy the Second. He combined absolute power with an uncurbed temper. Innumerable anecdotes, which the Odessites exchanged in whispers, circulated about him. At that time there appeared abroad, printed in a free plant, a whole book of tales of the heroic deeds of Admiral Zelenoy the Second. I saw him but once, and then only his back. But that was enough for me. The governor was standing in his carriage, fully erect, and was cursing in his throaty voice across the street, shaking his fist. Policemen with their hands at attention and janitors with their caps in hand passed by him in review, and from behind curtained windows frightened faces looked out. I adjusted my school kit and hurried home.

Whenever I want to restore in my memory the scene of official Russia in the years of my early youth, I visualize the back of that governor, his fist stretched into space, and I hear his throaty curses, not usually found in dictionaries.

4
Books and Early Conflicts

In my inner life, not only during my school years but throughout my youth, nature and individuals occupied a lesser place than books and ideas. Despite my country upbringing, I was not sensitive to nature. My interest in it and my understanding of it came in later years, when childhood and even early youth were far behind. For a long time people passed through my mind like random shadows. I looked into myself and into books, in which in turn I tried again to find myself and my future.

My reading commenced in 1887 after the arrival at Yanovka of Moissey Filippovich, who brought with him a pile of books, including some of Tolstoy's writings for the people. At first reading was more of a task than a pleasure. Every new book brought with it new obstacles, such as unfamiliar words, unintelligible human relationships, and the vagueness and instability which separate fancy from reality. Usually there was nobody at hand to answer my questions, and so I was often at sea – beginning a book, giving it up and beginning it again – joining the uncertain joy of knowledge with the fear of the unknown. One might perhaps liken my reading experiences during that period to a night drive on the steppes: squeaking wheels and voices crossing one another, bonfires along the road flaring up in the darkness; everything seems familiar and yet one does not quite grasp its meaning. What is happening? Who is driving past – and carrying what? Even oneself – where is one going, forwards or backwards? Nothing is clear, and there is nobody like Uncle Gregory to explain: 'These are drivers carrying wheat.'

In Odessa the choice of books was vastly greater, and with it went attentive and sympathetic guidance. I devoured books ravenously and had to be forced to go out for walks. On my walks I would live through again in my mind what I had read, and then would hurry home to resume the reading. In the evenings I would beg to be allowed to stay up another quarter of an hour, or even only five minutes to finish the chapter. Hardly an evening passed without an argument of this kind.

The awakened hunger to see, to know, to absorb, found relief in this insatiable swallowing of printed matter – in the hands and lips of a child ever reaching out for the cup of verbal fancy. Everything in my later life that was interesting or thrilling, gay or sad, was already present in my reading experiences as a hint, a promise, a slight and timid sketch in pencil or water-colour.

During the first years of my stay in Odessa, reading aloud in the evenings, after I finished my home work and until I went to bed, gave me my happiest hours, or rather half-hours.

Moissey Filippovich usually read Pushkin or Nekrassov, more often the latter. But at the hour set Fanny Solomonovna would say, 'It's time to go to bed, Lyova.' I would look at her with imploring eyes. 'It's time to sleep, little boy,' Moissey Filippovich would say. 'Another five minutes,' I begged, and the five minutes were granted. After that, I kissed them good-night and went off with the feeling that I could listen to their reading all night, though I had scarcely laid my head on the pillow before I was fast asleep.

A girl in the last grade of high school, a distant relative called Sophia, came to stay with the Schpentzers for a few weeks until her family got over an attack of scarlet fever. She was a very capable and well-read girl, although, since she lacked originality and character, she soon faded away for me. But I admired her tremendously, and every day found in her new stores of knowledge and new qualities; by contrast I appeared in my own eyes as utterly insignificant. I helped her by copying her examination programme, and generally in various other small ways. In return, when the grown-ups were resting after dinner, she would read aloud to me. Before long we began to compose together a satirical poem, 'A Journey to the Moon'. In this work I always lagged behind. No sooner had I made some modest suggestion than the senior collaborator would catch the idea 'on the wing', develop it, introduce variations, and pick up rhymes without effort, what time I was, so to speak, being hauled in tow. When the six weeks were up and Sophia returned to her home, I felt that I had grown older.

Among the more notable friends of the family there was Sergey Ivanovich Sychevsky, an old journalist and a romantic personality, who was known in the South of Russia as an authority on Shakespeare. He was a gifted man but was addicted to drink. Because of this weakness, he wore a guilty air towards people, even towards children. He had known Fanny Solomonovna since her early youth, and called her 'Fannyushka'. Sergey Ivanovich became attached to me at the very first meeting. After asking what we were studying at school, the old man told me to write a paper comparing Pushkin's 'Poet and Bookseller' with Nekrassov's 'Poet and Citizen'. This nearly took my breath away. I had never even read the second work and, what was still more important, I was intimidated by the fact that Sychevsky was an *author*. The very word 'author' sounded to me as if it was uttered from some unattainable height. 'We will read it right away,' said Sergey Ivanovich, and began instantly to read. He read superbly. 'Did you understand? Well, put it all into your essay.' They seated me in the study, gave me Pushkin's and Nekrassov's works, paper and ink.

'I tell you, I can't do it,' I swore in a tragic whisper to Fanny Solomonovna. 'What can I write here?'

'Now, don't you get excited,' she answered, stroking my head. 'You write just as you understand it – that's all.'

Her hand was tender, and so was her voice. I calmed down a little, or rather got my frightened vanity under control, and began to write. About an hour later, I was summoned to show the result. I brought in a large sheet of paper, written all over, and, shaking in my boots as I never did at school, handed it to the 'author'. Sergey Ivanovich ran over a few lines in silence, and, turning his sparkling eyes to me, exclaimed: 'Just listen to what he wrote. He is a smart fellow, I swear!' And then he read: ' "The poet lived with his beloved nature, whose every sound, both gay and sad, echoed in the Poet's heart." Didn't he word it beautifully, "whose every sound" – just listen to this – "both gay and sad, echoed in the Poet's heart".' And so deeply did those words engrave themselves that day on my own mind that I have remembered them ever since.

At dinner Sergey Ivanovich joked a great deal, delved into memories of the past, and told stories, finding inspiration in the glass of vodka which was always ready at his call. Now and again he looked at me across the table and said: 'Where ever did you learn to put it so well? Really, I must give you a kiss.' Then, wiping his moustache carefully with a napkin, he rose and with unsteady steps set out on a trip around the table. I sat as if waiting for some catastrophic blow; a gladsome blow, it is true, but catastrophic all the same. 'Go and meet him, Lyova,' Moissey Filippovich whispered to me. After dinner Sergey Ivanovich recited from memory the satirical 'Popóv's Dream'. Tensely I watched his grey moustache, from under which there escaped such funny words. The author's half-drunken state did not in the least impair his eminence in my eyes. Children possess a remarkable power of abstraction.

In the evenings before it was dark I sometimes went for walks with Moissey Filippovich, and when he was in a good humour we talked about all sorts of things. On one occasion he told me the story of the opera *Faust*, which he liked very much. As I eagerly followed the story, I hoped that one day I might hear the opera on the stage. From a change in his tone, however, I became aware that the story was approaching a delicate point. I was quite disturbed by his embarrassment and began to fear that I should not hear the end of the story. But Moissey Filippovich recovered his calm and continued: 'Then a baby was born to Gretchen before marriage ...' We both felt relieved when we had passed this point; after that the story was safely brought to its conclusion.

I was in bed with a bandaged throat, and by way of consolation was given Dickens's *Oliver Twist*. The remark of the doctor in the nursing home about the woman's not having a wedding-ring perplexed me utterly.

'What does it mean?' I asked Moissey Filippovich. 'What has the wedding-ring to do with it?'

'Oh,' said he, somewhat haltingly, 'it is simply that when people are not married, they wear no wedding-ring.'

I recalled Gretchen. And the fate of Oliver Twist was spun out in my imagination from a ring, a ring which did not exist. The forbidden world of human relations burst into my consciousness fitfully from books, and much that I had heard spoken of in a casual, and usually coarse and gross manner, now through literature became generalized and ennobled, rising to some higher plane.

At that time, public opinion was stirred up over Tolstoy's *Power of Darkness*, which had just appeared. People discussed it with great earnestness and were unable to come to any definite conclusion. Pobedonostzev succeeded in inducing Tsar Alexander III to prohibit the play from being performed. I knew that Moissey Filippovich and Fanny Solomonovna, after I had gone to bed, read the play in the adjoining room. I could hear the murmur of their voices. 'May I read it, too?' I asked. 'No, dear, you are too young for that,' came the answer, and it sounded so categorical that I made no attempt to argue. At the same time I noticed that the slim new volume found its way to the familiar bookshelf. Seizing an opportunity when my guardians were out, I read Tolstoy's play in a few hurried instalments. It impressed me much less vividly than my mentors apparently feared it would. The most tragic scenes, such as the strangling of the child and the conversation about the creaking bones, were accepted not as a terrible reality, but as a literary invention, a stage trick; in other words, I did not really grasp them at all.

During a vacation in the country, while I was exploring a bookshelf high up under the ceiling, I came across a booklet brought home from Elizavetgrad by my elder brother. I opened it and instantly sensed something extraordinary and secret. This was a court report of a murder case in which a little girl was the victim of a sexual crime. I read the book, strewn with medical and legal details, with my mind all astir and alarmed, as if I had found myself in a wood at night, stumbling against ghost-like, moonlit trees and not able to find my way out. Human psychology, particularly in the case of children, has its own buffers, brakes, and safety-valves – an extensive and well-devised system which stands guard against untimely and too drastic shocks.

My first visit to the theatre took place when I was in the

preparatory class at school. It was like no other experience, and beggars description. I was sent, under the chaperonage of the school janitor, Gregory Kholod, to see a Ukrainian play. I sat pale as a sheet – so Gregory afterwards reported to Fanny Solomonovna – and was tortured by a joy which was more than I could bear. During the intermissions I did not leave my seat, lest – God forbid! – I might miss something. The performance ended with a comic sketch: *The Tenant with a Trombone*. The tension of drama was now relieved by riotous laughter. I swayed in my seat, now throwing back my head, and now again riveting my eyes on the stage. At home I related the story of the tenant with a trombone, adding more and more details every time, hoping to arouse the laughter which I had just experienced. To my great disappointment, I found my efforts quite wasted. 'It seems you did not like the *Nazar Stodolya* at all – did you?' asked Moissey Filippovich. I felt these words as an inner reproach. I thought of Nazar's sufferings and said: 'No, it was quite remarkable.'

Before passing to the third grade, I lived for a short time outside Odessa in the summer home of my engineer uncle. There I attended an amateur theatrical in which a boy from our school, Kruglyakov, played the part of a servant. Kruglyakov was a weak-chested, freckled boy, with intelligent eyes, but in a very poor state of health. I became greatly attached to him and begged him to stage some play with me. We chose Pushkin's *The Niggardly Knight*. I had to act the rôle of the son, and Kruglyakov that of the father. I unreservedly accepted his guidance, and spent whole days learning Pushkin's lines. What delicious excitement this was! Soon, however, everything went to pieces: Kruglyakov's parents vetoed his participation in the theatrical on account of his health. When school opened again, he attended classes only the first few weeks. I always tried to catch him after school so that I could engage him in literary conversation on the way home. Soon after that Kruglyakov disappeared altogether. I learned that he was ill. A few months later came the report that he had died of consumption.

The magic of the theatre held its spell over me for several years. Later I developed a fondness for Italian opera, which was the pride of Odessa. In the sixth grade I even did some tutoring to earn money for the theatre. For several months I was mutely in love with the coloratura soprano bearing the mysterious name of Giuseppina Uget, who seemed to me to have descended from heaven to the stage-boards of the Odessa theatre.

I was not supposed to read newspapers. But the rule was not very strictly observed, and gradually, with a few setbacks, I won the right to read papers, more particularly the *feuilleton* columns. The centre of interest in the press of Odessa was occupied by the theatre, especially the opera, and such public divisions of opinion as occurred were mainly inspired by theatrical preferences. This was the only sphere in which the newspapers were allowed to display any semblance of temperament.

In those days the star of Doroshevich, the *feuilleton*- columnist, shone particularly brightly. Within a short time he became the idol of the city, although he wrote of small and, not infrequently, trivial things. But unquestionably he had talent, and by the daring form of his actually innocent articles he let fresh air into an Odessa oppressed to a state of strangulation by the governor, Zelenoy the Second. When I opened the morning paper, I immediately looked for the name of Doroshevich. This enthusiasm for his articles was then shared both by the moderate fathers and by their children who had not yet become immoderate.

From early years my love for words had now been losing, now gaining in force, but generally putting down ever firmer roots. In my eyes authors, journalists, and artists always stood for a world which was more attractive than any other, one open only to the elect.

In the second grade we started a magazine. Moissey Filippovich and I had many talks on this subject, and Moissey Filippovich even devised a title: *The Drop* – the idea being that the second grade of the St Paul *realschule* was contributing its 'drop' to the ocean of literature. I embodied this in a poem which took the place of an introductory article. There were other poems and stories, likewise mostly mine. One of our draftsmen decorated the cover with an involved ornamental design. Somebody suggested showing *The Drop* to Krizhanovsky. The commission was undertaken by the boy Y., who lived in Krizhanovsky's house. He performed his task with real brilliance: he rose from his seat, walked up to the master's desk, firmly laid *The Drop* upon it, ceremoniously bowed, and returned to his seat. We all held our breath. Krizhanovsky looked at the cover, made a few grimaces with his moustache, eyebrows, and beard, and silently began to read. There was complete quiet in the room; only the leaves of *The Drop* rustled. Then he got up from his desk and with great feeling read aloud my 'Pure little drop'. 'Good?' he asked. 'Good', answered the boys in chorus. 'Yes, it may be good, but the author knows nothing about versification. Now, tell me, what is a dactyl?' he turned to me, having guessed the author behind the thinly disguised *nom de plume*. 'I don't know,' I had to confess. 'Then I'll tell you.' And neglecting several lessons in grammar and syntax, Krizhanovsky explained to the little second-grade boys the mysteries of metric versification. 'And as for the magazine,' he said at the end, 'it will be better if you don't bother about it or the ocean of literature either, but let this be just your exercise-book.' It must be explained that school magazines were forbidden at that time. The question, however, found a different solution. The peaceful course of my studies was suddenly interrupted by my expulsion from the St Paul *realschule*.

From the days of my childhood I had many conflicts in life, which sprang, as a jurist would say, out of the struggle against injustice. The same motive not infrequently determined my making or breaking of friendships. It would take too long to go through all the numerous episodes. But there were two which assumed considerable proportions.

My biggest conflict occurred in the second grade with Burnande, whom we nicknamed 'The Frenchman', though he was really a Swiss. In the school the German language, to some extent, rivalled the Russian. Our French, on the other hand, showed very little progress. Most of the boys learned French for the first time at school, but the German colonists found it particularly difficult. Burnande waged a relentless war against the Germans. His favourite victim was Vakker. The latter was really a very poor scholar. But this time many if not all of us got the impression that the boy did not deserve the lowest marks that Burnande gave him. And that day Burnande was even more ferocious than ever, swallowing a double dose of dyspepsia tablets.

'Let's give him a concert,' the boys began whispering around, winking at and nudging one another. Among them I occupied not the least place, perhaps even the first. Such concerts had occasionally been arranged before, particularly in honour of the drawing-master, who was disliked for his spiteful stupidity. To give a concert meant to accompany the steps of the teacher while he was leaving the classroom with a howling sound made with a closed mouth, so that one could not tell who was actually doing it. Once or twice Burnande got it, but in a mild and considerably muffled form, as he was feared. This time, however, we mustered all our courage. The moment the Frenchman put the school 'journal' under his arm, there came, from the extreme flank, a howl which spread in a rolling wave to the desks in front. I for my part did what I could. Burnande, who had already stepped through the door, instantly turned back, and stood in the middle of the room, face to face with his enemies, his face pale-green and his eyes darting fire, but without uttering a word. The boys behind the desks, particularly those in the front seats, looked innocence itself. Those in the back seats were busy with their kits as if nothing had happened. After staring at us for half a minute Burnande turned to the door in such a fury that the tails of his coat blew out like sails. The Frenchman was accompanied this time by a unanimous and enthusiastic howl which followed him far down the corridor.

Before the next lesson began there came into the classroom Burnande, Schwannebach, and the class monitor Mayer, who was known among the boys as 'Ram' on account of his bulging eyes, strong forehead, and torpid brain. Schwannebach essayed something resembling an introductory speech, all the while circumnavigating with extreme care the hidden reefs of the Russian declensions and conjugations. Burnande breathed revenge. And Mayer scrutinized the boys' faces with his protruding eyes, calling out those known to be sportive, and saying: 'You are sure to have been in it.' Some boys mildly protested their innocence; others maintained silence. In this way ten or fifteen boys were picked out for detention 'without dinner', some for one hour, and some for two hours. The rest were allowed to go home, and I was of their number, although I believe I saw Burnande cast an intensely prying glance at me during the roll-call. I did nothing to obtain exemption. Neither did I accuse myself. I left the school rather with a feeling of regret, as staying with the other boys would have promised a jolly time.

Next morning, when I was on my way to school with the memory of the previous day's incident barely present in my mind, I was stopped at the gate by one of the punished boys. 'Look here,' he said, 'you're in for trouble. Yesterday Danilov accused you before Mayer, Mayer called Burnande, then the head master came, and they all tried to find out if you were the ringleader.'

My heart sank into my boots. And at the same moment the monitor, Peter Pavlovich, emerged. 'Go to the head master,' he said. The fact that he *had* waited for me at the entrance, and the tone in which he addressed me, augured ill. Inquiring of one doorman after another, I found my way into the mystery-wrapt corridor where the head master's room was, and there I stopped outside his door. The head master passed me, looked at me gravely and shook his head. I stood there, more dead than alive. The head master came out of his room again and only let fall: 'All right! All right!' I realized that in point of fact it was not all right at all. A few minutes later teachers began to come out of their room next door, the majority of them hurrying to their classrooms without so much as noticing me. Krizhanovsky answered my bow with a sly grimace which seemed to say: 'Got in a mess, my boy. I'm sorry for you, but such is fate.' And Burnande, after my courteous bow, came right up to me, bent his spiteful little beard over me, and waving his hands said: 'The star student of the second grade is a moral outcast,' then turned and walked away. A few minutes later the 'Ram' straddled up. 'That's the sort of bird you are,' he said with apparent satisfaction. 'We'll teach you a lesson.' Then my long torture commenced. In my classroom, from which I was kept away, there was no lesson: a cross-examination was going on there. Burnande, the head master, Mayer, and the 'inspector' Kaminsky formed a supreme investigating committee to inquire into the case of the moral outcast.

It began, as transpired afterwards, with one of the punished boys complaining to Mayer during the detention in school: 'We have been unjustly punished. The one who made the most noise went scot-free. B. egged the other boys on and shouted himself, and he was allowed to go home. And Carlson, he will tell you so, too.'

'I don't believe it,' said Mayer, 'B. is a well-behaved boy.' But Carlson, the boy who recommended Binneman to me as the cleverest man in Odessa, corroborated the accusation, as did a few others. Mayer called Burnande. Encouraged and urged on by their superiors, infecting one another with their example, there emerged ten or twelve informers from the entire body of boys.

They began to search their memories. A year before B. had said something during a walk about the head master. B. had repeated it to somebody else. B. had taken part in the 'concert' to Zmigordsky. Vakker, who was the cause of all the trouble, said in a moving voice: 'I cried, as you know, because Gustave Samoilovich gave me the lowest marks, and B. came up to me, put his hand on my shoulder and said: "Don't cry, Vakker, we will write the inspector-general such a letter that he will dismiss Burnande." '

'Write to whom?'

'The inspector-general.'

'Is that so! And what did you say?'

'I said nothing, of course.'

Danilox picked up the story: 'That's quite true. B. suggested writing a letter to the inspector-general, but not to sign it, so as not to get expelled, but to let everyone write one character in the letter in turn.'

'I see,' gloated Burnande, 'everyone a character in turn!'

All of the boys, without exception, were cross-examined. A number of them flatly denied everything – both what did not happen and what did. One of them was Kostya R., who wept bitterly at seeing his best friend, the star student, so shamefully betrayed. The informers denounced these stubborn deniers as my friends. Panic reigned in the classroom. The majority of the boys closed up and said nothing. For once Danilov was playing first-fiddle, which had never happened to him before and never did again. I stood in the corridor near the head master's room, next to a yellow polished cupboard, like a man who had committed a grave crime against the state. There the principal witnesses were brought in turn to confront the accused. In the end I was told to go home.

'Go and tell your parents to come here.'

'My parents are way down in the country.'

'Then tell your guardians.'

Only the day before I had held the undisputed rank of star student, quite a distance ahead of the next boy. Even Mayer had never so much as suspected me. Today I lay prostrate on the ground, and Danilov, who was known for his laziness and naughtiness, was reviling me in front of the entire class and the authorities of the school. What had happened? Had I come too rashly to the aid of an injured boy who was not my friend and for whom otherwise I had no feeling of sympathy? Or had I placed too much confidence in the united support of the class? I was in no mood for these generalizations, however, while I was returning to the Pokrovsky Alley. With a distorted face and beating heart, in a flood of words and tears, I related what happened. My guardians tried to console me as best they could, though they themselves were greatly perturbed. Fanny Solomonovna went to see the head master, the inspector Krizhanovsky, and Yurchenko, trying to explain, to persuade, and quoting her own experience as a teacher. All this was being done without my knowledge. I sat in my room, with my kit unopened on the table, and moped. Days passed. How would it end? The head master said: 'A meeting of the teachers' council will be called to consider the question in its entirety.' This sounded awe-inspiring.

The meeting took place. Moissey Filippovich went to hear the decision. I waited for his return with greater excitement than I did in later years for the sentence of the Tsar's court.

The entry downstairs resounded with the familiar bang, familiar footsteps mounted the iron staircase, the dining-room door opened, and simultaneously from another room appeared

Fanny Solomonovna. Gently I lifted my curtain. 'Expelled,' said Moissey Filippovich in a voice that betrayed fatigue. 'Expelled?' asked Fanny Solomonovna, catching her breath. 'Expelled,' repeated Moissey Filippovich in a still lower tone. I said nothing, only glanced at Moissey Filippovich and Fanny Solomonovna and withdrew behind my curtain. During the summer vacation, on a visit to Yanovka, Fanny Solomonovna described the scene: 'When this word was uttered he turned all green, so that I became very alarmed about him.' I did not cry. I merely pined.

At the teachers' council three degrees of expulsion were debated: without the right of joining any school; without the right of re-entering the St Paul *realschule*; and finally, *with* the right of re-entering the latter. The last and most lenient form was selected. I shuddered at the thought of the effect that breaking the news would have on my parents. My guardians did everything in their power to soften the blow. Fanny Solomonovna wrote a long letter to my elder sister, with instructions as to how the news should be broken. I stayed on in Odessa until the end of the school year and went home for the vacation as usual. During the long evenings, when my father and mother were already asleep, I would relate to my sister and oldest brother how it all happened, impersonating the teachers and the boys. The memory of their own school life was still fresh with my sister and brother. At the same time they regarded themselves as my superiors. Now they shook their heads, and then they burst out laughing over my story. From laughter my sister went on to tears and cried copiously, with her head resting on the table. It was decided then that I was to go on a visit somewhere for a week or two, and while I was away my sister would tell Father everything. She herself was rather frightened by her commission. After the academic failure of my oldest brother my father's ambition had centred in me. The first years seemed to bear out his hopes, and then suddenly all had gone down with a crash.

Returning to my home from the visit with a boy friend – Grisha, the grandson of Moissey Kharitonovich, the right-handed musician – I instantly perceived that everything was known. Mother welcomed Grisha very cordially, but pretended that she did not see me at all. On the contrary Father behaved as if nothing had happened. But a few days later, while he was resting in the cool hall after coming home from the fields, he suddenly asked me in the presence of Mother: 'Show me how you whistled at your head master. Like this? With two fingers in the mouth?' And, illustrating, he burst out laughing. Mother, greatly surprised, kept moving her eyes from Father to myself. On her face a smile struggled with indignation; how could one talk with such levity about such dreadful things? But Father persisted in his demand: 'Show how you whistled.' And his laughter grew still merrier. Pained as he was, he obviously relished the idea that his offspring, despite his title of the star student, had daring enough to whistle at high officials. In vain did I try to convince him that there was no whistling, but only a peaceful and perfectly innocent howl. He insisted that it was whistling. It ended up with Mother bursting into tears.

I made hardly any effort to prepare for the examinations. What had taken place made me lose, for the time being, all interest in study. I spent a restless summer with ever-recurring flare-ups of ill temper, and about a fortnight before the examinations returned to Odessa, but even there worked very badly. Perhaps the greatest effort I made was in the study of French. At the actual examination, however, Burnande confined himself to a few cursory questions. Other teachers asked even less. I was admitted to the third grade. There I met most of the boys who had either betrayed me, or defended me, or had remained neutral. This determined my personal relations for a long time. Some boys I cut completely; with others who had supported me during these trying moments I became even more friendly.

Such, one might say, was the first political test I underwent. These were the groups that resulted from that episode: the tale-bearers and the envious at one pole, the frank, courageous boys at the other, and the neutral, vacillating mass in the middle. These three groups never quite disappeared even during the years that followed. I met them again and again in my life in the most varied circumstances.

The snow was not yet all cleared from the streets – but it was already warm. The housetops, the trees, and the sparrows proclaimed the spring. The fourth-grade boy was walking home, carrying in his hand, against all regulations, a strap from his kit, the reason being that the hook was torn off. The long coat seemed useless and heavy, merely causing one's body to perspire. Fatigue went with it. The boy saw everything in a new light, himself above all. The spring sun stimulated the feeling that there was something immeasurably mightier than the school, the inspector, and the kit hanging aslant on the back – mightier than studying, chess, dinners and even reading and the theatre; in short, than all of one's everyday life. And the longing after this something unfathomed, commanding obedience and rising high above the individual, seized upon the boy's entire being down to the marrow of his bones and called forth the sweet pain of exhaustion.

He came home with a buzzing head, with painful music in his temples. Dropping the kit on the table, he lay down on the bed and, hardly realizing what he was doing, began to weep into the pillow. To find an excuse for his tears he recalled pitiful scenes from books and from his own life, as if to feed the furnace with fresh fuel, and wept and wept with tears of spring longing. He was in the fourteenth year of his life.

From his childhood the boy had suffered from a disease which the doctors in their official certificates described as chronic catarrh of the digestive tract, and which was closely intertwined with his entire life. Often he had to take medicine and go on a diet. Nervous shocks nearly always affected his digestion. In the fourth grade the disease became so acute that it crippled his studies. After a long but unsuccessful course of treatment the doctors passed sentence: the invalid must be sent to the country.

I received the doctors' verdict with pleasure rather than with regret. But it was necessary to gain the consent of my parents. It was necessary to get a tutor to stay with me in the country to avoid losing a year at school. This meant extra expense, and they did not like extra expense at Yanovka. With the help of Moissey Filippovich, however, the matter was finally arranged. The student G. was engaged as a tutor – a little man with a huge mane of hair, grown noticeably grey on the sides. He was slightly vain and slightly fantastic, very talkative and utterly lacking in character – one of that type of former undergraduate with an uncompleted education which never succeeds in life. He wrote verse and even had two poems published in the local paper. The two issues were always with him, and he was only too pleased to show them. His relations with me were subject to spasmodic outbursts tending constantly to get worse. At first G. established with me a relationship of ever-growing familiarity, insisting on every occasion that he wanted to be my friend. To this end he showed me the photograph of a certain Claudia and described their rather complicated relations. Then he would suddenly draw back and demand from me the respectful attitude due to the teacher from his pupil. This grotesque situation ended badly; there was a violent quarrel, and a final break between us. But even the episode with the tutor was not without effect, whatever one may think of it. Here was a man with greying hair confiding to me the secrets of his association with a woman who in her photograph looked very imposing. This made me feel older.

In the upper grades the teaching of literature passed from Krizhanovsky to the hands of Gamov. The latter was still a young man, fair-haired, rather plump, very short-sighted, and without the least spark of interest in his subject. We dismally tottered along after him from chapter to chapter. To top this off Gamov was also not punctual and would put off indefinitely the reviewing of our papers. In the fifth grade we were supposed to do four home papers on literature. I began to regard the task with an ever-growing attachment. I read not only the sources indicated by the teacher, but a number of other books as well, copying out facts and passages, altering and appropriating the sentences that caught my imagination, and in general working with a great enthusiasm which did not always stop at the threshold of innocent plagiarism. There were a few other boys who did not regard composition merely as an odious task.

Excitedly – some with fear, others with hope – the fifth-grade boys waited for the grading of their work. But the marks never arrived. The same thing happened in the second quarter of the school year. In the third quarter I handed in a paper which filled an entire pad. A week passed, then a second, and a third – but there was no trace of our work. Cautiously we brought the fact to Gamov's attention. His answer was evasive. At the next lesson Yablonovsky, also an eager composition-writer, put the question point-blank to Gamov: what was the reason for our never learning the fate of our papers, and what did actually happen to them? Gamov sharply told him to shut up. But Yablonovsky would not give up. Knitting his eyebrows still closer together, he began nervously to pull at the top of his desk, and, raising his voice, kept repeating that it was 'impossible to go on working like this'.

'I must ask you again to keep silent and sit down,' answered Gamov. But Yablonovsky would neither sit down nor stop talking. 'Please leave the room,' shouted Gamov. My relations with Yablonovsky had not been friendly for some time. The affair with Burnande in the second grade taught me to be more circumspect. But here I felt that I could not keep silent. 'Anton Mikailovich,' I cried, 'Yablonovsky is right and we all support him.'

'He's right, he's right,' echoed other boys. Gamov at first seemed somewhat taken aback, but immediately recovered, and flying into a rage shouted at the top of his voice: 'I know myself what to do and when to do it . . . I don't take orders from you. You are violating the rules . . .' We had evidently touched some sore spot.

'We only want to see our papers, that's all,' a third one chimed in. Gamov was fuming. 'Yablonovsky, leave the room at once!' he shouted. Yablonovsky did not budge. 'Go out, do go out,' came whispers from all sides. Shrugging his shoulders, rolling the whites of his eyes, and stamping heavily with his boots, Yablonovsky left the room, banging the door with all the force he could muster. At the beginning of recess Kaminsky slid into the room on his noiseless rubber soles. This was a bad omen. The room became very quiet. In a husky falsetto voice like a drunkard's, he administered a short, but very stern reproof containing a threat of expulsion from the school, and announced the punishment: Yablonovsky to be put in solitary confinement for twenty-four hours, and to be given a 'three' in conduct; for me, twenty-four hours in solitary confinement; and for the third protestant, twelve hours. That was the second hole on my academic road. The case brought no other important consequences. Gamov did not return our papers in spite of everything. And we too tried to forget the matter.

That year was marked by the death of the Tsar. The event seemed tremendous, even incredible, but very distant, like an earthquake in another country. Neither I nor the people about me were at all moved by the Tsar's illness, felt any sympathy for him, or any sorrow on account of his death. When I came to school the following morning, the place seemed gripped by something like a great, but causeless panic. 'The Tsar is dead,' said the boys one to another, and did not know what to say next, or how to express their feelings, for they did not realize themselves what this feeling was. But they knew well that there would be no classes, and, without showing it, were pleased at the prospect, particularly those who had not done their home work, or who were afraid of being called down. The janitor directed all comers into the big hall where requiem services were being arranged. The priest in gold spectacles said a few appropriate words: children are grieved when their father dies – how much greater must be the grief when the father of the whole people dies! But there was no grief. The requiem dragged on. It was trying and dull. Everybody was ordered to put a mourning-band around his left arm and to cover the badge on his cap with black muslin. Everything else went on as before.

In the fifth grade the boys were already exchanging views about going to college and choosing their vocations. A great deal of talk centred on the competitive entrance examinations, on the sternness of the St Petersburg professors towards the applicants, the tricky problems that were asked, and the specialists in St Petersburg who coached boys for their examinations. Among the older boys we knew there were some who went to St Petersburg year after year, flunked the examinations, prepared again, and again went through the same experience. At the thought of these future trials many a boy felt his heart freeze two years before the time.

The sixth grade passed without incident. Everybody was anxious to escape from the school drudgery as soon as possible. The matriculation examinations were staged with all pomp in the great hall, and with the participation of university professors sent especially by the educational authorities. The head master would open with great solemnity the package received from the inspector-general, which contained the subject for the papers. Its announcement was usually followed by a general sigh of fear, as if everybody had been dipped into icy water. The nervous suspense made one think that the task was utterly beyond one's powers. But further consideration soon revealed that the fears were much exaggerated. As the time drew towards the end of the two hours allotted for each paper, the teachers themselves would help us deceive the vigilance of the regional authorities. Having finished my paper, I did not hand it in immediately but remained in the hall, by a tacit agreement with the inspector Krizhanovsky, and engaged in animated correspondence with those who found themselves in difficulties.

The seventh grade was considered a supplementary one. There was no seventh grade in the St Paul *realschule* – and this necessitated a transfer to another school. In the interim we found ourselves free citizens. For the occasion everybody outfitted himself in civilian attire. The very evening of the day we received our diplomas a large group of us disported ourselves in the Summer Garden, where gay cabaret actresses sang on the open stage and where schoolboys were strictly forbidden to enter. We all wore neckties and smoked cigarettes, and there were two bottles of beer adorning the table. Deep in our hearts we were afraid of our own daring. No sooner had we opened the first bottle when the school monitor Wilhelm, nicknamed 'the goat' because of his bleating voice, sprang up right before our table. Instinctively we made an effort to rise and felt our hearts jump. But everything came off well. 'You are already here?' said Wilhelm with a tinge of regret in his voice, and graciously shook hands with us. The eldest of the boys, K., wearing a ring on his finger, nonchalantly invited the monitor to have a glass of beer with us. This was carrying it too far. Wilhelm, with a show of dignity, declined and, hurriedly saying 'good-bye', walked away in search of the boys who ventured to step over the forbidden threshold of the Garden. With redoubled awareness of our own status we attacked the beer.

The seven years I spent in the school, beginning with the preparatory class, had their joys too. But it would seem that these were not as plentiful as sorrows. The colour of my memory of the school, taken as a whole, has remained if not quite black, at least decidedly grey. Above all the episodes of school life, whether gay or sad, towered the régime of soulless, official formalism. It would be difficult to name a single teacher of whom I could think with genuine affection. And yet our school was not the worst. It certainly did teach me a few things: elementary knowledge, the habit of methodical work, and outward discipline. All these came in advantageously in my later life. The same school, however, sowed in me, contrary to its direct purpose, the seeds of enmity for the existing order. These seeds, at any rate, did not fall on barren ground.

5
Country and Town

The first nine years of my life, without a break, I spent in the country. During the next seven years I returned there every summer, sometimes also at Christmas and Easter. I was closely bound to Yanovka and all its environs until I was nearly eighteen. Throughout the early part of my childhood the influence of the country was paramount. In the next period, however, it had to defend itself against the influence of the town, and was forced to retreat all along the line.

The country made me familiar with agriculture, the flour-mill, and the American sheaf-binding machine. It brought me into close contact with peasants, the ones who lived near by and came to the flour-mill, and those far-away ones from the Ukrainian districts, who came with a scythe and a bag behind their backs. Much of my country life vanished from my memory or was shoved into the subconscious, but at every new turn some small part of it would emerge, often to help me greatly. The country brought me face to face with the various types of decadence in the gentry, and the types of capitalist aggrandizement. It revealed to me the natural coarseness of many aspects of human relationships, and intensified my feeling for that other urban type of culture, at once more advanced and more contradictory.

It was on my very first vacation that the contrast between town and country impressed itself on my mind. On my journey home I was all impatience. My heart was beating with joy. I longed to see everything again and to be seen. At Novy Bug I was met by my father. I showed him my school report, proudly displaying my high marks, and explained that now I was in the first grade and therefore I had to have a full-dress uniform. We were driving by night, in a covered wagon, with a young mill assistant in the place of the coachman. On the steppe, particularly in the dells, one felt a slight draught of cold, misty air, which made my father wrap me in a huge Cossack cloak. I was intoxicated with the change of environment, with the drive, the recollections, the new impressions, and was very talkative, running on about the school, the public baths, my friend Kostya R., the theatre, and so on. I gave full descriptions first of the *Nazar Stodolya*, and then of *The Tenant with a Trombone*. My father, sometimes awake, sometimes asleep, listened to me, and laughed quite a bit. The young assistant shook his head from time to time, and turning to my father said: 'What a story!'

Towards morning I fell asleep and woke up at Yanovka. Our house looked terribly small to me now; the home-made wheat bread seemed grey, and the whole routine of country life seemed at once familiar and strange. I described the theatre to my mother and sisters, but not nearly so fervently as I had to my father. In the workshop I found Victor and David so changed I could scarcely recognize them – they had grown bigger and stronger. But they thought me different, too. From the first they began to address me with the more respectful 'vy' (you), at which I protested. 'Well, what else can I call you?' retorted David. 'You are now a learned man.' During my absence Ivan Vasilyevich had married. The servants' kitchen had been rebuilt and served him as a house, while a new hut behind the machine-shop had been made over into a kitchen.

These were not the most important things, however. Something new had grown up like a wall between myself and the things bound up with my childhood. Everything seemed the same and yet quite different. Objects and people looked like counterfeits of themselves. Of course, certain things had changed during the year. But others seemed changed largely because I saw them with different eyes. After my first return home I began to grow away from my family. At first the breach revealed itself in trivialities, but as the years went on it became more and more serious and far-reaching.

The conflicting influences of town and country coloured the entire period of my school life. In the town my relations with other people were, I felt, more constant. With the exception of a few conflicts, however violent, such as those with the teachers of French and Russian, I got along peacefully under the school and family discipline. This should be attributed not only to the mode of life in the Schpentzer household, in which sensible strictness and comparatively high standards in personal relations were the rule, but also to the whole system of life in the city. To be sure, its contradictions were no less marked than those of country life – in fact they were greater – but in town they were more disguised, controlled, and regulated. People of different classes in town came into contact with one another only in their business relations; outside of these they did not exist for one another. In the country everybody lived in open view of everybody else. The relationship between a master and a servant stood out there like a spring in an old couch. My own behaviour in the country was more unbalanced and quarrelsome. There were several occasions when I quarrelled even with Fanny Solomonovna, who, on her visits to Yanovka, sometimes cautiously sided with my mother or sisters; and yet in town my relations with her were not only friendly but even affectionate. These clashes sometimes sprang up out of mere trifles. On other occasions, however, something much more important was at their source.

In a freshly laundered duck suit, with a leather belt that had a brass buckle, and a white cap with a glittering yellow badge, I felt that I was simply magnificent. And I had to show everybody. Together with my father I drove into the field on a day when the harvesting of winter wheat was at its peak. The head mower Arkhip, looking at once sullen and kindly, was leading the way over the hill, followed by eleven mowers and twelve women binders. Twelve scythes were cutting the wheat and the sultry air as well. Arkhip's feet were wrapped in pieces of cloth tightened by a button. The women binders wore torn skirts, or simply shirts of unbleached cotton. From a distance the sound of the mowing-scythes was as if the hot air itself were ringing.

'Well, well, let's see what this winter wheat is like,' said Father, taking Arkhip's scythe and stepping into his place. I watched him excitedly. Father made simple, homely movements, as if he were not actually working but only getting ready to begin, and his steps were light and tentative as if he were looking for a place to get a better swing. His scythe was also moving simply, without any swagger about it, and even – or so it seemed – not quite firmly. And yet it was cutting very low and very evenly, with each swift shave laying the ears in a straight belt running along on his left. Arkhip looked on with one eye, clearly approving Father's skill. The attitude of the others varied. Some seemed to be sympathetic, as if they thought the old fellow were no mere novice, while others were indifferent, as if feeling that it was no great achievement to mow what was one's own, and in order to show off, at that. Probably I did not translate their thoughts into exact words, but I had an intense realization of the complicated mechanics of their relations.

After Father had left for another field I also made an attempt to wield the scythe. 'Strike the hay on your heel, boy, on your heel; keep your toes free, don't press.' But in my excitement I couldn't quite see where that heel of mine actually was, and on the third swing of the scythe my toes dug right into the earth. 'That will soon finish the scythe, if you go on like this,' said Arkhip. 'You'd better learn from your father.' A woman binder, dark-faced and covered with dust, gave me a sneering look. I stepped out of the ranks with decided haste, still in my badge-adorned cap, from under which sweat was coming down in streams. 'Go and eat cakes with your mother,' came mockingly from behind. It was Mutuzka. I knew that mower, with a skin as dark as his boots. This was his third year at Yanovka. He lived in the village, had his wits about him, was sharp with his tongue, and on occasion in the preceding year, in my hearing and for my special benefit, had spoken nasty but very apt words about his masters. His smartness and daring appealed to my imagination, but his unbridled and shameless scoffing made me boil with impotent hatred. I should have liked to say something to him that would win him over to my side, or, on the contrary, to pull him up with a sharp word of command, but I did not know what to say.

As I returned home from the field I saw a barefooted woman at our doorstep. She was sitting on the ground, leaning against the wall, having apparently not courage enough to sit on the stone step. She was the mother of a half-witted shepherd boy, Ignatka, and she had walked seven versts to our house to get one rouble that was owed her. But there was no one in the house, and she could not get her rouble; so she had to wait until evening. It made my heart tighten to look at that figure – the embodiment of poverty and submission.

It was no better next year; in fact, it was worse. I was returning home after a game of croquet when I met my father in the courtyard. He had just arrived from the fields, all covered with dust, worn out and in a bad humour. A peasant, a piebald little man, was stumping behind him on bare, black-heeled feet. 'For the Lord's sake, please let me have my cow,' he kept saying, swearing that he would do everything to keep it away from the fields. Father answered: 'Your cow may eat only ten kopecks' worth of grain, but it will do ten roubles' worth of damage.' The peasant kept on beseeching, and in his pleas one could feel his hatred. The scene stirred me to my very marrow. The genial mood I had carried away from the croquet court with its fringe of pear-trees, where I had routed my sisters with flying colours, instantly gave way to a feeling of intense despair. I slipped past my father into my bedroom, and falling flat on the bed, gave myself up to tears, despite my status of a boy of the second grade. Father walked through the hall into the dining-room, with the little peasant pattering behind him up to the doorstep. I could hear their voices. Then the peasant left. Mother came from the mill – I could recognize her voice at once; the sound of plates being prepared for dinner came through, and I heard Mother calling me ... But I did not answer, and went on weeping. Tears were beginning to yield a sense of blissful pleasure. Then the door opened, and Mother bent over me.

'What's the matter, Lyovochka?'

I made no answer. Mother and Father whispered something to one another.

'Are you upset about that peasant? But we gave him back his cow, and we did not fine him.'

'I am not upset about that at all,' I answered from under the pillow, painfully ashamed of the cause of my tears.

'And we didn't fine him,' Mother said again, with emphasis.

It was Father who had guessed the cause of my sorrow and told Mother. Father noticed much in passing, with one quick glance.

One day, when Father was away, a police sergeant, a rude, greedy, and arrogant creature, came down and demanded the workers' passports. He found two overdue. Immediately he called their owners from the field and declared them under arrest for conveyance to their homes as prisoners. One of them was an old man whose brown neck was shrivelled into deep folds; the other was his young nephew. They dropped to their parched knees on the earthen floor of the hall, first the old man, then the younger one, and bowed their heads to the ground. They kept saying: 'Do be merciful – don't ruin us, sir!' The fat and sweating sergeant played with his sword, drank cold milk that had been brought to him from the cellar, and answered: 'I give mercy only on feast-days, and this is a weekday.' I felt as if I were sitting on fire and in a broken voice let fall some words of protest. 'You'd better mind your own business, young man,' the sergeant remarked with stern deliberation, while my elder sister waved her finger at me warningly. The sergeant left with the two labourers.

During my vacation I attended to the bookkeeping, that is, I took turn about with my elder brother and sister, entering in the books the names of labourers employed, the terms of employment, and payments made, whether in kind or in cash. I often assisted my father when wages were paid out, and on those occasions there were sudden, brief flashes of temper between us, which remained suppressed only because of the presence of the labourers. There was never any cheating in the making up of the accounts, but the terms of employment were always interpreted harshly. The labourers, particularly the older ones, sensed that the boy was on their side, and this annoyed Father.

After our clashes I would go out with a book and would stay away even through dinner. On one such occasion I was caught in a storm in the fields. There was a continuous cracking of thunder, the steppe rain was gurgling in rivulets, and lightning kept flashing from all sides as if trying to get at me. I went on pacing up and down, all soaked through, in shoes that yelped like dogs, and in a cap that looked like a waterspout. When I returned home I was greeted with sidelong glances and silence. Sister gave me a change of dry clothes and something to eat.

Returning to town after the vacations, I was usually accompanied by my father. As a rule we did not take a porter but carried our luggage ourselves. Father carried the heavier bags, and by his back and distended arms I could see that he was straining himself. I felt sorry for him and tried to carry as much as I could. But when we happened to have with us a heavy box full of gifts from home for the relatives in Odessa, we hired a porter. Father was stingy with his tips, the porter was dissatisfied, and shook his head angrily. I always felt very pained about this. When I travelled alone and had to resort to porters, I spent my pocket-money in no time, looking anxiously into the porter's eyes, and always afraid to give too little. This was a reaction against the closeness at home, and it has persisted throughout my life.

In the country as well as in the town I lived in a petty-bourgeois environment where the principal effort was directed towards acquisition. In this respect I cut myself off both from the country of my early childhood and from the town of my youth. The instinct of acquisition, the petty-bourgeois outlook and habits of life – from these I sailed away with a mighty push, and I did so never to return.

In the spheres of religion and nationality there was no opposition between the country and the town; on the contrary they complemented one another in various respects. In my father's family there was no strict observance of religion. At first appearances were kept up through sheer inertia: on holy days my parents journeyed to the synagogue in the colony; Mother abstained from sewing on Saturdays, at least within the sight of others. But all this ceremonial observance of religion lessened as years went on – as the children grew up and the prosperity of the family increased. Father did not believe in God from his youth, and in later years spoke openly about it in front of Mother and the children. Mother preferred to avoid the subject, but when occasion required would raise her eyes in prayer.

When I was about seven or eight years old, belief in God was still regarded in the family as something officially recognized. On one occasion a visiting guest before whom my parents, as was their wont, were boasting about their son, making me show my sketches and recite poetry, asked me the question:

'What do you know of God?'

'God is a sort of man,' I answered without hesitation.

But the guest shook his head: 'No, God is not a man.'

'What is God?' I asked him in my turn, for besides man I knew only animals and plants. The guest, my father, and my mother exchanged glances with an embarrassed smile, as always happens among grown-ups when children begin to shake the most firmly established conventions.

'God is spirit,' said the guest. Now it was I who looked with a smile of confusion at my seniors, trying to read in their faces whether they were serious or joking. But no, it was not a joke. I bowed my head before their knowledge. Soon I got used to the idea that God was spirit. As became a little savage, I connected God with my own 'spirit', calling it 'soul', and already knowing that 'soul', that is, 'breath', ends when death comes.* I did not yet know, however, that this doctrine bore the name of 'animism'.

On my first vacation at home, when I was getting ready to go to sleep on the sofa in the dining-room, I got into a discussion about God with the student Z., who was a visiting guest at Yanovka and slept on the divan. At that time I was not quite sure whether God did exist or not, and did not worry much about it, though I did not mind finding a definite answer.

'Where does the soul go after death?' I asked Z., bending over the pillow.

'Where does it go when a man is asleep?' came the answer.

'Well, it is then still . . .' I argued, trying to keep awake.

'And where does the soul of the horse go when he drops dead?' persisted Z. in his attack.

This answer satisfied me completely and I fell into a contented sleep.

In the Schpentzer family religion was not observed at all, not

---

*In Russian 'spirit', 'soul', and 'breath' – respectively 'dukh', 'dusha', and 'dykhaniyé' – derive from the same root. – *Translator*.

counting the old aunt, who did not matter. My father, however, wanted me to know the Bible in the original, this being one of the marks of his parental vanity, and therefore I took private lessons in the Bible from a very learned old man in Odessa. My studies lasted only a few months and did little to confirm me in the ancestral faith. A suggestion of a double meaning in the words of my teacher, concerning some text in the Bible which we were studying, prompted me to ask a question which I worded very cautiously and diplomatically: 'If we accept, as some do, that God does not exist, how did the world come to be?'

'Hm,' muttered the teacher, 'but you can turn this question against him as well.' In this ingenious way did the old man express himself. I realized that the instructor in religion did not believe in God, and this set my mind completely at rest.

The racial and religious composition of my *realschule* was very heterogeneous. Religion was taught respectively by a Russian orthodox priest, a Protestant parson, a Catholic priest, and a Jewish instructor. The Russian priest, a nephew of the archbishop, with the reputation of being a favourite with ladies, was a young and strikingly good-looking man, resembling the portraits of Christ – only of the drawing-room type; he had gold spectacles and abundant golden hair, and was, in brief, impossibly handsome. Before the lesson in religion was to begin boys of different persuasions would divide into separate groups, and those not of the orthodox Russian faith would leave the classroom, sometimes under the very nose of the Russian priest. On such occasions he put on a special expression, in which contempt was only slightly softened by true Christian forbearance, as he watched the boys walk out.

'Where are you going?' he would ask some boy.

'We are Catholics,' came the answer.

'Oh, Catholics!' he repeated, nodding his head, 'I see, I see . . . And you?'

'We are Jews.'

'Oh, Jews, I see, Jews! Just so, just so!'

The Catholic priest came like a black shadow, always appearing right against the wall and disappearing so inconspicuously that throughout all my years there I could never get a look at his shaven face. A good-natured man by the name of Ziegelman instructed the Jewish boys in the Bible and the history of the Jewish people. These lessons, conducted in Russian, were never taken seriously by the boys.

In my mental equipment nationality never occupied an independent place, as it was felt but little in everyday life. It is true that after the laws of 1881, which restricted the rights of Jews in Russia, my father was unable to buy more land, as he was so anxious to do, but could only lease it under cover. This, however, scarcely affected my own position. As son of a prosperous landowner I belonged to the privileged class rather than to the oppressed. The language in my family and household was Russian-Ukrainian. True enough, the number of Jewish boys allowed to join the schools was limited to a fixed percentage, on account of which I lost one year. But in the school I was always at the top of the grade and was not personally affected by the restrictions.

In my school there was no open baiting of nationalities. To some extent the variety of national elements, not only among the boys but among the masters as well, acted as an important check on such policies. One could sense, however, the existence of a suppressed chauvinism which now and again broke through to the surface. The teacher of history, Lyubimov, showed marked partisanship when questioning a Polish boy about the Catholic persecution of orthodox Russians in White Russia and Lithuania. Mizkevic, a lanky, dark-skinned boy, turned green and stood with his teeth set, without uttering a word. 'Well, why don't you speak?' Lyubimov encouraged him, with an expression of sadistic pleasure. One of the boys burst out: 'Mizkevic is a Pole and a Catholic.' Feigning surprise, Lyubimov drawled: 'Is that so? We don't differentiate between nationalities here.'

It hurt me quite as much to see the concealed cad in Lyubimov's attitude towards Poles, as to see the spiteful captiousness of Burnande with Germans, or the Russian priest's nodding of his head at the sight of Jews. This national inequality probably was one of the underlying causes of my dissatisfaction with the existing order, but it was lost among all the other phases of social injustice. It never played a leading part – not even a recognized one – in the lists of my grievances.

The feeling of the supremacy of general over particular, of law over fact, of theory over personal experience, took root in my mind at an early age and gained increasing strength as the years advanced. It was the town that played the major rôle in shaping this feeling, a feeling which later became the basis for a philosophic outlook on life. When I heard boys who were studying physics and natural history repeat the superstitious notions about 'unlucky' Monday, or about meeting a priest crossing the road, I was utterly indignant. I felt that my intelligence had been insulted, and I was on the verge of doing any mad thing to make them abandon their shameless superstitions.

While the Yanovka people were spending many weary hours trying to measure the area of a field which had the shape of a trapezoid, I would apply Euclid and get my answer in a couple of minutes. But my computation did not tally with the one obtained by 'practical' methods, and they refused to believe it. I would bring out my geometry text-book and swear in the name of science; I would get all excited and use harsh words – and all to no purpose. People refused to see the light of reason, and this drove me to despair.

I engaged in a frantic argument with our village mechanic, Ivan Vasilyevich, who persisted in his belief that he could build a perpetual-motion machine.

The law of the conservation of energy seemed to him merely a fanciful idea which had nothing to do with his problem. 'That is all book, and this is practice,' he would say. My mind refused to understand or reconcile itself to the fact that men could reject incontrovertible truths in order to accept errors and absurd fancies.

Later, the feeling of the supremacy of the general over the particular became an integral part of my literary and political work. The dull empiricism, the unashamed, cringing worship of the fact which is so often only imaginary, and falsely interpreted at that, were odious to me. Beyond the facts I looked for laws. Naturally this led me more than once into hasty and incorrect generalizations, especially in my younger years when my knowledge, book-acquired, and my experience in life were still inadequate. But in every sphere, barring none, I felt that I could move and act only when I held in my hand the thread of the general. The social-revolutionary radicalism which has become the permanent pivot for my whole inner life grew out of this intellectual enmity towards the striving for petty ends, towards out-and-out pragmatism, and towards all that is ideologically without form and theoretically ungeneralized.

I will try to look back, in retrospect, at myself. The boy no doubt was ambitious, quick-tempered, and probably a hard person to get along with. I do not think that he had a feeling of superiority over his schoolmates when he entered the school. Of course in the country they showed him off proudly to the guests; but then there was no one else to compare him with, and the town boys who came to Yanovka always had the superior advantage of being 'gymnasists'; they were older, as well, so that they could be seen only from below. The school, however, is a place where rivalry is bitter. From the moment that he found himself at the top of his grade, and quite a distance beyond the boy next behind him, the little visitor from Yanovka felt that he could do better than the others. The boys who became his friends acknowledged his leadership. This could not fail to have some effect on his character. The masters also approved of him, and some, like Krizhanovsky, even singled him out for special attention. On the whole, however, the masters treated him well but without any special interest. The boys were divided: there were good friends among them, there were also enemies.

The boy was not lacking in self-criticism. In this he was inclined to be a little too captious. He was dissatisfied with his intellectual equipment and with some of his peculiarities of character. With time this became even more aggravated. Fiercely, he would catch himself in the act of telling a lie; or he would taunt himself because he had not read all the books that the others mentioned so casually. It is obvious that this was very close to vanity. The thought that he must become better and more intelligent than the rest and acquire a wide knowledge of books weighed constantly on his mind. He thought about the purpose of Man, and of his own purpose.

One evening Moissey Filippovich, passing by, stopped and

asked me, with feigned solemnity: 'What do you think of life, old man?' He often resorted to this mock rhetorical manner that was both pompous and ironic. But this time I felt as if I were touched to the quick. Yes, I was indeed thinking of life, only I did not know enough to apply this name to my boyish fears for the future. My mentor must have overheard my thoughts. 'I seem to have touched the sore spot,' he said changing his tone. Then he slapped me gently on the shoulder, and went to his room.

Did the Schpentzer family have any political views? Those of Moissey Filippovich were moderately liberal in a humanitarian way. They were lightly touched by vague socialist sympathies, tinged with Populist and Tolstoyan ideas. Political subjects were never openly discussed, especially in my presence; probably that was because they were afraid that I might say something censurable at school, and get myself in trouble. And when casual reference to what was going on or had taken place within the revolutionary movement was made in the grown-ups' conversation, such as, for example, 'This was in the year of the assassination of Tsar Alexander II,' it had the ring of a past as far removed as if they had said, 'This was in the year Columbus discovered America.' The people who surrounded me were outside of politics.

During my school years I held no political views, nor for that matter had I any desire to acquire them. At the same time my subconscious strivings were tinged by a spirit of opposition. I had an intense hatred of the existing order, of injustice, of tyranny. Whence did it come? It came from the conditions existing during the reign of Alexander III; the high-handedness of the police; the exploitation practised by landlords; the grafting by officials; the nationalistic restrictions; the cases of injustice at school and in the street; the close contact with children, servants and labourers in the country; the conversations in the workshop; the humane spirit in the Schpentzer family; the reading of Nekrassov's poems and of all kinds of other books, and, in general, the entire social atmosphere of the time. This oppositional mood was revealed to me cuttingly in my contact with two classmates, Rodzevich and Kologrivov.

Vladimir Rodzevich was the son of a colonel, and was for a time the second highest in our grade. He persuaded his parents to allow him to invite me to their house on a Sunday. I was received with a certain dryness, but courteously. The colonel and his wife spoke to me very little and as if they were scrutinizing me. During the three or four hours which I spent with the family I stumbled several times upon something that was strange and disconcerting to me, and even inimical; it happened when the conversation casually touched on the subject of religion and the authorities. There was a tone of conservative piety about that house that I felt like a blow on the chest. Vladimir's parents did not let him visit me in my home, and the link between us was broken. After the first revolution in Odessa, the name of Rodzevich, a member of the Black Hundred, probably one of the members of this family, was fairly well known.

The case of Kologrivov was even more poignant. He entered the school in the second grade, after Christmas, and was conspicuous among the boys as a tall and awkward stranger. He was gifted with incredible industry; he learned things by heart, anything and everything, whenever he could. By the end of the first month his mind was completely groggy from incessant memorizing. When he was called on by the geography teacher to recite the map lesson, without even waiting for the question he started right in: 'Jesus Christ left his command to the world . . .' It is necessary only to mention that the following hour was to be a lesson in religion.

In conversation with this Kologrivov, who treated me, as the first in the grade, not without respect, I made some critical remarks about the principal and somebody else. 'How can you speak of the principal in this way?' asked Kologrivov, sincerely indignant. 'And why not?' I answered, with a surprise that was even more sincere. 'But he is our chief. If the chief orders you to walk on your head, it is your duty to do as you are told, and not criticize him.' He said it in just that way. I was astonished by this expression of a formula. It did not occur to me then that the boy was obviously repeating what he must have heard in his feudal home. And although I had no views of my own, I felt that it would be as impossible for me to accept certain views as to eat wormy food.

Along with the suppressed hostility to the political order in

Russia, I began to create, in my imagination, an idealized picture of the foreign world – of Western Europe and America. From scattered remarks and descriptions, I began to visualize a culture which was high in itself and included everybody without exception. Later this became part and parcel of my conception of ideal democracy. Rationalism implied that if anything was accepted as theory, it was of course carried out in practice. For this reason it seemed incredible that people in Europe could have superstitions, that the church could exercise a great influence there, that in America the whites could persecute the Negroes. This idealized picture of the Western world, imperceptibly absorbed from my environment of liberal smug citizenship, persisted later on when I was already formulating revolutionary views. I should probably have been greatly surprised in those years if I had heard – if it had been possible to hear it – that the German Republic which is crowned with a Social-Democratic government admits monarchists within its borders but refuses the right of asylum to revolutionaries. Fortunately, since that time many things have ceased to surprise me. Life has beaten rationalism out of me and has taught me the workings of dialectics. Even Hermann Mueller can no longer surprise me.

6
The Break

The political development of Russia, beginning with the middle of the last century, is measured by decades. The sixties – after the Crimean War – were an epoch of enlightenment, our short-lived eighteenth century. During the following decade the intelligentsia were already endeavouring to draw practical conclusions from the theories of enlightenment. The decade began with the movement of going down to the people with revolutionary propaganda; it ended with terrorism. The seventies passed into history mainly as the years of 'The People's Will'. The best elements of that generation went up in the blaze of the dynamite warfare. The enemy had held all its positions. Then followed a decade of decline, of disenchantment and pessimism, of religious and moral searchings – the eighties. Under the veil of reaction, however, the forces of capitalism were blindly at work. The nineties brought with them workers' strikes and Marxist ideas. The new tide reached its culmination in the first decade of the new century – in the year 1905.

The eighties passed bearing the mark of the Supreme Procurator of the Most Holy Synod, Pobedonostzev, the classical upholder of autocratic power and universal immutability. The liberals regarded him as the pure type of the bureaucrat who did not know life. But this was not true. Pobedonostzev evaluated the contradictions hidden in the depths of the national life far more soberly and seriously than did the liberals. He understood that, once the screws were loosened, the pressure from below would tear off the social roof in its entirety and all that not only Pobedonostzev but the liberals as well regarded as the pillars of culture and ethics would dissolve into dust. In his own way Pobedonostzev saw more profoundly than the liberals. It was not his fault that the processes of history proved mightier than the Byzantine system which he, the inspirer of Alexander III and Nicholas II, had defended with such force.

In the dead eighties, when the liberals thought that everything had become lifeless, Pobedonostzev still felt beneath his feet a ground-swell – subterranean rumblings. He was not calm even in the calmest years of the reign of Alexander III. 'It has been and still is hard, and it is bitter to confess that it will continue so,' he wrote to one of his trusted men. 'The burden upon my soul does not vanish, for I see and feel every hour the temper of the time and what has come over the people . . . Comparing the present with the distant past we feel that we are living in some strange world *where everything is going backward to primeval chaos* – and we feel ourselves helpless in the midst of all this ferment.' Pobedonostzev lived to see the year 1905, when the subterranean forces that had so greatly terrified him broke out, and the first deep cracks appeared in the foundation and walls of the entire old structure.

The year 1891, memorable for the crop failure and the famine, marks the official date of the political breaking-point in the country. The new decade centred around the labour question. And not in Russia alone – in 1901 the German Social-Democratic Party adopted its Erfurt programme. Pope Leo XIII issued his encyclical dealing with the condition of the working man. Wilhelm was obsessed by social ideas which consisted of a mixture of insane ignorance and bureaucratic romanticism. The *rapprochement* between the Tsar and France guaranteed the inflow of capital funds into Russia. The appointment of Witte to the post of Minister of Finance ushered in an era of industrial protectionism. The stormy development of capitalism bred that very 'temper of the time' which had tormented Pobedonostzev with uneasy forebodings.

The political shift in the direction of action cropped up first of all in the midst of the intelligentsia. More and more frequently and decisively did the young Marxists resort to action. At the same time the dormant populist movement began to show signs of awakening. In 1893 the first legally printed Marxist work, written by Struve, made its appearance. I was then in my fourteenth year, and still very remote from these matters.

In 1894 Alexander III died. As was usual on such occasions, the liberal hopes sought support from the heir to the throne. He replied with a kick. At the audience granted to the Zemstvo leaders, the young Tsar described their aspirations for a constitution as 'nonsensical dreams'. This speech was published in the press. The word-of-mouth report was that the paper from which the Tsar had read his speech said 'groundless dreams', but in his agitation the Tsar had expressed himself more harshly than he intended. I was fifteen at the time. I was unreservedly on the side of the nonsensical dreams, and not on that of the Tsar. Vaguely I believed in a gradual development which would bring backward Russia nearer to advanced Europe. Beyond that my political ideas did not go.

Commercial, multi-racial, loudly coloured and noisy Odessa remained, to an extraordinary degree, far behind other centres in a political sense. In St Petersburg, in Moscow, in Kiev, there were already in existence at that time numerous socialist circles in the educational institutions. Odessa had none. In 1895 Friedrich Engels died. Secret reports were read at meetings held in his memory by student groups in the various cities of Russia. I was then in my sixteenth year. But I did not know even the name of Engels, and could hardly say anything definite about Marx. As a matter of fact I probably had never heard of him.

My political frame of mind while at school was vaguely oppositionist, but no more than that. In my day revolutionary questions were still unknown among the students. It was whispered that certain groups met at the private *gymnasium* maintained by the Czech, Novak; that there had been arrests; that Novak, who was our instructor in athletics, had been dismissed and replaced by an army officer. In the environment surrounding the home of the Schpentzers there was dissatisfaction, but the régime was held to be unshakable. The boldest dreamed of a constitution as possible only after several decades. As for Yanovka, the subject was unmentionable there. When I returned to the village after my graduation from school, bringing with me dim democratic ideas, Father, immediately alert, remarked with hostility: 'This will not come to pass even in three hundred years.' He was convinced of the futility of all reformists' efforts and was apprehensive for his son. In 1921, when he came to me in the Kremlin, after having escaped the Red and White perils with his life, I jestingly asked: 'Do you remember what you used to say – that the Tsarist order was good for another three hundred years?' The old man smiled slyly and replied in Ukrainian: 'This time, let your truth prevail.'

In the early nineties the Tolstoyan tendencies began to die down among the intelligentsia. Marxism was victoriously marching upon the populist movement. Publications of all kinds were filled with the echoes of this ideological struggle. Everywhere there were references to the self-confident young people who called themselves materialists. I encountered all this for the first time in 1896.

The question of personal morals, so intimately connected with the passive ideology of the eighties, touched me in a period when 'self-perfection' was to me not so much a matter of theory as an organic demand of my spiritual growth. The problem of 'self-perfection', however, quickly became bound up with the question of my outlook on the world in general, which led, in turn, to the fundamental dilemma: populism or Marxism? The conflict of these trends engrossed me, but several years later than the general break in the intellectual concepts of the country. By the time I was approaching the alphabet of economic sciences, and was raising the question in my mind as to whether Russia must go through the stage of capitalism, the Marxists of the older generation had already succeeded in finding a path to the working man and in becoming Social Democrats.

I faced the first crossroads on my path, poorly equipped politically even for a seventeen-year-old boy of that period. Too many questions confronted me all at once, without the necessary sequence and order. Restlessly I cast about me. One thing is certain: even then life had stored within my consciousness a considerable load of social protest. What did it consist of? Sympathy for the down-trodden and indignation over injustice – the latter was perhaps the stronger feeling. Beginning with my earliest childhood, in all the impressions of my daily life human inequality stood out in exceptionally coarse and stark forms. Injustice often assumed the character of impudent licence; human dignity was under heel at every step. It is enough for me to recall the flogging of peasants. Even before I had any theories all these things imprinted themselves deeply on me and piled up a store of impressions of great explosive force. It was perhaps because of this that I seemed to hesitate for a while before reaching the great conclusions which I was impelled to draw from the observations of the first period of my life.

There was also another side to my development. When one generation succeeds another, the dead cling to the living. This was the case with the generation of Russian revolutionists whose early youth developed under the weight of the atmosphere of the eighties. In spite of the large perspectives held out by the new doctrines, the Marxists in reality remained imprisoned by the conservative mood of the eighties, displaying an inability to take bold initiatives, remaining inactive when confronted by obstacles, shoving the revolution into the indefinite future, and inclining generally to regard socialism as a task for centuries of evolution.

In such a home as the Schpentzers' political criticism would have been voiced far more loudly several years before my time or several years later. To my lot fell the most stagnant years. One heard almost no conversation on political topics. Big questions were evaded. It was the same at school. Undoubtedly I imbibed a great deal of the atmosphere of the eighties. And even afterwards, when my revolutionary ideas were already taking shape, I would catch myself in an attitude of mistrust of action by the masses, taking a bookish, abstract and therefore sceptical view of the revolution. I had to combat all this within myself, by my thinking, my reading, but mainly by means of experience, until the elements of psychic inertia had been conquered within me.

There is no evil without good. Perhaps the fact that I had consciously to overcome within me the reverberations of the eighties enabled me to approach fundamental problems of mass action in a more serious, concrete and profound manner. Only that is lasting which is gained through combat. All this, however, is related to chapters of my story which are still far ahead.

I attended the seventh grade not in Odessa but in Nikolayev.

It was a provincial town and the level of the school was lower there. But my year at Nikolayev – 1986 – was the turning-point of my youth, for it raised within me the question of my place in human society. I lived in a home where the children were more grown up, and already somewhat in the grip of the newer movements. It is remarkable that at first in conversations I was the stubbornest opponent of 'socialist utopias'. I played the part of the sceptic who had passed beyond all that. My reaction to political questions was always one of ironic superiority. The landlady in whose home I lodged regarded me with amazement and even cited me as a model – although not always quite confidently – to her own children, who were a little older than I and whose tendencies were towards the Left. But it was merely an unequal struggle on my part for independent judgement. I endeavoured to escape the personal influence of such young socialists as I would encounter. This losing battle lasted altogether a few months. The ideas filling the air proved stronger than I, especially since in the depths of my soul I wished for nothing better than to yield to them. My conduct underwent a radical change after several months in Nikolayev. I repudiated my assumption of conservatism and swung Leftwards with such speed that it even frightened away some of my new friends. 'How did it happen?' my landlady would remark. 'And it was all for nothing that I held you up to my children as a model!'

I neglected my studies. The store of knowledge which I had brought from Odessa enabled me, however, to retain somehow my official lead as a star student. More and more frequently I played truant. Once the inspector called on me at home to ascertain the cause of my non-attendance. I felt humiliated beyond words. But the inspector was courteous. He satisfied himself that the home in which I lived and my own room were orderly, and left peaceably. Under my mattress were several illegal political pamphlets.

In Nikolayev I met, in addition to the young people who were drawn towards Marxism, several former exiles who were under police surveillance. These were secondary figures of the period of the decline of the populist movement. At that time Social Democrats were not yet returning from exile, they were going into it. The two cross-movements gave rise to whirlpools of theory. For a time I too was drawn into them. There was an odour of putrefaction emanating from populism. Marxism repelled by its so-called 'narrowness'. Burning with impatience I tried to grasp the ideas instinctively, but they were not so easy to master. I found no one about me to offer sure guidance. Every new conversation, moreover, forced me to come to the bitter, painful and desperate conclusion that I was ignorant.

I became intimately acquainted with the gardener, Shvigovsky, who was a Czech by origin. He was the first working-man I had known who subscribed to newspapers, read German, knew the classics, and participated freely in the arguments between the Marxists and the populists. His one-room cabin in the garden was the meeting-place for visiting students, former exiles and the local youths. One could obtain a forbidden book through Shvigovsky. The conversations of the exiles were punctuated with the names of the populists, Zhelyabov, Perovskaya, Figner, who were treated not as legendary heroes but as real people with whom the older friends of these exiles – if not they themselves – were familiar. I had a feeling that I was joining a great chain as a tiny link.

I swallowed books, fearful that my entire life would not be long enough to prepare me for action. My reading was nervous, impatient and unsystematic. After wading through the illegal pamphlets of the preceding period, I passed on to *Logic* of John Stuart Mill, then took up Lippert's *Primitive Culture* without completing *Logic*. The utilitarianism of Bentham seemed to me the last word in human thought. For several months I was a staunch Benthamist. In the same manner I was carried away by the realistic aesthetics of Chernyshevsky. Without having finished Lippert, I threw myself upon the history of the French Revolution by Mignet. Each book lived separately for me, with no place in a unified system. My striving for a system became tense, sometimes savage. At the same time I would be repelled by Marxism partly because it seemed a completed system.

I began to read newspapers, not as I had read them in Odessa, but with a political mind. The most authoritative daily at the time was the liberal *Russkiya Vedomosti* of Moscow. We studied rather than read it, beginning with the impotent, professorial editorials and ending with the scientific articles. The foreign correspondence, especially from Berlin, was the pride of the newspaper. It was from the *Russkiya Vedomosti* that I first formed a picture of the political life of western Europe, especially of the parliamentary parties. It is difficult today to recall the agitation with which we followed the speeches of Bebel and even those of Eugene Richter. And to this day I remember the phrase which Dashinsky flung in the face of the police when they entered the house of parliament: 'I represent thirty thousand workers and peasants of Galicia – who will dare touch me?' We pictured the Galician revolutionist as a titanic figure. The theatrical stage of parliamentarism, alas! cruelly deceived us. The successes of German socialism, the presidential elections in the United States, the free-for-alls in the Austrian Reichsrat, the intrigues of the French royalists, all of this absorbed us far more than the personal fate of any one of us.

Meanwhile my relations with my family were growing worse. On one of his trips to Nikolayev to market grain my father somehow learned of my new acquaintances. He sensed the approach of danger, but hoped to prevent it by the power of his parental authority. We had several stormy scenes. I uncompromisingly defended my independence, my right to follow my own path. It ended with my refusing to accept material aid from home. I left my lodgings and went to live with Shvigovsky, who was now leasing another garden with a more spacious cottage. Here six of us led a communal life. During the summer one or two tubercular students seeking fresh air joined us. I began to give private lessons. We led a Spartan existence, without bed-linen, and got along on stews which we prepared ourselves. We wore blue smocks, round straw hats and black canes. In town it was rumoured that we had joined a secret organization. We read without method, we argued without restraint, we peered into the future passionately, and were happy in our own way.

After a while we organized a society for the distribution of useful books among the people. We collected dues and bought cheap editions, but were unable to disseminate them. In

Shvigovsky's garden there worked a hired labourer and an apprentice. We focused upon them, first of all, our efforts at enlightenment. But the labourer turned out to be a disguised gendarme who had been planted in our midst expressly to watch us. His name was Kirill Tkhorzhevsky. He had also put the apprentice in touch with the gendarmerie. The latter stole from us a large package of popular books and took it to headquarters. This beginning was clearly inauspicious, but we firmly hoped for success in the future.

I wrote a polemical article for a populist periodical in Odessa, taking issue with the first Marxist journal. The article had more epigraphs, quotations and venom than it had content. I mailed the article and a week later made a trip to find out its fate. The editor, through large glasses, eyed with sympathy an author whose head displayed an enormous mop of hair but whose face did not show a trace of beard. The article never saw the light. No one was the loser – least of all myself.

When the board of directors of the public library raised the annual fee from five to six roubles, we perceived an attempt to get away from democracy, and sounded an alarm. For several weeks we did nothing but prepare for a general meeting of the library members. We emptied all our democratic pockets, collecting roubles and half-roubles, and with this fund registered more radical members, many of whom not only lacked the six roubles but also were under the twenty-year age limit required by the constitution. We turned the library application-book into a collection of fiery leaflets. When the annual meeting was called, two parties appeared: on the one hand officials, teachers, liberal landlords, and naval officers; on the other hand we – the democracy. Victory was ours along the entire front. We restored the five-rouble fee and elected a new board.

Casting about for activities, we decided to organize a university on a basis of mutual instruction. There were about twenty students. My department was sociology. That was high-sounding. I prepared for my course with all my powers, but after two lectures, which came off satisfactorily, I suddenly realized that my resources had been exhausted. The second lecturer, whose course was the French Revolution, became confused as soon as he began and promised to deliver his lecture in writing. Of course he failed to fulfil his promise, and that was the end of the enterprise.

I then decided, with the second lecturer, the elder of the brothers Sokolovsky, to write a play. We even left the commune temporarily for that purpose, and hid ourselves in a room without leaving any address. Our play was full of social tendencies, against a background of the conflict of generations. Although the two dramatists regarded Marxism with only half-trust, nevertheless the populist in the play was a feeble character, while all the courage, youth and hope were with the young Marxists. Such is the power of time. The romantic element found expression in the love tendered by a revolutionist of the older generation, who had been crushed by life, to a young Marxist girl, but she handed it back with a merciless speech about the failure of populism.

The work on the play was no mean task. At times we wrote together, driving and correcting each other; at other times we divided the acts into sections, and each of us would devote his day to the preparation of a scene or a monologue. We had, it must be said, no shortage of monologues. Sokolovsky would return from his work towards evening, and then would proceed freely to revise the whimpering speeches of the hero of the seventies whose life had been crushed. I would return from my private lessons or from Shvigovsky's. The daughter of the landlady would put up a samovar for us. Sokolovsky would pull out from his pockets some bread and sausage. Separated by a mysterious armour from the rest of the world, the dramatists would spend the balance of the evening in intensive labour. We completed the first act, even providing the proper curtain effect. The remaining acts, four in number, were drafted. The further we got into it, however, the more we cooled. After a while we arrived at the conclusion that we must give up our mysterious room and postpone the completion of the drama to some future date. The roll of manuscripts was taken by Sokolovsky to another lodging. Later, when we found ourselves in the Odessa prison, Sokolovsky made an attempt through his relatives to locate the manuscript. Perhaps the thought occurred to him that exile would be favourable for the completion of our dramatic opus. But the manuscript was no more, having vanished without trace. In all probability the people in whose home it had been left considered it prudent to throw it in the fire upon the arrest of its ill-fated authors. It is not difficult for me to reconcile myself to its fate, especially since, in the course of my subsequent and none too smooth life, I have lost manuscripts of incomparably greater value.

7

My First Revolutionary Organization

In the autumn of 1896 I visited the country after all; but the visit resulted only in a brief truce. Father wanted me to become an engineer, whereas I hesitated between pure mathematics, to which I was very strongly attracted, and Revolution, which little by little was taking possession of me. Every time this question arose there was an acute family crisis. Everybody looked depressed, and seemed to suffer intensely; my elder sister would weep furtively, and nobody knew what to do about it. One of my uncles, an engineer and owner of a plant in Odessa, who was staying in the country with us, persuaded me to come and visit him in the city. This was at least a temporary relief from the impasse.

I stayed with my uncle for a few weeks. We were constantly discussing profit and surplus value. My uncle was better at acquiring profits than explaining them. And meanwhile I did nothing about registering for the course in mathematics in the University. I stayed on in Odessa, still looking for something. What was I trying to find? Actually, it was myself. I made casual acquaintances among workers, obtained illegal literature, tutored some private pupils, gave surreptitious lectures to the older boys of the Trade School, and engaged in arguments with the Marxists, still trying to hold fast to my old views. With the last autumn steamer I left for Nikolayev, and resumed my quarters with Shvigovsky in the garden.

And the same old business started in again. We discussed the latest numbers of the radical magazines and argued about Darwinism; we were vaguely preparing, and also waiting. What was it in particular that impelled us to start the revolutionary propaganda? It is difficult to say. The impulse originated within us.

In the intellectual circles in which I moved, nobody did any actual revolutionary work. We realized that between our endless tea-table discussions and revolutionary organization there was a vast gulf. We knew that any contacts with workers demanded secret, highly 'conspiratory' methods. And we pronounced the word solemnly, with a reverence that was almost mystic. We had no doubt that in the end we would go from the discussions at the tea-table to 'conspiratia'; but nobody was definite as to how and when the change would take place. In excusing our delay, we usually told each other that we must prepare; and we weren't so far wrong after all.

But apparently there had been some change in the air which brought us abruptly onto the road of revolutionary propaganda. The change did not actually take place in Nikolayev alone, but throughout the country, especially in the capitals. In 1896 the famous weavers' strikes broke out in St Petersburg. This put new life into the intelligentsia. The students gained courage, sensing the awakening of the heavy reserves. In the summer, at Christmas, and at Easter dozens of students came down to Nikolayev, bringing with them tales of the upheaval in St Petersburg, Moscow, and Kiev. Some of them had been expelled from universities – boys just out of the *gymnasium* returning with the haloes of heroes. In February 1897 a woman student, Vetrova, burned herself to death in the Peter-Paul fortress. This tragedy, which has never been fully explained, stirred everyone deeply. Disturbances took place in the university cities; arrests and banishments became more frequent.

I started my revolutionary work to the accompaniment of the Vetrova demonstrations. It happened in this way: I was walking along the street with a younger member of our commune, Grigory Sokolovsky, a boy about my age. 'It's about time we started,' I said.

'Yes, it is about time,' he answered.

'But how?'

'That's it, how?'

'We must find workers, not wait for anybody or ask anybody, but just find workers, and set to it.'

'I think we can find them,' said Sokolovsky. 'I used to know a watchman who worked on the boulevard. He belonged to the Bible Sect. I think I'll look him up.'

The same day Sokolovsky went to the boulevard to see the Biblist. He was no longer there. But he found there a woman who had a friend who also belonged to some religious sect. Through this friend of the woman he didn't know, Sokolovsky, on that very day, made the acquaintance of several workers, among them an electrician, Ivan Andreyevitch Mukhin, who soon became the most prominent figure in our organization. Sokolovsky returned from his search all on fire. 'Such men! They are the real thing!'

Next day five or six of us were sitting in an inn. The deafening music of the automatic organ screened our conversation from the rest. Mukhin, a thin man with a pointed beard and a sort of shrewd, apprehensive look, watched me through a half-closed left eye, amiably scanning my still beardless face. In detail, with well-calculated pauses, he explained: 'The Gospels for me, in this business, are just a peg. I begin with religion, and then switch off to life. The other day I explained the whole truth to the Stundists with navy-beans.'

'What do you mean, navy-beans?'

'It's very simple. I put a bean on the table and say, "This is the Tsar." Around it, I place more beans. "These are ministers, bishops, generals, and over there the gentry and merchants. And in this other heap, the plain people." Now, I ask, "Where is the Tsar?" They point to the centre. "Where are the ministers?" They point to those around. Just as I have told them, they answer. Now, wait,' and at this point Mukhin completely closed his left eye and paused. 'Then I scamble all the beans together,' he went on. 'I say, "Now tell me where is the Tsar? the ministers?" And they answer me, "Who can tell? You can't spot them now" ... "Just what I say. You can't spot them now." And so I say, "All beans should be scrambled." '

I was so thrilled at this story that I was all in a sweat. This was the real thing, whereas we had only been guessing and waiting and subtilizing. The music of the automatic organ was the 'conspiratia'; Mukhin's navy-beans, destroying the mechanics of the class system, were the revolutionary propaganda.

'Only how to scramble them, damn them, that's the problem,' Mukhin said, in a different tone, and looked sternly at me with both eyes. 'That's not navy-beans, is it?' And this time he waited for my answer.

From that day we plunged headlong into the work. We had no older men to direct us. Our own experience was inadequate. But not once did we run into difficulties or get confused. One thing evolved from another as inevitably as in our conversation with Mukhin at the inn.

At the end of the last century the pivot of the economic development of Russia was shifting swiftly to the south-east. Great plants were being built one after another in the South, two in Nikolayev. In 1897 the number of workers in the Nikolayev plants amounted to 8,000, in addition to which there were 2,000 workers in various trades. The intellectual level of the workers was comparatively high, as were their earnings. The illiterates were few. The place that the revolutionary organizations came to hold later was then filled to some extent by the religious sects which engaged in successful warfare with the official religion. In the absence of political disorders the secret police in Nikolayev were slumbering peacefully. They played into our hands admirably. If they had been awake, we would have been arrested during the very first weeks of our activity. But we were the pioneers and benefited by it. We shook up the police only after we had shaken up the workers.

When I made the acquaintance of Mukhin and his friends, I called myself by the name of Lvov. It was not easy for me to tell this first 'conspiratory' lie; in fact, it was really painful to 'deceive' people with whom one intended to be associated for such a great and noble cause. But the nickname of Lvov soon stuck to me, and I got used to it myself.

The workers streamed towards us as if they had been waiting for this. They all brought friends; some came with their wives, and a few older men joined the groups with their sons. We never sought them out; they looked for us. Young and inexperienced leaders that we were, we were soon overwhelmed by the movement we had started. Every word of ours met with a response. As many as twenty and twenty-five or more of the workers gathered at our secret readings and discussions, held in houses, in the woods, or on the river. The predominating element was composed of highly skilled workers who earned fairly good wages. They already had an eight-hour day at the Nikolayev ship-building yards; they were not interested in strikes; what they wanted was justice in social relations. They called themselves Baptists, or Stundists, or Evangelical Christians, but theirs was not a dogmatic sectarianism. The workers were simply breaking away from orthodoxy, and Baptism became a temporary phase for them in their progress towards revolution. During the first weeks of our conversations some of them still used sectarian expressions and often made comparisons with the period of the early Christians. But nearly all of them soon dropped this way of speaking when they found that they were only a laughing-stock for the younger men.

Even to this day the more striking figures among them seem alive to me. There was the cabinet-maker in his bowler, Korotkov, who had done with all mystics long ago, a jocular fellow and a rhymester who would say solemnly, 'I am a ratiolist', meaning a rationalist. And when Taras Savelyevitch, an old evangelist and a grandfather, would begin, for the hundredth time, to talk about the early Christians, who like ourselves met secretly, Korotkov would cut him short with 'A fig for your theology!' and toss his bowler indignantly up into the trees. He would wait for a while and then go into the woods in search of it. This all happened in the forest on the dunes.

Many of the workers were so infected by the new ideas that they began to compose verses. Korotkov wrote the 'Proletarian March' which began this way: 'We are the alphas and omegas, the beginnings and endings.' Nesterenko, a carpenter, who, like his son, was a member of the group of Alexandra Lvovna Sokolovskaya, composed a song about Karl Marx in Ukrainian, and we sang it in chorus. Nesterenko himself, however, ended very badly. He got in with the police and betrayed the whole organization.

A young labourer, Yefimov, a blond giant with blue eyes, who came of an officer's family and was not only literate but really well-read, lived in the slums of the town. I found him in an eating-place patronized by tramps. He worked in the harbour as a longshoreman; he neither smoked nor drank. He was reserved and well-mannered. But there must have been something mysterious about his life, despite the fact that he was only twenty-one, to account for his constant gloominess. He soon confided in me that he had been introduced to some members of the secret society of Narodovoltzi,* and offered to put me in touch with them. Three of us, Mukhin, Yefimov and I, were sitting drinking tea in the noisy 'Russia' inn, at the same time listening to the deafening music of the organ and waiting. At last Yefimov indicated to us with his eyes the figure of a big, stout man with a small beard. 'There he is.'

The man sat at a table by himself and kept on drinking tea. Then he began to put on his coat, and with a mechanical movement of his hand, crossed himself as he looked at the ikons. 'What! Is he the "Narodovoletz"?' Mukhin exclaimed in a hushed voice. The 'Narodovoletz' avoided meeting us, giving Yefimov some vague excuse. The incident has always remained a mystery to me. Yefimov himself soon squared his accounts with life by asphyxiating himself with coal-gas. It is quite possible that the blue-eyed giant was a tool for some spy – or conceivably something even worse.

Mukhin, who was an electrician by trade, installed a complicated system of signalling in his apartment for use in case of police raids. He was twenty-seven, but so full of practical wisdom and so rich in experience of life that he seemed almost old to me. A tubercular, he would cough blood. He remained a revolutionary throughout his life. After one exile and a prison term he was exiled again. I met him again after twenty-three years at the conference of the Ukrainian Communist Party at Kharkoff. We sat raking up the past as we told each other of the fate that had overtaken many of the group with whom we had been associated at the dawn of the revolution. At the conference Mukhin was elected to the central control committee of the Ukrainian Communist Party. He had surely earned the honour. But soon after that he was laid low by illness. He never recovered.

Immediately after we had come to know each other, Mukhin

---

*Members of the Terrorist Narodnaya Volya (The People's Will). – *Translator.*

introduced me to a friend of his, another sectarian, Babenko, who had a little house of his own with apple-trees in the courtyard. Babenko was lame; a slow man who was always sober. He taught me to drink tea with apple instead of lemon. He was arrested with others of our group and spent some time in prison before he returned to Nikolayev again. But Fate separated us. It was only in 1925 that I happened to read in some paper that a Babenko, a former member of the South Russian Labour Union, was living in the Province of Kuban. By then his legs were completely paralysed. Somehow I managed, at a time when things were already difficult for me, to have the old man transferred to Essentuki to take the cure. He regained the use of his legs. I visited him in the sanatorium. He didn't even know that Trotsky and Lvov were one and the same man. Again we drank tea with apple and talked about the past. I can just imagine his surprise when he heard that Trotsky was a counter-revolutionary.

There were many other interesting figures, too many to enumerate. There was the fine younger generation that had been trained in the technical school of the shipyards and was very cultured. A mere suggestion from the instructor was enough to enable them to grasp the whole trend of his thought. We found the workers more susceptible to revolutionary propaganda than we had ever in our wildest dreams imagined. The amazing effectiveness of our work fairly intoxicated us. From revolutionary tales we knew that the workers won over by propaganda were usually to be counted in single numbers. A revolutionary who converted two or three men to socialism thought he had done a good piece of work, whereas, with us, the number of workers who joined or wanted to join the groups seemed practically unlimited. The only shortage was in the matter of instructors and in literature. The teachers had to snatch from each other in turn the single soiled copy of the Communist Manifesto by Marx and Engels that had been transcribed by many hands in Odessa, with many gaps and mutilations of the text.

Soon we began to produce a literature of our own; this was, properly speaking, the beginning of my literary work, which almost coincided with the start of my revolutionary activities. I wrote proclamations and articles, and printed them all out in longhand for the hectograph. At that time we didn't even know of the existence of typewriters. I printed the letters with the utmost care, considering it a point of honour to make them clear enough so that even the less literate could read our proclamations without any trouble. It took me about two hours to a page. Sometimes I didn't even unbend my back for a week, cutting my work short only for meetings and study in the groups. But what a satisfied feeling I had when I received the information from mills and workshops that the workers read voraciously the mysterious sheets printed in purple ink, passing them about from hand to hand as they discussed them! They pictured the author as a strange and mighty person who in some mysterious way had penetrated into the mills and knew what was going on in the workshops, and twenty-four hours later passed his comments on events in newly printed handbills.

At first we made the hectograph and printed the proclamations in our rooms at night. One of us would stand guard in the court-yard. In the open stove we had kerosene and matches ready to burn the tell-tale things in case of danger. Everything was very crude, but the police of Nikolayev were no more experienced than we were. Later on we transferred the printing-press to the apartment of a middle-aged worker who had lost his sight through an accident in one of the shops. He placed his apartment at our disposal unhesitatingly. He would say with a low laugh, 'Everywhere is prison for a blind man.' Gradually we got to-gether at his place a large supply of glycerine, gelatine and paper. We worked at night. The slovenly room, with a ceiling that came low over our heads, had a poverty-stricken look about it. We cooked our revolutionary brew on his iron stove, pouring it out on a tin sheet. As he helped us the blind man moved about the half-dark room with more assurance than we did. Two of the workers, a young boy and girl, would watch reverently as I pulled the freshly printed sheets off the hectograph, and then would exchange glances. If it had been possible for anyone to look at all this with a 'sober' eye, at this group of young people scurrying about in the half-darkness around a miserable hecto-graph, what a sorry, fantastic thing it would have seemed to imagine that they could, in this way, overthrow a mighty state that was centuries old! And yet this sorry fantasy became a reality within a single generation; and only eight years separated those nights from 1905, and not quite twenty from 1917.

Word-of-mouth propaganda never gave me the same satisfaction as the printed bills did at that time. My knowledge was inadequate, and I didn't know how to present it effectively. We made no real speeches in the full sense of the word. Only once, in the woods on May Day, did I have to make one, and it embarrassed me greatly. Every word I uttered seemed horribly false. On the other hand, when I talked to the groups it wasn't so bad. As a rule, however, the revolutionary work went on at full speed. I established and developed contacts with Odessa. Evenings I would go to the pier, pay a rouble for a third-class ticket, and lie down on the deck of the steamer near the funnel, with my jacket under my head and overcoat to cover me; in the morning I would wake up in Odessa and seek out the people I knew there. Then I would return the next night, so as never to waste any time in travelling. My contacts in Odessa suddenly increased in number. At the entrance of the Public Library I met a spectacled worker. We looked at each other closely and understood. He was Albert Polyak, a compositor, who later organized the famous central printing-press of the party. My acquaintance with him marked an epoch in the life of our organization. Within a few days after I met him I brought back with me to Nikolayev a travelling-bag full of 'illegal' literature from abroad; new propaganda pamphlets in gaily coloured covers. We kept opening the bag to look admiringly at our treasure. The pamphlets were circulated in no time and increased our authority in labour circles.

From Polyak I accidentally learned in conversation that the mechanic Shrentsel, who had been posing as a full-fledged engineer and had been trying to wedge his way into our group, was an informer of long standing. This Shrentsel was a stupid and importunate fellow who always wore a uniform cap with a badge. Instinctively we never trusted him. But he did learn something about a few of us. I invited him to Mukhin's apartment, and told his life-story in detail, omitting his name. He became utterly frantic. We threatened to give him short shrift if he betrayed us. Apparently it had its effect, because he left us alone for three months after that. But when we were arrested, as if to get even with us, Shrentsel piled horror on horror in his evidence against us.

We called our organization the South Russian Workers' Union, intending to include workers from other towns. I drafted our constitution along Social-Democratic lines. The mill authorities tried to offset our influence through speakers of their own. We would answer them the next day with new proclamations. This duel of words aroused not only the workers but a great many of the citizens as well. The whole town was alive with talk about revolutionaries who were flooding the mills with their handbills. Our names were on every tongue. Still the police delayed. They refused to believe that 'those young brats from the garden' were capable of carrying on any such campaign. They suspected that there were more experienced leaders behind us, probably old exiles. This gave us two or three additional months in which to work. Finally our movements were so closely watched that the police couldn't help but discover one group after another. So we decided to leave Nikolayev for a few weeks, to put the police off our track. I was supposed to go to my family in the country; Sokolovskaya, with her brother, to Ekaterinoslav, and so on. At the same time, we firmly resolved not to hide in case of wholesale arrests, but to let ourselves be taken, so that the police could not say to the workers: 'Your leaders have deserted you.'

Some time before I was supposed to leave, Nesterenko insisted that I should hand over a bundle of proclamations to him in person. He fixed as the meeting-place behind the cemetery, late at night. There was deep snow on the ground; the moon was shining. Beyond the cemetery you could see a wide desert-like expanse. I found him at the appointed spot. Just as I was handing him a packet that I took out from under my coat, some-one detached himself from the cemetery wall and walked past us, touching Nesterenko with his elbow.

'Who is that?' I asked, in surprise.

'I don't know,' answered Nesterenko as he watched the other

man walk off. At that time he was already working with the police, but it never entered my mind to suspect him.

On 28 January 1898 there were mass arrests. Altogether over two hundred people were taken. The police applied the scourge. One of those arrested, a soldier named Sokolov, was driven to throw himself from the second floor of the prison; he was merely badly bruised. Another, Levandovsky, went insane. There were still other victims.

Among those arrested there were many who got there by accident. A few of those on whom we were relying deserted us, and even in some instances betrayed us. On the other hand, some who had been quite inconspicuous in our ranks showed great strength of character. For instance, there was a turner, a German named August Dorn, a man about fifty years old, who for some unknown reason was detained in prison for a long time, although he had only visited our group a few times. He behaved magnificently, and kept singing gay and, one must admit, not always puritanical German songs at the top of his voice. He made jokes in pidgin-Russian, and kept up the spirits of the young. In the Moscow transfer prison where we were detained, all of us in the same cell, Dorn would address the samovar mockingly, ask it to come over, and then retort, 'You won't? Well, then Dorn will come to you.' Although this was repeated every day, we always good-naturedly laughed at it.

The Nikolayev organization was hard hit, but it did not disappear. Others soon replaced us. Both the revolutionaries and the police were growing in experience.

During the raids of January 1898 I was arrested, not in Nikolayev but on the estate of a wealthy landowner, Sokovnin, where Shvigovsky had found a job as a gardener. I had stopped off there on the way from Yanovka to Nikolayev with a large brief-case filled with manuscripts, drawings, letters, and all manner of other 'illegal' material. Shvigovsky hid the dangerous pack-ages for the night in a hole, along with cabbages; and, at sunrise, when he was going out to plant his trees, he took it out again to turn it over to me for our work. It was just at that very moment that the police suddenly invaded the place. Shvigovsky managed to drop the package behind a water-barrel when he was in the hall, and whispered to the housekeeper, who gave us our dinner under supervision of the police, to take it away from there and hide it. The old woman decided that the best thing was to bury it under the snow in the garden. We were quite sure that the papers would never get into the hands of our enemies. When spring came the snow melted away, but a fresh crop of green grass covered the package, which had swollen somewhat with the spring rains.

We were still in prison. It was summer. A workman was cut-ting the grass in the garden when two of his boys who were playing there stumbled on the package and gave it to their father. And he, in turn, took it to the landowner, who was so terrified at the sight of it that he went to Nikolayev at once and turned it over to the chief of the secret police. The handwriting on the manuscripts was evidence against many of our people.

The old prison in Nikolayev had no decent accommodation for political prisoners, especially for so many of them. I was put into the same cell with a young bookbinder named Yavitch. The cell was a very large one; it could hold about thirty, but there was no furniture of any sort, and it had very little heat. There was a big square opening in the door that looked out on an open corridor leading straight into the courtyard. The January frosts were very bitter. A straw mattress was spread on the floor for us to sleep on at night and was taken away at six o'clock in the morning. It was torture to get up and dress ourselves. Yavitch and I would sit on the floor, in hats, overcoats and rubbers, pressing close to one another and leaning against the stove, which was barely warm, and would dream away for two hours or more at a time. It was the happiest part of the day for us. We were not being called up for cross-examination, so we would run back and forth from one corner to the other, trying to keep warm; we talked about the past and hoped wonderingly about our future. I began to teach Yavitch something about the sciences. Three weeks passed in this way.

Then there was a change. With all my belongings, I was summoned to the prison office and given over to two tall gendarmes, who drove me by horse to a prison at Kherson. It was a building even older than the other. My cell was roomy, but it had only a narrow window that did not open, and was protected by heavy iron bars through which little light could enter. My isolation was absolute and hopeless. There was no walking, nor were there any neighbours. I couldn't see anything through my window, which had been entirely sealed up for the winter. I got no parcels from outside and I had no tea or sugar. Prisoner's stew was given to me once a day, for dinner. A ration of rye bread with salt was breakfast and supper. I had long discussions with myself as to whether I should increase my morning portion at the expense of the evening one. The morning arguments in favour of an increase seemed quite senseless and criminal at night; at supper-time I hated the person who had treated himself at breakfast. I didn't have a change of linen. For three months I had to wear the same underwear and I had no soap. The vermin there were eating me alive. I would set myself to taking one thousand, one hundred and eleven steps on the diagonal. That was my nineteenth year. The solitude was unbroken, worse than any I ever experienced afterwards, although I served time in nearly twenty prisons. I didn't have even a book, a piece of paper or a pencil. The cell was never aired. The only way I could gauge the comparative purity of the air was by the grimace that twisted the face of the assistant warden when he sometimes visited me.

Biting off a piece of the prison bread, I would compose verses while I walked on the diagonal. I turned the populist song 'Dubinushka' into a proletarian 'Machinushka', and I composed a revolutionary 'Kamarinsky'. Although they were most mediocre, these verses became very popular later on. They are reprinted in the songbooks even today. There were times, however, when I was sick with loneliness. And on such occasions I would be exaggeratedly firm with myself and count out another one thousand, one hundred and eleven steps in shoes already worn out.

At the end of the third month, when a straw-filled bag, prison-bread, and lice were the fixed elements of existence, as much so as day and night, one evening the guards brought me a great bundle of things from that other, utterly fantastic world; there were fresh linen, covers and a pillow, white bread, tea, sugar, ham, canned foods, apples, oranges – yes, big bright-coloured oranges! Even today, after thirty-one years, I list all these marvellous things with emotion, and I even pull myself up for having forgotten the jar of jam, the soap and the comb for my hair. 'Your mother sent them,' said the assistant warden. And, little as I knew about reading the thoughts of people in those days, I could tell from his tone that he had been bribed.

A little while later I was taken on a steamer to Odessa, where I was put into solitary confinement in a prison built only a few years before, and the last word in technical equipment. After Nikolayev and Kherson the Odessa prison seemed a perfect place. Tapping, notes, 'telephone', and shouting through windows – in other words, communication service – were continuous. I tapped my verses written at Kherson to my neighbours, and they sent me news in return. By way of the window Shvigovsky managed to tell me of the discovery of the brief-case, so that I had no trouble in avoiding the trap that Lieutenant-Colonel Dremlyuga set for me. At that time, I must explain, we had no. yet begun to refuse to give evidence, as we did a few years latert

The prison was overcrowded after the thoroughgoing spring arrests. On 1 March 1898, while I was still at Kherson, the first congress of the Social Democratic Party met at Minsk and drew up its constitution. There were nine members there, and most of them were caught in a wave of arrests that followed their meeting. A few months afterwards no one talked about the congress any more. But what followed it affected the history of man. The manifesto adopted there limned the future of political struggle as follows: 'The farther we go to the East of Europe, the more cowardly and dishonest, in a political sense, do we find the bourgeoisie; and the greater, correspondingly, becomes the political and cultural task confronting the proletariat.' There is a certain historical piquancy in the fact that the author of the manifesto was the notorious Peter Struve, who later became the leader of liberalism, and still later the publicist of the clerical and monarchist reaction.

During the first few months of my stay in the prison in Odessa I received no books from the outside, and so I had to be content with the prison library, which was made up mostly of conservative historical and religious magazines covering several years. I studied them insatiably, and learned through them to know all the sects and heresies of ancient and modern times, all the advantages of the orthodox church service, and the best arguments against Catholicism, Protestantism, Tolstoyism, and Darwinism. 'The Christian consciousness', I read in the *Orthodox Review*, 'loves true sciences, including natural sciences, as the intellectual kinsmen of faith.' The miracle of Balaam's ass, who entered into an argument with a prophet, could not be disproved even from the point of view of natural science. 'Isn't it a fact, for instance, that parrots and even canary-birds can talk?' This argument by the archbishop Nikanor occupied my mind for several days, even in my dreams.

The investigations of devils and their chief, the Prince of Darkness, and of their kingdom, were constantly amazing to me, and diverted my rationalist mind with their codified stupidities of thousand of years. The exhaustive description and study of Paradise, with detailed bits about its location and inner structure, ended melancholically with: 'The precise location of paradise is not known.' And, at tea, at dinner, and during my walks, I repeated this sentence: 'Regarding the geographical longitude of the felicitous paradise, there is no precise information.' I seized on every opportunity to indulge in theological bickering with the police sergeant Miklin, a greedy, malicious fellow and an inveterate liar, who was extremely pious and well read in the holy books. He used to hum hymns as he hurried from cell to cell, his dangling keys ringing out as he climbed the iron stairs.

'Only for one single word, "Christ's mother" instead of "God's mother",' he instructed me, 'the heretic Arius's belly burst.'

'And why are the bellies of the heretics today still intact?' I retorted. 'These are . . . these are different times,' he replied, in an offended tone.

Through my sister, who had come from the country, I managed to get four copies of the Bible in different languages. So I read the Gospels, verse by verse, with the help of the little knowledge of German and French that I had acquired in school, and side by side with this a parallel reading in English and Italian. In a few months I made excellent progress in this way. I must admit, however, that my linguistic talents are very mediocre. Even now I do not know a single foreign language well, although I stayed for some time in various European countries.

For their meeting with relatives the prisoners were transferred to narrow wooden cages separated from the visitors by a double grating. When my father came to see me for the first time, he imagined that I was always kept in that narrow box and was so overcome at the thought that he could not speak. In answer to my questions he only moved his bloodless lips in silence. Never will I forget his face. My mother came forewarned and was much calmer.

Echoes of what was taking place in the outside world reached us in bits. The South African war hardly touched us. We were still provincials in the full sense of the word. We were inclined to interpret the struggle between the Boers and the English chiefly as an instance of the inevitable victory of large capital over small. The Dreyfus case, which was then at its climax, thrilled us by its drama. Once, a rumour reached us that a *coup d'état* had been carried out in France and that monarchy had been restored. We all felt deeply ashamed. The guards went rushing through the iron corridors and up and down the staircases trying to stop our banging and shouting. They thought we had been served inedible food. But no! It was the political wing of the prison protesting excitedly against the restoration of monarchy in France.

The articles dealing with freemasonry in the theological magazines aroused my interest. Where did this strange movement come from? I asked myself. How would Marxism explain it? I resisted the theory of historical materialism for quite a long time, and held to that of the multiplicity of historical factors, which, as we know, even today is the most widely accepted theory in social science. People denote as 'factors' the various aspects of their social activity, endow this concept with a suprasocial character, and then superstitiously interpret their own activity as the result of the interaction of these independent forces. Where did the factors come from, that is, under the influence of what conditions did they evolve from primitive human society? With these questions, the official eclectic theory does not concern itself.

It was in my cell that I read with delight two well-known essays by an old Italian Hegelian-Marxist, Antonio Labriola, which reached the prison in a French translation. Unlike most Latin writers, Labriola had mastered the materialist dialectics, if not in politics – in which he was helpless – at least in the philosophy of history. The brilliant dilettantism of his exposition actually concealed a very profound insight. He made short work, and in marvellous style, of the theory of multiple factors which were supposed to dwell on the Olympus of history and rule our fates from there.

Although thirty years have gone by since I read his essays, the general trend of his argument is still firmly entrenched in my memory, together with his continuous refrain of 'Ideas do not drop from the sky'. After Labriola, all the Russian proponents of the multiplicity of factors, Lavrov, Mikhaylovsky, Kareyev, and others, seemed utterly ineffectual to me. Many years later I was wholly at a loss to understand some of the

Marxists who had succumbed to the influence of the sterile treatise on *Economics and the Law*, written by the German professor, Stammler. It was just another of the innumerable attempts to force the great stream of natural and human history, from the amoeba to present-day man and beyond, through the closed rings of the eternal categories – rings which have reality only as marks on the brain of a pedant.

It was during that period that I became interested in freemasonry. For several months I avidly studied books on its history, books given to me by relatives and friends in the town. Why had the merchants, artists, bankers, officials, and lawyers, from the first quarter of the seventeenth century on, begun to call themselves masons and tried to recreate the ritual of the medieval guilds? What was all this strange masquerade about? Gradually the picture grew clearer. The old guild was more than a producing organization; it regulated the ethics and mode of life of its members as well. It completely embraced the life of the urban population, especially the guilds of semi-artisans and semi-artists of the building trades. The break-up of the guild system brought a moral crisis in a society which had barely emerged from medievalism. The new morality was taking shape much more slowly than the old was being cut down. Hence, the attempt, so common in history, to preserve a form of moral discipline when its social foundations, which in this instance were those of the industrial guilds, had long since been undermined by the processes of history. Active masonry became theoretical masonry. But the old moral ways of living, which men were trying to keep just for the sake of keeping them, acquired a new meaning. In certain branches of freemasonry elements of an obvious reactionary feudalism were prominent, as in the Scottish system. In the eighteenth century freemasonry became expressive of a militant policy of enlightenment, as in the case of the Illuminati, who were the forerunners of revolution; on its left it culminated in the Carbonari. Freemasons counted among their members both Louis XVI and the Dr Guillotin who invented the guillotine. In southern Germany freemasonry assumed an openly revolutionary character, whereas at the court of Catherine the Great it was a masquerade reflecting the aristocratic and bureaucratic hierarchy. A freemason Novikov was exiled to Siberia by a freemason empress.

Although in our day of cheap and ready-made clothing hardly anybody is still wearing his grandfather's *surtout*, in the world of ideas the *surtout* and the crinoline are still in fashion. Ideas are handed down from generation to generation, although, like grandmother's pillows and covers, they reek of staleness. Even those who are obliged to change the substance of their opinions force them into ancient moulds. The revolution in industry has been much more far-reaching than it has in ideas, where piece-work is preferred to new structures. That is why the French parliamentarians of the petty bourgeoisie could find no better way of creating moral ties to hold the people together against the disruptiveness of modern relations than to put on white aprons and arm themselves with a pair of compasses or a plumb-line. They were really thinking less of erecting a new building than of finding their way back into the old one of parliament or ministry.

As the prison rules demanded that a prisoner give up his old exercise-book when he was given a new one, I got for my studies on freemasonry an exercise-book with a thousand numbered pages, and entered in it, in tiny characters, excerpts from many books, interspersed with my own reflections on freemasonry, as well as on the materialist conception of history. This took up the better part of a year. I edited each chapter carefully, copied it into a note-book which had been smuggled in to me, and then sent that out to friends in other cells to read. For contriving this we had a complicated system which we called the 'telephone'. The person for whom the package was intended – that is, if his cell was not too far away – would attach a weight to a piece of string, and then, holding his hand as far as he could out of the window, would swing the weight in a circle. As previously arranged through tapping, I would stick my broom out so that the weight could swing around it. Then I would draw the broom in and tie the manuscript to the string. When the person to whom I wanted to send it was too far away, we managed it by a series of stages, which of course made things more complicated.

Towards the end of my stay in the Odessa prison the fat

exercise-book, protected by the signature of the senior police sergeant, Usov, had become a veritable well of historical erudition and philosophic thought. I don't know whether it could be printed today as I wrote it then. I was learning too much at a time, from too many different spheres, epochs, and countries, and I am afraid that I was too anxious to tell everything at once in my first work. But I think that its main ideas and conclusions were correct. I felt, even at that time, that I was standing firmly on my own feet, and as the work progressed, I had the feeling even more strongly. I would give a great deal today to find that manuscript. It went with me into exile, although there I discontinued my work on freemasonry to take up the study of Marxian economics. After my escape abroad Alexandra Lvovna* forwarded the script to me from Siberia, through my parents, when they visited me in Paris in 1903. Later on, when I went on a secret mission to Russia, it was left in Geneva with the rest of my modest émigré archives, to become part of the *Iskra's* archives and to find there an untimely grave. After my second escape from Siberia I tried to recover it, but in vain. Apparently it had been used to light fires or some such thing by the Swiss landlady who had been entrusted with the custody of the archives. I can't refrain here from conveying my reproaches to that worthy woman.

The way in which my work on freemasonry had to be carried on, in prison, where literary resources at my disposal were of course very limited, served me in good stead. At that time I was still comparatively ignorant of the basic literature of the Marxists. The essays by Labriola were really philosophic pamphlets and presumed a knowledge that I didn't have, and for which I had to substitute guesswork. I finished them with a bunch of hypotheses in my head. The work on freemasonry acted as a test for these hypotheses. I made no new discoveries; all the methodological conclusions at which I had arrived had been made long ago and were being applied in practice. But I groped my way to them, and somewhat independently. I think this influenced the whole course of my subsequent intellectual develop-

*Alexandra Lvovna Sokolovskaya, who was exiled to Siberia with the author, and became his wife. – *Translator*.

ment. In the writings of Marx, Engels, Plekhanov and Mehring I later found confirmation for what in prison seemed to me only a guess needing verification and theoretical justification. I did not absorb historical materialism at once, dogmatically. The dialectic method revealed itself to me for the first time not as abstract definitions but as a living spring which I had found in the historical process as I tried to understand it.

Meanwhile, the tide of revolution was beginning to rise all through the country. The historical dialectics were also working marvellously there, only in a practical sense, and on a huge scale. The student movement vented itself in demonstrations. The Cossacks knouted the students. The liberals were indignant at this treatment of their sons. The Social Democracy was getting stronger, and was becoming an integral part of the labour movement. Revolution was no longer a privileged avocation in intellectual circles. The number of workers arrested was increasing. It was easier to breathe in the prisons, despite the overcrowding. By the end of the second year the verdict in the case of the South Russian Workers' Union was announced: the four principal defendants were sentenced to exile in eastern Siberia for four years. After this we were still kept for over six months in the Moscow transfer prison. I used the interim for intensive studies in theory. Then for the first time I heard of Lenin, and studied his book on the development of Russian capitalism, which had just appeared, from cover to cover. Then I wrote and smuggled out of prison a pamphlet on the labour movement at Nikolayev, which was published soon after that in Geneva. We were sent away from the Moscow prison in the summer. There were interludes in other prisons. It wasn't until the autumn of 1900 that we reached our place of banishment.

9

My First Exile

We were going down the river Lena, a few barges of convicts with a convoy of soldiers, drifting slowly along with the current. It was cold at night, and the heavy coats with which we covered ourselves were thick with frost in the morning. All along the way, at villages decided on beforehand, one or two convicts were put ashore. As well as I can remember it took about three weeks before we came to the village of Ust-Kut. There I was put ashore with one of the woman prisoners, a close associate of mine from Nikolayev. Alexandra Lvovna had one of the most important positions in the South Russian Workers' Union. Her utter loyalty to socialism and her complete lack of any personal ambition gave her an unquestioned moral authority. The work that we were doing bound us closely together, and so, to avoid being separated, we had been married in the transfer prison in Moscow.

The village comprised about a hundred peasant huts. We settled down in one of them on the very edge of the village. About us were the woods; below us, the river. Farther north, down the Lena, there were gold-mines. The reflection of the gold seemed to hover about the river. Ust-Kut had known lusher times, days of wild debauches, robberies, and murders. When we were there the village was very quiet, but there was still plenty of drunkenness. The couple who owned the hut that we took were inveterate tipplers. Life was dark and repressed, utterly remote from the rest of the world. At night the cockroaches filled the house with their rustlings as they crawled over table and bed, and even over our faces. From time to time we had to move out of the hut for a day or so and keep the door wide open, at a temperature of thirty-five degrees (Fahrenheit) below zero.

In the summer our lives were made wretched by midges. They even bit to death a cow which had lost its way in the woods. The peasants wore nets of tarred horsehair over their heads. In the spring and autumn the village was buried in mud. To be sure, the country was beautiful, but during those years it left me cold. I hated to waste interest and time on it. I lived between the woods and the river, and I almost never noticed them – I was so busy with my books and personal relations. I was studying Marx, brushing the cockroaches off the page.

The Lena was the great water route of the exiled. Those who had completed their terms returned to the South by way of the river. But commnnication was continuous between these various nests of the banished which kept growing with the rise of the revolutionary tide. The exiles exchanged letters with each other, some of them so long that they were really theoretical treatises. It was comparatively easy to get a transfer from one place to another from the governor of Irkutsk. Alexandra Lvovna and I moved to a place 250 versts east on the river Ilim, where we had friends. I found a job there for a while, as clerk to a millionaire merchant. His fur depots, stores and saloons were scattered over a territory as big as Belgium and Holland put together. He was a powerful merchant-lord. He referred to the thousands of Tunguses under him as 'my little Tunguses'. He couldn't even write his name; he had to mark it with a cross. He lived in niggardly fashion the whole year round, and then would squander tens of thousands of roubles at the annual fair at Nijni-Novgorod. I worked under him for a month and a half. Then one day I entered on a bill a pound of red-lead as 'one pood' (forty pounds), and sent this huge bill to a distant store. This completely ruined my reputation with my employer and I was discharged.

So we went back to Ust-Kut. The cold was terrific; the temperature dropped as low as fifty-five degrees (Fahrenheit) below zero. The coachman had to break the icicles off the horses' muzzles as we drove along. I held a ten-months-old baby girl on my knees. We had made a fur funnel to put over her head, arranged so that she could breathe through it and at every stop we removed her fearfully from her coverings, to see if she was still alive. Nothing untoward happened on that trip, however. We didn't stay long at Ust-Kut. After a few months, the governor gave us permission to move a little farther south, to a place called Verkholensk, where we had friends.

The aristocracy among the exiles was made up of the old Populists who had more or less succeeded in establishing themselves during the long years they had been away. The young Marxists formed a distinct section by themselves. It was not until my time that the striking workers, often illiterates who by some freak of fate had been separated from the great mass, began to drift to the north. For them, exile proved an invaluable school for politics and general culture. Intellectual disagreements were made the more bitter by squabbles over personal matters, as is natural where a great many people are forcibly confined. Private, and especially romantic, conflicts frequently took on the proportions of drama. There were even suicides on this account. At Verkholensk we took turns at guarding a student from Kiev. I noticed a pile of shining metal shavings on his table. We found out later that he had made lead bullets for his shotgun. Our guarding him was in vain. With the barrel of the gun against his breast, he pulled the trigger with his foot. We buried him in silence on the hill. At that time we were still shy about making speeches, as if there were something artificial about them. In all the big exile colonies there were graves of suicides. Some of the exiles became absorbed into the local populations, especially in the towns; others took to drink. In exile, as in prison, only hard intellectual work could save one. The Marxists, I must admit, were the only ones who did any of it under these conditions.

It was on the great Lena route, at that time, that I met Dzerzhinsky, Uritzky, and other young revolutionaries who were destined to play such important rôles in the future. We awaited each arriving party eagerly. On a dark spring night, as we sat around a bonfire on the banks of the Lena, Dzerzhinsky read one of his poems, in Polish. His face and voice were beautiful, but the poem was a slight thing. The life of the man was to prove to be one of the sternest of poems.

Soon after our arrival at Ust-Kut, I began to contribute articles to an Irkutsk newspaper, the *Vostochnoye Obozreniye*

(*The Eastern Review*). It was a provincial organ within the law, started by the old Populist exiles, but occasionally it fell into the hands of Marxists. I began as a village correspondent, and I waited anxiously for my first article to appear. The editor encouraged my contributions, and I soon began to write about literature, as well as about public questions. One day when I was trying to think of a pen-name, I opened the Italian dictionary and 'antidoto' was the first word that met my eye. So for several years I signed myself 'Antid Oto', and jestingly explained to my friends that I wanted to inject the Marxist antidote into the legitimate newspapers. After a while my pay jumped suddenly from two kopecks a line to four. It was the best proof of success. I wrote about the peasantry; about the Russian classic authors; about Ibsen, Hauptmann and Nietzsche; de Maupassant, Andreyev and Gorky. I sat up night after night scratching up my manuscripts, as I tried to find the exact idea or the right word to express it. I was becoming a writer.

Since 1896, when I had tried to ward off revolutionary ideas, and the following year, when I had done the same to Marxist doctrines even though I was already carrying on revolutionary work, I had travelled far. At the time of my exile Marxism had definitely become the basis of my philosophy. During the exile I tried to consider, from the new point of view I had acquired, the so-called 'eternal' problems of life: love, death, friendship, optimism, pessimism, and so forth. In different epochs, and in varying social surroundings, man loves and hates and hopes differently. Just as the tree feeds its leaves, flowers, and fruits with the extracts absorbed from the soil by its roots, so does the individual find food for his sentiment and ideas, even the most 'sublime' ones, in the economic roots of society. In my literary articles written in this period I developed virtually one theme only: the relations between the individual and society. Not very long ago these articles were published in a single volume, and when I saw them collected I realized that, although I might have written them differently today, I should not have had to change the substance of them.

At that time official or so-called 'legal' Russian Marxism was in the throes of a crisis. I could see then from actual experience how brazenly new social requirements create for themselves intellectual garments from the cloth of a theory that was intended for something quite different. Until the nineties the greater part of the Russian intelligentsia was stagnating in Populist theories with their rejection of capitalist development and idealization of peasant communal ownership of the land. And capitalism in the meantime was holding out to the intelligentsia the promise of all sorts of material blessings and political influence. The sharp knife of Marxism was the instrument by which the bourgeois intelligentsia cut the Populist umbilical cord, and severed itself from a hated past. It was this that accounted for the swift and victorious spread of Marxism during the latter years of the last century.

As soon as Marxism had accomplished this, however, it began to irk this same intelligentsia. Its dialectics were convenient for demonstrating the progress of capitalist methods of development, but finding that it led to a revolutionary rejection of the whole capitalist system, they adjudged it an impediment and declared it out of date. At the turn of the century, at the time when I was in prison and exile, the Russian intelligentsia was going through a phase of widespread criticism of Marxism. They accepted its historical justification of capitalism, but discarded its rejection of capitalism by revolutionary means. In this roundabout way the old Populist intelligentsia, with its archaic sympathies, was slowly being transformed into a liberal bourgeois intelligentsia.

European criticisms of Marxism now found a ready hearing in Russia, irrespective of their quality. It is enough to say that Eduard Bernstein became one of the most popular guides from socialism to liberalism. The normative philosophy, shouting victory with more and more assurance, was ousting the materialist dialectics. Bourgeois public opinion, in its formative stages, needed inflexible norms, not only to protect it against the tyrannies of the autocratic bureaucracy, but against the wild revolutionism of the masses. Kant, although he overthrew Hegel, did not in turn hold his position very long. Russian liberalism came very late, and from the first lived on volcanic soil. The categorical imperative, it found, gave it too abstract and unreliable a security. Much stronger measures were needed to resist the revolutionary masses. The transcendental idealists became orthodox Christians. Bulgakov, a professor of political economy, began with a revision of Marxism on the agrarian question, went on to idealism, and ended by becoming a priest. But this last stage was not reached until some years later.

In the early years of this century Russia was a vast laboratory of social thinking. My work on the history of freemasonry had fortified me in a realization of the subordinate place of ideas in the historical process. 'Ideas do not drop from the sky,' I repeated after old Labriola. Now it was no longer a question of pure scientific study, but of the choice of a political path. The revision of Marxism that was going on in all directions helped me as it did many another young Marxist – it helped us to make up our minds and sharpen our weapons. We needed Marxism, not only to rid ourselves of Populism, which touched us but slightly, but actually to begin a stout war against capitalism in its own territory. The struggles against the Revisionists toughened us politically, as well as in the field of theory. We were becoming proletarian revolutionaries.

During this same period we met with a great deal of criticism from our left. In one of the northern colonies – I think it was Viluysk – lived an exile called Makhaisky, whose name soon became generally known. Makhaisky began as a critic of Social Democratic opportunism. His first hectographed essay, devoted to an exposure of the opportunism of the German Social Democracy, had a great vogue among the exiles. His second essay criticized the economic system of Marx and ended with the amazing conclusion that Socialism is a social order based on the exploitation of the workers by a professional intelligentsia. The third essay advocated the rejection of political struggle in the spirit of anarchist syndicalism. For several months the work of Makhaisky held first place in the interest of the Lena exiles. It gave me a powerful inoculation against anarchism, a theory very sweeping in its verbal negations, but lifeless and cowardly in its practical conclusions.

The first time I ever met a living anarchist was in the Moscow transfer prison. He was a village school-teacher, Luzin, a man reserved and uncommunicative, even cruel. In prison he always preferred to be with the criminals and would listen intently to their tales of robbery and murder. He avoided discussions of theory. But once when I pressed him to tell me how railways would be managed by autonomous communities, he answered: 'Why the hell should I want to travel on railways under anarchism?' That answer was enough for me. Luzin tried to win the workers over, and we carried on a concealed warfare which was not devoid of hostility.

We made the journey to Siberia together. During the high floods on the river, Luzin decided to cross the Lena in a boat. He was not quite sober and challenged me to go with him. I agreed. Loose timber and dead animals were floating on the surface of the swollen river; there were many whirlpools. We made the crossing safely, though not without exciting moments. Luzin gave me a sort of verbal testimonial: a 'good comrade', or something to that effect, and we became friendlier. Soon after, however, he was transferred to a place farther north. A few months later he stabbed the local police-chief with a knife. The policeman was not a bad sort of fellow and the wound did not prove dangerous. At the trial Luzin declared that he had nothing against the man personally, but that he wanted, through him, to strike at the tyranny of the state. He was sentenced to hard-labour.

While hot discussions were seething in the far-flung, snow-covered Siberian exile colonies – discussions of such things as the differentiation of the Russian peasantry, the English trades-unions, the relationship between the categorical imperative and the class interests, and between Marxism and Darwinism – a struggle of a special sort was taking place in government spheres. In February 1901 the Holy Synod excommunicated Leo Tolstoy.

The edict was published in all the papers. Tolstoy was accused of six crimes: 1. 'He rejects the personal, living God, glorified in the Holy Trinity.' 2. 'He denies Christ as the God-man risen from the dead.' 3. 'He denies the Immaculate Conception and the virginity, before and after the birth, of the God-mother.' 4. 'He does not recognize life after death and retribution for sins.' 5. 'He rejects the benefaction of the Holy Ghost.' 6. 'He mocks

at the sacrament of the Eucharist.' The grey-bearded metro-
politans, Pobedonostzev, who was inspiring them, and all the
other pillars of the state who looked upon us revolutionaries as
half-mad fanatics, not to say criminals – whereas they, in their
own eyes, were the representatives of sober thought based on the
historical experience of man – it was these people who demanded
that the great artist-realist subscribe to the faith in the Immaculate Conception, and in the transubstantiation of the Holy
Ghost through wafers. We read the list of Tolstoy's heresies
over and over again, each time with fresh astonishment, and
said to ourselves: No, it is we who rest on the experience of man,
it is we who represent the future, while those men at the top are
not merely criminals but maniacs as well. We were absolutely
sure that we would get the better of that lunatic asylum.

The old structure of the state was cracking all through its
foundations. The students were still the ringleaders in the
struggle, and in their impatience began to employ the methods
of terrorism. After the shots fired by Karpovich and Balmashov*
all the exiles were as much aroused as if they had heard the
bugle-call of alarm. Arguments about the use of terrorist
methods began. After individual vacillations the Marxist section
of the exiled went on record against terrorism. The chemistry of
high explosives cannot take the place of mass action, we said.
Individuals may be destroyed in a heroic struggle, but that will
not rouse the working class to action. Our task is not the assassination of the Tsar's ministers, but the revolutionary overthrow
of Tsarism. This is where the line was drawn between the Social
Democrats and the Socialist-Revolutionists. While my theoretical views were formed in prison, my political self-determination
was achieved in exile.

Two years had passed in this way and much water had flowed
under the bridges of St Petersburg, Moscow, and Warsaw. A
movement begun underground was now walking the streets of
the cities. In some districts the peasantry was beginning to stir.
Social-Democratic organizations sprang up even in Siberia along
the line of the Trans-Siberian railway. They got in touch with

* Karpovich shot Bogolyepov, Minister of Education, in 1901. Balmashov
shot Sipyagin, Minister of the Interior, in 1902. – *Translator.*

me, and I wrote proclamations and leaflets for them. After a three years' interval I was rejoining the ranks for active struggle.

The exiles were no longer willing to stay in their places of confinement, and there was an epidemic of escapes. We had to arrange a system of rotation. In almost every village there were individual peasants who as youths had come under the influence of the older generation of revolutionaries. They would carry the 'politicals' away secretly in boats, in carts, or on sledges, and pass them along from one to another. The police in Siberia were as helpless as we were. The vastness of the country was an ally, but an enemy as well. It was very hard to catch a runaway, but the chances were that he would be drowned in the river or frozen to death in the primeval forests.

The revolutionary movement had spread far and wide, but it still lacked unity. Every district and every town was carrying on its individual struggle. Tsarism had the invaluable advantage of concerted action. The necessity for creating a centralized party was engaging the minds of many revolutionaries. I devoted an essay to this and copies of it were circulated throughout the colonies; it was discussed with avidity. It seemed to us that our fellow Social Democrats in Russia and abroad were not giving this question enough thought. But they did think and act. In the summer of 1902 I received, by way of Irkutsk, a number of books in the binding of which were concealed the latest publications from abroad, printed on extremely fine paper. We learned from them that there was a Marxian newspaper published abroad, the *Iskra*, which had as its object the creation of a centralized organization of professional revolutionaries who would be bound together by the iron discipline of action. A book by Lenin also reached us, a book published in Geneva, entitled *What Is to Be Done?* which dealt exclusively with the same problem. My hand-written essays, newspaper articles, and proclamations for the Siberian Union immediately looked small and provincial to me in the face of the new and tremendous task which confronted us. I had to look for another field of activity. I had to escape from exile.

At that time we already had two daughters. The younger was four months old. Life under conditions in Siberia was not easy, and my escape would place a double burden on the shoulders of Alexandra Lvovna. But she met this objection with the two words: 'You must.' Duty to the revolution overshadowed everything else for her, personal considerations especially. She was the first to broach the idea of my escape when we realized the great new tasks. She brushed away all my doubts.

For several days after I had escaped she concealed my absence from the police. From abroad I could hardly keep up a correspondence with her. Then she was exiled for a second time; after this we met only occasionally. Life separated us, but nothing could destroy our friendship and our intellectual kinship.

My First Escape

Autumn was drawing near with its threat of impassable roads. To speed my escape we decided to kill two birds with one stone. A peasant friend agreed to drive me out of Verkholensk, together with E. G., a woman translator of Marx. At night, in the fields, he hid us under hay and matting in his cart, as if we were mere cargo. At the same time, to ward off the suspicions of the police, they kept a dummy of a supposedly sick man in the bed in my house for a few days. The driver sped on in the Siberian fashion, making as much as twenty versts an hour. I counted all the bumps with my back, to the accompaniment of the groans of my companion. During the trip the horses were changed twice. Before we reached the railway, my companion and I went our separate ways, so that each of us would not have to suffer the mishaps and risks incurred by the other. I got into the railway-carriage in safety. There my friends from Irkutsk provided me with a travelling-case filled with starched shirts, neckties and other attributes of civilization. In my hands I had a copy of the 'Iliad' in the Russian hexameter of Gnyeditch; in my pocket, a passport made out in the name of Trotsky, which I wrote in it at random, without even imagining that it would become my name for the rest of my life. I was following the Siberian line towards the West. The station police let me pass with indifference.

At the stations along the way the tall Siberian women sold roast chickens and suckling pigs, bottled milk and great heaps of bread. Every one of the stations was like an exhibition of Siberian produce. Throughout the journey the entire carful of passengers drank tea and ate cheap Siberian buns. I read the hexameter and dreamed of the life abroad. The escape proved to be quite without romantic glamour; it dissolved into nothing but an endless drinking of tea.

I made a halt at Samara, where the interior general staff of the *Iskra*, as distinct from the foreign-émigré staff, was concentrated. At the head of it was a certain Kler, the name which the engineer Krzhizhanovsky, who is the present chairman of the State Planning Committee, had assumed as a disguise. He and his wife were friends of Lenin, and had been associated with him in the Social Democratic work in St Petersburg in the years of 1894-5, and in the exile in Siberia. After the defeat of the revolution in 1905, Kler, together with many other thousands of revolutionists, withdrew from the party, and as an engineer achieved an important place in the industrial world. The revolutionaries, who continued to work in secret, complained that he refused to give such help as even the liberals had given earlier. After an interval of from ten to twelve years Krzhizhanovsky rejoined the party, after it had already come into power. This was the course of many of the intelligentsia who are the backbone of Stalin's régime today.

In Samara I joined – officially, as it were – the *Iskra* organization under the name of Pero (Pen), assigned to me by Kler as a tribute to my successes as a journalist in Siberia. The organization was building up the party all over again. The first party congress, held in Minsk in 1898, had failed to establish a centralized party. Wholesale arrests destroyed an incipient organization which was not rooted firmly enough throughout the country. After this, the revolutionary movement continued to grow in scattered centres, maintaining its provincial character. Simultaneously, its intellectual level showed signs of lowering. The Social Democrats, in their effort to win the masses, let their political slogans recede into the background. And thus the so-called 'Economic' school of Social Democratic policy was evolved. It drew its strength from the industrial boom and the preponderance of strikes. Towards the end of the century, a crisis developed that accentuated the antagonisms all over the country, and gave the political movement a strong impetus. The *Iskra* launched a militant campaign against the provincial 'Economists', and advocated a centralized revolutionary party.

The general staff of the *Iskra* was established abroad, so that the organization, which was being carefully recruited from among the so-called 'professional' revolutionaries, would be assured of an ideological stability, and would be bound together by unity in theory and in practical method. At the same time, most of the adherents of the *Iskra* still belonged to the intelligentsia. They fought for the control over local Social Democratic committees, and for a party congress which would ensure a victory for the ideas and methods of the *Iskra*. This was really a draft outline of the revolutionary organization, which, as it developed and hardened, advanced and retreated, became more and more closely bound to the masses of workers, set before them ever more far-reaching tasks, and fifteen years later overthrew the bourgeoisie and assumed power.

At the request of the Samara organization, I visited Kharkoff, Poltava and Kiev, to meet a number of revolutionaries who had already joined the *Iskra* or who had still to be won over. I returned to Samara with little accomplished; the connections with the South were still very ineffectual; in Kharkoff the address given me proved false, and in Poltava I ran into a sort of local patriotism. It was obvious that a single trip to the provinces could achieve nothing; it was persistent work that was needed. Meanwhile Lenin, with whom the Samara bureau kept up a lively correspondence, urged me to hasten my departure for abroad. Kler supplied me with the money for the trip, and the necessary information for crossing the Austrian frontier near Kamenetz-Podolsk.

A whole train of adventures more amusing than tragic began at the station at Samara. To avoid meeting the station-police a second time, I decided to board the train at the last possible moment. My seat was to be held for me and my travelling-bag brought to the railway-carriage by a student named Solovyov, who is today one of the heads of the Oil Syndicate. I was walking peacefully back and forth in the field far away from the station, keeping my eye on the clock, when I suddenly heard the second bell. I realized that I had been given the wrong time for the departure of the train and dashed to the station for all I was worth. Solovyov, who had been waiting for me in the car, as he had promised, and had to jump off the train after it had begun to move, was standing surrounded by the station-police and officials. The sight of a breathless man arriving post-haste after the train had started attracted general attention. The police threatened to take action against Solovyov, but it only ended in sarcastic jokes at our expense.

I reached the frontier zone without any trouble. At the last station the policeman asked for my passport. I was genuinely surprised when he found the paper that I had fabricated myself perfectly in order. A boy who was studying at the *gymnasium* had charge of smuggling me across the frontier. He is now a prominent chemist at the head of one of the science institutes of the Soviet Republic. In his political views he favoured the Socialist-Revolutionists. When he heard that I belonged to the *Iskra* organization, he said: 'Do you know that *Iskra*, in its last issues, had been engaging in shameful polemics against terrorism?'

I was about to begin a theoretical discussion when the young fellow added with a great show of temper: 'I won't conduct you across the frontier.' This argument amazed me because it was so unexpected. And yet it was perfectly legitimate. Fifteen years later we had to fight the power of the Socialist-Revolutionists with arms in hand. At that moment, however, I was not interested in historical prospects. I argued that it was not fair to punish me for an article in the *Iskra*, and finally declared that I would not budge until I had obtained a guide. The boy relented. 'Well,' he said, 'I will help you. But tell them over there that this is the last time.'

The fellow put me up for the night in the empty house of a commercial traveller who was to return the next day. I remember vaguely that I had to make my way into the locked house through a window. At night I was awakened suddenly by a flash of light. A strange little man in a bowler hat was bending over me with a candle in one hand and a stick in the other. From the ceiling a huge shadow of a man was crawling towards me. 'Who are you?' I asked indignantly. 'I like that!' answered the stranger. 'He is lying in my bed and asks me who I am!' Obviously, this was the owner of the house. My attempt to explain to him that he wasn't supposed to return until the next day made not the slightest impression on him. 'I know when I am supposed to return,' he rejoined, not unreasonably. The situation was getting complicated. 'I understand,' exclaimed the host. 'This is one of Alexander's little jokes. But I shall talk it over with him to-morrow.' I readily chimed in with his happy thought that the cause of all the trouble was the absent Alexander. I spent the rest of the night with the commercial traveller, who even graciously treated me to tea.

Next morning the student at the *gymnasium*, after a stormy time of explaining everything to my host, handed me over to the smugglers of the village of Brody. I whiled away the day in a barn, while its owner, a Ukrainian peasant, fed me liberally on watermelons. At night, in a rain-storm, he led me across the frontier. For a long time we had to wade in the dark, stumbling every now and then. 'Now, get on my back,' said my guide, 'there is water farther on.' I protested. 'You can't possibly appear on the other side all wet,' he insisted. So I had to continue the journey on the man's back, which didn't save me, however, from getting water in my shoes.

About a quarter of an hour later we were drying ourselves out in a Jewish hut in the Austrian section of Brody. The people there informed me that the guide had purposely led me into deep water to get more money from me. For his part, the Ukrainian, as he was taking his leave, warned me in a friendly way against the Jews, who always like to make one pay three times more than one owes them. And, indeed, my resources were swiftly melting away. I still had another eight kilometres to make before I could reach the railway-station. For one or two kilometres along the frontier, on a road whipped into mud by the rain, until we reached the main road, the going was not only difficult, but dangerous as well. I was riding in a little two-wheeled cart with an old Jewish workman for a driver.

'One day I shall lose my life in this business,' he muttered.

'Why?'

'Because soldiers keep calling out and if you don't answer them, they shoot. You can see their light over there. Fortunately, this is a fine night.'

The night was fine indeed! A cutting and impenetrable autumn darkness, an interminable rain hitting one in the face, and mud sloshing under the horse's hoofs. We were going uphill; the wheels kept slipping; the old man was cajoling the horse in a gruff half-whisper; the wheels sank, the light cart tilted more and more, and suddenly went right over. The October mud was cold and deep. I fell down flat, sinking half into it. And, to top it all, I lost my glasses. But the most awful thing was that just after we had fallen, there was a terrible piercing cry, right where we were, at our very side, a cry of despair, imploring help – a mystic appeal to heaven. It was beyond the power of reason to say, in that dark, wet night, to whom that mysterious voice belonged – a voice so expressive and yet not human.

'I tell you, he will ruin us,' muttered the old man in despair. 'He will ruin us!'

'Who is it?' I asked, almost afraid to breathe.

'It's the rooster, curse him, the rooster that my mistress gave me to take to the rabbi to have killed for Saturday.' The penetrating shrieks continued at regular intervals. 'He will ruin us. It's only two hundred steps to the post; the soldiers will rush out in a moment.'

'Strangle him,' I hissed in a rage.

'Who? The rooster? Where am I to find him? He must have got pinned under something!'

We both crawled around in the dark and grubbed in the mud with our hands, while the rain lashed us from above. We cursed the rooster and our fate. Finally, the old man freed the miserable sufferer from under my blanket, and the grateful bird immediately stopped crying. We lifted the cart together, and continued our journey. At the station I spent three hours drying out and cleaning myself up before the train arrived.

After I had changed my money, I found that I shouldn't have enough to reach my destination, which was Zurich, where I was to present myself to Axelrod. I bought a ticket to Vienna, and decided that there I would arrange for the next lap.

Vienna surprised me most of all by the fact that I could understand no one, despite my study of German at school. Most of the passers-by found me equally difficult. Nevertheless, I managed finally to tell an old man in a red cap that I wanted to get to the offices of the *Arbeiter-Zeitung*. I had made up my mind that I would explain to no one less than Victor Adler, the leader of the Austrian Social Democracy, that the interests of the Russian revolution demanded my immediate presence in Zurich. The guide agreed to take me there. We walked for an hour. Then we found out that two years earlier the paper had moved its offices to a new address. We walked for another half-hour. Then the doorman informed us that visiting hours were over. I had no money to pay the guide, I was hungry, and what was most important of all, I *had* to get to Zurich. A gentleman who didn't look too amiable was coming down the steps. I addressed myself to him with a query about Adler.

'Do you know what day it is?' he asked me sternly.

I did not know; in the train, in the cart, in the house of the commercial traveller, in the Ukrainian's barn, in the midnight struggle with the rooster, I had lost track of time.

'Today is Sunday,' the old gentleman announced, and tried to pass by me.

'No matter – I want to see Adler.'

At this, my interrogator answered me in the voice of one giving orders to a battalion of troops in a storm: 'I am telling you, Dr Adler cannot be seen on Sundays.'

'But I have important business with him,' I persisted.

'Even if your business were ten times as important – do you understand?' It was Fritz Austerlitz himself speaking, the terror of his office, a man whose conversation, as Hugo would have said, consisted only of lightning. 'Even if you had brought the news – you hear me? – that your Tsar had been assassinated, that a revolution had broken out in your country – do you hear – even this would not give you the right to disturb the Doctor's Sunday rest.'

I was beginning to be impressed by the thunders of the gentleman's voice. All the same I thought he was talking nonsense. It was inconceivable that a Sunday's rest should be rated above the demands of revolution. I decided not to give in. I had to get to Zurich. The editors of the *Iskra* were waiting for me. Besides, I had escaped from Siberia – surely that was of some importance.

Finally, by standing at the bottom of the staircase and barring the stern gentleman's way, I got what I wanted. Austerlitz gave me the address. Accompanied by the same guide, I went to Adler's house.

A short man, with a pronounced stoop, almost a hunch, and with swollen eyes in a tired face, came out to see me. At the time there was an Landtag election in Vienna. Adler had made speeches at several meetings the day before and during the night had written his articles and exhortations. I learned all this a quarter of an hour later from his daughter-in-law.

'Pardon me for disturbing your Sunday rest, Doctor.'

'Go on, go on,' he said with seeming sternness, but in a tone that did not frighten but encouraged me instead. One could see intelligence emanating from each wrinkle of the man.

'I am Russian.'

'You need not tell me that, I have had enough time to guess it.'

I told the Doctor, while he studied me with swift glances, about my conversation at the entrance to his office.

'Is that so? Did they tell you that? Who could it have been? A tall man? Shouts? Oh, that was Austerlitz. You said he shouted? Oh, yes, it was Austerlitz. Don't take it too seriously. If you ever bring news of a revolution in Russia, you may ring my bell, even at night. Katya, Katya,' he called out suddenly. His Russian daughter-in-law came out. 'Now we shall get along better,' he said, leaving us.

My further travel was assured.

II

An Émigré for the First Time

I arrived in London from Zurich by way of Paris, in the autumn of 1902. I think it was in October, early in the morning, when a cab, engaged after I had resorted to all sorts of pantomime, drove me to the address written on a slip of paper. My destination was Lenin's house. I had been instructed before I left Zurich to knock on the door three times. The door was opened by Nadyezhda Konstantinovna, who had probably been wakened by my knocking. It was early, and anyone used to civilized ways would have waited quietly at the station for an hour or two, instead of knocking at the door of a strange house at such an unearthly hour. But I was still impelled by the force that had set me off on my journey from Verkholensk. I had disturbed Axelrod in Zurich in the same barbarous way, although that was in the middle of the night, instead of at dawn. Lenin was still in bed, and the kindly expression of his face was tinged with a justifiable amazement. Such was the setting for our first meeting and conversation. Both Vladimir Ilyich* and Nadyezhda Konstantinovna already knew of me from Kler's letter, and had been waiting for me.

I was greeted with: 'The Pero has arrived!' At once I unloaded my modest list of impressions of Russia: the connections in the South are bad, the secret *Iskra* address in Kharkov is wrong, the editors of the *Southern Worker* oppose amalgamation, the crossing at the Austrian frontier is in the hands of a student at the *gymnasium* who refuses help to followers of the *Iskra*. The facts in themselves were not of a sort to fill one with much hope,

*Lenin's full original name is Vladimir Ilyich Ulyanov, Nikolay Lenin being his party- and pen-name. Since the revolution it has become customary to refer to him as Vladimir Ilyich Lenin, and more familiarly as Ilyich. His wife's maiden name is Nadyezhda Konstantinovna Krupskaya. – *Translator.*

but there was faith enough to make up for it, and to spare.

Either the same or the next morning Vladimir Ilyich and I went for a long walk around London. From a bridge, Lenin pointed out Westminster and some other famous buildings. I don't remember the exact words he used, but what he conveyed was: 'This is their famous Westminster,' and 'their' referred of course not to the English but to the ruling classes. This implication, which was not in the least emphasized, but coming as it did from the very innermost depths of the man, and expressed more by the tone of his voice than by anything else, was always present, whether Lenin was speaking of the treasures of culture, of new achievements, of the wealth of books in the British Museum, of the information of the larger European newspapers, or, years later, of German artillery or French aviation. They know this or they have that, they have made this or achieved that – but what enemies they are! To his eyes, the invisible shadow of the ruling classes always overlay the whole of human culture – a shadow that was as real to him as daylight.

The architecture of London scarcely attracted my attention at that time. Transferred bodily from Verkholensk to countries beyond the Russian border which I was seeing for the first time, I absorbed Vienna, Paris and London in a most summary fashion, and details like the Westminster Palace seemed quite superfluous. It wasn't for that, of course, that Lenin had taken me out for this long walk. His object was to become acquainted with me, and to question me. His examination, it must be admitted, was very thorough indeed.

I told him all about our Siberian discussions, especially on the question of a centralized organization; about my essay on the subject; about the violent encounters I had had with the old Populists in Irkutsk, where I had stayed for a few weeks; about the three essays by Makhaysky, and so forth. Lenin knew how to listen.

'And how did you fare in questions of theory?'

I told him how we, as a group, had studied his book, *The Development of Capitalism in Russia*, in the transfer-prison in Moscow, and how in exile we had worked on Marx's *Capital*, but had stopped at the second volume. We had studied the controversy between Bernstein and Kautsky intently, using the original sources. There were no followers of Bernstein among us. In philosophy we had been much impressed by Bogdanov's book, which combined Marxism with the theory of knowledge put forward by Mach and Avenarius. Lenin also thought, at the time, that Bogdanov's theories were right. 'I am not a philosopher,' he said, with a slightly timorous expression, 'but Plekhanov denounces Bogdanov's philosophy as a disguised sort of idealism.' A few years later, Lenin dedicated a big volume to the discussion of Mach and Avenarius; his criticism of their theories was fundamentally identical with that voiced by Plekhanov.

I mentioned, during our conversation, that the Siberian exiles had been greatly impressed by the enormous amount of statistical data analysed in Lenin's book on Russian capitalism. 'Well, it was not done all at once, you know,' he answered, as if somewhat embarrassed. He was apparently greatly pleased that the younger comrades appreciated the tremendous amount of work he had put into his principal opus on economics. My own future work was discussed then only in a very general way. We assumed that I would stay abroad for a time, get acquainted with current literature, look around, and the rest would be discussed afterwards. At any event, I intended to return illegally to Russia for revolutionary work some time later.

Nadyezhda Konstantinovna took me to a house a few blocks away, where lived Vera Zasulitch, Martov, and Blumenfeld, the *Iskra* printing-press manager, and where they found a room for me. According to the English custom, the rooms were arranged vertically, and not on the same floor, as in Russia: the lowest room was occupied by the landlady, and the lodgers had rooms one above another. There was also a common room in which we drank coffee, smoked, and engaged in endless discussions. This room, thanks chiefly to Zasulitch, but not without help from Martov, was always in a state of rank disorder. Plekhanov, after his first visit to the room, described it as a 'den'.

That was the beginning of my brief London episode. I took to studying the published issues of the *Iskra*, and the review of *Zarya*, which came from the same offices. These were brilliant periodicals, combining scientific profundity with revolutionary passion. I actually fell in love with the *Iskra*, and was so ashamed of my ignorance that I strained every nerve in my effort to overcome it. Soon I began to write for the *Iskra*. At first it was only short notes, but a little later I wrote political articles and even editorials.

At that time, too, I gave a public lecture in Whitechapel, when I had a passage-at-arms with the patriarch of the Russian émigrés, Tchaikovsky, and with the anarchist Tcherkezov, also a man of advanced years. I was honestly amazed at the infantile arguments with which these worthy elders were trying to crush Marxism. I returned home, I remember, as if I were walking on air. In my contacts with Whitechapel and with the outside world in general my go-between was an old Londoner, Alexeyev, an émigré Marxist who was closely allied with the editors of the *Iskra*. He initiated me into the mysteries of English life, and in general was my source of information on all sorts of things. Of Lenin, Alexeyev spoke with very great respect. 'I believe,' he said to me once, 'that Lenin is more important for the revolution than Plekhanov.' I did not mention this to Lenin, of course, but I did to Martov. Martov made no comment.

One Sunday I went with Lenin and Krupskaya to a Social-Democratic meeting in a church, where speeches alternated with the singing of hymns. The principal speaker was a compositor who had just returned from Australia. He spoke of the Social revolution. Then everybody rose and sang: 'Lord Almighty, let there be no more kings or rich men!' I could scarcely believe my eyes or ears. When we came out of the church, Lenin said: 'There are many revolutionary and socialistic elements among the English proletariat, but they are mixed up with conservatism, religion, and prejudices, and can't somehow break through to the surface and unite.'

After attending the Social-Democratic church, we had dinner in the tiny kitchen of a two-room apartment. My friends jested as usual about my finding my way home. I was very bad at making my way about the streets and, with my usual penchant for systematic thinking, called this defect 'a topographic cretinism'. Later I did better in this respect, but my improvement was not won without a great deal of effort.

My modest knowledge of English acquired in the prison at Odessa was increased very little by my stay in London. I was too much absorbed in Russian affairs. British Marxism was not interesting. The intellectual centre of the Social Democracy at that time was Germany, and we watched intently the struggle then going on between the 'orthodox' Marxists and the 're-visionists'.

In London, as well as later on in Geneva, I met Zasulitch and Martov much more often than Lenin. Since we lived in the same house in London, and in Geneva usually had our meals in the same restaurants, I was with Martov and Zasulitch several times a day, whereas Lenin led the life of a family man, and every meeting with him, aside from the official meetings, was a small event. The Bohemian habits and tastes which weighed so heavily with Martov were utterly alien to Lenin. He knew that time, be it ever so relative, was the most absolute of gifts. He spent a great deal of time in the library of the British Museum, where he carried on his theoretical studies, and where he usually wrote his newspaper articles. With his assistance, I obtained admission to that sanctuary too. I was insatiable, and simply gorged myself on the super-abundance of books there. Soon, however, I had to leave for the continent.

After my 'test' public appearance in Whitechapel, I was sent on a lecture tour of Brussels, Liège and Paris. My lecture was devoted to the defence of historical materialism against the criticisms of the so-called 'Russian subjective school'. Lenin was very much interested in my subject. I gave him my detailed synopsis to look over, and he advised me to revise the lecture so that it could be published in an article in the next issue of the *Zarya*. But I didn't have the courage to appear by the side of Plekhanov and the others with a strictly theoretical essay.

From Paris I was soon summoned by cable to London. They were planning to smuggle me over to Russia again, as reports from there complained about wholesale arrests and the shortage of men, and demanded my return. But I had hardly set foot in London when the plan was changed. Deutsch, who lived in London then and treated me very kindly, told me afterwards how he had stood up for me, urging that the 'youth' (he had no other name for me) needed a stay abroad for a while to improve his education, and how Lenin had agreed with him. The prospect of working in the Russian organization of the *Iskra* was tempting, but nevertheless I was very glad to be able to stay abroad a little longer.

I returned to Paris, where, unlike London, the Russian student colony was very large. The revolutionary parties were fighting each other bitterly to win over the mass of the students. Here is an excerpt from the recollections of that period by N. I. Sedova:

The autumn of 1902 was marked by frequent lectures in the Russian colony in Paris. The *Iskra* group, to which I belonged, saw first Martov, and then Lenin. A war was being fought against the 'Economists' and the Socialist-Revolutionists. In our group there was some talk about the arrival of a young comrade who had escaped from Siberia. He called at the house of E. M. Alexandrova, formerly one of the Narodovoltsi, who had joined the *Iskra*. We of the younger generation were very fond of Ekaterina Mikhailovna, listened to her talks with great interest, and were much under her influence. When the young contributor to the *Iskra* made his appearance in Paris, Ekaterina Mikhailovna bade me find out if there was a vacant room near by. There happened to be one in the house where I lived. The rent for it was twelve francs a month, but the room was small, dark and narrow, just like a prison cell. When I began describing the room to her, Ekaterina Mikhailovna cut me short with: 'That's enough describing – it will do. Let him take it.'

After the young comrade (whose name was not revealed to us) established himself in the room, Ekaterina Mikhailovna asked me: 'Is he preparing for his lecture?'

'I don't know, I suppose so,' I answered. 'Last night as I was coming upstairs I heard him whistling in his room.'

'Then tell him to work hard and not whistle.' She was very anxious that 'he' should be successful. But her anxiety was uncalled for. The lecture went off very well and the colony was delighted, as the young follower of the *Iskra* exceeded all expectations.

I was much more interested in learning about Paris than I had been about London. This was because of the influence of N. I. Sedova. I was born and brought up in the country, but it was in Paris that I began to draw close to nature. And there, too, I came face to face with real art. I learned to appreciate painting, as well as nature, with great difficulty. One of Sedova's later entries says: 'He expressed his general impression of Paris in this way: "Resembles Odessa, but Odessa is better." This absurd conclusion can be explained by the fact that L. D. was utterly absorbed in political life, and could see something else only when it forced itself upon him. He reacted to it as if it were a bother, something unavoidable. I did not agree with him in his estimate of Paris, and twitted him a little for this.'

Yes, it was just like that. I was entering the atmosphere of a world centre with an obstinate and antagonistic attitude. At first, I 'denied' Paris, and even tried to ignore it. Rightly considered, it was the case of a barbarian struggling for self-preservation. I felt that in order to get close to Paris and understand it fully, I would have to spend a great deal of mental energy. But I had my own world of revolution, and this was very exacting and brooked no rival interests. With difficulty, and by degrees, I was getting closer to art. I resisted the Louvre, the Luxembourg, and the exhibitions. Rubens seemed to me too well-fed and self-satisfied, Puvis de Chavannes too ascetic and faded, Carrière's portraits irritated me with their twilight ambiguousness. The same applied to sculpture and architecture. In point of fact I was resisting art as I had resisted revolution earlier in life, and later, Marxism; as I had resisted, for several years, Lenin and his methods. The revolution of 1905 soon interrupted the progress of my communings with Europe and its culture. It was only during my second exile from Russia that I came closer to art – saw things, read, and even wrote a little about it. I never went beyond the stage of pure dilettantism, however.

In Paris I heard Jaurès. It was at a time when Waldeck-Rousseau was at the head of the government, with Millerand as the minister of the Posts and General Galliffet as the minister of war. I took part in a street demonstration of the Guesdists and shouted diligently, with the rest, all sorts of unpleasant things against Millerand. Jaurès did not make any great impression on me then. I felt too intensely that he was an enemy. Only several years later did I learn to appreciate that magnificent figure, even if my attitude towards Jaurèsism remained as hostile as before.

Pressed by the Marxist section of the students, Lenin agreed to give three lectures on the agrarian question at the Higher School organized in Paris by professors expelled from Russian universities. The liberal professors asked the undesirable lecturer to refrain from polemics as far as possible. But Lenin made no promise on this score, and began his first lecture with the statement that Marxism is a revolutionary theory, and therefore fundamentally polemical. I remember that Vladimir Ilyich was considerably excited before his first lecture, but as soon as he was on the platform he completely mastered himself, at least to all outward appearances. Professor Gambarov, who came to hear him speak, gave his impression to Deutsch in these words: 'A perfect professor.' He obviously thought this the highest praise.

Once we decided to take Lenin to the opera. All arrangements were entrusted to Sedova. Lenin went to the Opéra Comique with the same brief-case that accompanied him to his lectures. We sat in a group in the top gallery. Besides Lenin, Sedova, and myself, I believe the company included also Martov. An utterly unmusical reminiscence is always associated in my mind with this visit to the opera. In Paris Lenin had bought himself a pair of shoes that had turned out to be too tight. As fate would have it I badly needed a new pair of shoes just then. I was given Lenin's, and at first I thought they fitted me perfectly. The trip to the opera was all right. But in the theatre I began to have pains. On the way home I suffered agonies, while Lenin twitted me all the more mercilessly because he had gone through the same thing for several hours in those very shoes.

From Paris I went on a lecture tour of the Russian student colonies in Brussels, Liège, in Switzerland, and in some German towns. In Heidelberg I listened to old Kuno Fischer, but I wasn't tempted by his Kantian teaching. The normative philosophy was foreign to my whole being. How could one prefer dry hay when next to it there was soft, juicy grass? Heidelberg had the name of being the centre of philosophical idealism among Russian students. One of their numbers was Avksentiev, the future minister of the Interior under the Kerensky government. I broke more than one lance there in my hot defence of materialist dialectics.

12

The Party Congress and the Split

When Lenin went abroad at the age of thirty, he was already fully mature. In Russia, in the students' circles, in the Social-Democratic groups, and in the exile colonies, he held first place. He could not fail to realize his power, if only because everyone he met or worked with so clearly did. When he left Russia, he was already in possession of a full theoretical equipment and of a solid store of revolutionary experience. Abroad there were collaborators waiting for him: 'The Group of Liberation of Labour', and chief among them, Plekhanov, the brilliant Marxist interpreter, teacher of several generations, theorist, politician, publicist, and orator, with a European reputation and European connections. Side by side with Plekhanov were two other prominent authorities, Zasulitch and Axelrod. It was not only her heroic past that had placed Vera Zasulitch in the front ranks: she had an exceedingly sharp mind, an extensive background, chiefly historical, and a rare psychological insight. It was through Zasulitch that the 'Group' in its day became connected with old Engels.

Unlike Plekhanov and Zasulitch, who were more closely bound to Latin socialism, Axelrod represented in the 'Group' the ideas and experience of the German Social Democracy. In that period, however, Plekhanov was already beginning to enter upon a state of decline. His strength was being undermined by the very thing that was giving strength to Lenin – the approach of the revolution. All of Plekhanov's activity took place during the preparatory, theoretical days. He was Marxian propagandist and polemist-in-chief, but not a revolutionary politician of the proletariat. The nearer the shadow of the revolution crept the more evident it became that Plekhanov was losing ground. He couldn't help seeing it himself, and that was the cause of his irritability towards the younger men.

The political leader of the *Iskra* was Lenin. Martov was the literary power; he wrote as easily and as continuously as he spoke. Working side by side with Lenin, Martov, his closest companion in arms, was already beginning to feel not quite at his ease. They were still addressing each other as 'ty' (thou), but a certain coldness was beginning to creep into their mutual relations. Martov lived much more in the present, in its events, in his current literary work, in the political problems of the day, in the news and conversations; Lenin, on the other hand, although he was firmly entrenched in the present, was always trying to pierce the veil of the future. Martov evolved innumerable and often ingenious guesses, hypotheses, and propositions which even he promptly forgot; whereas Lenin waited until the moment when he needed them. The elaborate subtlety of Martov's ideas sometimes made Lenin shake his head in alarm. The different political lines had not yet had time to form; in fact they had not even begun to make themselves felt. Later on, through the split at the Second Congress of the party, the *Iskra* adherents were divided into two groups, the 'hard' and the 'soft'. These names were much in vogue at first. They indicated that, although no marked divisions really existed, there was a difference in point of view, in resoluteness and readiness to go on to the end.

One can say of Lenin and Martov that, even before the split, even before the congress, Lenin was 'hard' and Martov 'soft'. And they both knew it. Lenin would glance at Martov, whom he estimated highly, with a critical and somewhat suspicious look, and Martov, feeling his glance, would look down and move his thin shoulders nervously. When they met or conversed afterwards, at least when I was present, one missed the friendly inflection and the jests. Lenin would look beyond Martov as he talked, while Martov's eyes would grow glassy under his drooping and never quite clean *pince-nez*. And when Lenin spoke to me of Martov, there was a peculiar intonation in his voice: 'Who said that? Julius?' – and the name Julius was pronounced in a special way, with a slight emphasis, as if to give warning:

'A good man, no question about it, even a remarkable one, but much too soft.' At the same time Martov was also coming under the influence of Vera Ivanovna Zasulitch, who was drawing him away from Lenin, not so much politically as psychologically.

Lenin concentrated all connections with Russia in his own hands. The secretary of the editorial board was his wife, Nadyezhda Konstantinovna Krupskaya. She was at the very centre of all the organization work; she received comrades when they arrived, instructed them when they left, established connections, supplied secret addresses, wrote letters, and coded and decoded correspondence. In her room there was always a smell of burned paper from the secret letters she heated over the fire to read. She often complained in her gently insistent way that people did not write enough, or that they got the code all mixed up, or wrote in chemical ink in such a way that one line covered another, and so forth.

Lenin was trying, in the everyday work of political organization, to achieve a maximum of independence from the older members and above all from Plekhanov, with whom he had had many bitter struggles, especially in the drafting of the party programme. Lenin's original draft, submitted as a counter-proposal to Plekhanov's, received from the latter a sharply unfavourable estimate, in the jesting and superior manner characteristic of Geórgy Valentinovitch on such occasions. But of course Lenin could not be confused or intimidated by such methods. The struggle took on a very dramatic aspect. Zasulitch and Martov acted as intermediaries; the former on behalf of Plekhanov, the latter of Lenin. Both intermediaries were in a most conciliatory mood and, besides this, they were friends. Vera Ivanovna, according to her own account, once said to Lenin: 'George [Plekhanov] is a hound – he will shake a thing for a while, and then drop it; whereas you are a bulldog – yours is the death-grip.' When she repeated this conversation to me later, Vera Ivanovna added: 'This appealed to Lenin very much – "a death-grip", he repeated, with obvious delight.' As she said this, she good-naturedly mimicked Lenin's intonation and accent. (He could not pronounce the sound of 'r' clearly.)

All these disagreements took place before I arrived from

Russia. I never suspected them. Nor did I know that the relations among the editors of the *Iskra* had been aggravated even more by my coming. Four months after my arrival, Lenin wrote to Plekhanov:

2 March 1903. PARIS.

I suggest to all the members of the editorial board that they co-opt 'Pero' as a member of the board on the same basis as other members. I believe co-optation demands not merely a majority of votes, but a unanimous decision. We *very much need* a seventh member, both as a convenience in voting (six being an even number), and as an addition to our forces. 'Pero' has been contributing to every issue for several months now; he works in general most energetically for the *Iskra*; he gives lectures (in which he has been very successful). In the section of articles and notes on the events of the day he will not only be very useful, but absolutely necessary. Unquestionably a man of rare abilities, he has conviction and energy, and he will go much farther. Furthermore, in the field of translations and of popular literature he will be able to do a great deal. Possible objections: (1) His youth; (2) his leaving for Russia, possibly in a short time; (3) his pen [pero], this time without the quotation, which shows traces of the feuilleton style and is excessively florid, etc.

Re (1) 'Pero' is proposed not for any independent post, but only as a member of the board. There he will acquire his experience. He has unquestionably the 'sense' of a party man, of a man of faction, and knowledge and experience are a matter of time. The co-optation is necessary in order to tie him down and encourage him.

Re (2) If 'Pero' does enter into an intimate contact with all of our work, he will probably not leave so early. If he does leave, his organized connection with the board and his working under its instruction will not constitute a minus, but an enormous plus.

Re (3) The defects of style are not a matter of importance. He will outgrow them. At present, he accepts 'corrections' in silence (and not very readily). On the board there will be discussions, votings, and the 'instructions' will have a more definite and obligatory character.

To sum up. I propose: (1) to pass a vote by all the six members of the board for a full co-optation of 'Pero'; (2) to start, if he is accepted, on the definite formulation of the relations among the editors, of the rules of voting, and on the drafting of a precise constitution. *This is necessary for ourselves*, as well as for the congress.

P.S. I consider that it would be *very inconvenient* and awkward *to put off* the co-optation, as it has been made clear to me that 'Pero' is *considerably* annoyed – though of course he does not show it openly – about his being still up in the air, and about his being treated, as it seems to him, as a 'youth'. If we do not accept 'Pero' at once, and he goes away, say, a month from now, to Russia, I am convinced that he will interpret this as our *direct unwillingness* to accept him on the board. He will slip away and this will be very undesirable.

I quote this letter, which I discovered only recently, almost in its entirety (excepting only technical details) because it is extremely characteristic of the situation within the editorial board, characteristic of Lenin himself, and of his attitude towards me. As I have already said, I was completely ignorant of the struggle that was going on behind the scenes with regard to my joining the board. Lenin's idea that I was 'considerably annoyed' about my not being included on the board is incorrect and not in the least characteristic of my mood at that time. In point of fact it never entered my mind. My attitude towards the board was that of a pupil towards his masters. I was only twenty-three years old. The youngest of the editors was Martov, who was seven years older than I, and Lenin himself was ten years my senior. I was much pleased with the fate that had placed me so close to this remarkable group of people. I could learn much from each of them, and I did, most diligently.

Where did Lenin get the idea that I was annoyed? I think it was simply a tactical trick. The entire letter is imbued with the desire to prove, to convince, and to get what he wanted. Lenin purposely tried to scare the other editors with my supposed annoyance and possible estrangement from the *Iskra*. He used this merely as an additional argument, and nothing more. The same also applies to his argument about my being referred to as a 'youth'. This was the name by which old Deutsch frequently addressed me but no one else did. And to Deutsch, who never had and never could have any political influence over me, I was only bound by genuine friendship. Lenin used the argument merely to impress on the older ones the necessity of reckoning with me, as with a man who was politically mature.

Ten days after Lenin's letter had been sent Martov wrote to Axelrod:

10 March 1903. LONDON.

Vladimir Ilyich has proposed to us that we admit 'Pero', whom you know, to the board of editors, with full rights. His literary work shows undeniable talent, he is quite 'ours' in thought, he has wholly identified himself with the interests of the *Iskra*, and here, abroad, he wields considerable influence, thanks to his exceptional eloquence. He speaks magnificently; he could not do better. Of this, both Vladimir Ilyich and I have had occasion to convince ourselves. He has knowledge and works hard to increase it. I unreservedly subscribe to Vladimir Ilyich's proposal.

In this letter Martov shows himself only as a true echo of Lenin. But he does not repeat the argument about my annoyance. I lived with Martov, side by side in the same house. He had observed me too closely to suspect any impatient desire on my part to become a member of the board.

Why did Lenin insist so eagerly on the necessity of my joining the board? He wanted to obtain a stable majority. On a number of important questions the editors were divided into two equal groups: the older ones (Plekhanov, Zasulitch, Axelrod), and the younger generation (Lenin, Martov, Potresov). Lenin felt sure that on the most critical questions I would be with him. On one occasion, when it was necessary to oppose Plekhanov, Lenin called me aside and said slyly: 'Let Martov speak. He will smooth it over, whereas you will hit straight from the shoulder.' Observing an expression of surprise on my face, he added immediately: 'For my part, I prefer to hit from the shoulder, but with Plekhanov it would be better this time to smooth things over.'

Lenin's proposal that I be put on the board was wrecked by Plekhanov's opposition. Worse still, this proposal became the chief cause of an extremely unfriendly attitude on Plekhanov's part towards me, because he guessed that Lenin was looking for a firm majority against him. The question of reorganizing the editorial board was deferred until the congress. The board decided, however, without waiting for the congress, to invite me to the editorial meetings in an advisory capacity. Plekhanov resolutely opposed even this. But Vera Ivanovna said to him, 'I'll bring him, no matter what you say.' And she did actually 'bring' me to the next meeting. As I knew nothing about what had happened behind the scenes, I was much put out by the studied coldness with which Geórgy Valentinovitch shook hands with me, a thing at which he was past-master. Plekhanov's dislike of me lasted for a long time; in fact, it never disappeared. In April 1904 Martov, in writing to Axelrod, referred to 'his [Plekhanov's] personal hatred of the said person [myself] – a hatred that is degrading to himself and ignoble'.

The reference in Lenin's letter to my literary style at that time is interesting. It is true in both respects, that is, regarding my tendency to florid writing, and also my disinclination to accept corrections. My writing was an affair of only about two years' standing at that time, and the question of style held an important and independent place with me. I was just beginning to appreciate the flavour of words. Just as children rub their gums when they are teething, sometimes with quite inappropriate objects, I would pursue words, formulas, or an image in my literary teething-stage. Only time would purify my style. And as the struggle for form was neither an accidental nor an external thing, but a reflection of my intellectual processes, it is no wonder that, with all my respect for editors, I instinctively protected my still-shaping individuality as a writer against the inroads of men who were already mature but differently constituted.

Meanwhile, the day set for the congress was drawing near, and eventually it was decided to transfer the editorial board to Geneva in Switzerland, where living was cheaper and contact with Russia easier. Lenin agreed to this with a heavy heart. 'In Geneva we were put up in two tiny attic rooms,' writes Sedova. 'L. D. was engrossed in the work for the congress, while I was getting ready to leave for party work in Russia.' The first delegates to the congress began to arrive, and there were continuous conferences. In this preparatory work the leadership unquestionably belonged to Lenin, although the fact was not always obvious. Some delegates arrived with doubts or with pretensions. The work of preparation took a great deal of time. Much time was given to the consideration of the proposed constitution, since one of the important points in the scheme of organization was the relationship to be established between the central organ (the *Iskra*), and the Central Committee which was to function in Russia. I arrived abroad with the belief that the editorial board should be made subordinate to the Central Committee. That was the prevailing attitude of the majority of the *Iskra* followers.

'It can't be done,' objected Lenin. 'The correlation of forces is different. How can they guide us from Russia? No, it can't be done. We are the stable centre, we are stronger in ideas, and we must exercise the guidance from here.'

'Then this will mean a complete dictatorship of the editorial board?' I asked.

'Well, what's wrong with that?' retorted Lenin. 'In the present situation it must be so.'

Lenin's schemes of organization aroused certain doubts in me. But nothing was farther from my mind than the thought that the congress would blow up on those very questions.

I was made the delegate of the Siberian Union, with which I had been closely associated during my exile. To avoid spies, I set out for the congress with the Tula delegate, Dr Ulyanov, who was Lenin's younger brother, not from Geneva but from the adjoining quiet little station of Nion where the express-train stopped for only half a minute. Like good Russian provincials we waited for the train on the wrong side of the track, and when the express pulled in we dashed to our carriage over the buffers. Before we could climb inside, the train started. The station-master saw two passengers between the buffers, blew his whistle, and the train stopped. As soon as we had been conducted to our car, the guard told us that it was the first time he had ever seen such stupid fellows and that we would have to pay fifty francs for stopping the train. And we, in turn, told him that we didn't understand a word of French. As a matter of fact this was not strictly true, but it answered our purpose. After shouting at us for another three minutes the fat Swiss left us in peace, and that was all the more sensible because we didn't have fifty francs between us. Later on, when he was checking the tickets, he again aired, to the rest of the train, his contemptuous opinion of the two travellers who had to be taken off the buffers. The poor fellow did not know that we were travelling to create a party.

The congress opened in Brussels at the headquarters of a labour cooperative society in the Maison du Peuple. The store-room, which had been assigned for our work, and which was sufficiently hidden away from alien eyes, contained bales of wool; as a result we were constantly being attacked by huge numbers of fleas. We referred to them as 'Ansele's army',* mobilized for its attack on bourgeois society. The meetings were an actual physical torture. Still worse was the persistent dogging of the delegates' steps, from the very first day of their stay.

I lived on the strength of a passport issued to Samokovliyev, a Bulgarian about whom I knew nothing. One night during the second week I came out of a little restaurant, 'The Golden Pheasant', with Zasulitch. A delegate from Odessa, Z., crossed our path, and without even looking at us, hissed between his teeth: 'There's a detective behind you. Separate, and he will follow the man.' Z. was an expert on detectives and possessed an eye as precise as an astronomical instrument. He lived near the 'Pheasant', on the top floor, and made his window an obser-vation tower.

I immediately said good-bye to Zasulitch and walked straight ahead. In my pocket there were my Bulgarian passport and five francs. The sleuth, a tall slim Fleming with a nose like a duck's bill, followed me. It was after midnight and there was not a soul on the street. I turned back sharply.

'M'sieu, what's the name of this street?' The Fleming seemed frightened and pressed back against the wall.

'Je ne sais pas.' He no doubt expected a revolver-shot. I walked on, straight along the boulevard. A clock struck one. At the first side street I turned and ran for all I was worth, the Fleming after me. So there we were, two strangers, racing after each other in the streets of Brussels after midnight. Even now I can hear the clatter of feet. After I had run around the three

*Ansele was one of the leaders of the Socialist party in Belgium, par-ticularly prominent in the cooperative movement. – *Translator.*

sides of the block, I came to the boulevard again, with the Fleming. We were both tired and furious. We kept on walking. We passed a few cabs standing at the kerb. It would have been useless to take one of them, because the detective would have followed in another. We continued to walk. The interminable boulevard seemed to be approaching what looked like an end, and we were going out of town. I saw a solitary cab near a bar that was open all night. With a swift push, I was in the cab.

'Go, I'm in a hurry!'

'Where do you want to go?' The detective was listening intently. I gave the name of a park a few minutes' walk from my place.

'A hundred sous.'

'Go!'

The driver pulled in the reins. The detective rushed into the bar and came out again with a *garçon*, pointing his finger at his disappearing enemy.

Half an hour later I was in my own room. As soon as I lit the candle I noticed a letter on the dressing-table, addressed to me under my Bulgarian name. Who could have written me here? It turned out to be an invitation to 'Sieur Samokovliyev' to appear with his passport the next morning at ten at the police station. So another detective must have tracked me there the day before, and all that night-chase on the boulevard was nothing but a little disinterested exercise for both parties. Similar invitations were extended to other delegates that night, too. Those who visited the police were ordered to leave Belgium in twenty-four hours. I did not go to the police station but simply left for London, to which the congress was transferred.

The head of the Russian secret service in Berlin, a man named Harting, afterwards reported to the Police Department that 'the Brussels police were surprised to see such an influx of foreigners, and suspected ten men of an anarchist conspiracy'. As a matter of fact the Brussels police were surprised by Harting himself. His real name was Hekkelmann, a bombist *agent-provocateur* sentenced in a state of contumacy to hard-labour by the French courts, who later became a general of the Tsar's secret police, and, under a false name, a Chevalier of the Légion d'Honneur in France. Harting in turn obtained his information through another *agent-provocateur*, Dr Zhitomirsky, who, working from Berlin, had taken an active part in the organization of the congress. But all this came out several years later. It would seem as if Tsarism held all the strings. And yet even this did not save it.

As the congress progressed the differences between the foremost adherents of the *Iskra* came to a head. The division between the 'hard' and the 'soft' was apparent. At first, the disagreements centred about the first paragraph of the constitution: the question of who was to be considered a member of the party. Lenin insisted on identifying the party with the underground organization. Martov wanted to consider as members also those who worked under the direction of the underground organization. The difference was of no immediate practical importance, as both formulas conferred the right of voting only on members of the underground organizations. Nevertheless, the two divergent tendencies were unmistakable. Lenin wanted clear-cut, perfectly definite relationships within the party. Martov tended towards diffuse forms. The grouping of the members determined the whole subsequent course of the congress, and, among other things, the composition of the directing centres of the party.

Behind the scenes there was a struggle for the support of every individual delegate. Lenin lost no opportunity to win me over to his side. He, another delegate, Krasikov, and I, all three had a long walk together, during which they both tried to persuade me that Martov and I could not follow the same road, for Martov was a 'soft' one. Krasikov's descriptions of the other editors of the *Iskra* were so unceremonious that they made Lenin frown, while I shivered. My attitude towards the editors of the *Iskra* was still touched with the sentimentality of youth.

That conversation repelled rather than attracted me. The differences were still intangible; everybody was merely groping about and working with impalpable things. We decided to hold a meeting of the proved *Iskra* men to clear the whole business up. But even the selection of the chairman was full of difficulties. 'I suggest electing your Benjamin,' said Deutsch, in an attempt to find a way out. So I had to occupy the chair at the very meeting of the *Iskra* followers in which the future split between the Bolsheviks and the Mensheviks first took shape. Everybody's nerves were strained to the breaking-point.

Lenin left the meeting, banging the door behind him. That was the only time I ever saw him lose his self-control during the bitter struggle inside the party. The situation became even more aggravated. The differences all came to the surface at the congress itself. Lenin made another attempt to win me over to the 'hard' faction by sending to me a woman delegate, Z., as well as his younger brother, Dmitry. My conversation with them, which was carried on in the park, lasted for several hours. The emissaries would not let me go. 'We have orders', they said, 'to bring you with us at any cost.' In the end I flatly refused to follow them.

The split came unexpectedly for all the members of the congress. Lenin, the most active figure in the struggle, did not foresee it, nor had he ever desired it. Both sides were greatly upset by the course of events. After the congress Lenin was sick for several weeks with a nervous illness. 'From London, L. D. wrote almost daily,' writes Sedova in her memoirs. 'His letters were expressive of a growing alarm, and finally there was a letter reporting the split, that said with despair that the *Iskra* was no more, that it was dead . . . The split in the *Iskra* upset us dreadfully. After L. D.'s return from the congress I soon left for St Petersburg with reports of the congress written in a microscopic hand on thin paper, and inserted inside of the binding of a Larousse French dictionary.'

How did I come to be with the 'softs' at the congress? Of the *Iskra* editors, my closest connections were with Martov, Zasulitch and Axelrod. Their influence over me was unquestionable. Before the congress there were various shades of opinion on the editorial board, but no sharp differences. I stood farthest from Plekhanov, who, after the first really trivial encounters, had taken an intense dislike to me. Lenin's attitude towards me was unexceptionally kind. But now it was he who, in my eyes, was attacking the editorial board, a body which was, in my opinion, a single unit, and which bore the exciting name of *Iskra*. The idea of a split within the board seemed nothing short of sacrilegious to me.

Revolutionary centralism is a harsh, imperative and exacting principle. It often takes the guise of absolute ruthlessness in its relation to individual members, to whole groups of former associates. It is not without significance that the words 'irreconcilable' and 'relentless' are among Lenin's favourites. It is only the most impassioned, revolutionary striving for a definite end – a striving that is utterly free from anything base or personal – that can justify such a personal ruthlessness. In 1903 the whole point at issue was nothing more than Lenin's desire to get Axelrod and Zasulitch off the editorial board. My attitude towards them was full of respect, and there was an element of personal affection as well. Lenin also thought highly of them for what they had done in the past. But he believed that they were becoming an impediment for the future. This led him to conclude that they must be removed from their position of leadership. I could not agree. My whole being seemed to protest against this merciless cutting off of the older ones when they were at last on the threshold of an organized party. It was my indignation at his attitude that really led to my parting with him at the Second Congress. His behaviour seemed unpardonable to me, both horrible and outrageous. And yet, politically it was right and necessary, from the point of view of organization. The break with the older ones, who remained in the preparatory stages, was inevitable in any case. Lenin understood this before anyone else did. He made an attempt to keep Plekhanov by separating him from Zasulitch and Axelrod. But this, too, was quite futile, as subsequent events soon proved.

My break with Lenin occurred on what might be considered 'moral' or even personal grounds. But this was merely on the surface. At bottom the separation was of a political nature and merely expressed itself in the realm of organization methods. I thought of myself as a centralist. But there is no doubt that at that time I did not fully realize what an intense and imperious centralism the revolutionary party would need to lead millions of people in a war against the old order. My early years were passed in the dismal atmosphere of a reaction which prolonged its stay in Odessa for an extra five years. Lenin's youthful years dated back to the 'Narodnaya Volya'. Those who came a few years after me were brought up in an environment that was influenced by the new political upheaval. At the time of the London Congress in 1903 revolution was still largely a theoretical abstraction to me. Independently I still could not see Lenin's centralism as the logical conclusion of a clear revolutionary concept. And the desire to see a problem independently, and to draw all the necessary conclusions from it, has always been my most imperious intellectual necessity.

The seriousness of the conflict which blazed up at the congress, apart from the impact of principles, which was still very incipient, was also caused by the failure of the older ones to recognize the stature and importance of Lenin. During the congress and immediately after, the indignation of Axelrod and others on the board at Lenin's conduct was coupled with amazement: 'How could he have the nerve to do it?'

'Was it so long ago that he came abroad as a mere pupil and behaved as a pupil?' the older ones argued. 'Where, then, did he get that supreme self-confidence? Where did he get the nerve?'

But Lenin had the nerve. All he needed was to be convinced that the older ones were incapable of assuming direct leadership of the militant organization of the proletarian vanguard in the revolution which was clearly approaching. The older ones – and they were not alone – erred in their judgement; Lenin was not merely a remarkable party worker, but a leader, a man with every fibre of his being bent on one particular end, one who finally realized that he was himself a leader after he had stood side by side with the elders and had been convinced that he was stronger and more necessary than they. In the midst of the still-vague moods that were common in the group that upheld the *Iskra* banner, Lenin alone, and with finality, envisaged 'tomorrow', with all its stern tasks, its cruel conflicts and countless victims.

At the congress Lenin won Plekhanov over, although only for a time. At the same time he lost Martov; this loss was for ever. Plekhanov apparently sensed something at the congress. At least he told Axelrod, in discussing Lenin: 'Of such stuff

Robespierres are made.' Plekhanov himself did not play an enviable part at the congress. Only once did I see and hear Plekhanov in all his power. That was on the programme committee of the congress. With a clear, scientifically exact scheme of the programme in mind, sure of himself, of his knowledge and superiority, with a gay ironic sparkle in his eyes, his greying moustache alert and bristling, with slightly theatrical but lively and expressive gestures, Plekhanov as chairman illumined the entire large gathering with his personality, like a live fireworks of erudition and wit.

The leader of the Mensheviks,* Martov, must be counted as one of the most tragic figures of the revolutionary movement. A gifted writer, an ingenious politician, a penetrating thinker, Martov stood far above the intellectual movement of which he became the leader. But his thought lacked courage; his insight was devoid of will. Sheer doggedness was no substitute. Martov's initial reaction to events always showed a revolutionary trend of thought. Immediately, however, his thought, which lacked the support of a live will, died down. My friendship with him did not survive the test of the first important events precipitated by the approaching revolution.

Whatever I may say about it, however, the Second Congress was a landmark in my life, if only because it separated me from Lenin for several years. As I look back now on the past, I am not sorry. I came to Lenin for the second time later than many others, but I came in my own way, after I had gone through and had weighed the experience of the revolution, the counter-revolution and the Imperialist war. I came, as a result, more surely and seriously than those 'disciples' who, during the master's life, repeated his words and gestures – not always at the right moment – but, after his death, proved to be nothing but helpless epigones and unconscious tools in the hands of hostile forces.

*As the result of the split at the Second Congress of the Russian Social Democratic Party, the two factions came to be known as 'Bolsheviks', meaning 'of the majority', and 'Mensheviks', meaning 'of the minority'. – *Translator.*

13
The Return to Russia

This connection with the minority of the Second Congress was brief. Before many months had passed, two tendencies had become conspicuous within the minority. I advocated taking steps to bring about a union with the majority as soon as possible, because I thought of the split as an outstanding episode but nothing more. For others, the split at the Second Congress was the beginning of the evolution towards opportunism. I spent the whole year of 1904 arguing with the leading group of Mensheviks on questions of policy and organization. The arguments were concentrated on two issues: the attitude towards liberalism and that towards the Bolsheviks. I was for an uncompromising resistance to the attempts of the liberals to lean upon the masses, and at the same time, because of it, I demanded with increasing determination the union of the two Social Democratic factions.

In September I formally renounced my membership in the minority; I had ceased being an active member in April of that year. During that period I spent a few months away from Russian émigré circles, in Munich, which was then considered the most democratic and most artistic city in Germany. I came to know the Bavarian Social Democracy quite well, as well as the galleries of Munich and the cartoonists of *Simplicissimus*.

Even at the time of the party congress the entire southern part of Russia was in the throes of a great strike. Peasant disturbances grew more and more frequent. The universities were seething. For a little while the Russo–Japanese war stopped the movement, but the military *débâcle* of Tsarism promptly provided a formidable lever for revolution. The press was becoming more daring, the terrorist acts more frequent; the liberals began to wake up and launched a campaign of political banquets. The fundamental questions of revolution came swiftly to the front. Abstractions were beginning in my eyes to acquire actual social flesh. The Mensheviks, Zasulitch especially, were placing great hopes in the liberals.

Even before the congress, after one of the editorial meetings in the café 'Landolt', Zasulitch began to complain, in the peculiar, timidly insistent tone which she always assumed for such occasions, that we were attacking the liberals too much. That was a sore point with her.

'See how eager they are about it,' she would say, looking past Lenin, though it was really Lenin whom she was aiming at. 'Struve demands that the Russian liberals should not renounce Socialism, because if they do they will be threatened with the fate of the German liberals; he says they should follow the example of the French Radical Socialists.'

'We should strike them all the more,' said Lenin with a gay smile, as if he were teasing Vera Ivanovna.

'That's nice!' she exclaimed in utter despair. 'They come to meet us and we strike them down.'

I was with Lenin unreservedly in this discussion, which became more crucial the deeper it went. In 1904 during the liberal banquet campaign, which quickly reached an impasse, I put forward the question, 'What next?' and answered it in this way: the way out can be opened only by means of a general strike, followed by an uprising of the proletariat which will march at the head of the masses against liberalism. This aggravated my disagreements with the Mensheviks.

On the morning of 23 January 1905 I returned to Geneva from a lecture tour, exhausted after a sleepless night on the train. A newsboy sold me a paper of the day before. It referred in the future tense to the march of the workers to the Winter Palace. I decided that it had failed to take place. An hour or so later I called at the *Iskra* office. Martov was all excitement.

'So it did not come off?'

'What do you mean, did not come off?' he pounced on me. 'We spent the whole night in a café reading fresh cables. Haven't you heard anything? Here it is, here, here . . .' and he pushed the paper into my hands. I ran through the first ten lines of the telegraphed report of the bloody Sunday.* A dull, burning sensation seemed to overpower me.

I could not stay abroad any longer. My connections with the Bolsheviks had ended with the congress. I broke away from the Mensheviks; I had to act at my own risk. Through a student I got a new passport and, with my wife,† who had come abroad again in the autumn of 1904, I took the train to Munich. Parvus put us up in his own house. There he read my manuscript dealing with the events of 22 January and was much excited by it. 'The events have fully confirmed this analysis. Now no one can deny that the general strike is the most important means of fighting. The twenty-second of January was the first political strike, even if it was disguised under a priest's cloak. One need only add that revolution in Russia may place a democratic workers' government in power.' It was after this fashion that Parvus wrote a preface to my pamphlet.

Parvus was unquestionably one of the most important of the Marxists at the turn of the century. He used the Marxian methods skilfully, was possessed of wide vision, and kept a keen eye on everything of importance in world events. This, coupled with his fearless thinking and his virile, muscular style, made him a remarkable writer. His early studies brought me closer to the problems of the Social Revolution, and, for me, definitely transformed the conquest of power by the proletariat from an astronomical 'final' goal to a practical task for our own day.

And yet there was always something mad and unreliable about Parvus. In addition to all his other ambitions, this revolutionary was torn by an amazing desire to get rich. Even this he connected, in those years at least, with his social-revolutionary ideas. 'The party apparatus has become petrified,' he would

*On 22 January 1905 great masses of workers in St Petersburg, led by the priest Gapon and carrying church banners and the portrait of the Tsar, marched to the Winter Palace to submit a petition in which they set forth their grievances and appealed to the Tsar to help improve their lot. The men, their wives and children proceeded to the Palace Square, but were met by government troops who shot and sabred them, killing or wounding thousands. The day has become known in Russia as 'The Bloody Sunday'. – *Translator.*

†Natalia Ivanovna Sedova, the author's second wife. – *Translator.*

complain. 'It is hard to get anything into even Bebel's head. What we revolutionary Marxists need is a great daily newspaper published in three European languages. But for this we must have money, and lots of it.' Thus were thoughts of the revolution and of wealth intermingled in the heavy, fleshy head of this bulldog. He made an attempt to set up a publishing house of his own in Munich, but it ended rather badly for him. Then he went to Russia and took part in the revolution of 1905. In spite of his originality and ingenuity of thought, he failed utterly as a leader. After the defeat of the revolution of 1905, he went into a decline. From Germany he moved to Vienna, and from there to Constantinople, where eventually the World War found him. During the war he achieved wealth immediately through military commercial enterprises. At the same time he came out publicly as a defender of the progressive mission of German militarism, broke definitely with the revolutionaries, and became one of the intellectual leaders of the right wing of the German Social Democracy. It goes without saying that since the war I have not had any political or personal contact with him.

From Munich, Sedova and I went to Vienna. The émigré tide was already rolling back to Russia. Victor Adler was completely engrossed in Russian affairs, and was obtaining money, passports, addresses and the like for the émigrés. In his house, a hairdresser wrought a change in my appearance – an appearance that had already become too familiar to the Russian police-agents abroad.

'I have just received a telegram from Axelrod,' Adler informed me, 'saying that Gapon has arrived abroad and announced himself a Social Democrat. It's a pity. If he had disappeared altogether there would have remained a beautiful legend, whereas as an émigré he will be a comical figure. You know,' he added, with a sparkle in his eye that dulled the edge of his irony, 'such men are better as historical martyrs than as comrades in a party.'

While I was in Vienna, I heard the news of the assassination of Grand Duke Sergius. Events were crowding each other. The Social Democratic press turned its eyes to the east. My wife went ahead of me to arrange for living quarters and connections in Kiev. With a passport in the name of a retired corporal, Arbuzov, I arrived in Kiev in February, and for several weeks moved about from house to house. I stayed first with a young lawyer who was afraid of his own shadow, then with a professor at the Technological Institute, then with some widow who had liberal views. At one time I even found refuge in an ophthalmic hospital. Under instructions from the physician in charge, who understood my situation, the nurse, to my great embarrassment, gave me foot-baths and applied some harmless drops to my eyes. I had to be doubly secretive because of that, and write my proclamations out of her sight – she watched me so rigidly to prevent me from tiring my eyes. During the rounds of inspection, the doctor would get away from one of his assistants who was not considered reliable, rush into my room with a woman assistant whom he trusted, and quickly lock the doors and draw the curtains as if he were preparing to examine my eyes. After this, all three of us would break out into gay but cautious laughter.

'Have you cigarettes?' the doctor would ask. 'Yes,' I would reply. 'Quantum satis?' he continued. 'Quantum satis,' I answered. And then we all laughed again. That was the end of the examination, and I would go back to writing proclamations. I was highly amused by this life. The only thing that made me feel a little ashamed of myself was having to deceive the amiable old nurse who treated me so conscientiously with foot-baths.

The famous underground printing-press was then in operation in Kiev, and, despite the many raids and arrests on every hand, managed to keep going for several years under the very nose of the chief of the secret police, Novitsky. It was in that same press that I had many of my proclamations printed in the spring of 1905. My longer writings I began to entrust to a young engineer named Krassin whom I met in Kiev. He was a member of the Bolshevik Central Committee and had at his disposal a large and well-equipped secret printing-press somewhere in the Caucasus. In Kiev I wrote a number of leaflets for his press, which printed them clearly, an extraordinary thing in those underground conditions.

The party, like the revolution, was still young at that time, and one was struck by the inexperience and lack of finish revealed both by the members and by their actions in general. Krassin likewise was not wholly free from this fault. But there was something firm, resolute and 'administrative' about him. He was an engineer of some experience, he held a paying job and filled it well; he was valued by his employers, and had a circle of acquaintances that was much larger and more varied than that of any of the young revolutionaries of the day. In workers' rooms, in engineers' apartments, in the mansions of the liberal Moscow industrialists, in literary circles – everywhere, Krassin had connections. He managed them all with great skill and, consequently, practical possibilities that were quite closed to the others were opened to him. In 1905, in addition to participating in the general work of the party, Krassin had charge of the most dangerous fields of the work, such as armed units, the purchase of arms, the preparing of stocks of explosives, and the like. In spite of his broad outlook he was primarily a man of immediate achievements, in politics as well as in life. That was his strength, but it was also his heel of Achilles. For long years of laborious gathering of forces, of political training, of theoretical analysis and experience – for all this he had no call, and when the revolution of 1905 failed to realize its hopes, electrotechnics and industry in general became his first consideration. Even in that phase Krassin excelled as a man who realized his aims, who could show exceptional achievements. There is no doubt that his greatest successes in engineering gave him the sort of personal satisfaction that he had earlier found in the revolutionary struggle. He received the Bolshevik revolution with hostile bewilderment, as an adventure foredoomed to failure. For a long time, he refused to believe in our ability to overcome the breakdown of the country. Later, however, he was carried away by the vista of work that was opened up before him.

As for myself, my connection with Krassin in 1905 was a godsend. We arranged to meet in St Petersburg; he also supplied me with secret addresses there. The first and most important was that of the Konstantinovsky School of Artillery, where I was to meet the chief medical officer, Alexander Alexandrovitch Litkens, to whose family fate bound me for a long time after. It was in Litkens's house on Zabalkansky Prospect, in the school building, that I sought secret refuge more than once in the restless days and nights of 1905. Sometimes under the very eyes of the military doorman the house of the chief physician was visited by such people as the school courtyard and its staircases had never seen. But the lower functionaries were very friendly to the doctor, no reports were made to the police, and everything went off smoothly. The doctor's elder son, Alexander, who was about eighteen, was then a member of the party, and a few months later led the peasant movement in the Orlov district. But he could not stand the terrific nervous strain, and fell ill and died. The doctor's younger son, Evgraf, then a student in the *gymnasium*, later played an important part in the civil war and in the educational work of the Soviet Government, but was killed by bandits in the Crimea in 1921.

In St Petersburg I lived officially on the passport of a landowner named Vikentiev. In revolutionary circles I was known as Petr Petrovitch. I was not formally a member of either of the two factions. I continued to work with Krassin, who was at that time a Bolshevik conciliator. This, in view of my interfactional position, brought us even closer together. At the same time I kept in touch with the local Menshevik group, which was following a very revolutionary policy. Under my influence the group advocated boycott of the first advisory Duma, which brought it into conflict with the Menshevik centre abroad. This group was soon trapped by the government, however. It was betrayed by one of its active members, Dobroskok, known as 'Nikolay of the Gold Spectacles', who turned out to be a professional *agent-provocateur*. He knew that I was in St Petersburg, and he knew me by sight. My wife was arrested at the May Day meeting in the woods. I had to hide for a while, and so, in the summer, I left for Finland. Then there was a short interval of peace in which I did intensive literary work and took short walks in the country. I read the papers with avidity, watched the parties take shape, clipped newspapers, and grouped and sifted facts. During that period I finally formulated my conception of the inner forces of Russian society and of the prospects of the Russian revolution.

Russia, I wrote then, is facing a bourgeois-democratic revolution. The basis of the revolution is the land question. Power will be captured by the class or the party which will lead the peasantry against Tsarism and the landowners. Neither the liberals nor the democratic intelligentsia will be able to do so; their historical time has passed. The revolutionary foreground is already occupied by the proletariat. Only the Social Democracy, acting through workers, can make the peasantry follow its lead. This opens to the Russian Social Democracy the prospect of capturing the power before that can possibly take place in the countries of the West. The immediate task of the Social Democracy will be to bring the democratic revolution to completion. But once in control the proletariat party will not be able to confine itself merely to the democratic programme; it will be obliged to adopt Socialist measures. How far it will go in that direction will depend not only on the correlation of forces in Russia itself, but on the entire international situation as well. Hence the chief strategic line of action consequently demands that the Social Democracy, while fighting liberalism for the leadership of the peasantry, shall also set itself the task of seizing the power even during the progress of the bourgeois revolution.

The question of the general prospects of revolution was most intimately bound up with tactical problems. The central political slogan of the party was the demand for a constituent assembly. But the course of the revolutionary struggle raised the question of who would summon the constituent assembly and how. From the prospect of a popular uprising directed by the proletariat there followed logically the creation of a provisional revolutionary government. The leading rôle of the proletariat in the revolution was bound to secure for it a decisive part in the provisional government.

This question caused animated discussions in the upper circles of the party, as well as between Krassin and me. I wrote theses in which I argued that a complete victory of revolution over Tsarism would mean either a proletariat in power, supported by the peasantry, or a direct step towards such power. This decisive statement frightened Krassin. He accepted the slogan of provisional revolutionary government, and the programme of its activities as I outlined them. But he refused to lay down in advance any rules on the subject of a Social Democratic majority in the government. In this form my theses were printed in St Petersburg, and Krassin took it upon himself to defend them at the all-party congress which was to meet abroad in May. The congress, however, failed to occur. Krassin took an active part in the discussion of the question of provisional government at the Bolshevik congress and submitted my theses as an amendment to Lenin's resolution. This episode is so interesting, politically, that I feel obliged to quote the minutes of the Bolshevik Congress.

'As regards the resolution of Comrade Lenin,' said Krassin,

I see its weak point in its failure to stress the question of provisional government, and to indicate, with sufficient clarity, the connection between provisional government and armed uprising. As a matter of fact the provisional government is established by the popular uprising as its own organ ... I further find in the resolution the incorrect opinion that the provisional revolutionary government will appear only *after* the final victory of the armed uprising and after the overthrow of autocracy. No – it arises in the very process of the uprising and takes the most active part in the conduct of the uprising, ensuring the latter's victory by its organized action. It is naïve to think that the Social Democracy will be able to take part in the provisional revolutionary government the moment the autocracy is completely overthrown; when the chestnuts have been removed from the fire by other hands than ours, nobody will ever dream of sharing them with us.

All this was an almost verbatim statement of my theses.

Lenin, who in his introductory report had raised the question in its purely theoretical form, received Krassin's point of view with great sympathy. This is what he said:

Taking it by and large, I subscribe to the opinion of Comrade Krassin. It is natural that as a literary man I should concentrate my attention on the literary shaping of the question. The importance of the object of the struggle is pointed out by Comrade Krassin very exactly, and I wholly subscribe to his view. One cannot engage in a struggle without expecting to capture the position for which one is fighting.

The resolution was correspondingly amended. It may not

be superfluous to remark that during the polemics of the last few years, the resolution of the Third Congress on the question of provisional government has been quoted hundreds of times as something opposed to 'Trotskyism'. The 'red professors' of the Stalin school have not the ghost of an idea that they are quoting against me, as an example of Leninism, the very lines that I wrote myself.

The environment in which I lived in Finland, with its hills, pine-trees and lakes, its transparent autumn air, and its peace, was scarcely a reminder of a permanent revolution. At the end of September I moved still farther into the Finnish interior and took up my quarters in the woods on the shore of a lake, in an isolated *pension*, 'Rauha'. This name in Finnish means 'peace'. The huge *pension* was almost empty in the autumn. A Swedish writer was staying there during these last days with an English actress, and they left without paying their bill. The proprietor rushed after them to Helsingfors. His wife was very ill; they could only keep her heart beating by means of champagne. I never saw her. She died while the proprietor was still away. Her body was in a room above me. The head waiter went to Helsingfors to look for her husband. There was only a young boy left for service. A heavy snow fell. The pine-trees were wrapped in a white shroud. The *pension* was like death.

The young boy was away down in the kitchen, somewhere below the ground. Above me the dead woman was lying. I was alone. All in all it was 'rauha' – peace. Not a soul, not even a sound. I wrote and walked. In the evening the postman brought a bunch of St Petersburg papers. I opened them, one after another. It was like a raging storm coming in through an open window. The strike was growing, and spreading from town to town. In the silence of the hotel, the rustling of the papers echoed in one's ears like the rumble of an avalanche. The revolution was in full swing.

I demanded my bill from the boy, ordered horses, and left my 'peace' to meet the avalanche. That same evening I was making a speech in the great hall of the Polytechnic Institute in St Petersburg.

14
The Year 1905

The October strike did not develop according to plan. It began with the printers in Moscow, and then subsided slowly. The decisive fights had been planned by the parties for the anniversary of the Bloody Sunday (22 January). That is why I was completing my work in my Finnish refuge without haste. But an accidental strike that was already in its last gasps suddenly spread to the railways and went off at a gallop. After 10 October of that year, the strike, now with political slogans, spread from Moscow throughout the country. No such general strike had ever been seen anywhere before. In many towns there were clashes with the troops. But, taken by and large, the October events remained on the plane of a political strike and never took on the character of an armed uprising. Absolutism lost its head, however, and retreated. On 17 October* it announced the Constitutional Manifesto. It is true that injured Tsarism retained the apparatus of power. The government policy was more than ever, to use the words of Witte, 'a mixture of cowardice, blindness, treachery and stupidity'. Nevertheless, the revolution won its first victory, a victory not complete in itself, but one which promised much.

'The most important part of the Russian revolution of 1905', the same Witte wrote later, 'was, of course, in the slogan of the peasantry: "Give us land."' With this one can agree. But Witte goes on to say: 'I did not attribute much importance to the Soviet of Workers. Nor did it have any.' This only proves that even the most gifted of bureaucrats did not understand the

*The date is according to the Julian calendar which was in use in Russia before the revolution, and corresponds to 30 October in the Gregorian calendar – a difference of thirteen days. Where a double date is quoted the one in parentheses represents the Gregorian calendar. – *Translator*.

significance of the events which were the last warning to the ruling classes. Witte died in time to avoid having to revise his views on the importance of the workers' Soviets.

I arrived in St Petersburg when the October strike was at its peak. The wave of strikes was sweeping farther and farther, but there was danger that the movement, not being controlled by a central organization, would die down without any results. I came from Finland with a plan for an elected non-party organization, with delegates who represented each a thousand workers. From a writer named Iordansky (later, the Soviet ambassador to Italy) I learned on the day of my arrival that the Mensheviks had already launched the slogan of an elected revolutionary organization on the basis of one delegate to five hundred men. This was the right thing to do. The part of the Bolshevik Central Committee then in St Petersburg resolutely opposed an elected non-party organization because it was afraid of competition with the party. At the same time the Bolshevik workers were entirely free of this fear. The sectarian attitude of the Bolshevik leaders towards the Soviet lasted until Lenin's arrival in November.

One could write an instructive chapter on the leadership of the Leninists without Lenin. The latter towered so high above his nearest disciples that in his presence they felt that there was no need of their solving theoretical and tactical problems independently. When they happened to be separated from Lenin at a critical moment, they amazed one by their utter helplessness. This was the situation in the autumn of 1905, and again in the spring of 1917. In both instances, as in others of less importance historically, the rank-and-file of the party sensed the correct line of action much better than did their semi-leaders when the latter were thrown on their own resources. Lenin's delay in arriving from abroad was one of the things that prevented the Bolshevik faction from gaining a leading position in the events of the first revolution.

I have already mentioned the fact that N. I. Sedova had been made prisoner during a cavalry raid on a May Day meeting in the woods. She served about six months in prison and was then sent to live under police supervision at Tver. After the October Manifesto, she returned to St Petersburg. Under the names of

Mr and Mrs Vikentiyev, we rented a room in the apartment of a man who turned out to be a gambler on the stock exchange. Business in the stock-market was bad, and many a speculator had to take in roomers. Newsboys brought us all the published papers every morning. Our landlord would sometimes borrow them from my wife, read them, and gnash his teeth. His affairs were constantly getting worse. One day he burst into our room waving a newspaper wildly. 'Look,' he yelled, as he pointed his finger at my newly written article 'Good morning, St Petersburg janitors!' 'Look, they are now reaching out for the janitors! If I came across the jailbird I would shoot him with this gun!' And he pulled a gun out of his pocket and shook it in the air. He looked like a maniac. He wanted sympathy. My wife came to my office at the newspaper with this disturbing news. We felt we had to look for new quarters. But we didn't have a free minute; so we trusted to fate. We stayed on with this despairing speculator until my arrest. Fortunately, neither he nor the police ever learned the identity of Vikentiyev. After my arrest our room was not even searched.

In the Soviet I was known by the name of Yanovsky, after the village in which I was born. In the press I wrote as Trotsky. I had to work for three newspapers. With Parvus I took over the tiny *Russian Gazette* and transformed it into a fighting organ for the masses. Within a few days the circulation rose from thirty thousand to one hundred thousand. A month later it had reached the half-million mark. But our technical resources could not keep up with the growth of the paper. We were finally extricated from our difficulties by the government raid.

On 13 (26), November in alliance with the Mensheviks, we had started a big political organ, *Nachalo* (*The Beginning*). The paper's circulation was jumping by leaps and bounds. Without Lenin, the Bolshevik *Novaya Zhizn* (*The New Life*) was rather drab. The *Nachalo*, on the other hand, had a tremendous success. I think this paper, more than any other publication of the past half-century, resembled its classic prototype, the *Neue Rheinische Zeitung*, which was published by Marx in 1848. Kamenev, one of the editors of the *Novaya Zhizn*, told me afterwards how he watched the sale of newspapers at the stations when he was passing through by train. The St Petersburg train was awaited by endless lines. The demand was only for revolutionary papers. '*Nachalo, Nachalo, Nachalo*', came the cry of the waiting crowds. '*Novaya Zhizn*', and then again, '*Nachalo, Nachalo, Nachalo.*'

'Then I said to myself, with a feeling of resentment,' Kamenev confessed, 'they do write better in the *Nachalo* than we do.'

Besides the *Russian Gazette* and *Nachalo*, I also wrote editorials for the *Izvestia* (*The News*), the official Soviet organ, as well as numerous appeals, manifestos and resolutions. The fifty-two days of the existence of the first Soviet were filled to the brim with work – the Soviet, the Executive Committee, endless meetings, and three newspapers. How we managed to live in this whirlpool is still not clear, even to me. But much of the past seems inconceivable because as we remember it we lose the element of activity; we look at ourselves from outside. Whereas in those days we were sufficiently active. We not only whirled in the vortex, but we helped to create it. Everything was done in a hurry, but, after all, not so badly, and some things were even done very well. Our accountable editor, an old democrat, Dr D. M. Hertzenstein, would drop in sometimes at the *Nachalo* offices, dressed in an immaculate Prince Albert coat. He would stand in the middle of the room and watch our chaos affectionately. A year later he had to answer in court the charges brought against him for the revolutionary fury of a newspaper over which he had not the least influence. The old man did not renounce us. On the contrary, with tears in his eyes, he told the court how, while editing the most popular paper, we fed ourselves between work on stale 'pirozhki' which the doorman brought, wrapped in paper, from the nearest bakery. The old man had to serve a year in prison for the revolution which did not succeed, for the émigré fraternity, and for stale 'pirozhki'.

In his memoirs Witte wrote afterwards that in 1905 'the vast majority of the people seemed to go mad'. Revolution appears to a conservative as collective madness only because it raises the 'normal' insanity of social contradictions to the highest possible tension. Just as people dislike to recognize themselves in a bold caricature. And yet the entire modern development condenses,

strains, and accentuates the contradictions and makes them unbearable, consequently preparing that state of mind when the
great majority 'goes mad'. But in such cases, the insane majority
puts the strait jacket on the sane minority. Thanks to this,
history keeps moving along.

A revolutionary chaos is not at all like an earthquake or a
flood. In the confusion of a revolution a new order begins to
take shape instantly; men and ideas distribute themselves naturally in new channels. Revolution appears as utter madness only
to those whom it sweeps aside and overthrows. To us it was
different. We were in our own element, albeit a very stormy one.
A time and place was found for everything. Some were even
able to lead personal lives, to fall in love, to make new friends
and actually to visit revolutionary theatres. Parvus, for instance,
was so taken with a new satirical play that he bought fifty tickets
for the next performance and invited his friends. (I must explain
that the day before he had been paid for his books.) When he
was arrested, the police found fifty theatre-tickets in his pockets,
and for a long time racked their brains over this revolutionary
puzzle. They did not know that Parvus did everything on a
large scale.

The Soviet roused great masses of people. The workers supported it to a man. In the country disturbances continued, as
they did among the troops who were returning home from the
Far East after the Peace of Portsmouth. But the guards and the
Cossack regiments stood firm. All the elements that go to make
a successful revolution were there, but they did not mature.

On 18 October, the day after the promulgation of the manifesto, tens of thousands of people were standing in front of the
University of St Petersburg, aroused by the struggle and intoxicated with the joy of their first victory. I shouted to them
from the balcony not to trust an incomplete victory, that the
enemy was stubborn, that there were traps ahead; I tore the
Tsar's manifesto into pieces and scattered them to the winds.
But such political warnings only scratch the surface of the mass
consciousness. The masses need the schooling of big events.

In this connection I remember two scenes during the life of
the St Petersburg Soviet. One was on 29 October when the city

was filled with rumours of pogroms being prepared by the Black Hundred. The delegates came straight from their workshops to the meeting, and showed samples of the weapons that were being made by the workers against the Black Hundred. They shook their knives, knuckles, daggers and wire whips in the air, but more in good humour than seriously, and with much jesting. They seemed to believe that their readiness to face the enemy was enough to solve the problem. Most of them did not seem to realize that it was a life-or-death struggle. But that they learned in the December days.

On the evening of 3 December the St Petersburg Soviet was surrounded by troops. All the exits and entrances were closed. From the balcony where the Executive Committee was in session, I shouted down to the hundreds of delegates who were crowding the hall: 'No resistance to be made, no arms to be surrendered.' The arms were revolvers. And then, in the meeting-hall, already surrounded on all sides by detachments of infantry, cavalry and artillery, the workers began to wreck their arms. They did it with practised hands, striking a Mauser with a Browning and a Browning with a Mauser. And this time it did not have the sound of a jest, as it had on 29 October. In the clashing and creaking of twisting metal one heard the gnashing teeth of a proletariat who for the first time fully realized that a more formidable and more ruthless effort was necessary to overthrow and crush the enemy.

The partial victory of the October strike had for me a tremendous theoretical as well as political importance. It was not the opposition of the liberal bourgeoisie, not the elemental risings of the peasantry or the terrorist acts of the intelligentsia, but the strike of the workers that for the first time brought Tsarism to its knees. The revolutionary leadership of the proletariat revealed itself as an incontrovertible fact. I felt that the theory of permanent revolution had withstood its first test successfully. Revolution was obviously opening up to the proletariat the prospect of seizing the power. The years of reaction which soon followed failed to make me move from this position. But from these premises I also drew my conclusions about the West. If the young proletariat of Russia could be so formidable, how mighty the revolutionary power of the proletariat of the more advanced countries would be!

Writing afterwards in the inexact and slovenly manner which is peculiar to him, Lunacharsky described my revolutionary concept as follows:

Comrade Trotsky held in 1905 that the two revolutions (the bourgeois and socialist), although they do not coincide, are bound to each other in such a way that they make a permanent revolution. After they have entered upon the revolutionary period through a bourgeois political revolution, the Russian section of the world, along with the rest, will not be able to escape from this period until the Social Revolution has been completed. It cannot be denied that in formulating this view Comrade Trotsky showed great insight and vision, albeit he erred to the extent of fifteen years.

The remark about my error of fifteen years does not become any more profound through its later repetitions by Radek. All our estimates and slogans of 1905 were based on the assumption of a victorious revolution, and not of a defeat. We achieved then neither a republic nor a transfer of land, nor even an eight-hour day. Does it mean that we erred in putting these demands forward? The defeat of the revolution blanketed all prospects – not merely those which I had been expounding. The question was not of the dates of revolution but of the analysis of its inner forces and of foreseeing its progress as a whole.

What were the relations between Lenin and me during the revolution of 1905? Since his death the official history has been revised, and, for 1905 as well, a struggle has been established between the powers of good and evil. What were the facts? Lenin took no active part in the work of the Soviet, and he never spoke there. It goes without saying that he watched its every step intently; he influenced its policies through the representatives of the Bolshevik faction and expounded its work in his paper. There was not a question in which he disagreed with the Soviet policies. And yet – the documents are witnesses – all the decisions of the Soviet, with the exception perhaps of a few that were accidental and unimportant, were shaped by me; I submitted them first to the Executive Committee, and then, in its name, I placed them before the Soviet. When the federative commission was formed of representatives of the Bolsheviks and Mensheviks, again it was I who had to appear as its representative before the Executive Committee. And there was never a conflict in that connection.

The first president of the Soviet was elected before my arrival from Finland. He was a young lawyer, Khrustalyov, an accidental figure in the revolution, representing an intermediate stage between Gapon and the Social Democracy. Khrustalyov presided, but he had no real political leadership. After his arrest a 'presidium' was elected, and I was at the head of it. Sverchkov, one of the prominent members of the Soviet, writes in his memoirs: 'The intellectual leader of the Soviet was L. D. Trotsky. The president of the Soviet, Nosar-Khrustalyov, was really a screen, for he was never able to solve a single question of principle himself. A man with an exaggerated vanity which was almost an illness with him, he came to hate L. D. Trotsky because of the very necessity of referring to him for advice and direction.' Lunacharsky relates in his memoirs: 'I remember somebody saying in Lenin's presence: "The star of Khrustalyov is setting. Today the strong man in the Soviet is Trotsky." For a moment Lenin's expression seemed to darken; then he said, "Well, Trotsky has won this by his tireless and striking work."'

The relations between the editors of the two papers were most friendly. They engaged in no polemics against each other. 'The first number of the *Nachalo* has come out,' wrote the Bolshevik *Novaya Zhizn*. 'We welcome a comrade in the struggle. The first issue is notable for the brilliant description of the October strike written by Comrade Trotsky.' People don't write in this way when they are fighting with each other. But there was no fighting. On the contrary, the papers defended each other against bourgeois criticism. The *Novaya Zhizn*, even after the arrival of Lenin, came out with a defence of my articles on the permanent revolution. Both newspapers, as well as the two factions, followed the line of the restoration of party unity. The central committee of the Bolsheviks, with Lenin participating, passed a unanimous resolution to the effect that the split was merely the result of the conditions of foreign exile, and the events of the revolution had deprived the factional struggle of any reasonable grounds. I defended the same line in the *Nachalo*, with only a passive resistance from Martov.

Under the pressure of the masses, the Mensheviks in the Soviet during its first period did their utmost to keep in line with the left flank. A change in their position took place only after the first blow of the reaction. In February 1906 the leader of the Mensheviks, Martov, complained in a letter to Axelrod: 'For two months now . . . I have not been able to finish any of the writing I have started. It is either neurasthenia or mental fatigue – but I cannot gather my thoughts together.' Martov did not know what to call his illness. But it has quite a definite name: '*Menshevism*'. In an epoch of revolution, opportunism means, first of all, vacillation and inability 'to gather one's thoughts'.

While the Mensheviks were beginning to repent publicly and to criticize the policy of the Soviet, I defended that policy in the Russian press, and later in the German publications, as well as in the Polish magazine edited by Rosa Luxemburg. Out of this struggle for the methods and traditions of 1905 came my book, at first entitled *Russia in the Revolution*, and later reprinted many times in various countries under the title of *1905*. After the October revolution, this book was regarded as the official text-book of the party, not only in Russia, but among the communist parties in the West as well. Only after Lenin's death, when a carefully prepared campaign was started against me, did this book of mine on 1905 come under fire. At first the attack was confined to a few captious remarks, which were sorry and trivial. But gradually the criticism became more daring; it grew and multiplied, became more involved and arrogant, and seemed all the noisier because it had to silence its own distress. In this way was created the legend of the struggle of Lenin's and Trotsky's policies during the revolution of 1905.

The revolution of 1905 made a break in the life of the country, in the life of the party, and in my own life. The break was in the direction of greater maturity. My first revolutionary work in Nikolayev was a provincial experiment gropingly carried out. The experiment did not go without leaving a trace. Never in

my later life, it seems, did I come into such intimate contact
with the plain workers as in Nikolayev. At that time I had no
'name', and there was nothing to stand between us. The principal types of the Russian proletariat impressed themselves on
my consciousness forever. In the years that followed, I encountered almost no one who was not a variant of one of these types.
In prison I had to start my revolutionary education almost from
the A B Cs. Two and a half years in prison and two years of exile
in Siberia gave me the theoretical foundations for a revolutionary
view of life. My first stay abroad was my school for political
education. Under the guidance of distinguished Marxist revolutionaries, I was learning to understand events in a wide
historical perspective and in their international connection.
Towards the end of my foreign stay, I cut myself adrift from
both of the leading groups, the Bolsheviks and the Mensheviks.
I came to Russia in February of 1905; the other émigré leaders
did not come until October and November. Among the Russian
comrades there was not one from whom I could learn anything.
On the contrary, I had to assume the position of teacher myself.
The events of the stormy years were coming swiftly, one upon
the heels of another. One had to occupy one's position there on
the spot. A proclamation with the ink barely dry on it went
straight to the underground printers. The theoretical foundations laid in prison and in exile, the political method assimilated
abroad, now for the first time found practical application in war.
I was confident in the face of events. I understood their inner
mechanism, or at least so I believed. I visualized their effect on
the minds of the workers, and envisaged, in its main features,
the next day to come. From February to October my participation in the events was chiefly of a literary nature. In October
I plunged headlong into the gigantic whirlpool, which, in a
personal sense, was the greatest test for my powers. Decisions
had to be made under fire. I can't help noting here that those
decisions came to me quite obviously. I did not turn back to see
what others might say, and I very seldom had opportunity to
consult anybody; everything had to be done in such a hurry.
Later I observed with astonishment and a sense of estrangement
how every event caught the cleverest of the Mensheviks, Martov,

unawares and threw him into confusion. Without thinking about it – there was too little time left for self-examination – I organically felt that my years of apprenticeship were over, although not in the sense that I stopped learning. No – the urge and willingness to learn I have carried through my whole life in all their first intensity. But in the years that followed I have been learning as a master learns, and not as a pupil. At the time of my second arrest I was twenty-six. And the acknowledgement of my maturity came from old Deutsch, who, in prison, solemnly foreswore calling me 'youth', and addressed me by my full name.

In his book *Silhouettes*, already quoted here, and which is now under a ban, Lunacharsky gives the following estimate of the parts played by the leaders of the first revolution:

His [Trotsky's] popularity among the St Petersburg proletariat was very great by the time of his arrest, and was increased still further by his strikingly effective [?] and heroic [?] behaviour at the trial. I must say that Trotsky, of all the Social Democratic leaders of 1905–6, undoubtedly showed himself, in spite of his youth, the best prepared; and he was the least stamped by the narrow émigré outlook which, as I said before, handicapped even Lenin. He realized better than the others what a state struggle is. He came out of the revolution, too, with the greatest gains in popularity; neither Lenin nor Martov gained much. Plekhanov lost a great deal because of the semi-liberal tendencies which he revealed. But Trotsky from then on was in the front rank.

These lines, written in 1923, are all the more expressive because today Lunacharsky, not very 'effectively' and not very 'heroically', is writing their exact opposite.

No great work is possible without intuition – that is, without that subconscious sense which, although it may be developed and enriched by theoretical and practical work, must be ingrained in the very nature of the individual. Neither theoretical education nor practical routine can replace the political insight which enables one to apprehend a situation, weigh it as a whole, and foresee the future. This gift takes on decisive importance at a time of abrupt changes and breaks – the conditions of revolution. The events of 1905 revealed in me, I believe, this revolutionary intuition, and enabled me to rely on its assured support during my later life. I must add here that the errors which I have committed, however important they may have been – and some of them were of extreme importance – always referred to questions that were not fundamental or strategic, but dealt rather with such derivative matters as organization and policy. In all conscientiousness, I cannot, in the appreciation of the political situation as a whole and of its revolutionary perspectives, accuse myself of any serious errors of judgement.

In Russian life the revolution of 1905 was the dress rehearsal for the revolution of 1917. That was its significance in my personal life as well. I took part in the events of 1917 with absolute resolution and confidence, because they were merely a continuation and development of the revolutionary activity which had been interrupted by the arrest of the St Petersburg Soviet on 3 December 1905.

The arrest took place a day after we had published our so-called financial manifesto, which proclaimed that the financial bankruptcy of Tsarism was inevitable, and issued a categorical warning that the debts incurred by the Romanovs would not be recognized by the victorious nation. 'The autocracy never enjoyed the confidence of the people,' said the manifesto of the Soviet of Workers' Delegates, 'and was never granted any authority by the people. We have therefore decided not to allow the repayment of such loans as have been made by the Tsarist government when openly engaged in a war with the entire people.'

The French *Bourse* answered our manifesto a few months later with a new loan of three quarters of a million francs. The liberal and reactionary press poured sarcasm over the important threat of the Soviet against the Tsar's finances and the European bankers. In later years, the manifesto was successfully forgotten – but it recalled itself to mind. The financial bankruptcy of Tsarism, prepared for by its whole past history, coincided with the military *débâcle*. And later, after the victories of the revolution, the decree of the Soviet of People's Commissaries, issued on 10 February 1918, declared all the Tsarist debts annulled. This decree remains in force even to this day. It is wrong to say, as some do, that the October revolution does not recognize any obligations: *its own* obligations the revolution recognizes to the full. The obligation that it took upon itself on 2 December 1905, it carried out on 10 February 1917. The revolution is fully entitled to remind the creditors of Tsarism: 'Gentlemen, you were warned in ample time.'

In this respect, as in others, the year 1905 was a preparation for the year 1917.

15
Trial, Exile, Escape

The second prison cycle began. It was much easier to bear than the first, and the conditions were infinitely more tolerable than those of eight years before. I was in the 'Kresty' prison for a short time, then in the Peter-Paul fortress, and finally in the House of Preliminary Detention. Before we were sent to Siberia we were moved to a transfer-prison.

Altogether I was in prison for fifteen months. Each prison had its peculiar features to which one had to adapt oneself. But it would be too dull to dwell on them, for, different as they were, prisons are really all alike. Again I entered on a period of systematic scientific and literary work. I studied the theory of rent and the history of social relations in Russia. The big work on rent, though still unfinished, was lost during the first years after the October revolution. To me this was a most tragic loss, next to that of my work on freemasonry. My studies of the social history of Russia were embodied in an article, 'The Results of the Revolution and Its Prospects' ('Itogi i Perspectivi'), which represents, for that period, the most finished statement in proof of the theory of permanent revolution.

After our transfer to the House of Preliminary Detention, lawyers were allowed to visit us. The first Duma brought with it a stimulation of political life. The newspapers again grew daring. Marxist publishing enterprises took a new lease on life. The new conditions made it possible to return to militant political writing. I wrote a great deal in prison; the lawyers would carry my manuscripts out in their brief-cases. My pamphlet, 'Peter Struve in Politics', belongs to this period. I worked over it with such zeal that the walks in the prison yard seemed an annoying duty to me. The pamphlet, which was directed against liberalism, was essentially a defence of the St Petersburg

Soviet, of the December armed uprising in Moscow, and of the revolutionary policy in general, as opposed to the criticism by the opportunists. The Bolshevik press received the pamphlet in a decidedly friendly manner; the Menshevik press was silent. Tens of thousands of copies of the pamphlet were sold within a few weeks.

D. Sverchkov, who shared my imprisonment with me, later described the prison period in his book *At the Dawn of the Revolution*. He wrote:

L. D. Trotsky, working under great pressure, wrote and handed in for printing parts of his book, *Russia and the Revolution*, a book in which he definitely advanced for the first time* the idea that the revolution which had started in Russia could not end until the Socialist régime was fulfilled. His theory of 'permanent revolution', as it was called, was accepted by few, but he held firmly to his position, and even then discerned in the state of the world all the symptoms of decomposition of the bourgeois-capitalist economy, and the relative nearness of the Socialist Revolution . . .

'Trotsky's prison cell', continued Sverchkov, 'soon became transformed into a sort of library. He was supplied with all the new books that deserved attention; he read them all, and the entire day, from morning until late at night, he was occupied with his literary work. "I feel splendid," he would say to us. "I sit and work and feel perfectly sure that I can't be arrested. You will agree that under the conditions in Tsarist Russia, that is rather an unusual sensation."'

For relaxation I read the European classics. As I lay in my prison bunk I absorbed them with the same sense of physical delight that the gourmet has in sipping choice wines or in inhaling the fragrant smoke of a fine cigar. These were my best hours. The traces of my classical studies, in the shape of epigraphs and quotations, were evident in all of my political writings at that time. It was then for the first time that I really acquainted myself with the 'grands seigneurs' of the French novel in their original French. The art of story-telling is primarily French. Although I know German perhaps somewhat

*Inexact. – *L. D. Trotsky*.

better than French, especially as regards scientific terminology, I read French fiction more easily than German. To this day I have retained my love for the French novel. Even in a railway-car during the civil war, I found time to read the latest ones.

Taking it all in all, I can hardly complain about my life in prison. It was a good school for me. I left the hermetically sealed cell of solitary confinement in the Peter-Paul fortress with a tinge of regret; it was so quiet there, so eventless, so perfect for intellectual work. The House of Preliminary Detention was, on the contrary, filled with people and bustle. Not a few there were sentenced to death; terrorist acts and so-called armed 'expropriations' were sweeping the country. The prison régime, on account of the first Duma, was very liberal; the cells were not locked during the day, and we could take our walks all together. For hours at a time we would go into raptures over playing leap-frog. The men condemned to death would leap and offer their backs as well as the rest of us. My wife came to visit me twice a week. The officials on duty winked at our exchange of letters and manuscripts. One of them, a middle-aged man, was especially well disposed towards us. At his request I presented him with a copy of my book and my photograph with an inscription. 'My daughters are all college students,' he whispered delightedly, as he winked mysteriously at me. I met him later under the Soviet, and did what I could for him in those years of famine.

Parvus walked with old Deutsch in the prison yard. I joined them occasionally. There is a photograph showing all three of us in the prison kitchen. The indefatigable Deutsch was planning a wholesale escape for us and easily won Parvus over, insisting that I join them too. I resisted because I was attracted by the political importance of the trial ahead. Too many people were included in the plans, however. In the prison library where they conspired, one of the guards discovered a set of tools. The prison administration hushed the affair up, because the secret police were suspected of planting the tools there to bring about a change in the prison régime. And, after all, Deutsch had to effect his fourth escape not from the prison but from Siberia.

The factional disagreements in the party were sharply re-newed after the defeat in December. The high-handed disso-lution of the Duma raised all the problems of the revolution anew. I made them the subject of a pamphlet on tactics, which Lenin published through a Bolshevik publishing house. The Mensheviks were already beating a retreat along the entire front. In prison, however, the factional relations had not yet reached the acute stage which they had in the world outside, and we were able to publish a collective work dealing with the St Petersburg Soviet in which some of the Mensheviks still appeared as contributors.

The trial of the Soviet of Workers' Delegates opened on 19 September 1906, in the early days of Stolypin's court-martial justice. The yard of the court building and the adjoining streets were turned into a military camp. All the police of St Petersburg were mobilized. But the trial itself was carried on with a certain amount of freedom; the reactionary government was out to disgrace Witte by exposing his 'liberalism', his weakness in dealing with the revolution. About four hundred witnesses were called; and more than two hundred witnesses came and offered evidence. Workers, manufacturers, members of the secret police, engineers, servants, citizens, journalists, post-office officials, police chiefs, *gymnasium* students, municipal councillors, jani-tors, senators, hooligans, deputies, professors, soldiers, all passed in file during the month of the trial, and, under the cross-fire of the judges' bench, of the prosecution, of the attorneys for the defence, and of the defendants – especially the latter – recon-structed, line by line, and stroke by stroke, the activity of the workers' Soviet. The defendants gave their explanations. I spoke of the importance in the revolution of an armed uprising. The chief objective was therefore obtained, and when the court re-fused our demand to call to the witness-stand Senator Lopukhin, who in the autumn of 1905 had opened a printing-press in the Police Department to disseminate pogrom literature, we broke up the trial by forcing the court to take us back to prison. The counsel for the defence, the witnesses and the public all left the court-room after us; the judges remained alone with the prose-cutor. They passed the verdict in our absence. The stenographic report of this unique trial, which lasted for a month, has not been published, and it seems that to this day it has not even been located. The most essential facts about the trial I related in my book *1905*.

My father and mother were at the trial. Their thoughts and emotions were divided. It was now impossible to explain away my conduct as a boy's foolishness, as they had in my Nikolayev days when I lived in Shvigovsky's garden. I was an editor of newspapers, the chairman of the Soviet, and I had a name as a writer. The old couple were impressed by all this. My mother tried to talk with the lawyers for the defence, hoping to hear further complimentary remarks about me from them. During my speech, which she could scarcely understand, she wept silently. She wept more when a score of attorneys for the defence came up to shake my hand. One of the lawyers for the defence had demanded a temporary adjournment before that, because of the general excitement caused by my speech. This was A. Z. Zarudny; in Kerensky's government, he was the Minister of Justice and kept me in prison on a charge of state treason. But that happened ten years later.

During the intervals of the trial the old folks looked at me happily. My mother was sure that I would not only be acquitted, but even given some mark of distinction. I tried to persuade her to prepare for a sentence to hard labour. Somewhat frightened and puzzled by all this, she kept looking from me to the lawyers as if trying to understand how such a thing could be possible. My father was pale, silent, happy and distressed, all in one.

We were deprived of all civic rights and sentenced to enforced settlement in exile. This was a comparatively mild punishment. We were expecting hard labour. But enforced settlement in exile is quite a different thing from the administrative exile to which I had been sentenced the first time. The enforced settlement was for an indefinite period, and every attempt at escape carried the additional punishment of three years at hard-labour. The forty-five strokes with the lash which used to go with this had been abolished several years before.

'It is about two or three hours since we came to the transfer-prison,' I wrote to my wife on 3 January 1907.

I confess I parted with my cell in the Detention House not without nervousness. I had become so used to that tiny cubicle in which there was every chance for me to work. In the transfer-prison we knew we would all be placed in the same cell – what could be more tiresome? And after that – the familiar dirt, the bustle, and the stupid muddling of the journey to exile. Who knows how long it will take before we reach our destination? And who can tell when we will return? Wouldn't it have been better if I could have stayed as I was in cell No. 462, reading, writing and waiting?

We have been brought here today unexpectedly, without notice. In the reception-hall we were ordered to change into the prison clothes. We did so with all the curiosity of schoolboys. It was interesting to see one another in the grey trousers, the grey coats, and grey caps. There was no diamond of classic fame on the backs of these, however. We were allowed to keep our own underwear and boots. We returned to our cell in our new costumes, a great, excited crowd.

My keeping my boots was of no small importance to me, for in the sole of one I had a fine passport, and in the high heels gold pieces. We were all to be sent to the village of Obdorsk, far within the Arctic circle. The distance from Obdorsk to the railway-line was fifteen hundred versts, and to the nearest telegraph-station eight hundred. The mail comes once a fortnight there. When the roads are bad, in spring and autumn, it does not come at all for six or eight weeks.

Exceptional measures were taken to guard us during the journey. A St Petersburg convoy was not considered reliable. And, indeed, the sergeant on guard, his sword unsheathed, declaimed the latest revolutionary poems to us in our convict car. The adjoining car carried a platoon of secret police who surrounded our car at every stop. At the same time the prison officials treated us with the utmost consideration. Revolution and counter-revolution were still in the balance, and nobody knew which side was to win. The officer of the convoy began by showing us the order from his superiors authorizing him not to handcuff us, as the law demands.

On 11 January during the journey, I wrote to my wife:

If the officer is considerate and civil, the lower ranks are even more so; nearly all of them have read the reports of our trial, and they treat us with extreme sympathy. The soldiers did not know whom they would be taking, or where they would be taking them, until the last moment. From the precautionary measures which accompanied their sudden transfer from Moscow to St Petersburg, they concluded that they were to take some prisoners condemned to death to Schlüsselburg. In the reception-hall of the transfer-prison, I noticed that the soldiers of the convoy were very excited, and seemed, in rather an odd way, anxious to be obliging, as if they felt guilty of something. It was only in the train that I learned why. They were terribly pleased when they discovered that their charges were workers' delegates sentenced only to exile. The secret police who act as a super-convoy never show themselves in our car. They keep guard outside, surround the car at the station, stand at the outside door, but it would seem that their especial watch is the convoy-men.

Our letters from the road were secretly mailed by the soldiers of the convoy.

On the railway we went as far as Tiumen. From there we continued by horse. To guard the fourteen prisoners there were fifty-two soldiers, in addition to a captain, a senior police officer, and a police sergeant. The party had about forty sleighs. The route from Tiumen via Tobolsk was by way of the river Ob. 'Every day,' I wrote to my wife, 'we have been going from ninety to 100 versts farther north, that is, nearly one degree. Owing to this continuous advance, the lessening of culture, if one may speak of culture in this case, becomes strikingly evident. Every day we descend one degree farther into the kingdom of cold and barbarism.'

After we had crossed districts completely infected with typhus, on 12 February, the thirty-third day of our journey, we reached Berezov, the place in which Prince Menshikov, Tsar Peter's right-hand man at one time, had lived in exile. In Berezov a two-day halt was announced. There was still another 500 versts to be made before we got to Obdorsk. We walked about in complete freedom. Our guardians had no fear of attempts at escape. The only way back was by the river Ob, along the telegraph-line; any runaway would have been caught. Among the residents in Berezov was the land-surveyor, Roshkovsky. I discussed the question of escape with him, and he told me that one might try to follow a straight course due west along the river Sosva in the direction of the Urals, going by deer as far as the mining settlements, then getting on to a narrow-gauge railway at the Bogoslovsky mines and travelling to Kushva, the junction with the Perm line. And then – Perm, Viatka, Vologda, St Petersburg, Helsingfors . . .

There were no roads along the Sosva, however. Beyond Berezov the country is utterly wild. For thousands of versts there are no police, and not a single Russian settlement, only occasional Ostyak huts. No sign of a telegraph. There are no horses along the entire route, as the track is exclusively for deer-travel. The police could not overtake one, but there was the possibility of getting lost in the wilderness and perishing in the snow. And it was February, the month of blizzards.

Dr Feit, an old revolutionary and a member of our group of prisoners, taught me how to simulate sciatica in order to be able to stay in Berezov for a few more days. I carried out this modest part of the plan successfully. Sciatica, as is known, cannot be verified. I was placed in a hospital. The régime there imposed no restriction whatever on me. When I felt 'better', I would go out for several hours at a time. The doctor encouraged me to walk. As I said, nobody was afraid of any attempt to escape at this time of the year.

I had to make up my mind. I decided in favour of the western route, straight across to the Urals. Roshkovsky obtained the advice of a local peasant nicknamed 'The Goat's Foot'. This dry, intelligent little man organized the escape, quite disinterestedly. When his part was discovered later on, he was severely punished. After the October revolution, 'The Goat's Foot' did not learn for some time that I was the man he had helped to escape ten years before. Only in 1923 did he come to me in Moscow, and our meeting was very friendly. He was given the full-dress uniform of the Red Army, taken around to the theatres, and presented with a gramophone and other gifts. Shortly after this the old man died in his far-away North.

The journey from Berezov had to be made by deer. The difficulty was to find a guide who would risk the certain danger of a trip at that time of year. 'The Goat's Foot' found a Zyryan, a clever and experienced fellow, like all the Zyryans.

'Is he a tippler?'

'Of course, a frightful tippler. But he speaks Russian and Zyryan fluently, and two Ostyak dialects which barely resemble each other. Another driver like him is not to be found – a shrewd one, he is.' It was this shrewd fellow who afterwards gave 'The Goat's Foot' away. But he got me away successfully.*

The departure was set for Sunday at midnight. That day the officials were having amateur theatricals. I appeared at the barracks, which served as the improvised theatre, and when I met the local chief of police I told him that I felt much better and would be able to leave shortly for Obdorsk. This was a ruse, but a necessary one.

When the church-bells struck twelve, I stole into 'The Goat's Foot's' yard. The sleigh was waiting. I stretched myself on the bottom and lay on my spare fur coat; 'The Goat's Foot' spread frozen hay over me, bound it with a rope, and we set off. The hay thawed, and cold water dripped on my face. After we had driven for a few versts, we stopped. 'The Goat's Foot' unbound the hay and I got out. Then he whistled.

Several men answered him, in voices that were – alas! – quite unmistakably drunken. The Zyryan was drunk, and he had brought his friends with him. This was a bad start, but there was no choice. I was transferred with my small luggage to a light deer-sleigh. I had on two fur coats – one had fur inside, the other outside – fur stockings, fur boots, a double-lined fur cap, and fur gloves; in short, the complete winter outfit of an Ostyak. In my bag I carried a few bottles of liquor, the best medium of exchange in a desert of snow.

'From the fire lookout in Berezov', Sverchkov relates in his memoirs,

one could see all movements to and from the town over the white expanse of snow for at least a verst around. It was only reasonable to

*In my book *1905* this part of my escape was purposely described in a different way. At that time to tell the truth would have meant putting the Tsar's police on the track of my accomplices. Today I still hope that Stalin will not prosecute them either, especially since their sentences would have expired, and since Lenin himself helped me at the last stage of my escape, as I will later show.

expect the police to question the fireman on duty whether he had seen anybody driving out of town that night. Acting on this presumption, Roshkovsky arranged for one of the local men to take a slaughtered calf down the Tobolsk road. As we anticipated, the move was detected, and when Trotsky's escape was discovered two days later, the police rushed after the calf and lost two more days in this way.

But I only learned of this much later.

We took the course along the Sosva. The deer that my guide had bought were the pick of a herd of several hundred. Early in the journey the drunken driver had a way of falling asleep frequently, and then the deer would stop. This promised trouble for both of us. In the end he did not even answer when I poked him. Then I took off his cap, his hair quickly froze, and he began to sober up.

We drove on. It was a magnificent ride through a desert of virgin snow all covered with fir-trees and marked with the foot-prints of animals. The deer kept up a lively trot, their tongues out at the side, breathing heavily with a 'chu-chu-chu-chu'. The track was narrow, the beasts herded close together, and it was a wonder they did not get in each other's way. Amazing creatures, knowing no hunger or fatigue! They had had no food for twenty-four hours before our sudden departure, and it was another twenty-four hours from the time we started before they got any. According to the driver, they were just getting into their stride. They ran evenly, without effort, at a speed of eight to ten versts an hour. They found their own food. A log of wood was tied about their necks, and they were let loose; they chose a place where they sensed the presence of moss under the snow, dug deep holes with their hoofs, going in almost to the tops of their ears, and then fed themselves. I had the same feeling for these animals that an aviator must have for his motor when he flies over an ocean at an altitude of several hundred feet.

The leader of the three deer went lame. We were much upset about it; he had to be changed. We looked around for an Ostyak settlement. They are scattered here, many versts away from each other. My guide would find camps by almost imper-ceptible signs – several versts away he could smell the odour of smoke. The changing of the deer lost us another full day. But on the other hand I was lucky enough to see a beautiful thing at dawn: three Ostyaks, riding full-tilt, lassoed some deer, already marked, from their herd of several hundred while the dogs drove the deer towards them.

We drove on again through woods, over snow-covered swamps, and through vast forests that had been destroyed by fires. We boiled snow for water, sat on the snow and drank tea. My guide preferred liquor, but I saw to it that he did not over-indulge.

Although it looks always the same, the road is constantly changing, and the deer know it. Now we are going through an open field, between the birch woods and the river. The road is terrible. Behind us the wind blows away the narrow track which the sleigh has left. The third deer keeps missing the trail. He sinks in the snow up to his belly and even deeper, makes a few desperate leaps, climbs to the road, pushes against the middle one and knocks the leader off the track. In another place the road, warmed by the sun, is so difficult that the straps on the front sled snap twice, and at each stop the sleds freeze to the track; it is only with much effort that they can be made to move again. After the first two runs, the deer seem tired.

But now the sun has set, the road is frozen over, and driving is better again. Soft, but not mushy – the most 'business-like' road, as the driver expresses it. The deer trot on almost noise-lessly, and pull the sleigh without effort. In the end we have to unharness the third deer and tie him behind because easy driving makes them prance about, and they might smash the sleigh. The sleigh glides smoothly and in silence, like a boat on a crystal-clear lake. In the darkening twilight the woods seem even more gigantic. I cannot see the road; the movement of the sleigh is hardly perceptible. The enchanted trees rush towards us, the bushes run away on the sides, slim birches and old stumps covered with snow fly past us. Everything is filled with mystery. Chu-chu-chu-chu resounds the even breathing of the deer in the wooded silence of the night.

The journey lasted a week. We had done 700 kilometres and were nearing the Urals; we were meeting whole trains of sleighs more often now. I posed as an engineer and a member of the polar expedition of Baron Tol. Near the Urals we met a clerk who had worked on this expedition and knew its members. He overwhelmed me with questions. Fortunately he was not quite sober. I tried to get out of this fix with the aid of a bottle of rum which I had taken for use in emergency. Everything went off beautifully. Once in the Urals I travelled by horse. Now I posed as an official and, together with an excise controller who was surveying his district, finally reached the narrow-gauge railway. The secret police at the station looked on indifferently as I extricated myself from my Ostyak fur coats.

My position on the local Ural line was still far from secure; on that line, where every 'stranger' is noticed, I might easily be arrested by cabled instructions from Tobolsk. I went on fearfully. But a day later, when I found myself in a comfortable car of the Perm railway, I began at once to feel as if my case were won. The train passed through the same stations at which we had been received with such solemn ceremonies by the secret police, guards, and local police chiefs, not so long ago. But now my way lay in a different direction, and I was travelling with different emotions. For the first few minutes the almost empty car seemed too crowded and stuffy, and I went out onto the front platform, where the wind was blowing, and it was dark. A loud cry burst from me spontaneously – a cry of joy and freedom.

At one of the nearest stops I telegraphed my wife to await me at the station at the junction-point. She had not been expecting this telegram, at least not so soon. And no wonder! Our trip to Berezov had taken over a month. St Petersburg papers were full of reports of our progress towards the North; reports were still arriving by mail. Everybody thought that I was on my way to Obdorsk. And yet I had made the entire return journey in eleven days. Obviously, the possibility of meeting me near St Petersburg must have seemed utterly incredible to my wife. That was all the better, and the meeting took place just the same.

This is how N. I. Sedova described it:

When I received the telegram in Terioki, a Finnish village near St Petersburg where I was staying alone with my baby son, I was beside myself with joy and excitement. That same day I received a long letter from L. D. written on his way to exile, in which, aside from its description of the journey, he asked me to take with me when I left for Obdorsk a number of articles necessary in the north, among them certain books. It now looked as if he had changed his mind and was flying back in some mysterious way, and was even arranging for me to meet him at a station where the trains cross. But strangely enough, the name of the station was left out of the telegram. Next day I went to St Petersburg and tried to find out from the railway guide what station I had to book a ticket for. I was afraid to make inquiries, and finally set off on my journey without knowing the name of the station. I booked for Viatka and left in the evening. The car was full of land-owners returning to their estates from St Petersburg, with parcels of table delicacies for the feast of Carnival week. The conversations were about pancakes, caviare, smoked sturgeon, wine, and such things. I could scarcely endure this talk – I was so excited about the meeting ahead of me, and I was worried by the fear of possible accidents . . . And yet, I felt sure that we would meet.

I could hardly wait for the morning when the train was to arrive at the station of Samino – I had found out its name on the way, and memorized it forever. The trains stopped; ours and the other. I ran out to the station. Nobody there. I jumped into the other train, ran through one car after another, and he was not there. Suddenly I recognized L. D.'s fur coat in a compartment. So he had come with the train. But where was he? I leaped out of the car, and immediately ran into L. D., who was rushing out of the station looking for me. He was indignant about the mutilation of the cable and wanted to make a complaint about it right away. I could stop him from doing so only with difficulty. After he had sent me the cable, he of course realized that instead of me, he might be met by the secret police, but he felt that being with me would make it easier for him in St Petersburg, and he trusted to his lucky star. We took our seats in the compartment, and continued our journey together. I could not help being amazed at L. D.'s freedom and ease as he laughed and chatted aloud in the train and at the station. I wanted to keep him invisible, to hide him away, because of the threat of hard-labour hanging over him for his escape. But he was in full view and said that it was his best protection.

From the station in St Petersburg we went straight to our loyal friends at the School of Artillery. I never saw people so startled as Dr Litkens's family. I stood like a ghost in the large dining-room, while they all looked at me breathless. After we had kissed each other they still could not believe their eyes and kept expressing their surprise. Finally they were convinced that it was I. Even now I feel that those were happy hours. But I was not out of danger yet. The doctor was the first to remind us of this. In a sense the danger was just beginning. There was no doubt that the authorities of Berezov had already sent telegrams about my disappearance. In St Petersburg, I was known to a great many people, thanks to my work at the Soviet of Delegates. So I decided to go with my wife to Finland, where the liberties won by the revolution were in operation much longer than in St Petersburg. The most dangerous place was the Finnish terminal in St Petersburg. Before the train started several secret police entered our car to look over the passengers. My wife sat facing the entrance-door, and I could tell from her eyes what danger we were in. We lived through a minute of terrific nervous tension. The police looked us over indifferently and walked on. That was all they were capable of.

Lenin and Martov had left St Petersburg long before, and were living in Finland. The union of the two factions that had been effected at the Stockholm congress was again showing a breach. The tide of the revolution was still ebbing. The Mensheviks were recanting the mad acts of 1905. The Bolsheviks were not recanting anything, and were getting ready for a new revolution. I visited both Lenin and Martov, who lived in neighbouring villages. Martov's room, as usual, was in a state of unutterable disorder. In the corner newspapers were piled as high as a man. During my conversation with him, Martov dived into the pile now and again to bring out an article that he wanted. Manuscripts covered with ashes lay on his table. The *pince-nez* that was never quite clean drooped on his thin nose. As always Martov had many ideas, brilliant and subtle ones, but he had not the one idea that was more important than any other: he did not know what to do next.

Lenin's room was the usual picture of order. Lenin did not smoke. The necessary newspapers, earmarked, lay close at hand. And above all there was in his prosaic but extraordinary face that expression of indomitably biding his time. It was then not yet clear whether the tide of revolution had definitely turned back, or had only slowed down before rising again. But in either case it was equally necessary to fight the sceptics, to review the experience of 1905 theoretically, to educate the rank-and-file for a new turn of the tide, or for a second revolution. Lenin spoke approvingly of my work in prison, but he taunted me for not drawing the necessary conclusions, in other words, for not going over to the Bolsheviks. He was right in this. As we parted he gave me some addresses in Helsingfors which proved invaluable to me.

The friends to whom Lenin directed me helped me to establish myself with my family in a comfortable little place in Oglbu, near Helsingfors, where some time afterwards Lenin also came to stay. The chief of police in Helsingfors was an activist, or revolutionary Finnish nationalist. He promised to give me due warning in case of any danger from St Petersburg. I stayed several weeks in Oglbu with my wife and infant son, who had been born while I was in prison. In the solitude of this village I described my journey in a book entitled *There and Back*, and with the money that I received from it went abroad by way of Stockholm. My wife and son stayed in Russia for the time being. I was accompanied to the frontier by a young Finnish woman who was also an activist. At that time the activists were friendly. In 1917 they became Fascists and bitter enemies of the October revolution.

On a Scandinavian steamer I set forth on a new foreign exile which was to last for ten years.

16

My Second Foreign Exile: German Socialism

The party congress of 1907 held its meetings in a socialist church in London. It was a protracted, crowded, stormy, and chaotic congress. The second Duma was still alive in St Petersburg. The revolution was subsiding, but it was still arousing great interest, even in English political circles. Prominent liberals invited the better-known delegates to their houses to show them off to their guests. The ebbing tide of the revolution was already evident in the lessening of the party funds. There was not enough money for the return journey, or even to carry the congress to its conclusion. When this sad news re-echoed under the arches of the church, cutting into the discussion on armed uprisings as it did, the delegates looked at one another in alarm and amazement. What was to be done? We could not stay in the church, of course. But a way out was found, and in quite unexpected form. An English liberal agreed to lend the Russian revolution three thousand pounds, as nearly as I can remember the figure. He demanded, however, that the revolutionary promissory note be signed by all the delegates at the congress, and so the Englishman received a document bearing several hundred signatures, in the characteristic signs of all the races of Russia. He had to wait a long time, however, for the payment of the note. During the years of the reaction and the war, the party could not even dream of such huge sums. It was the Soviet government that bought back the promissory note of the London congress. Revolution carries out its obligations, although usually not without delay.

On one of the first days of the congress I was stopped in the church vestibule by a tall, angular man with a round face and high cheek-bones, who wore a round hat. 'I am your admirer,' he said, with an amiable chuckle.

'Admirer?' I echoed in astonishment. It seemed that the compliment referred to my political pamphlets that had been written in prison. My interlocutor was Maxim Gorky, and this was the first time I ever saw him. 'I hope it is not necessary for me to say that I am your admirer,' I said, answering the compliment with another. In that period Gorky was close to the Bolsheviks. With him was the well-known actress Andreyeva. We went about London together.

'Would you believe it?' said Gorky, as he glanced at Andreyeva in amazement, 'she speaks all languages.' He himself spoke only Russian, but well. When some beggar would shut the door of the cab behind us, Gorky would plead: 'We ought to give him some of those pence.' To which Andreyeva would answer, 'They have been given, Alyosha dear, they have been given.'

At the London congress I renewed acquaintance with Rosa Luxemburg, whom I had known since 1904. She was a little woman, frail, and even sickly looking, but with a noble face, and beautiful eyes that radiated intelligence; she captivated one by the sheer courage of her mind and character. Her style, which was at once precise, intense and merciless, will always be the mirror of her heroic spirit. Hers was a many-sided nature, rich in subtle shadings. Revolution and its passions, man and art, nature, birds and growing things – all these could play on the many strings of her soul. 'I must have somebody', she wrote to Luise Kautsky, 'who believes me when I say that it is only through misunderstanding that I am in the midst of this whirlpool of world history, whereas in reality I was born to look after the geese in the fields.' My relations with Rosa were not marked by any personal friendship; our meetings were too brief and too infrequent. I admired her from a distance. And yet I probably did not appreciate her enough at that time. On the question of the so-called permanent revolution Rosa took the same stand as I did. In this connection Lenin and I once had a half-humorous conversation in the lobby. The delegates stood about us in a close ring. 'It is all because she does not speak Russian too well,' he said, referring to Rosa. 'But then, she speaks excellent Marxian,' I retorted. The delegates laughed, and so did we.

At the congress I had occasion to set forth again my view of the proletariat's part in the bourgeois revolution, and, in particular, of its relationship to the peasantry. In concluding the debate Lenin said in reference to this: 'Trotsky holds the view that the proletariat and the peasantry have common interests in the revolution of today.' Consequently: 'We have solidarity of views here as regards the fundamentals of our attitude towards the bourgeois parties.' How little does this resemble the legend that in 1905 I ignored the peasantry! I need only add that my London programme speech in 1907, which to this day I think is absolutely right, was reprinted separately after the October revolution as an example of the Bolshevik attitude towards the peasantry and the bourgeoisie.

From London I went to Berlin to meet my wife, who was to come from St Petersburg. By that time Parvus had also escaped from Siberia. In Dresden he arranged for the publication of my little book, *There and Back*, by Kaden's Social Democratic publishing company. For this booklet dealing with my escape I agreed to write a preface on the Russian revolution itself. Out of that preface, in the course of a few months there grew my book, *Russland in der Revolution*. My wife, Parvus and I went all three for a tramp through Saxon Switzerland. It was the end of the summer, the weather was magnificent, and the mornings were crisp; we drank quantities of milk as well as mountain air. An attempt to descend into a valley off the road nearly cost my wife and me our lives. Later we went to Bohemia, to a little hamlet called Hirschberg, a summer residence for petty officials, and stayed there several weeks. When our funds were getting low, and this happened periodically, either Parvus or I would dash off an article for the Social Democratic papers. While I was in Hirschberg, I wrote a book on the German Social Democracy for a Bolshevik printing house in St Petersburg. There, for the second time – the first was in 1905 – I set forth the idea that the gigantic machine of the German Social Democracy might, at a critical moment for the bourgeois society, prove to be the mainstay of the conservative order. At that time, however, I did not foresee to what extent this theoretical presumption would be confirmed by the facts. From Hirschberg we all went our separate ways – I to the congress at Stuttgart, my wife to Russia to get our child, and Parvus to Germany.

There still hovered over the congress of the Socialist International the echo of the storms of the Russian revolution of 1905. Everyone tried to keep in line with the left flank. But one noticed already a disappointment with revolutionary methods. Russian revolutionaries still aroused interest, but there was a touch of irony in it, as if people were saying: 'Here they are, back again.' When in February 1905 I was passing through Vienna on my way to Russia, I asked Victor Adler what he thought of the participation of the Social Democracy in the provisional government. Adler answered me in the Adler way: 'Your hands are too full with the *existing* government to puzzle your brains over the *future* one.' At Stuttgart I reminded him of his words. 'I confess that you came nearer to provisional government than I expected,' he said. Adler was generally very friendly to me – and if you look deeper, was not universal suffrage in Austria won by the St Petersburg Soviet of Workers' Delegates?

The English delegate at Stuttgart, Quelch, who had got me admission to the British Museum in 1902, at the congress referred disrespectfully to the diplomatic conference as a meeting of robbers. This did not find favour with Prince von Bülow. Under pressure from Berlin the Wurtemberg government expelled Quelch. Bebel immediately became ill at ease. The party could not pluck up enough courage to take steps against Quelch's expulsion. There was not even a single protest demonstration. The international congress was like a schoolroom: the rude boy is told to leave the room, and the rest keep silent. Behind the power in numbers of the German Social Democracy one could discern, all too clearly, the shadow of impotence.

In October 1907 I was already in Vienna. Soon my wife came with our child. While we were waiting for a new tide of revolution, we took up our quarters outside the city, at Hütteldorf. We had long to wait. We were carried away from Vienna seven years later by a very different tide – that one which soaked the soil of Europe with blood. Why did we choose Vienna when the rest of the foreign exiles were concentrated in Switzerland and

Paris? At that period my closest contacts were with German political life, but we could not settle down in Berlin because of the police. So we made Vienna our home. But during all those seven years I watched German life more attentively than I did Austrian, which reminded me too much of a squirrel in a cage.

Victor Adler, the recognized leader of the party, I had known since 1902. Now it was time for me to get acquainted with those who were around him, and with his party as a whole. I made the acquaintance of Hilferding in the summer of 1907, in Kautsky's house. He was then at the peak of his revolutionism, which did not prevent him from hating Rosa Luxemburg and from being contemptuous of Karl Liebknecht. But for Russia, in those days he was ready, like many another, to accept the most radical conclusions. He praised my articles which the *Neue Zeit* had managed to translate from the Russian periodicals even before I came abroad, and, quite unexpectedly for me, he insisted from the very first that we address each other as 'thou'. Because of this our outward relations took on the semblance of intimacy. But there was no moral or political basis for it.

Hilferding regarded the staid and passive German Social Democracy of that time with great contempt, and contrasted it with the activity of the Austrian party. This criticism, however, retained its fireside character. In practice Hilferding remained a literary official in the service of the German party – and nothing more. On his visits to Vienna he would come to see me and in the evenings would introduce me in the cafés to his friends among the Austrian Marxists. On my trips to Berlin I called on Hilferding. We once met Macdonald in one of the Berlin cafés. Eduard Bernstein acted as the interpreter. Hilferding asked the questions, Macdonald answered. Today I do not remember either the questions or the answers; they were distinguished only by their triteness. I asked myself which of these three men stood farthest from what I had been accustomed to call socialism. And I was at a loss for an answer.

During the Brest peace negotiations, I received a letter from Hilferding. Nothing of significance was to be expected from him, but nevertheless I opened the letter with interest. After the October revolution, this was the first direct voice from the socialist West. And what did I find? In his letter Hilferding asked me to free some war prisoner, one of the inescapable varieties of Viennese 'doctor'. *Of the revolution, the letter contained not a single word.* And yet he addressed me in the letter as 'thou'. I knew well enough the sort of person Hilferding was. I thought I had no illusions about him. But I could not believe my own eyes.

I remember the lively interest with which Lenin asked me: 'I hear that you had a letter from Hilferding?'

'I did.'

'Well?'

'He asks us to help his relative, a prisoner.'

'And what does he say about the revolution?'

'Nothing about the revolution.'

'Nothing?'

'Nothing.'

'Incredible,' said Lenin, staring at me. I was less at a loss because I had already accepted the thought that the October revolution and the tragedy at Brest were for Hilferding merely an occasion to ask favours for a relative. I will spare the reader the two or three epithets with with Lenin vented his amazement.

It was Hilferding who first introduced me to his friends in Vienna, Otto Bauer, Max Adler, and Karl Renner. They were well-educated people whose knowledge of various subjects was superior to mine. I listened with intense and, one might almost say, respectful interest to their conversation in the 'Central' café. But very soon I grew puzzled. These people were not revolutionaries. Moreover, they represented the type that was furthest from that of the revolutionary. This expressed itself in everything – in their approach to subjects, in their political remarks and psychological appreciations, in their self-satisfaction – not self-assurance, but self-satisfaction. I even thought I sensed philistinism in the quality of their voices.

I was surprised to find that these educated Marxists were absolutely incapable of applying Marx's method as soon as they came to the big problems of politics, especially its revolutionary turns. I first became convinced of this with regard to Renner. We sat very late in a café; it was too late to catch a street-car to

Hütteldorf where I was living, and so Renner invited me to spend the night at his place. At that time it never entered the head of this educated and talented Hapsburg official that the unhappy destiny of Austria-Hungary, whose historical advocate he then was, would make him, ten years later, the chancellor of the Austrian republic. On the way from the café we spoke of the possible developments in Russia, where the counter-revolution was then firmly in the saddle. Renner discussed these questions with the civility and indifference of an educated foreigner. The Austrian ministry of the day, under Baron Beck, interested him much more. His view of Russia was substantially this: that the alliance between the landlords and the bourgeoisie which found its expression in Stolypin's constitution after the *coup d'état* of 3 June 1907 fully corresponded to the stage of development of the productive forces of the country, and consequently had every chance of surviving. I retorted that, as I saw it, the ruling bloc of the landlords and the bourgeoisie was paving the way for a second revolution, which in all likelihood would transfer the power to the Russian proletariat. I remember Renner's fleeting, puzzled, and at the same time condescending glance at me under the lamp-post. He probably considered my prognosis as ignorant raving, rather like the apocalyptic prophecies of an Australian mystic who, a few months earlier, at the International Socialist Congress at Stuttgart, had prophesied the date and hour of the coming world revolution.

'You think so?' he asked, adding with deadly civility: 'Probably I am not sufficiently well acquainted with the conditions in Russia.' We had no common ground for continuing our conversation. I saw clearly that the man was as far from revolutionary dialectics as the most conservative Egyptian pharaoh.

My first impressions were only intensified by further observations. These men knew a great deal, and they were capable, within the limits of political routine, of writing good Marxist articles. But to me they were strangers. I was more firmly convinced of this, the more extensive my connections became and the keener my observations grew. In informal talks among themselves, they revealed, much more frankly than in their articles and speeches, either undisguised chauvinism, or the bragging of a petty proprietor, or holy terror of the police, or vileness towards women. In amazement I often exclaimed, 'What revolutionaries!' I am not referring here to the workers who, of course, also have many philistine traits, though of a more naïve and simple sort. No, I was meeting the flower of the pre-war Austrian Marxists, members of parliament, writers, and journalists. At those meetings, I learned to understand the extraordinary variety of the elements that can be comprised within the mind of one man, and the great distance which separates the mere passive assimilation of certain parts of a system from its complete psychological re-creation as a whole, from re-educating oneself in the spirit of a system. The psychological type of Marxist can develop only in an epoch of social cataclysms, of a revolutionary break with traditions and habits; whereas an Austrian Marxist too often revealed himself a philistine who had learned certain parts of Marx's theory as one might study law, and had lived on the interest that *Das Kapital* yielded him. In the old imperial, hierarchic, vain and futile Vienna, the academic Marxists would refer to each other with a sort of sensuous delight as 'Herr Doktor'. Workers often called the academicians, 'Genosse Herr Doktor'. During all the seven years that I lived in Vienna, I never had a heart-to-heart talk with any one of this upper group, although I was a member of the Austrian Social Democracy, attended their meetings, took part in their demonstrations, contributed to their publications, and sometimes made short speeches in German. I felt that the leaders of the Social Democrats were alien, whereas I found, quite easily, a mutual language with the Social Democratic workers at meetings or at May Day demonstrations.

In this atmosphere the correspondence between Marx and Engels was one of the books that I needed most, and one that stood closest to me. It supplied me with the greatest and most unfailing test for my own ideas as well as for my entire personal attitude towards the rest of the world. The Viennese leaders of the Social Democracy used the same formulas that I did. But one had only to turn any of them five degrees around on their axes to discover that we gave quite different meanings to the same concepts. Our agreement was a temporary one, superficial and unreal. The correspondence between Marx and Engels was for me not a theoretical one, but a psychological revelation. *Toutes proportions gardées*, I found proof on every page that to these two I was bound by a direct psychological affinity. Their attitude to men and ideas was mine. I guessed what they did not express, shared their sympathies, was indignant and hated as they did. Marx and Engels were revolutionaries through and through. But they had not the slightest trace of sectarianism or asceticism. Both of them, and especially Engels, could at any time say of themselves that nothing human was strange to them. But their revolutionary outlook lifted them always above the hazards of fate and the works of men. Pettiness was incompatible not only with their personalities, but with their presences. Vulgarity could not stick even to the soles of their boots. Their appreciations, sympathies, jests – even when most commonplace – are always touched by the rarefied air of spiritual nobility. They may pass deadly criticism on a man, but they will never deal in tittle-tattle. They can be ruthless, but not treacherous. For outward glamour, titles, or rank they have nothing but a cool contempt. What philistines and vulgarians considered aristocratic in them was really only their revolutionary superiority. Its most important characteristic is a complete and ingrained independence of official public opinion at all times and under all conditions. When I read their letters, I felt, even more than when I read their writings, that the same thing which bound me so closely to the world of Marx and Engels placed me in irreconcilable opposition to the Austrian Marxists.

These people prided themselves on being realists and on being business-like. But even here they swam in shallow water. In 1907, to increase its income, the party set out to establish its own bread-factory. This was the crudest adventure possible, one that was dangerous in principle and utterly hopeless in any practical sense. I fought against the venture from the start, but I was met with a smile of condescending superiority from the Vienna Marxists. Nearly twenty years later, after many vagaries and losses, the Austrian party had shamefacedly to hand it over to private hands. In defending themselves against the displeasure of the workers who had made so many futile sacrifices, Otto Bauer tried to prove the necessity of abandoning the factory by afterwards quoting, among others, the warnings I had given them at the outset. But he did not explain to the workers why he had failed to see what I had seen, and why he did not act upon my warnings, which were not all the result of my personal powers of insight. I based my opinions neither on the situation in the bread-market nor on the state of the membership of the party, but on the position of the proletariat party in capitalist society. This seemed like dogmatic theorizing, but it proved to be the best criterion. The confirming of my warnings only meant the superiority of the Marxist method over its Austrian counterfeit.

Victor Adler was in all respects far above the rest of his colleagues. But he had long been a sceptic. In the Austrian scramble his fighting temper was wasted on little things. The vistas of the future were obscure, and Adler turned his back on them, sometimes demonstratively. 'The business of a prophet is a thankless one, and especially in Austria' – this was the constant refrain of his speeches. 'You may say what you like,' he said in the lobby of the Stuttgart congress, apropos of the above-mentioned Australian prophecy, 'but for my part I prefer political predictions based on the Apocalypse to those supported by a materialistic interpretation of history.'

This was, of course, a jest. And yet not merely that. It was this that placed Adler and me at opposite poles in the things that were most vital to me; without a broad political view of the future I cannot conceive either of political activity or of intellectual life in general. Victor Adler became a sceptic, and as such he tolerated everything and adapted himself to everything, especially to the nationalist spirit which had corroded the Austrian Social Democracy to the very core.

My relations with the leaders of the party were even more strained when I came out openly against the chauvinism of the Austro-German Social Democracy. This was in 1909. During my meetings with the Balkan Socialists, and especially with the Serbs – one of whom was Dmitry Tutsovitch who later was killed as an officer of the Balkan war – I had heard indignant complaints to the effect that all the Serbian bourgeois press was quoting the chauvinist outbursts of the *Arbeiter-Zeitung* with a sort of malicious delight, in proof of the fact that the international solidarity of workers was no more than a fraudulent tale. I wrote a very cautious and tempered article against the chauvinism of the *Arbeiter-Zeitung* and sent it to the *Neue Zeit*. After much hesitation, Kautsky published the article. The next day an old Russian émigré, Klyachko, with whom I was very friendly, informed me that the leaders of the party were angry with me . . . 'How dared he?'

Otto Bauer and other Austrian Marxists privately admitted that Leitner, the foreign-news editor, had gone too far. In this they were simply echoing Adler himself, who, although he tolerated extremes of chauvinism, did not approve of them. But in the face of daring interference from outside the leaders became united in sentiment. On one of the following Saturdays Otto Bauer came up to the table at which Klyachko and I were sitting and began to rail at me. I confess that under his torrent of words I did not know what to say. I was astounded not so much by his lecturing tone as by the nature of his arguments.

'What importance have Leitner's articles?' he demanded with an amusing haughtiness. 'Foreign policy does not exist for Austria-Hungary. No worker ever reads about it. It has not the slightest importance.'

I listened with wide-open eyes. These men, it seemed, believed neither in revolution nor in war. They wrote about war and revolution in their May Day manifestos, but they never took them seriously; they did not perceive that history had already poised its gigantic soldier's boot over the ant-heap in which they were rushing about with such self-abandon. Six years later they learned that foreign policy existed even for Austria-Hungary. And at the same time they began to speak in that same shameless language which they had learned from Leitner and other chauvinists like him.

In Berlin the atmosphere was different – though essentially perhaps not much better, still, different. The ridiculous mandarin attitude of the Vienna academists scarcely existed there. Relations were simpler. There was less nationalism, or at least it had not the incentive to reveal itself as often or as vociferously as it had in many-nationed Austria. For the time being nationalist sentiment seemed to have dissolved in the pride of the party – the most powerful Social Democracy, the first fiddle of the International!

For us Russians the German Social Democracy was mother, teacher, and living example. We idealized it from a distance. The names of Bebel and Kautsky were pronounced reverently. In spite of my disturbing theoretical premonitions about the German Social Democracy, already mentioned, at that period I was undeniably under its spell. This was heightened by the fact that I lived in Vienna, and when I visited Berlin off and on, I would compare with two Social Democratic capitals and console myself: No, Berlin is not Vienna.

In Berlin I attended two of the weekly meetings of the left-wingers. They were held on Fridays in the 'Rheingold' restaurant. The principal figure at these gatherings was Franz Mehring. Karl Liebknecht also came there; he always arrived late and left before the rest. I was taken there the first time by Hilferding. Then he still regarded himself as of the 'left', although he hated Rosa Luxemburg with the same fierce passion that Dashinsky was cultivating against her in Austria. My memory has retained nothing significant from these conversations. Mehring asked me ironically, with a twitch of his cheek – he suffered from a tic – which of his 'immortal works' had been translated into Russian. Hilferding, in conversation, referred to the German left-wingers as revolutionaries. 'We are revolutionaries? Bah!' Mehring interrupted him. 'Those are revolutionaries,' and he nodded in my direction. I knew Mehring too little and I had met philistines who spoke mockingly of the Russian revolution too often to be able to make out whether he was jesting or serious. But he was serious, as his subsequent life showed.

I met Kautsky for the first time in 1907. Parvus took me to his house. It was with much excitement that I walked up the steps of a neat little house in Friedenau, near Berlin. A white-haired and very jolly old man with clear blue eyes greeted me with the Russian: 'Zdravstvuyte'. With what I already knew of Kautsky from his books, this served to complete a very charming personality. The thing that appealed to me most was the absence of fuss, which, as I later discovered, was the result of his undisputed authority at that time and of the inner calm which it gave him. His opponents called him the 'papa' of the International. Sometimes he was called that by his friends, too, in a genial way. Kautsky's old mother, who wrote problem novels which she dedicated to 'her son and teacher', on her seventy-fifth birthday received a greeting from Italian socialists that read 'alla mamma del papa' (to papa's mama).

Kautsky saw his principal theoretical mission as the reconciling of reform and revolution. But he achieved his intellectual maturity during an era of reform. Reality was simply reform for him, revolution a misty historical prospect. After he had accepted Marxism as a complete system, Kautsky popularized it like a school-teacher. Great events were beyond his ken. His decline set in as early as the days of the revolution of 1905. One got little from conversation with Kautsky. His mind was too angular and dry, too lacking in nimbleness and psychological insight. His evaluations were schematic, his jokes trite. For the same reason he was a poor speaker.

Kautsky's friendship with Rosa Luxemburg coincided with the best period of his intellectual activity. But soon after the 1905 revolution appeared the first signs of a growing coolness between them. Kautsky warmly sympathized with the Russian revolution, and could interpret it fairly well – from afar. But he was by nature hostile to a transfer of revolutionary methods to German soil. When I came to his house before the demonstration in Treptow Park, I found Rosa engaged in a heated argument with him. Although they still addressed each other as 'thou', and spoke as intimate friends, in Rosa's retorts one could hear suppressed indignation, and in Kautsky's answers one sensed a profound inner embarrassment disguised by rather uncertain jokes. We went to the demonstration together – Rosa, Kautsky, his wife, Hilferding, the late Gustav Eckstein, and I. There were more sharp clashes on the way. Kautsky wanted to remain an onlooker, whereas Rosa was anxious to join the demonstration.

The antagonism between them burst out in 1910 over the

question of the struggle for suffrage in Prussia. Kautsky developed at that time the strategic philosophy of wearing out the enemy (*Ermattungsstrategie*) as opposed to the strategy of overthrowing the enemy (*Niederwerfungsstrategie*). It was a case of two irreconcilable tendencies. Kautsky's line was that of an increasingly firm adaptation to the existing system. In the process what was 'worn out' was not bourgeois society, but the revolutionary idealism of the masses of workers. All the philistines, all the officials, all the climbers sided with Kautsky, who was weaving for them the intellectual garments with which to hide their nakedness.

Then came the war; the political strategy of exhaustion was ousted by the trench variety. Kautsky was adapting himself to the war in the same way that he had been adapting himself to peace. But Rosa showed how she interpreted loyalty to her ideas.

I remember the celebration in Kautsky's house of Ledebour's sixtieth birthday. Among the guests was August Bebel, already past his seventieth year. It was at the time when the party was at its peak; they were united in policy; the elders recorded the successes and looked into the future with assurance. During the supper Ledebour, the centre of the festivity, drew amusing caricatures. It was at this party that I first met Bebel and his Julia. Everyone there, including Kautsky, listened avidly to every word that old Bebel uttered. Needless to say, I did too.

Bebel personified the slow and stubborn movement of a new class that was rising from below. This withered old man seemed to have been cut out of patient but adamantine will directed towards a single end. In his reasoning, in his eloquence, in his articles and books, Bebel knew no such thing as expending mental energy on an object which did not immediately serve some practical purpose. The quiet magnificence of his political pathos lay in this. He reflected the class that gets its learning during its spare hours, values every minute, and absorbs voraciously only what is strictly necessary – an incomparable portrait of a *man*. Bebel died during the Bucharest peace conference in the interval between the Balkan war and the World war. The news reached me at the station in Ploesci, Roumania. It seemed incredible: Bebel dead! What would happen to the Social

Democracy? Ledebour's words about the core of the German party instantly flashed through my mind: twenty per cent radicals, thirty per cent opportunists – and the rest follow Bebel.

Bebel's fond hopes for a successor centred in Haase. The old man was doubtless attracted by Haase's idealism – not broad revolutionary idealism, which Haase did not possess, but a narrower, more personal, everyday sort of idealism; one might instance his readiness to sacrifice a rich legal practice at Königsberg to party interests. To the great embarrassment of the Russian revolutionaries, Bebel referred to this not very heroic sacrifice even in his speech at the party congress – I think it was in Jena – and insistently recommended Haase for the post of second chairman of the party's central committee. I knew Haase fairly well. After one of the party congresses we joined each other for a tour of some parts of Germany, and saw Nuremberg together. Gentle and considerate as he was in personal relations, in politics Haase remained to the end what his nature intended him to be – an honest mediocrity, a provincial democrat without revolutionary temperament or theoretical outlook. In the realm of philosophy he called himself, somewhat shyly, a Kantian. Whenever the situation was critical, he was inclined to refrain from final decisions; he would resort to half-measures and wait. No wonder the party of the independents later chose him as its leader.

Karl Liebknecht was entirely different. I knew him for many years, but there were long intervals between our meetings. Liebknecht's Berlin house was the headquarters of the Russian émigrés. Every time it was necessary to raise a voice of protest against the friendly assistance the German police gave Tsarism, we referred first to Liebknecht, and he rapped at all the doors and at all the skulls. Although he was an educated Marxist, he was not a theorist but a man of action. His was an impulsive, passionate and heroic nature; he had, moreover, real political intuition, a sense of the masses and of the situation, and an incomparable courage of initiative. He was a revolutionary. It was because of this that he was always a half-stranger in the house of the German Social Democracy, with its bureaucratic faith in measured progress and its ever-present readiness to draw back.

What a group of philistines and shallow vulgarians were they, who, under my own eyes, looked down ironically at Liebknecht!

At the Social Democratic congress at Jena in the early part of September 1911 I was asked at Liebknecht's suggestion to speak on the tyrannies of the Tsarist government in Finland. But before my turn came a report was received of the assassination of Stolypin in Kiev. Bebel immediately began to question me: What did the assassination mean? Which party was responsible for it? Would not my proposed speech attract unwelcome attention from the German police?

'Do you fear,' I asked the old man cautiously, remembering Quelch's case in Stuttgart, 'that my making a speech may cause trouble?'

'I do,' answered Bebel. 'I should prefer, I confess, that you do not speak.'

'In that case there can be no question of my speaking.'

Bebel sighed with relief. A minute later Liebknecht came rushing over to me with a disturbed look on his face. 'Is it true that you have been asked not to speak? And that you agreed?'

'How could I refuse?' I answered, trying to excuse myself. 'The host here is Bebel, not I.'

Liebknecht gave vent to his indignation in a speech in which he lashed the Tsar's government mercilessly, ignoring the signals of the presidium, who did not want to create complications by *lèse-majesté*. All the subsequent developments had their germ in these small episodes.

When the Czech trade unions opposed the German leadership, the Austrian Marxists advanced, against the split in the trade organizations, arguments which skilfully counterfeited internationalism. At the International Congress in Copenhagen the report on the question was read by Plekhanov. Like all of the Russians, he completely and unreservedly supported the German point of view as opposed to the Czech. Plekhanov's candidacy as chairman of the committee was put forward by old Adler, who found it more convenient in such a delicate matter to have a Russian for the principal accuser of Slavic chauvinism. For my part I of course could have nothing in common with the sorry national narrowness of such men as Nemec, Soukup, or Smeral, who tried hard to convince me of the justice of the Czech case. At the same time I had watched the inner life of the Austrian labour movement too closely to throw all or even the principal blame upon the Czechs. There was plenty of evidence that the rank and file of the Czech party were more radical than the Austro-German party, and that the legitimate dissatisfaction of the Czech workers with the opportunist leadership of Vienna would be cleverly utilized by Czech chauvinists like Nemec.

On the way from Vienna to the congress at Copenhagen at one of the stations where I had to change trains, I suddenly met Lenin on his way from Paris. We had to wait about an hour, and a significant conversation took place there, in its first stages very friendly, later quite the opposite. I argued that if anyone was to blame for the secession of the Czech trade unions, it was first of all the Vienna leaders, who made high-sounding appeals to fight to the workers of all countries, including the Czechs, and then always ended in deals behind the scenes with the monarchy. Lenin listened to me with great interest. He had a peculiar capacity for attention, watching the speech of his interlocutor for the exact thing he wanted, and meanwhile looking past him into space.

Our conversation assumed a very different character, however, when I told Lenin of my latest article in the *Vorwaerts* about the Russian Social Democracy. The article was written for the congress, and was severely criticized by both the Mensheviks and the Bolsheviks. The most prickly question in the article was that of so-called 'expropriations'. After the defeat of the revolution, armed 'expropriations' and terrorist acts inevitably tended to disorganize the revolutionary party itself. The London Congress, by a majority of votes composed of Mensheviks, Poles and some Bolsheviks, banned 'expropriations'. When the delegates shouted from their seats: 'What does Lenin say? We want to hear Lenin,' the latter only chuckled, with a somewhat cryptic expression. After the London Congress, 'expropriations' continued; they were harmful to the party. That was the point on which I had centred my attack in the *Vorwaerts*.

'Did you really write like this?' Lenin asked me reproachfully.

At his request I repeated to him from memory the principal ideas as I had formulated them in the article.

'Could it be stopped by telegraph?'

'No,' I answered. 'The article was to appear this morning – and what's the use of holding it up? It is perfectly right.'

As a matter of fact, the article was not right, for it assumed that the party would take shape by the union of the Bolsheviks and the Mensheviks, cutting off the extremes, whereas in reality the party was formed by a merciless war of the Bolsheviks against the Mensheviks. Lenin tried to induce the Russian delegation at the congress to condemn my article. This was the sharpest conflict with Lenin in my whole life. He was unwell at the time; he was suffering from a violent toothache, and his head was all bandaged. In the Russian delegation the attitude towards the article and its author was rather hostile; the Mensheviks were no less displeased with another article in which the main ideas were directed chiefly against them.

'What a disgusting article he has in the *Neue Zeit*!' Axelrod wrote Martov in October 1910. 'Perhaps even more disgusting than the one in the *Vorwaerts*.'

'Plekhanov, who disliked Trotsky intensely,' Lunarcharsky writes, 'took advantage of the situation and tried to engineer bringing him to trial. I thought this was not fair and spoke for Trotsky. Together with Ryazanov, we helped to collapse Plekhanov's plan.' The majority of the Russian delegation knew the article only from indirect reports. I demanded that it be read. Zinoviev argued that there was no need of reading the article to condemn it. The majority did not agree with him. The article was read aloud and translated, if my memory serves me, by Ryazanov. The previous account of the article pictured it as such a monstrous thing that its reading was an anticlimax; it sounded perfectly harmless. By an overwhelming majority of votes, the delegation declined to condemn it. This does not prevent me today from condemning the article as an incorrect evaluation of the Bolshevik faction.

On the question of the Czech trade-unions, the Russian delegation voted at the congress for the Vienna resolution as opposed to the one moved by Prague. I tried to move an amendment, but with no success. After all, I was not yet sure of the sort of amendment that must be made to the entire policy of the Social Democracy. The amendment should have been in the nature of a declaration of a holy war against it. This move we did not make until 1914.

17

Preparing for a New Revolution

During the years of the reaction my work consisted chiefly of interpreting the revolution of 1905, and of paving the way for the next revolution by theoretical research. Shortly after my arrival abroad I toured the Russian émigré and student colonies with two lectures: 'The Fate of the Russian Revolution: Apropos the Present Political Situation', and 'Capitalism and Socialism: Social Revolutionary Prospects'. The first lecture aimed to show that the prospect of the Russian Revolution as a permanent revolution was confirmed by the experience of 1905. The second lecture connected the Russian with the world revolution.

In October 1908 I began to publish in Vienna a Russian paper, *Pravda* (*The Truth*), a paper with an appeal to the masses of workers. It was smuggled into Russia either across the Galician frontier or by way of the Black Sea. The paper was published for three and a half years as a bi-monthly, but even at that it involved a great deal of work. The secret correspondence with Russia took a lot of time. In addition I was in contact with the underground union of Black Sea seamen and helped them to publish their organ.

My chief contributor to the *Pravda* was A. A. Joffe, who later became a well-known Soviet diplomatist. The Vienna days were the beginning of our friendship. Joffe was a man of great intellectual ardour, very genial in all personal relations, and unswervingly loyal to the cause. He gave to the *Pravda* both money and all his strength. Joffe suffered from a nervous complaint and was then being psychoanalysed by the well-known Viennese specialist, Alfred Adler, who began as a pupil of Freud but later opposed his master and founded his own school of individual psychology. Through Joffe I became acquainted with the problems of psychoanalysis, which fascinated me, although much in this field is still vague and unstable and opens the way for fanciful and arbitrary ideas. My other contributor was a student named Skobelev, who later became the minister of labour in Kerensky's government; we met in 1917 as enemies. I had Victor Kopp for a while as secretary of the *Pravda*; he is now Soviet ambassador to Sweden.

In connection with the activities of the *Pravda* Joffe went to Russia for revolutionary work. He was arrested in Odessa, spent a long time in prison, and was later exiled to Siberia. He was not set free until February 1917, as a result of the revolution of that month. In the October revolution which followed he played one of the most active parts. The personal bravery of this very sick man was really magnificent. I can still see him in the autumn of 1919 – as clearly as if it were today – with his rather thick-set figure on the shell-ridden field below St Petersburg. In the immaculate dress of a diplomat, with a gentle smile on his calm face and a cane in his hand, as if he were merely walking along Unter den Linden, Joffe watched the shells exploding near by, curiously, without speeding or slowing his steps. He was a good speaker, thoughtful and earnest in appeal, and he showed the same qualities as a writer. In everything he did, he paid the most exacting attention to detail – a quality that not many revolutionaries have. Lenin had a very high opinion of his diplomatic work. For a great many years I was bound to him more closely than anyone else. His loyalty to friendship as well as to principle was unequalled. Joffe ended his life tragically. Grave hereditary diseases were undermining his health. Just as seriously, too, he was being undermined by the unbridled baiting of Marxists led by the epigones. Deprived of the chance of fighting his illness, and so deprived of the political struggle, Joffe committed suicide in the autumn of 1927. The letter he wrote me before his death was stolen from his dressing-table by Stalin's agents. Lines intended for the eyes of a friend were torn from their context, distorted and belied by Yaroslavsky and others intrinsically demoralized. But this will not prevent Joffe from being inscribed as one of the noblest names in the book of the revolution.

In the darkest days of the reaction Joffe and I were confidently waiting for a new revolution, and we pictured it in the very way in which it actually evolved in 1917. Sverchkov, at that time a Menshevik and today a follower of Stalin, writes of the Vienna *Pravda* in his memoirs:

In this paper, he [Trotsky] continued to advocate, insistently and unswervingly, the idea of the 'permanency' of the Russian revolution, which argues that after the revolution has begun it cannot come to an end until it effects the overthrow of capitalism and establishes the socialist system throughout the world. He was laughed at, accused of romanticism and the seven mortal sins by both the Bolsheviks and the Mensheviks. But he stuck to his point with tenacity and firmness, impervious to the attacks.

In 1909, writing in the Polish magazine of Rosa Luxemburg, I characterized the revolutionary relationship between the proletariat and the peasantry in the following words:

Local cretinism is the historical curse of the peasant movements. It was on the circumscribed political intelligence of the peasant who while in his village plundered his landlord in order to seize his land, but then, decked out in a soldier's coat, shot down the workers, that the first wave of the Russian revolution (1905) broke. The events of that revolution may be regarded as a series of ruthless object-lessons by means of which history is hammering into the head of the peasant the consciousness of the ties which connect his local demand for land with the central problem of the state power.

Quoting the example of Finland, where the Social Democracy won great influence among the peasants by its stand on the question of the small farmer, I concluded: 'What great influence will our party then wield over the peasantry, in the exercise of its leadership of a new and much more widespread movement of the masses in town and country! Provided, of course, that we do not lay down our arms in our fear of the temptations of political power to which we will inevitably be subjected by the new wave to come.'

How much like 'ignoring the peasantry' or 'jumping over the agrarian question' that is!

On 4 December 1909, at a time when the revolution seemed

to have been hopelessly and permanently trampled under, I wrote in the *Pravda*: 'Even today, through the black clouds of the reaction which have surrounded us, we envisage the victorious reflection of the new October.' Not only the liberals but the Mensheviks as well ridiculed these words, which they regarded as a mere slogan for agitation, as a phrase without content. Professor Miliukoff, to whom the honour of coining the term 'Trotskyism' belongs, retorted: 'The idea of dictatorship by the proletariat is purely childish, and there is not a man in Europe who will support it.' And yet there were events in 1917 which must have shaken the magnificent confidence of the liberal professor.

During the years of the reaction I studied the questions of trade and industry both on a world scale and a national scale. I was prompted by a revolutionary interest. I wanted to find out the relationship between the fluctuations of trade and industry on the one hand, and the progressive stages of the labour movement and revolutionary struggle on the other. In this, as in all other questions like it, I was especially on my guard to avoid establishing an automatic dependence of politics on economics. The interaction must necessarily be the result of the whole process considered in its entirety.

I was still living in the little Bohemian town of Hirschberg when the New York stock exchange suffered the 'Black Friday' catastrophe. This was the harbinger of a world crisis which was bound to engulf Russia as well, shaken to her foundations as she was by the Russo–Japanese war and by the ensuing revolution. What consequences could be expected? The point of view generally accepted in the party, without distinction of faction, was that the crisis would serve to heighten the revolutionary struggle. I took a different stand. After a period of big battles and defeats, a crisis has the effect of depressing rather than arousing the working class. It undermines the workers' confidence in their powers and demoralizes them politically. Under such conditions, only an industrial revival can close the ranks of the proletariat, pour fresh blood into its veins, restore its confidence in itself and make it capable of further struggle.

This analysis was met with criticism and incredulity. The official party economists also put forward the idea that under the counter-revolution a trade boom was impossible. In opposition, I based my argument on the inevitability of an economic revival and of the new wave of strikes it would bring in its wake, after which a new economic crisis would be likely to provide the impetus for a revolutionary struggle. This prognosis was confirmed to the letter. An industrial boom came in 1910, in spite of the counter-revolution – and with it came strikes. The shooting down of the workers at the Lena gold mines in 1912 gave rise to great protests all over the country. In 1914, when the crisis was unmistakable, St Petersburg again became an arena of workers' barricades. They were witnessed by Poincaré, who visited the Tsar on the eve of the war.

This theoretical and political test was invaluable in my future activities. At the Third Congress of the Communist International I had an overwhelming majority of the delegates against me when I insisted on the inevitability of an economic revival in post-war Europe as a condition for further revolutionary crises. And again in recent times I had to bring against the Sixth Congress of the Communist International the charge of utter failure to understand the break in the economic and political situation in China, a failure which found expression in unwarranted hopes that the Chinese revolution, in spite of the disastrous defeats it had suffered, would continue to progress because of the country's growing economic crisis.

The dialectics of the process are really not very complex. But they are easier to formulate than to discover every time in the living facts. At any rate, in the discussions of this question I am constantly coming across the most tenacious prejudices, which lead in politics to grave errors and painful consequences.

In its view of the future of Menshevism and of the problems of organization within the party, the *Pravda* never arrived at the preciseness of Lenin's attitude. I was still hoping that the new revolution would force the Mensheviks – as had that of 1905 – to follow a revolutionary path. But I underestimated the importance of preparatory ideological selection and of political case-hardening. In questions of the inner development of the party I was guilty of a sort of *social-revolutionary* fatalism. This was a mistaken stand, but it was vastly superior to that *bureaucratic* fatalism, devoid of ideas, which distinguishes the majority of my present-day critics in the camp of the Communist International.

In 1912, when the political curve in Russia took an unmistakable upward turn, I made an attempt to call a union conference of representatives of all the Social Democratic factions. To show that I was not alone in the hope of restoring the unity of the Russian Social Democracy, I can cite Rosa Luxemburg. In the summer of 1911 she wrote: 'Despite everything the unity of the party could still be saved if both sides could be *forced* to call a conference together.' In August 1911 she reiterated: 'The only way to save the unity is to bring about a general conference of people sent from Russia, for the people in Russia all want peace and unity, and they represent the only force that can bring the fighting-cocks abroad to their senses.'

Among the Bolsheviks themselves conciliatory tendencies were then still very strong, and I had hoped that this would induce Lenin also to take part in a general conference. Lenin, however, came out with all his force against union. The entire course of the events that followed proved conclusively that Lenin was right. The conference met in Vienna in August 1912, without the Bolsheviks, and I found myself formally in a 'bloc' with the Mensheviks and a few disparate groups of Bolshevik dissenters. This 'bloc' had no common political basis, because in all important matters I disagreed with the Mensheviks. My struggle against them was resumed immediately after the conference. Every day, bitter conflicts grew out of the deep-rooted opposition of the two tendencies, the social-revolutionary and the democratic-reformist.

'From Trotsky's letter', writes Axelrod on 4 May, shortly before the conference, 'I got the very painful impression that he had not the slightest desire to come to a real and friendly understanding with us and our friends in Russia . . . for a joint fight against the common enemy.' Nor had I, in fact, nor could I possibly have had, an intention of allying myself with the Mensheviks to fight against the Bolsheviks. After the conference Martov complained in a letter to Axelrod that Trotsky was reviving the 'worst habits of the Lenin–Plekhanov literary individualism'. The correspondence between Axelrod and Martov, published a few years ago, testifies to this perfectly unfeigned hatred of me. Despite the great gulf which separated me from them, I never had any such feeling towards them. Even today I gratefully remember that in earlier years I was indebted to them for many things.

The episode of the August bloc has been included in all the 'anti-Trotsky' text-books of the epigone period. For the benefit of the novices and the ignorant the past is there presented in such a way as to suggest that Bolshevism came out of the laboratory of history fully armed – whereas the history of the struggle of the Bolsheviks against the Mensheviks is also a history of ceaseless efforts towards unity. After his return to Russia in 1917, Lenin made the last effort to come to terms with the Mensheviks-Internationalists. When I arrived from America in May of the same year, the majority of the Social Democratic organizations in the provinces consisted of united Bolsheviks and Mensheviks. At the party conference in March 1917, a few days before Lenin's arrival, Stalin was preaching union with the party of Tzereteli. Even after the October revolution Zinoviev, Kamenev, Rykov, Lunacharsky and dozens of others were fighting madly for a coalition with the Social Revolutionaries and the Mensheviks. And these are the men who are now trying to sustain their ideological existence by hair-raising stories about the Vienna unity conference of 1912!

The *Kievskaya Mysl* (*The Kiev Thought*) made me an offer to go to the Balkans as its military correspondent. The proposal was all the more timely because the August conference had already proved to be abortive. I felt that I must break away, if only for a short time, from the interests of the Russian émigrés. The few months that I spent in the Balkans were the months of the war, and they taught me much.

In September 1912 I was on my way to the East, believing that war was not only probable but inevitable. But when I found myself on the pavements of Belgrade, and saw long lines of reservists; when I saw with my own eyes that there was no way back, that war was coming, almost any day; when I learned that a number of men whom I knew well were already in arms on the frontier and that they would be the first to kill or be killed – then war, which I had treated so lightly in my thoughts and my articles, seemed utterly incredible and impossible. I watched, as if it were a phantom, a regiment going to war – the eighteenth infantry regiment, in uniforms of protective colouring and bark sandals, and wearing a sprig of green in their caps. The ssndals on their feet and the little sprig of green in their caps, in combination with the full fighting outfit, gave the soldiers the look of men doomed for sacrifice. At that moment nothing so deeply burned the madness of war into my consciousness as those sprigs and bark sandals. How far the present generation has come from the habits and moods of 1912! I understood even then that the humanitarian, the moral, point of view of the historical process was the most sterile one. But it was the emotion, not its explanation, that mattered then. A sense of the tragedy of history, which words cannot suggest, was taking possession of me; a feeling of impotence before fate, a burning compassion for the human locust.

War was declared two or three days later. 'You in Russia know it, and believe in it,' I wrote, 'but here, on the spot, I do not believe in it. My mind does not accept this combination of the things of everyday life, of chicken, cigarettes, bare-footed and smut-nosed boys, with the incredibly tragic fact of war. I know that war has been declared, and that it has already begun, but I have not yet learned to believe in it.' I had to learn this, however, decisively and for a long time.

The years 1912–13 gave me a close acquaintance with Serbia, Bulgaria, Roumania – and with war. In many respects this was an important preparation not only for 1914 but for 1917 as well. In my articles I launched attacks on the falsity of Slavophilism, on chauvinism in general, on the illusions of war, on the scientifically organized system for duping public opinion. The editors of the *Kievskaya Mysl* had the courage to print my article describing the Bulgarian atrocities on the wounded and captured Turks, and exposing the conspiracy of silence on the part of the Russian press. This brought forth a storm of indignant protests from the liberal papers. On 30 January 1913 I published in the newspaper an 'ex-parliamentary question' to Miliukoff concerning the Slav atrocities to the Turks. Miliukoff, the permanent defence-attorney of official Bulgaria, was cornered and answered stammeringly. The controversy lasted for several weeks, with the government papers – as was inevitable – dropping hints that the pen name 'Antid Oto' disguised not only an émigré but also an agent of Austria-Hungary.

The month I spent in Roumania brought me into close contact with Dobrudjanu-Gherea, and cemented my friendship with Rakovsky, whom I had known since 1903, for ever.

A Russian revolutionary of the seventies stopped in Roumania in passing, on the very eve of the Russo–Turkish war; he was detained for a while by circumstances beyond his control; a few years later, under the name of Gherea, he had won far-reaching influence over the Roumanian intelligentsia, extending it later to the more advanced among the workers as well. Literary criticism on a social basis was Gherea's chief medium for shaping the more advanced groups among the Roumanian intelligentsia. Then, from questions of aesthetics and personal ethics, he led them to scientific socialism. The majority of Roumanian politicians of almost every party passed through, at least in their younger days, a brief school of Marxism under Gherea's guidance. It did not prevent them, however, from pursuing a policy of reactionary banditry in their riper age.

Ch. G. Rakovsky is, internationally, one of the best-known figures in the European socialist movement. A Bulgarian by birth, Rakovsky comes from the town of Kotel in the very heart of Bulgaria, but he is a Roumanian subject by dint of the Balkan map, a French physician by education, a Russian by connections, by sympathies and literary work. He speaks all the Balkan and four European languages; he has at various times played an active part in the inner workings of four Socialist parties – the Bulgarian, Russian, French, and Roumanian – to become eventually one of the leaders of the Soviet Federation, a founder of the Communist International, president of the Ukrainian Soviet of People's Commissaries, and the diplomatic Soviet representative in England and France – only to share finally the fate of all the 'left' opposition. Rakovsky's personal traits, his broad international outlook, his profound nobility of character, have made him particularly odious to Stalin, who personifies the exact opposite of these qualities.

In 1913 Rakovsky was the organizer and leader of the Roumanian Socialist party, which later joined the Communist International. The party was showing considerable growth. Rakovsky edited a daily paper, which he financed as well. On the coast of the Black Sea, not far from Mangalia, he owned a small estate which he had inherited, and with the income from it he supported the Roumanian Socialist party and several revolutionary groups and individuals in other countries. Every week he spent three days in Bucharest, writing articles, directing the sessions of the Central Committee, and speaking at meetings and street demonstrations. Then he would dash over to the Black Sea coast by train, carrying with him to his estate binder-twine, nails and other appurtenances of country life; he would drive out into the fields, watching the work of a new tractor, running behind it along the furrow in his frock-coat; then, a day later, he would be speeding back to town so as not to be late for a public meeting or for some private session. I accompanied him on one of his trips, and could not but admire his superabundant energy, his tirelessness, his constant spiritual alertness, and his kindness to and concern for unimportant people. Within fifteen minutes on a street in Mangalia Rakovsky would switch from Roumanian to Turkish, from Turkish to Bulgarian, and then to German and French when he was talking to colonists or to commercial agents; then, finally, he would speak Russian with the Russian Skoptsi, who are numerous in the adjoining district. He would carry on conversations as a landlord, as a doctor, as a Bulgarian, as a Roumanian subject and, chiefly, as a Socialist. In these aspects he passed before my eyes like a living miracle on the streets of this remote, leisurely and carefree little maritime town. And the same night he would again be dashing to the field of battle by train. He was always at ease and self-confident, whether he was in Bucharest or Sophia, in Paris, St Petersburg, or Kharkoff.

The years of my second foreign exile were years spent in

writing for the Russian democratic press. I made my *début* in the *Kievskaya Mysl* with a long article on the Munich journal, *Simplicissimus*, which at one time interested me so much that I went through all its issues from the very first one, when the cartoons by T. T. Heine were still impregnated with a poignant social feeling. My closer acquaintance with the new German fiction belongs to the same period. I even wrote a long social-critical essay on Wedekind, because interest in him was increasing in Russia with the decline of the revolutionary moods.

In the south of Russia the *Kievskaya Mysl* was the most popular radical paper of the Marxist hue. A paper like it could exist only in Kiev, with its feeble industrial life, its undeveloped class contradictions, and its long-standing traditions of intellectual radicalism. *Mutatis mutandis*, one can say that a radical paper appeared in Kiev for the same reason that *Simplicissimus* appeared in Munich. I wrote there on the most diverse subjects, sometimes very risky as regards censorship. Short articles were often the result of long preparatory work. Of course I couldn't say all that I wanted to in a legally published, non-partisan paper. But I never wrote what I did not want to say. My articles in the *Kievskaya Mysl* have been republished by a Soviet publishing house in several volumes; I didn't have to recant a thing. It may not be superfluous for the present moment to mention that I contributed to the bourgeois press with the formal consent of the Central Committee, on which Lenin had a majority.

I have already mentioned that immediately after our arrival in Vienna, we took quarters out of town. 'Hütteldorf pleased me,' wrote my wife.

The house was better than we could usually get, as the villas here were usually rented in the spring, and we rented ours for the autumn and winter. From the windows we could see the mountains, all dark-red autumn colours. One could get into the open country through a back gate without going to the street. In the winter, on Sundays, the Viennese came by on their way to the mountains, with sleds and skis, in little coloured caps and sweaters. In April, when we had to leave our house because of the doubling of the rent, the violets were already blooming in the garden and their fragrance filled the rooms from the open windows. Here Seryozha was born. We had to move to the more democratic Sievering.

The children spoke Russian and German. In the kindergarten and school they spoke German, and for this reason they continued to talk German when they were playing at home. But if their father or I started talking to them, it was enough to make them change instantly to Russian. If we addressed them in German, they were embarrassed, and answered us in Russian. In later years they also acquired the Viennese dialect and spoke it excellently.

They liked to visit the Klyachko family, where they received great attention from everybody – the head of the family, his wife, and the grown-up children – and were shown many interesting things and treated to others. The children were also fond of Ryazanov, the well-known Marxian scholar, who was then living in Vienna. He caught the imagination of the boys with his gymnastic feats, and appealed to them with his boisterous manner. Once when the younger boy Seryozha was having his hair cut by a barber and I was sitting near him, he beckoned to me to come over and then whispered in my ear: 'I want him to cut my hair like Ryazanov's.' He had been impressed by Ryazanov's huge smooth bald patch; it was not like everyone else's hair, but much better.

When Lyovik entered the school, the question of religion came up. According to the Austrian law then in force, children up to the age of fourteen had to have religious instruction in the faith of their parents. As no religion was listed in our documents, we chose the Lutheran for the children because it was a religion which seemed easier on the children's shoulders as well as their souls. It was taught in the hours after school by a woman teacher, in the schoolhouse; Lyovik liked this lesson, as one could see by his little face, but he did not think it necessary to talk about it. One evening I heard him muttering something when he was in bed. When I questioned him, he said, 'It's a prayer. You know prayers can be very pretty, like poems.'

Ever since my first foreign exile my parents had been coming abroad. They visited me in Paris; then they came to Vienna with my oldest daughter,* who was living with them in the country. In 1910 they came to Berlin. By that time they had become fully reconciled to my fate. The final argument was probably my first book in German.

My mother was suffering from a very grave illness (actinomy-

* By the author's first marriage. – *Translator*.

cosis). For the last ten years of her life she bore it as if it were simply another burden, without stopping her work. One of her kidneys was removed in Berlin; she was sixty then. For a few months after the operation her health was marvellous, and the case became famous in medical circles. But her illness returned soon after, and in a few months she passed away. She died at Yanovka, where she had spent her working life and had brought up her children.

The long Vienna episode in my life would not be complete without mention of the fact that our closest friends there were the family of an old émigré, S. L. Klyachko. The whole history of my second foreign exile is closely intertwined with this family. It was a centre of political and intellectual interests, of love of music, of four European languages, of various European connections. The death, in April 1914, of the head of the family, Semyon Lvovich, was a great loss to me and my wife. Leo Tolstoy once wrote of his very talented brother, Sergey, that he lacked only a few small defects to make him a great artist. One could say the same of Semyon Lvovich. He had all the abilities necessary to attain great prominence in politics, except that he hadn't the necessary defects. In the Klyachko family we always found friendship and help, and we often needed both.

My earnings at the *Kievskaya Mysl* were quite enough for our modest living. But there were months when my work for the *Pravda* left me no time to write a single paying line. The crisis set in. My wife learned the road to the pawn-shops, and I had to resell to the booksellers books bought in more affluent days. There were times when our modest possessions were confiscated to pay the house-rent. We had two babies and no nurse; our life was a double burden on my wife. But she still found time and energy to help me in revolutionary work.

18
The Beginning of the War

In Vienna the inscription 'Alle Serben müssen sterben' appeared on the hoardings, and the words became the cry of the street boys. Our youngest son, Seryozha, prompted, as usual, by an instinct for being contradictory, shouted on the Sievering Common: 'Hoch Serbien!' He came home with a black eye and experience in international politics.

Buchanan, the former British ambassador to St Petersburg, speaks with exaltation in his memoirs of 'those wonderful early August days' when 'Russia seemed to have been completely transformed'. There is similar exaltation in the memoirs of other statesmen, although they may not embody the self-satisfied fatuity of the ruling classes with the completeness of Buchanan. All the European capitals were having equally 'wonderful' days in August. They were all entirely 'transformed' for the business of mutual extermination.

The patriotic enthusiasm of the masses in Austria-Hungary seemed especially surprising. What was it that drew to the square in front of the War Ministry the Viennese bootmaker's apprentice, Pospischil, half German, half Czech; or our greengrocer, Frau Maresch; or the cabman Frankl? What sort of an idea? The national idea? But Austria-Hungary was the very negation of any national idea. No, the moving force was something different.

The people whose lives, day in and day out, pass in a monotony of hopelessness are many; they are the mainstay of modern society. The alarm of mobilization breaks into their lives like a promise; the familiar and long-hated is overthrown, and the new and unusual reigns in its place. Changes still more incredible are in store for them in the future. For better or worse?

For the better, of course – what can seem worse to Popischil than 'normal' conditions?

I strode along the main streets of the familiar Vienna and watched a most amazing crowd fill the fashionable Ring, a crowd in which hopes had been awakened. But wasn't a small part of these hopes already being realized? Would it have been possible at any other time for porters, laundresses, shoemakers, apprentices and youngsters from the suburbs to feel themselves masters of the situation in the Ring? War affects everybody, and those who are oppressed and deceived by life consequently feel that they are on an equal footing with the rich and powerful. It may seem a paradox, but in the moods of the Viennese crowd that was demonstrating the glory of the Hapsburg arms I detected something familiar to me from the October days of 1905 in St Petersburg. No wonder that in history war has often been the mother of revolution.

And yet how different, or, to be more precise, how contrasting, were the attitudes of the ruling classes to the one and to the other! To Buchanan those days seemed wonderful, and Russia transformed. On the other hand Witte wrote about the most pathetic days of the revolution of 1905: 'The overwhelming majority of Russians seem to have gone mad.'

Like revolution, war forces life, from top to bottom, away from the beaten track. But revolution directs its blows against the established power. War, on the contrary, at first strengthens the state power which, in the chaos engendered by war, appears to be the only firm support – and then undermines it. Hopes of strong social and national movements, whether it be in Prague or in Trieste, in Warsaw or Tiflis, are utterly groundless at the outset of a war. In September 1914 I wrote to Russia: 'The mobilization and declaration of war have veritably swept off the face of the earth all the national and social contradictions in the country. But this is only a political delay, a sort of political moratorium. The notes have been extended to a new date, but they will have to be paid.' In these censored lines, I referred, of course, not only to Austria-Hungary, but to Russia as well – in fact, to Russia most of all.

Events were crowding one another. There came the report of

the assassination of Jaurès. The newspapers were so full of malicious lies that there was still a possibility, for a few hours at least, of doubt and hope. But soon even this disappeared. Jaurès had been killed by his enemies and betrayed by his own party.

What attitude towards the war did I find in the leading circles of the Austrian Social Democracy? Some were quite obviously pleased with it, and spoke abusively of Serbians and Russians, making little distinction between the governments and the people. These were really nationalists, barely disguised under the veneer of a socialist culture which was now melting away as fast as it could. I remember Hans Deutsch, in later years some sort of a war minister, talking openly of the inevitability and the salutary nature of this war, which was at last to rid Austria of the Serbian 'nightmare'. Others, with Victor Adler at their head, regarded the war as an external catastrophe which they had to put up with. Their passive waiting, however, only served as a cover for the active nationalist wing. Some, with an air of being very profound, remembered the German victory of 1871, which gave an impetus to German industry, and, along with it, to the Social Democracy.

On 1 August Germany declared war against Russia. Even before then, Russians had begun to leave Vienna. On the morning of 3 August I went to the Wienzeile to take counsel with the Socialist deputies as to what we Russian émigrés should do. Friedrich Adler continued, through sheer inertia, to busy himself in his room with books, papers, and stamps for the International Socialist Congress soon to have met in Vienna. But the congress had already been relegated to the past – other forces were occupying the field. Old Adler suggested that he take me with him, at once, to headquarters, that is, to Geyer, the chief of the political police. On our way to the prefecture by automobile I drew Adler's attention to the festal mood that war alone had caused. 'It is those who do not have to go to war who show their joy,' he answered promptly. 'Besides, all the unbalanced, all the madmen now come out into the streets; it is their day. The murder of Jaurès is only the beginning. War opens the door for all instincts, all forms of madness.'

A psychiatrist by profession, Adler often approached political events – 'especially Austrian', he would remark ironically – from the psycho-pathological point of view. How far he then was from thinking that his own son would commit a political murder! On the very eve of the war I published an article in the *Kampf* magazine, edited by Adler's son, showing the futility of individual terrorism. It is significant that the editor warmly approved the article. The terrorist act committed by Friedrich Adler was merely an outburst of opportunism in despair, nothing more.* After he had vented his despair, he returned to his old rut.

Geyer cautiously indicated the possibility that all Russians and Serbians might be put under arrest the following morning.

'Then your advice is to leave?'

'The sooner, the better.'

'Good. I will leave with my family for Switzerland tomorrow.'

'Hm . . . I should prefer that you do it today.'

This conversation took place at three o'clock; at 6.10 that evening I was already sitting with my family in the train bound for Zurich. Behind us, we had left the ties of seven years, and books, papers, and unfinished writings, including a polemic against Professor Masaryk on the future prospects of Russian culture.

The telegram telling of the capitulation of the German Social Democracy shocked me even more than the declaration of war, in spite of the fact that I was far from a naïve idealizing of German socialism. 'The European socialist parties', I wrote as early as 1905, and reiterated more than once afterwards, 'have developed their own conservatism, which grows stronger the more the masses are captured by socialism. In view of this the Social Democracy can become, at a definite moment, an actual obstacle in the way of an open conflict between the workers and the bourgeois reaction. In other words the propagandist socialist conservatism of the proletariat party may at a certain moment obstruct the direct struggle for power by the proletariat.' I did

---

*Friedrich Adler, son of Victor Adler, shot Count Stuergkh, the Austro-Hungarian premier, on 21 October 1916. He received the death-sentence, later commuted to imprisonment. He was released from prison by the revolution of 1918. – *Translator.*

not expect the official leaders of the International, in case of war, to prove themselves capable of serious revolutionary initiative. At the same time I could not even admit the idea that the Social Democracy would simply cower on its belly before a nationalist militarism.

When the issue of the *Vorwaerts* that contained the report of the meeting of the Reichstag on 4 August arrived in Switzerland, Lenin decided that it was a faked number published by the German general staff to deceive and frighten their enemies. For, despite his critical mind, Lenin's faith in the German Social Democracy was still as strong as that. At the same time the Vienna *Arbeiter-Zeitung* proclaimed the day of the capitulation of German Socialism as 'the great day of the German nation'. This was the cap-sheaf of Austerlitz – his own 'Austerlitz'! I did not think the *Vorwaerts* a fake; my first personal impressions in Vienna had already prepared me for the worst. Nevertheless the vote of 4 August has remained one of the tragic experiences of my life. What would Engels have said? I asked myself. To me, the answer was obvious. And how would Bebel have acted? Here, I was not so certain. But Bebel was dead. There was only Haase, an honest provincial democrat, with no theoretical outlook or revolutionary temper. In every critical situation he was inclined to refrain from decisive solutions; he preferred to resort to half-measures and to wait. Events were too great for him. And beyond him one saw the Scheidemanns, the Eberts, the Welses.

Switzerland reflected Germany and France only in a neutral, that is to say, a subdued, way and also on a much-reduced scale. As if to make the situation more obvious, the Swiss parliament had as members two Socialist deputies with identical names: one was Johann Sigg from Zurich, the other Jean Sigg from Geneva. Johann was a rabid Germanophile and Jean a still more rabid Francophile. Such was the Swiss mirror of the International.

About the second month of the war, in a street in Zurich I met old Molkenbuhr, who had come there to mould public opinion. To my question as to how his party visualized the course of the world war, the old member of the *Vorstand* answered: 'During the next two months we will finish France; then we will turn to the east and finish the Tsar's armies; and three, or at most, four months later, we will give Europe a lasting peace.' This answer is entered in my diary word for word. Molkenbuhr was stating, of course, not his own estimate of the situation; he was simply expressing the official opinion of the Social Democracy. At the same time the French ambassador to St Petersburg wagered Buchanan five pounds sterling that the war would be over before Christmas. No, we 'utopians' foresaw things a little better than these realistic gentlemen from the Social Democracy and the diplomatic circles.

Switzerland, our refuge from the war, reminded me of my Finnish *pension*, 'Rauha', where, in the autumn of 1905, I had received news of the revolution in Russia. Of course the Swiss army was also mobilized, and in Basel one could even hear the noise of cannonading. But the huge Helvetian *pension* worried chiefly over the surplus of cheese and the shortage of potatoes and resembled a quiet oasis surrounded by the fiery echoes of war. Perhaps the hour is not so far off, I suggested to myself, when I can leave the Swiss oasis 'Rauha' (Peace) to return again to the St Petersburg workers in the hall of the Technological Institute. But that hour did not come until thirty-three months later.

A desire to clarify my thoughts about what was happening made me turn to a diary. As early as 9 August I wrote in it:

It is perfectly obvious that the question here is not one of mistakes, of certain opportunist acts, of confused statements from the parliamentary tribune, of the voting of the budget by the Social Democrats of the Grand Duchy of Baden, of the experiments of French militarism, of certain leaders turning renegade – it is a question of the *collapse of the International*, at the time of greatest responsibility, a time for which all the preceding work was only preparation.

On 11 August I entered this: 'Only an awakening of the revolutionary socialist movement, an awakening which will need to be very warlike from the start, will lay the foundations for a new International. The years to come will be the period of a social revolution.'

I entered actively into the life of the Swiss Socialist party. In its lower or labour strata, Internationalism was regarded with almost boundless sympathy. I carried away from every party meeting a double store of assurance in the rightness of my stand. I found my first stanchion of support in the workers' union, 'Eintracht', which was international in its membership. By agreement with the directorate of the union, in the early part of September I drafted a manifesto against war and socialist patriotism. The directorate invited the leaders of the party to the meeting where I was to read a paper in German in support of the manifesto. The leaders did not arrive. They thought it was dangerous to take a definite stand on such a bristling question; they preferred to wait and confine themselves, for the time being, to fireside criticizings of the 'extremes' of German and French chauvinism. The meeting of the 'Eintracht' almost unanimously adopted the manifesto, which, for all its ambiguities, gave a decided impetus to public opinion in the party. This was probably the first internationalist document on behalf of a labour organization after the outbreak of the war.

In those days I came for the first time into close contact with Radek, who had come to Switzerland from Germany at the beginning of the war. In the German party he belonged to the extreme left and I hoped to find in him one who shared my views. Indeed, Radek condemned the ruling section of the German Socialist Democracy in fiercely militant tones. In this I was with him. But I was surprised to learn from our conversations that he never conceded the possibility of a proletarian revolution in connection with the war and, generally speaking, in the near future. 'No,' he replied, 'for this the productive forces of mankind, taken as a whole, are not sufficiently developed.' I was quite used to hearing that the productive forces of Russia were not sufficient for the conquest of power by the working class. But I did not imagine that such an answer could come from a revolutionary politician of a progressive capitalist country. Shortly after my departure from Zurich, Radek read a long paper in the very same 'Eintracht', arguing that the capitalist world was not yet ready for the Social Revolution.

Radek's paper, and Zurich as the general socialist crossroads at the outset of the war, are described in the rather interesting memoirs of a Swiss writer, Brupbacher. Curiously enough he refers to my views at that time as 'pacifist'. What he means by the word it is difficult to understand. He expresses his own progress at that time in the title of one of his books, *From a Smug Citizen to a Bolshevik*. I got a clear enough idea of his views at that time to subscribe unreservedly to the first half of the title. For the second half I take no responsibility.

When the German and French socialist newspapers had made clear the picture of the moral and political catastrophe of official Socialism, I put aside my diary to write a political pamphlet on the subject of war and the International. Impressed by my first conversation with Radek, I added a preface to the pamphlet in which I emphasized even more energetically my view that the present war was nothing but an uprising of the productive forces of capitalism on a world scale, against private property on the one hand and state boundaries on the other.

The booklet, *The War and the International*, like all my other books, had its own peculiar destiny, first in Switzerland, then in Germany and France, later in America, and finally in Soviet Russia. A few words must be said about all this. My work was translated from the Russian manuscript by a Russian whose command of German was far from perfect. A professor in Zurich, Ragaz, took it upon himself to edit the translation, and this gave me an opportunity to know an original personality.

Ragaz, although a believing Christian, being moreover a theologian by education and profession, occupied a position on the extreme left of the Swiss socialism, recognized the most extreme methods of struggle against the war, and expressed himself in favour of the proletarian revolution. He and his wife attracted me by the profound moral earnestness of their attitude towards political problems, an attitude which distinguished them so favourably from the Austrian, the German, Swiss and other officials of the Social Democracy, who were so utterly devoid of ideals. As far as I know he was forced later on to sacrifice his chair at the University because of his ideas. For the class that he belonged to this was considerable. And yet in the conversations I had with him I would sense, along with my great respect for this unusual man, an almost physical sensation as of a thin but utterly impenetrable veil separating us from each other. He was an out-and-out mystic, and although he did not press his beliefs on me or even mention them, still in his speech even an armed uprising would become invested with some sort of vapours from another world which produced in me nothing but an uncomfortable shiver. From the very moment that I began to think for myself I was an intuitive and then a conscious material-ist. I not only never felt the necessity of other worlds, but I could not find any psychological contact with the people who managed to recognize both Darwin and the Holy Trinity at the same time.

But the book, thanks to Ragaz, came out in good German. From Switzerland it found its way, as early as December 1914, to Austria and Germany. The Swiss Left-wingers – F. Platten and others – saw to that. Intended for German countries, the pamphlet was directed first of all against the German Social Democracy, the leading party of the Second International. I remember that a journalist named Heilmann, who played first-violin in the orchestra of chauvinism, called my book mad, but quite logical in its madness. I could not have wished for greater praise. There was, of course, no lack of hints that my book was an artful tool of Entente propaganda.

Later on, in France, I came unexpectedly across a report in the French papers, by way of Switzerland, that one of the German courts had sentenced me in a state of contumacy to im-prisonment for the Zurich pamphlet. From this I concluded that the pamphlet had hit the mark. The Hohenzollern judges did me a very good turn by their sentence, a sentence that I was not in any hurry to serve. For the slanderers and spies of the Entente this German court-sentence was always a stumbling-block in their noble efforts to prove that I was nothing more than an agent of the German general staff.

This did not keep the French authorities, however, from holding up my book at the frontier on the strength of its 'German origin'. An ambiguous note defending my pamphlet against the French censorship appeared in the newspaper published by Hervé. I believe that it was written by Ch. Rappaport, a man of some note, who was almost a Marxist; at any rate, he was the author of the greatest number of puns ever invented by any man who has devoted a long life to them.

After the October revolution an enterprising New York publisher brought out my German pamphlet as an imposing American book. According to his own statement, President Wilson asked him, by telephone from the White House, to send the proofs of the book to him; at that time the President was composing his Fourteen Points and, according to reports from people who were informed, could not get over the fact that a Bolshevik had forestalled him in his best formulas. Within two months the sales of the book in America reached 16,000 copies. Then came the days of the Brest-Litovsk peace. The American press raised a furious campaign against me, and the book instantly disappeared from the market.

In the Soviet Republic my Zurich pamphlet had by that time gone through several editions, serving as a text-book for the study of the Marxist attitude towards the war. It disappeared from the 'market' of the Communist International only after 1924, the year when 'Trotskyism' was discovered. At present the pamphlet is still under a ban, as it was before the revolution.

Indeed, it would seem that books have their own destiny.

19
Paris and Zimmerwald

On 19 November 1914 I crossed the French frontier as a war-correspondent for the *Kievskaya Mysl*. I accepted the offer from the paper all the more eagerly because it would give me a chance to get closer to war. Paris was sad; in the evening the streets were lost in pitch-black darkness. Now and then the Zeppelins would pay their flying visits. After the checking of the German advance on the Marne, the war became constantly more exacting and ruthless. In the boundless chaos that was enveloping Europe, with silence from the masses of workers, deceived and betrayed by the Social Democracy, the engines of destruction were developing their automatic power. Capitalist civilization was reducing itself to an absurdity while it strove to break the thick skulls of men.

At the time when the Germans were nearing Paris and the bourgeois French patriots were deserting it, two émigré Russians set up a tiny daily paper published in Russian. Its object was to explain current events to the Russians whom fate had isolated in Paris, and to see that the spirit of international solidarity was not utterly extinguished. Before the first number appeared the capital of the paper amounted to exactly thirty francs. No 'sane' person could believe it possible to publish a daily paper on so little capital. As a matter of fact, in spite of work donated by the editors and other contributors, at least once a week the paper went through a crisis so acute that there seemed to be no way out. But somehow a way out was found. The compositors, faithful to the paper, went hungry; the editors scoured the town in search of francs, and the issue that was due appeared. In this way, withstanding the constant buffets of deficit and censorship, disappearing and reappearing again under a new name, the paper managed to exist for two years and a half, until the revolution of

February 1917. Arriving in Paris, I began to work actively for the *Nashe Slovo* (*Our Word*) which then was called the *Golos* (*The Voice*). A daily paper proved a valuable aid in orienting myself in the midst of the events that were unfolding. My experience on the *Nashe Slovo* was useful to me later, when I had to deal with military affairs more closely.

My family came to France in May 1915. We settled down in Sèvres, in a little house lent to us for a few months by a young friend of ours, an Italian artist, René Parece. Our boys went to the school in Sèvres. The spring was very lovely; its greenness seemed especially caressing. But the number of women in black was growing constantly – the school-children were losing their fathers. The two armies dug themselves into the ground. One could see no way out. Clémenceau was launching attacks against Joffre in his paper. In the reactionary underground circles a *coup d'état* was being prepared; reports of it were passing by word of mouth. In the pages of *Le Temps*, the parliament for several days was referred to only by the name of 'ass'. But *Le Temps* still sternly demanded of the Socialists that they preserve the national unity.

Jaurès was no more. I visited the Café du Croissant where he was killed; I wanted to find a trace of him there. Politically I had been far removed from him. But one could not help feeling the pull of his powerful personality. Jaurès's mind, which was a composite of national traditions, of the metaphysics of moral principles, of love for the oppressed, and of poetic imagination, showed the mark of the aristocrat as clearly as Bebel's revealed the great simplicity of the plebeian. They were both, however, head and shoulders above the legacy which they left.

I had heard Jaurès at popular meetings in Paris, at international congresses, and on committees, and on each occasion it was as if I heard him for the first time. He did not fall into routine; fundamentally he never repeated himself, but was always finding himself again, and mobilizing the latent resources of his spirit. With a mighty force as elemental as a waterfall, he combined great gentleness, which shone in his face like a reflection of a higher spiritual culture. He would send rocks tumbling down, he would thunder and bring the earthquake, but himself he never deafened. He stood always on guard, watched intently for every objection, quick to pick it up and parry it. Sometimes he swept all resistance before him as relentlessly as a hurricane, sometimes as generously and gently as a tutor or elder brother. Jaurès and Bebel were at opposite poles, and yet at the same time they were the twin peaks of the Second International. Both were intensely national, Jaurès with his fiery Latin rhetoric, and Bebel with his touch of Protestant dryness. I loved them both, but with a difference. Bebel exhausted himself physically, whereas Jaurès fell in his prime. But both of them died in time. Their deaths marked the line where the progressive historical mission of the Second International ended.

The French Socialist party was in a state of complete demoralization. There was no one to take the place Jaurès had left. Vaillant, the old 'antimilitarist', was putting out daily articles in a spirit of intensest chauvinism. I once met the old man in the Committee of Action, which was made up of delegates of the party and the trade unions. Vaillant looked like a shadow of himself – a shadow of Blanquism, with the traditions of sans-culotte warfare, in an epoch of Raymond Poincaré. Pre-war France, with her arrested growth in population, her conservative economic life and thought, seemed to Vaillant the only country of progress or movement, the chosen, liberating nation whose contact alone awakens others to spiritual life. His socialism was chauvinistic, just as his chauvinism was messianic. Jules Guesde, the leader of the Marxist wing, who had exhausted himself in a long and trying struggle against the fetishes of democracy, proved to be capable only of laying down his untarnished moral authority on the 'altar' of national defence.

Everything was topsy turvy. Marcel Sembat, the author of the book, *Make a King, or Make Peace*, seconded Guesde in the ministry of – Briand. Pierre Renaudel found himself for a time the 'leader' of the Socialist party – after all, somebody had to occupy the place left vacant by Jaurès. Renaudel strained himself to the utmost to imitate the gestures and thundering voice of the murdered leader. Behind him trailed Longuet, with a certain diffidence which he passed off for extreme radicalism. His ways were a constant reminder that Marx was not responsible for his grandsons. The official syndicalism, represented by the president of the Confédération Générale, Jouhaux, faded away in twenty-four hours. He 'denied' the state in peace-time, only to kneel before it in time of war. That revolutionary buffoon, Hervé, the extreme antimilitarist of the day before, turned himself inside out, but remained, as an extreme chauvinist, the identical, self-satisfied buffoon. As if to make his mockery of his own ideas of yesterday doubly painful, his paper continued to call itself *La Guerre sociale*.

Taken all in all, it seemed like making a masquerade of mourning, a carnival of death. One could not help saying to oneself: 'No, we are made of sterner stuff; events did not catch us unawares; we foresaw something of this, and we foresee much now, and we are prepared for much of what lies ahead of us.' How often we clenched our fists when the Renaudels, the Hervés, and their like tried to fraternize, from a distance, with Karl Liebknecht! There were elements of opposition scattered about in the party and in the syndicates, but they showed few signs of life.

The outstanding figure among the Russian émigrés in Paris without a doubt was Martov, the leader of the Mensheviks, and one of the most talented men I have ever come across. The man's misfortune was that fate made him a politician in a time of revolution without endowing him with the necessary resources of will-power. The lack of balance in his spiritual household was tragically revealed whenever great events took place. I watched him through three historical cataclysms: 1905, 1914, and 1917. Martov's first reaction to events was nearly always revolutionary, but before he could put his ideas on paper his mind would be besieged by doubts from all sides. His rich, pliant, and multiform intelligence lacked the support of will. In his letters to Axelrod in 1905 he complained ruefully that he could not gather his thoughts together. And he never really did, up to the very day when the reactionaries assumed power. At the beginning of the war he again complained to Axelrod that events had driven him to the very verge of insanity. Finally in 1917 he made a hesitant step towards the left and then, within his own faction, yielded the leadership to Tzereteli and Dan, men not even knee-high to him in intellect – in Dan's case, not in any respect.

On 14 October 1914 Martov wrote to Axelrod: 'More readily than with Plekhanov, we could probably come to an understanding with Lenin who, it seems, is preparing to appear in the rôle of a fighter against opportunism in the International.' But this mood did not last long with Martov. When I arrived in Paris, I found him already fading. From the very first our collaboration in the *Nashe Slovo* developed into nothing more nor less than a bitter struggle, which ended with Martov's resigning from the editorial board and finally from the contributing staff.

Soon after I arrived in Paris Martov and I sought out Monatte, one of the editors of the syndicalist journal, *La Vie ouvrière*. A former teacher, later a proofreader, Monatte in appearance was a typical Paris worker, a man of brains as well as character, and he never for a moment inclined towards reconciliation with militarism or the bourgeois state. But how was one to find a way out? We differed. Monatte 'denied' the state and political struggle, but the state ignored his denial and made him don the red trousers after he had come out with an open protest against syndicalist chauvinism. Through Monatte I came into close touch with the journalist Rosmer, who also belonged to the anarchist-syndicalist school, but, as events proved, even then stood closer to Marxism fundamentally than to the Guesdists. Since those days I have been bound to Rosmer by ties of friendship which have stood the test of war, of revolution, of Soviet power, and of the demolition of the opposition. About this time I came to know several active workers in the French labour movement whom I had not known before. They included the secretary of the union of metal-workers, Merrheim, a cautious, slyly ingratiating, and calculating man, whose end was in every respect unhappy; the journalist Guilbeaux, later condemned to death in contumacy for a treason he had not committed; the secretary of the coopers' syndicate, 'Papa' Bourderon; the teacher Loriot, who was trying to find the way to the road of revolutionary socialism; and many others. We met every week on the Quai de Jemmapes, and sometimes in greater numbers on the Grange-aux-Belles, exchanged 'inside' news of the war and the diplomatic goings-on, criticized official socialism, seized upon signs of a socialist reawakening, encouraged the falterers, and mapped out the future.

On 4 August 1915 I wrote in the *Nashe Slovo*: 'And in spite of everything we meet the bloody anniversary without mental distress or political scepticism. In the midst of the greatest catastrophe we revolutionary internationalists have held to our standards of analysis, criticism, and forethought. We have refused to view things through the "national" spectacles that the general staffs have been offering us, not merely cheaply but even with a bonus attached. We have continued to see things as they are, to call them by their real names, and to foresee their logical consequences.'

And now, thirteen years later, I can only repeat those words. That feeling of being superior to the official political thought, including patriotic socialism – a feeling that never left us – was not the fruit of unjustified presumption. There was nothing personal in it; it was the natural result of our theoretical position, for we were standing on a higher peak. Our critical view-point enabled us first of all to see the war in clearer perspective. Each side, as everybody knows, was counting on an early victory. One could quote innumerable evidences of such optimistic lightness of judgement. 'My French colleague', Buchanan relates in his memoirs, 'was at one moment so optimistic that he even bet me £5 that the war would be over by Christmas.' In his own heart Buchanan himself did not postpone the end of the war any later than Easter. In opposition to this view we reiterated day in and day out in our paper, from the autumn of 1914 on, that the war, regardless of all the official prophecies, would be hopelessly protracted and that all Europe would emerge from it utterly broken. Time after time we said in the *Nashe Slovo* that even in case of victory by the Allies France would find herself, when the smoke and fumes had cleared away, only a larger Belgium in the international arena. We definitely foresaw the coming world-dictatorship of the United States. 'Imperialism,' we wrote for the hundredth time on 5 September 1916, 'by virtue of this war, has placed its stakes on the strong; they will own the world.'

Long before this my family had moved from Sèvres to Paris,

to the little rue Oudry. Paris was growing more and more deserted. One by one the street clocks stopped. The Lion de Belfort, for some reason, had dirty straw sticking out of its mouth. The war went on digging farther and farther into the ground. Let us get out of the trenches, out of this stagnation, this immobility! – that was the cry of patriotism. Movement! Movement! And out of this there grew the terrible madness of the Battle of Verdun. In those days, writing in such a way as to elude the lightning of the military censors, I said in the *Nashe Slovo*: 'However great the military significance of the Battle of Verdun may be, the political significance is infinitely greater. In Berlin and other places [*sic*!] they have been wanting "movement" – and they will have it. Hark! under Verdun there is being forged *our* tomorrow.'

In the summer of 1915 there arrived in Paris the Italian deputy Morgari, the secretary of the Socialist faction of the Rome parliament, and a naïve eclectic, who had come to secure the participation of French and English socialists in an international conference. On the *terrasse* of a café on one of the Grands Boulevards we held a meeting attended by a few socialist deputies who for some reason thought themselves 'lefts', and Morgari. As long as the conversation held to pacifist talk and to repeating generalities about the necessity of restoring international connections, everything went smoothly. But when Morgari spoke in a tragic whisper of the necessity of getting false passports for the trip to Switzerland – he was obviously fascinated by the 'carbonari' aspect of the affair – the deputies made long faces, and one of them – I don't remember which – hurriedly called for the waiter and paid for all the coffee we had had. The ghost of Molière stalked across the *terrasse* and, I think, the ghost of Rabelais too. That was the end of the meeting. As we walked back with Martov we laughed a lot, gaily, but not without a certain anger.

Monatte and Rosmer had already been called up for the army and could not go to Switzerland. I went to the conference with Merrheim and Bourderon, both very moderate pacifists. We did not need the false passports, after all, because the government, which had not completely shed its pre-war customs, issued legal ones. The organization of the conference was in the hands of the Berne socialist leader, Grimm, who was then trying his utmost to raise himself above the philistine level of his party, which was also his own inherent level. He had arranged to hold the meeting in a little village called Zimmerwald, high in the mountains and about ten kilometres distant from Berne. The delegates, filling four stage-coaches, set off for the mountains. The passers-by looked on curiously at the strange procession. The delegates themselves joked about the fact that half a century after the founding of the first International, it was still possible to seat all the internationalists in four coaches. But they were not sceptical. The thread of history often breaks – then a new knot must be tied. And that is what we were doing in Zimmerwald.

The days of the conference, 5 to 8 September, were stormy ones. The revolutionary wing, led by Lenin, and the pacifist wing, which comprised the majority of the delegates, agreed with difficulty on a common manifesto of which I had prepared the draft. The manifesto was far from saying all that it should have said, but, even so, it was a long step forward. Lenin was on the extreme left at the conference. In many questions he was in a minority of one, even within the Zimmerwald left wing, to which I did not formally belong, although I was close to it on all important questions. In Zimmerwald Lenin was tightening up the spring of the future international action. In a Swiss mountain village he was laying the corner-stone of the revolutionary International.

The French delegates noted in their report the value of the *Nashe Slovo* in establishing a contact of ideas with the international movement in other countries. Rakovsky pointed out that the *Nashe Slovo* had played an important part in setting forth the development of the international position of the Balkan Social Democratic parties. The Italian party was acquainted with the *Nashe Slovo*, thanks to the many translations by Balabanova. The German press, including the government papers, quoted the *Nashe Slovo* oftenest of all; just as Renaudel tried to lean on Liebknecht, so Scheidemann was not averse to listing us as his allies.

Liebknecht himself was not in Zimmerwald; he had been imprisoned in the Hohenzollern army before he became a captive in prison. Liebknecht sent a letter to the conference which proclaimed his abrupt about-face from pacifism to revolution. His name was mentioned on many occasions at the conference. It was already a watchword in the struggle that was rending world socialism.

The conference put a strict ban on all reports of its proceedings written from Zimmerwald, so that news could not reach the press prematurely and create difficulties for the returning delegates when they were crossing the frontier. A few days later, however, the hitherto unknown name of Zimmerwald was echoed throughout the world. This had a staggering effect on the hotel proprietor – the valiant Swiss told Grimm that he looked for a great increase in the value of his property and accordingly was ready to subscribe a certain sum to the funds of the Third International. I suspect, however, that he soon changed his mind.

The conference at Zimmerwald gave to the development of the anti-war movement in many countries a powerful impetus. In Germany the Spartacists expanded their activities. In France a 'Committee for the Restoration of International Connections' was established. The labour section of the Russian colony in Paris tightened its ranks about the *Nashe Slovo*, giving it the support needed to keep it afloat through constant financial and other difficulties. Martov, who had taken an active part in the work of the *Nashe Slovo* in the first period, now drew away from it. The essentially unimportant differences that still separated me from Lenin at Zimmerwald dwindled into nothing during the next few months.

But in the meantime clouds were gathering overhead, and during 1916 they grew very dark. The reactionary *La Liberté* was publishing, as advertisements, anonymous communications accusing us of being Germanophiles. We were constantly receiving anonymous letters containing threats. Both the accusations and the threats clearly had their source in the Russian embassy. Suspicious-looking persons were always prowling about our printing-works. Hervé was threatening us with the arm of the police. Professor Durckheim, who was chairman of the government committee on Russian exiles, was heard to say that there was talk in government circles of closing down the *Nashe Slovo* and expelling the editors from the country. The action was being delayed, however. They had nothing to base it on, because I had not infringed upon the law, not even the censor's infractions of the law. But there had to be a reasonable excuse, and so in the end it was found, or, to be more exact, manufactured.

20

My Expulsion from France

Certain French newspapers recently reported, when I was already in Constantinople, that the order for my expulsion from France is still in force today, after thirteen years. If that be true, it is added evidence that not all values were destroyed in the most terrible of world catastrophes. During those years, whole generations have been wiped out by shells, entire cities have been razed; imperial and royal crowns have been strewn about the waste lands of Europe; the boundaries of states have changed; the frontiers of France, forbidden to me, have moved. And yet in the midst of this tremendous cataclysm the order signed by Malvy in the early autumn of 1916 has happily been preserved. What of the fact that Malvy himself has since managed to be exiled and to come back? In history the work of a man's hands has often proved more formidable than its creator.

True, a strict jurist might object that he fails to see why there need be continuity in the life of the order. Thus, in 1918 the French military mission in Moscow placed its acting officers at my disposal. This could hardly have been done for an 'undesirable' alien deprived of admission to France. Again, on 10 October 1922 M. Herriot paid me a visit in Moscow, not at all to remind me of the order for my expulsion from France. On the contrary it was I who recalled it to him, when M. Herriot courteously inquired when I planned to visit Paris. But my reminder was in the nature of a jest. We both laughed, for different reasons, it is true, but we laughed together all the same. True, too, that in 1925 the ambassador of France, M. Herbette, on behalf of the diplomats present at the opening of the Shatura power station, replied to my speech with a most amiable greeting, in which even the most captious ear could not have detected the slightest echo of M. Malvy's order. But what of that? There is significance in the fact that one of the two police inspectors who were conducting me from Paris to Irun in the autumn of 1916 explained to me: 'Governments come and go, but the police remain.'

For the better understanding of the circumstances of my expulsion from France it is necessary for me to dwell for a moment on the conditions under which the tiny Russian paper existed during my editorship. Its chief enemy was, of course, the Russian embassy. There the articles of the *Nashe Slovo* were diligently translated into French and forwarded with appropriate comments to the Quai d'Orsay and the Ministry of War. Thereupon, telephone calls of alarm would go to our military censor, M. Chasles, who had spent several years in Russia as a French teacher before the war. Chasles was not distinguished for any quality of resolution. He always solved his hesitations by crossing out rather than leaving in. (What a pity that he did not apply this rule to the unusually poor biography of Lenin that he wrote several years later!) As a timorous censor, Chasles extended his protection not only to the Tsar, Tsarina, Sazonov, the Dardanelles dreams of Miliukoff, but to Rasputin as well. It would require no great effort to prove that the whole war against the *Nashe Slovo* – a veritable war of attrition – was waged not against the paper's internationalism, but against its revolutionary spirit in opposition to Tsarism.

We ran into the first acid bit of censorship at the time of the Russian successes in Galicia. At the least military success the Tsar's embassy would become arrogant to an extreme. This time the censor went so far as to cross out the entire obituary notice of Count Witte and even the title of the article, consisting only of five letters: WITTE. At that very time the official organ of the St Petersburg Navy Department was publishing uncommonly insolent articles aimed at the French republic, sneering at the parliament and its 'sorry little tsars', the deputies. With a copy of the St Petersburg journal in my hand I went to the censor's office to ask for an explanation.

'I have nothing to do with this,' M. Chasles said to me. 'All the instructions concerning your publication come from the

Ministry of Foreign Affairs. Would you like to speak to one of our diplomats?'

Half an hour later a grey-haired diplomat arrived at the War Ministry. The conversation between us, which I wrote down soon after it was over, was something like this:

'Could you explain to me why an article in our paper dealing with a Russian bureaucrat, who was in retirement and also in disfavour, and, moreover, already deceased, has been crossed out? And what relation this measure has to military operations?'

'Well, you know such articles are displeasing to them,' the diplomat said, as he inclined his head vaguely – presumably in the direction of the Russian embassy.

'But it is precisely to displease them that we write them.'

The diplomat smiled condescendingly at this answer, as if it were a charming joke. 'We are at war. We depend on our allies.'

'Do you mean to say that the internal affairs of France are controlled by the Tsar's diplomacy? Didn't your ancestors make a mistake then in chopping off Louis Capet's head?'

'Oh, you exaggerate. And besides, please don't forget; we are at war.'

Our further conversation was fruitless. The diplomat explained to me with a suave smile that since statesmen are mortal the living ones do not like to hear the dead spoken of disparagingly. After the meeting everything went on as before. The censor continued to blue-pencil. Instead of a newspaper often all that appeared was a sheet of white paper. We were never guilty of disregarding M. Chasles's will; he, in turn, was even less inclined to disregard the will of his masters.

Nevertheless, in September 1916, the prefecture handed me the order for my expulsion from French territory. What was the reason for it? But they told me nothing. Gradually, however, it became apparent that the cause was a malicious frame-up organized by the Russian secret police in France.

When deputy Jean Longuet came to Briand to protest, or, to be more precise, to grieve (Longuet's protests always sounded like the gentlest of tunes) about my expulsion, the French prime minister answered him: 'Do you know that the *Nashe Slovo* was found on the persons of the Russian soldiers who murdered their colonel at Marseilles?' Longuet had not been expecting this. He knew of the 'Zimmerwald' policy of the paper; he could reconcile himself more or less to that, but the murder of a colonel could not but find him at a loss. He turned to inquire of my French friends there, and they in turn asked me, but I knew no more about the murder at Marseilles than they did. Correspondents of the Russian liberal press who were patriotic enemies of the *Nashe Slovo* accidentally came into the affair and cleared up the whole Marseilles incident.

It happened that when the Tsar's government brought troops to the soil of the republic – troops called 'symbolical' because of their slim numbers – they also mobilized in haste the requisite number of spies and *agents-provocateurs*. Among these was a certain Vining (I believe that was his name) who arrived from London with a letter of introduction to the Russian consul. To start things going, Vining tried to induce the most moderate of the Russian correspondents to take part in the 'revolutionary' propaganda among the Russian soldiers. They refused. He did not dare address himself to the editors of the *Nashe Slovo*, and consequently we did not even know of him. After his failure in Paris Vining went to Toulon, where it seems he had some success among the Russian sailors, who were unable to see through him. 'The soil is very favourable for our work here. Send me revolutionary books and papers,' he wrote to certain Russian journalists, whom he chose at random; but he received no answer. Serious mutinies broke out on the Russian cruiser *Askold*, stationed at Toulon, and were cruelly suppressed. Vining's part in the business was only too obvious, and he decided that it was an opportune time to transfer his activities to Marseilles. The soil proved 'favourable' there, too. Not without his cooperation, mutinies broke out among the Russian soldiers and culminated in the stoning to death of the Russian colonel, Krause, in the courtyard of the barracks. When the soldiers concerned in the affair were arrested, copies of the same issue of the *Nashe Slovo* were found on them. The Russian correspondents, coming to Marseilles to investigate, were told by the officers that during the disturbances a certain Vining had distributed the *Nashe Slovo* to all soldiers, whether they wanted it or not. And that was the only reason why the paper was found on the arrested soldiers, who had not even had a chance to read it.

Immediately after Longuet's interview with Briand concerning my expulsion – that is, before Vining's part in the affair had been disclosed – I wrote an open letter to Jules Guesde in which I suggested that the *Nashe Slovo* might have been intentionally distributed among the soldiers at the right moment by some *agent-provocateur*. This surmise was completely confirmed by bitter opponents of the paper, sooner than I could have hoped for. But it did not matter. The Tsar's diplomacy gave the government of the republic to understand, only too clearly, that if France wanted Russian soldiers the nest of Russian revolutionaries must be destroyed at once. The object was achieved; the French government, hesitant until then, closed down the *Nashe Slovo*, and the minister of the interior, Malvy, signed the order, previously prepared by the prefect of police, expelling me from France.

Now the ministry felt that it was well covered. Briand quoted the Marseilles incident as the reason for my expulsion, not only to Jean Longuet, but to a number of other deputies as well, among them the chairman of the parliamentary committee, Leysgues. This could not fail to have its effect. But since the *Nashe Slovo* was a censored paper sold openly on the newsstands, and could not call upon soldiers to kill their colonel, the case remained a mystery until the frame-up was disclosed. It became known even in the Chamber of Deputies. I was told that Painlevé, then the minister of education, when he was told the 'inside' story exclaimed: 'It's a shame . . . things must not be left at that. . .' But there was a war on. The Tsar was an ally. Vining could not be exposed. There was nothing to do but to carry out Malvy's order.

The Paris prefecture informed me that I was being expelled from France to any other country I might choose. I was also informed that England and Italy declined the honour of having me as a guest. My only choice was to go back to Switzerland. Alas! the Swiss legation flatly refused to issue a visa to me. I telegraphed my Swiss friends and received a reassuring answer from them: the question would be decided favourably. The Swiss legation, however, continued to refuse me a visa. I found out later that the Russian embassy, with the help of the Allies, put on the screws in Berne when it seemed necessary, and the Swiss authorities deliberately delayed the solution of the question hoping that in the meantime I would have been expelled from France. I could get to Holland and Scandinavia only through England, but the English government refused me the right of passage. Spain was the only country left. But now it was my turn to refuse to go voluntarily to the Iberian peninsula.

Arguments with the Paris police continued for about six weeks. Detectives followed me wherever I went; they stood on guard outside my home and the offices of our paper, never once letting me out of their sight. Finally the Paris authorities decided to take firm measures. The prefect of police, Laurent, invited me to his office and told me that since I refused to leave voluntarily, two police inspectors – in 'plain clothes' however, he added with the utmost consideration – would be sent to conduct me to the frontier. The Tsar's embassy achieved its end; I was expelled from France.

The details of this account, which is based on the entries I made at that time, may show some slight inaccuracies. But all the main facts are absolutely irrefutable. Besides, most of the people who had anything to do with the episode are still alive; many of them are in France now. There are documents as well. It would therefore be quite easy to establish the facts. For my part I have no doubt that if Malvy's order for my expulsion were resurrected from the police archives and if the document were subjected to a dactyloscopic examination, it would be found to bear somewhere in a corner the finger-prints of Monsieur Vining.

21

Through Spain

Two police inspectors were waiting for me in my home in the little rue Oudry. One of them was short and looked rather elderly; the other was enormous and bald, about forty-five and as swarthy as pitch. The plain clothes they wore hung awkwardly on them, and when they spoke they raised their hands as if in salute. While I was saying good-bye to my friends and the family, the police, with excessive politeness, hid behind the doors. The older man, when he left, kept taking off his hat and saying, '*Excusez, Madame!*'

One of the two detectives who had been pursuing me so tirelessly and vehemently during the past two months was waiting outside the door. In a friendly way, as if there were nothing at all between us, he arranged the rug and shut the door of the car. He reminded me of a hunter who was handing his game over to the buyer. We set off.

A fast train. A third-class compartment. The older inspector proved to be a geographer; Tomsk, Kasan, the Nijni-Novgorod fair – he knew them all. He spoke Spanish and knew the country. The other, tall and dark, was silent for a long time, and sat sullenly a little distance away. But presently he unburdened himself. 'The Latin race is marking time; the rest are leaving it behind,' he remarked suddenly, as he cut a piece of fat pork with a knife held in a hairy hand adorned with heavy rings. 'What have you in literature? Decadence in everything. The same in philosophy. There has been no movement since Descartes and Pascal ... The Latin race is marking time ...' I waited, in astonishment, to see what would come next. But he lapsed into silence and began to chew the fat and a bun. 'You had Tolstoy, not so long ago, but we understand Ibsen better than Tolstoy.' And he was silent again.

The old man, piqued by this sudden show of erudition, began to explain to me the importance of the Trans-Siberian railway. Then, at once supporting and softening the pessimistic conclusions of his colleague, he added: 'Yes, we suffer from lack of initiative. Everybody wants to be a government official. It is sad, but one cannot deny it.' I listened to them both humbly and not without interest.

'Shadowing a person? Today it is impossible. Shadowing is efficient when it isn't noticed, isn't it? I must say candidly the metro kills shadowing. People being watched should be ordered never to use the metro, only then would shadowing be possible.' And the dark one laughed grimly.

The older man added, to soften the effect, 'We often watch, alas, without even knowing why.'

'We policemen are sceptics,' the dark one resumed abruptly, changing the subject, 'You have your ideas. But we preserve the existing order. Take the Great Revolution. What a movement of ideas! Fourteen years after the revolution, the people were more miserable than ever before. Read Taine ... We policemen are conservatives from the very nature of our duties. Scepticism is the only philosophy possible for our profession. After all, no one chooses his own path. There is no freedom of will. Everything is predetermined by the course of things.'

He began to drink wine with the air of a stoic, straight from the bottle. Then, corking the bottle: 'Renan said that new ideas always come too early. And that is true.'

With this, he cast a suspicious glance at my hand, which I had placed casually on the door-knob. To reassure him I hid my hand in my pocket. By that time the old man was again having his revenge: he was talking about the Basques, their language, women, head-dress, and so forth. We were approaching the station of Hendaye.

'This is where Déroulède, our national romantic, lived. He needed only to see the mountains of France. A Don Quixote in his Spanish abode.' The dark fellow smiled with a sort of solid condescension. 'If you please, monsieur, follow me to the station commissariat.'

At Irun a French gendarme addressed a question to me, but

my guardian made a masonic sign to him and led me hurriedly through the station corridors.

'*C'est fait avec discrétion, n'est-ce pas?*' the dark one asked me. 'You can take a trolley-car from Irun to San Sebastian. You must try and look like a tourist so as not to arouse the suspicions of the Spanish police, who are very distrustful. And from now on, I don't know you, do I?'

We parted coldly.

From San Sebastian, where I was delighted by the sea and appalled by the prices, I went to Madrid and found myself in a city in which I knew no one, not a single soul, and no one knew me. And since I did not speak Spanish, I could not have been lonelier even in the Sahara or in the Peter-Paul fortress. There remained only the language of art. The two years of war had made one forget that such a thing as art still existed. With the eagerness of a starved man, I viewed the priceless treasures of the Museum of Madrid and felt again the 'eternal' element in this art. The Rembrandts, the Riberas. The paintings of Bosch were works of genius in their naïve joy of life. The old caretaker gave me a lens so that I might see the tiny figures of the peasants, little donkeys and dogs in the pictures of Miel. Here there was no feeling of war; everything was securely in its place. The colours had their own life, uncontrolled.

This is what I wrote in my notebook in the museum:

Between us and these old artists – without in the least obscuring them or lessening their importance – there grew up before the war a new art, more intimate, more individualistic, one with greater nuances, at once more subjective and more intense. The war, by its mass passions and suffering, will probably wash away this mood and this manner for a long time – but that can never mean a simple return to the old form, however beautiful – to the anatomic and botanic perfection, to the Rubens thighs (though thighs are apt to play a great rôle in the new post-war art, which will be so eager for life). It is difficult to prophesy, but out of the unprecedented experiences filling the lives of almost all civilized humans, surely a new art must be born.

In my hotel I read the Spanish papers with the aid of a dictionary, and waited for an answer to the letters I had sent to

Switzerland and Italy. I was still hoping to get there. On the fourth day of my stay in Madrid I received a letter from Paris giving me the address of a French Socialist, Gabier. He was the director of an insurance company, but in spite of his bourgeois social standing, I found him in firm opposition to the patriotic policy of his party. From Gabier I learned that the Spanish party was completely under the influence of the French patriotic socialism. There was serious opposition only in Barcelona, among the syndicalists. The secretary of the Socialist party, Anguillano, whom I intended to visit, was serving a prison sentence of fifteen days for a disrespectful reference to some Catholic saint. In bygone days Anguillano would simply have been burned in an *auto-da-fé*.

I was waiting for an answer from Switzerland, meanwhile memorizing Spanish words and visiting the Museum. On 9 November, the maid at the small *pension* in which Gabier had placed me called me out into the corridor with a frightened air. There I found two young men of unmistakable appearance who invited me, in not very friendly fashion, to follow them. Where to? But of course, to the Madrid prefecture of police. Once there, they seated me in a corner.

'Am I under arrest, then?' I asked.

'Si, para una hora, dos horas (for an hour or two).'

Without changing my position, I sat there in the prefecture for seven hours. At nine o'clock in the evening, I was taken upstairs. I found myself before a fairly well-thronged Olympus.

'What it is that you have arrested me for, precisely?'

This simple question nonplussed the Olympians. They offered various hypotheses in turn. One of them referred to the passport difficulties that the Russian government raised for foreigners going to Russia.

'If you could only know the amount of money we spend in prosecuting our anarchists,' said another, appealing to my sympathy.

'But surely I cannot be held answerable at the same time for both the Russian police and the Spanish anarchists?'

'Of course, of course, that is only to give you an example.'

'What are your ideas?' the chief asked me at last, after deliberating for a while.

I stated my views in as popular language as I could.

'There, you see!' they said.

In the end the chief informed me through the interpreter that I was invited to leave Spain at once, and until I left my freedom would be subjected to 'certain limitations'. 'Your ideas are too advanced for Spain,' he told me candidly, still through the interpreter.

At midnight a police agent took me to the prison in a cab. There was the inevitable examination of my belongings in the centre of the prison 'star', at the intersection of five wings, each of them four storeys high. The staircases were of iron and were suspended. The peculiar prison night-silence, saturated with heavy vapours and nightmarishness. Pale electric lights in the corridors. Everything familiar, everything the same. The rumbling of the iron-bound door when it opened; a large room, semi-darkness, heavy prison odours, a miserable and repulsive bed. Then the rumbling of the door as it was locked. How many imprisonments did this make? I opened the small aperture in the window behind the grating. A draft of cool air blew in. Without undressing, with my clothes all buttoned up, I lay down on the bed and covered myself with my overcoat. Only then did I begin to realize the full incongruity of what had happened. In a prison – in Madrid! I had never dreamed of such a thing. Izvolsky had done his job well. In Madrid! I lay on the bed in the Madrid 'model' prison and laughed with all my might, laughed until I fell asleep.

When I was taking my walk, the convicts explained to me that there were two kinds of cells in the prison – the free cells and those for which one paid. A cell of the first class cost one and a half pesetas a day; one of the second class, seventy-five centimes. Every prisoner was entitled to occupy a paid cell, but he had no right to refuse a free one. My cell was a paid one of the first class. I again laughed heartily. But after all, it was only logical. Why should there be equality in prison in a society built entirely on inequality? I also learned that the occupants of paid cells walk out twice a day for an hour at a time, whereas the others have only a half-hour. Again, this was perfectly right. The lungs of a government thief who pays a franc and a half a day are entitled to a larger portion of air than the lungs of a striker who gets his breathing free of charge.

On the third day I was called up for anthropometric measurements, and was told to paint my fingers with printer's ink and impress their marks on cards. I refused. Then 'force' was resorted to, but with a studied politeness. I looked out the window while the guard courteously painted my hand, finger after finger, and pressed it about ten times on various cards and sheets, first the right hand, then the left. Next I was invited to sit down and take off my boots. I refused. The feet proved more difficult to manage, and the administration presently was walking about me in confusion. In the end I was unexpectedly allowed to go and talk to Gabier and Anguillano, who had come to see me. Anguillano had been released from prison – another one – the day before. They told me that all the agencies to bring about my release had been set in motion. In the corridor I met the prison chaplain, who expressed his Catholic sympathies with my pacificism and added consolingly: '*Paciencia, paciencia.*' There was nothing else possible for me anyway.

On the morning of the twelfth the police agent informed me that I was to leave for Cadiz that same evening, and asked if I wanted to pay for my railway ticket. But I had no desire to go to Cadiz and I firmly refused to pay for the ticket. It was enough that one had to pay for accommodation in the 'model' prison.

And so, in the evening, we left Madrid for Cadiz. The travelling costs were at the expense of the Spanish king. But why Cadiz? Again I looked at the map. Cadiz is the farthest extremity of the south-western peninsula of Europe; from Berezov by deer via the Urals and St Petersburg, thence by a circular route to Austria, from Austria through Switzerland to France, from France to Spain, and finally across the entire Iberian peninsula to Cadiz, the general direction being from North-east to South-west. There the continent ends and the ocean begins. *Paciencia!*

The police agents who accompanied me did not make the slightest attempt to invest the journey with mystery. On the contrary they told my story in complete detail to everyone interested, giving me, at the same time, the best of characters: not a counterfeiter of money but a *caballero*, unfortunately one who held unsuitable views. Everybody consoled me with the prospect of a very fine climate in Cadiz.

'How did you get to me?' I asked the agents.

'Very easily. By telegram from Paris.'

Just as I had thought. The Madrid police had received a telegram from the Paris prefecture: 'A dangerous anarchist, so-and-so, crossed the frontier at San Sebastian. Intends to settle down in Madrid.' So the Madrid police had been waiting for me, had looked everywhere for me, and were upset because they could not find me for a whole week. The French policemen had politely escorted me across the frontier; the admirer of Montaigne and Renan had even asked me: '*C'est fait avec discrétion, n'est-ce pas?*' – and then the same police had telegraphed to Madrid that a dangerous 'anarchist' had passed through Irun to San Sebastian!

In all this the chief of the so-called juridical police, Bidet-'Fauxpas', played an important part. He was the heart and soul of my shadowing and expulsion; he was distinguishable from his colleagues only by his exceptional rudeness and malice. He tried to speak to me in a tone that even the Tsar's officers of the secret police never allowed themselves to assume. My conversations with him always ended in explosions. As I was leaving him, I would feel a look of hate behind my back. At the prison meeting with Gabier, I expressed my conviction that my arrest had been prearranged by Bidet-'Fauxpas', and the name, started by my lucky stroke, circulated through the Spanish press.

Less than two years later the fates willed me an entirely unexpected satisfaction at M. Bidet's expense. In the summer of 1918 a telephone call to the War Commissariat informed me that Bidet – the Thunderer, Bidet! – was under arrest in one of the Soviet prisons. I could not believe my ears. But it seemed that the French government had put him on the staff of the military mission to engage in spying and conspiracy in the Soviet republic, and he had been so careless as to get caught. One could hardly ask for a greater satisfaction from Nemesis, especially if one adds the fact that Malvy, the French Minister of the Interior who signed the order for my expulsion, was himself soon after expelled from France by the Clémenceau government on a charge of pacifist intrigues. What a concurrence of circumstances, as if intended for a film plot!

When Bidet was brought to me at the Commissariat, I could not recognize him at first. The Thunderer had become transformed into an ordinary mortal, and a seedy one at that. I looked at him in amazement.

'*Mais oui, monsieur,*' he said as he bowed his head, '*c'est moi.*'

Yes, it was Bidet. But how had it happened? I was genuinely astonished. Bidet spread out his hands philosophically, and with the assurance of a police stoic, remarked, '*C'est la marche des événements.*' Exactly – a magnificent formula! There floated before my eyes the figure of the dark fatalist who had conducted me to San Sebastian: 'There is no freedom of choice; everything is predetermined.'

'But, Monsieur Bidet, you were not very polite to me in Paris.'

'Alas, I must admit it, Mr People's Commissary, sorry as I am. I have thought often of it as I sat in my cell. It does a man good sometimes', he added significantly, 'to get acquainted with prison from the inside. But I still hope that my Paris behaviour will not have any unpleasant consequences for me.'

I reassured him.

'When I return to France, I will change my occupation.'

'Will you, Monsieur Bidet? *On revient toujours à ses premiers amours.*' (I have described this scene to my friends so often that I remember our dialogue as if it took place yesterday.) Later Bidet was allowed to go back to France as one of the exchange prisoners. I have no information as to his subsequent fate.

But we must go back from the War Commissariat to Cadiz.

After consulting the governor the Cadiz prefect informed me that at eight o'clock the following morning I would be sent to Havana, for which, by happy chance, a steamer was sailing that day.

'Where?'

'To Havana.'

'Ha-van-a?'

'Havana.'

'I won't go voluntarily.'

'Then we shall be compelled to place you in the hold of the vessel.'

The secretary of the German consul, a friend of the prefect's who was present at the conversation as an interpreter, advised me to 'accept realities' (*sich mit den Realitäten abzufinden*).

Paciencia, paciencia! But this was a little too much. I told them again that it wouldn't do. Accompanied by detectives, I rushed to the telegraph office through the streets of an enchanting town, noticing it but little, and sent telegrams '*urgente*' to Gabier, to Anguillano, to the chief of the secret police, the Minister of the Interior, Premier Romanones, the liberal papers, to the republican deputies, mobilizing all the arguments that one could find room for in a telegram. After this I wrote letters in every possible direction. 'Just imagine, dear friend,' I wrote to the Italian deputy, Serrati, 'that you are at the moment in Tver under the supervision of the Russian police, and that you are about to be expelled to Tokyo, to a place that you have never had any intention of going – such is approximately my position in Cadiz on the eve of a forced journey to Havana.' Then I dashed back with the detectives to the prefecture. At my insistence and my expense the latter telegraphed to Madrid that, rather than go to Havana, I preferred to stay in the Cadiz prison until the New York boat arrived. I did not want to surrender. It was an exciting day.

In the meantime the republican deputy Castrovido interrogated the government in the Cortes regarding my arrest and deportation. A controversy began in the papers. The left attacked the police, but, as francophiles, condemned my pacifism. The right sympathized with my 'germanophilism' (had I not been expelled from France?), but they were afraid of my anarchism. In this confusion nobody could understand anything. Still, I was permitted to stay in Cadiz until the next boat arrived for New York. This was a considerable victory.

For a few weeks after this I was under the observation of the Cadiz police. But this was a perfectly peaceful, paternal sort of

observation, quite unlike the one in Paris. There, during the last
two months of my stay, I had spent a great deal of energy trying
to dodge the sleuths. I would drive away in a solitary taxi, go
into a dark cinema theatre, jump into a metro train at the very
last moment, jump out of it just as suddenly, and so on. The
detectives were on the alert, too, and kept up the chase in every
possible fashion. They would snatch taxis under my nose, keep
watch at the entrance of the cinema, and would bolt out like a
rocket from a trolley-car or from the metro, to the great indignation of passengers and conductor. Properly speaking, it was
on my part a case of art for art's sake. My political activity lay
open to the eyes of the police, but the pursuit by the detectives
irritated me and roused my sporting instincts.

In Cadiz, on the other hand, the detective informed me that
he would return at a certain hour, and I had to wait patiently
for him in the hotel. He, for his part, firmly protected my
interests, helped me in my purchases, drew my attention to all
the hollows in the sidewalks. When the pedlar of boiled shrimps
demanded two *reals* a dozen for them, my spy swore at the man
in a rage, shook his fists threateningly at him, and even ran out of
the café after him and kicked up such a rumpus under the windows that a crowd gathered about them.

I tried not to waste my time; I worked in the library on the
history of Spain, memorized Spanish conjugations, and renewed
my stock of English words in preparation for going to America.
The days passed almost imperceptibly, and often, towards evening, I would note sadly that the day for my departure was drawing nearer, while I was making very little headway in my studies.
I was always alone in the library – not counting the bookworms
that had eaten away many an eighteenth-century volume; sometimes it took a great deal of effort to decipher a name or a number.

In my notebook for that time I find the following entry:

A historian of the Spanish revolution tells of politicians who
branded it as crime and madness five minutes before the victory of
the popular movement, but afterwards pushed themselves to the front.
These clever gentlemen, the old historian tells us, appeared in all the
subsequent revolutions and outshouted the others. The Spaniards

call these smart fellows 'panzistas' – from the word 'belly'. As is well known, the name of our old friend Sancho Panza derives from the same word. The name is hard to translate, but the difficulty is linguistic rather than political. The type itself is quite international.

Since 1917 I have had many occasions to find that out.

It is remarkable that the Cadiz paper carried no information about the war, just as if it did not exist. When I drew my companions' attention to the utter absence of military reports in the most popular paper, *El Diario de Cadiz*, they answered in surprise, 'Is that so? Really? Why, yes, it's true!' Before then they had not even noticed it themselves. After all, the fighting was going on somewhere beyond the Pyrenees. Even I began to forget the war.

The boat for New York sailed from Barcelona. I managed to wrest permission to go there to meet my family. In Barcelona there were new difficulties with the prefecture, new protests and telegrams, and new detectives. My family arrived – they too had had difficulties in Paris. But now everything was all right. We went sightseeing in Barcelona, accompanied by detectives. The boys approved of the sea and the fruit. We had all become reconciled to the idea of going over to America. My attempts to secure permission to go to Switzerland by way of Italy brought no result. It is true the permission was finally granted under the pressure of Italian and Swiss socialists, but it came only after my family and I had already embarked on the Spanish boat that was to sail from Barcelona on 25 December. The delay was intentional, of course. In this detail Izvolsky arranged things very well.

The doors of Europe shut behind me in Barcelona. The police put me and my family on board the Spanish Transatlantic Company's steamer *Monserrat*, which delivered its live and dead cargo at New York after seventeen days. Seventeen days! The time would have seemed tempting in the days of Christopher Columbus, whose monument towers over the harbour at Barcelona. But the sea was very rough at this time of the year, and our boat did everything to remind us of the frailty of human life. The *Monserrat* was an old tub little suited for ocean voyages. But during the war the neutral Spanish flag lessened the chances of being sunk. The Spanish company charged high fares, and provided bad accommodation and even worse food.

The population of the steamer is multicoloured, and not very attractive in its variety. There are quite a few deserters from different countries, for the most part men of fairly high standing. An artist is carrying away his paintings, his talent, his family and his property under the chaperonage of his old father, in order to get as far away as possible from the firing-line. A boxer, who is also a novelist and a cousin of Oscar Wilde, confesses openly that he prefers crashing Yankee jaws in a noble sport to letting some German stab him in the midriff. A billiard champion, an immaculate gentleman, waxes indignant about extending conscription to men of his age. And all for what? For this senseless butchery! And he expresses his sympathy – with the ideas of Zimmerwald. The others are of much the same sort: deserters, adventurers, speculators, or simply 'undesirables' thrown out of Europe. Who would ever dream of crossing the Atlantic at this time of year on a wretched little Spanish boat from choice?

It is more difficult to make out the third-class passengers. They lie close together, move about very little, say very little – for they have not much to eat – and are very sullen as they sail from a poverty that is bitter and hateful to another that for the moment is shrouded in uncertainty. America works for fighting Europe, and needs new labour, but it must be labour without trachoma, without anarchism and other diseases of the sort.

The boat opens to the boys an endless field for observation. They are always discovering something new.

'Do you know, the fireman is very nice? He is a "republicker".' Thanks to their constant moving about from one country to another, they speak a peculiar language of their own.

'A republican? How could you understand him?'

'Oh, he explains everything fine. He said, "Alfonso!" and then went "Piff-piff".'

'Oh, then he is certainly a republican,' I agree. The boys take the fireman some dried Malaga grapes and other delicacies. We are introduced to each other. The republican is about twenty, and he seems to have most definite views about the monarchy.

1 January 1917: Every one on the boat congratulates every one else on the New Year. Two New Years of the war I have spent in France, the third is spent on the ocean. What has 1917 in store for us?

Sunday, 13 January: We are nearing New York. At three o'clock in the morning, everybody wakes up. We have stopped. It is dark. Cold. Wind. Rain. On land, a wet mountain of buildings. The New World!

Here I was in New York, city of prose and fantasy, of capitalist automatism, its streets a triumph of cubism, its moral philosophy that of the dollar. New York impressed me tremendously because, more than any other city in the world, it is the fullest expression of our modern age.

Of the legends that have sprung up about me, the greater number have to do with my life in New York. In Norway, which I only touched in passing, the resourceful journalists had me working as a codfish cleaner. In New York, where I stayed for two months, the newspapers had me engaged in any number of occupations, each more fantastic than the one before. If all the adventures that the newspapers ascribed to me were banded together in a book, they would make a far more entertaining biography than the one I am writing here.

But I must disappoint my American readers. My only profession in New York was that of a revolutionary socialist. This was before the war for 'liberty' and 'democracy', and in those days mine was a profession no more reprehensible than that of a bootlegger. I wrote articles, edited a newspaper, and addressed labour meetings. I was up to my neck in work, and consequently I did not feel at all like a stranger. In one of the New York libraries I studied the economic history of the United States assiduously. The figures showing the growth of American exports during the war astounded me; they were, in fact, a complete revelation. And it was those same figures that not only predetermined America's intervention in the war, but the decisive part that the United States would play in the world after the war as well. I wrote several articles about this at the time, and gave several lectures. Since that time the problem of 'America versus Europe' has been one of my chief interests. And even now I am studying the question with the utmost care, hoping to devote a separate book to it. If one is to understand the future destiny of humanity, this is the most important of all subjects.

The day after I arrived in New York I wrote in the Russian paper, the *Novy Mir* (*The New World*): 'I left a Europe wallowing in blood, but I left with a profound faith in a coming revolution. And it was with no democratic "illusions" that I stepped on the soil of this old-enough New World.' Ten days later I addressed the international meeting of welcome as follows:

It is a fact of supreme importance that the economic life of Europe is being blasted to its very foundations, whereas America is increasing in wealth. As I look enviously at New York – I who still think of myself as a European – I ask myself: 'Will Europe be able to stand it? Will it not sink into nothing but a cemetery? And will the economic and cultural centres of gravity not shift to America?'

And despite the success of what is called 'European stabilization', this question is just as pertinent today.

I lectured in Russian and German in various sections of New York, Philadelphia and other near-by cities. My English was even worse than it is today, so that I never even thought of making public addresses in English. And yet I have often come across references to my speeches in English in New York. Only the other day an editor of a Constantinople paper described one of those mythical public appearances which he witnessed as a student in America. I confess that I didn't have the courage to tell him that he was the dupe of his own imagination. But alas! with even greater assurance, he repeated these same recollections of his in his paper.

We rented an apartment in a workers' district, and furnished it on the instalment plan. That apartment, at eighteen dollars a month, was equipped with all sorts of conveniences that we Europeans were quite unused to: electric lights, gas cooking-range, bath, telephone, automatic service-elevator, and even a chute for the garbage. These things completely won the boys over to New York. For a time the telephone was their main interest; we had not had this mysterious instrument either in Vienna or Paris.

The janitor of the house was a Negro. My wife paid him three months' rent in advance, but he gave her no receipt because the landlord had taken the receipt-book away the day before, to verify the accounts. When we moved into the house two days later, we discovered that the Negro had absconded with the rent of several of the tenants. Besides the money, we had entrusted to him the storage of some of our belongings. The whole incident upset us; it was such a bad beginning. But we found our property after all, and when we opened the wooden box that contained our crockery, we were surprised to find our money hidden away in it, carefully wrapped up in paper. The janitor had taken the money of the tenants who had already received their receipts; he did not mind robbing the landlord, but he was considerate enough not to rob the tenants. A delicate fellow, indeed. My wife and I were deeply touched by his consideration, and we always think of him gratefully. This little incident took on a symptomatic significance for me – it seemed as if a corner of the veil that concealed the 'black' problem in the United States had lifted.

During those months America was busily getting ready for war. As ever, the greatest help came from the pacifists. Their vulgar speeches about the advantages of peace as opposed to war invariably ended in a promise to support war if it became 'necessary'. This was the spirit of the Bryan campaign. The socialists sang in tune with the pacifists. It is a well-known axiom that pacifists think of war as an enemy only in time of peace. After the Germans came out for unrestricted submarine warfare, mountains of military supplies blocked the railways and filled all the eastern stations and ports. Prices instantly soared, and I saw thousands of women – mothers, in the wealthiest city of the world – come out into the streets, upset the stalls, and break into shops. What will it be like in the rest of the world after the war? I asked myself.

On 3 February came the long-awaited break in diplomatic relations with Germany. The volume of the chauvinistic music was increasing daily. The tenor of the pacifists and the falsetto of the socialists did not disrupt the general harmony. But I had seen the same thing in Europe, and the mobilization of American patriotism was simply a repetition of what I had seen before. I

noted the stages of the process in my Russian paper, and medi-
tated on the stupidity of men who were so slow to learn their
lessons.

I once saw, through the window of my newspaper office, an
old man with suppurating eyes and a straggling grey beard stop
before a garbage-can and fish out a crust of bread. He tried the
crust with his hands, then he touched the petrified thing with his
teeth, and finally he struck it several times against the can. But
the bread did not yield. Finally he looked about him as if he were
afraid or embarrassed, thrust his find under his faded coat, and
shambled along down St Mark's Place. This little episode took
place on 2 March 1917. But it did not in any way interfere with
the plans of the ruling class. War was inevitable, and the pacifists
had to support it.

Bukharin was one of the first people I met in New York; he
had been deported from Scandinavia only a short time before.
He had known us in the Vienna days, and welcomed us with the
childish exuberance characteristic of him. Although it was late,
and we were very tired, Bukharin insisted on dragging us off to
the Public Library the very first day. That was the beginning of
a close association that warmed – on Bukharin's part – into an
attachment for me that grew steadily more intense until 1923,
when it suddenly changed to an opposite sentiment.

Bukharin's nature is such that he must always attach himself
to someone. He becomes, in such circumstances, nothing more
than a medium for someone else's actions and speeches. You
must always keep your eyes on him, or else he will succumb
quite imperceptibly to the influence of someone directly opposed
to you, as other people fall under an automobile. And then he
will deride his former idol with that same boundless enthusiasm
with which he has just been lauding him to the skies. I never
took Bukharin too seriously and I left him to himself, which
really means, to others. After the death of Lenin he became
Zinoviev's medium, and then Stalin's. At the very moment that
these lines are being written Bukharin is passing through still
another crisis, and other fluids, as yet not known to me, are
filtering through him.

Madame Kolontay was in America at that time, but she

travelled a great deal and I did not meet her very often. During the war, she veered sharply to the left, without transition abandoning the ranks of the Mensheviks for the extreme left wing of the Bolsheviks. Her knowledge of foreign languages and her temperament made her a valuable agitator. Her theoretical views have always been somewhat confused, however. In her New York period nothing was revolutionary enough for her. She was in correspondence with Lenin and kept him informed of what was happening in America, my own activities included, seeing all facts and ideas through the prism of her ultra-radicalism. Lenin's replies to her reflected this utterly worthless information. Later, in their fight against me, the epigones have not hesitated to make use of mistaken utterances by Lenin, utterances that he himself recanted both by word and by deed. In Russia Kolontay took from the very first an ultra-left stand, not only towards me but towards Lenin as well. She waged many a battle against the 'Lenin–Trotsky' régime, only to bow most movingly later on to the Stalin régime.

In ideas the Socialist party of the United States lagged far behind even European patriotic Socialism. But the superior airs of the American press – still neutral at the time – towards an 'insensate' Europe, were reflected also in the opinions of American socialists. Men like Hillquit welcomed the chance to play the socialist American 'uncle' who would appear in Europe at the crucial moment and make peace between the warring factions of the Second International. To this day I smile as I recall the leaders of American Socialism. Immigrants who had played some rôle in Europe in their youth, they very quickly lost the theoretical premise they had brought with them in the confusion of their struggle for success. In the United States there is a large class of successful and semi-successful doctors, lawyers, dentists, engineers and the like, who divide their precious hours of rest between concerts by European celebrities and the American Socialist party. Their attitude towards life is composed of shreds and fragments of the wisdom they absorbed in their student days. Since they all have automobiles, they are invariably elected to the important committees, commissions, and delegations of the party. It is this vain public that impresses the stamp of its mentality on American Socialism. They think that Wilson was infinitely more authoritative than Marx. And, properly speaking, they are simply variants of 'Babbitt', who supplements his commercial activities with dull Sunday meditations on the future of humanity. These people live in small national clans, in which the solidarity of ideas usually serves as a screen for business connections. Each clan has its own leader, usually the most prosperous of the Babbitts. They tolerate all ideas, provided they do not undermine their traditional authority, and do not threaten – God forbid! – their personal comfort. A Babbitt of Babbitts is Hillquit, the ideal Socialist leader for successful dentists.

My first contact with these men was enough to call forth their candid hatred of me. My feelings towards them, though probably less intense, were likewise not especially sympathetic. We belonged to different worlds. To me they seemed the rottenest part of that world with which I was and still am at war.

Old Eugene Debs stood out prominently among the older generation because of the quenchless inner flame of his socialist idealism. Although he was a romantic and a preacher, and not at all a politician or a leader, he was a sincere revolutionary; yet he succumbed to the influence of people who were in every respect his inferiors. Hillquit's art lay in keeping Debs on his left flank while he maintained a business friendship with Gompers. Debs had a captivating personality. Whenever we met, he embraced and kissed me; the old man did not belong to the 'drys'. When the Babbitts proclaimed a blockade against me, Debs took no part in it; he simply drew aside, sorrowfully.

I joined the editorial board of the *Novy Mir* at the very outset. The staff included, besides Bukharin and myself, Volodarsky, who later was killed by the Socialist-Revolutionists in Petrograd, and Chudnovsky, who later was wounded outside Petrograd, and eventually was killed in the Ukraine. The paper was the headquarters for internationalist revolutionary propaganda. In all of the national federations of the Socialist party there were members who spoke Russian, and many of the Russian federation spoke English. In this way the ideas of the *Novy Mir* found their way out into the wider circles of American workers. The mandarins of official Socialism grew alarmed. Intrigues waxed hot against the European immigrant who, it was said, had set foot on American soil only the day before, did not understand the psychology of the American, and was trying to foist his fantastic methods on American workers. The struggle grew bitter. In the Russian federation the 'tried and trusted' Babbitts were promptly shouldered aside. In the German federation old Schlueter, the editor-in-chief of the *Volkszeitung*, and a comrade in arms of Hillquit's, was more and more yielding his influence to the young editor Lore, who shared our views. The Letts were with us to a man. The Finnish federation gravitated towards us. We were penetrating by degrees into the powerful Jewish federation, with its fourteen-storey palace from which two hundred thousand copies of the *Forward* were daily disgorged – a newspaper with the stale odour of sentimentally philistine socialism, always ready for the most perfidious betrayals.

Among the American workers the connections and influence of the Socialist party as a whole, and of our revolutionary wing in particular, were less effective. The English organ of the party, *The Call*, was edited in a spirit of innocuous pacifist neutrality. We decided to begin by establishing a militant Marxist weekly. The preparations for it were in full swing – when the Russian revolution intervened!

After the mysterious silence of the cables for two or three days came the first confused reports of the uprising in Petrograd. The cosmopolitan working-class in New York was all excited. Men hoped and were afraid to hope. The American press was in a state of utter bewilderment. Journalists, interviewers, reporters, came from all sides to the offices of the *Novy Mir*. For a time our paper was the centre of interest of the New York press. Telephone calls from the Socialist newspaper offices and organizations never stopped.

'A cablegram has arrived saying that Petrograd has appointed a Guchkov–Miliukoff ministry. What does it mean?'

'That tomorrow there will be a ministry of Miliukoff and Kerensky.'

'Is that so? And what next?'

'Next? We shall be the next.'

'Oho!'

This sort of thing was repeated dozens of times. Almost everyone I talked with took my words as a joke. At a special meeting of 'worthy and most worthy' Russian Social Democrats I read a paper in which I argued that the proletariat party inevitably would assume power in the second stage of the Russian revolution. This produced about the same sort of impression as a stone thrown into a puddle alive with pompous and phlegmatic frogs. Dr Ingermann did not hesitate to explain that I was ignorant of the four first rules of political arithmetic and that it was not worth while wasting five minutes to refute my nonsensical dreams.

The working-masses took the prospects of revolution quite differently. Meetings, extraordinary for their size and enthusiasm, were held all over New York. Everywhere, the news that the red flag was flying over the Winter Palace brought an excited cheer. Not only the Russian immigrants, but their children, who knew hardly any Russian, came to these meetings to breathe in the reflected joy of the revolution.

At home they saw me only in abrupt flashes. They had a complex life of their own there. My wife was building a nest and the children had new friends. The closest was the chauffeur of Dr M. The doctor's wife took my wife and the boys out driving and was very kind to them. But she was a mere mortal, whereas the chauffeur was a magician, a titan, a superman! With a wave of his hand, he made the machine obey his slightest command. To sit beside him was the supreme delight. When they went into a tea-room, the boys would anxiously demand of their mother, 'Why doesn't the chauffeur come in?'

Children have an amazing capacity for adapting themselves to new surroundings. In Vienna we had lived for the most part in the workers' districts, and my boys mastered the Viennese dialect to perfection, besides speaking Russian and German. Dr Alfred Adler observed with great satisfaction that they spoke the dialect like the good old Viennese cabmen. In the school in Zurich the boys had to switch to the Zurich dialect, which was the language in use in the lower grades, German being studied as a foreign language. In Paris the boys changed abruptly to

French, and within a few months had mastered it. Many times I envied them their ease in French conversation. Although they spent, in all, less than a month in Spain and on the Spanish boat, it was long enough for them to pick up the most useful words and expressions. And then in New York they went to an American school for two months and acquired a rough-and-ready command of English. After the February revolution they went to school in Petrograd. But school life there was disorganized, and foreign languages vanished from their memory even more quickly than they had been acquired. But they spoke Russian like foreigners. We were often surprised to notice that they would build up a Russian sentence as if it were an exact translation from the French – and yet they could not form the sentence in French. Thus the story of our foreign wanderings was written on the brains of the children as indelibly as if they were palimpsests.

When I telephoned my wife from the newspaper office that Petrograd was in the midst of revolution, the younger boy was in bed with diphtheria. He was nine years old, but he realized definitely – and had for a long time – that revolution meant an amnesty, a return to Russia and a thousand other blessings. He jumped to his feet and danced on the bed in honour of the revolution. It was a sign of his recovery.

We were anxious to leave by the first boat. I rushed from consulate to consulate for papers and visas. On the eve of our departure the doctor allowed the convalescent boy to go out for a walk. My wife let him go for half an hour, and began to pack. How many times she had gone through that same operation! But there was no sign of the boy. I was at the office. Three anxious hours; then came a telephone call to my wife. First, an unfamiliar masculine voice, and then Seryozha's voice: 'I am here.' 'Here' meant a police station at the other end of New York. The boy had taken advantage of his first walk to settle a question that had been worrying him for a long time: Was there really a First Street? (We lived on 164th Street, if I am not mistaken.) But he had lost his way, had begun to make inquiries, and was taken to the police station. Fortunately he remembered our telephone number.

When my wife arrived at the station an hour later with our older son, she was greeted gaily, like a long-awaited guest. Seryozha was playing chequers with the policemen, and his face was quite red. To hide his embarrassment over an excess of official attention he was diligently chewing some black American cud with his new friends. He still remembers the telephone number of our New York apartment.

It would be a gross exaggeration to say that I learned much about New York. I plunged into the affairs of American Socialism too quickly and I was straightway up to my neck in work for it. The Russian revolution came so soon that I only managed to catch the general life-rhythm of the monster known as New York. I was leaving for Europe with the feeling of a man who has had only a peep into the foundry in which the fate of man is to be forged. My only consolation was the thought that I might return. Even now I have not given up that hope.

In a Concentration Camp

On 25 March I called at the office of the Russian Consul-General in New York. By that time the portrait of Tsar Nicholas had been removed from the wall, but the heavy atmosphere of a Russian police station under the old régime still hung about the place. After the usual delays and arguments the Consul-General ordered that papers be issued to me for the passage to Russia. In the British consulate, as well, they told me, when I filled out the questionnaire, that the British authorities would put no obstacles in the way of my return to Russia. Everything was in good order.

I sailed with my family and a few other Russians on the Norwegian boat *Christianiafjord* on 27 March. We had been sent off in a deluge of flowers and speeches, for we were going to the country of the revolution. We had passports and visas. Revolution, flowers and visas were balm to our nomad souls. At Halifax the British naval authorities inspected the steamer, and police officers made a perfunctory examination of the papers of the American, Norwegian and Dutch passengers. They subjected the Russians, however, to a downright cross-examination, asking us about our convictions, our political plans, and so forth. I absolutely refused to enter into a discussion of such matters with them. 'You may have all the information you want as to my identity, but nothing else.' Russian politics were not yet under the control of the British naval police. But that did not prevent the detectives, Machen and Westwood, from making inquiries about me among the other passengers after the double attempt to cross-examine me had proved futile. They insisted that I was a dangerous socialist.

The whole business was so offensive, so clearly a discrimination against the Russian revolutionaries, in contrast to the treatment accorded other passengers not so unfortunate as to belong to a nation allied to England, that some of the Russians sent a violent protest to the British authorities. I did not join with them because I saw little use in complaining to Beelzebub about Satan. But at the time we did not foresee the future.

On 3 April British officers, accompanied by bluejackets, came aboard the *Christianiafjord* and demanded, in the name of the local admiral, that I, my family, and five other passengers leave the boat. We were assured that the whole incident would be cleared up in Halifax. We declared that the order was illegal and refused to obey, whereupon armed bluejackets pounced on us, and amid shouts of 'shame' from a large part of the passengers, carried us bodily to a naval cutter, which delivered us in Halifax under the convoy of a cruiser. While a group of sailors were holding me fast, my older boy ran to help me and struck an officer with his little fist. 'Shall I hit him again, papa?' he shouted. He was eleven then, and it was his first lesson in British democracy.

The police left my wife and children in Halifax; the rest of us were taken by train to Amherst, a camp for German prisoners. And there, in the office, we were put through an examination the like of which I had never before experienced, even in the Peter-Paul fortress. For in the Tsar's fortress the police stripped me and searched me in privacy, whereas here our democratic allies subjected us to this shameful humiliation before a dozen men. I still remember Sergeant Olsen, a Swedish-Canadian with a red head of the criminal-police type, who was the leader of the search. The *canaille* who had arranged all this from a distance knew well enough that we were irreproachable Russian revolutionaries returning to our country, liberated by the revolution.

Not until the next morning did the camp commander, Colonel Morris, in answer to our repeated demands and protests, tell us the official reason for the arrest. 'You are dangerous to the present Russian government,' he said briefly. The colonel, obviously not a man of eloquence, had worn an air of rather suspicious excitement since early morning. 'But the New York agents of the Russian government issued us passports into Russia,' we protested, 'and after all the Russian government should be allowed to take care of itself.' Colonel Morris thought for a while, moving his jaws, then added, 'You are dangerous to the Allies in general.'

No written orders for our arrest were ever produced. But, speaking for himself, the colonel explained that since we were political emigrants who obviously had left the country for good reason, we ought not to be surprised at what had happened. For him the Russian revolution simply did not exist. We tried to explain that the Tsar's ministers, who in their day had made us political emigrants, were themselves now in prison, excepting those who had escaped to other countries. But this was too complicated for the colonel, who had made his career in the British colonies and in the Boer war. I did not show proper respect when I spoke to him, which made him growl behind my back, 'If I only had him on the South African coast!' That was his pet expression.

My wife was not formally a political emigrant because she had left Russia on a legal passport. But she was arrested just the same with both our boys, respectively nine and eleven years old. I am not exaggerating when I say that the children were arrested. At first the Canadian authorities tried to separate them from their mother and put them in a children's home. Overwhelmed by such a prospect, my wife declared that she would never allow them to separate her from her boys. And it was only because of her protest that the boys were placed with her in the house of an Anglo-Russian police agent. To prevent 'illegal' dispatch of letters and telegrams, this functionary allowed the children to go out only with an escort, even when they were not with their mother. It was not until eleven days later that my wife and the children were allowed to move to a hotel, on condition that they report each day at the police station.

The Amherst concentration camp was located in an old and very dilapidated iron-foundry that had been confiscated from its German owner. The sleeping bunks were arranged in three tiers, two deep, on each side of the hall. About eight hundred of us lived in these conditions. The air in this improvised dormitory at night can be imagined. Men hopelessly clogged the passages, elbowed their way through, lay down or got up, played cards or chess. Many of them practised crafts, some with extraordinary skill. I still have, stored in Moscow, some things made by Amherst prisoners. And yet, in spite of the heroic efforts of the prisoners to keep themselves physically and morally fit, five of them had gone insane. We had to eat and sleep in the same room with these madmen.

Of these eight hundred prisoners, in whose company I spent almost a month, perhaps five hundred were sailors from German boats sunk by the British; about two hundred were workers caught by the war in Canada, and a hundred more were officers and civilian prisoners of the bourgeois class. Our relations with the German prisoners became clearly defined according to their reaction to the fact that we had been arrested as revolutionary socialists. The officers and petty officers, whose quarters were behind a wooden partition, immediately set us down as enemies; the rank-and-file, on the other hand, surrounded us with an ever-increasing friendliness.

The whole month I was there was like one continuous mass-meeting. I told the prisoners about the Russian revolution, about Liebknecht, about Lenin, and about the causes of the collapse of the old International, and the intervention of the United States in the war. Besides these speeches we had constant group discussions. Our friendship grew warmer everyday. By their attitudes one could class the rank-and-file of the prisoners in two groups: those who said, 'No more of that, we must end it once and for all' – they were the ones who had dreams of coming out into the streets and squares – and those others who said, 'What have they to do with me? No, they won't get me again.'

'How will you hide yourself from them?' others would ask them. The coal-miner, Babinsky, a tall, blue-eyed Silesian, would say, 'I and my wife and children will set our home in a thick forest, and around us I will build traps, and I will never go out without a gun. Let no one dare to come near!'

'Won't you let *me* in, Babinsky?'

'No, not even you. I don't trust anybody.'

The sailors did everything they could to make my life easier, and it was only by constant protests that I kept my right to stand in line for dinner and to do my share of the compulsory work of sweeping floors, peeling potatoes, washing crockery, and cleaning the common lavatory.

The relations between the rank-and-file and the officers, some of whom, even in prison, were still keeping a sort of conduct-book for their men, were hostile. The officers ended by complaining to the camp commander, Colonel Morris, about my anti-patriotic propaganda. The British colonel instantly sided with the Hohenzollern patriots and forbade me to make any more public speeches. But this did not happen until the last few days of our stay at the camp and served only to cement my friendship with the sailors and workers, who responded to the colonel's order by a written protest bearing five hundred and thirty signatures. A plebiscite like this, carried out in the very face of Sergeant Olsen's heavy-handed supervision, was more than ample compensation for all the hardships of the Amherst imprisonment.

All the time we were confined in the camp the authorities steadfastly refused us the right to communicate with the Russian government. Our telegrams to Petrograd were not forwarded. We made an attempt to cable Lloyd George, the British prime minister, protesting against this prohibition, but the cable was held up. Colonel Morris had become accustomed to a simplified form of 'habeas corpus' in the colonies. The war gave him still more protection. He went so far as to stipulate that I refrain from trying to communicate through my wife with the Russian consul before he would let me meet her again. That may sound incredible but it is true. On such a condition I declined to meet my wife. Of course the consul was in no hurry to help us either. He was waiting for instructions, and the instructions, it seemed, were slow in coming.

I must admit that even today the secret machinery of our arrest and our release is not clear to me. The British government must have put me on its black-list when I was still active in France. It did everything it could to help the Tsar's government oust me from Europe, and it must have been on the strength of this black-list, supported by reports of my antipatriotic activities in America, that the British arrested me in Halifax. When the news of my arrest found its way into the revolutionary Russian press, the British embassy in Petrograd, which apparently was not expecting my early return, issued an official statement to the Petrograd press that the Russians who had been arrested in Canada were travelling 'under a subsidy from the German embassy, to overthrow the Provisional Russian government'. This, at least, was plain speaking. The *Pravda*, which was published under Lenin's direction, answered Buchanan on 16 April, doubtless by Lenin's own hand:

Can one even for a moment believe the trustworthiness of the statement that Trotsky, the chairman of the Soviet of Workers' Delegates in St Petersburg in 1905 – a revolutionary who has sacrificed years to a disinterested service of revolution – that this man had anything to do with a scheme subsidized by the German government? This is a patent, unheard-of, and malicious slander of a revolutionary. From whom did you get your information, Mr Buchanan? Why don't you disclose that? Six men dragged Comrade Trotsky away by his legs and arms, all in the name of friendship for the Provisional Russian government!

The part played by the Provisional government in all this is less clear. One needs no proof to show that Miliukoff, then minister of foreign affairs, was heart and soul in favour of my arrest; as early as 1905 he was waging bitter war against 'Trotskyism'; the very term is of his coining. But he was dependent on the Soviet, and had to be all the more circumspect because his social-patriotic allies had not yet begun the baiting of the Bolsheviks.

Buchanan in his memoirs says that 'Trotsky and other Russian refugees were being detained at Halifax until the wishes of the Provisional government with regard to them had been ascertained.' According to the British ambassador, Miliukoff was immediately informed of our arrest. As early as 8 April the British ambassador claims he conveyed Miliukoff's request for our release to his government. Two days later, however, the same Miliukoff withdrew his request and expressed the hope that our stay in Halifax would be prolonged. 'It was the Provisional government, therefore,' concludes Buchanan, 'that was responsible for their further detention.' This all sounds very much like the truth. The only thing that Buchanan forgot to explain in his memoirs is: What became of the German subsidy that I was supposed to have accepted to overthrow the Provisional government? And no wonder – for as soon as I arrived in Petrograd, Buchanan was forced to state in the press that he knew nothing at all about the subsidy. Never before did people lie as much as they did during the 'great war for liberty'. If lies could explode, our planet would have been blown to dust long before the treaty of Versailles.

In the end, the Soviet stepped in and Miliukoff had to bow. On 29 April came the hour for our release from the concentration camp. But even in release we were subjected to violence. We were ordered to pack our things and proceed under convoy. When we demanded the why and wherefore, they refused to say anything. The prisoners became excited because they thought we were being taken to a fortress. We asked for the nearest Russian consul; they refused us again. We had reason enough for not trusting these highwaymen of the sea, and so we insisted that we would not go voluntarily until they told us where we were going. The commander ordered forcible measures. Soldiers of the convoy carried out our luggage, but we stayed stubbornly in our bunks. It was only when the convoy was faced with the task of carrying us out bodily, just as we had been taken off the steamer a month earlier, and of doing it in the midst of a crowd of excited sailors, that the commander relented and told us, in his characteristic Anglo-Colonial way, that we were to sail on a Danish boat for Russia. The colonel's purple face twitched convulsively. He could not bear the thought that we were escaping him. If only it had been on the African coast!

As we were being taken away from the camp, our fellow prisoners gave us a most impressive send-off. Although the officers shut themselves up in their compartment, and only a few poked their noses through the chinks, the sailors and workers lined the passage on both sides, an improvised band played the revolutionary march, and friendly hands were extended to us from every quarter. One of the prisoners delivered a short speech acclaiming the Russian revolution and cursing the German monarchy. Even now it makes me happy to remember that in the very midst of the war we were fraternizing with German sailors in Amherst. In later years I received friendly letters from many of them, sent from Germany.

Machen, the British police officer who had brought about our arrest, was present at our departure. As a parting shot I warned him that my first business in the Constituent Assembly would be to question foreign minister Miliukoff about the outrageous treatment of Russian citizens by the Anglo-Canadian police. 'I hope,' said Machen in quick retort, 'that you will never get into the Constituent Assembly.'

The journey from Halifax to Petrograd passed monotonously, like going through a tunnel – and it really was a tunnel into the revolution. Of my trip through Sweden, I remember nothing but bread-cards, the first I had ever seen. In Finland I met Vandervelde and De Man on a train; they also were going to Petrograd.

'Do you recognize us?' De Man asked.

'I do – although people change a lot in time of war.' And our conversation ended with that not very courteous retort.

In his younger days De Man had tried to be a Marxist and had fought Vandervelde well. During the war he shed the innocent infatuations of his youth in politics; after the war he shed them in theory. He became an agent of his government and nothing more. As for Vandervelde – he was the least important of the leading group of the International. He was elected chairman because neither a German nor a Frenchman could hold the post. As a theorist he was simply a compiler; he manoeuvred his way about among the various socialistic currents as his government did among the Great Powers. He never had any authority among Russian Marxists; as an orator he was never more than a brilliant mediocrity. When the war came along, he exchanged the chairmanship of the International for a post as royal minister. I fought Vandervelde implacably in my Paris paper; by way of answer, he appealed to the Russian revolutionaries to make peace with Tsardom. Now he was going to Petrograd to invite the Russian revolution to take Tsardom's place in the ranks of the Allies. We had nothing to say to each other.

At Belöostrov, the station on the Finnish border, we were welcomed by a delegation of the United Internationalists and the Central Committee of the Bolsheviks. No one was there from the Mensheviks – not even from their 'internationalist' wing (Martov, etc.). I embraced my old friend Uritzky, whom I had met in Siberia at the beginning of the century. He had been the permanent correspondent of the Paris *Nashe Slovo* for Scandinavia, and had acted as our connecting link with Russia during the war. A year after we met at Belöostrov Uritzky was assassinated by a young Socialist-Revolutionist.* It was in the welcoming delegation that I first met Karakhan, who later became famous as a Soviet diplomatist. The Bolsheviks were represented by Fyodorov, a metal-worker who soon after became the chairman of the workers' section of the Petrograd Soviet.

Even before we reached Belöostrov I had learned from the Russian papers that Chernov, Tzereteli and Skobelev had joined the coalition Provisional government. The alignment of the political groups became perfectly clear at once. Looming ahead of us, as something that must be launched promptly, was an implacable fight, allied with the Bolsheviks, against the Mensheviks and the Populists.

We were given a tremendous welcome at the Finnish terminal in Petrograd. Uritzky and Fyodorov made speeches, and I answered with a plea for the necessity of preparing a second revolution – our own. And when they suddenly lifted me into the air, I thought of Halifax, where I had had the same experience; but this time the arms were those of friends. There were many banners around us. I noticed my wife's excited look, and the pale disturbed faces of my boys, who were not certain whether this was a good or a bad sign; they had already been deceived once by the revolution.

At the end of the platform, right behind me, I noticed De Man and Vandervelde. They kept back on purpose, apparently because they were afraid to mix with the crowd. The new Socialist ministers of Russia had not arranged any welcome for their Belgian colleague. Vandervelde's rôle of the day before was still too fresh in everyone's memory.

*The Socialist-Revolutionist Party represented the left wing of the Populist movement. It differed from the Social Democrats and the Marxists in general in its insistence on the identity of the interests of the proletariat and the peasantry, and in its use of terrorist methods against the Tsarist government. – *Translator*.

Immediately after the welcome at the station I found myself in a whirlpool in which men and events swept by me as swiftly as litter on a rushing stream. The most important events are now the least charged with personal memories, for thus does memory guard against burdening itself too heavily. I think that I went from the station straight to the meeting of the Executive Committee of the Soviet. Chiedze, who, at that time was invariably the chairman, greeted me rather dryly. The Bolsheviks moved that I be elected to the Executive Committee, on the strength of my having been chairman of the Soviet in 1905. This threw the committee into confusion. The Mensheviks and the Populists began whispering to one another. They had then an overwhelming majority in all the revolutionary institutions. Finally it was decided to include me in an advisory capacity. I was given my membership card and my glass of tea with black bread.

Even my wife and I shared a bit in the bewilderment of our boys in the streets of Petrograd at hearing Russian and seeing the Russian signs on the shops. We had been away from the capital for ten years. When we left our oldest boy was only a little over a year old; the younger one had been born in Vienna.

The Petrograd garrison was enormous, but it was no longer solid in its allegiances. The soldiers sang revolutionary songs as they marched, and sported red ribbons on their tunics. It all seemed as incredible as a dream. The tram-cars were full of soldiers. Military training was still going on in the wider streets. Riflemen would squat to charge, run a distance in a line, and then squat again. War, the gigantic monster, was still standing behind the revolution, throwing its shadow upon it. But the masses no longer believed in the war, and it seemed as if the training were going on only because no one had thought of stopping it. The war had become impossible, but the liberals (Kadets) had not yet begun to understand that, nor had the leaders of the so-called 'revolutionary democracy'. They were mortally afraid to let go of the skirts of the Entente.

I knew Tzereteli only slightly, Kerensky not at all, and Chiedze somewhat better. Skobelev was an old pupil of mine. With Chernov I had had many passages at arms in the debates abroad. Gotz I now met for the first time. And this was the ruling group of the Soviet democracy.

Tzereteli was unquestionably head and shoulders above the others. I first met him at the London Congress of 1907, when he represented the Social Democratic faction in the Second Duma. Even in those early days he was a splendid speaker whose moral integrity made a strong appeal. His years of hard labour in Siberia advanced his political authority. He returned to the revolutionary arena a mature man and immediately took a foremost place among his confrères and allies. He was the only one of my opponents to be taken seriously. But, as is often the case in history, it took a revolution to prove that Tzereteli was not a revolutionary. One had to approach the Russian revolution from the world point of view rather than from that of Russia, to avoid getting lost in complexities. Yet Tzereteli approached it with the background of his experience in Georgia, supplemented by that in the Second Duma. His political outlook proved to be hopelessly narrow, his education superficially literary. He had a profound respect for liberalism; he viewed the irresistible dynamics of revolution with the eyes of a half-educated bourgeois, terrified for the safety of culture. The awakened masses seemed to him more and more like a mutinous mob. From his very first words, I realized that he was an enemy. Lenin called him a 'dullard'. It was cruel, but apt – Tzereteli was a gifted and honest but limited man.

Lenin called Kerensky a 'petty braggart'. Even now there is little one can add to that. Kerensky was and still is an adventitious figure, a ruling favourite of the historical moment. Every mighty wave of revolution, as it draws in the virgin masses not yet trained to discrimination, inevitably raises on its crest such heroes for a day, heroes who are instantly blinded by their own effulgence. Kerensky followed in the direct line of Father Gapon and Khrustalyov. He personified the accidental in an otherwise continuous causation. His best speeches were merely a sumptuous pounding of water in a mortar. In 1917 the water boiled and sent up steam, and the clouds of steam provided a halo.

Skobelev first entered politics under my guidance when he was a student in Vienna. He left the editorial staff of the Vienna

Pravda to go home to the Caucasus to try to get elected to the Fourth Duma. In this he was successful. In the Duma he came under the influence of the Mensheviks, and entered the February revolution with them. Our connections had long ago been broken off. I found him in Petrograd as a newly created minister of labour. He came swaggering up to me in the Executive Committee and asked me what I thought of it all. I answered: 'I think we shall get the better of you very soon.' It was not very long ago that Skobelev laughingly reminded me of this friendly forecast, which came true six months later. Soon after the October victory he declared himself a Bolshevik. Lenin and I were opposed to his admission to the party. At present of course he is a Stalinite – and in this things are as they should be.

With my wife and children I found with great difficulty a room in the Kiev Hostelry. On our second day there a resplendent young officer called to see us. 'You don't recognize me?' I did not. 'I am Loghinov.' And as I looked at the debonair young officer I remembered a young blacksmith of 1905, a member of a fighting unit, who had engaged in street fights with the police, and had attached himself to me with all the fervour of youth. I lost track of him after 1905. It was only now, in Petrograd, that I learned from him that he was not really the proletarian Loghinov, but a student at the technology institute, a man named Serebrovsky, who came of a wealthy family, but in his younger years had become affiliated with the workers. In the reactionary period he became a qualified engineer and drew away from the revolution; during the war he had been a government director of two of the biggest plants in Petrograd. The February revolution shook him up and made him remember his past. He had heard through the newspapers of my return, and now he was standing before me insisting that my family and I move to his apartment, and that without delay. After some hesitation we consented.

Serebrovsky and his young wife occupied an enormous and luxurious apartment becoming to a director. They had no children; everything was waiting for us there. In a half-starved and dilapidated city we felt as if we were in heaven. But things changed suddenly when we began to talk politics. Serebrovsky was a patriot; we found out afterwards that he hated the Bolsheviks bitterly and considered Lenin a German agent. At the outset he met with opposition from me, and he immediately became more circumspect. But it was impossible to live in the same house with him; so we left the home of these hospitable but, as far as we were concerned, alien people, and returned to our room in the Kiev Hostelry. Some time later Serebrovsky once again got our boys to visit him at his house. He treated them to tea and preserves and the boys gratefully told him their impressions of Lenin's speech at a public meeting, their faces flushed with pleasure over the chatter and the preserves.

'But Lenin is a German spy,' said their host.

What was that? Could anyone have said those words? The boys relinquished their tea and preserves and jumped to their feet. 'Well, that is certainly a dirty thing to say,' declared the elder of the two, as he searched his meagre vocabulary for an appropriate word. It was the host's turn to feel offended, and with this their acquaintance came to an end. After our victory in October I induced Serebrovsky to join in the Soviet work. The Soviet service brought him, as it did so many others, into the Communist party. At present he is a member of Stalin's Central Committee of the party and one of the mainstays of the régime. If he could pass for a proletarian in 1905, it is even easier for him to pass for a Bolshevik now.

After the July days, of which I will say more later, the streets of the capital teemed with slander against the Bolsheviks. I was arrested by Kerensky's government and, two months after my return from exile, found myself once again in the familiar Kresty prison. Colonel Morris of Amherst must have read the news in his morning paper with great satisfaction, and he was not the only one who felt that way about it. But the boys were disgruntled. What sort of a revolution was this, they asked their mother reproachfully, if Dad could first be put in a concentration camp and then in prison? Their mother assured them that this was not yet the real revolution. But the bitterness of scepticism had crept into their souls.

After my release from the prison of the 'revolutionary democracy', we settled down in a little apartment, rented from the widow of a liberal journalist, in a big bourgeois house. Preparations for the October revolution were in full swing. I was made the chairman of the Petrograd Soviet. The press attacked me in every conceivable way. At home we were surrounded by a wall of growing enmity and hatred. Our cook, Anna Osipovna, had to endure the attacks of the housewives whenever she went to the house committee for our ration of bread. My son was hounded at school, and dubbed 'chairman', after his father. When my wife came home from her work at the Wood-Workers' Trade Union, the head janitor watched her go by, with eyes full of hatred. It was torture to walk up the stairs. Our landlady kept asking us over the telephone whether her furniture was safe. We wanted to leave the house – but where could we go? There were no apartments available in the entire city.

The situation was growing more and more intolerable, but one fine day the house blockade ceased as abruptly as if somebody had lifted it with an all-powerful hand. When the head janitor met my wife he would make a bow such as only the most important tenants were privileged to receive. At the house committee the bread was issued without delays or threats. No one banged doors in our faces now. Who had achieved this change – what magician? It was Nikolay Markin. I must give an account of him, because through him, or rather through a collective Markin, the October revolution was victorious.

Markin was a sailor in the Baltic navy, a gunner and a Bolshevik. At the outset we did not know of his existence – it was not his way to push himself forward. Markin was not a speaker; words came to him with difficulty. Moreover, he was shy and sullen, with the sullenness of a force driven in deep. He was cut all of one piece, and of the purest dye. I did not even know that he existed when he undertook to care for my family. He got to know our boys, treated them to tea and sandwiches at the canteen of the Smolny and, in general, provided them with the little pleasures that were so hard to get in that grim period. Without ever showing himself, he would drop in to inquire if everything was all right. I did not even suspect his existence. From the boys and from Anna Osipovna he learned that we were living in the camp of the enemy. Markin called on the head janitor and the house committee, not alone, I think, but with a group of sailors. He must have used some very persuasive words, for suddenly everything about us was changed. And thus, even before the October revolution, there was a dictatorship of the proletariat in our house. Not until much later did we learn that the sailor, our children's friend, was responsible for all this.

As soon as the Soviet turned Bolshevik the Central Executive Committee opposed to the Bolsheviks used the support of the owners of the printing works to deprive the Soviet of its paper. We needed a new organ. I consulted Markin. He vanished into the abyss, made the necessary calls, had his say with the printers, and in a few days we had a newspaper. We called it *The Worker and the Soldier*. Markin spent day and night in the office arranging things. During the October days his solid figure, with its dark and sullen head, was always turning up in the most dangerous places at the most crucial moment. He called to see me only to say that everything was all right and ask if I needed anything. He had widened his sphere – he was establishing the dictatorship of the proletariat in Petrograd.

The looting of the rich wine stores of the capital by the rabble of the streets was beginning. Behind this dangerous movement was someone who was trying to consume the revolution in the flames of alcohol. Markin instantly sensed the danger and went to fight it. He guarded the wine stores; when it was impossible to guard them, he destroyed them. In high boots, he would wade to his knees in precious wines full of broken bottles. The wine flowed down the open street sewers into the Neva and stained the snow; tipplers lapped it up from the gutters. With revolver in hand, Markin fought for a sober October. Soaked to the skin, exuding the fragrance of the choicest wines, he would return home, where our two boys were waiting breathlessly for him. Markin beat off the alcoholic attack of the counter-revolution.

When I was entrusted with the ministry of foreign affairs, it seemed quite impossible to start anything. The entire staff, from the assistant minister to the typist, were practising sabotage against us. The cases were locked and the keys were missing. I called in Markin, who knew the secret of direct action. Two or three diplomats spent twenty-four hours in locked rooms, and the next day Markin brought me the keys and invited me to the ministry. But I was still busy at the Smolny with the general work of the revolution, and so, for a time, Markin became an unofficial minister of foreign affairs. He learned the mechanism of the commissariat quickly, carried on the weeding-out of the high-born and thieving diplomats with a firm hand, reorganized the office, confiscated for the benefit of the homeless the contraband which was still coming through from abroad in the valises of diplomats, extracted the more instructive secret documents from the archives, and published them on his own responsibility and with his own commentaries in separate pamphlets. Markin had no academic degree, and his writing was not free from grammatical errors. His comments were sometimes quite unexpected. But on the whole he drove the diplomatic nails in firmly, and at the very points where they were most needed. Baron von Kühlmann and Count Tsernin read Markin's yellow pamphlets at Brest-Litovsk eagerly.

Then the civil war began. Markin filled many breaches. Now he was establishing the dictatorship far to the east, commanding a flotilla on the Volga, and driving the enemy before him. Whenever I heard that the man at the danger-point was Markin, I felt relieved and heartened. But his hour had struck. On the Kama an enemy's bullet overtook Nikolay Georgiyevich Markin and knocked him off his strong seaman's feet. When the telegram telling of his death reached me, I felt as if a column of granite had come crashing down in front of me. His photograph stood on the children's table in a sailor cap with ribbons.

'Boys, boys, Markin is dead!'

Two pale faces were twisted with sudden pain before me. They had been on an equal footing with the sullen Nikolay. He had initiated them into his plans and into the secrets of his life. With tears in his eyes he had told the nine-year-old Seryozha that the woman he had loved so dearly and so long had deserted him, and that was why there was often darkness and sullenness in his soul. In a frightened whisper and with tears in his eyes, Seryozha had confided this secret to his mother. This tender friend, who had opened his soul to the boys as if they had been his equals, was at the same time an old sea-wolf and revolutionary, a true hero, like those of the most marvellous fairy-tales. Could it really be true that the Markin who, in the basement of the ministry, had taught them how to use revolver and gun was now dead? In the silence of the night, two little bodies shook under their blankets after the black news came. Only their mother heard their disconsolate sobs.

Life was a whirl of mass meetings. When I arrived in Petrograd, I found all the revolutionary orators either hoarse or voiceless. The revolution of 1905 had taught me to guard my voice with care, and thanks to this I was hardly ever out of the ranks. Meetings were held in plants, schools, and colleges, in theatres, circuses, streets, and squares. I usually reached home exhausted after midnight; half-asleep I would discover the best arguments against my opponents, and about seven in the morning, or sometimes even earlier, I would be pulled painfully from my bed by the hateful, intolerable knocking on the door, calling me to a meeting in Peterhof, or to go to Kronstadt on a tug sent for me by the navy boys there. Each time it would seem to me as if I could never get through this new meeting, but some hidden reserve of nervous energy would come to the surface, and I would speak for an hour, sometimes two, while delegations from other plants or districts, surrounding me in a close ring, would tell me that thousands of workers in three or perhaps five different places had been waiting for me for hours on end. How patiently that awakening mass was waiting for the new word in those days!

The mass meetings in the Modern Circus were for me quite special. My opponents likewise considered them so, but in a different light. They regarded the circus as my particular fortress, and never even attempted to speak in it. But whenever I attacked the conciliationists in the Soviet, I was interrupted by bitter shouts: 'This is not your Modern Circus.' It became quite a refrain.

I usually spoke in the Circus in the evening, sometimes quite late at night. My audience was composed of workers, soldiers, hard-working mothers, street urchins – the oppressed underdogs of the capital. Every square inch was filled, every human body compressed to its limit. Young boys sat on their fathers' shoulders; infants were at their mothers' breasts. No one smoked.

The balconies threatened to fall under the excessive weight of human bodies. I made my way to the platform through a narrow human trench, sometimes I was borne overhead. The air, intense with breathing and waiting, fairly exploded with shouts and with the passionate yells peculiar to the Modern Circus. Above and around me was a press of elbows, chests, and heads. I spoke from out of a warm cavern of human bodies; whenever I streched out my hands I would touch someone, and a grateful movement in response would give me to understand that I was not to worry about it, not to break off my speech, but to keep on. No speaker, no matter how exhausted, could resist the electric tension of that impassioned human throng. They wanted to know, to understand, to find their way. At times it seemed as if I felt, with my lips, the stern inquisitiveness of this crowd that had become merged into a single whole. Then all the arguments and words thought out in advance would break and recede under the imperative pressure of sympathy, and other words, other arguments, utterly unexpected by the orator but needed by these people, would emerge in full array from my subconsciousness. On such occasions I felt as if I were listening to the speaker from the outside, trying to keep pace with his ideas, afraid that, like a somnambulist, he might fall off the edge of the roof at the sound of my conscious reasoning.

Such was the Modern Circus. It had its own contours, fiery, tender, and frenzied. The infants were peacefully sucking the breasts from which approving or threatening shouts were coming. The whole crowd was like that, like infants clinging with their dry lips to the nipples of the revolution. But this infant matured quickly.

Leaving the Modern Circus was even more difficult than entering it. The crowd was unwilling to break up its new-found unity; it would refuse to disperse. In a semi-consciousness of exhaustion I had to float on countless arms above the heads of the people to reach the exit. Sometimes I would recognize among them the faces of my two daughters, who lived near by with their mother. The elder was sixteen, the younger fifteen. I would barely manage to beckon to them in answer to their excited glances, or to press their warm hands on the way out, before the crowd would separate us again. When I found myself outside the gate, the Circus followed me. The street became alive with shouts and the tramping of feet. Then some gate would open, suck me in, and close after me. This would be the doing of my friends, who pushed me into the palace of the dancer Kseshinskaya, a palace built for her by Tsar Nicholas. There the general staff of the Bolsheviks had firmly entrenched itself, and men in grey soldiers' coats sat on the silk-upholstered furniture or tramped the long-unpolished floors in their heavy boots. One could wait there until the crowd cleared away, and then go out again.

Walking in the dark along the deserted streets after the meeting, I caught the sound of footsteps behind me. The same thing had happened the night before and, as it now seemed, the night before that. With my hand on my Browning I turned sharply and walked back a few steps.

'What do you want?' I ask sternly. I saw a young, devoted face before me.

'Allow me to protect you. Some of those who come to the Circus are enemies.' It was the student Poznansky. From then on he was always with me. Through all the years of the revolution he was attached to me for special missions, of varying sorts but always involving great responsibility. He guarded my personal safety, organized secretarial help during military campaigns, sought out forgotten war stores, got the necessary books, built fighting squadrons out of nothing, fought at the front himself, and later on in the ranks of the opposition. He is now in exile. I hope that the future will bring us together again.

On 3 December, when I was speaking before the audience of the Modern Circus, I made a report on the work of the Soviet government. I explained the significance of our publishing the diplomatic correspondence of Tsarism and Kerensky. I told my faithful listeners how, in reply to my assertion that the people cannot shed their blood for agreements which they do not conclude, do not read, and do not see, the conciliationists in the Soviet had cried out to me: 'Don't speak to us in this language. This is not your Modern Circus.' And I repeated my answer to the conciliationists: 'I know only one tongue, one revolutionary language. I speak it to the people at their meetings, and I shall speak it to the Allies and the Germans.' The newspaper report of this speech records prolonged applause at this point. My connection with the Modern Circus ended only in February, when I went to Moscow.

25
Concerning Slanderers

When I arrived in Petrograd in the early part of May 1917, the campaign about the 'sealed car' in which Lenin had made his way through Germany was in full blast. The new Socialist ministers were in alliance with Lloyd George, who had refused to let Lenin pass into Russia. And the same gentlemen were hounding Lenin for passing through Germany. My own experience on the return journey supplemented Lenin's experience with a proof from the contrary. But that didn't save me from being made the butt of the same slander. Buchanan was the first to set the ball rolling. In an open letter to the minister of foreign affairs (in May, it was no longer Miliukoff, but Teryeschenko) I described my Atlantic Odyssey. My argument culminated in this question: 'Do you, Mr Minister, consider it in order that England should be represented by a man who has disgraced himself by such shameless calumny and who has not moved a finger to rehabilitate himself?'

There was no answer, nor did I expect one. But Miliukoff's paper stepped in to defend the ambassador of an ally, and repeated the charge on its own behalf. I decided to brand the calumniators as solemnly as I could. The first all-Russian congress of Soviets was then in session. On 5 June the hall was full to the brim. At the close of the meeting I rose to make a personal statement. Gorky's paper, which was hostile to the Bolsheviks, next day reported my concluding words and the scene as a whole as follows:

'Miliukoff charges us with being hired agents of the German government. From this tribunal of the revolutionary democracy I ask the honest Russian press [Trotsky here turns to the press table] to reproduce my exact words: Until Miliukoff withdraws his accusation, the brand of a dishonourable slander will remain on his forehead.'

'Trotsky's statement', the report continues, 'uttered with force and dignity, was received with a unanimous ovation from the entire gathering. The whole congress, without distinction of faction, applauded stormily for several minutes.'

And nine tenths of the congress were our opponents. But this success, as subsequent events proved, was fleeting. It was one of the paradoxes peculiar to parliamentarism. Next day the *Rech* (*The Speech*) tried to pick up the glove by publishing the statement that the German patriotic *Verein* in New York had given me $10,000 to overthrow the Provisional government. This at least was plain speaking. I must explain that two days before I left for Europe, the German workers in New York, to whom I had lectured many times, together with my American, Russian, Lettish, Jewish, Lithuanian, and Finnish friends and followers, had given me a farewell meeting at which a collection was taken up for the Russian revolution. The sum collected amounted to $310, of which $100 was contributed by the German workers through their chairman at the meeting. On the following day, with the consent of those who organized the meeting, I distributed the $310 among five emigrants who were returning to Russia and were short of money for the trip. That was the history of the $10,000. I recounted it at the time in Gorky's paper, the *Novaya Zhizn* (27 June), ending the article with this moral:

To provide the necessary corrective for future occasions, I feel that it is pertinent for me to state, for the benefit of liars, slanderers, Kadet* reporters and blackguards in general, that in my entire life I have not only never had at my disposal, at one time, $10,000, but even a tenth of that sum. Such a confession, I am afraid, may ruin my reputation among the Kadet public more completely than all the insinuations of M. Miliukoff, but I have long since become reconciled to the thought of living without the approval of the liberal bourgeois.

After this the slanderous tales died down. I summed up the whole campaign in a pamphlet, 'To the Slanderers', and sent it

---

*The Constitutional-Democratic Party, founded by Prof. Miliukoff, is known colloquially as the 'Kadet' party (after the first letters, K–D) and its members as the 'Kadets'. In Russian usage the term is almost synonymous with 'liberal'. – *Translator*.

to the printers. A week later the July days were upon us, and on 23 July I was imprisoned by the Provisional government on the charge of being in the service of the German Kaiser. The investigation was in the hands of practitioners of justice seasoned under the régime of the Tsar. They were unaccustomed to treating facts or arguments honestly. This was a turbulent time too. When I learned what the prosecution's material was, I was so amused at its helpless stupidity that it took the edge off my wrath at the villainy of the accusation itself. I wrote in the record of the preliminary investigation of 1 September:

In view of the fact that the very first document produced (the deposition of corporal Yermolyenko, which so far has played the leading rôle in the persecution of my party and me, a persecution undertaken with the aid of members of the Department of Justice) is unquestionably a purposely fabricated document, not intended to clear up the case, but maliciously to cloud things over; in view also of the fact that M. Alexandrov, the court-examiner, has wilfully ignored the most important questions and circumstances concerning this document, the examination of which would inevitably expose the falsity of the evidence submitted by Yermolyenko, a person whom I do not know; in view of all this, I consider it morally and politically debasing for me to take any part in the procedure of investigation, while I reserve the right to expose the true meaning of the accusation before the public by every means at my disposal.

The accusation was soon lost in the larger events that swallowed up not only the investigators but all of old Russia, with her 'new' heroes, like Kerensky.

I did not think that I should have to return to this subject. But there is a writer who in 1928 picked up and supported the old slander. His name is Kerensky. In 1928, eleven years after the revolutionary happenings that lifted him so suddenly to the crest and washed him as inevitably away, Kerensky assured us that Lenin and other Bolsheviks were agents of the German government, were connected with the German general staff, were receiving sums of money from it, and were carrying out its secret instructions with a view to bringing about the defeat of the Russian army and the dismemberment of the Russian state. This is all told in great detail in his amusing book,* and with especial emphasis on pages 290-310. I had formed a pretty clear idea of Kerensky's intellectual and moral stature from the events of 1917, but I never would have thought it possible that at this time, after all that has happened, he could have the audacity to repeat the accusation. But that is exactly what he did.

He writes: 'Lenin's betrayal of Russia, at the most crucial moment in the war, is *an indubitable, established historical fact.*' Who, then, supplied these indubitable proofs, and when? Kerensky starts off with a pretentious story about how the German general staff recruited candidates for its espionage among the Russian prisoners of war and shoved them into the Russian armies. One of these spies, either actual or self-constituted (often they themselves did not know), presented himself to Kerensky to tell him of the entire espionage system. But, remarks Kerensky with a melancholy air, 'these disclosures had no particular importance'. Precisely. Even from his own account one can see that some petty adventurer tried to lead him by the nose. Did this episode have any relation to Lenin or to the Bolsheviks in general? None whatsoever. The episode, as Kerensky himself admits, had no particular importance. Then why does he tell it? Only because he wants to fill in his narrative and make his further disclosures appear more important. Like his informer Kerensky simply wants to lead the reader by the nose.

Yes, he says, the first case had no importance, but then, from another source, they received information of 'great value', and that information '*proved beyond the possibility of a doubt* that the Bolsheviks were in contact with the German general staff'. Please note that 'beyond the possibility of a doubt'. Next follows: 'The ways and means, too, by which this contact was maintained, could be established.' *Could* be established? This sounds equivo-

---

*The quotations in the above text are translated directly from the Russian edition of Kerensky's book, and the pages cited refer to that edition. An English translation is published in New York by D. Appleton & Co. under the title of *The Catastrophe*. In that translation the passages discussed will be found on pp. 229-33. – *Translator*.

cal. Were they established? We will know presently. Let us be patient: it took eleven years for the disclosure to ripen in the depths of its creator's soul.

'In April, a Ukranian officer by the name of Yarmolyenko came to General Alexeyev at Headquarters.' We had heard this name. He is the decisive figure in all this business. One notes too that Kerensky cannot be exact even when he has no interest in being inexact. The name of the petty rogue whom he brings out on the stage is not 'Yarmolyenko', but 'Yermolyenko'.* This, at least, was the name under which he was listed by Mr Kerensky's court investigators.

And so corporal Yermolyenko (Kerensky refers to him as 'officer' with intentional vagueness) presented himself at headquarters as a pretended German agent, to expose the real German agents. The evidence given by this great patriot, whom even the bourgeois press – bitterly hostile to the Bolsheviks – was soon obliged to characterize as a dark and suspicious person, proved conclusively, once and for all, that Lenin was not one of history's greatest figures, but only a paid agent of Ludendorff's. How did corporal Yermolyenko discover this secret, and what proofs did he submit to captivate Kerensky? Yermolyenko, according to his statement, had received instructions from the German staff to carry on separatist propaganda in the Ukraine. 'He was given,' Kerensky relates, 'all (!) the necessary information regarding the ways and means of maintaining contact with the directing (!) German representatives, regarding the banks (!) through which the necessary funds had been forwarded, and the names of the more important agents, which included several Ukrainian separatists and Lenin.'

All this is printed word for word on pages 295–6 of the great opus. Now we at least know how the German general staff behaved towards its spies. When it found an unknown and semi-literate corporal as a candidate for espionage work, it did not put him under the observation of a junior officer of the German intelligence service, but connected him with the 'directing German representatives', acquainted him at once with the entire

* In Russian, the diphthongs 'ya' and 'ye' are represented by two different characters: 'Я' and 'Е', respectively. – *Translator.*

network of German agents and even gave him the list of banks – not one, but all the banks – through which it forwarded its secret German funds. Say what you will, you cannot dispel the impression that the German staff acted with arrant stupidity. This impression is the result, however, of our seeing the German staff not as it really was, but as pictured by 'Max and Moritz', the two corporals – the military corporal Yermolyenko and the political corporal Kerensky.

But, in spite of his being unknown, unintelligent, and low in rank, could Yermolyenko perhaps have held some high post in the German espionage system? Kerensky would like to make us think so. But we happen to know not only Kerensky's book but his sources as well. Yermolyenko himself is simpler than Kerensky. In his evidence, given in the tone of a stupid little adventurer, Yermolyenko himself quotes his price: The German general staff gave him exactly 1,500 roubles – the highly depreciated roubles of that time – for all the expenses incurred in arranging for the secession of the Ukraine and Kerensky's overthrow. He candidly adds in his evidence (it has now been published) that he had complained bitterly but in vain about the stinginess of the Germans. 'Why so little?' protested Yermolyenko, but the 'directing personages' were deaf to all his pleas. Yermolyenko does not tell us, however, whether he conducted his negotiations with Ludendorff, Hindenburg, the Crown Prince or the Kaiser himself. He stubbornly refrains from naming the 'directing' gentlemen who had given him his 1,500 roubles for the breaking up of Russia, travelling expenses, tobacco, and liquor. We venture the hypothesis that the money was spent mostly on liquor, and that after the German funds had melted from the corporal's pockets, without resorting to the banks of which he had been told in Berlin, he bravely presented himself at the headquarters of the Russian general staff to find further patriotic help. It is quite probable that on his way there he was picked up by some officer of the Russian intelligence service engaged in hounding out Bolsheviks, and it was from just such an officer that he probably got his inspiration. As a result, two views of life, so to speak, were lodged in the corporal's incapacious head: on the one hand he could not suppress his sense of injury against the German lieutenant who had thrown down 1,500 roubles and not a kopeck more; on the other he did not dare forget that he had been initiated by the 'directing German representatives' into the whole German espionage system, including all its agents and banks.

And who were the 'several Ukrainian separatists' whom Yermolyenko disclosed to Kerensky? Kerensky's book says nothing about this. To give additional weight to some of Yermolyenko's sorry lies, Kerensky simply adds a few of his own. According to his testimony, the only separatist Yermolyenko mentioned was Skoropis-Ioltukhovksy. But Kerensky is silent about this name, because his very mention of it would have compelled him to admit that Yermolyenko had no disclosures to make. The name of Ioltukhovksy was no secret to anyone. During the war the papers had mentioned it several times. And he himself did not try to conceal his connection with the German general staff. In the Paris *Nashe Slovo*, as early as the close of 1914, I had branded that small group of Ukrainian separatists who associated themselves with the German military authorities. I named all of them, including Ioltukhovksy. But we are also told that Yermolyenko had mentioned not only 'several Ukrainian separatists', but Lenin as well. Why separatists were mentioned one can perhaps understand; Yermolyenko himself was being sent for separatist propaganda. But why mention Lenin to him? Kerensky does not answer that; and it is not through oversight, either.

Yermolyenko drags the name of Lenin in senselessly and without any connection. The man who inspired Kerensky tells how he was recruited as a paid German spy with 'patriotic' aims; how he demanded an increase in his 'secret funds' (1,500 war roubles); how he was informed of his future duties, such as espionage, blowing up bridges, etc. Then, according to his testimony, – and all this has nothing at all to do with the story he has just been telling – he was told (by whom?) that he would be working in Russia but 'not alone'; that 'Lenin and his followers were working in the same (!) direction there'. This is the verbatim text of his deposition. It seems that a petty agent engaged in blowing up bridges is initiated, for no practical reason, into such a secret as the relationship between Lenin and

Ludendorff. Yermolyenko suddenly adds at the end of his evidence, still with no apparent connection with the rest of the tale, but obviously at the crude prompting of some other person: 'I was told [by whom?] that Lenin took part in conferences in Berlin (with the representatives of the German general staff) and that he stayed at the home of Skoropis-Ioltukhovksy, *as I later learned for myself.*' And that's all. Not a word to explain *how* he had found out.

The court examiner, Alexandrov, showed not the slightest interest in this single 'factual' bit of Yermolyenko's testimony. He did not ask him the plainest question as to *how* the corporal found out that Lenin was in Berlin during the war and that he had stayed with Skoropis-Ioltukhovsky. Or perhaps Alexandrov did ask this question – he could hardly help asking it – but, receiving an answer as inarticulate as a cow's moo, decided not to keep the episode on record at all. Probably! Are we not entitled to ask about this cock-and-bull story: what fool will believe it? But it seems there are so-called statesmen who pretend that they believe it and invite their readers to believe it, too.

And is that all? It is. The military corporal has nothing more to say. The political corporal has only hypotheses and guesses. We will follow him. 'The Provisional government,' Kerensky relates, 'saw itself confronted with a difficult problem – that of further investigating the threads indicated by Yermolyenko, following on the heels of the agents who were going back and forth between Lenin and Ludendorff, and catching them red-handed with the most incriminating material.'

This high-sounding sentence is woven of two threads: falsehood and cowardice. This is the first time the name of Ludendorff is introduced. Yermolyenko does not mention a single German name: the corporal's head was remarkable for its small capacity. Kerensky speaks with studied ambiguousness of the agents who went to and fro between Lenin and Ludendorff. On the one hand it sounds as if the reference is too definite, already known agents who had only to be caught red-handed; on the other it looks as if Kerensky simply had a platonic idea of agents. If he intended to 'follow on their heels', his problem was that of following unknown, anonymous, transcendental heels. By his verbal artifices, he only discloses his own Achilles' heel, or, to put it in less classical language, his own 'ass's hoof'.

According to Kerensky, the investigation was conducted so secretly that no one but four ministers knew anything about it. Even the poor minister of justice, Perevyerzev, was not informed of it. That is the meaning of a really 'statesmanlike' approach! At a time when the German general staff was disclosing to every Tom, Dick and Harry not only the names of its trusted banks, but even its connection with the leaders of the greatest revolutionary party, Kerensky was doing the exact opposite; aside from himself, he could find only three ministers case-hardened enough to follow on the heels of Ludendorff's agents.

'The task was very difficult, complicated and long drawn-out,' is Kerensky's plaint. We are ready to believe that. But finally his patriotic efforts were crowned with success. Kerensky says it in so many words: 'Our success, at any rate, was simply annihilating for Lenin. His connection with Germany was established unquestionably.'

Let us remember that 'established unquestionably'. How and by whom?

It is at this point in his crime novel that Kerensky introduces two well-known Polish revolutionaries, Ganetsky and Kozlovsky, and a certain Madame Sumenson, of whom no one could give any information and whose very existence has not yet been proved. These three, it is alleged, were the contact agents in question. What are Kerensky's grounds for representing the now defunct Kozlovsky, and Ganetsky, who is still alive, as intermediaries between Ludendorff and Lenin? No information is given. Yermolyenko did not even mention these names. They crop up in Kerensky's pages just as they cropped up in the newspaper pages of the July days of 1917, as suddenly as *dei ex machina*, with the Tsarist intelligence service playing the part of the machine.

Here is Kerensky's story: 'The Bolshevik German agent from Stockholm, who was carrying with him documents which proved incontrovertibly the connection between Lenin and the German high command, was to be arrested on the Russo-Swedish border. The documents were known to us, exactly.'

This agent, it transpires, was Ganetsky. We see that the four ministers, of whom the prime minister was naturally the wisest, did not work in vain: the Bolshevik agent from Stockholm was carrying with him documents that were known beforehand ('known exactly') to Kerensky – documents containing incontrovertible proof that Lenin was the agent for Ludendorff. But why doesn't Kerensky let us share his secret knowledge of these documents? Why doesn't he throw some light, if only in a few words, on what they were about? Why doesn't he say, or even intimate, how he learned of the contents of these documents? Why doesn't he explain what the idea of the Bolshevik agent was in carrying documents that proved the Bolsheviks to be agents of Germany? Kerensky doesn't say a word about all this. Once again, may we not ask: what fool will believe him?

But it turns out that the Stockholm agent was never actually arrested. The remarkable documents, 'known exactly' to.Kerensky in 1917 but still unknown to his readers in 1928, were never captured. The Bolshevik agent was proceeding towards the Swedish frontier, but he never reached it. Why? Because the minister of justice, Perevyerzev, who could not follow on his heels, bolted out corporal Yermolyenko's great secret too soon. And success was so near, and so easy!

'The two months' work of the Provisional government (chiefly of Teryeschenko) directed towards the exposure of the Bolshevik intrigues, ended in *failure*.' Yes, those are Kerensky's exact words: 'ended in failure'. On a previous page it was said that 'the success of this work was simply annihilating for Lenin'; his connection with Ludendorff was 'incontrovertibly established'; and now we read that 'the two months' work ended in *failure*'. Doesn't all of this seem like rather questionable clowning?

Yet despite the failure of the four ministers who followed on the heels of the legendary Madame Sumenson, Kerensky does not lose heart. He proudly declares of the connection of the Bolsheviks with Ludendorff: '*in complete consciousness of my responsibility before history*, I can only repeat the words of the Prosecuting Attorney of the Petrograd Regional court'. This is his culmination. It was thus that he appeared on the public platform in 1927 to charm the bourgeois volunteers, the Left lieutenants, the *gymnasium* students and the democratic young ladies: 'in complete consciousness of my responsibility before history'. Here he is, in his full stature, the inimitable political corporal, Narcissus Kerensky. And a few pages after this solemn oath, another deadly confession: 'We, the Provisional government, in this way lost for ever (!) the possibility of proving Lenin's treason decisively, and on the basis of documentary material.'

'Lost for ever.' Of the whole structure founded on Yermolyenko's shoulders, nothing is left, after all, except the word of honour before history.

But even this is not the end. Kerensky's falsehood and cowardice reveal themselves perhaps more strikingly than ever in his treatment of my case. Concluding his list of German agents who were to be arrested by his orders, he modestly remarks: 'A few days later Trotsky and Lunacharsky were arrested.' That is the only place where he includes me in the German espionage system. He does it with studied vagueness, without any elocutionary bouquets, and saving his 'words of honour'. There is reason enough for this. Kerensky cannot avoid mentioning me altogether, because his government did arrest me on the same charge as that preferred against Lenin. But he does not want to – nor is he able to – dwell on the evidence against me, because in my case his government disclosed its aforementioned 'ass's hoof' in a very spectacular way.

The only evidence against me that the court examiner Alexandrov produced was the allegation that I together with Lenin had passed through Germany in a sealed car. The old watch-dog of Tsarist justice had not the ghost of an idea that Lenin's companion in the sealed car was not I but the leader of the Mensheviks, Martov; whereas I arrived a month after Lenin from New York, travelling by way of a Canadian concentration camp and Scandinavia. The charges against the Bolsheviks were being compiled by such sorry and contemptible dealers in lies that they did not even think it necessary to find out from the newspapers when and by what route Trotsky had come back to Russia. I showed the court examiner up then and there. I flung his dirty little papers in his face and turned my back on him. Then I sent a protest to the Provisional government. Kerensky's criminal guilt towards his readers is all the more obvious in its crudeness on this point. He knows how disgracefully his court justice collapsed in its charges against me. And that is why, although he includes me, in passing, in the German espionage system, he does not say a word about how he himself and his three other ministers had been following on my heels across Germany at the time that I was in a concentration camp in Canada.

'If Lenin had not had the support of all the material and technical power of the German propaganda apparatus and the espionage system,' the slanderer generalizes, 'he would never have succeeded in destroying Russia.' Kerensky wants to believe that the old régime (and he, along with it) was overthrown by German spies rather than by the revolutionary people. How consoling it must be to have a historical philosophy that represents the life of a great country as a toy in the hands of an organization of spies maintained by that country's neighbours! But if the military and technical power of Germany was able to overthrow Kerensky's democracy in a few months and plant Bolshevism in its place by artificial means, why has the material and technical apparatus of all the countries of the Entente failed in twelve years to overthrow this artificially fostered Bolshevism? But let us not be drawn into the realm of historical philosophy; let us stick to the world of facts. In what did the technical and financial assistance of Germany actually find expression? Kerensky does not say a word about that. In 1917 the Bolsheviks in Petrograd were publishing a tiny newspaper, like the one they had published in 1912 before the war. They were issuing handbills. They had agitators. In other words we were a revolutionary party. Where, then, did the help of the German espionage system express itself? Of this, too, there is no word in Kerensky's book. But what could one say of this, anyway?

We have examined Kerensky's evidence 'before history', suppressing our disgust and resorting to the support of a saving irony that is sometimes as necessary as a lemon in seasickness. We have not ignored a single argument or a single consideration, in spite of the doubt that kept plaguing us throughout this examination: whether it was generally worth while to rake up this garbage. Ludendorff, Hindenburg, and many other heads and workers of the German staff are still alive. They are all enemies of the Bolsheviks. What prevents them from giving away the old secret? In Germany the power is now in the hands of the Social Democracy, which has access to all the old archives. If Ludendorff did not hide his connection with Lenin from Yermolyenko, there are surely many people in Germany who knew at least as much as was confided to the Russian corporal. Why do all these implacable enemies of the Bolsheviks and the October revolution keep silent?

It is true that Kerensky mentions Ludendorff's memoirs. But only one fact emerges from these memoirs: Ludendorff hoped that the revolution in Russia would lead to a disintegration of the Russian army – first the February revolution, and later the October one. No memoirs were necessary to disclose this scheme of his. The fact that he allowed a group of Russian revolutionaries to pass through Germany was enough. On Ludendorff's part this was an adventure dictated by the grave military situation in Germany. Lenin took advantage of Ludendorff's plans to further thereby his own. Ludendorff was saying to himself: 'Lenin will overthrow the patriots, and then I will strangle Lenin and his friends.' And Lenin was saying to himself: 'I shall pass through in Ludendorff's car, but for his service I shall pay him in my own way.'

No detective talents like Kerensky's were necessary to prove that two opposing historical plans crossed each other's paths at a certain point, and that this point was the 'sealed car'. The fact is history. Since then history has already had time to check up on both reckonings. On 25 October (7 November) 1917 the Bolsheviks seized power. Exactly a year later, under the mighty influence of the Russian revolution, the revolutionary masses of Germany overthrew Ludendorff and his masters. And ten years after that the democratic Narcissus whose feelings history had hurt tried to give fresh life to a stupid calumny – not against Lenin, but against a great nation and its revolution.

26

From July to October

On 4 June, a declaration that I had submitted concerning Kerensky's preparation for an offensive at the front was read by the Bolshevik faction at the congress of the Soviets. We had pointed out that the offensive was an adventure that threatened the very existence of the army. But the Provisional government was growing intoxicated with its own speechifying. The ministers thought of the masses of soldiers, stirred to their very depths by the revolution, as so much soft clay to be moulded as they pleased. Kerensky toured the front, adjured and threatened the troops, kneeled, kissed the earth – in a word, clowned it in every possible way, while he failed to answer any of the questions tormenting the soldiers. He had deceived himself by his cheap effects, and, assured of the support of the congress of the Soviets, ordered the offensive. When the calamity that the Bolsheviks had warned against came, the Bolsheviks were made the scapegoats. They were hounded furiously. The reaction, which the Kadet party was shielding, pressed in from all sides, demanding our heads.

The faith of the masses in the Provisional government was hopelessly undermined. At this second stage of the revolution Petrograd was again too far in the van. In the July days this vanguard came to an open clash with Kerensky's government. It was not yet an uprising, but only a reconnaissance that went deep. But it had already become obvious in the July encounter that Kerensky had no 'democratic' army behind him; that the forces supporting him against us were those of a counter-revolution.

During the session in the Taurid Palace on 3 July I learned of the demonstration of the machine-gun regiment and its appeal to other troops and to factory workers. The news came as a surprise to me. The demonstration had been spontaneous, at the initiative of the masses, but next day it went farther, now with the participation of our party. The Taurid Palace was overrun by the people. They had only one slogan: 'Power to the Soviets.'

In front of the palace a suspicious-looking group of men who had kept aloof from the crowd seized the minister of agriculture, Chernov, and put him in an automobile. The crowd watched indifferently; at any rate their sympathy was not with him. The news of Chernov's seizure and of the danger that threatened him reached the palace. The Populists decided to use machine-gun armoured cars to rescue their leader. The decline of their popularity was making them nervous; they wanted to show a firm hand. I decided to try to go with Chernov in the automobile away from the crowd, in order that I might release him afterwards. But a Bolshevik, Raskolnikov, a lieutenant in the Baltic navy, who had brought the Kronstadt sailors to the demonstration, excitedly insisted on releasing Chernov at once, to prevent people from saying that he had been arrested by the Kronstadt men. I decided to try to carry out Raskolnikov's wish. I will let him speak for himself.

'It is difficult to say how long the turbulence of the masses would have continued,' the impulsive lieutenant says in his memoirs,

but for the intervention of Comrade Trotsky. He jumped on the front of the automobile, and with an energetic wave of his hand, like a man who was tired of waiting, gave the signal for silence. Instantly, everything calmed down, and there was dead quiet. In a loud, clear and ringing voice, Lev Davydovich made a short speech, ending with 'those in favour of violence to Chernov raise their hands!' Nobody even opened his mouth [continues Raskolnikov]; no one uttered a word of protest. 'Citizen Chernov, you are free,' Trotsky said, as he turned around solemnly to the minister of agriculture and with a wave of his hand, invited him to leave the automobile. Chernov was half-dead and half-alive. I helped him to get out of the automobile, and with an exhausted, expressionless look and a hesitating, unsteady walk, he went up the steps and disappeared into the vestibule of the palace. Satisfied with his victory, Lev Davydovich walked away with him.

If one discounts the unnecessarily pathetic tone, the scene is described correctly. It did not keep the hostile press from asserting that I had Chernov seized to have him lynched. Chernov shyly kept silent; how could a 'People's' minister confess his indebtedness not to his own popularity, but to the intervention of a Bolshevik for the safety of his head?

Delegation after delegation demanded, in the name of the demonstrants, that the Executive Committee take the power. Chiedze, Tzereteli, Dan, and Gotz were sitting in the presidium like statues. They did not answer the delegations, and looked blankly off into space or exchanged perturbed and cryptic glances. Bolsheviks spoke one after another in support of the delegations of workers and soldiers. The members of the presidium were silent. They were waiting – but for what? Hours passed in this way. Then, in the middle of the night, the halls of the palace resounded suddenly with the triumphant blare of trumpets. The members of the presidium came to life as if they had been touched by an electric current. Someone solemnly reported that the Volyn regiment had arrived from the front to put itself at the disposal of the Central Executive Committee. In all of the Petrograd garrison the 'democracy' had not had a single unit that it could rely on. And so it had had to wait until an armed force could come from the front.

Now the whole setting changed immediately. The delegations were driven out; Bolsheviks were not allowed to speak. The leaders of the democracy were wreaking on us their vengeance for the fear that the masses had made them suffer. Speeches from the platform of the Executive Committee told of an armed mutiny suppressed by the loyal troops of the revolution. The Bolsheviks were declared a counter-revolutionary party. The arrival of that one Volyn regiment had done all this. Three and a half months later, the same regiment cooperated whole-heartedly in the overthrow of Kerensky's government.

On the morning of the fifth I met Lenin. The offensive by the masses had been beaten off. 'Now they will shoot us down, one by one,' said Lenin. 'This is the right time for them.' But he overestimated the opponent – not his venom, but his courage and ability to act. They did not shoot us down one by one, although they were not far from it. Bolsheviks were being beaten down in the streets and killed. Military students sacked the Kseshinskaya Palace and the printing-works of the *Pravda*. The whole street in front of the works was littered with manuscripts, and among those destroyed was my pamphlet 'To the Slanderers'. The deep reconnaissance of July had been transformed into a one-sided battle. The enemy were easily victorious, because we did not fight. The party was paying dearly for it. Lenin and Zinoviev were in hiding. General arrests, followed by beatings, were the order of the day. Cossacks and military students confiscated the money of those arrested, on the ground that it was 'German money'. Many of our sympathizers and half-friends turned their backs on us. In the Taurid Palace we were proclaimed counter-revolutionists and were actually put outside the law.

The situation in the ruling circles of the party was bad. Lenin was away; Kamenev's wing was raising its head. Many – and these included Stalin – simply let events take their own course, so that they might show their wisdom the day after. The Bolshevik faction in the Central Executive Committee felt orphaned in the Taurid Palace. It sent a delegation to ask me if I would speak to them about the situation, although I was not yet a member of the party; my formal joining had been delayed until the party congress, soon to meet. I agreed readily of course. My talk with the Bolshevik faction established moral bonds of the sort that are forged only under the enemy's heaviest blows. I said then that after this crisis we were to expect a rapid upswing; that the masses would become twice as strongly attached to us when they had verified the truth of our declaration by facts; that it was necessary to keep a strict watch on every revolutionary, for at such moments men are weighed on scales that do not err. Even now I recall with pleasure the warmth and gratitude that the members showed me when I left them. 'Lenin is away,' Muralov said, 'and of the others, only Trotsky has kept his head.'

If I had been writing these memoirs under different circumstances – although in other circumstances I should hardly have been writing them at all – I should have hesitated to include much of what I say in these pages. But now I cannot forget that widely organized lying about the past which is one of the chief activities of the epigones. My friends are in prison or in exile. I am obliged to speak of myself in a way that I should never have done under other conditions. For me it is a question not merely of historical truth but also of a political struggle that is still going on.

My unbroken fighting friendship as well as my political friendship with Muralov began then. I must say at least a few words about the man. Muralov is an old Bolshevik who went through the revolution of 1905 in Moscow. In Serpukhov in 1906 he was caught in the pogrom of the Black Hundred – carried out, as usual, under the protection of the police. Muralov is a magnificent giant, as fearless as he is kind. With a few others he found himself in a ring of enemies who had surrounded the building of the Zemstvo administration. Muralov came out of the building with a revolver in his hand and walked evenly towards the crowd. It moved back a little. But the shock company of the Black Hundred blocked his path, and the cabmen began to howl taunts at him. 'Clear a way,' ordered the giant without slackening his advance, as he raised the hand holding the revolver. Several men pounced on him. He shot one of them down and wounded another. The crowd drew back again. With the same even step, cutting his way through the crowd like an ice-breaker, Muralov walked on and on towards Moscow.

His subsequent trial lasted for two years, and, in spite of the frenzy of the reaction that swept over the country, he was acquitted. An agricultural expert by training, a soldier in an automobile detachment during the imperialist war, a leader of the October fighting in Moscow, Muralov became the first commander of the Moscow military region after the victory. He was a fearless marshal of the revolutionary war, always steady, simple, and unaffected. In his campaigning he was a tireless living example; he gave agricultural advice, mowed grain, and in his free moments gave medical treatment to both men and cows. In the most difficult situations he radiated calm, warmth, and confidence. After the close of the war Muralov and I always tried to spend our free days together. We were united too by our love of hunting. We scoured North and South for bears and wolves, or for pheasants and bustards. At present Muralov is hunting in Siberia as an exiled oppositionist.

In the July days of 1917 Muralov held his head up, as usual, and encouraged many others. In those days we all needed a lot of self-control to stride along the corridors and halls of the Taurid Palace without bowing our heads, as we ran the gauntlet of furious glances, venomous whispers, grinding of teeth, and a demonstrative elbowing that seemed to say: 'Look! Look!' There is no fury greater than that of a vain and pampered 'revolutionary' philistine when he begins to perceive that the revolution which has suddenly lifted him to the top is about to threaten his temporary splendour.

The route to the canteen of the Executive Committee was a little Golgotha in those days. Tea was dispensed there, and sandwiches of black bread and cheese or red caviar; the latter was plentiful in the Smolny and later in the Kremlin. For dinner the fare was a vegetable soup with a chunk of meat. The canteen was in charge of a soldier named Grafov. When the baiting of the Bolsheviks was at its worst, when Lenin was declared a German spy and had to hide in a hut, I noticed that Grafov would slip me a hotter glass of tea or a sandwich better than the rest, trying meanwhile not to look at me. He obviously sympathized with the Bolsheviks but had to keep it from his superiors. I began to look about me more attentively. Grafov was not the only one: the whole lower staff of the Smolny – porters, messengers, watchmen – were unmistakably with the Bolsheviks. Then I felt that our cause was half won. But so far, only half.

The press was conducting an exceptionally venomous and dishonest campaign against the Bolsheviks, a campaign surpassed in this respect only by Stalin's campaign against the opposition a few years later. In July Lunacharsky made a few equivocal statements which the press naturally interpreted as a renunciation of Bolshevism. Some papers attributed similar statements to me. On 10 July, I addressed a letter to the Provisional government in which I stated my complete agreement with Lenin and which I ended as follows: 'You can have no grounds for exempting me from the action of the decree by virtue of which Lenin, Zinoviev and Kamenev are subject to arrest; you can have no grounds for doubting that I am as irreconcilably opposed to the general policy of the Provisional government as my above-mentioned comrades.' Messrs the ministers drew the due conclusion from this letter and arrested me as a German agent.

In May, when Tzereteli was hounding the sailors and disarming the machine-gun companies, I warned him that the day was probably not far distant when he would have to seek help from the sailors against some general who would be soaping the hangman's rope for the revolution. In August such a general made his appearance in the person of Kornilov. Tzereteli called for the help of the Kronstadt bluejackets; they did not refuse it. The cruiser *Aurora* entered the waters of the Neva. I was already in the Kresty prison when I saw this quick fulfilment of my prophecy. The sailors from the *Aurora* sent a special delegation to the prison to ask my advice: should they defend the Winter Palace or take it by assault? I advised them to put off the squaring of their account with Kerensky until they had finished Kornilov. 'What's ours will not escape us.'

'It won't?'

'It will not.'

While I was in prison my wife and boys called to see me. The boys had by that time acquired some political experience of their own. They were spending the summer in the country house of the family of a retired colonel. Visitors often came there, mostly officers, and as they helped themselves to vodka they would rail at the Bolsheviks. In the July days this railing reached its climax. (Some of these officers left soon after that for the South, where the future 'White' forces were being gathered.) When, in the course of a meal, a certain young patriot called Lenin and Trotsky German spies, my older boy dashed at him with a chair and the younger one with a table-knife. The grown-ups separated them, and the boys, sobbing hysterically, locked themselves in their room. They were secretly planning to make their way on foot to Petrograd to find out what was happening to the Bolsheviks there, but fortunately their mother came, pacified them, and took them away. But in the city things seemed hardly better. The newspapers were denouncing the Bolsheviks, their father was in prison – the revolution was definitely disappointing. But that did not prevent them from delightedly watching my wife furtively slip me a pen-knife through the grating in the prison reception-room. I continued to console them by saying that the real revolution was still to come.

My daughters were being drawn more actively into political life. They attended the meetings in the Modern Circus and took part in demonstrations. During the July days they were both shaken up in a mob, one of them lost her glasses, both lost their hats, and both were afraid that they would lose the father who had just reappeared on their horizon.

During the days of Kornilov's advance on Petrograd, the prison régime was hanging by a thread. Everybody realized that if Kornilov entered the city he would immediately slaughter all the Bolsheviks arrested by Kerensky. The Central Executive Committee was afraid too that the prisons might be raided by the White Guard elements in the capital. A large detachment of troops was detailed to guard the Kresty. Of course it proved to be not 'democratic' but Bolshevik, and ready to release us at any moment. But an act like that would have been the signal for an immediate uprising, and the time for that had not yet come. Meanwhile, the government itself began to release us, for the same reason that it had called in the Bolshevik sailors to guard the Winter Palace. I went straight from the Kresty to the newly organized committee for the defence of the revolution, where I sat with the same gentlemen who had put me in prison as an agent of the Hohenzollerns, and who had not yet withdrawn the accusation against me. I must candidly confess that the Populists and Mensheviks by their very appearance made one wish that Kornilov might grip them by the scruffs of their necks and shake them in the air. But this wish was not only irreverent, it was unpolitical. The Bolsheviks stepped into the harness, and were everywhere in the first line of the defence. The experience of Kornilov's mutiny completed that of the July days: once more Kerensky and Co. revealed the fact that they had no forces of their own to back them. The army that rose against Kornilov was the army-to-be of the October revolution. We took advantage of the danger to arm the workers whom Tzereteli had been disarming with such restless industry.

The capital quieted down in those days. Kornilov's entry was awaited with hope by some and with terror by others. Our boys heard someone say, 'He may come tomorrow,' and in the morning, before they were dressed, they peered out of the window to see if he had arrived. But Kornilov did not arrive. The revolutionary upswing of the masses was so powerful that his mutiny simply melted away and evaporated. But not without leaving its trace; the mutiny was all grist to the Bolshevik mill.

'Retribution is not slow in coming,' I wrote in the Kornilov days. 'Hounded, persecuted, slandered, our party never grew as rapidly as it is growing now. And this process will spread from the capitals to the provinces, from the towns to the country and the army . . . Without ceasing for a moment to be the class organization of the proletariat, our party will be transformed in the fire of persecution into a true leader of all the oppressed, downtrodden, deceived and hounded masses.'

We were hardly able to keep pace with the rising tide. The number of Bolsheviks in the Petrograd Soviet was increasing daily. We represented almost half of the membership, and yet there was not a single Bolshevik in the presidium. We raised the question of re-electing the Soviet presidium. We offered to form a coalition presidium with the Mensheviks and the Populists. Lenin, as we afterwards found out, was displeased at that, because he was afraid that it implied conciliatory tendencies on our part. But no compromise was effected. Despite our recent joint struggle against Kornilov, Tzereteli declined the coalition presidium.

We had hoped for this; nothing but a vote on the lists of candidates along party lines could solve the problem now. I asked whether the list of our opponents included Kerensky; formally, he was a member of the presidium, though he did not attend the Soviet, and showed his disregard of it in every way. The question took the presidium by surprise. Kerensky was neither liked nor respected, but it was impossible to disavow one's prime minister. After consulting one another the members of the presidium answered: 'Of course, he is included.' We wanted nothing better. Here is an extract from the minutes:

We were convinced that Kerensky was no longer in the presidium [tumultuous applause], but we see now that we have been mistaken. The shadow of Kerensky is hovering between Chiedze and Zavadye. When you are asked to approve the political line-up of the presidium, remember that you are asked in this way to approve the policies of Kerensky [tumultuous applause].

This threw over to our side another hundred or so of the delegates who had been vacillating.

The Soviet numbered considerably more than a thousand members. The voting was performed by going out the door. There was tremendous excitement, for the question at issue was not the presidium, but the revolution. I was walking about in the lobbies with a group of friends. We reckoned that we should be a hundred votes short of half, and were ready to consider that a success. But it happened that we received a hundred votes more than the coalition of the Socialist-Revolutionists and the Mensheviks. We were the victors. I took the chair. Tzereteli, taking his leave, expressed his wish that we might stay in the Soviet at least half as long as they had been leading the revolution. In other words our opponents opened for us a credit account of not more than three months.

They made a gross miscalculation. We were undeviating in our march to power.

27

The Deciding Night

The twelfth hour of the revolution was near. The Smolny was being transformed into a fortress. In its garret there were a dozen or two machine-guns, a legacy from the old Executive Committee. Captain Grekov, commandant of the Smolny, was an undisguised enemy. On the other hand the chief of the machine-gun company came to tell me that his men were all on the side of the Bolsheviks. I instructed someone – perhaps Markin – to inspect the machine-guns. They proved to be in poor condition as a result of continuous neglect – the soldiers had grown slack because they had no intention of defending Kerensky. I had a new and more reliable machine-gun detachment brought to the Smolny.

24 October,* a grey morning, early. I roamed about the building from one floor to another, partly for the sake of movement and partly to make sure that everything was in order and to encourage those who needed it. Along the stone floors of the interminable and still half-dark corridors of the Smolny, the soldiers were dragging their machine-guns, with a hearty clangour and tramping of feet – this was the new detachment I had summoned. The few Socialist-Revolutionists and Mensheviks still in the Smolny could be seen poking sleepy, frightened faces out at us. The music of the guns was ominous in their ears, and they left the Smolny in a hurry, one after the other. We were now in full command of the building that was preparing to rear a Bolshevist head over the city and the country.

Early in the morning two workers, a man and a woman,

*By the Julian calendar which at the time was still the official calendar in Russia; 6 November, by the calendar used in the rest of Europe. This accounts for the revolution being called sometimes the October, sometimes the November revolution. – *L. D. Trotsky.*

panting after their run from the party printing-works, bumped into me on the staircase. The government had closed down the central organ of the party and the paper of the Petrograd Soviet. Government agents, accompanied by military students, had put seals on the printing-works. For a moment the news startled us; such is the power exercised over the mind by legal formality.

'Couldn't we break the seals?' the woman asked.

'Break them,' I answered, 'and to make it safe for you we will give you a dependable escort.'

'There is a battalion of sappers next door to us; the soldiers are sure to back us,' said the woman printer confidently.

The Military-Revolutionary Committee immediately issued an order: '(1) The printing-works of revolutionary newspapers to be reopened. (2) The editorial staffs and compositors to be invited to continue publishing the papers. (3) The honorary duty of protecting the revolutionary printing-works from counter revolutionary attacks to be entrusted to the gallant soldiers of the Litovsky regiment and the Sixth Sapper Reserve Battalion.' And from that time on the printing-works ran without interruption and both newspapers continued publication.

On the twenty-fourth, there was difficulty at the telephone exchange. Military students had entrenched themselves there, and under their protection the telephone operators went into opposition to the Soviet and refused to make our connections. This was the first, sporadic instance of sabotage. The Military-Revolutionary Committee sent a detachment of sailors to the telephone exchange, and the detachment placed two small guns at the entrance. The telephone service was restored. Thus began the taking over of the organs of administration.

On the third floor of the Smolny in a small corner room, the Committee was in continuous session. All the reports about the movements of troops, the attitude of soldiers and workers, the agitation in the barracks, the designs of organizers of pogroms, the intrigues of the bourgeois politicians and the foreign embassies, the happenings in the Winter Palace – all these came to this centre, as did the reports of the conferences of the parties formerly in the Soviet. Informants came from all sides – workers, soldiers, officers, porters, socialist military students, servants, wives of petty officials. Many of them told us utter rubbish, but some supplied us with serious and very valuable information.

All that week I had hardly stepped out of the Smolny; I spent the nights on a leather couch without undressing, sleeping in snatches, and constantly being roused by couriers, scouts, messenger-cyclists, telegraphists, and ceaseless telephone calls. The decisive moment was close at hand. It was obvious that there could now be no turning back.

On the night of the twenty-fourth the members of the Revolutionary Committee went out into the various districts, and I was left alone. Later on Kamenev came in. He was opposed to the uprising, but he had come to spend that deciding night with me, and together we stayed in the tiny corner room on the third floor, so like the captain's bridge on that deciding night of the revolution.

There is a telephone booth in the large empty room adjoining us, and the bell rings incessantly about important things and trifles. Each ring heightens the alertness of the silence. One can readily picture the deserted streets of Petrograd, dimly lit, and whipped by the autumn winds from the sea; the bourgeois and officials cowering in their beds, trying to guess what is going on in those dangerous and mysterious streets; the workers' quarters quiet with the tense sleep of a war-camp. Commissions and conferences of the government parties are exhausting themselves in impotence in the Tsar's palaces, where the living ghosts of democracy rub shoulders with the still hovering ghosts of the monarchy. Now and again the silks and gildings of the halls are plunged into darkness – the supplies of coal have run short. In the various districts detachments of workers, soldiers, and sailors are keeping watch. The young proletarians have rifles and machine-gun belts across their shoulders. Street pickets are warming themselves at fires in the streets. The life of the capital, thrusting its head from one epoch into another on this autumn night, is concentrated about a group of telephones.

Reports from all the districts, suburbs, and approaches to the capital are focused in the room on the third floor. It seems that everything has been foreseen; the leaders are in their places; the contacts are assured; nothing seems to have been forgotten.

Once more, let us go over it in our minds. This night decides. Only this evening in my report to the delegates of the second congress of the Soviets, I said with conviction: 'If you stand firm, there will be no civil war, our enemies will capitulate at once, and you will take the place that belongs to you by right.' There can be no doubt about victory; it is as assured as the victory of any uprising can be. And yet these hours are still tense and full of alarm, for the coming night decides. The government, while mobilizing cadets yesterday, gave orders to the cruiser *Aurora* to steam out of the Neva. They were the same Bolshevik sailors whom Skobelev, coming hat in hand, in August begged to protect the Winter Palace from Kornilov. The sailors referred to the Military-Revolutionary Committee for instructions, and consequently the *Aurora* is standing tonight where she was yesterday. A telephone call from Pavlovsk informs me that the government is bringing up from there a detachment of artillery, a battalion of shock troops from Tsarskoye Syelo, and student-officers from the Peterhof military school. Into the Winter Palace Kerensky has drawn military students, officers, and the women shock troops. I order the commissaries to place dependable military defences along the approaches to Petrograd and to send agitators to meet the detachments called out by the government. All our instructions and reports are sent by telephone and the government agents are in a position to intercept them. But can they still control our communications?

'If you fail to stop them with words, use arms. You will answer for this with your life.'

I repeat this sentence time and time again. But I do not yet believe in the force of my order. The revolution is still too trusting, too generous, optimistic and light-hearted. It prefers to threaten with arms rather than really use them. It still hopes that all questions can be solved by words, and so far it has been successful in this – hostile elements evaporate before its hot breath. Earlier in the day (the twenty-fourth) an order was issued to use arms and to stop at nothing at the first sign of street pogroms. Our enemies don't even dare think of the streets; they have gone into hiding. The streets are ours; our commissaries are watching all the approaches to Petrograd. The officers' school and the gunners have not responded to the call of the government. Only a section of the Oraniembaum military students have succeeded in making their way through our defences, but I have been watching their movements by telephone. They end by sending envoys to the Smolny. The government has been seeking support in vain. The ground is slipping from under its feet.

The outer guard of the Smolny has been reinforced by a new machine-gun detachment. The contact with all sections of the garrison is uninterrupted. The companies on duty are on watch in all the regiments. The commissaries are in their places. Delegations from each garrison unit are in the Smolny, at the disposal of the Military-Revolutionary Committee, to be used in case the contact with that unit should be broken off. Armed detachments from the districts march along the streets, ring the bells at the gates or open the gates without ringing, and take possession of one institution after another. Nearly everywhere these detachments are met by friends who have been waiting impatiently for them. At the railway terminals, specially appointed commissaries are watching the incoming and outgoing trains, and in particular the movement of troops. No disturbing news comes from there. All the more important points in the city are given over into our hands almost without resistance, without fighting, without casualties. The telephone alone informs us: 'We are here!'

All is well. It could not have gone better. Now I may leave the telephone. I sit down on the couch. The nervous tension lessens. A dull sensation of fatigue comes over me.

'Give me a cigarette,' I say to Kamenev. (In those years I still smoked, but only spasmodically.) I take one or two puffs, but suddenly with the words, 'Only this was lacking!' I faint. (I inherited from my mother a certain susceptibility to fainting spells when suffering from physical pain or illness. That was why some American physician described me as an epileptic.) As I come to, I see Kamenev's frightened face bending over me.

'Shall I get some medicine?' he asks.

'It would be much better,' I answer after a moment's reflection, 'if you got something to eat.' I try to remember when I last had food, but I can't. At all events it was not yesterday.

Next morning I pounced upon the bourgeois and Menshevik-Populist papers. They had not even a word about the uprising. The newspapers had been making such a to-do about the coming action by armed soldiers, about the sacking, the inevitable rivers of blood, about an insurrection, that now they simply had failed to notice an uprising that was actually taking place. The press was taking our negotiations with the general staff at their face value, and our diplomatic statements as signs of vacillation. In the meantime, without confusion, without street-fights, almost without firing or bloodshed, one institution after another was being occupied by detachments of soldiers, sailors, and the Red Guards, on orders issuing from the Smolny Institute.

The citizen of Petrograd was rubbing his frightened eyes under a new régime. Was it really possible that the Bolsheviks had seized the power? A delegation from the municipal Duma called to see me, and asked me a few inimitable questions. 'Do you propose military action? If so, what, and when?' The Duma would have to know of this 'not less than twenty-four hours in advance'. What measures had the Soviet taken to ensure safety and order? And so on, and so forth.

I replied by expounding the dialectic view of the revolution, and invited the Duma to send a delegate to the Military-Revolutionary Committee to take part in its work. This scared them more than the uprising itself. I ended, as usual, in the spirit of armed self-defence: 'If the government uses iron, it will be answered with steel.'

'Will you dissolve us for being opposed to the transfer of power to the Soviets?'

I replied: 'The present Duma reflects yesterday: if a conflict arises, we will propose to the people that they elect a new Duma on the issue of power.' The delegation left as it had come, but it left behind it the feeling of an assured victory. Something had changed during the night. Three weeks ago we had gained a majority in the Petrograd Soviet. We were hardly more than a banner – with no printing-works, no funds, no branches. No longer ago than last night, the government ordered the arrest of the Military-Revolutionary Committee, and was engaged in tracing our addresses. Today a delegation from the city Duma comes to the 'arrested' Military-Revolutionary Committee to inquire about the fate of the Duma.

The government was still in session at the Winter Palace, but it was no more than a shadow. Politically it had ceased to exist. During the day of the twenty-fifth the Winter Palace was being surrounded on all sides by our troops. At one o'clock midday I made a statement of the situation to the Petrograd Soviet. The newspaper account reports it as follows:

On behalf of the Military-Revolutionary Committee, I declare that the Provisional government is no longer existent. [Applause.] Some ministers have been arrested. ['Bravo.'] Others will be arrested in the course of a few days or hours. [Applause.] The revolutionary garrison, at the disposal of the Military-Revolutionary Committee, has dissolved the session of the Pre-parliament. [Loud applause.] We have been on the watch here throughout the night and have followed the detachments of revolutionary soldiers and the workers' guards by telephone as they silently carried out their tasks. The citizen slept in peace, ignorant of the change from one power to another. Railway-stations, the post-office, the telegraph, the Petrograd Telegraph Agency, the State Bank, have been occupied. [Loud applause.] The Winter Palace has not yet been taken, but its fate will be decided during the next few minutes. [Applause.]

This bare account may give a wrong impression of the mood of the gathering. My memory supplies these particulars. When I reported the change of power effected during the night, there was tense silence for a few seconds. Then applause began, a not very stormy, rather thoughtful applause. The assembly was feeling intensely and waiting. While they were preparing for the struggle, the working class had been seized by an indescribable enthusiasm, but when we stepped over the threshold of power, this unthinking enthusiasm gave way to a disturbed thoughtfulness. A sure historical instinct revealed itself here. Ahead of us there was probably the greatest resistance from the old world; there were struggle, starvation, cold, destruction, blood and death. 'Will we overcome all this?' many asked themselves.

That was the cause of the moments of disturbed reflection. 'We will overcome it!' they all answered. New dangers were looming in the far distance. But now we felt a sense of a great victory, and it sang in our blood. It found its expression in the tumultuous welcome accorded to Lenin, who at that meeting made his first appearance after a four months' absence.

Late that evening, as we were waiting for the opening of the congress of the Soviets, Lenin and I were resting in a room adjoining the meeting-hall, a room entirely empty except for chairs. Someone had spread a blanket on the floor for us; someone else, I think it was Lenin's sister, had brought us pillows. We were lying side by side; body and soul were relaxing like overtaut strings. It was a well-earned rest. We could not sleep, so we talked in low voices. Only now did Lenin become reconciled to the postponement of the uprising. His fears had been dispelled. There was a rare sincerity in his voice. He was interested in knowing all about the mixed pickets of the Red Guards, sailors, and soldiers that had been stationed everywhere. 'What a wonderful sight: a worker with a rifle, side by side with a soldier, standing before a street fire!' he repeated with deep feeling. At last the soldier and the worker had been brought together!

Then he started suddenly. 'And what about the Winter Palace? It has not been taken yet. Isn't there danger in that?' I got up to ask on the telephone about the progress of the operations there, but he tried to stop me. 'Lie still, I will send someone to find out.' But we could not rest for long. The session of the congress of the Soviets was opening in the next hall. Ulyanova, Lenin's sister, came running to get me.

'Dan is speaking. They are asking for you.'

In a voice that was breaking repeatedly, Dan was railing at the conspirators and prophesying the inevitable collapse of the uprising. He demanded that we form a coalition with the Socialist-Revolutionists and the Mensheviks. The parties that had been in power only the day before, that had hounded us and thrown us into prison, now that we had overthrown them were demanding that we come to an agreement with them.

I replied to Dan and, in him, to the yesterday of the revolution:

What has taken place is an uprising, not a conspiracy. An uprising of the masses of the people needs no justification. We have been strengthening the revolutionary energy of the workers and soldiers. We have been forging, openly, the will of the masses for an uprising. Our uprising has won. And now we are being asked to give up our victory, to come to an agreement. With whom? You are wretched, disunited individuals; you are bankrupts; your part is over. Go to the place where you belong from now on – the dust-bin of history!

This was the last retort in that long dialogue that had begun on 3 April, with the day and hour of Lenin's arrival in Petrograd.

After 1904 I stood outside of both the Social Democratic factions. I went through the revolution of 1905–7 arm-in-arm with the Bolsheviks. During the years of the reaction I defended revolutionary methods in the international Marxist publications against the Mensheviks. I still hoped, however, that the Mensheviks would move further to the left, and I made several attempts to bring about a union in the party. It was not until the war that I became finally convinced of the utter hopelessness of the Mensheviks. In New York at the beginning of March 1917 I wrote a series of articles dealing with the class forces and perspectives of the Russian revolution. At that very time Lenin, in Geneva, was sending to Petrograd his *Letters from Afar*. And both of us, though we were writing in different parts of the world and were separated by an ocean, gave the same analysis and the same forecast. On every one of the principal questions, such as the attitude towards the peasantry, towards the bourgeoisie, the Provisional government, the war, and the world revolution, our views were completely identical. Here a test of the relations between 'Trotskyism' and Leninism was made on the very touchstone of history. And it was carried out under the conditions of a chemically pure experiment. At that time I knew nothing of Lenin's stand; I argued on the basis of my own premises and my own revolutionary experience, and I drew the same perspective and suggested the same line of strategy as Lenin.

But perhaps the question was quite clear to everyone at that time, and the solution universally accepted? On the contrary; Lenin's stand at that period, that is, before 4 April 1917, when he first appeared on the Petrograd stage, was his own personal one, shared by no one else. Not one of those leaders of the party who were in Russia had any intention of making the dictatorship of the proletariat – the social revolution – the immediate object of his policy. A party conference which met on the eve of Lenin's arrival and counted among its numbers about thirty Bolsheviks showed that none of them even imagined anything beyond democracy. No wonder the minutes of that conference are still kept a secret! Stalin was in favour of supporting the Provisional government of Guchkov and Miliukoff, and of merging the Bolsheviks with the Mensheviks. The same stand, or rather an even more opportunist one, was taken by Rykov, Kamenev, Molotov, Tomsky, Kalinin, and all the rest of the leaders and half-leaders of today. During the February revolution Yaroslavsky, Ordzhonikidze, chairman Petrovsky of the Ukrainian Executive Committee, and others were publishing with the Mensheviks at Yakutsk a paper called *The Social Democrat*, in which they expounded the most vulgar and provincial sort of opportunism. If those articles in the Yakutsk *Social Democrat*, edited by Yaroslavsky, were to be reprinted today they would kill him as a political thinker, if such a death were possible for him. Such are the present guards of 'Leninism'.

I realize, of course, that at various times in their lives they have repeated Lenin's words and gestures after him. But the beginning of 1917 found them left to their own resources. The political situation was difficult. Here was their chance to show what they had learned in Lenin's school and what they could do without Lenin. Let them name one of their number who arrived independently at the position achieved identically by Lenin in Geneva and by me in New York. They cannot name a single one. The Petrograd *Pravda*, which was edited by Stalin and Kamenev until Lenin's arrival, will always remain a document of limited understanding, blindness, and opportunism. And yet the mass membership of the party, like the working class as a whole, was moving spontaneously towards the fight for power. There was no other path for either the party or the country.

In the years of reaction one needed theoretical foresight in order to hold fast to the prospect of a permanent revolution. Probably nothing more than political sense was needed to advance the slogan of a fight for power in March 1917. Not a single one of the present leaders revealed such a foresight or such a sense. Not one of them went beyond the point of view of the left petty-bourgeois democrat in March 1917. Not one of them stood the test of history.

I arrived in Petrograd a month after Lenin – it was exactly that long that I had been detained in Canada by Lloyd George. By that time the situation in the party had changed substantially. Lenin had appealed to the masses against their sorry leaders. He had launched a systematic fight against 'the old Bolsheviks who', as he wrote in those days, 'more than once have played a sorry part in the history of our party by repeating a formula, unintelligently learned, instead of studying the peculiar nature of the new and living reality.' Kamenev and Rykov tried to resist. Stalin silently stepped aside. Not one of his articles written about that period shows that Stalin made any attempt to estimate his previous policy and win his way to Lenin's stand. He simply kept silent, because he had been too much compromised by his unfortunate leadership during the first month of the revolution. He preferred to withdraw into the background. He never made any public appearance to defend Lenin's views; he merely stood back and waited. During the most responsible months of the theoretical and political preparation for the uprising, Stalin simply did not exist in the political sense.

At the time of my arrival there were in the country many Social-Democratic organizations which included both Bolsheviks and Mensheviks. This was the natural result of the stand that Stalin, as well as Kamenev and others, had taken, not only in the early stages of the revolution but also during the war – although one must admit that Stalin's position during the war was known to no one: to this rather important question he had never devoted a line. Today the Communist International textbooks all over the world – among the Communist Youths of Scandinavia and the Pioneers of Australia – keep pounding it in that Trotsky made an attempt in 1912 to bring about the union of the Bolsheviks with the Mensheviks. But they never once mention the fact that in March 1917 Stalin was advocating union with Tzereteli's party, and that it was not until the middle of the year 1917 that Lenin was able to pull the party out of the morass into which its temporary leaders – the epigones of today – had driven it. The fact that not one of them understood the significance and direction of the revolution at its outset is now represented as a special dialectic profundity, in contrast with the heresy of Trotskyism, which was audacious enough not only to understand the day before, but to foresee the day after as well.

When I told Kamenev on my arrival in Petrograd that nothing separated me from Lenin's famous 'April theses' that determined the new course of his party, the former's only reply was, 'I should say not!' Before formally joining the party I took part in drafting the most important Bolshevist documents. It never entered anyone's head to ask if I had renounced 'Trotskyism', as I was asked thousands of times during the period of the epigone decline, by the Cachins, Thälmanns, and others of the hangers-on of the October revolution. The only juxtaposition of Trotskyism and Leninism to be heard in those days was in the leading group of the party, where they accused LENIN of Trotskyism during the month of April. Kamenev did this openly and with much insistence. Others did it more cautiously behind the scenes. Many 'old Bolsheviks' said to me after I arrived in Russia: 'Now the celebration is on *your* street.' I had to argue that Lenin had not come over to my point of view, but had developed his own, and that the course of events, by substituting arithmetic for algebra, had revealed the essential identity of our views. And that is what really happened.

At those first meetings of ours, and even more after the July days, Lenin gave one the sense of a terrific inner concentration under a surface of calm and 'prosaic' simplicity. The movement that had found its symbol in Kerensky seemed all-powerful in those days. Bolshevism seemed nothing more than an 'insignificant group', and officially it was being treated as such. The party itself did not realize the power it was to have on the day after, but Lenin was leading it firmly towards its greatest tasks. I harnessed myself to the work and helped him.

Two months before the October revolution I wrote: 'To us internationalism is not an abstract idea existing only to be betrayed on every opportune occasion (as it is to Tzereteli and Chernov), but is a real guiding and wholly practical principle. A lasting, decisive success is inconceivable for us without a revolution in Europe.' At that time I could not yet place the name of Stalin, the philosopher of 'socialism in a single country', beside the names of Tzereteli and Chernov. I concluded my article with the words: 'A permanent revolution versus a permanent slaughter: that is the struggle, in which the stake is the future of man.' This was published in the central organ of our party on 7 September, and later reissued as a separate pamphlet. Why did my present critics keep silent then about my heretical slogan of permanent revolution? Where were they? Some, like Stalin, were waiting cautiously, peering about them. Others, like Zinoviev, were hiding under the table. But the more important question is: How could Lenin have tolerated my heretical propaganda in silence? In questions of theory he recognized no such thing as indifference or indulgence; how did he happen to allow the preaching of 'Trotskyism' in the central organ of the party?

On 1 November 1917 at the meeting of the Petrograd committee (the minutes of this historical meeting – historical in every sense of the word – are still kept secret) Lenin said that after Trotsky had become convinced of the impossibility of union with the Mensheviks 'there has been no better Bolshevik'. And in this he proved very clearly – and not for the first time, either – that it had not been the theory of permanent revolution that had separated us, but the narrower, though very important question of the attitude towards Menshevism.

Looking back, two years after the revolution, Lenin wrote: 'At the moment when it seized the power and created the Soviet republic, Bolshevism drew to itself all the best elements in the currents of Socialist thought that were nearest to it.' Can there be even a shadow of a doubt that when he spoke so deliberately of the best representatives of *the currents closest to Bolshevism*, Lenin had foremost in mind what is now called the 'historical Trotskyism'? For what was nearer to it than the current that I represented? And whom else could Lenin have had in mind? Perhaps Marcel Cachin? Or Thälmann? To Lenin, when he surveyed the past development of the party as a whole, Trotskyism was no hostile and alien current of Socialist thought, but on the contrary the one that was closest to Bolshevism.

The actual course of the development of ideas in the party, as we can see, did not at all resemble the false caricature that the epigones, taking advantage of Lenin's death and the tide of reaction, have been creating.

29

In Power

In the life of the country and in the life of the individual, those were extraordinary days. In social passions as well as in personal powers tension reached its highest point. The masses were creating an epoch and their leaders felt their steps merging with those of history. On the decisions made and the orders given in those days depended the fate of the nation for an entire historical era. And yet those decisions were made with very little discussion. I can hardly say that they were even properly weighed and considered; they were almost improvised on the moment. But they were none the worse for that. The pressure of events was so terrific, and the work to be done so clear before us, that the most important decisions came naturally, as a matter of course, and were received in the same spirit. The path had been predetermined; all that was required was to indicate the work. No arguments were necessary, and very few appeals. Without hesitation or doubt the masses picked up what was suggested to them by the nature of the situation. Under the strain of events their 'leaders' did no more than formulate what answered the requirements of the people and the demands of history.

Marxism considers itself the conscious expression of the unconscious historical process. But the 'unconscious' process, in the historico-philosophical sense of the term – not in the psychological – coincides with its conscious expression only at its highest point, when the masses, by sheer elemental pressure, break through the social routine and give victorious expression to the deepest needs of historical development. And at such moments the highest theoretical consciousness of the epoch merges with the immediate action of those oppressed masses who are furthest away from theory. The creative union of the conscious with the unconscious is what one usually calls 'inspiration'. Revolution is the inspired frenzy of history.

Every real writer knows creative moments, when something stronger than himself is guiding his hand; every real orator experiences moments when someone stronger than the self of his everyday existence speaks through him. This is 'inspiration'. It derives from the highest creative effort of all one's forces. The unconscious rises from its deep well and bends the conscious mind to its will, merging it with itself in some greater synthesis.

The utmost spiritual vigour likewise infuses at times all personal activity connected with the movement of the masses. This was true for the leaders in the October days. The hidden strength of the organism, its most deeply rooted instincts, its power of scent inherited from animal forbears – all these rose and broke through the psychic routine to join forces with the higher historico-philosophical abstractions in the service of the revolution. Both these processes, affecting the individual and the mass, were based on the union of the conscious with the unconscious: the union of instinct – the mainspring of the will – with the higher theories of thought.

Outwardly it did not look very imposing: men went about tired, hungry, and unwashed, with inflamed eyes and unshaven beards. And afterwards none of them could recall much about those most critical days and hours.

Here is an extract from notes made considerably later by my wife:

During the last days of the preparation for October, we were staying in Taurid street. Lev Davydovich lived for whole days at the Smolny. I was still working at the union of wood-workers, where the Bolsheviks were in charge, and the atmosphere was tense. All the working hours were spent in talking about the uprising. The chairman of the union upheld 'the point of view of Lenin–Trotsky' (as it was called then), and we carried on our agitation together. The question of the uprising was discussed everywhere – in the streets, at meal-time, at casual meetings on the stairs of the Smolny. We ate little, slept little, and worked almost twenty-four hours a day. Most of the time we were separated from our boys, and during the October days I worried about them. Lyova and Seryozha were the only 'Bolsheviks' in their school except for a third, a 'sympathizer', as they called him. Against them these three had a compact group of off-shoots of the ruling democracy – Kadets and Socialist-Revolutionists. And, as usually happens in such cases, criticism was supplemented by practical arguments. On more than one occasion the head master had to extricate my sons from under the piled-up 'democrats' who were pummelling them. The boys, after all, were only following the example of their fathers. The head master was a Kadet, and consequently always punished my sons with 'Take your hats and go home.' After the revolution it was quite impossible for the boys to remain in that school, and so they went to a 'people's school' instead. Everything was much simpler and cruder there, but one could breathe more freely.

L. D. and I very seldom were at home. The boys would come home from school and, finding that we weren't in, would think it unnecessary for them to stay within the four walls either. In those days of demonstrations, clashes and shootings we were worried for their safety, because they were then in such a revolutionary mood . . . At our brief meetings they would tell us with the greatest joy: 'Today we were with some Cossacks in a street-car and saw them read Dad's appeal, "Brother Cossacks!"'

'Well?'

'They read it and passed it on to others; it was fine!'

'Fine?'

'Fine.'

An acquaintance of L. D.'s, the engineer K., who had a large family of children of all ages, with a governess and so forth, offered to keep the boys in his home, where there would be someone to look after them. I jumped at this as a saving grace. I had to call at the Smolny about five times a day to carry out different commissions for L. D. We would return to Taurid street late at night; in the morning we would separate again, L. D. going to the Smolny, and I to the union. At the culmination of events we almost never left the Smolny. For days at a time L. D. would not come to Taurid street even to sleep. And I often stayed at the Smolny, as well. We slept on sofas and chairs without undressing. The weather was not exactly warm; it was autumn; the days were dry and lowering, and the wind blew in sharp, cold gusts. The main streets were quiet and deserted. And in this stillness one felt an intense watchfulness. The Smolny was bubbling over. The enormous hall sparkled with the thousands of lights from the magnificent chandeliers; day and night it was filled to the brim with people. Life in the mills and factories was strained, but the streets had quieted down. They were as still as if the city, in fright, had drawn its head down between its shoulders.

I remember that on the morning of the second or third day after the uprising, I dropped into a room at the Smolny and found Vladimir Ilyich [Lenin] there with Lev Davydovich. With them, if I remember correctly, were Dzerzhinsky, Joffe, and a crowd of others. Their faces were a greyish-green from lack of sleep; their eyes were inflamed, their collars soiled, and the room was full of smoke . . . Someone was sitting at a table surrounded by people waiting for orders. Lenin and Trotsky were also in the midst of a waiting mob. It seemed to me that orders were being given as if by people who were asleep. There was something of the somnambulist in the way they talked and moved about. For a moment I felt as if I were seeing it all in a dream, and that the revolution was in danger of being lost if 'they' didn't get a good sleep and put on clean collars; the dream was closely bound up with those collars. I remember that next day I met Lenin's sister, Marya Ilinishna, and reminded her hurriedly that Vladimir Ilyich needed a clean collar. 'Oh, yes, of course,' she replied, laughing. But by that time this matter of clean collars had lost its nightmarish significance for me.

The power is taken over, at least in Petrograd. Lenin has not yet had time to change his collar, but his eyes are very wide-awake, even though his face looks so tired. He looks softly at me, with that sort of awkward shyness that with him indicates intimacy. 'You know,' he says hesitatingly, 'from persecution and a life underground, to come so suddenly into power. . .' He pauses for the right word. '*Es schwindelt*,' he concludes, changing suddenly to German, and circling his hand around his head. We look at each other and laugh a little. All this takes only a minute or two; then a simple 'passing to next business'.

The government must be formed. We number among us a few members of the Central Committee. A quick session opens over in a corner of the room.

'What shall we call them?' asks Lenin, thinking aloud. 'Anything but ministers – that's such a vile, hackneyed word.'

'We might call them commissaries,' I suggest, 'but there are too many commissaries just now. Perhaps "supreme comissaries"? No, "supreme" does not sound well, either. What about "people's commissaries"?'

"'People's commissaries"? Well, that might do, I think,' Lenin agrees. 'And the government as a whole?'

'A Soviet, of course . . . the Soviet of People's Commissaries, eh?'

'The Soviet of People's Commissaries?' Lenin picks it up. 'That's splendid; smells terribly of revolution!'

Lenin was not much inclined towards the aesthetics of revolution, or towards relishing its 'romantic quality'. But all the more deeply did he feel the revolution as a whole, and all the more unmistakably did he define its 'smell'.

'And what,' Vladimir Ilyich once asked me quite unexpectedly, during those first days – 'what if the White Guards kill you and me? Will Svyerdlov and Bukharin be able to manage?'

'Perhaps they won't kill us,' I rejoined, laughing.

'The devil knows what they might do,' said Lenin, laughing in turn.

In 1924, in my recollections of Lenin, I described this incident for the first time. I learned afterwards that the members of what was then a 'trio' – Stalin, Zinoviev and Kamenev – felt terribly offended by it, although they did not dare contradict it. But the fact remains that Lenin only mentioned Svyerdlov and Bukharin. He did not think of any others.

Since he had spent fifteen years in his two exiles abroad, with only short intervals between, Lenin knew the main figures of the party who were living in Russia only from his correspondence with them or from his few meetings with them abroad. It was not until after the revolution that he was able to see them at close range and actually at work. And consequently he had to revise the old opinions, based on indirect reports, or else form new ones. A man of great moral passion, Lenin could not imagine such a thing as indifference towards people. A thinker, observer, and strategist, he was subject to spasms of enthusiasm for people. Krupskaya also mentions this trait of his in her memoirs. Lenin never weighed a man at a glance, forming some average estimate of him. His eye was like a microscope; it would magnify many times the trait that came within its field of vision at a particular moment. He would often fall in love with people, in the full sense of the word. And on such occasions I would tease him: 'I know, I know, you are having a new romance.' Lenin realized this characteristic of his, and would laugh by way of reply, a little embarrassed but a little angry, too.

Lenin's attitude towards me changed several times during 1917. He met me first with a certain reserve, cautiously. The July days brought us very close together quite suddenly. When, in opposition to the majority of the leading Bolshevists, I proposed boycotting the pre-parliament, Lenin wrote me from his refuge: 'Bravo, Comrade Trotsky!' Later on, judging from some accidental and quite erroneous indications, he concluded that I was being too dilatory in the matter of an armed uprising, and this suspicion was reflected in several of his letters during October. By contrast, his attitude towards me on the day of the revolution, when we were resting on the floor of a half-dark, empty room, became all the more unmistakable in its warmth and friendliness. The next day, at the meeting of the Central Committee of the party, he proposed that I be elected chairman of the Soviet of People's Commissaries. I sprang to my feet, protesting – the proposal seemed to me so unexpected and inappropriate. 'Why not?' Lenin insisted. 'You were at the head of the Petrograd Soviet that seized the power.' I moved to reject his proposal, without debating it. The motion was carried. On the first of November, during the impassioned discussions that took place at the meeting of the Petrograd party committee, Lenin exclaimed: 'There is no better Bolshevik than Trotsky.' Coming from him the words meant a great deal. It is no wonder that the minutes of the meeting at which they were pronounced are still withheld from the public.

The conquest of the power brought up the question of my government work. Strangely enough I had never even given a thought to it; in spite of the experience of 1905 there was never an occasion when I connected the question of my future with that of power. From my youth on, or, to be more precise, from my childhood on, I had dreamed of being a writer. Later, I subordinated my literary work, as I did everything else, to the revolution. The question of the party's conquest of power was always before me. Times without number I wrote and spoke about the programme of the revolutionary government, but the question of my personal work after the conquest never entered my mind. And so it caught me unawares.

After the seizure of power I tried to stay out of the government, and offered to undertake the direction of the press. It is quite possible that the nervous reaction after the victory had something to do with that; the months that had preceded it had been too closely tied up with the preparatory work for the revolution. Every fibre of my entire being was strained to its limit. Lunacharsky wrote somewhere in the papers that Trotsky walked about like an electric battery and that each contact with him brought forth a discharge. The twenty-fifth of October brought the let-down. I felt like a surgeon who has finished a difficult and dangerous operation – I must wash my hands, take off my apron, and rest.

Lenin was in a different position. He had just arrived from his refuge, after spending three and a half months cut off from real, practical direction. One thing coincided with the other, and this only added to my desire to retire behind the scenes for a while. Lenin would not hear of it, however. He insisted that I take over the commissariat of the interior, saying that the most important task at the moment was to fight off a counter-revolution. I objected, and brought up, among other arguments, the question of nationality. Was it worth while to put into our enemies' hands such an additional weapon as my Jewish origin?

Lenin almost lost his temper. 'We are having a great international revolution. Of what importance are such trifles?'

A good-humoured bickering began. 'No doubt the revolution is great,' I answered, 'but there are still a good many fools left.'

'But surely we don't keep step with the fools?'

'Probably we don't, but sometimes one has to make some allowance for stupidity. Why create additional complications at the outset?'

I have already had occasion to observe that the national question, so important in the life of Russia, had practically no personal significance for me. Even in my early youth the national bias and national prejudices had only bewildered my sense of reason, in some cases stirring in me nothing but disdain and even a moral nausea. My Marxist education deepened this feeling, and changed my attitude to that of an active internationalism. My life in so many countries, my acquaintance with so many different languages, political systems and cultures only helped me to absorb that internationalism into my very flesh and blood. If, in 1917 and later, I occasionally pointed to my Jewish origin as an argument against some appointment, it was simply because of political considerations.

Svyerdlov and other members of the Central Committee were won over to my side. Lenin was in the minority. He shrugged his shoulders, sighed, shook his head reproachfully, and consoled himself with the thought that we should all have to fight the counter-revolution anyway, no matter what departments of the government we were in. But my going over to the press was also firmly opposed by Svyerdlov; Bukharin, he said, was the man for that. 'Lev Davydovich should be set up against the rest of Europe. Let him take charge of foreign affairs.'

'What foreign affairs will we have now?' retorted Lenin. But reluctantly he finally agreed, and I, likewise with reluctance, consented. And thus, at the instigation of Svyerdlov, I came to head the Soviet diplomacy for a quarter of a year.

The commissariat of foreign affairs actually meant freedom from departmental work. To comrades who offered their help I almost invariably suggested that they look for a more gratifying field for their energy. One of them later gave, in his memoirs, a fairly juicy report of a conversation he had with me soon after the Soviet government was formed. 'What diplomatic work are we apt to have?' I said to him, according to his account. 'I will issue a few revolutionary proclamations to the peoples of the world, and then shut up shop.' My interlocutor was genuinely hurt by my lack of diplomatic consciousness. I had of course intentionally exaggerated my point of view, because I wanted to emphasize the fact that the centre of gravity was not in diplomacy at that time.

The principal tasks were to develop the October revolution further, extend it to the entire country, beat off the raid against Petrograd by Kerensky and General Krasnov, and fight the counter-revolution. These problems we were solving outside of the departments, and my collaboration with Lenin was most intimate and continuous at all times.

Lenin's room in the Smolny was at the opposite end of the building from my own. The corridor that connected, or rather divided, them was so long that Lenin jestingly suggested that we establish communication by bicycle. We were connected by telephone, and several times each day I would walk the endless corridor that looked like an ant-hill to Lenin's room for our conferences. A young sailor who was known as Lenin's secretary was constantly running between us, bringing me Lenin's notes, which consisted of two or three firmly expressed sentences, with the more important words underscored two or three times and the final question aimed pointblank. Often the notes were accompanied by drafts of decrees that required immediate comment. The archives of the Soviet of People's Commissaries hold a great many documents of that period, some written by Lenin, some by me – Lenin's texts with my amendments or my proposals with Lenin's additions.

During the first period – roughly speaking until August 1918 – I was active in the general work of the Soviet of People's Commissaries. During the Smolny period, Lenin was eagerly impatient to answer all problems of economic, political, administrative and cultural life by decrees. In this he was guided not by any passion for bureaucratic method, but rather by a desire to unfold the party's programme in the language of power. He knew that revolutionary decrees were only partially carried out. But to ensure full execution and control for these measures, a properly functioning machine was required, as well as time and experience. No one could tell how much time we would have at our disposal. During that first period the decrees were really more propaganda than actual administrative measures. Lenin was in a hurry to tell the people what the new power was, what it was after, and how it intended to accomplish its aims. He went from question to question with a magnificent tirelessness; he called small conferences, commissioned experts to make inquiries, and dug into books himself. And I helped him.

Lenin's conviction of continuity in the work that he was doing was very strong. As a great revolutionary, he understood the meaning of historical tradition. It was impossible to tell in advance whether we were to stay in power or be overthrown. And so it was necessary, whatever happened, to make our revolutionary experience as clear as possible for all men. Others would come, and, with the help of what we had outlined and begun, would take another step forwards. That was the meaning of the legislative work during the first period. That was why Lenin insisted impatiently on the earliest possible publication of the classics of socialism and materialism in Russian translation. He was anxious to have as many revolutionary monuments erected as possible, even if they were of the simplest sort, like busts or memorial tablets to be placed in all the towns, and, if it could be managed, in the villages as well, so that what had happened might be fixed in the people's imagination, and leave the deepest possible furrow in memory.

Every meeting of the Soviet of People's Commissaries,* which changed its membership often at first, presented a picture of an immense legislative improvisation. Everything had to proceed from the beginning. There were no 'precedents', since history had none to offer. Lenin presided indefatigably at the Soviet for five and six hours on end, and the meetings of the People's Commissaries were held every day. As a rule matters were brought up for consideration without previous preparation, and almost always as urgent business. Often the substance of the question discussed was not known either to the members of the Soviet or to the chairman before the meeting opened. The debates were always condensed, only ten minutes being allowed for the opening report. Nevertheless Lenin always sensed the necessary course. To save time he would send very short notes to the members present, asking for information on this or that subject. These notes would reveal a large and very interesting epistolary element in the legislative technic of Lenin's Soviet of Com-

*The Soviet (Council) of People's Commissaries is the executive and directive organ of the Central Executive Committee of the USSR. The Central Executive Committee acts as a legislative body between the sessions of the Congresses of Soviets. The Central Executive Committee, or, as it is sometimes called, the All-Union Central Executive Committee, is not to be confused with the 'Central Committee', often mentioned in the text; the latter is that of the Russian Communist Party. – *Translator.*

missaries. But unfortunately the majority have disappeared, because the reply in most cases was written on the reverse side of the paper, and the note was usually destroyed at once by the chairman. At the proper moment Lenin would announce his resolutions, always with an intentional sharpness; after that the debates would cease or else would give way to practical suggestions. In the end Lenin's 'points' were usually taken as the basis for the decree.

Besides other qualities a great creative imagination was necessary to guide this work. One of the most valuable powers of such an imagination is the ability to visualize people, objects, and events as they really are, even if one has never seen them. To combine separate little strokes caught on the wing, to supplement them by means of unformulated laws of correspondence and likelihood, and in this way to recreate a certain sphere of human life in all its concrete reality, basing everything upon experience in life and upon theory – that is the imagination that a legislator, an administrator, a leader must have, especially in a period of revolution. Lenin's strength was chiefly this power of realistic imagination.

It is hardly necessary to say that in this fever of creative legislation there were many blunders and contradictions. But, taken as a whole, Lenin's decrees of the Smolny period, that is, of the most stormy and chaotic period of the revolution, will be preserved forever in history as the proclamations of a new world. Not only sociologists and historians, but future legislators as well, will draw repeatedly from this source.

In the meantime practical problems – especially problems of civil war, food-supply and transport – were coming more and more urgently to the fore. Special extraordinary commissions were created to face these new questions for the first time and to set in motion some department or other that was helplessly marking time at the threshold of the problem. I had to preside over many of these commissions: the food-supply commission – of which Tzyurupa, enrolled for the first time in government work, was a member – the transport commission, the one for publications, and others.

The diplomatic department, with the exception of the Brest-

Litovsk peace negotiations, took very little of my time. The business proved a bit more complicated than I had expected, however. Even in the very first days, I found myself unexpectedly in diplomatic negotiations with the Eiffel Tower! During the uprising, we had been too rushed to pay heed to the foreign radios. But now, as the People's Commissary for foreign affairs, I had to watch the reaction of the capitalist world towards the revolution. It is quite unnecessary to say that no greetings reached us from anywhere. The Berlin government, although it was ready to flirt with the Bolsheviks, set up interference from its Nauen station when the Tsarskoye Syelo station was broadcasting my statement about our victory over Kerensky's troops. But if Berlin and Vienna were still vacillating between enmity to the revolution and the hope of concluding a profitable peace, the rest of the world – not only those countries engaged in war, but the neutral ones as well – echoed, in their respective languages, the sentiments of the ruling classes of the old Russia which we had overthrown. In this chorus the Eiffel Tower stood out for its very fury. In those days it spoke even in Russian, obviously seeking some direct appeal to the hearts of the Russian people. Sometimes, when I read the Paris radios, I thought that Clémenceau himself must be sitting on top of the tower. I knew him as a journalist well enough to recognize his spirit, if not his style. The hatred in those radios almost choked in its own venom; malice reached its utmost limit. Sometimes it seemed as if the radio-scorpion on the Eiffel Tower would sting its head with its own tail.

We had the Tsarskoye Syelo station at our disposal, and so there was nothing to impose silence upon us. For several days I dictated answers to Clémenceau's abuse. I knew enough of the political history of France to characterize the principal *dramatis personae* none too flatteringly. I reminded them of certain forgotten facts in their past history, beginning with the Panama business. For several days a tense duel raged between Paris and the Tsarskoye Syelo station. Ether, being a neutral agent, conscientiously transmitted the arguments of both sides. And what happened? Even I had not expected such quick results. Paris changed its tone abruptly; henceforth it expressed itself in a still hostile but civil manner. Later I often remembered with pleasure that I had begun my diplomatic activity by teaching the Eiffel Tower good manners.

On 18 November General Judson, the chief of the American mission, made an unexpected call on me at the Smolny. He informed me that he was not yet able to speak in the name of the American government, but he hoped that everything would be 'all right'. Did the Soviet government intend to work towards the conclusion of the war in conjunction with the Allies? I replied that in view of the complete publicity of the forthcoming negotiations, the Allies would be able to watch their progress and join them at any stage. In conclusion the peace-loving General said: 'The time for protests and threats against the Soviet power has passed, if there ever was such a time.' But, as we know, one swallow, even if it has the rank of general, does not make a summer.

My first and last meeting with the French ambassador, Noulens, took place early in December. A former Radical deputy, he had been sent to establish friendly relations with the February revolution, in place of the declared monarchist, Paléologue, a Byzantine in more than name, whom the Republic had used to keep her friendship with the Tsar. Why Noulens and not some one else was chosen, I do not know. But he did not raise my opinion of the rulers of human destiny. The conference, arranged at his initiative, brought no results. After vacillating for a while, Clémenceau finally went over to the barbed-wire régime.

I did not have a friendly interview with the head of the French mission, General Niessel, in my office at the Smolny. He had been exercising his aggressiveness in rear-guard actions. Under Kerensky he had been accustomed to command, and he did not want to unlearn this bad habit. To begin with I had to ask him to leave the Smolny. Presently, relations with the French mission became even more difficult. The information bureau attached to the mission became a factory for the most disgusting insinuations against the revolution. In all the hostile papers cabled reports 'from Stockholm' began to appear daily, reports that excelled each other in fantastic invention, malice, and sheer stupidity. When questioned as to the source of the 'Stockholm' telegrams, the editors of the papers pointed to the French military mission. I asked for an official explanation from General Niessel, and on 22 December he replied in a truly remarkable document.

'Numerous journalists of various shades of opinion,' wrote the General,

call at the military mission for information. I am authorized to give them information as to military events on the western front of the war, as to Salonika, Asia, and as to the situation in France. At one [?] of these interviews, one [?] of the young officers allowed himself to communicate a rumour which spread through the city [?] and whose origin was attributed to Stockholm . . .

In conclusion, the General promised vaguely 'to take steps to prevent such oversights [?] in the future'.

This was too much. We had not taught the Paris radio station the rules of decency only to allow General Niessel to create a subsidiary tower of lies in Moscow. The same day I wrote to Niessel:

1. In view of the fact that the propaganda bureau called the bureau of 'information' at the French military mission has acted as a source for the dissemination of wilfully false rumours, with the object of spreading confusion and chaos in the public mind, this bureau is to be closed at once.

2. The 'young officer' who fabricated lying reports is requested to leave Russian territory at once. I request you to communicate the name of this officer to me without delay.

3. The receiving installation of the radio telegraph is to be removed from the mission.

4. The French officers in the civil-war zone are to be recalled immediately to Petrograd, by an order to be published in the press.

5. I request you to inform me of all steps undertaken by the mission in connection with this letter.

People's Commissary for Foreign Affairs
L. TROTSKY.

The 'young officer' was brought out of his anonymity and left Russia as a scapegoat. The radio receiving installation was removed. The information bureau was closed. The officers were recalled to the centre. But this was only petty, front-line skirmishing. It gave way to a brief and unstable truce, after I had gone over to the Commissariat of War. The too forthright General Niessel was replaced by the insinuating General Lavergne. The truce did not last long, however. The French military mission, like the French diplomacy, soon became the centre of every plot and armed attack against the Soviet power. But this did not develop openly until after Brest-Litovsk, during the Moscow period in the spring and summer of 1918.

30

In Moscow

The signing of the Brest-Litovsk peace treaty divested my withdrawal from the commissariat for foreign affairs of any political significance. Chicherin had meanwhile arrived from London to succeed me. I had known Chicherin for a long time. In the years of the first revolution he gave up his position as a diplomatic official and went over to the Social Democracy. As a Menshevik he engaged actively in the work of the party 'groups of assistance' abroad. At the outbreak of the war he assumed a stiffly patriotic stand and tried to defend it in his many letters from London. One or two of these letters fell to my lot. Very soon, however, he drew nearer to the internationalists and became an active correspondent for the *Nashe Slovo*, which I was editing in Paris. In the end he got into an English prison. I demanded his release: the negotiations were dragging on. I threatened reprisals against Englishmen. 'There is, after all, something in Trotsky's argument,' Buchanan, the British ambassador, said in his diary, 'that if we claim the right to arrest Russians for making a pacifist propaganda in a country bent on continuing the war, he has an equal right to arrest British subjects who are conducting a war propaganda in a country bent on peace.'

Chicherin was released. He arrived in Moscow at the most opportune moment, and with a sigh of relief I handed the diplomatic helm over to him. I was not appearing at the ministry at all then. On rare occasions Chicherin would consult me by telephone. Not until 13 March was there a public announcement of my resignation from the commissariat of foreign affairs, coinciding with the announcement of my appointment as war commissary and as chairman of the Supreme War Council, formed only a little while before on my initiative.

Thus Lenin achieved his end after all. He used my offer to resign in connection with the Brest-Litovsk disagreements only to carry out his original idea, modified to meet changed circumstances. As the enemy within changed from plotting to the creating of armies and battle fronts, Lenin expressed the wish that I take charge of military operations. He had now won over Svyerdlov to his side. I tried to argue against it. 'Whom else can we appoint? Name them,' Lenin pressed his attack. I thought it over for a moment, and consented.

Was I prepared to do military work? Of course not. I had not even had the benefit of service in the Tsar's army. My army-service years I had spent in prison, in exile, and abroad. In 1906 the court sentence deprived me of all civil and military rights. While spending a few months during the Balkan wars in Serbia, Bulgaria, and later in Roumania, I came closer to military affairs. But my approach to these questions was by nature still political rather than military. The World War brought everyone – myself included – close to the questions of militarism. My everyday work on the *Nashe Slovo* and my writing for the *Kievskaya Mysl* gave me the needed stimulus to systematize my new knowledge and observations. But there the important thing was war as the continuation of politics, and the army as the instrument of the latter. The problems of military organization and technique were still in the background as far as I was concerned. On the other hand the psychology of an army, in its barracks, trenches, battles, hospitals, and the like, deeply stirred my interest. This was later very useful.

In parliamentary countries war and navy ministries are often given over to lawyers and journalists who, like myself, see the army chiefly from the window of their editorial offices – although they are more comfortable than mine were. And yet there was an obvious difference. In capitalist countries the problem is that of maintaining the existing army – strictly speaking, of maintaining a political cover for a self-sustaining system of militarism. With us, the problem was to make a clean sweep of the remains of the old army, and in its place to build, under fire, a new army, whose plan was not to be discovered in any book. This explains sufficiently why I felt uncertain about my military work, and consented to take it over only because there was no one else to do it.

I did not think of myself as in any sense a strategist, and had little patience with the sort of strategist-dilettantism that flooded the party as a result of the revolution. It is true that on three occasions – in the war with Denikin, in the defence of Petrograd, and in the war with Pilsudski – I took an independent strategic position and defended it first against the high command, and again against the majority of the Central Committee. But in these cases my strategic position was determined by political and economic considerations, rather than by those relating to pure strategy. It may be pointed out, however, that questions of high strategy cannot be solved in any other way, after all.

The change in my work coincided with the change of the seat of the government. The transfer of the central government to Moscow was, of course, a blow to Petrograd. There was almost general opposition to the transfer, headed by Zinoviev, who by that time had become the chairman of the Petrograd Soviet. He was supported by Lunacharsky, who had resigned from the government a few days after the revolution, on the ground that he did not wish to bear the responsibility for the destruction (imaginary) of St Basil's Church in Moscow. Now, back at his post, he was unwilling to part with the Smolny as 'the symbol of the revolution'.

Others brought forward more serious arguments. The majority feared chiefly the bad effect of the transfer on the Petrograd workers. Our enemies at that time were circulating the rumour that we had undertaken to hand Petrograd over to Kaiser Wilhelm. On the contrary Lenin and I insisted that the transfer of the government to Moscow was to ensure not only the safety of the government but of Petrograd itself. The temptation to seize the revolutionary capital and its government with it in one swift blow could not fail to appeal strongly to both Germany and the Allies. To seize a starving Petrograd without the government would be quite another matter. In the end resistance broke down and the majority of the Central Committee voted for the transfer. The government actually left for Moscow on 12 March 1918. To soften the impression that we were demoting the

October capital, I remained in Petrograd for another week or two. The railway administration detained me at the station for a few extra hours; the sabotage was diminishing, but it was still considerable. I arrived in Moscow the day after I was appointed war commissary.

With its medieval wall and its countless gilded cupolas, the Kremlin seemed an utter paradox as a fortress for the revolutionary dictatorship. To be sure, no more had the Smolny, formerly a private school for girls of the nobility, been intended for workers, soldiers, and peasants' deputies. Until March 1918 I had never been inside the Kremlin, nor did I know Moscow in general, with the exception of one solitary building, the Butyrsky transfer-prison, in the tower of which I had spent six months during the cold winter of 1898 to 1899. As a visitor I might admiringly have contemplated the antiquities of the Kremlin, the palace of Ivan the Terrible, with its throne-room. But we had to settle down here for a long time. The close, day-by-day contact of those two historical poles, the two irreconcilable cultures, was at once bewildering and amusing. As I drove along the wood-paved road past the Nikolayevsky Palace, I often looked sideways at the Tsar-gun and the Tsar-bell. The heavy barbarism of Moscow stared from the breach in the bell and from the muzzle of the gun. Prince Hamlet would have repeated on this spot: 'The time is out of joint; – O cursed spite, that ever I was born to set it right!' But there was nothing Hamletish about us. Even when the more important questions were being discussed, Lenin allowed the speakers only two minutes apiece. One could probably meditate on the contradictions in the development of a backward country for a minute or two when dashing off at a tangent to the Kremlin past, on the way from one meeting to another – but no longer than that.

The Kavalersky building, opposite the Potyeshny Palace, before the revolution was the living-quarters of the officials of the Kremlin. The entire lower floor was occupied by the commanding officer. His apartment had now been made into several smaller ones. Lenin and I took quarters across the corridor sharing the same dining-room. The food at the Kremlin was then very bad. Instead of fresh meat they served corned beef.

The flour and the barley had sand in them. Only the red Ket caviare was plentiful, because its export had ceased. This inevitable caviare coloured the first years of the revolution, and not for me alone.

The musical clock on the Spassky tower was rebuilt. Now the old bells, instead of ringing out 'God Save the Tsar', slowly and pensively rang out the 'International', at quarter-hour intervals. The automobile entrance was under the Spassky tower, through an arched tunnel. Over the tunnel there was an ancient ikon with a top of broken glass; in front of the ikon was a lamp long since extinguished. Often, when one came out of the Kremlin, one's eyes would fasten on the ikon, while one's ears would catch the peal of the 'International' from overhead. And over the tower, with its bell, was a double-headed gilt eagle which rose just as before, except that its crown had been removed. I advised setting the hammer-and-sickle up above the eagle, so that the breach in the times might look down from the height of the Spassky tower. But for one reason or another it was never done.

Lenin and I met a dozen times a day in the corridor, and called on each other to talk things over. Sometimes these talks lasted as long as ten or even fifteen minutes – a long time for us. In that period Lenin was rather talkative – judged, of course, by his own standard. There were so many new things, things utterly strange to us, to prepare for. We had to create ourselves and the others to fit in with the new conditions, and accordingly we felt the need of passing from the particular to the general and the other way about. The little cloud of the Brest-Litovsk disagreements* had dispersed, leaving never a trace. Lenin was very cordial and considerate both to me and to my family. He often stopped our boys in the corridor to play with them.

The furniture in my room was Karelian birch. Over the fireplace a clock struck the hours in a thin, silver voice from beneath a Cupid and Psyche. Everything in the room was incompatible with work. The aroma of the idle life of the master class emanated from every chair. But I took even my apartment on the wing; this was all the more true because during those years I

*Explained in the ensuing chapters. – *Translator.*

M.L. – 18

slept in it only on my brief visits to Moscow from the front.

I think it was the very first day of my arrival from Petrograd, while Lenin and I were having a chat in the midst of all that Karelian birch, that the Cupid and his Psyche interrupted us with their singing, silver bells. We looked at each other as if we had both caught ourselves thinking the same thing; we were being overheard by the past, lurking over there in the corner. Surrounded by it on all sides as we were, we treated it without respect, but without hostility either, rather with a touch of irony. It would be incorrect to imply that we got used to the surroundings in the Kremlin. Our lives were too dynamic for that; we had no time to get used to anything. We saw the surroundings out of the corners of our eyes, and said in imagination to the Cupids and Psyches, in a tone at once ironical and encouraging: 'You did not expect us? Can't be helped! Get used to us, now!' We were making our surroundings accustom themselves to us.

The lower ranks of the old staff were retained at their posts. They received us a little fearfully. The régime here had been a stern one, dating from the days of serfdom, and the service had passed from father to son. Among the countless flunkeys and other attendants at the Kremlin were many old men who had waited on several emperors in their time. One of them, Stupishin, a little, clean-shaven man, was a dutiful fellow who had been feared by all the attendants in his day. Now the younger ones looked at him with a respect that was mingled with a new challenge. He shuffled tirelessly along the corridors, putting chairs in their places, dusting them off, and generally keeping up the appearance of the old order. At dinner we were given thin vegetable soup and unpolished buckwheat, served on plates adorned with eagles. 'What is he doing? Look!' whispered Seryozha to his mother. The old man was moving like a shadow behind the chairs and silently turning the plates this way or that. Seryozha was the first to guess it: the double-headed eagle on the rim of the plate must be right-side-up to face the guest.

'Did you notice old Stupishin?' I asked Lenin.

'How can you help noticing him?' he replied, in a tone of gentle irony.

Sometimes one felt sorry for these old men who had been

pulled, root and branch, from their element. Stupishin was soon firmly attached to Lenin; when the latter moved to another building nearer to the Soviet of Commissaries, he transferred his devotion to my wife and me, observing that we appreciated order and valued his care.

The entire staff of attendants was soon dissolved. The young ones quickly adapted themselves to the new conditions. Stupishin did not want to be put on a pension, and so he was transferred to a great palace that had been changed into a museum. He would often call at the Kavalersky building to look us up. Afterwards he was doorman in front of the Andreyevsky hall in the palace, during the congresses and conferences. Around him there was always order; he performed the same duties that he had at the receptions of the Tsars and the Grand Dukes, except that now it was the Communist International. He was fated, like the clock-bells in the Spassky tower, to change his tune from the Tsar's hymn to the hymn of the revolution. In 1926, when the old man was dying a lingering death in a hospital, my wife sent him presents and he wept with gratitude.

Soviet Moscow received us chaotically. Moscow, it seemed, had its own Soviet of People's Commissaries under the chairmanship of the historian Pokrovsky, the last man in the world to hold such a post. The authority of the Moscow Soviet extended all through the Moscow region, whose boundaries no one could define. In the north, it claimed the Archangel province; in the south, the province of Kursk. And so in Moscow we discovered a government that had authority, doubtful as it was, over the main section of the Soviet territory. The traditional antagonism between Moscow and Petrograd survived the October revolution. Once upon a time Moscow had been a big village, and Petrograd a city. Moscow represented the landowners and merchants, Petrograd the military and the officials. Moscow was regarded as full-blooded Russian, Slavophile, hospitable – in other words, the very heart of Russia. Petrograd was European, impersonal, egotistic, the bureaucratic brains of the country. Moscow developed the textile industries, Petrograd those of metal-working. The antitheses represented literary exaggerations of actual differences. We felt them at once. The local patriotism extended even to the native Moscow Bolshevists. A special commission was set up, with me as chairman, to regulate relations with the Moscow Soviet of Commissaries. It was a curious sort of work. We dissected the regional commissariats patiently, and took for the central government what properly belonged to it. As we progressed with the work it became quite evident that the second Moscow government was unnecessary. The Muscovites themselves realized the need of winding up their Soviet of Commissaries.

The Moscow period, for the second time in Russian history, became one of gathering the state together and of creating organs of administration. Lenin now was showing impatience, irony, and sometimes downright bitter mockery in brushing aside people who continued to answer all questions in terms of propagandist formulas. 'Where do you think you are, my man? In the Smolny?' he would shoot at them, with a ferocity softened by his good humour. 'The veriest Smolny,' he would interrupt a speaker who was not talking business. 'Please wake up; we are not at the Smolny, we have gone ahead since then.' Lenin never spared vigorous words about the past, when it was necessary to prepare for the next day. We were arm in arm in this work. Lenin was very methodical; I was even pedantic. We waged a tireless fight against slovenliness and laxity of any sort. At my suggestion strict rules against late comers and the late opening of meetings were passed. Step by step chaos yielded to order.

Before the sessions at which questions of principle or matters deriving importance from the conflicts between departments were to be discussed, Lenin would insist by telephone that I acquaint myself with the subject in advance. The current literature on the disagreements between Lenin and Trotsky is full of apocrypha. Of course there were sometimes disagreements. But far more often we came to the same conclusion after we had exchanged a few words by telephone, or else independently of each other. When it was obvious that we both had the same opinion about a certain matter, we knew that we would get the necessary decision adopted. But at times, when Lenin was afraid that there might be serious opposition to one of his projects, he would remind me by telephone: 'Don't fail to come to the meeting! I'll have you speak first.' I would talk for a few minutes, and Lenin would say 'Right!' perhaps twice during my speech, and that would decide the vote. Not because the others were afraid to oppose us – at that time there was no sign of the present practice of keeping in line with your superiors and of the revolting fear of compromising yourself by an inappropriate word or vote – but because the less the bureaucratic subservience the greater the authority of leadership.

When I disagreed with Lenin, a fevered discussion not only could but sometimes did develop. But when we agreed the discussion was always brief. If, for some reason, we were unable to talk things over in advance, we would exchange notes during the meeting, and if these revealed some disagreement between us, Lenin would so guide discussion as to defer the issue. Sometimes in notes stating my disagreement with him I would write in a humorous vein, and Lenin's whole body would shake while he read them. He was very susceptible to laughter, especially when he was tired. It was one of his child-like traits; in that manliest of all men there were many child-like traits. I would watch him in delight as he struggled so hard to overcome a fit of laughter while trying to direct the meeting with the utmost seriousness. His cheek-bones then would bulge even more under the strain.

The war commissariat, where most of my work was done – not only my military work but party and literary work, or any other task there was for me – was situated outside of the Kremlin. I had only my living quarters in the Kavalersky building. No one came to see us there. People who came to see me on business came to the commissariat. As for social visits – no one ever thought of such a thing; we were much too busy for that. We returned home from work at about five o'clock. By seven I was back at the commissariat for the evening sessions. When, much later, the revolution had settled down a little, I devoted my evenings to theoretical and literary work.

My wife joined the commissariat of education and was placed in charge of museums and ancient monuments. It was her duty to fight for the monuments of the past against the conditions of civil war. It was a difficult matter. Neither the White nor the Red troops were much inclined to look out for historical estates, provincial Kremlins, or ancient churches. This led to many arguments between the war commissariat and the department of museums. The guardians of the palaces and churches accused the troops of lack of respect for culture; the military commissaries accused the guardians of preferring dead objects to living people. Formally, it looked as if I were engaged in an endless departmental quarrel with my wife. Many jokes were made about us on this score.

I now communicated with Lenin chiefly by telephone. His calls to me and mine to him were very frequent, and referred to an infinite number of things. The departments often bothered him with complaints against the Red army; Lenin would immediately call me. Five minutes later he would want to know if I could meet a new candidate for the people's commissary of agriculture for inspection, and tell him what I thought of him. An hour later he was interested to know if I had watched the theoretical discussion on proletarian culture, and whether I intended to make a counter-attack on Bukharin. Then the question would be: Could the war department on the southern front allot motor-trucks for the transport of food-supplies to the stations? Another half-hour would bring Lenin's inquiry whether I was following the disagreements in the Swedish communist party. And that was the way it went every day that I was in Moscow.

From the moment of the German advance the behaviour of the French – at least the more sensible of them – changed suddenly; they had realized the stupidity of the talk about our secret deal with the Hohenzollerns. It was just as clear to them that we could not engage in a war. Some of the French officers even insisted on our signing the peace in order to gain time. This idea was defended with special energy by a French intelligence officer, an aristocrat and royalist with an artificial eye, who offered me his services for the most dangerous commissions.

General Lavergne, who had replaced Niessel, gave me frequent advice in a cautious and rather soft-spoken manner – advice of little value but in appearance well meant. According to him, the French government now accepted the conclusion of the peace of Brest-Litovsk, and was anxious only to lend us its disinterested help in the building up of the army. He offered to place at my disposal the officers of the many French missions returning from Roumania. Two of them, a colonel and a captain, took quarters opposite the building of the war commissariat, so that I might always have them close at hand. I must confess that I suspected them of being more competent in military espionage than in military administration. They submitted written reports to me which, in the confusion of those days, I had not even time to look over.

One of the episodes of that brief 'truce' was the presentation to me of the military missions of the Allies. There were many of them, and each was composed of a number of men. About twenty of their representatives came into my tiny room. Lavergne made the presentations. Some of them uttered little pleasantries. A soft-looking Italian general distinguished himself by congratulating me on our success in ridding Moscow of bandits. 'Now', he said with a charming smile, 'one can live in Moscow as safely as in any other capital.' I remarked that this was rather an exaggeration. After this we literally did not know what to say to each other. The visitors could not brace themselves to get up and leave, and I did not know how to get rid of them. Finally, General Lavergne rescued us from this difficult situation by asking if I would object if the military representatives were to take no more of my time. I answered that, although I was loath to part with so select a company, I would not dare to object. Everyone has had scenes in his life that he can recall only with a somewhat embarrassed laugh. My meeting with the military missions of the Allies was that sort.

Gradually military affairs absorbed most of my time, the more so because I had myself to start with the A B Cs. In the technical sphere and in that of operations I saw my task chiefly as a matter of putting the right man in the right place, and then letting him exercise his abilities. My political and organization work in creating the army merged completely with the work of the party. Success would never have been possible in any other way.

Among the party workers at the war commissariat I found the army doctor Sklyansky. In spite of his youth (in 1918 he was barely twenty-six) he was conspicuous for his businesslike methods, his industry, and his talent for appraising people and circumstances – in other words, for the qualities that make an administrator. After consulting Svyerdlov, who was invaluable in such matters, I chose Sklyansky as my deputy. I never had any occasion to regret it afterwards. The duty of deputizing for me involved great responsibility because I was at the front most of the time. In my absence Sklyansky presided over the Military-Revolutionary Council, directed all the current work of the commissariat, which consisted chiefly of attending to the needs of the front, and finally represented the war commissariat on the Council of Defence, of which Lenin was chairman.

If any one could be compared with Lazare Carnot of the French Revolution, it is Sklyansky. He was always exact, indefatigable, alert, and well-informed. Most of the orders from the war commissariat were issued over his signature. And since these orders were published in the central organs and local publications, Sklyansky's name became widely known. Like every serious and rigorous administrator, he had many enemies. His youthful abilities irritated not a few mediocre worthies; Stalin stirred them up behind the scenes. Attacks against Sklyansky were made surreptitiously, and especially when I was away. Lenin knew Sklyansky well, through the Council of Defence, and always defended him with great zeal. 'A splendid worker', he would invariably say, 'a remarkable worker'. Sklyansky kept away from all these intrigues and worked; he listened to the reports of the quartermasters, gathered information from the industries, kept count of cartridges, of which there was always a shortage. Smoking endlessly, he spoke by direct wire, called on the telephone the chief officers, and prepared data for the Council of Defence. One could call him at two or three in the morning and find him still at his desk in the commissariat. 'When do you sleep?' I would ask him. He would reply with a jest.

It makes me happy to remember that the war department was almost free from the personal cliques and squabbles that affected the other departments so gravely. The strenuous nature of the work, the authority of leadership, the correct choice of workers (without nepotism or leniency) – the spirit of exacting loyalty – it was these that ensured uninterrupted work from a mechanism that was cumbersome, not very well balanced, and very heterogeneous in its composition. Much of the credit for this is due to Sklyansky.

The civil war kept me away from the work in the Soviet of Commissaries. I lived now in a railway-carriage or in an automobile. After weeks and months of such travelling I got so completely out of touch with the current government business that I could not pick up the threads again in my brief visits to Moscow. The most important questions, however, were decided at the Politbureau.* Sometimes I would return specially for the meeting of the Politbureau, in answer to Lenin's summons. Or sometimes, through Svyerdlov, I would call an extraordinary meeting of the Politbureau to discuss important questions that I had brought with me from the front. During these years my correspondence with Lenin was largely confined to matters relating to the civil war; there were short notes or long telegrams either to supplement previous conversations or to lay the groundwork for future ones. In spite of their businesslike brevity these documents show, better than anything else, the actual relations within the leading group of the Bolsheviks. I will publish this extensive correspondence in the near future, with the necessary commentaries. It will appear as a deadly rebuttal of the work of the historians of the Stalin school.

When Wilson was planning – among his other anaemic professorial utopias – a conciliation conference of all the governments of Russia, Lenin, on 24 January 1919, sent a coded telegram to me on the southern front: 'Wilson proposes truce and invites all the governments of Russia to a conference... It will be you who will probably have to go to Wilson.' The difference at the time of the Brest-Litovsk negotiations did not prevent Lenin from turning to me again when an important diplomatic task had to be met, although at that time I was completely absorbed in my military work. As everybody knows, nothing came of Wilson's peacemaking efforts, and so I had no occasion to go to the conference.

---

*The Politbureau (an abbreviation of the 'Political Bureau') is an organization within the Central Committee of the Communist Party which controls the policy. – *Translator*.

Aside from the hundreds of testimonials by Lenin himself, there is a vivid account by Maxim Gorky of his attitude towards my war work: 'Striking the table with his hand, he [Lenin] said: "Could anyone point out to me another man who could organize an almost model army in a year and even win the respect of military experts? We have such a man! We have everything. And there will be miracles."'

According to Gorky, Lenin said to him in the same conversation: 'Yes, yes. I know. Some lies are being told about my relations to him. Too many lies are being told, and especially about me and Trotsky.' What would Lenin have said today, when the lying about our mutual relations, despite facts, documents and logic, has become a state cult?

When I was declining the commissariat of home affairs on the second day after the revolution, I brought up, among other things, the question of race. It would seem that in war business this consideration should have involved even greater complications than in civil administration. But Lenin proved to be right. In the years of the revolutionary *ascendancy* this question never had the slightest importance. Of course the Whites tried to develop anti-Semitic motifs in their propaganda in the Red army, but they failed signally. There are many testimonials to this, even in the White press. In *Archives of the Russian Revolution*, published in Berlin, a White Guard writer relates the following striking episode: 'A Cossack who came to see us was hurt by someone's taunt that he not only served under, but fought under the command of a Jew – Trotsky – and retorted with warm conviction: "Nothing of the sort. Trotsky is not a Jew. Trotsky is a fighter. He's ours ... Russian! ... It is Lenin who is a communist, a Jew, but Trotsky is ours ... a fighter ... Russian ... our own!"'

The same motif will be found in *The Horse Army*, by Babel, the most talented of our younger writers. The question of my Jewish origin acquired importance only after I had become a subject for political baiting. Anti-Semitism raised its head with that of anti-Trotskyism. They both derived from the same source – the petty bourgeois reaction against October.

31

Negotiations at Brest-Litovsk

The decree that announced our willingness to make peace was passed by the Congress of Soviets on 26 October when only Petrograd was in our hands. On 7 November, I sent an appeal by radio to the Allied countries and to the Central Powers, inviting them to conclude a general peace. Through their agents the Allied governments replied to General Dukhonin, the Russian Commander-in-Chief, that any further steps in the direction of separate negotiations would entail 'the gravest consequences'. I replied to this threat with an appeal to all workers, soldiers and peasants. It was a categorical appeal: When we overthrow our bourgeoisie, it was not to make our army shed its blood at the order of a foreign bourgeoisie.

On 22 November we signed an agreement for a truce along the entire front, from the Baltic to the Black Sea. Once more we invited the Allies to join us in the peace negotiations. No reply was forthcoming, but neither were any more threats; the Allied governments seemed to have learned something. The peace negotiations began on 9 December, six weeks after the adoption of the decree of peace, which left the countries of the Entente sufficient time to determine their attitude on this question. At the outset our delegation made a formal declaration stating the principles of democratic peace.

The opposing side demanded an adjournment. The resumption of the conference was put off time and again. The delegations of the quadruple alliance had to cope with all kinds of internal difficulties in framing their reply to us, finally given on 25 December. The governments of the quadruple alliance 'subscribed' to the democratic formula of peace – no annexations, no indemnities, and self-determination for the peoples. On 28 December a huge demonstration was held in Petrograd, in honour of democratic peace. Though the masses mistrusted the German reply they accepted it as a great moral victory for the revolution. The next morning our delegation returned from Brest-Litovsk, bringing with it the monstrous demands that Kühlmann had submitted on behalf of the Central Powers.

'To delay negotiations, there must be some one to do the delaying,' said Lenin. At his insistence I set off for Brest-Litovsk. I confess I felt as if I were being led to the torture chamber. Being with strange and alien people always had aroused my fears; it did especially on this occasion. I absolutely cannot understand revolutionaries who willingly accept posts as ambassadors and feel like fish in water in their new surroundings.

At Brest-Litovsk the first Soviet delegation, headed by Joffe, was treated in a most ingratiating way by the Germans. Prince Leopold of Bavaria received them as his 'guests'. All the delegations had dinner and supper together. General Hoffmann must have observed with considerable interest the woman delegate Vitzenko, who had assassinated General Sakharov. The Germans took their seats between our men and tried to worm out of them whatever information they wanted. The first delegation included a worker, a peasant, and a soldier. They were delegates by mere accident and they were little prepared for that sort of trickery. The peasant, an old man, was even encouraged to drink more wine than was good for him.

General Hoffman's staff was publishing a paper called *Russky Vyestnik* (*The Russian Messenger*) for the benefit of the Russian prisoners; in its early phases it always spoke of the Bolsheviks with the most touching sympathy. 'Our readers ask us who Trotsky is,' Hoffmann informed his Russian prisoners in his paper and with admiring affection told them of my struggle against Tsarism, and of my German book *Russland in der Revolution*. 'The whole revolutionary world was thrilled by his successful escape.' And further on: 'When Tsarism was overthrown, its secret friends threw Trotsky into prison soon after he had returned from a long exile.' In a word, there were no more ardent revolutionaries than Leopold of Bavaria and Hoffmann of Prussia.

But this idyll did not last long. At the meeting of the Brest-Litovsk conference of 7 February, which bore the least possible resemblance to an idyll, I remarked, referring to the past: 'We are inclined to regret the premature compliments paid us by the official German and Austro-Hungarian press. This was quite unnecessary for the successful progress of peace negotiations.'

In this affair the Social Democracy was again no more than the shadow of the Hohenzollern and Hapsburg governments. Schiedemann, Ebert and others tried at first to slap us patronizingly on the back. The Vienna *Arbeiter-Zeitung* wrote eloquently on 15 December that 'the duel between Trotsky and Buchanan is the symbol of the great struggle of our day, the struggle of the proletariat against capital'. In the days when Kühlmann and Czernin were trying to strangle the Russian revolution at Brest-Litovsk the Austrian Marxists were able to see nothing but a 'duel' between Trotsky and – Buchanan! Even today one views such hypocrisy only with disgust.

'Trotsky', wrote the Hapsburg Marxists, 'is the authorized representative of the peaceful will of the Russian working class that is trying to break the iron-gold chain with which it has been bound by English capital.' The leaders of the Social Democracy voluntarily chained themselves to Austro–German capital, and were helping their governments forcibly to chain the Russian revolution. At the most difficult stages of the Brest-Litovsk negotiations, when Lenin or I would come across a copy of the Berlin *Vorwärts*, or the Vienna *Arbeiter-Zeitung*, we would silently point out to each other the lines underscored with a coloured pencil, lift our eyes to one another for a moment, and then turn away with an inordinate sense of shame for the men who, only the day before, had been our comrades in the International. Everyone who consciously passed through this stage realized forever that, whatever the fluctuations of the political situation, the Social Democracy was historically dead.

To end this improper masquerade, I asked in our own papers if the German staff would not be so good as to tell the German soldiers something about Karl Liebknecht and Rosa Luxemburg. We published a special leaflet on the subject for the German soldiers, and the *Vyestnik* of General Hoffmann bit its tongue.

Immediately after my arrival at Brest-Litovsk Hoffmann protested against our propaganda among the troops. I refused to
discuss the matter, and suggested that the General continue his
own propaganda among the Russian troops – the conditions
were the same, the only difference being in the kind of propaganda. I also reminded him that the dissimilarity of our views
on certain rather important questions had long been known, and
had even been certified to by one of the German courts – the
one that during the war had sentenced me in contumacy to
prison. This indecorous reminder created a great sensation.
Many of the titled gentlemen almost gasped. Turning to Hoffmann, Kühlmann asked, 'Would you like to reply?' To which
Hoffmann retorted, 'No, that's enough.'

As chairman of the Soviet delegation I decided to put an
immediate stop to the familiarity that had quite imperceptibly
been established during the early stages. Through our military
representatives I made it known that I had no desire to be
presented to the Prince of Bavaria. This was noted. I next
demanded separate dinners and suppers, under the pretext that
we had to hold conferences during the intervals. This was also
accepted in silence. In his diary for 7 January, Czernin wrote:
'All the Russians, under the leadership of Trotsky, arrived before
dinner-time. They immediately asked to be excused if, in the
future, they did not join in the meals in common. And they
generally kept out of sight; this time it seems that quite a
different wind is blowing than on the last occasion.' The feigned
friendliness of relations gave way to an official formality.This
was all the more opportune since we had to pass from academic
preliminaries to the concrete questions of a peace treaty.

Kühlmann was head and shoulders above Czernin, and probably above all the rest of the diplomats whom I met in the years
after the war. He impressed me as a man of character, with a
practical mind far above the average, and with malice enough
to cover not only us – here he met his match – but his dear allies
as well. During the discussion of the question of occupied
territories Kühlmann, stretching himself to his full height and
raising his voice, said: '*Our* German territory, thank God, is
not being held by foreign troops anywhere!' whereupon Czer-

nin's face went green and his figure shrank. Kühlmann was deliberately aiming at him. Their relationship was far from that of a serene friendship. Later, when the discussion turned to Persia, which was occupied on both sides by foreign armies, I remarked that since Persia, unlike Austria-Hungary, was not in alliance with anyone, it did not cause any of us pious rejoicing that it was Persia's territory, and not ours, that was occupied. At this Czernin almost jumped as he exclaimed, '*Unerhört!*' ('unheard of'). Ostensibly this exclamation was addressed to me, although it was really for Kühlmann. Episodes like this were frequent.

Like a good chess-player who for a long time has met weaker players, and who has lost some of his skill, Kühlmann, having met only his Austro-Hungarian, Turkish, Bulgarian and neutral diplomatic vassals during the war, was inclined to underestimate his revolutionary opponents and play his game in a slovenly manner. He often astonished me, especially at the outset, by the primitiveness of his methods and by his lack of understanding of his opponent's psychology.

I was considerably and quite unpleasantly agitated when I went to my first meeting with the diplomats. When I was hanging up my coat in the hall, I came face to face with Kühlmann. I did not know him by sight. He introduced himself and immediately added that he was 'very pleased' at my coming, since it was better to deal directly with the master than with his emissary. His face bore witness to his satisfaction with this 'fine' move, so calculated to impress an upstart. This made me feel exactly as if I had stepped on something unclean. I even started back involuntarily. Kühlmann realized his blunder, put himself on his guard, and his tone became instantly more formal. But that did not prevent him from following the same method, in my presence, with the head of the Turkish delegation, an old court diplomatist. As he was introducing his colleagues to me Kühlmann waited until the Turkish delegate walked a step away and then said to me in a confidential stage whisper, certain that the other would hear him: 'He is the best diplomatist in Europe.' When I told this to Joffe, he answered laughing: 'At my first meeting with Kühlmann he did exactly the same thing.'

It looked very much as if Kühlmann was giving the 'best diplomatist' a platonic compensation for certain unplatonic extortions. It is also possible that he was trying to kill two birds with one stone, by making it known to Czernin that he did not consider him the best diplomatist – next to himself. On 28 December, Kühlmann said to Czernin, according to the latter's account: 'The emperor is the only intelligent man in all Germany.' One imagines that these words were not intended so much for Czernin's ears as for those of the emperor himself. In transmitting flatteries to their destination, the diplomatists no doubt were helping each other. *Flattez, flattez, il en restera toujours quelque chose!*

This was the first time that I had come face to face with this social circle. Of course, even before, I had never had any illusions about it. I had a fairly strong suspicion that 'pots were not baked by gods'. But I must admit that I had thought the general level much higher. My impressions of that first meeting were something like this: men rate others cheaply and rate themselves not much dearer.

In this connection the following episode may be of some interest. At Victor Adler's instigation – Adler tried in those days to show his personal sympathy for me in every possible way – Count Czernin suggested casually that my library, which had been left in Vienna at the beginning of the war, be sent to Moscow. The library was of considerable interest, for during the long years of foreign exile I had gathered together a large collection of Russian revolutionary literature. I had hardly had time to express my thanks, with a little reserve, before the diplomat was asking me to inquire into the case of two Austrian prisoners who, he alleged, were being badly treated. This direct and underscored transition from the library to the prisoners, who were of course not privates but officers from the circles closest to Count Czernin, seemed altogether too brazen. I answered succinctly that if Czernin's information should prove correct, it would of course be my duty to do everything necessary, but that this matter had nothing to do with my library. In his memoirs Czernin gives a fairly exact account of this incident, without denying that he had tried to connect the business of the prisoners with that of the library. On the contrary he seems to consider this quite natural. He ends his story with the ambiguous phrase: 'He obviously wants to have the library.' I might add that immediately after receiving the library I handed it over to one of the learned institutions in Moscow.

The circumstances of history willed that the delegates of the most revolutionary régime ever known to humanity should sit at the same diplomatic table with the representatives of the most reactionary caste among all the ruling classes. How greatly our opponents feared the explosive power of their negotiations with the Bolsheviks was shown by their readiness to break off the negotiations rather than transfer them to a neutral country. In his memoirs Czernin says quite plainly that in a neutral country, with the help of their international friends the Bolsheviks would have taken the reins in their own hands. Officially he used the excuse that in a neutral country England and France would immediately have launched their intrigues, 'both openly and behind the scenes'. I retorted that our political practice had no use for anything behind the scenes, because this weapon of the old diplomacy had been eradicated by the Russian people, together with many other things, in the victorious uprising of 25 October. But we had to bow to an ultimatum, and so we remained at Brest-Litovsk.

Barring a few buildings that stood apart from the old town and were occupied by the German staff, Brest-Litovsk strictly speaking no longer existed. The town had been burned to the ground in impotent rage by the Tsar's troops during their retreat. Hoffmann must have chosen this place for his staff because he knew that he could keep its members within his grasp. The furnishings, like the food, were of the simplest, and German soldiers acted as attendants. For them we were messengers of peace and they looked to us with hope. A high, barbed-wire fence surrounded the staff buildings. On my morning walks I kept running into notices: 'Any Russian found in this place will be shot.' This referred to prisoners, of course, but I would ask myself if it did not apply also to us, who were semi-prisoners here, and would turn back again. There was a fine, strategic road running through the town of Brest-Litovsk. During the first days of our stay there we went out for drives in the staff automobiles, and, as a result, a conflict developed one day between one of the members of our delegation and a German sergeant. Hoffmann sent a formal complaint to me; I answered that we declined, with thanks, to make any further use of the automobiles placed at our disposal. The negotiations dragged on. All of us had to communicate with our respective governments by direct wires, and frequently these wires did not work. Whether this was actually due to physical causes or whether the breakdown was feigned to enable our opponents to gain time, we were unable to say. At any rate the intervals between meetings were frequent, and sometimes lasted as long as several days. During one of these I made a trip to Warsaw. The city was living under the rule of the German bayonet. The inhabitants evinced a great interest in the Soviet diplomatists, but expressed it very cautiously, because no one knew how it was all going to end.

The delay in negotiations was to our interest. That was my real object in going to Brest-Litovsk. But I can claim no credit for myself on this score; my partners helped me as best they could. 'Time is plentiful here,' Czernin writes melancholically in his diary. 'Now it is the Turks who are not ready, now it is the Bulgarians, and now the Russians – and the meetings are adjourned again, or else broken off when they have only begun.' The Austrians, in turn, began to delay the negotiations when they struck their difficulties with the Ukrainian delegation. Of course this did not restrain Kühlmann and Czernin in their public statements from accusing the Russian delegation alone of trying to protract the negotiations. I protested against this insistently, but quite in vain.

Not a trace of the clumsy compliments which the officially inspired German press had indulged in towards the Bolsheviks – and except for the underground sheets it was all officially inspired – was left as the negotiations drew to their close. The *Tägliche Rundschau*, for instance, not only complained that 'in Brest-Litovsk, Trotsky has created for himself a platform from which his voice is carried throughout the world', and accordingly demanded an end to it as soon as possible – it also stated that 'neither Lenin nor Trotsky wants peace, which would in all probability mean either the gallows or prison for them'. The tone of the Social-Democratic press was substantially the same. The Scheidemanns, Eberts and Stampfers saw our hope for a revolution in Germany as our greatest crime. These gentlemen were far from thinking that in a few months the revolution would seize them by the scruff of their necks and put them in power.

After the long vacation from reading German papers I took them up again at Brest-Litovsk with great interest. The peace negotiations figured in them in a way that showed a very thorough propagandist treatment. But the papers alone were not enough to take all of my time. I decided to make the fullest possible use of my enforced leisure, which I could foresee would not happen again in the near future. We had with us a good many stenographers who had once been on the staff of the State Duma, and so I began dictating to them, from memory, a historical sketch of the October revolution. From a few sessions there grew a book intended primarily for foreign workers. The necessity of explaining to them what had happened was most imperative; Lenin and I had discussed this necessity more than once but no one had any time to spare. And I had been farthest from supposing that Brest-Litovsk would become a seat for my literary work. Lenin was very happy when I brought back with me a finished manuscript on the Russian revolution. In it we both saw one of the modest pledges of a future revolutionary recompense for the harsh peace. The book was soon translated into a dozen European and Asiatic languages.

Although all the parties included in the Communist International had followed the lead of the Russians and had printed innumerable editions of the book, that did not prevent the epigones, after 1923, from declaring it a poisoned offshoot of Trotskyism. Today it is on Stalin's black-list. In this little incident the ideological preparation for the Thermidor found one of its many expressions. The only way to achieve victory was to cut the umbilical cord of the continuity with October.

The diplomatists who opposed us also found ways of taking up their spare time at Brest-Litovsk. Count Czernin, according to his diary, not only went hunting but also increased his store of knowledge by reading memoirs of the period of the French Revolution. He compared the Bolsheviks with the Jacobins, trying thereby to console himself. The Hapsburg diplomatist wrote: 'Charlotte Corday said: "I killed a wild beast, not a man." These Bolsheviks will disappear again and – who knows? – perhaps there will yet be a Corday for Trotsky.' In those days of course I didn't know about these soulful meditations of the pious Count. But I can easily believe in their sincerity.

At first it may seem difficult to discover exactly what German diplomacy was aiming at when it proposed its democratic formulas on 25 December, only to uncover its wolfish appetites a few days later. It was obvious that there was quite a risk to the German government in allowing the theoretical debate on the self-determination of nationalities, which developed chiefly through Kühlmann's own initiative. It must have been clear to the Hohenzollern diplomatists even before they began that they were not likely to achieve any great triumphs in that direction. Kühlmann, for instance, was anxious to show that the German seizure of Poland, Lithuania, the Baltic provinces and Finland was nothing more than a form of 'self-determination' on the part of each of these countries, since their will was being expressed through 'national' organs created by the German authorities of occupation. This was not so easy to prove. But Kühlmann would not give up. He asked me, insistently, if I would not recognize that the Nizam of Haidarabad, for instance, expressed the will of his own people. I replied that if India were cleared of British troops, it was quite improbable that the worthy Nizam would stand on his feet more than twenty-four hours. Kühlmann shrugged his shoulders rudely. General Hoffmann grunted. The interpreter translated. The stenographers took down notes, and the discussion went on *ad infinitum*.

The secret of this conduct on the part of the German diplomatists lay in Kühlmann's apparent conviction that we were ready to play his game. He must have reasoned it out in this way: 'The Bolsheviks got their power through advocating peace. They can retain it only on condition that they make peace. It is true that they have committed themselves to peace on democratic terms. But then, what are diplomatists for? If I, Kühlmann, give the Bolsheviks their revolutionary formulas in appropriate diplomatic transcriptions, they will give me the chance to take possession – under another name, of course – of provinces and peoples. In the eyes of the world the German annexations will carry the sanction of the Russian revolution. As for the Bolsheviks, they will have their peace.' In cherishing these hopes, Kühlmann no doubt was misled by the statements of our liberals, Mensheviks, and Populists, who had been representing the Brest-Litovsk negotiations as a comedy with rôles assigned in advance.

When we made it quite clear to our partners at Brest-Litovsk – and in no equivocal manner – that with us it was not a matter of a hypocritical disguise for a back-stairs deal, but a question of the principles governing the mutual relations of peoples, Kühlmann, who had already bound himself by his first stand, reacted to us almost as if we had broken some tacit agreement, one that really existed only in his own imagination. He persisted stubbornly in holding fast to the democratic principles of 25 December. Confident of his considerable gift for casuistry, he hoped to show the world that white was just the same as black. Count Czernin, in his own clumsy way, played second-fiddle to Kühlmann, and under his direction took it upon himself to make even more arrogant and cynical statements whenever the situation had become critical. He hoped in this way to conceal his own weakness. General Hoffmann on the other hand brought a refreshing element into the negotiations. With a quite obvious lack of sympathy for the subtleties of diplomacy, the General on several occasions put his soldier's boot on the table around which the discussion was taking place. For our part we never for a moment doubted that in these negotiations Hoffmann's boot was the only reality to take seriously.

There were times, however, when the General made incursions into discussions that were purely political, and did it in his own way. When he had completely lost patience with all the dreary palaver about the self-determination of peoples, he appeared one fine morning – it was 14 January – with a brief-case packed with Russian newspapers, mostly of the Socialist-Revolutionist party. Hoffmann read Russian easily. In short, staccato sentences, as if he were snarling at someone or giving orders, the General charged the Bolsheviks with suppressing freedom of speech and of assembly, and with violating the principles of democracy, meanwhile quoting approvingly from the articles by the Russian terrorist party that since 1902 had sent to the other world quite a number of Russians of the General's way of thinking. The General denounced us indignantly because our government was supported by force. Coming from him, that sounded really magnificent. An entry in Czernin's diary says: 'Hoffmann made his unfortunate speech. He had been working on it for several days, and is very proud of his success.'

I replied to Hoffmann that in a society based on classes every government rests on force. The only difference was that General Hoffmann applied repression to protect big property-owners, whereas we did it in defence of the workers. For a few minutes the peace conference was transformed into a Marxian propagandist class for beginners. 'The thing that surprises and repels the governments of other countries,' I said, 'is that we do not arrest strikers, but capitalists who subject workers to lock-outs; that we do not shoot peasants who demand land but arrest the landowners and officers who try to shoot the peasants.' At this point Hoffmann's face grew purple.

After every incident of the sort Kühlmann would inquire with malicious courtesy whether Hoffmann wanted to say something on the subject under discussion, and the General would reply abruptly: 'No, no more!' and look out of the window in a rage. There was something delightfully piquant in this discussion of the revolutionary use of force in that gathering of Hohenzollern, Hapsburg, Sultanic and Coburg diplomatists, generals, and admirals. Some of the titled and decorated gentlemen could do nothing at all during these discussions but look bewildered and glance at me and then at Kühlmann and Czernin. They wanted someone to explain to them what, for heaven's sake, all this meant! Behind the scenes, no doubt, Kühlmann was hammering it into them that our length of life was now measured in weeks, and that this brief time must be utilized to conclude a 'German' peace, so that the successors of the Bolsheviks would have to accept the consequences.

In debates of matters on principle my position was as much superior to that of Kühlmann as, in matters of military fact, General Hoffmann's was superior to mine. That is why the General was trying so impatiently to reduce all questions to the comparative strength of our forces, whereas Kühlmann was making futile attempts to make a peace based on the war-map look as if it were based on principle. On one occasion, to soften the impression made by Hoffmann's speeches, Külhmann said that a soldier inevitably expressed himself more pungently than a diplomatist. I replied that 'we members of the Russian delegation do not belong to the diplomatic school, but consider ourselves rather as soldiers of the revolution' and consequently preferred the rough language of the soldier.

But Kühlmann's diplomatic civility was entirely relative. The problem he had set himself was obviously insoluble without co-operation from us, and it was just that that was missing. 'We are revolutionaries,' I explained to Kühlmann, 'but we are realists too, and we prefer to talk plainly about annexations rather than to substitute pseudonyms for real names.' After that it was little wonder that Kühlmann would occasionally throw off his diplomatic mask and snarl viciously. I still remember the intonation of his voice when he said that Germany was sincerely anxious to restore friendly relations with its *powerful* eastern neighbour. The word 'powerful' was uttered in a tone of mockery so provocative that even Kühlmann's allies winced. And besides, Czernin was mortally afraid of a rupture of negotiations. I picked up the glove and reminded them, once more, of what I had said in my first speech. 'We are not in a position, nor do we desire,' I said on 10 January, 'to dispute the fact of our country's having been weakened by the policies of the classes that ruled it until recently. But the world position of a country is determined not by the condition of its technical apparatus today, but by the possibilities latent in it, just as the economic power of Germany cannot be measured by the present condition of its food-supplies. A broad and far-sighted policy rests on capacity for development; on the inner forces that, once awakened, will sooner or later reveal their power.'

Less than nine full months after this, on 3 October 1918, I

said at a meeting of the All-Union Central Executive Committee, recalling Kühlmann's Brest-Litovsk challenge: 'No one of us has any feeling of malicious joy because Germany is now passing through a terrible catastrophe.' It is unnecessary to adduce proofs that the major part of this catastrophe was prepared by German diplomacy, military as well as civil, at Brest-Litovsk.

The more precisely we framed our questions the greater was Hoffmann's ascendancy over Kühlmann. They no longer concealed their antagonism – especially the General. When, in reply to one of his periodical attacks, I mentioned the German government with no hidden motive in mind, Hoffmann interrupted me in a voice that was hoarse with anger: 'I do not represent the German government here, but the German High Command.' This sounded as if someone had crushed a stone through glass. I looked about the table at our opponents. Kühlmann's face was all screwed up; he sat looking down. Czernin's expression was a combination of embarrassment and a sort of vicious rejoicing. I replied that I did not think that I was entitled to judge the mutual relationship between the government of the German empire and its high command, but that I was authorized to conduct negotiations only with its government. Kühlmann crunched his teeth as he noted my declaration and expressed his agreement with it.

It would be difficult to exaggerate the extent of the disagreements between the German diplomacy and the high command. Kühlmann was trying to prove that the occupied territories had already 'self-determined' themselves in favour of Germany through their authorized national organs. On the other hand Hoffmann explained that in view of the absence of authorized organs in those territories there would be no question of withdrawing German troops. The arguments were diametrically opposed to each other, but the practical conclusion was the same.

In this connection Kühlmann tried a stratagem that at first seems almost incredible. In a written reply (announced by von Rosenberg) to a list of questions that we had submitted, a statement was made to the effect that the German troops could not be withdrawn from the occupied territories until the termination of the war on the Western front. I concluded from this that the troops would be withdrawn *after* the termination of the war, and demanded a more precise indication of the time. Kühlmann got very excited. He had obviously relied on the soporific effect of his formula; in other words he wanted to disguise annexation by means of – a play on words! When this failed, he explained, through Hoffmann, that the troops were not going to be withdrawn either *before* or *after*.

I made an attempt towards the end of January – though I did not hope for success – to obtain permission from the Austrian government to visit Vienna for a talk with the representatives of the Austrian proletariat. The Austrian Social Democracy was, I think, more frightened than anyone else at the idea of such a visit. Of course my application was refused for the quite incredible reason that I had no authority to carry out such negotiations. I replied to Czernin in the following letter:

Mr Minister: In forwarding herewith a copy of the letter from Legation-Councillor Count Czakki, dated 26 inst., which is apparently to be considered your reply to my telegram of the 24 inst., I hereby beg to inform you that I note the refusal, stated therein, to grant me permission to visit Vienna to conduct negotiations with the representatives of the Austrian proletariat in the interests of bringing about a democratic peace. I am obliged to record that, under considerations of a formal character, this reply conceals your unwillingness to allow personal negotiations between the representatives of the workers' and the peasants' Government of Russia and those of the Austrian proletariat. With regard to the reference in the letter to my lack of plenipotentiary powers for conducting such negotiations – a reference that is inadmissable either in form or in fact – I should like to draw your attention, Mr Minister, to the fact that the right of determining the scope and character of my powers belongs exclusively to my Government.

During the last stages of the negotiations Kühlmann's and Czernin's trump card was the independent action of the Kiev Rada,* which was hostile to Moscow. Its leaders represented the

---

*The Rada, an assembly of representatives of various public organizations in the Ukraine, was formed after the February revolution and claimed to be the spokesman for the Ukrainian nation. After its overthrow by the Bolsheviks, the Rada favoured the German occupancy, which, when established, dissolved the Rada government and made Hetman Skoropadsky the sole ruler of the country. – *Translator.*

Ukrainian variety of Kerenskyism, and differed from their Great Russian prototype only in that they were even more provincial. The Brest-Litovsk delegates of the Rada were never intended by nature for any other fate than to be led by the nose by any capitalist diplomatist. Kühlmann and Czernin both engaged in this business with disdainful condescension. The democratic simpletons felt as if they were walking on air, so elated were they at the thought of the two stalwart firms of Hohenzollern and Hapsburg taking them seriously. When the head of the Ukrainian delegation, Golubovich, after making his due comments, sat down in his chair, carefully separating the long skirts of his black frock coat, one was afraid that he would melt on the spot from the intense joy and admiration that were simmering inside him.

Czernin eventually succeeded, as he himself records in his diary, in inciting the Ukrainians to come out against the Soviet delegation with an openly hostile statement. But the Ukrainians overdid it. For a quarter of an hour their speaker heaped rudeness on arrogance, even embarrassing the conscientious German interpreter, who could not quite take his pitch from this sort of tuning-fork. In describing this scene, the Hapsburg count speaks of my bewilderment, pallor, convulsions, and of the drops of cold sweat that gathered on my face. These exaggerations aside, I must admit that the scene was most distressing – the distressing thing about it being not, as Czernin thinks, that our fellow countrymen were insulting us in the presence of foreigners, but the frantic self-humiliation of what was after all a representative body of the revolution before vain aristocrats who only despised them. A grandiloquent baseness and a servility that choked with its raptures flowed like a fountain from the tongues of these miserable national democrats who for a moment had been touched with power. Kühlmann, Czernin, Hoffmann and the rest were breathing heavily, like gamblers at a race-course who have placed bets on the winning horse. With a glance at his patrons after each sentence, as if he were looking for encouragement, the Ukrainian delegate read from his notes all the vituperation that his delegation had prepared in forty-eight hours of collective effort. There is no denying that it was one of the vilest scenes that I have ever witnessed. But even under the cross-fire of insults and the maliciously rejoicing glances, I never for a moment doubted that these over-zealous flunkies would soon be thrown out-of-doors by their triumphant masters, who in turn were soon to be ejected from the seats they had been holding for centuries.

At that time revolutionary Soviet detachments were victoriously advancing through the Ukraine, fighting their way through to the Dnieper. And on the very day when the matter came to a head, and it was obvious that the Ukrainian delegates had struck up a deal with Kühlmann and Czernin for the sale of the Ukraine, the Soviet troops took possession of Kiev. When Radek inquired over the direct wire about the situation in the Ukrainian capital, the German telegraph-operator, mistaking the person he was addressing for someone else, announced: 'Kiev is dead.' On 7 February I called the attention of the delegations of the Central Powers to the telegram from Lenin informing us that the Soviet troops had occupied Kiev on 29 January; that the government of the Rada, now deserted by everyone, was already in hiding; that the Central Executive Committee of the Soviets of the Ukraine had been proclaimed the supreme power in the country and had taken its seat at Kiev; and that the Ukrainian government had adopted a federative connection with Russia, with complete unity in home and foreign policies. At the next meeting I told Kühlmann and Czernin that they were treating with the delegation of a government whose entire territory was confined to Brest-Litovsk. (By the treaty this town was to be restored to the Ukraine.) But the German government, or rather the German high command, had already decided by that time to occupy the Ukraine with German troops. The diplomacy of the Central Powers was merely drawing up a passport for their admission. Ludendorff worked magnificently to prepare the final agony of the Hohenzollern army.

During those days, confined in a German prison, was a man whom the politicians of the Social Democracy were accusing of crazy utopian ideas, and the Hohenzollern judges of state treason. This prisoner wrote:* 'The result of Brest-Litovsk is

*Karl Liebknecht, *Politische Aufzeichnungen aus seinem Nachlass*, Die Aktion, 1921, page 51.

not nil, even if it comes to a peace of forced capitulation. Thanks to the Russian delegates Brest-Litovsk has become a revolutionary tribunal whose decrees are heard far and wide. It has brought about the exposé of the Central Powers; it has exposed German avidity, its cunning lies and hypocrisy. It has passed an annihilating verdict upon the peace policy of the German [Social-Democratic] majority – a policy which is not so much a pious hypocrisy as it is cynicism. It has proved powerful enough to bring forth numerous mass movements in various countries. And its tragic last act – the intervention against the revolution – has made socialism tremble in every fibre of its being. Time will show what harvest will ripen for the present victors from this sowing. They will not be pleased with it.'

32
Peace

All through the autumn delegates from the front appeared daily before the Petrograd Soviet to say that unless peace was signed by 1 November the soldiers themselves would come from the trenches to make peace in their own way. This became the slogan at the front. Soldiers left the trenches in droves. The October revolution gave a temporary check to this, but not for long.

Thanks to the February revolution the soldiers had discovered that they had been ruled by the Rasputin gang, which had dragged them into a heinous and futile war; they saw no reason for continuing it because they were asked to do so by a certain young lawyer named Kerensky. They wanted to get back to their homes, their families, the land, and the revolution, which had promised them land and freedom but so far had done nothing but keep them in cold and verminous holes at the front. Kerensky took offence at the soldiers, workers and peasants, and called them 'mutinous slaves'. He failed to understand one little thing – that revolution consists in exactly this: in slaves mutinying and refusing to be slaves. Buchanan, the patron and the power behind Kerensky, was incautious enough to tell us in his memoirs what war and revolution meant to him and to his sort. Several months after the October revolution Buchanan wrote the following description of Russia in 1916 – the terrible year of the defeat of the Tsar's armies and the breakdown of the economic life, a year of bread-lines, with a government leap-frogging at Rasputin's command. 'At one of the many beautiful villas which we visited' (Buchanan is writing of his trip to the Crimea in 1916),

we were not only presented with bread and salt on a silver platter, but found in our motor, on leaving, a case with a dozen bottles of old

Burgundy, whose praises I had sung while drinking it at luncheon. It is terribly sad to look back on those happy by-gone days [!] and to think of all the misery and misfortunes which have befallen those who showed us such kindness and hospitality.

Buchanan refers not to the sufferings of the soldiers in the trenches, or to the starving mothers in the bread-lines, but to the misfortune of the former owners of beautiful villas in the Crimea, owners of silver platters and Burgundy. Reading those blissfully shameless lines one can only say: the October revolution was not in vain. Not in vain did it sweep away not only the Romanoffs but the Buchanans and Kerenskys as well.

When I was crossing the front line for the first time on my way to Brest-Litovsk, our sympathizers in the trenches could not muster up much of a protest against the monstrous demands of Germany because the trenches were almost deserted. After the experiments of Buchanan and Kerensky no one dared to speak even conditionally of continuing the war. Peace, peace, at any price! Later, on one of my return trips from Brest-Litovsk to Moscow, I tried to persuade one of the representatives from the front on the Central Executive Committee to give a little support to our delegation by a vigorous speech. 'Impossible,' he replied, 'absolutely impossible. We shouldn't be able to return to the trenches. They wouldn't understand us, and would say that we were continuing to deceive them as Kerensky did.'

It was obvious that going on with the war was impossible. On this point there was not even a shadow of disagreement between Lenin and me. We were both equally bewildered at Bukharin and the other apostles of a 'revolutionary war'. But there was another question, quite as important. How far could the Hohenzollern government go in their struggle against us? In a letter to one of his friends Czernin wrote that if they had been strong enough, they would have sent their troops against Petrograd to establish order there, instead of negotiating with the Bolsheviks. There was certainly no lack of ill-will. But was there strength enough? Could Hohenzollern send his troops against revolutionaries who wanted peace? How had the February revolution, and, later on, the October revolution, affected the German army?

How soon would any effect show itself? To these questions no answer could as yet be given. We had to try to find it in the course of the negotiations. Accordingly we had to delay the negotiations as long as we could. It was necessary to give the European workers time to absorb properly the very fact of the Soviet revolution, including its policy of peace. And this was all the more important since the press of the Entente, like the Russian 'conciliatory' and bourgeois press, was portraying the peace negotiations in advance as a comedy with the roles ingeniously distributed.

Even in Germany among the Social Democratic opposition of that period, which was apt to see its own weaknesses reflected in us, people were talking about the Bolsheviks working hand in hand with the German government. And this version must have been even more credible in France and in England. It was obvious that if the bourgeoisie of the Entente and the Social Democracy succeeded in spreading the wrong idea about us among the masses of workers, the future military intervention of the Allies would be made all the simpler. So I insisted that before signing a separate peace – if that proved absolutely unavoidable – we must at all costs give the workers of Europe a striking and incontestable proof of the deadly enmity existing between us and the German ruling classes. It was these considerations that gave me the idea of a political demonstration at Brest-Litovsk expressing the slogan: 'We end war, we demobilize the army, but we do not sign peace.' If German imperialism finds itself unable to send troops against us – I reasoned – it will mean that we have achieved a tremendous victory of far-reaching consequences. But if it were still possible for the Hohenzollerns to strike against us we should always be able to capitulate early enough. I consulted the other members of the delegation, among them Kamenev, and found them in sympathy with me, and wrote Lenin to that effect. His reply was: 'When you come to Moscow we will talk it over.'

'One could want nothing better,' Lenin answered my arguments, 'if it turns out that Hoffmann is not strong enough to send troops against us. But there is little hope of that. He will find specially selected regiments of rich Bavarian farmers for it.

And then, how many of them does he need? You say yourself that the trenches are empty. What if the Germans resume fighting?'

'Then we will be compelled to sign the peace, but everyone will realize that we had no choice. By this act alone we will deal a decisive blow at the story of our secret connection with the Hohenzollerns.'

'Of course, there are certain advantages in that. But it is too risky. If it were necessary for us to go under to assure the success of the German revolution, we should have to do it. The German revolution is vastly more important than ours. But when will it come? No one knows. And at the moment there is nothing so important as our revolution. It must be safe-guarded against danger at any price.'

The difficulties of the question were further aggravated by the inner state of the party. The prevalent attitude in the party, at least among its leading elements, was that of irreconcilable hostility to signing the Brest-Litovsk peace terms. The stenographic reports of the negotiations published in our press intensified this mood; it found its most acute expression in the 'left' communist group, which put forward a slogan of revolutionary war.

The inner struggle grew more intense every day. Contrary to the tale later spread about, it was not between Lenin and me, but between Lenin and the overwhelming majority of the chief organizations of the party. On the most important questions, such as whether we were then in a position to carry on a revolutionary war and whether it was generally admissible for the revolutionary power to sign agreements with the imperialists, I was unreservedly with Lenin, and answered, as he did, the first question in the negative and the second in the positive.

The first discussion of the differences before a wider audience took place on 21 January, at the meeting of the active party workers. Three points of view came to the fore then. Lenin held that we should try to delay negotiations, and in case of an ultimatum capitulate immediately. I considered it necessary to break off negotiations even at the risk of a new German advance, so that we might capitulate – if we had to do so – only in the face of an obvious use of force. Bukharin demanded war to extend the arena of revolution. Lenin waged a bitter fight against the advocates of revolutionary war at that meeting, although he made only a slight criticism of my proposal. The supporters of revolutionary war obtained thirty-two votes, Lenin fifteen, and I sixteen. But these figures are not really indicative of the mood of the party. In the upper stratum, if not in the masses, the 'left wing' was even stronger than at this particular meeting. It was this fact that ensured the temporary victory of my formula. Those who shared Bukharin's view regarded my proposal as a step in their own direction. On the other hand Lenin believed, and rightly, that postponement of the final decision would work for his eventual victory.

At this time our own party, no less than the workers of western Europe, was much in need of some visual demonstration of the actual state of things. In all the directing institutions of the party and state Lenin was in a minority. Over two hundred local Soviets, in response to the invitation of the Soviet of Commissaries, stated their views on war and peace. Of them all, only two large Soviets – Petrograd and Sebastopol (the latter with reservations) – went on record as being in favour of peace. On the other hand several of the big workers' centres, such as Moscow, Ekaterinburg, Kharkoff, Ekaterinoslav, Ivanovo-Voznesensk, Kronstadt, etc. voted by overwhelming majorites to break off negotiations. The same attitude prevailed among our party organizations, and of course among the left Socialist-Revolutionists. Lenin's point could have been carried out by means of a split in the party and a *coup d'état*, but not otherwise. And yet every day was bound to increase the number of Lenin's followers. In these circumstances the formula of 'neither war nor peace' actually served as a bridge to Lenin's stand. And it was the bridge over which the majority of the party, or at least of its directing elements, made the crossing.

'All right, let's suppose that we have actually refused to sign a peace, and that the Germans answer it by an advance. What are you going to do then?' Lenin questioned me.

'We will sign peace at the point of a bayonet. The situation will be clear to all the world.'

'But in that case you won't support the slogan of revolutionary war, will you?'

'Under no circumstances.'

'In that case the experiment will probably not be so dangerous. We will only risk losing Estonia or Latvia.' And with a sly chuckle, Lenin added: 'For the sake of a good peace with Trotsky, Latvia and Estonia are worth losing.' For several days that was his favourite refrain.

It was at this decisive session of 22 January that the Central Committee adopted my proposals: to delay negotiations; in the event of a German ultimatum, to declare war at an end, but to refuse to sign peace; to act, thereafter, according to the demands of circumstance. Late at night, on 25 January, a joint session of the Central Committees of the Bolsheviks and the 'left' Socialist-Revolutionists (our allies then) was held, and the same formula was voted by an overwhelming majority. As we often did then, we declared that this decision of both the Central Committees should stand as that of the Soviet of People's Commissaries.

On 31 January, I telegraphed Lenin at the Smolny over a direct wire from Brest-Litovsk:

Among the countless rumours and reports reaching the German press, there has appeared the absurd statement that we intend to refuse, demonstratively, to sign the peace treaty; that there are dis-agreements among the Bolsheviks on this score, and so forth and so on. I am referring to a telegram of this sort that came from Stockholm and quoted the *Politiken* as its authority. If I am not mistaken, the *Politiken* is the organ of Höglund. Could you ask him why his editors publish such absurd nonsense, in case it is true that a report of this nature appeared in the paper? Inasmuch as the bourgeois press is full of all sorts of malicious gossip, the Germans are not likely to attach much significance to this report. But, in this case, the source is a news-paper of the left wing, one of whose editors is in Petrograd. This gives the report a certain authoritativeness that can only confuse the minds of our opponents.

The Austrian and German press are full of reports of horrors in Petrograd, Moscow, and throughout Russia, of hundreds and thou-sands of dead, of the rattle of machine-guns, etc. It is absolutely necessary to appoint a level-headed man to issue daily reports on the state of the country, and to make them public through the Petrograd telegraph agency and the radio. It would be a good thing if Comrade Zinoviev would take this upon himself. It is extremely important, and the reports should be sent, first of all, to Vorovsky and Litvinov; this could be done through Chicherin.

We have only had one formal meeting so far. The Germans are delaying negotiations, apparently because of their own internal crisis. The German press has begun to shout that we really do not want peace and are only anxious to spread the revolution to other countries. These jackasses are incapable of understanding that is it simply because we want to further European revolution that the earliest peace possible is of the utmost importance to us.

Have any measures been taken towards expelling the Roumanian embassy? I believe that the King of Roumania is in Austria. According to a report in one of the German papers, we have, stored in Moscow, not the national Roumanian fund, but the gold fund of the national bank of Roumania. The sympathies of official Germany are, of course, entirely on the Roumanian side.

Yours, TROTSKY.

This note demands a little explanation. Cable dispatches from Brest-Litovsk were regarded as safe from listening-in or tapping. But we had every reason to believe that the Germans at Brest-Litovsk were reading our correspondence over the direct wire; we had enough respect for their technical resourcefulness to believe this. It was impossible for us to code all our messages, and we did not consider coding a sufficient protection. At the same time the newspaper *Politiken* was doing us no service by spreading its inopportune but authentic information. For this reason my dispatch was written not so much to warn Lenin that the secret of our decision had been blabbed abroad, but to try to put the Germans off the track. I used the very discourteous word 'jackasses' in referring to the newspaper men only to make the message read quite 'naturally'. I can't say to what extent my stratagem succeeded in deceiving Kühlmann. At any event my declaration on 10 February seemed to impress our opponents as something quite unexpected. In Czernin's diary for 11 February, we read: 'Trotsky refuses to sign. War is over, but there is no peace.'

It is hard to believe, but in 1924 the school of Stalin and Zinoviev made an attempt so to represent this matter as to make me seem to have acted at Brest-Litovsk *contrary* to the decision of the party and the government. The falsifiers did not even bother to look up the old minutes and read their own statements. Zinoviev spoke at the Petrograd Soviet on 11 February, the day after I had made the declaration at Brest-Litovsk, and averred that 'our delegation has found the only correct way out of the situation as it now stands'. And it was Zinoviev who moved the resolution which was adopted by the majority of all against one – with the Mensheviks and Socialist-Revolutionists abstaining – and approved the refusal to sign the peace treaty.

On 14 February, after I had made my report to the Central Executive Committee, Svyerdlov, on behalf of the Bolshevik faction, moved a resolution that began with the words: 'Having heard and fully considered the report of the peace delegation, the Central Executive Committee fully approves of the action of its representatives at Brest-Litovsk.' There was not a single party or Soviet local organization that did not express its approval of the conduct of the Soviet delegation during the interval between 11 and 15 February. At the party congress in March 1918 Zinoviev declared: 'Trotsky is right when he says that he acted in accordance with the decision of the majority of the Central Committee. No one tried to deny that.' Lastly, Lenin himself reported at the same congress that 'at the Central Committee . . . a decision was adopted not to sign peace'. All this has not prevented the establishing, in the Communist International, of the new dogma that Trotsky alone was responsible for the refusal to sign peace at Brest-Litovsk.

After the October strikes in Germany and Austria the question of whether the German government would decide on an offensive was not as obvious, either to us or to the German government, as it is being represented today after the fact by many 'intelligent' persons. On 10 February the delegations of Germany and Austria-Hungary at Brest-Litovsk arrived at the conclusion that 'the situation proposed in Trotsky's declarations must be accepted'. Only General Hoffmann opposed it. At their concluding conference next day, according to Czernin, Kühlmann spoke with complete assurance of the necessity of accepting the *de facto* peace. Echoes of this reached us at once. All of our delegation returned to Moscow under the impression that the Germans would not start an offensive. Lenin was very pleased with the result.

'And perhaps they will deceive us?' he was still asking.

We shrugged our shoulders. To all appearances it did not look that way.

'Well, if it is so, it's all to the good,' said Lenin. 'Appearances are saved and the war is over.'

However, two days before the expiration of the week fixed for the German reply a cabled dispatch from General Samoylo, who had remained at Brest-Litovsk, informed us that the Germans had announced, through General Hoffmann, that from midnight of 18 February, they would consider themselves in a state of war with Russia, and had therefore invited him to leave Brest-Litovsk. Lenin got the telegram first. I was in his room at the time, where a conference was being held with the left Socialist-Revolutionists. Without saying a word Lenin handed me the telegram. His face made me realize instantly that something was up. He hurried the conversation with the Socialist-Revolutionists, so that he could discuss the situation after they had left.

'They have deceived us, after all ... Gained five days ... This wild beast will let nothing escape it. There is nothing left, then, but to sign the old terms, provided that the Germans will agree to leave them exactly as they are.'

As before I insisted that Hoffmann be allowed actually to start an offensive, so that the workers of Germany, as well as of the countries of the Allies, would learn of the offensive as a fact rather than as a threat.

'No,' rejoined Lenin, 'we can't afford to lose a single hour now. The test has been made. Hoffmann wants to and can fight. Delay is impossible. The beast jumps fast.'

In March at the party congress Lenin said: 'It was agreed between us [that is, Lenin and me] that we hold out until a German ultimatum, but that after the ultimatum we were to surrender.' I described the agreement above. Lenin consented not to attack my point of view before the party only because

I promised him not to support the advocates of a revolutionary war. The official representatives of that group – Uritzky, Radek, and, I believe, Ossinsky – came to me with an offer of a 'single front'. I made it quite clear to them that our positions had nothing in common. When the German high command gave notice of the expiration of the truce, Lenin reminded me of our agreement. I answered that by an ultimatum I had not meant simply a verbal statement, but an actual German offensive that would leave no doubt as to the real relations between the countries.

At the meeting of the Central Committee on 17 February Lenin put the preliminary question to a vote: 'If the German offensive becomes a fact and no revolutionary upheaval takes place in Germany, are we still to sign peace?' Bukharin and his followers answered this cardinal question by abstaining from voting. Krestinsky acted in the same way. Joffe voted against peace. Lenin and I voted in favour of it. The next day I voted against the immediate dispatch of the telegram stating our readiness to sign peace, as Lenin proposed. During the day, however, telegraphic reports informed us that the Germans had opened an offensive, had seized our military supplies and were advancing in the direction of Dvinsk. That evening I voted for Lenin's telegram; now there was no possible doubt that the German offensive would be broadcast to the entire world.

On 21 February, we received new terms from Germany, framed, apparently, with the direct object of making the signing of peace impossible. By the time our delegation returned to Brest-Litovsk, these terms, as is well known, had been made even harsher. All of us, including Lenin, were of the impression that the Germans had come to an agreement with the Allies about crushing the Soviets, and that a peace on the western front was to be built on the bones of the Russian revolution. If this was true, it was obvious that no concessions from us would have been of any use. The developments in Finland and the Ukraine tipped the scales strongly in favour of war. Every hour brought something unfavourable. The news of a German landing in Finland and of the routing of the Finnish workers reached us. I met Lenin in the corridor near his room. He was terribly excited; never before had I seen him like that, nor did I again.

'Yes, we shall have to fight,' he said, 'though we have nothing to fight with. There does not seem to be any other way out.'

But ten or fifteen minutes later, when I called at his room, he said: 'No, we must not change our policy. Military action on our part would not be able to save the revolution in Finland, but it would most certainly ruin us. We will help the Finnish workers in every way we can, but we must do it without abandoning peace. I am not sure that this will save us now. But at any rate it is the only way in which salvation is still possible.'

I was very sceptical about the possibility of securing peace even at the price of complete capitulation. But Lenin decided to try the capitulation idea to the utmost. Since he had no majority in the Central Committee, and the decision depended on my vote, I abstained from voting to ensure for him the majority of one vote. I stated this explicitly when I explained my reasons for not voting. If the surrender should fail to obtain peace for us, I reasoned, we would straighten out our party front in armed defence of the revolution thrust on us by the enemy.

'It seems to me,' I told Lenin, privately, 'that it would be politically wise if I submitted my resignation as commissary for foreign affairs.'

'What for? I hope that we aren't going to introduce these parliamentarian methods.'

'But my resignation would imply for the Germans a radical change in our policy, and would strengthen their confidence in our willingness actually to sign the peace treaty this time.'

'There is something in that,' Lenin answered, thinking it over. 'That is a serious political reason.'

On 22 February at the meeting of the Central Committee I reported that the French military mission had conveyed the French and English offers to help us in a war with Germany. I expressed myself as in favour of accepting the offer, on condition, of course, that we be completely independent in matters of foreign policy. Bukharin insisted that it was inadmissible for us to enter into any arrangements with the imperialists. Lenin came vigorously to my aid and the Central Committee adopted my resolution by six votes against five. As far as I can remember now Lenin dictated the resolution in these words: 'That Comrade Trotsky be authorized to accept the assistance of the brigands of the French imperialism against the German brigands.' He always preferred formulas that left no room for doubt.

After I left the meeting Bukharin overtook me in the long corridor of the Smolny, threw his arms about me, and began to weep. 'What are we doing?' he exclaimed. 'We are turning the party into a dung-heap.' Bukharin is generally ready with his tears, and likes realistic expressions. But at this time the situation was becoming really tragic. The revolution was between the hammer and the anvil.

On 3 March our delegation signed the peace treaty without even reading it. Forestalling many of the ideas of Clémenceau, the Brest-Litovsk peace was like the hangman's noose. On 22 March the treaty was ratified by the German Reichstag. The German Social Democrats gave their approval in advance to the future principles of Versailles. The Independents voted against it; they were just beginning to describe the futile curve that eventually brought them back to their starting-point.

Reviewing the way already covered at the Seventh Congress of the party (March 1918), I described my position with detail and clarity enough: Had we really wanted to obtain the most favourable peace, we would have agreed to it as early as last November. But no one [except Zinoviev] raised his voice to do it. We were all in favour of agitation, of revolutionizing the working classes of Germany, Austria-Hungary and all of Europe. But all our previous negotiations with the Germans had revolutionary significance only in so far as they were received as genuine. I had already reported to the Bolshevik faction of the All-Russian Congress of Soviets how the former Austrian minister, Gratz, said that the Germans only needed some pretext to present us with an ultimatum. They believed that we ourselves were inviting it ... that we understood in advance that we were to sign *anything*; that we were just playing in a revolutionary comedy.

In these circumstances, if we had refused to sign peace, we should have been threatened with the loss of Reval and other territories, whereas, on the other hand, if we had signed too hastily, we should have risked the loss of the sympathy of the world proletariat, or at least of the larger part of it. I was one of those who thought that the Germans were not likely to advance, but that if they did, we should always have time to sign the peace, even if it involved still harsher terms. In due course of time,

I said then, 'everyone would have become convinced that there was no other way out.'

It is remarkable that Liebknecht wrote at the same time from prison:

In no sense can it be said that the present solution of the problem is not as favourable for future development as a surrender at Brest-Litovsk would have been at the beginning of February. Quite the contrary. A surrender like that would have thrown the worst light on all preceding resistance and would have made the subsequent submission to force appear as '*vis haud ingrata*'. The cynicism that cries to heaven and the brutal character of the ultimate German action *have driven all suspicions into the background.*

Liebknecht grew amazingly during the war; he learned to establish a gulf between himself and the honest characterlessness of Haase. It is unnecessary to say that Liebknecht was a revolutionary of endless courage. But he was only now developing himself into a strategist. This disclosed itself in questions of his personal life as well as of revolutionary policy. Considerations of personal safety were absolutely alien to him. After his arrest many friends shook their heads at his self-sacrificing 'recklessness'. Lenin on the contrary was always much concerned about the safety of the leadership. He was the head of the general staff and always remembered that, during war, he had to ensure the functioning of the high command. Liebknecht was like a general who himself leads his troops to battle.

For this reason, as well as for various others, it was hard for him to understand our strategy at Brest-Litovsk. At first he wanted us simply to challenge fate and advance to meet it. In that period he repeatedly condemned the 'policy of Lenin–Trotsky', quite reasonably making no distinction in this basic question between Lenin's stand and my own. But later on he began to see the policy of Brest-Litovsk in a different light. Early in May he wrote: 'One thing over and above all is necessary for the Russian Soviets – and that is certainly not demonstrations and decorations, but a stern, harsh power. For this they need intelligence and time as well as energy; intelligence so that they may gain the time that is necessary for even the most intelligent energy.' This is a complete recognition of the rightness of Lenin's Brest-Litovsk policy, which was wholly directed towards gaining time.

Truth makes its way, but nonsense is just as tenacious. Professor Fisher of America, in a big book describing the first years of Soviet Russia, *The Famine in Soviet Russia*,* attributed to me the idea that the Soviets will never enter into a war with the bourgeois governments, nor make peace with them. Fisher, like many another, copied this nonsensical formula from Zinoviev and the epigones in general, adding to it some of his own lack of understanding. My belated critics have long since taken my Brest-Litovsk proposal from the context of its time and place and turned it into a universal formula in order to reduce it more easily to absurdity. In doing so, however, they have failed to notice that the state of 'no peace, no war', or, more precisely, of neither peace *treaty* nor war, held nothing unnatural in itself. Exactly these relations exist today between Soviet Russia and the greatest countries of the world – the United States and Great Britain.† True, it was not by our wish that they became established as such, but that does not alter matters.

Moreover, there is a country with which we have established exactly those relations of 'no peace, no war' on our own initiative – I refer to Roumania. While attributing to me a universal formula which they portray as sheer absurdity, my critics seem to be very ignorant of the fact that they are reproducing the 'absurd' formula in the existing relations of the Soviet Union with many other countries.

---

* *The Famine in Soviet Russia, 1919–1923; the Operations of the American Relief Administration*', H. H. Fisher, Macmillan Company, New York, 1927.

† Written before the recent resumption of diplomatic relations between Soviet Russia and Great Britain. – *Translator*.

How did Lenin himself regard the Brest-Litovsk episode when it was a thing of the past? Lenin generally considered occasional differences of opinion with me as not worth mentioning. But more than once he spoke of 'the tremendous propagandist importance of the Brest-Litovsk negotiations'. (For instance, in his speech of 17 May 1918.) At the congress of the party a year after the peace Lenin remarked:

Our extreme isolation from Western Europe and all the other countries deprived us of any objective materials for judging the possible rate of development, or the forms of growth, of the proletarian revolution in the West. The result of all this complicated situation was that the question of the Brest-Litovsk peace brought out many differences of opinion in our party.

(The speech of 18 March 1919.)

There remains the question of the behaviour, during those days, of my later critics and accusers. For almost a year Bukharin had fought furiously with Lenin and me, threatening to split the party. Kuybyshev, Yaroslavsky, Bubnov, and many of the other current pillars of Stalinism were with him. Zinoviev, on the contrary, demanded an immediate signing of the peace, forswearing the propagandist possibilities of Brest-Litovsk. Lenin and I were unanimous in condemning this stand. Kamenev agreed with my formula while he was at Brest-Litovsk, but joined Lenin on his return to Moscow. Rykov was not on the Central Committee at the time, and so took no part in the deciding conferences. Dzerzhinsky was against Lenin, but on the last vote went over to him. What was Stalin's position? As usual he had none. He was simply waiting and calculating. 'The old man is still hoping for peace,' he would nod to me, referring to Lenin. 'He won't get any.' Afterwards he would go to Lenin and probably make the same sort of observation about me. He never spoke in public. Nobody was much interested in his contradictions, either. My principal object – to make our conduct in the question of peace understood by the world proletariat in the best possible light – was no doubt a matter of secondary importance to Stalin. He was interested in 'peace in one country', as he later was in 'socialism in one country'. In the deciding vote he joined Lenin. It was not until several years later that he worked out a semblance of a 'point of view' for himself on the events of Brest-Litovsk, and that was simply in the interests of his struggle against Trotskyism.

It is hardly necessary to dwell much longer on all this. As it is I have devoted a disproportionately large space to the disagreements at Brest-Litovsk. But it seemed necessary to disclose at least one of the debatable episodes in all its completeness to show what really happened, and how it was represented later. And with this I wanted to put the epigones in their places. As regards Lenin – no serious person will suspect that I am guided in my attitude toward him by the sentiment known in German as 'Rechthaberei'. Long before anyone else, I made a public appreciation of Lenin's part in the Brest-Litovsk days. On 3 October 1918 at the extraordinary joint meeting of the higher organs of the Soviet government I said: 'I deem it my duty to say, in this authoritative assembly, that at the hour when many of us, including myself, were doubtful as to whether it was admissible for us to sign the Brest-Litovsk peace, only Comrade Lenin maintained stubbornly, with amazing foresight and against our opposition, that we had to go through with it to tide us over until the revolution of the world proletariat. And now we must admit that we were wrong.'

I did not wait for the delayed revelations from the epigones to recognize the political courage of Lenin's genius, which had saved the dictatorship of the proletariat in the Brest-Litovsk days. In the words I have just quoted I took upon myself a larger share of responsibility for the errors of others than was really my due. I did it as an example to the others. At this point the stenographic report notes 'prolonged ovation'. The party wanted to show in this way that it understood and appreciated my attitude towards Lenin, an attitude devoid of jealousy or pettiness. I realized only too well what Lenin meant to the revolution, to history, and to me. He was my master. This does not mean that I repeated his words and gestures a bit late, but that I learned from him to arrive independently at the same decision.

33
A Month at Sviyazhsk

The spring and summer of 1918 were unusually hard. All the aftermath of the war was then just beginning to make itself felt. At times it seemed as if everything were slipping and crumbling, as if there were nothing to hold to, nothing to lean upon. One wondered if a country so despairing, so economically exhausted, so devastated, had enough sap left in it to support a new régime and preserve its independence. There was no food. There was no army. The railways were completely disorganized. The machinery of state was just beginning to take shape. Conspiracies were being hatched everywhere.

In the West the Germans occupied Poland, Lithuania, Latvia, White Russia and a large section of Great Russia. Pskov was in their hands. The Ukraine became an Austro-German colony. On the Volga in the summer of 1918 agents of France and England engineered a rebellion of Czecho-Slovak regiments, made up of former war prisoners. The German high command let me know, through their military representatives, that if the Whites approached Moscow from the east, the Germans would come from the west, from the direction of Orsha and Pskov, to prevent the forming of a new eastern front. We were between hammer and anvil. In the North the French and English occupied Murmansk and Archangel, and threatened an advance on Vologda. In Yaroslavl there broke out an insurrection of the White Guards, organized by Savinkov at the instigation of the French ambassador Noulens and the English representative Lockhart, with the object of connecting the northern troops with the Czecho-Slovaks and White Guards on the Volga, by way of Vologda and Yaroslavl. In the Urals Dutov's bands were at large. In the South on the Don an uprising was spreading under the leadership of General Krasnov, then in actual alliance with the Germans. The left Socialist-Revolutionists organized a conspiracy in July and murdered Count Mirbach; they tried at the same time to start an uprising on the eastern front. They wanted to force us into war with Germany. The civil-war front was taking more and more the shape of a noose closing ever tighter about Moscow.

After the fall of Simbirsk it was decided that I should go to the Volga, where we were facing the greatest danger. I began to get a special train ready – in those days not so simple a matter. Everything was missing, or, to be more exact, no one knew where to find anything. The simplest task became a complicated improvisation. I never imagined then that I would have to live in that train for two years and a half. I left Moscow on 7 August still ignorant of the fall of Kazan the day before; only en route did I hear that very disturbing news. Red units hastily drawn up for service had left their posts without a struggle and had bared the defences of Kazan. Part of the staff proved to be traitors; the others had been caught off guard and had to run for safety as best they could, under a rain of bullets. No one knew where the commander-in-chief or the other commanding officers were. My train stopped at Sviyazhsk, the nearest sizable station to Kazan. There for a whole month the fate of the revolution hung again in the balance. That month was a great training school for me.

The army at Sviyazhsk was made up of detachments which had retreated from Simbirsk and Kazan, and of assisting units rushed in from all directions. Each unit lived its own distinct life, sharing in common only a readiness to retreat – so superior were the enemy in both organization and experience. Some White companies made up exclusively of officers performed miracles. The soil itself seemed to be infected with panic. The fresh Red detachments, arriving in vigorous mood, were immediately engulfed by the inertia of retreat. A rumour began to spread among the local peasantry that the Soviets were doomed. Priests and tradesmen lifted their heads. The revolutionary elements in the villages went into hiding. Everything was crumbling; there was nothing to hold to. The situation seemed hopeless.

Here, before Kazan, one could see on a small stretch of land the multiple diversity of the factors in human history, and could draw up arguments against that cowardly historical fatalism which, on all concrete questions, hides behind the passive working of the law of cause and effect, ignoring the while that most important factor -- the living and active man. Could much more be needed to overthrow the revolution? Its territory was now reduced to the size of the ancient Moscow principality. It had hardly any army; it was surrounded by enemies on all sides. After Kazan would have come the turn of Nijni-Novgorod from which a practically unobstructed road lay open to Moscow. The fate of the revolution was being decided here at Sviyazhsk. And here, at the most critical moment, it rested on a single battalion, on one company, on the courage of one commissary. In short, it really was hanging by a thread. And thus it went, day in and day out.

Despite all this the revolution was saved. What was needed for that? Very little. The front ranks of the masses had to realize the mortal danger in the situation. The first requisite for success was to hide nothing, our weakness least of all; not to trifle with the masses but to call everything by its right name. The revolution was still very irresponsible; the October victory had been won very easily. At the same time the revolution had not removed, by a single stroke, all the hardships that had fostered it. The spontaneous pressure had relaxed. The enemy was gaining its successes through military organization, the very thing we did not have. But the revolution was achieving it, before Kazan.

The propaganda throughout the country was being fed by telegrams from Sviyazhsk. The Soviets, the party, the trades-unions, all devoted themselves to raising new detachments, and sent thousands of communists to the Kazan front. Most of the youth of the party did not know how to handle arms, but they had the will to win, and that was the most important thing. They put backbone into the soft body of the army.

The commander-in-chief on the eastern front was Colonel Vatzetis, who had been in command of a division of Latvian Rifles. This was the only unit left over from the old army. The Latvian farm-hands, labourers, and poor peasants hated the

Baltic barons. Tsarism had capitalized this antagonism in the war with the Germans, and the Latvian regiments had been the best troops in the Tsar's army. After the February revolution they came almost to a man under the Bolshevik influence and played an important role in the October revolution. Vatzetis was enterprising, energetic and resourceful. He had distinguished himself during the insurrection of the left Socialist-Revolutionists. Under his direction light guns were placed in front of the conspirators' headquarters, and two or three volleys, merely to frighten them without casualties, were enough to make them take to their heels. Vatzetis replaced Muravyov after the treason of the adventurer in the east. Unlike the other officers trained at the military academy, he never lost himself in the chaos of the revolution, but plunged cheerfully in, blowing bubbles, appealing, exhorting, giving orders even when there was little hope of their being carried out. While other 'specialists' in government service were more fearful of overstepping their authority than of anything else, Vatzetis in his moments of inspiration would issue orders as if the Soviet of Commissaries and the Central Executive Committee did not exist. About a year later he was accused of dubious schemes and connections and had to be dismissed, but there was really nothing serious about the accusations. Perhaps before going to sleep the chap had been reading Napoleon's biography, and confided his ambitious dreams to two or three young officers. Today Vatzetis is a professor in the military academy.

In the retreat from Kazan on 6 August he was one of the last to leave the staff headquarters when the Whites were already entering the building. He managed to make his escape and arrived at Sviyazhsk by way of a circuitous route, having lost Kazan but not his optimism. We considered the more important questions together, appointed the Latvian officer Slavin commander of the Fifth army and said good-bye to each other. Vatzetis left for his staff headquarters and I remained at Sviyazhsk.

Among the party workers who arrived on the same train with me was a man named Gusev. He was called an 'old Bolshevik' because of his share in the revolution of 1905. He had retired to bourgeois life for the next ten years, but, like many others, returned to revolution in 1917. Later Lenin and I removed him from military work because of some petty intrigues, and he was immediately picked up by Stalin. His special vocation today is chiefly that of falsifying the history of the civil war, for which his main qualification is his apathetic cynicism. Like the rest of the Stalin school he never looks back over what he has written or said before. At the beginning of 1924, when the campaign against me was already quite overt, Gusev played his rôle of phlegmatic slanderer. But the memory of those days at Sviyazhsk, despite the six intervening years, was still too fresh, and acted as a check on even him. This is what he said then of the events before Kazan:

> The arrival of Comrade Trotsky worked a decisive change in the situation. In Comrade Trotsky's train to the obscure station of Sviyazhsk there came a firm will to victory, a sense of initiative, and resolute pressure in all phases of the army work.
>
> From the very first days everyone began to feel that some abrupt change had taken place, not only at the station – the active campaign headquarters of the political section and the army supply staff, crammed with the supply trains of countless regiments – but even in army units stationed about fifteen versts away. It was first apparent in the matter of discipline. Comrade Trotsky's harsh methods ... were most expedient and necessary for that period of undisciplined and irregular warfare. Persuasion counted for nothing, and there was no time for it. And so, during the twenty-five days that Comrade Trotsky spent at Sviyazhsk, a tremendous amount of work was done, with the result that the disorganized and demoralized units of the Fifth army were changed into the fighting units that later recaptured Kazan.

Treason had nests among the staff and the commanding officers; in fact everywhere. The enemy knew where to strike and almost always did so with certainty. It was discouraging. Soon after my arrival I visited the front-line batteries. The disposition of the artillery was being explained to me by an experienced officer, a man with a face roughened by wind and with impenetrable eyes. He asked for permission to leave me for a moment, to give some orders over the field-telephone. A few minutes later two shells dropped, forkwise, fifty steps away from where we were standing; a third dropped quite close to us. I had barely time to lie down, and was covered with earth. The officer stood motionless some distance away, his face showing pale through his tan. Strangely enough I suspected nothing at the moment; I thought it was simply an accident. Two years later I suddenly remembered the whole affair, and, as I recalled it in its smallest detail, it dawned on me that the officer was an enemy, and that through some intermediate point he had communicated with the enemy battery by telephone, and had told them where to fire. He ran a double risk – of getting killed along with me by a White shell, or being shot by the Reds. I have no idea what happened to him later.

I had no sooner returned to my carriage than I heard rifle-shots all about me. I rushed to the door. A White aeroplane was circling above us, obviously trying to hit the train. Three bombs dropped on a wide curve, one after another, but did no damage. From the roofs of our train rifles and machine-guns were shooting at the enemy. The aeroplane rose out of reach, but the fusillade went on – it seemed as if everyone were drunk. With considerable difficulty I managed to stop the shooting. Possibly the same artillery officer had sent word as to the time of my return to the train. But there may have been other sources as well.

The more hopeless the military situation of the revolution, the more active the treason. It was necessary, no matter what the cost, to overcome as quickly as possible the automatic inertia of retreat, in which men no longer believe that they can stop, face about, and strike the enemy in the chest. I brought about fifty young party men from Moscow with me on the train. They simply outdid themselves, stepping into the breach and fairly melting away before my very eyes through the recklessness of their heroism and sheer inexperience. The posts next to theirs were held by the Fourth Latvian regiment. Of all the regiments of the Latvian division that had been so badly pulled to pieces, this was the worst. The men lay in the mud under the rain and demanded relief, but there was no relief available. The commander of the regiment and the regimental committee sent me a statement to the effect that unless the regiment was relieved at once 'consequences dangerous for the revolution' would follow. It was a threat. I summoned the commander of the regiment and the chairman of the committee to my car. They sullenly held to their statement. I declared them under arrest. The communications officer of the train, who is now the commander of the Kremlin, disarmed them in my compartment. There were only two of us on the train staff; the rest were fighting at the front. If the men arrested had showed any resistance, or if their regiment had decided to defend them and had left the front line, the situation might have been desperate. We should have had to surrender Sviyazhsk and the bridge across the Volga. The capture of my train by the enemy would undoubtedly have had its effect on the army. The road to Moscow would have been left open. But the arrest came off safely. In an order to the army I announced the commitment of the commander of the regiment to trial before the revolutionary tribunal. The regiment remained at its post. The commander was merely sentenced to prison.

The communists were explaining, exhorting, and offering example, but agitation alone could not radically change the attitude of the troops, and the situation did not allow sufficient time for that. We had to decide on sterner measures. I issued an order which was printed on the press in my train and distributed throughout the army:

I give warning that if any unit retreats without orders, the first to be shot down will be the commissary of the unit, and next the commander. Brave and gallant soldiers will be appointed in their places. Cowards, dastards and traitors will not escape the bullet. This I solemnly promise in the presence of the entire Red Army.

Of course the change did not come all at once. Individual detachments continued to retreat without cause, or else would break under the first strong onset. Sviyazhsk was open to attack. On the Volga a steamboat was held ready for the staff. Ten men of my train crew, mounted on bicycles, were on guard over the pathway between the staff headquarters and the steamship landing. The military Soviet of the Fifth army proposed that I move to the river. It was a wise suggestion, but I was afraid of the bad effect on an army already nervous and lacking in assurance. Just at that time the situation at the front suddenly grew worse. The fresh regiment on which we had been banking left its post, with its commissary and commander at its head, and seized the steamer by threat of arms, intending to steam to Nijni-Novgorod.

A wave of alarm swept over the front. Everyone began to look towards the river. The situation seemed almost hopeless. The staff remained at its post, though the enemy was only a kilometre or two away and shells were bursting close at hand. I had a talk with the indispensable Markin. Boarding an improvised gunboat with a score of tested men, he sailed up to the steamer held by the deserters, and at the point of a gun demanded their surrender. Everything depended on that one moment; a single rifle-shot would have been enough to bring on a catastrophe. But the deserters surrendered without resisting. The steamer docked alongside the pier, the deserters disembarked. I appointed a field-tribunal which passed death-sentences on the commander, the commissary, and several privates – to a gangrenous wound a red-hot iron was applied. I explained the situation to the regiment without hiding or softening anything. A number of communists were injected into the regiment, which returned to the battle front with new commanding officers and a new spirit. Everything happened so quickly that the enemy did not have time to take advantage of the disturbance in our ranks.

It was necessary to organize an aviation service. I called up an engineer-pilot. Akashev, who, though an anarchist by conviction, was working with us. Akashev showed his initiative and quickly rounded up an air squadron. At last we got with its help a full picture of the enemy front; the command of the Fifth army had come out of the dark. The fliers made daily air raids on Kazan and a frenzy of alarm took hold of the city. Some time later after Kazan had been taken I received some documents that included the diary of a bourgeois girl who went through the siege of Kazan. Pages were given over to descriptions of the panic that our airmen caused, and alternated with pages describing the girl's affairs of the heart. Life went on. Czech officers vied with Russian. Affairs begun in the drawing-rooms of Kazan ran their course and reached their finale in the cellars that served as shelters from the bombs.

On 28 August the Whites launched an outflanking movement. Colonel Kappel, later a celebrated White general, penetrated to our rear under cover of darkness, with a strong detachment behind him, and seized a small railway station, destroyed the tracks, and cut down the telegraph-poles. When he had cut off our retreat in this way, he advanced to attack Sviyazhsk. If I am not mistaken, Kappel's staff included Savinkov. This move caught us quite off our guard. We were afraid to disrupt the already shaky front, and so we withdrew only two or three companies. The commander of my train again mobilized everyone he could lay his hands on, both in the train and at the station, including even the cook. We had a good stock of rifles, machine-guns and hand-grenades. The train crew was made up of good fighters. The men took their posts about a verst from the train. The battle went on for about eight hours, and both sides had losses. Finally, after they had spent themselves, the enemy withdrew. Meanwhile the break in the connection with Sviyazhsk had stirred up Moscow and the whole line. Small units were rushed to our relief. The line was quickly repaired; fresh detachments poured into the army. At that time the Kazan papers were reporting that I had been cut off, taken prisoner, killed, had flown away in an aeroplane – but that my dog was captured as a trophy. This faithful animal later was captured on all the civil-war fronts. In most cases it was a chocolate-coloured dog, but sometimes a Saint Bernard. I got off all the cheaper because I never had any dog.

While I was making the rounds of the staff quarters at three o'clock in the morning, on the most critical night at Sviyazhsk, I heard a familiar voice from the staff-room saying: 'He will play this game until he is taken prisoner, and will ruin himself and all of us. You mark my words.' I stopped at the threshold. There, facing me, were two young officers of the general staff, sitting at a table and poring over a map. The man who was speaking stood with his back to me, bent over the table. He must have read something like alarm on his companions' faces, for he turned sharply around towards the door. It was Blagonravov, former lieutenant in the Tsar's army, a young Bolshevik. An expression of mingled terror and shame seemed to freeze on his face. As a commissary it was his duty to keep up the morale of the specialists attached to the army. Instead of that, here he was, at this critical moment, stirring them against me and actually suggesting that they desert! I had caught him red-handed, and I could scarcely believe my eyes or ears.

During 1917 Blagonravov had proved himself a fighting revolutionary. He was the commissary of the Peter-Paul fortress during the revolution, and later on he took part in the suppression of the military students' uprising. I entrusted him with important commissions during the Smolny period, and he carried them out well. 'Out of such a lieutenant,' I had once said jokingly to Lenin, 'even a Napoleon may come some day. He even has the right name for it: Blago-nravov,* almost like Bonaparte.' Lenin laughed at this unexpected comparison, then he grew thoughtful, and, with his cheek-bones bulging even more, said very seriously, almost threateningly, 'Well, I think we'll manage the Bonapartes, don't you?'

'Everything is in the hands of God,' I answered him in jest. It was this same Blagonravov whom I had sent to the East when the people there had been asleep to the treachery of Muravyov. When, in Lenin's reception-room in the Kremlin, I explained his task to Blagonravov, he answered as if he were depressed: 'The whole point of the thing is that the revolution has entered upon a decline.' That was in the middle of 1918. 'Is it possible that you are spent so quickly?' I asked him, indignantly. Blagonravov pulled himself up, changed his tone, and promised to do everything that needed to be done. I was reassured.

And now I had caught him on the verge of downright treason at our most critical time!

We walked into the corridor so that we need not discuss it in front of the officers. Blagonravov was pale and trembling, with his hand raised to his cap. 'Please don't commit me to the tribunal,' he kept repeating despairingly. 'I will earn my reprieve if you send me into the lines as a private.' My prophecy had not come true; here was my candidate for a Napoleon standing before me like a wet hen. He was dismissed from his post and sent to do less responsible work.

*In Russian this means 'good-natured' or 'good-mannered.' – *Translator.*

Revolution is a great devourer of men and character. It leads the brave to their destruction and destroys the souls of those who are less hardy. Today Blagonravov is a member of the ruling staff of the State Political Board ('GPU'),* and one of the pillars of the present régime. He must have learned to hate the 'permanent revolution' when he was still at Sviyazhsk.

The fate of the revolution was trembling in the balance between Sviyazhsk and Kazan. No retreat was open, except into the Volga. The revolutionary Soviet of the army informed me that the problem of my safety at Sviyazhsk restricted the freedom of their action and demanded that I move at once aboard a ship on the river. They were entitled to make this demand – from the outset I had made it a rule that my presence at Sviyazhsk should in no way embarrass or restrict the high command of the army. I stuck to this rule all through my stops at various fronts. So I complied with the demand and moved over to the river, not, however, to the passenger-steamer that had been made ready for me, but to a torpedo-boat. Four small torpedo-boats had been brought up to the Volga, with great difficulty, by way of the Mariinsk canal system. By that time a few of the river steamers also had been armed with guns and machine-guns.

The flotilla under the command of Raskolnikov was planning a raid on Kazan that night. It had to pass two high headlands on which the Whites had mounted their batteries. Beyond the headlands the river curved and broadened out, and there the enemy's flotilla was stationed. On the opposite bank Kazan lay open. The plan was to pass the headlands under cover of darkness, destroy the enemy's flotilla and shore batteries, and shell the city.

The flotilla set out in battle formation with lights out, like a thief in the night. Two old Volga pilots, both with thin little beards, stood next to the captain. Having been forced to come aboard, they were in mortal fear every minute, and were hating us and cursing their fate, trembling the while like aspens. Now everything depended on them. The captain reminded them from time to time that he would shoot both of them on the spot if

*The GPU, which is the abbreviation of 'Gosudarstvennoye Politicheskoye Upravleniye', *i.e.*, 'State Political Board', is the Soviet organization of secret police. – *Translator.*

they drove the ship aground. We had just come abreast of the headland, rising dimly out of the dark, when a shot from a machine-gun lashed across the river like a whip. A gunshot followed it from the hill. We went on silently. Behind us, from below, answering shots followed. Several bullets drummed on the iron sheet that protected us to the waist on the captain's bridge. We crouched, and the boatswains shrank down, searching the darkness with piercing eyes and exchanging words in tense whispers with the captain. Once past the headland we entered the reach. Beyond us on the opposite shore the lights of Kazan were visible. Heavy firing was going on behind us from above and below.

Not more than two hundred yards away at the right, under cover of the hilly banks, the enemy flotilla was lying, the boats looming up as a vague mass. Raskolnikov ordered the guns to open fire on the boats. The metal body of our torpedo-boat groaned and shrieked with the first shot from its own gun. We were moving in jerks, as if that iron womb were giving birth to shells in grinding pain. Suddenly the darkness of the night was stripped naked by a flare – one of our shells had set fire to an oil-barge. An unexpected, unwelcome, but resplendent torch rose above the Volga. Now we began to fire at the pier. We could see the guns on it clearly, but they did not answer. The gunners apparently had simply fled. The whole expanse of river was lit up. There was no one behind us. We were alone; the enemy's artillery obviously had cut off the passage of the rest of our boats. Our torpedo-boat stood out on that bright river like a fly on a white plate. In another moment we would find ourselves under the cross-fire from the headlands and the pier. It gave one the creeps. And on top of this we lost control of our boat. The steering-gear had been broken, probably by a shot. We tried to turn the rudder by hand, but the broken chain got tangled around it and the rudder became useless. We had to stop the engines. The boat was slowly drifting toward the Kazan bank when it ran into an old, half-submerged barge. The firing ceased altogether. It was as light as day and as silent as night.

We were in a trap. The only thing that seemed incomprehensible was the fact that we were not being pounded by shells.

We did not realize the destruction and panic caused by our raid. Finally the young commanders decided to push away from the barge and regulate the movement of the boat by running the right and left engines alternately. It proved successful. With the oil torch still blazing we went on to the headland. There were no shots. Around the headland we sank into darkness again. A sailor who had fainted was brought up from the engine-room. The battery stationed on the hill did not fire a single shot. Obviously we were not being watched and probably there was no one there to watch us. We were saved. An easy word to write, 'saved'. Cigarettes were lighted. The charred remains of one of our improvised gunboats were lying sadly on the shore. We found a few wounded men on the other boats. Only then did we notice that the bow of our torpedo-boat had been neatly pierced by a three-inch shell. It was the hour before dawn. We all felt as if we had been born a second time.

One thing followed another. A flier who had just come down with welcome news was brought to me. A detachment of the Second army under the command of the Cossack Azin had come right up to Kazan from the north-east. They had captured two armoured cars, had disabled two guns, routed an enemy detachment, and occupied two villages twelve versts away from Kazan. The airman flew back at once with instructions and an appeal. Kazan was being squeezed in the clutch of the pincers. Our night raid, as we soon learned through our reconnaissance men, had cracked the White resistance. The enemy flotilla had been almost completely destroyed, and the shore batteries had been reduced to silence. The word 'torpedo-boat', on the Volga, had the effect on the Whites that the word 'tank' had on the young Red troops before Petrograd some time later. Rumours were spread about to the effect that the Bolsheviks had Germans fighting with them. The prosperous classes began to flee in hordes from Kazan. The workers' districts lifted their heads again. A revolt broke out in the powder-works. An aggressive spirit became apparent among our troops.

The month at Sviyazhsk was crammed full of exciting episodes. Something happened every day. In this respect the nights quite often were not far behind the days. It was the first time that war had unrolled before me so intimately. This was a small war; on our side there were only about 25,000 to 30,000 men engaged. But the small war differed from a big one only in scale. It was like a living model of a war. That is why its fluctuations and surprises were felt so directly. The small war was a big school.

Meanwhile the situation before Kazan changed beyond recognition. Heterogeneous detachments became regular units, buttressed by worker-communists from Petrograd, Moscow and other places. The regiments stiffened up. Inside the units the commissaries acquired the importance of revolutionary leaders, of direct representatives of the dictatorship. The tribunals demonstrated to everyone that revolution, when threatened by mortal danger, demands the highest sacrifice. Propaganda, organization, revolutionary example and repression produced the necessary change in a few weeks. A vacillating, unreliable and crumbling mass was transformed into a real army. Our artillery had emphatically established its superiority. Our flotilla controlled the river. Our airmen dominated the air. No longer did I doubt that we would take Kazan.

Suddenly on 1 September I received a code telegram from Moscow: 'Come at once. Vladimir Ilyich wounded, how dangerously not yet known. Complete order prevails. 31 August 1918. Svyerdlov.' I left at once. The mood of the party circles in Moscow was sullen and dismal, but they were absolutely unshakable. The best expression of this determination was Svyerdlov. The physicians declared that Lenin's life was not in danger and promised an early recovery. I encouraged the party with the prospects of success in the East, and returned at once to Sviyazhsk.

Kazan was taken on 10 September. Two days later Simbirsk was occupied by our First army. This was no surprise to me. The commander of the First army, Tukhachevsky, had promised at the end of August that we would take Simbirsk not later than 12 September. When the town was taken, he sent a telegram. 'Order carried out. Simbirsk taken.' Meanwhile Lenin had been recovering. He sent a jubilant telegram of greetings. Things were improving all along the line.

The Fifth army was now headed by Ivan Nikitich Smirnov.

This was vastly important. Smirnov represented the most complete and finished revolutionary type; he had entered the ranks thirty years before, and had neither known nor sought for relief. In the darkest years of the reaction Smirnov went on digging underground passages. When they caved in, he did not lose heart but began all over again. Ivan Nikitich was always a man of duty. In this respect a revolutionary resembles a good soldier, and that is why a revolutionary can become a fine one. Obeying only the demands of his own nature, Ivan Nikitich was always a model of firmness and bravery, without that cruelty which so often accompanies them. All the finest workers of the army began to take him as their example. 'No one was more respected than Ivan Nikitich,' wrote Larissa Reisner in her description of the siege of Kazan. 'One felt that at the most critical moment he would be the strongest and the bravest.' Smirnov has not a trace of pedantry. He is the most sociable, cheerful, and witty of men. People submit to his authority all the more readily because it is not at all obvious or peremptory, even though quite indisputable.

As they grouped themselves about Smirnov, the communists of the Fifth army formed a separate political family which even today, several years after the liquidation of that Fifth army, plays a part in the life of the country. 'A Fifth-army man', in the lexicon of the revolution, carries a special meaning; it denotes a true revolutionary, a man of duty and, above all, a scrupulous one. With Ivan Nikitich the men of the Fifth army, after the termination of the civil war, transferred all their heroism to economics, and almost without exception found themselves in the ranks of the opposition. Smirnov stood at the head of the military industry, then he held the office of commissary of post and telegraph. Today he is in exile in the Caucasus. In prisons and in Siberia you will find many of his fellow heroes of the Fifth army. But revolution is a great devourer of men and character! The latest reports have it that even Smirnov has been broken by the struggle and is preaching surrender.

Larissa Reisner, who called Ivan Nikitich 'the conscience of Sviyazhsk', was herself prominent in the Fifth army, as well as in the revolution as a whole. This fine young woman flashed across the revolutionary sky like a burning meteor, blinding many. With her appearance of an Olympian goddess, she combined a subtle and ironical mind and the courage of a warrior. After the capture of Kazan by the Whites she went into the enemy camp to reconnoitre, disguised as a peasant woman. But her appearance was too extraordinary, and she was arrested. While she was being cross-examined by a Japanese intelligence officer, she took advantage of an interval to slip through the carelessly guarded door and disappear. After that she engaged in intelligence work. Later she sailed on war-boats and took part in battles. Her sketches about the civil war are literature. With equal gusto she would write about the Ural industries and the rising of the workers in the Ruhr. She was anxious to know and to see all and to take part in everything. In a few brief years she became a writer of the first rank. But after coming unscathed through fire and water this Pallas of the revolution suddenly burned up with typhus in the peaceful surroundings of Moscow, before she was even thirty.

One good worker joined another. Under fire men learned in a week. The army was taking shape magnificently. The lowest ebb of the revolution – the moment of the fall of Kazan – was now behind us. Along with this a tremendous change was taking place in the peasantry. The Whites were teaching the mouzhiks their political ABCs. During the ensuing seven months the Red Army cleared a territory of nearly a million square kilometres, with a population of forty millions. The revolution was again advancing. When they fled from Kazan, the Whites carried away with them the gold reserves of the republic, which had been stored there since the February offensive of General Hoffmann. We recaptured them considerably later, and with them Admiral Kolchak.

When I was at last able to take my eyes from Sviyazhsk, I observed that certain changes had taken place in Europe. The German army was in a hopeless position.

34
The Train

Now it is time to speak of 'The train of the Predrevoyensoviet'.*
During the most strenuous years of the revolution my own
personal life was bound up inseparably with the life of that train.
The train, on the other hand, was inseparably bound up with
the life of the Red Army. The train linked the front with the
base, solved urgent problems on the spot, educated, appealed,
supplied, rewarded, and punished.

An army cannot be built without reprisals. Masses of men
cannot be led to death unless the army command has the death-
penalty in its arsenal. So long as those malicious tailless apes
that are so proud of their technical achievements – the animals
that we call men – will build armies and wage wars, the command will always be obliged to place the soldiers between the
possible death in the front and the inevitable one in the rear.
And yet armies are not built on fear. The Tsar's army fell to
pieces not because of any lack of reprisals. In his attempt to
save it by restoring the death penalty Kerensky only finished
it. Upon the ashes of the great war the Bolsheviks created a
new army. These facts demand no explanation for anyone who
has even the slightest knowledge of the language of history.
The strongest cement in the new army was the ideas of the
October revolution, and the train supplied the front with this
cement.

In the provinces of Kaluga, Voronezh, and Ryazan tens of
thousands of young peasants had failed to answer the first recruiting summons by the Soviets. The war was going on far from
their provinces, the registration of conscripts was inefficient,
and consequently the draft to service was not taken seriously.

*The train of the Chairman of the Military Revolutionary Council.
– Translator

Those who failed to present themselves were known as deserters. It became necessary to launch a strong campaign against these absentees. The war commissariat of Ryazan succeeded in gathering in some fifteen thousand of such deserters. While passing through Ryazan I decided to take a look at them. Some of our men tried to dissuade me. 'Something might happen,' they warned me. But everything went off beautifully. The men were called out of their barracks. 'Comrade-deserters – come to the meeting. Comrade Trotsky has come to speak to you.' They ran out excited, boisterous, as curious as schoolboys. I had imagined them much worse, and they had imagined me as more terrible. In a few minutes I was surrounded by a huge crowd of unbridled, utterly undisciplined, but not at all hostile men. The 'comrade-deserters' were looking at me with such curiosity that it seemed as if their eyes would pop out of their heads. I climbed on a table there in the yard and spoke to them for about an hour and a half. It was a most responsive audience. I tried to raise them in their own eyes; concluding, I asked them to lift their hands in token of their loyalty to the revolution. The new ideas infected them before my very eyes. They were genuinely enthusiastic; they followed me to the automobile, devoured me with their eyes, not fearfully, as before, but rapturously, and shouted at the tops of their voices. They would hardly let me go. I learned afterwards, with some pride, that one of the best ways to educate them was to remind them: 'What did you promise Comrade Trotsky?' Later on regiments of Ryazan 'deserters' fought well at the fronts.

I recall to mind the second grade of the St Paul *realschule* in Odessa. The forty boys there did not differ materially from any other group of forty boys. But when Burnande, with the mysterious cross on his forehead, superintendent Mayer, superintendent Wilhelm, inspector Kaminsky, and director Schwannebach struck with all their force at the daring and more critical group of boys, the tale-bearers and envious dullards promptly reared their heads and led the others after them.

Every regiment, every company, comprises men of different qualities. The intelligent and self-sacrificing are in the minority. At the opposite pole is an insignificant number of the completely demoralized, the skulkers, and the consciously hostile. Between these two minorities is a large middle group, the undecided, the vacillating. And when the better elements have been lost in fighting or shoved aside, and the skulkers and enemies gain the upper hand, the unit goes to pieces. In such cases the large middle group do not know whom to follow and, in the moment of danger, succumb to panic. On 24 February 1919 I said to the young commanders gathered in the Hall of Columns in Moscow: 'Give me three thousand deserters, call them a regiment; I will give them a fighting commander, a good commissary, fit officers for battalions, companies and platoons – and these three thousand deserters in the course of four weeks in our revolutionary country will produce a splendid regiment... During the last few weeks,' I added, 'we tested this again by experience in the Narva and Pskov sections of the front, where we succeeded in making fine fighting units out of a few scattered fragments.'

For two and a half years except for comparatively short intervals I lived in a railway-coach that had formerly been used by one of the ministers of communication. The car was well fitted out from the point of view of ministerial comfort, but it was scarcely adapted to work. There I received those who brought reports, held conferences with local military and civil authorities, studied telegraphic dispatches, dictated orders and articles. From it I made long trips along the front in automobiles with my co-workers. In my spare time I dictated my book against Kautsky, and various other works. In those years I accustomed myself, seemingly forever, to writing and thinking to the accompaniment of Pullman wheels and springs.

My train was hurriedly organized in Moscow on the night of 7 August 1918. In the morning I left in it for Sviyazhsk, bound for the Czecho-Slovak front. The train was continually being reorganized and improved upon, and extended in its functions. As early as 1918 it had already become a flying apparatus of administration. Its sections included a secretariat, a printing-press, a telegraph station, a radio station, an electric-power station, a library, a garage, and a bath. The train was so heavy that it needed two engines; later it was divided into two trains. When we had to stop for some time at some one section of the front, one of the engines would do service as courier and the other was always under steam. The front was shifting constantly and one could take no chances.

I haven't the history of the train at hand. It is buried in the archives of the war department. At one time it was painstakingly worked over by my young assistants. The diagram of the train's movements prepared for the civil-war exhibition used to attract a great many visitors, as the newspapers reported at the time. Later it was put in the civil-war museum. Today it must be hidden away with hundreds and thousands of other exhibits, such as placards, proclamations, orders, flags, photographs, films, books and speeches reflecting the most important moments of the civil war and connected in some way or other with my part in it.

During the years of 1922 to 1924, that is, before repressions were begun against the opposition, the military publishing house managed to bring out five volumes of my works relating to the army and the civil war. The history of the train is not dealt with in these volumes. I can only partially reconstruct the orbit of the train's movements from the place names under the leading articles in the train newspaper, *En Route* – Samara, Chelyabinsk, Vyatka, Petrograd, Balashov, Smolensk, Samara again, Rostov-on-Don, Novocherkask, Kiev, Zhitomir, and so on, without end. I haven't even the exact figures of the total distance covered by the train during the civil war. One of the notes to my military books mentions thirty-six trips, with a total run of over 105,000 kilometres. One of my former fellow travellers writes that he reckons from memory that in three years we circled the earth five and a half times – he gives, that is, a figure twice as large as the one mentioned above. This does not include thousands of kilometres done by automobile from the railway line into the heart of the front lines. Since the train always went to the most critical points, the diagram of its journeyings gives a fairly exact and comprehensive picture of the relative importance of the different fronts. The greatest number of trips was in 1920, the last year of the war. My trips to the southern front were especially frequent, because all during that period it was the most stubborn, dangerous and extended of all the fronts.

What was the train of the Chairman of the Military Revolutionary Council seeking on the civil-war fronts? The general answer is obvious: it was seeking victory. But what did it give the fronts? What methods did it follow? What were the immediate objects of its endless runs from one end of the country to the other? They were not mere trips of inspection. No, the work of the train was all bound up with the building-up of the army, with its education, its administration, and its supply. We were constructing an army all over again, and under fire at that. This was true not only at Sviyazhsk, where the train recorded its first month, but on all the fronts. Out of bands of irregulars, of refugees escaping from the Whites, of peasants mobilized in the neighbouring districts, of detachments of workers sent by the industrial centres, of groups of communists and trade-unionists – out of these we formed at the front companies, battalions, new regiments, and sometimes even entire divisions. Even after defeats and retreats the flabby, panicky mob would be transformed in two or three weeks into an efficient fighting force. What was needed for this? At once much and little. It needed good commanders, a few dozen experienced fighters, a dozen or so of communists ready to make any sacrifice, boots for the barefooted, a bath-house, an energetic propaganda campaign, food, underwear, tobacco and matches. The train took care of all this. We always had in reserve a few zealous communists to fill in the breaches, a hundred or so of good fighting men, a small stock of boots, leather jackets, medicaments, machine-guns, field-glasses, maps, watches and all sorts of gifts. Of course the actual material resources of the train were slight in comparison with the needs of the army, but they were constantly being replenished.

But – what is even more important – tens and hundreds of times they played the part of the shovelful of coal that is necessary at a particular moment to keep the fire from going out. A telegraph station was in operation on the train. We made our connections with Moscow by direct wire, and my deputy there, Sklyansky, took down my demands for supplies urgently needed for the army, sometimes for a single division or even for a regiment. They were delivered with a dispatch that would have been absolutely impossible without my intervention. Of course this is not exactly a proper way of doing things – a pedant would tell us that in the supply service, as in military departments in general, the most important thing is system. That is absolutely true. I am myself rather inclined to err on the side of pedantry. But the point is that we did not want to perish before we could build up a smoothly running system. That is why, especially in that early period, we had to substitute improvisations for a system – so that later on we might develop a system on their foundations.

On all of my trips I was accompanied by the chief workers in all the principal departments of the army, especially in those connected with the supply service. We had inherited, from the old army, supply service officers who tried to work in the old way or in even worse fashion, for the conditions became infinitely more difficult. On these trips many of the old specialists had to learn new ways, and new ones received their training in live experience. After making the round of a division and ascertaining its needs on the spot I would hold a conference in the staff-car or the dining-car, inviting as many representatives as possible, including those from the lower commanding force and from the ranks, as well as from the local party organizations, the Soviet administration, and the trades-unions. In this way I got a picture of the situation that was neither false nor highly coloured. These conferences always had immediate practical results. No matter how poor the organs of the local administration might be they always managed to squeeze a little tighter and cut down some of their own needs to contribute something to the army.

The most important sacrifices came from institutions. A new group of communists would be drawn from the institutions and put immediately into an unreliable regiment. Stuff would be found for shirts and for wrappings for the feet, leather for new soles, and an extra hundredweight of fat. But of course the local sources were not enough. After the conference I would send orders to Moscow by direct wire, estimating our needs according to the resources of the centre, and, as a result, the division would get what it desperately needed, and that in good time. The commanders and commissaries of the front learned from their experience on the train to approach their own work – whether they were commanding, educating, supplying or administering justice – not from above, from the standpoint of the pinnacle of the staff, but from below, from the standpoint of the company or platoon, of the young and inexperienced new recruit.

Gradually, more or less efficient machinery for a centralized supply service for the front and the armies was established. But, alone, it did not and could not satisfy all needs. Even the most ideal organization will occasionally miss fire during a war, and especially during a war of manoeuvres based entirely on movement – sometimes, alas! in quite unforeseen directions. And one must not forget that we fought without supplies. As early as 1919 there was nothing left in the central depots. Shirts were sent to the front direct from the workshop. But the supply of rifles and cartridges was most difficult of all. The Tula munition factories worked for the needs of the current day. Not a carload of cartridges could be sent anywhere without the special authorization of the Commander-in-Chief. The supply of munitions was always as taut as a string. Sometimes the string would break and then we lost men and territory.

Without constant changes and improvisations the war would have been utterly impossible for us. The train initiated these, and at the same time regulated them. If we gave an impulse of initiative to the front and its immediate rear, we took care to direct it into the channels of the general system. I do not want to say that we always succeeded in this. But, as the civil war has demonstrated, we did achieve the principal thing – victory.

The trips to the sections of the front where often the treason of the commanding officers had created catastrophes were especially important. On 23 August 1918 during the most critical period before Kazan I received a coded telegram from Lenin and Svyerdlov:

Sviyazhsk Trotsky. Treason on the Saratov front, though discovered in time, has yet produced very dangerous wavering. We consider your going there at once absolutely necessary, for your appearance at the front has an effect on soldiers and the entire army. Let us together arrange for your visits to other fronts. Reply stating date of your departure, all by code, 22 August 1918. Lenin. Svyerdlov.

I thought it quite impossible to leave Sviyazhsk, as the departure of the train would have shaken the Kazan front, which was having a difficult enough time as it was. Kazan was in all respects more important than Saratov. Lenin and Svyerdlov themselves soon agreed with me on this. I went to Saratov only after the recapture of Kazan. But telegrams like this reached the train at all stages of its travel. Kiev and Vyatka, Siberia and the Crimea would complain of their difficult positions and would demand, in turn or at the same time, that the train hasten to their rescue.

The war unrolled on the periphery of the country, often in the most remote parts of a front that stretched for eight thousand kilometres. Regiments and divisions were cut off from the rest of the world for months at a time. Very often they had not enough telephone equipment even for their own intercommunication, and would then succumb to hopelessness. The train, for them, was a messenger from other worlds. We always had a stock of telephone apparatus and wires. A wireless aerial had been arranged over a particular car in our train, so that we could receive radio messages from the Eiffel Tower, from Nauen, and from other stations, thirteen in all, with Moscow, of course, foremost. The train was always informed of what was going on in the rest of the world. The more important telegraphic reports were published in the train newspaper, and given passing comment in articles, leaflets and orders. Kapp's raid, conspiracies at home, the English elections, the progress of grain collections, and feats of the Italian Fascismo were interpreted while the footprints of events were still warm, and were linked up with the fates of the Astrakhan or Archangel fronts.

These articles were simultaneously transmitted to Moscow by direct wire, and radioed from there to the press of the entire country. The arrival of the train put the most isolated unit in touch with the whole army, and brought it into the life not only of the country, but of the entire world. Alarmist rumours and doubts were dispelled, and the spirit of the men grew firm. This change of morale would last for several weeks, sometimes until the next visit of the train. In the intervals members of the Military-Revolutionary Council of the front or the army would make trips similar in character, but on a smaller scale.

All my work in the train, literary and otherwise, would have been impossible without my assisting stenographers, Glazman and Syermuks, and the younger assistant, Nechayev. They worked all day and all night in the moving train, which, disregarding all rules of safety in the fever of war, would rush over shaken ties at a speed of seventy or more kilometres an hours, so that the map that hung from the ceiling of the car would rock like a swing. I would watch in wondering gratitude the movements of the hand that, despite the incessant jerking and shaking, could inscribe the finely shaped symbols so clearly. When I was handed the typed script half an hour later, no corrections were necessary. This was not ordinary work; it took on a character of heroic sacrifice. Afterwards, Glazman and Syermuks paid dearly for their sacrifices in the service of the revolution. Glazman was driven to suicide by the Stalinites, and Syermuks has been shut away in the wilds of Siberia.

Part of the train was a huge garage holding several automobiles and a gasoline tank. This made it possible for us to travel away from the railway line for several hundred versts. A squad of picked sharpshooters and machine-gunners, amounting to from twenty to thirty men, occupied the trucks and light cars. A couple of hand machine-guns had also been placed in my car. A war of movement is full of surprises. On the steppes we always ran the risk of running into some Cossack band. Automobiles with machine-guns insured one against this, at least when the steppe had not been transformed into a sea of mud. Once, during the autumn of 1919, in the province of Voronezh, we could move at a speed of only three kilometres an hour. The automobiles sank deep into the black, rain-soaked earth. Thirty men had to keep jumping off their cars to push them along. And once, when we were fording a river, we got stuck in midstream. In a rage I blamed everything on the low-built machine which my excellent chauffeur, an Estonian named Puvi, considered the very best machine in the world. He turned round to me, and raising his hand to his cap, said in broken Russian:

'I beg to state that the engineers never foresaw that we should have to sail on water.'

In spite of the difficulty of the moment I felt like embracing him for the cold aptness of his irony.

The train was not only a military-administrative and political institution, but a fighting institution as well. In many of its features it was more like an armoured train than a staff head-quarters on wheels. In fact it was armoured, or at least its engines and machine-gun cars were. All the crew could handle arms. They all wore leather uniforms, which always make men look heavily imposing. On the left arm, just below the shoulder, each wore a large metal badge, carefully cast at the mint, which had acquired great popularity in the army. The cars were connected by telephone and by a system of signals. To keep the men on the alert while we were travelling, there were frequent alarms, both by day and by night. Armed detachments would be put off the train as 'landing parties'. The appearance of a leather-coated detachment in a dangerous place invariably had an overwhelming effect. When they were aware of the presence of the train just a few kilometres behind the firing-line, even the most nervous units, their commanding officers especially, would summon up all their strength. In the unstable poise of a scale only a small weight is enough to decide. The rôle of that weight was played by the train and its detachments a great many times during its two-and-a-half years of travel. When we took the returned 'landing party' aboard, we usually found someone missing. Altogether the train lost about fifteen men in killed and wounded, not counting the ones who joined the units in the field and disappeared from our view. For instance a squad was made up from our train crew for the model armoured train named for Lenin; another joined the troops in the field before Petrograd. For its share in the battles against Yudenich the train as a whole was decorated with the order of the Red Flag.

Sometimes the train was cut off and shelled or bombed from the air. No wonder it was surrounded by a legend woven of victories both real and imagined. Time and again the commander of a division, of a brigade, or even of a regiment would ask me to stay at his staff headquarters for an extra half-hour, just whiling away the time, or to drive with him by automobile or on horseback to some distant sector, or even to send a few men from the train there with supplies and gifts, so that the news of the train's arrival might be spread far and wide. 'This will be as good as a division in reserve,' commanders would say. The news of the arrival of the train would reach the enemy lines as well. There people imagined a mysterious train infinitely more awful than it really was. But that only served to increase its influence on morale.

The train earned the hatred of its enemies and was proud of it. More than once the Socialist-Revolutionists made plans to wreck it. At the trial of the Socialist-Revolutionists the story was told in detail by Semyonov, who organized the assassination of Volodarsky and the attempt on Lenin's life and who also took part in the preparations to wreck the train. As a matter of fact such an enterprise presented no great difficulty, except that by that time the Socialist-Revolutionists, weakened politically, had lost faith in themselves and no longer had much influence with the younger generation.

On one of our trips south the train was wrecked at the station of Gorki. In the middle of the night I was suddenly jerked out of bed, and was seized by that creepy feeling one has during an earthquake of the ground slipping away under one's feet with no firm support anywhere. Still half-asleep, I clutched the sides of the bed. The familiar rumbling had stopped at once; the car had turned on its edge and stood stock-still. In the silence of the night, a single, pitiful voice was the only thing to be heard. The heavy car-doors were so bent that they could not even be opened, and I could not get out. No one appeared, which alarmed me. Was it the enemy? With a revolver in my hand I jumped out of the window and ran into a man with a lantern. It was the commander of the train, unable to get to me.

The car was standing on a slope, with three wheels buried deep in the embankment, and the other three rising high above the rails. The rear and front of the car had crumpled. The front grating had pinned down a sentry, and it was his pitiful little voice, like the crying of a child, that I had heard in the darkness. It was no easy matter to release him from the grating covering him so tightly. To everyone's surprise, he got off with nothing but bruises and a scare. In all, eight cars were destroyed. The restaurant car, which was used as the club for the train, was a heap of polished splinters. A number of men had been reading or playing chess while they waited for their turn to go on duty, but they had left the club at midnight, ten minutes before the accident. The trucks with books, equipment and gifts for the front were all badly damaged as well. None of the men was seriously hurt. The accident was due to faulty switching, whether because of negligence or deliberate action we never found out. Fortunately for us the train was passing a station at the time, running at a speed of only thirty kilometres.

The train crew performed many other tasks besides their special duties. They lent their help in time of famine, during epidemics of disease, in propaganda campaigns, and at international congresses. The train was the honorary head of a rural district and of several children's homes. Its communist local published its own paper, *On Guard*. Many an incident of adventure and battle is recorded in its pages, but unfortunately this, like many other records, is not in my present travelling archives.

When I was leaving to prepare an offensive against Wrangel, who had entrenched himself in the Crimea, I wrote in the train newspaper *En Route* on 27 October 1920:

Our train is again bound for the front.

The fighting men of our train were before the walls of Kazan in the grave weeks of 1918, when we were fighting for the control of the Volga. That fight ended long ago. Today the Soviet power is approach-the Pacific Ocean.

The fighting men of our train fought gallantly before the walls of Petrograd. Petrograd has been saved and has since been visited by many representatives of the world proletariat.

Our train visited the western front more than once. Today, a preliminary peace has been signed with Poland.

The fighting men of our train were on the steppes of the Don when Krasnov and, later, Denikin advanced against Soviet Russia from the south. The days of Krasnov and Denikin are long since past.

There now is left only the Crimea, which the French government has made its fortress. The White Guard garrison of this French fortress is under the command of a hired German-Russian general, Baron Wrangel.

The friendly family of our train is starting on a new campaign. Let this campaign be the last.

The Crimean campaign was actually the last campaign of the civil war. A few months later the train was disbanded. From these pages I send fraternal greetings to all my former comrades-in-arms.

35
The Defence of Petrograd

There were sixteen armies fighting on the revolutionary fronts of the Soviet Republic. The Great French Revolution had almost as many – fourteen. And every one of the sixteen Soviet armies had its own brief but striking history. The mere mention of the number of any one army is enough to evoke scores of remarkable stories. Each of the armies had its own clear-cut, though ever-changing, physiognomy.

The Seventh army held the western approaches to Petrograd. The prolonged standstill had impaired its morale. Its watchfulness became dulled; its best workers, even whole detachments, were taken away and sent to the more active sectors of the front. For a revolutionary army, which needs constant charges of enthusiasm, marking time almost always ends in mishap, and often in disaster. The Seventh army was no exception.

In June 1919 an important fort called 'Krasnaya Gorka' (The Red Hill), in the Gulf of Finland, was captured by a detachment of Whites. A few days later it was recaptured by a force of Red marines. Then it was discovered that the chief of the staff of the Seventh army, Colonel Lundkvist, was transmitting all information to the Whites. There were other conspirators working hand-in-glove with him. This shook the army to its very core.

In July General Yudenich was made Commander-in-Chief of the North-Western army of the Whites, and was recognized by Kolchak as his representative. In August, with the aid of England and Estonia, the Russian 'north-western government' was established. The English navy in the Gulf of Finland promised Yudenich its support. Yudenich's offensive was timed for a moment when we were desperately pressed on the other fronts. Denikin had occupied Orel and was threatening Tula, the munitions-manufacturing centre. From there it was only a short distance to Moscow. The South demanded all our attention. Just then the first strong blow from the west threw the Seventh army completely off its balance, and it began to roll back with hardly a show of resistance, abandoning its arms and supplies as it went. The Petrograd leaders, Zinoviev in particular, kept telling Lenin about the enemy's excellent equipment – the automatic rifles, tanks, aeroplanes, the British monitors on their flanks, and so forth. Lenin concluded that we could fight Yudenich's army of officers, armed with the latest technical devices, only at the cost of denuding and weakening our other fronts, the southern one most of all. But this was impossible, and so, in his opinion, there was only one thing to do: abandon Petrograd and shorten the front line. After he decided that such an amputation was essential Lenin began to try to win over other leaders. When I arrived in Moscow, I firmly opposed this plan. Yudenich and his masters would not have been satisfied with Petrograd alone; they wanted to meet Denikin in Moscow. In Petrograd Yudenich would have found enormous industrial resources and manpower; moreover there would be no serious obstacles in his way from Petrograd to Moscow. So I decided that we had to save Petrograd at any cost, and found support first of all among the citizens of Petrograd. Krestinsky, at that time a member of the Politbureau, sided with me. I believe that Stalin also supported my stand. Several times during those twenty-four hours I attacked Lenin, until he said at last: 'Very well, let us try!'

On 15 October the Politbureau adopted my resolution on the situation at the fronts:

Recognizing the existence of an acute military danger, we must take steps really to transform Soviet Russia into a military camp. With the help of the party and the trade-unions a registration must be carried out listing every member of the party, of the Soviet institutions and the trade-unions, with a view to using them for military service.

This was followed by a list of practical measures. Regarding Petrograd, the resolution said: 'Not to be evacuated.' The same day I submitted the draft of a decree to the Council of Defence: 'To defend Petrograd to the last ounce of blood, to refuse to

yield a foot, and to carry the struggle into the streets of the city.'
I had no doubt that even if the White army of 25,000 fighting
men could manage to force its way into the city of a million inhabitants, it would be doomed to extinction if it met serious and
well-organized resistance in the streets. At the same time, with
an eye especially on the possible intervention of Estonia and
Finland, I thought it necessary to plan for the withdrawal of the
army and workers towards the south-east, since that was the
only way to save the flower of the Petrograd proletariat from
wholesale extermination.

On the sixteenth I left for Petrograd. The next day Lenin
wrote me:

17 October 1919. Comrade Trotsky: Last night transmitted in code
. . . the decision of the Council of Defence. As you will see, your plan
has been accepted. But the withdrawal of the Petrograd workers to
the south is, of course, not rejected (I am told that you expounded it
to Krassin and Rykov), but to discuss it before the need arises would
distract attention from the fight-to-the-finish. An attempt to outflank
and cut off Petrograd will, of course, bring corresponding changes
which you will carry out on the spot . . . I enclose a proclamation
which I wrote at the suggestion of the Council of Defence. I did it
hastily, and it did not turn out well. You had better put my name
under your own text. Greetings.

LENIN.

This letter, it seems to me, definitely shows how the most violent disagreements between Lenin and me, inevitable in a work
of such scope, were overcome in practice and left no trace on
our personal relations or on our joint work. It occurs to me that
if it had been me against Lenin, instead of Lenin against me,
who in October 1919 defended the idea of surrendering Petrograd, there would have been plenty of literature today, in every
known language, exposing this destructive manifestation of
'Trotskyism'.

During the course of the year 1918 the Allies were forcing a
civil war on us, supposedly in the interests of victory over the
Kaiser. But now it was 1919. Germany had long since been defeated. Yet the Allies continued to spend hundreds of millions
to spread death, famine, and disease in the country of the revo-

lution. Yudenich was one of the *condottieri* in the pay of England and France. His rear was propped up by Estonia, his left flank was covered by Finland. The Allies demanded that both these countries, freed by the revolution, should help to butcher it. There were endless negotiations in Helsingfors, as there were in Reval; the scales tipped this way and that. We watched in alarm the two little states that constituted a hostile pincers about the head of Petrograd.

On 1 September I wrote in the *Pravda*, by way of warning: 'Among the divisions we are now bringing over to the Petrograd front, the part of the Bashkir horsemen will not be least important, and if the bourgeois Finns attempt to attack Petrograd, the Red Bashkirs will advance with the battle-cry: "To Helsingfors!"'

The Bashkir cavalry division had been formed only a short time before. From the outset I had planned to transfer it to Petrograd for a few months, so that the men from the steppes might have a chance to live for a time amid the cultural surroundings of the city, come into closer contact with the workers, and visit clubs, meetings and theatres. To this a new and still more urgent consideration was now added – that of frightening the Finnish bourgeoisie with the spectre of a Bashkir invasion.

But our warnings carried less weight than the swift successes of Yudenich. He took Luga on the thirteenth of October, Krasnoye Syelo and Gatchina on the sixteenth, directing his blow at Petrograd in such a way that he could cut off the railway line connecting Petrograd and Moscow. On the tenth day of his offensive Yudenich advanced as far as Tsarskoye Syelo. His scouts on horseback could see the gilded dome of St Isaac's cathedral from the hill.

The Finnish radio, forestalling the event, reported the occupation of Petrograd by Yudenich's troops. The ambassadors of the Allies in Helsingfors reported this officially to their governments. All through Europe and the rest of the world the news spread that the Red Petrograd had fallen. A Swedish newspaper wrote of 'a world-week of Petrograd fever'. The ruling circles in Finland were especially excited. The government, as well as the military, was advocating intervention. No one wanted to let the quarry slip out of his hands. As was to be expected, the Finnish Social Democracy promised to observe 'neutrality'. A White historian writes: 'The question of intervention was now discussed only from the financial side.' All that remained was to ratify the guarantee of fifty million francs – that was the price of the blood of Petrograd in the Allied markets.

The question of Estonia was no less acute. I wrote to Lenin on 17 October: 'If we save Petrograd, as I hope, we shall be in a position to make an end of Yudenich. The difficulty will be his right of asylum in Estonia. Estonia must close its frontiers to him. In case he does enter we must retain the right of invading Estonia on Yudenich's heels.' This proposal was accepted after our army had begun to drive Yudenich, but it took some time to start the drive.

In Petrograd I found the leaders in a state of utmost demoralization. Everything was slipping. The troops were rolling back and breaking up into separate units. The commanding officers looked to the communists, the communists to Zinoviev, and Zinoviev was the very centre of utter confusion. Svyerdlov said to me: 'Zinoviev is panic itself.' And Svyerdlov knew men. In favourable periods, when, in Lenin's phrase, 'there was nothing to fear', Zinoviev climbed easily to the seventh heaven. But when things took a bad turn, he usually stretched himself out on a sofa – literally, not metaphorically – and sighed. Since 1917 I had had many opportunities to convince myself that Zinoviev had no intermediate moods; it was either the seventh heaven or the sofa. This time I found him on the sofa. And yet there were brave men about him – Lashevich, for example – but even their hands hung limp. Everyone felt it, and it had its effect everywhere. I ordered an automobile from a military garage by telephone from the Smolny. It did not come on time, and in the voice of the garage man in charge I sensed that apathy, hopelessless, and submission to fate which had infected even the lower ranks of the administrative staff. Exceptional measures were necessary; the enemy was at the very gates. As usual in such straits I turned to my train force – men who could be depended on under any circumstances. They checked up, put on pressure, established connections, removed those who were unfit, and filled in the gaps. From the official apparatus, which had become completely demoralized, I descended two or three floors to the district organizations of the party, the mills, the factories and the barracks.

Everyone expected an early surrender of the city to the Whites, and so people were afraid of becoming too conspicuous. But as soon as the masses began to feel that Petrograd was not to be surrendered, and if necessary would be defended from within, in the streets and squares, the spirit changed at once. The more courageous and self-sacrificing lifted up their heads. Detachments of men and women, with trenching-tools on their shoulders, filed out of the mills and factories. The workers of Petrograd looked badly then; their faces were grey from under-nourishment; their clothes were in tatters; their shoes, sometimes not even mates, were gaping with holes.

'We will not give up Petrograd, comrades!'

'No.' The eyes of the women burned with especial fervour. Mothers, wives, daughters, were loath to abandon their dingy but warm nests. 'No, we won't give it up,' the high-pitched voices of the women cried in answer, and they grasped their spades like rifles. Not a few of them actually armed themselves with rifles or took their places at the machine-guns. The whole city was divided into sections, controlled by staffs of workers. The more important points were surrounded by barbed wire. A number of positions were chosen for artillery, with a firing-range marked off in advance. About sixty guns were placed behind cover on the open squares and at the more important street-crossings. Canals, gardens, walls, fences and houses were fortified. Trenches were dug in the suburbs and along the Neva. The whole southern part of the city was transformed into a fortress. Barricades were raised on many of the streets and squares. A new spirit was breathing from the workers' districts to the barracks, the rear units, and even to the army in the field.

Yudenich was only from ten to fifteen versts away from Petrograd, on the same Pulkovo heights where I had gone two years before, when the revolution which had just assumed power was fighting for its life against the troops of Kerensky and Krasnov. Once more the fate of Petrograd was hanging by a thread, and we had to break the inertia of retreat, instantly and at any cost.

On 18 October I issued an order 'not to send in false reports of hard fights when the actual truth was bitter panic. Lies will be punished as treason. Military work admits errors, but not lies, deception and self-deception.' As usual, in moments of stress I thought it necessary to bare the grim truth before the army and the country, and I made public the senseless retreat that took place that very day.

A company of the rifle regiment took alarm because of an enemy threat against its flank. The regimental commander gave the order to withdraw. The regiment ran at a trot for eight or ten versts and reached Alexandrovka. A check-up disclosed that the troops on the flank belonged to one of our own units ... But the stampeding regiment was not so bad, after all. With its self-confidence restored, it turned back at once, and at a rapid pace or a trot, sweating despite the cold, covered eight versts in an hour, dislodged the enemy, who were few in number, and recovered its old position with only a small loss.

In this brief episode, for the one and only time during the entire war, I had to play the role of a regimental commander. When the retreating lines came up against the division headquarters at Alexandrovka, I mounted the first horse I could lay my hands on and turned the lines back. For the first few minutes there was nothing but confusion. Not all of them understood what was happening, and some of them continued to retreat. But I chased one soldier after another, on horseback, and made them all turn back. Only then did I notice that my orderly Kozlov, a Muscovite peasant, and an old soldier himself, was racing at my heels. He was beside himself with excitement. Brandishing a revolver, he ran wildly along the line, repeating my appeals and yelling for all he was worth: 'Courage, boys, Comrade Trotsky is leading you.' The men were now advancing at the pace at which they had been retreating before. Not one of them remained behind. After two versts, the bullets began their sweetish, nauseating whistling, and the first wounded began to drop. The regimental commander changed beyond recognition. He appeared at the most dangerous points, and before the regiment had recovered the positions it had previously abandoned he was wounded in both legs. I returned to the staff headquarters on a truck. On the way we picked up the wounded. The impetus had been given, and with my whole being I felt that we would save Petrograd.

At this point I should like to dwell for a moment on a question the reader must already have asked himself several times: When a man is in charge of a whole army, has he the right to expose himself to the danger of actual fighting? My answer is that there are no absolute rules of conduct, either in peace or in war. Everything depends on circumstances. Officers who accompanied me in my trips along the front frequently would remark: 'In the old days even divisional commanders never poked their noses into places like these.' The bourgeois journalists wrote of this as a 'pursuit of self-advertisement', and in this way translated into their familiar language something that was beyond their ken. In point of fact the conditions under which the Red army was created, its personal composition, and the very nature of the civil war demanded exactly this sort of behaviour. Everything was built up anew – discipline, fighting tradition, and military authority. Just as it was not in our power, especially in the first period, to supply the army with all its needs from a single centre and according to plan, just so were we unable by means of circulars or semi-anonymous appeals to inspire this army, got together under fire, with revolutionary enthusiasm. It was necessary to win authority in the eyes of the soldiers, so that next day one could justify to them the stern demands of the higher command. Where tradition is lacking, a striking example is essential. Personal risk was the unavoidable hazard on the road to victory.

The commanding staff, which had been drawn into a series of failures, needed to be shaken up, refreshed and renewed. Greater changes had to be made among commissaries. All the units were strengthened from the inside by adding communists, and fresh units were also beginning to arrive. The military schools were sent to the front posts. In two or three days the supply service, which had gone completely slack, was tightened up. The rank-

and-file of the Red army got some heartier food, changed their linen and boots, listened to a speech or two, pulled themselves together, and became quite different men.

21 October was a critical day. Our troops had retired to the Pulkovo heights. Further retreat from there would have meant transferring the struggle to the streets of the city. Until then the Whites had advanced without meeting serious opposition. On the twenty-first our army took a firm stand on the Pulkovo line and offered vigorous resistance. The advance of the enemy was checked. On the twenty-second, the Red army assumed the offensive; Yudenich had time to bring up reserves and strengthen his line; the fighting grew very bitter, but by the evening of the twenty-third we had retaken Tsarskoye Syelo and Pavlovsk. In the meantime the neighbouring Fifteenth army was beginning to press in from the south, threatening the White rear and right flank. Then came the turning-point. Our units, caught unawares by the offensive, and embittered by their reverses, now began to vie with each other in self-sacrifice and acts of heroism. They suffered many losses. The White high command stated that our losses were greater than theirs. It is quite possible; they had had more experience and had more arms. But there was more self-sacrifice on our side. Young workers and peasants, military students from Moscow and Petrograd, were utterly reckless with their lives. They advanced against machine-gun fire and attacked tanks with revolvers in their hands. The general staff of the Whites wrote of the 'heroic frenzy' of the Reds.

In the preceding days hardly any prisoners had been taken; White deserters were rare. Now the number of deserters and prisoners suddenly increased. On 24 October, when I realized the bitterness of the struggle, I issued an order: 'Woe to the unworthy soldier who raises his knife over a defenceless prisoner or deserter!'

Our advance continued. The Estonians and Finns were no longer thinking of intervention. The routed Whites were rolled back in two weeks to the Estonian frontier, completely demoralized. As they crossed the boundary-line the Estonian government disarmed them. In London and Paris no one gave them a thought. What only yesterday had been the 'north-western army' of the Entente was now perishing of cold and starvation. Fourteen thousand Whites were stricken with typhus and poured into the camp hospitals. That was the end of the 'world-week of Petrograd fever'.

The White leaders later complained loudly against Admiral Cowan, who, they said, had broken his promise to lend them sufficient support from the Gulf of Finland. These complaints are, to say the least, exaggerated. Three of our torpedo-boats were sunk by mines during a night expedition, carrying down with them 550 young seamen. The British admiral should at least be given credit for this. The order to the army and navy mourning the grave loss said that day:

Red warriors! On all the fronts you meet the hostile plots of the English. The counter-revolutionary troops shoot you with English guns. In the depots of Shenkursk and Onega, on the southern and western fronts, you find supplies of English manufacture. The prisoners you have captured are dressed in uniforms made in England. The women and children of Archangel and Astrakhan are maimed and killed by English airmen with the aid of English explosives. English ships bomb our shores ...

But, even today, when we are engaged in a bitter fight with Yudenich, the hireling of England, I demand that you never forget that there are two Englands. Besides the England of profits, of violence, bribery and blood-thirstiness, there is the England of labour, of spiritual power, of high ideals of international solidarity. It is the base and dishonest England of the stock-exchange manipulators that is fighting us. The England of labour and the people is with us.

(The order to the army and navy, 24 October 1919, No. 159.)

For us, the tasks of education in socialism were closely integrated with those of fighting. Ideas that enter the mind under fire remain there securely and forever.

In Shakespeare tragedy alternates with comedy, for the same reason that in life the sublime is mingled with the petty and vulgar. Zinoviev, who had by that time managed to rise from his sofa and to climb to the second or third heaven, handed me the following document on behalf of the Communist International:

The saving of the Red Petrograd meant an invaluable service to the world proletariat, and consequently to the Communist International. To you, dear Comrade Trotsky, belongs of course the first place in the struggle for Petrograd. In the name of the Executive Committee of the Communist International, I hand over to you the banners, with the request that you give them to the most deserving units of the glorious Red Army under your leadership. Chairman of the Executive Committee of the Communist International – G. ZINOVIEV.

I received documents like this from the Petrograd Soviet, from trades-unions and various other organizations. I handed the banners over to the regiments and the documents were put away by my secretaries in the archives, where they stayed until, some time later, they were removed when Zinoviev began to sing new songs and in quite a different key.

Today it is difficult to describe, or even to recall, the outburst of joy over the victory before Petrograd, rejoicing that was all the greater because we had just begun to win decisive successes on the southern front as well. The revolution was again holding its head high. In Lenin's eyes our victory over Yudenich took on even greater importance, because towards the middle of October he had thought it quite out of the question. The Polit-bureau decided to confer on me the order of the Red Flag for the defence of Petrograd. This placed me in a very difficult position. I had been rather hesitant about introducing the revolutionary order because it was not very long since we had abolished the orders of the old régime. In introducing the order of the Red Flag, I hoped that it might be an added stimulus for those for whom the consciousness of revolutionary duty was not enough. Lenin supported me in this. The decoration became established, and it was awarded, at least in those days, for actual service under fire. And now it was being given to me. I could not decline it without disparaging the mark of distinction that I had so often given to others. There was nothing for me but to yield to the convention.

Apropos of this, I remember an episode that I saw in its proper light only some time later. At the close of the meeting of the Politbureau, Kamenev, considerably embarrassed, introduced a proposal to award the decoration to Stalin. 'For what?' Kalinin inquired, sincerely indignant. 'I can't understand why it should be awarded to Stalin.' They pacified him with a jest, and the proposal was accepted. After the meeting Bukharin pounced on Kalinin. 'Can't you understand? This is Lenin's idea. Stalin can't live unless he has what someone else has. He will never forgive it.' I understood Lenin, and inwardly agreed with him.

The award of the decoration was very impressively staged in the Grand Opera theatre, where I made a report on the military situation before the joint session of the major Soviet institutions. When, towards the end, the chairman named Stalin, I tried to applaud. Two or three hesitant hand-claps followed mine. A sort of cold bewilderment crept through the hall; it was especially noticeable after the ovations that had gone before. Stalin himself was wisely absent.

I was infinitely more pleased with the award of the decoration of the Red Flag to my train as a whole. 'In the heroic fight of the Seventh army from 17 October to 3 November', I stated in the order of 4 November, 'the members of our train played a deserving part. Comrades Kliger, Ivanov, and Zastar fell in battle. Comrades Prede, Draudin, Purin, Chernyavtzev, Kuprievich, and Tesnek were wounded. Comrades Adamson, Purin, and Kiselis are suffering from shell-shock. I do not mention other names, because, if I did, everyone would be mentioned. In the striking change that came over the front the members of our train played a most important part.'

Some months later Lenin asked me by telephone: 'Have you read Kirdetzov's book?' The name suggested nothing to me. 'He is a White, an enemy. He writes about Yudenich's advance on Petrograd.' I must add here that Lenin generally watched the White publications more closely than I. A day later he asked me again: 'Have you read it?'

'No.'

'Would you like me to send it over to you?' But I decided that I had the book, since Lenin and I received the same new publications from Berlin. 'You must read the last chapter. It is an appreciation of the enemy. It says something about you, too.' But somehow I didn't find opportunity to read the book. Strangely enough, I came across it in Constantinople, and remembered Lenin's insistence that I read the last chapter. Here is the appreciation from the enemy as given by one of Yudenich's ministers:

On 16 October Trotsky arrived in haste at the Petrograd front, and the confusion of the Red Staff gave away before his burning energy. A few hours before the fall of Gatchina, he was still trying to check the advance of the Whites; but when he saw how impossible that was he left the town in a hurry to organize the defence of Tsarskoye Syelo. The heavy reserves had not yet come up, but he quickly concentrated all the Petrograd military students, mobilized the entire male population of Petrograd, and with machine-guns [? !] drove all the Red army units back to their positions, and by means of his energetic measures established defences on all the approaches to Petrograd . . .

Trotsky succeeded in organizing detachments of worker-communists, men who were strong in spirit, in Petrograd itself, and threw them into the thick of the fight. According to the evidence of Yudenich's staff, these detachments but not [?] the Red army units, together with the marine battalions and military students, fought like lions. They attacked the tanks with their bayonets, and, although they were mowed down in rows by the devastating fire of the steel monsters, they continued to defend their positions.

We never drove the men of the Red army with machine-guns. But we did save Petrograd.

36

The Military Opposition

The foundation for the successful upbuilding of the Red army was the proper relationship between the proletariat and the peasantry throughout the country. Later, in 1923, a stupid legend was invented to the effect that I 'underestimated' the peasantry. As a matter of fact, from 1918 to 1921 I had to deal with the problems of rural life more closely and directly than anyone else, because the army was being raised chiefly from among the peasants, and carried on its work in constant touch with peasant life. The question is too large to be discussed here at length. So I shall confine myself to two or three sufficiently outstanding examples.

On 22 March 1919 I demanded over the direct wire that the Central Committee

decide the question of an official inquiry by the Central Executive Committee in the Volga region, and of the appointment of an authoritative commission from the Central Committee and the Central Executive Committee. The commission's job should be to strengthen the faith of the Volga peasantry in the central Soviet power, to correct the most conspicuous local illegalities, and punish the guilty representatives of the Soviet power; to gather complaints and materials to be used as the basis of demonstrative decrees in favour of the 'middle' peasant.

It is interesting to note that I held this conversation over the direct wire with no one other than Stalin; and it was to him that I explained the importance of the question of the middle peasant. In the same year Kalinin, at my instigation, was elected chairman of the Central Executive Committee as a man who was close to the middle peasants and familiar with their peculiar needs. But more important is the fact that as early as February 1920, influenced by my own observation of the lives of the Ural peasants, I insistently advocated a change in the new economic policy. In the Central Committee I mustered only four votes against an opposing eleven. At that time Lenin was irreconcilably against abolishing the food levy. Of course Stalin voted against me. The change to the new economic policy went into effect just a year later, unanimously, but to the tune of the rumblings of the Kronstadt rebellion and in an atmosphere of threatening moods in the entire army.

Most of the questions of principle and the difficulties in connection with the constructive work of the Soviets during the years that followed were encountered first of all in the military sphere, and in most concentrated form at that. As a rule solutions had to be found on the spur of the moment, and mistakes were followed by immediate retribution. Whatever opposition there might be was tested in action, right on the spot. Hence, by and large, the inner logic of the development of the Red army, and the absence of wild leaps from one system to another. If we had had more time for discussion, we should probably have made a great many more mistakes.

And yet there was fighting within the party, often very bitter. Things could not have been otherwise. The work was too new, the difficulties much too great. The old army was still breaking up and sowing hatred of war over the country at the time when we were obliged to raise new regiments. The Tsar's officers were being driven out of the old army, sometimes quite ruthlessly; we had to enrol these very officers as instructors for the Red army. Committees came into existence in the old regiments as the very embodiment of the revolution, at least during its first period. In the new regiments the committee system was not to be tolerated; it stood for disintegration. The curses against the old discipline were still ringing in our ears when we began to introduce the new. In a short time we had to go from voluntary enlistment to conscription, from detachments of irregulars to a proper military organization. We had continuously to fight the methods of the irregulars – a fight that demanded the utmost persistence and unwillingness to compromise, sometimes even the sternest measures. The chaos of irregular warfare expressed the peasant element that lay beneath the revolution, whereas the struggle against it was also a struggle in favour of the proletarian state organization as opposed to the elemental, petty-bourgeois anarchy that was undermining it. But the methods and ways of the irregular fighting found an echo in the ranks of the party as well.

On the military question the opposition assumed a more or less definite form during the first months of the organizing of the Red army. Its fundamental ideas found expression in a defence of the electoral method and in protest against the enlistment of experts, the introduction of military discipline, the centralizing of the army, and so on. The opposition tried to find some general theoretical formula for their stand. They insisted that a centralized army was characteristic of a capitalist state; revolution had to blot out not only positional war, but a centralized army as well. The very essence of revolution was its ability to move about, to deliver swift attacks, and to carry out manoeuvres; its fighting force was embodied in a small, independent detachment made up of various arms; it was not bound to a base; in its operations it relied wholly on the support of a sympathetic populace; it could emerge freely in the enemy's rear, etc. In short the tactics of a *small war* were proclaimed the tactics of revolution.

This was all very abstract and was really nothing but an idealization of our weakness. The serious experience of the civil war very soon disproved these prejudices. The superiority of central organization and strategy over local improvisations, military separatism and federalism, revealed itself only too soon and too clearly in the experiences of the struggle.

The Red army had in its service thousands, and, later on, tens of thousands of old officers. In their own words many of them only two years before had thought of moderate liberals as extreme revolutionaries, while the Bolsheviks, in their eyes, belonged to the fourth dimension. 'We should indeed have a low opinion of ourselves and of our party,' I wrote against the opposition at that time, 'of the moral force of our idea, of the drawing power of our revolutionary morale, if we thought ourselves incapable of winning over thousands and thousands of "specialists", including military ones.' We certainly achieved our end, but not without difficulty and friction.

The communists adapted themselves to the military work with some difficulty. Here selection and training were essential. Even when we were before Kazan in August 1918, I telegraphed Lenin: 'Only communists who know how to obey should be sent here, the ones who are ready to suffer hardships and are prepared to die. Feather-weight agitators are not wanted here.' A year later in the Ukraine, where anarchy was rampant even in the party ranks, I wrote in an order to the Fourteenth army:

I give warning that every communist delegated by the party to join the ranks of the army becomes thereby a part of the Red army and has the same rights and duties as every other soldier of the Red army. Communists found guilty of misdemeanours and crimes against the revolutionary military duty will be doubly punished, for offences that may be condoned in a benighted, uneducated man cannot be condoned in a member of the party that leads the working classes of the world.

Obviously, much friction arose on this score, and there was no dearth of malcontents.

The military oppositionists included, for example, Pyatakov, the present director of the State Bank. He usually joined every opposition only to wind up as a government official. Three or four years ago, when Pyatakov belonged to the same group as I did, I prophesied in jest that in the event of a Bonapartist *coup d'état*, Payatkov would go to the office the next day with his brief-case. Now I can add more earnestly that if this fails to come about, it will be only through lack of a Bonapartist *coup d'état*, and not through any fault of Pyatakov's. In the Ukraine he enjoyed considerable influence, not by accident but because he is a fairly well-educated Marxist, especially in the realm of economics, and is undoubtedly a good administrator with a reserve of will. In the early years Pyatakov showed revolutionary energy, but it later changed to a bureaucratic conservatism. In fighting his semi-anarchist views, I resorted to giving him an important post from the very outset, so that he would have to change from words to deeds. This method is not new, but often is very efficacious. His administrative sense soon prompted him to apply the very methods against which he had been waging his war of words. Such changes were common.

All the best elements of the military opposition were soon

drawn into the work. At the same time I offered the most implacable an opportunity to organize a few regiments according to their own principles, promising for my part to give them all the necessary resources. Only one district group on the Volga accepted the challenge, and organized a regiment that was in no way different from the rest. The Red army was winning on all the fronts and the opposition eventually melted away.

Tsaritsin, where the military workers were grouped around Voroshilov, held a special place in the Red army and in the military opposition. There revolutionary detachments were headed chiefly by former non-commissioned officers from among the peasants of the northern Caucasus. The deep antagonism between the Cossacks and the peasants of the southern steppes imparted a vicious ferocity to the civil war in that region; it penetrated far into the villages and led to the wholesale extermination of entire families. This was a peasant war with its roots deep in local soil, and, in its mouzhik ferocity, it far surpassed the revolutionary struggle in all other parts of the country. This war brought forward a good many stalwart irregulars who excelled in local skirmishing but usually failed when they had to undertake military tasks of larger scope.

The life of Voroshilov illustrates the career of a worker-revolutionist, with its leadership in strikes, underground work, imprisonment, and exile. Like many of the other rulers of today Voroshilov was merely a national revolutionary democrat from among the workers, nothing more; this was most apparent in the imperialist Great War, and later on in the February revolution. In the official biographies of Voroshilov the years 1914 to 1917 are a great blank, as is true of most of the present leaders. The secret of this blank is that during the war most of these men were patriots, and discontinued their revolutionary work. In the February revolution Voroshilov, like Stalin, supported the government of Guchkov and Miliukoff from the left. They were extreme revolutionary democrats, but in no sense internationalists. As a rule the Bolsheviks who were patriots during the war were democrats after the February revolution, and are today followers of Stalin's national socialism. Voroshilov is no exception.

Although he was one of the Lugansk workers, from their privileged top section, in his habits and tastes Voroshilov always resembled a small proprietor more than he did a proletarian. After the October revolution he became the natural centre of the opposition of non-commissioned officers and irregulars against a centralized military organization demanding military knowledge and a wider outlook. Such was the origin of the Tsaritsin opposition.

In Voroshilov's circles 'specialists', graduates of the military academy, high staffs, and Moscow were mentioned with hatred. But since the chiefs of the irregulars had no military knowledge of their own, everyone had close at hand his own 'specialist' who, being naturally of the second order, held tenaciously to his post against the more capable and better informed. The attitude of the Tsaritsin military heads towards the command of the southern military front scarcely differed from their attitude towards the Whites. Their contact with the Moscow centre did not go beyond a constant demand for munitions. Our resources were very slight; everything produced by the factories was immediately sent to the armies. Not one of them, however, absorbed as many rifles or cartridges as the Tsaritsin army. Whenever its demands were refused, Tsaritsin would raise the cry of 'treason by the Moscow specialists'. It kept a special representative in Moscow, a sailor named Zhivodyor, to extort supplies for its army. When we tightened up on the discipline, Zhivodyor turned bandit. I believe that later he was caught and shot.

Stalin stayed in Tsaritsin for a few months, shaping his intrigue against me with the aid of the home-bred opposition of Voroshilov and his closest associates; even then it was assuming a very prominent place in his activities. He so conducted himself, however, as to be able to withdraw at any moment.

Every day I would receive from the high command or the front commands such complaints against Tsaritsin as: it is impossible to get executions of an order, it is impossible to find out what is going on there, it is even impossible to get an answer to an inquiry. Lenin watched the conflict develop with alarm. He knew Stalin better than I did, and obviously suspected that the stubbornness of Tsaritsin was being secretly staged by Stalin. The situation became intolerable; I decided to enforce order in Tsaritsin. After a new clash between the high command and Tsaritsin I obtained Stalin's recall. It was done through the medium of Svyerdlov, who went in a special train to bring Stalin back. Lenin was anxious to reduce the conflict to its minimum, and in this he of course was right. I, for my part, scarcely ever gave Stalin a thought. In 1917 he flashed before me as a barely perceptible shadow. In the heat of the fight I usually forgot his existence. I thought of the Tsaritsin army because I needed a dependable left flank on the southern front, and I set out for Tsaritsin to arrange it at any cost. On my way there I met Svyerdlov. He inquired cautiously about my intentions, and then suggested that I have a talk with Stalin, who, as it happened, was returning in the same car with Svyerdlov.

' 'Do you really wish to dismiss them all?' Stalin asked me, in a tone of exaggerated humility. 'They are fine boys!'

'Those fine boys will ruin the revolution, which can't wait for them to grow out of their adolescence,' I answered him. 'All I want is to draw Tsaritsin into Soviet Russia.'

A few hours later I met Voroshilov. The staff was in a state of alarm. The rumour was that Trotsky was coming with a big broom and his score of Tsarist generals to replace the irregular chiefs, who, I must add, had all hurriedly renamed themselves as commanders of regiments, brigades, and divisions by the time I arrived there. I put the question to Voroshilov: how did he regard the orders from the front and the high command? He opened his heart to me: Tsaritsin thought it necessary to execute only such orders as it considered right. That was too much. I retorted that if he did not undertake to carry out the orders and military tasks exactly and absolutely as they were given to him, I would immediately send him under convoy to Moscow for committal before the revolutionary tribunal. I dismissed no one, satisfied with the formal assurance of obedience. Most of the communists of the Tsaritsin army supported me with utter sincerity, not merely out of fear. I visited all the units and encouraged the irregulars, among whom there were many excellent soldiers who needed only proper leadership. With this, I returned to Moscow.

In all this affair I had no feeling of personal prejudice or ill will. I think I can rightly say that in all my political activity personal considerations have never played a part. But in the great struggle that we were carrying on, the stakes were too big to permit me to consider side issues. As a result I frequently trod on the toes of personal prejudice, friendly favouritism, or vanity. Stalin carefully picked up the men whose toes had been trodden on; he had the time and the personal interest to do it. From that time on the Tsaritsin ruling circle became one of his chief weapons. As soon as Lenin fell ill Stalin with the help of his allies had Tsaritsin renamed Stalingrad. The mass of the people had not the ghost of an idea what the name meant. And if Voroshilov is today a member of the Politbureau, the only reason – I see no other – is that in 1918 I forced his submission by the threat of sending him under convoy to Moscow.

I feel that it will be interesting to illustrate the chapter on our military work, or rather on the struggle connected with it within the party, by a few excerpts from the party correspondence of that time, hitherto unpublished anywhere. On 4 October 1918 I said to Lenin and Svyerdlov over a direct wire from Tambov:

I insist categorically on Stalin's recall. The Tsaritsin front is in a bad way, despite the abundance of troops. I leave him (Voroshilov) as commander of the Tenth (Tsaritsin) army on condition of obedience to the commander of the southern front. Until now the men there have not even sent reports of operations to Kozlov. I made them undertake to send in reports of operations and reconnoitring twice a day. If this is not done tomorrow, I will commit Voroshilov to trial and announce this in an order to the army. There is only a short time left for an offensive before the roads become impassable either by foot or by horse. We have no time for diplomatic negotiations.

Stalin was recalled. Lenin understood that I was guided only by military considerations. At the same time he was naturally disturbed by the disagreement and tried to smooth out our relations. On 23 October he wrote to me at Balashov:

Today Stalin returned bringing with him news of three big victories by our troops before Tsaritsin. [The 'victories' actually had merely episodic importance. – L. T.] Stalin has persuaded Voroshilov and Minin, whom he considers very valuable and quite irreplaceable workers not to leave, and to obey in full the orders of the centre. The only cause of their dissatisfaction, according to him, is the extreme delay or even failure in sending them shells and cartridges, for lack of which the two hundred thousand strong of the Caucasian army, which is in fine fettle, are also perishing. [This army of irregulars crumbled away at a single blow shortly after, and revealed its complete incompetence. – L. T.] Stalin is anxious to work on the southern front . . . He hopes that in actual work he will be able to demonstrate the correctness of his view . . . In informing you, Lev Davydovich, of all these statements of Stalin's, I request that you consider them and reply; first, as to your willingness to talk the matter over with Stalin personally – for this he agrees to visit you – and, second, if you think it possible to remove the friction by certain concrete terms and to arrange for the joint work which Stalin so much desires. As for me I think it necessary to make every effort to arrange to work in conjunction with Stalin. LENIN.

I replied stating my complete accord, and Stalin was appointed a member of the Military-Revolutionary Council of the southern front. Alas, the compromise brought no results. In Tsaritsin things did not improve a bit. On 14 December I telegraphed Lenin from Kursk: 'It is impossible to leave Voroshilov at his post after he has nullified all attempts at compromise. It is necessary to send a new Military-Revolutionary Council with a new commander to Tsaritsin and to transfer Voroshilov to the Ukraine.'

This proposal was accepted without opposition. But matters in the Ukraine did not improve either. Even as it was the anarchy that reigned there had made regular military work very difficult, and now Voroshilov's opposition, with Stalin again behind him, made the work quite impossible.

On 10 January 1919 I transmitted the following message to Svyerdlov, then chairman of the Central Executive Committee, from the station of Gryazi: 'I must categorically state that the Tsaritsin policy, which led to the complete disintegration of the Tsaritsin army, cannot be tolerated in the Ukraine. . . The line pursued by Stalin, Voroshilov and Co. means the ruin of the entire enterprise. TROTSKY.'

Lenin and Svyerdlov, who were watching the work of the Tsaritsin group from a distance, were still trying to achieve a compromise. Unfortunately I haven't their telegram, but on 11 January I answered Lenin: 'A compromise is of course necessary, but not one that is rotten. In point of actual fact all the Tsaritsin men are gathered now at Kharkoff... I consider Stalin's patronage of the Tsaritsin policy a most dangerous ulcer, worse than any treason or betrayal by military specialists ... TROTSKY.'

'*A compromise is necessary, but not one that is rotten.*' Four years later Lenin returned this phrase, almost word for word, apropos of the same Stalin. It was before the Twelfth Party Congress. Lenin was getting ready to rout the Stalin group, and opened his attack on the line of the question of nationality. When I suggested a compromise, Lenin answered: 'Stalin will make a rotten compromise and then he will deceive us.'

In a letter to the Central Committee in March 1919 I replied to Zinoviev, who was flirting equivocally with the military opposition:

I cannot engage in investigations of individual psychology to determine which group of the military opposition Voroshilov should be included in, but I will say that the only thing I can blame myself for, in regard to him, is my protracted attempt, extending over two or three months, to proceed by means of negotiations, persuasions, and personal combinations, when the interests of the work demanded instead a firm, administrative decision. For, after all, the problem of the Tenth army was not one of changing Voroshilov's views, but of securing military success in the shortest possible time.

On 30 May an insistent demand reached Lenin from Kharkoff to form a separate Ukrainian group of armies under Voroshilov's command. Lenin communicated this to me at the station of Kantemirovka, over the direct wire. On 1 June I replied to him:

The insistent demands of certain Ukrainians to merge the Second, Eighth and Thirteenth armies under Voroshilov are utterly indefensible. What we need is not an operative unity in the Donyetzk district but a general unity against Denikin ... The idea of a military and food dictatorship by Voroshilov (in the Ukraine) is the result of

he Donyetzk separatism directed against Kiev (*i.e.*, against the
Ukrainian government) and the southern front. I have no doubt that
the realization of this plan would only increase the chaos and would
utterly kill the direction of operations. Please demand that Voroshilov
and Mezhlauk carry out the real task that has been given them.
TROTSKY.

On 1 June Lenin telegraphed Voroshilov: 'It is absolutely
imperative that all agitation be stopped immediately, and that
all work be placed on a military basis; that no more time be
wasted on all the fine projects about separate groups and similar
attempts at restoring the Ukrainian front. LENIN.'

Having learned from experience how difficult it was to manage
the undisciplined separatists, Lenin called a meeting of the
Politbureau the same day and got the following decision adopted;
it was sent immediately to Voroshilov and to all interested persons:

The Politbureau of the Central Committee met on 1 June and in
complete agreement with Trotsky rejected decisively the Ukrainian
plan to create a separate Donyetzk unity. We demand that Voroshilov
and Mezhlauk carry out their immediate work ... or the day after
tomorrow Trotsky will call you to Izyum and make his decisions more
detailed ... By the instruction of the Bureau of the Central Committee. LENIN.

Next day the Central Committee took up the question of the
army commander, Voroshilov, who had arbitrarily taken for the
use of his army the greater part of the military supplies captured
from the enemy. The Central Committee resolved: 'To instruct
Comrade Rakovsky to telegraph this to Comrade Trotsky at
Izyum and ask him to take the most energetic measures to
transfer these supplies for the disposal of the Military-
Revolutionary Council of the Republic.' On the same day Lenin
informed me by direct wire: 'Dybenko and Voroshilov making
free with military property. Complete chaos, no serious help
given the Donyetsk base. LENIN.' In other words, what was
going on in the Ukraine was simply a repetition of the practices
against which I had fought in Tsaritsin.

It is no wonder that my military work created so many enemies
for me. I did not look to the side; I elbowed away those who in-

terfered with military success, or in the haste of the work trod on the toes of the unheeding and was too busy even to apologize. Some people remember such things. The dissatisfied and those whose feelings had been hurt found their way to Stalin or Zinoviev, for these two also nourished hurts. Every reverse at the front led the malcontents to increase their pressure on Lenin. Behind the scenes these machinations were even then being managed by Stalin. Memoranda were submitted criticizing our military policy, my patronage of the 'specialists', the harsh treatment of the communists and so on. Commanders who had been compelled to resign or frustrated Red 'marshals' sent in one report after another pointing out the precariousness of our strategy, the sabotage by the high command, and much else besides.

Lenin was too much absorbed in the general question of direction to make trips to the fronts or to enter into the everyday work of the military department. I stayed at the fronts most of the time, which facilitated the activities of the Moscow whisperers. Their insistent criticisms could not but occasionally disturb Lenin. By the time I paid my visit to Moscow he had accumulated many doubts and questions. But after half an hour's talk with me our mutual understanding and complete solidarity were again restored. During our reverses in the East, when Kolchak was approaching the Volga, at one of the meetings of the Soviet of Commissaries to which I had come straight from the train, Lenin wrote me a note: 'What if we fire all the specialists and appoint Lashevich as commader-in-chief?' Lashevich was an old Bolshevik who had earned his promotion to the rank of a sergeant in the 'German' war. I replied on the same note: 'Child's play!' Lenin looked slyly at me from under his heavy brows, with a very expressive grimace that seemed to say: 'You are very harsh with me.' But, deep down, he really liked abrupt answers that left no room for doubt. We came together after the meeting. Lenin asked me various things about the front.

'You ask me' I said, 'if it would not be better to kick out all the old officers? But do you know how many of them we have in the army now?'

'No.'

'Not even approximately?'

'I don't know.'

'Not less than thirty thousand.'

'What?'

'Not less than thirty thousand. For every traitor there are a hundred who are dependable; for every one who deserts there are two or three who get killed. How are we to replace them all?'

A few days later Lenin was making a speech on the problems of constructing the socialist commonwealth. This is what he said: 'When Comrade Trotsky recently informed me that in our military department the officers are numbered in tens of thousands, I gained a concrete conception of what constitutes the secret of making proper use of our enemy . . . of how to build communism out of the bricks that the capitalists had gathered to use against us.'

At the party congress held about the same time Lenin in my absence – I was at the front – came forward with an impassioned defence of the military policy that I was carrying out, against the criticisms of the opposition. For this reason the minutes of the military section of the Eighth Congress of the party have never to this day been published.

At the front I was once visited by Menzhinsky. I had known him for a long time. In the years of the reaction he belonged to the group of the extreme left, or the Vperyodovists, as they were called from the name of their paper (Bogdanov, Lunacharsky, and others). Menzhinsky himself inclined to French Syndicalism. The Vperyodovists organized a Marxist school in Bologna for ten to fifteen Russian workers who had come over in the 'illegal' revolutionary fashion from Russia. This was in 1910. For about two weeks I gave a course there on the press, and also conducted conferences on questions of party tactics. There I met Menzhinsky, who had come from Paris. The impression he made on me could best be described by saying that he made none at all. He seemed more like the shadow of some other unrealized man, or rather like a poor sketch for an unfinished portrait. There are such people. Only now and then would an ingratiating smile or a secret play of the eyes betray his eagerness to emerge from his insignificance. I do not know what his conduct was during the October days or whether he had any at all. But after the seizure of power in the hustle-bustle of the period he was sent to the ministry of finance. He showed no active enterprise of his own, or rather only enough to reveal his incompetence. Later on Dzerzhinsky took him over. Dzerzhinsky was a man of tremendous will, passion, and high moral tension. His figure dominated the Che-Ka.* No one took any notice of Menzhinsky, so quietly toiling away over his papers. It was not until Dzerzhinsky, towards the end of his life, parted company with his deputy Unschlicht that he suggested appointing Menzhinsky to the vacant post, not being able to find anyone else. The proposal caused general surprise. 'But who else?' Dzerzhinsky said in excuse. 'There is no one.' But Stalin supported Menzhinsky. Stalin generally gave his support to people who existed politically only through the grace of the government apparatus. And so Menzhinsky became the true shadow of Stalin in the GPU. After Dzerzhinsky's death Menzhinsky became not only the head of the GPU. but a member of the Central Committee as well. Thus may the shadow of an unrealized man pass on the bureaucratic screen for that of a real one.

Ten years ago, however, Menzhinsky tried to find a different orbit for himself. He came to me in the train with a report about the special departments of the army. After he had finished the official visit he began to stammer and shuffle about, with that ingratiating smile of his that makes one feel alarmed and puzzled at the same time. He ended by putting a question to me: Was I aware that Stalin was conducting a very complicated intrigue against me?

'What!' I said in sheer bewilderment – I was so far from thoughts or apprehensions of anything of the sort.

'Yes, he is insinuating to Lenin and some others that you

---

*The 'Chrezvychaynaya Komissia' (the Extraordinary Commission), known in short as the Che-Ka, performed police and judicial duties, chiefly in connection with the defence of the revolution. The functions of the Che-Ka, after its reorganization, have been taken over by the GPU. (the State Political Board). – *Translator*.

are grouping men about you who are especially hostile to Lenin.'

'You must be mad, Menzhinsky. Please wake up. And as for me I don't even want to talk about it.' Menzhinsky left coughing, with shoulders hunched in embarrassment. After that very day I think he began to look for other fields.

After an hour or so of work I began to feel as if something were the matter with me. This man, with his indistinct speech, had disquieted me as surely as if I had swallowed a piece of glass with my food. I began to recall definite incidents, coupling them together, and there, before my eyes, Stalin emerged in a new light. Considerably later Krestinsky said to me of Stalin: 'He is a bad man, with yellow eyes.' It was this *moral yellowness* of his that flashed through my mind for the first time after Menzhinsky's call. When I went to Moscow later for a short visit, I went as usual first to Lenin. We talked about the front. Lenin liked concrete details of life, little facts and casual observations which conducted him, without any beating around the bush, to the heart of things. He couldn't bear approaching real life at a tangent. Leaping over all intermediate steps, he would put his own particular questions, and I would answer him, all the time admiring the skill with which he drilled through to the facts. We laughed. Lenin was usually in a gay mood. Nor would I describe myself as a gloomy person. In the end I told him about Menzhinsky's visit at the southern front: 'It is really possible that there is any truth in it?' I asked. I noticed that Lenin immediately became excited and that the blood rushed to his face. 'All trifles,' he kept repeating, although not in a very convincing way.

'I am interested in knowing only one thing,' I said. 'Could you possibly entertain, if only for a moment, such a horrible thought as that I was picking up men to oppose you?'

'Trifles,' replied Lenin, but this time with a firmness that instantly reassured me. The little cloud that had hung over us seemed to melt away, and our parting was unusually friendly. But I realized that Menzhinsky was not talking through his hat. If Lenin denied it without telling me everything, it was only because he wanted to avoid a conflict, a personal quarrel.

In this I was fully in accord with him.

But Stalin was obviously sowing trouble. Not until much later did I realize how systematically he had been doing that – almost nothing but that. For Stalin never did any serious work. 'Stalin's first quality is laziness,' Bukharin had once told me, 'and his second is an implacable jealousy of any one who knows more or does things better than he. He even tried to dig under Ilyich.'

37

Disagreements over War Strategy

In these pages I am not recounting the history of the Red army or of its battles. Both these themes, so inseparably bound up with the history of the revolution, and going far beyond the scope of an autobiography, will probably make the subject-matter for another book. But I cannot pass by the political-strategic disagreements that sprang up in the progress of the civil war. The fate of the revolution depended on the course of military operations. As time went on the Central Committee of the party was more and more absorbed in the problems of war, among them the questions of strategy. The chief commanding posts were occupied by military experts of the old school who lacked an understanding of social and political conditions. The experienced revolutionary politicians who comprised the Central Committee of the party lacked military knowledge. The strategic conceptions on a large scale were usually the result of collective work and, as always in such cases, gave rise to dissension and conflict.

There were four instances when the Central Committee was divided by strategic disagreements; in other words there were as many disagreements as there were main fronts. Here I can deal with these only very briefly, merely introducing the reader to the essence of the problems that presented themselves to the military leadership, and at the same time disposing, in passing, of the later inventions about me.

The first acute argument in the Central Committee took place in the summer of 1919, apropos of the situation on the eastern front. The commander-in-chief at the time was Vatzetis, of whom I spoke in the chapter on Sviyazhsk. I directed my efforts towards making Vatzetis sure of himself, of his rights and his authority. Without this command is impossible. Vatzetis's point of view was that after our great successes against Kolchak we abstain from rushing too far into the East, to the other side of the Urals. He wanted the eastern front to stay at the mountains for the winter. This would have enabled us to withdraw a few divisions from the East and switch them to the South, where Denikin was getting more dangerous. I supported this plan. But it met with rigorous opposition from Kamenev, the commander of the eastern front and a colonel of the general staff in the Tsar's army, as well as from two members of the Military Council, both old Bolsheviks – Smilga and Lashevich. They insisted that Kolchak was so far defeated that only a few men were necessary to follow him, and that the most important thing was that he be prevented from getting a breathing-spell, because in that case he would recover during the winter and we would have to start the eastern campaign all over again in the spring. The entire question hinged, therefore, on a true estimate of the condition of Kolchak's army and rear. Even then I considered the southern front far more important and dangerous than the eastern. Later on this was fully confirmed.

But it proved to be the command of the eastern front that was right in appraising Kolchak's army. The Central Committee adopted a decision against the high command, and therefore against me, because I supported Vatzetis on the ground that this strategic equation had several unknowns in it, but that one of the important and known quantities was the need of maintaining the still-new authority of the commander-in-chief. The decision of the Central Committee proved right. The eastern armies released some troops for the southern front and continued at the same time their advance on the heels of Kolchak into the heart of Siberia. This brought about a change in the high command. Vatzetis was dismissed and Kamenev put in his place.

The disagreement, in itself, was of a practical nature, and of course had not the slightest bearing on my relations with Lenin. But out of these small episodic disagreements the intrigue was weaving its nets. On 4 June 1919 Stalin, writing from the South, was trying to scare Lenin with the dangers of the military direction. 'The whole question now is', he wrote, 'whether the

Central Committee can find enough courage to draw the proper conclusions. Has the Central Committee sufficient character and firmness?' The meaning of the above lines is quite obvious. Their tone proves that Stalin had raised the question more than once, and just as many times had met with Lenin's opposition. I was ignorant of all this at the time. But I sensed some intrigue afoot. Being without time or desire to go into the matter, I offered my resignation to the Central Committee, so as to make an end of it. On 5 July the Central Committee replied as follows:

The Organizational and Political Bureau of the Central Committee, after considering the statement of Comrade Trotsky and discussing it in full, has unanimously come to the conclusion that it is quite unable to accept Comrade Trotsky's resignation and comply with his request. The Organizational and Political Bureau of the Central Committee will do everything in its power to make the work on the southern front, now the most difficult, dangerous, and significant, and which Comrade Trotsky himself has chosen, most convenient for him and profitable for the Republic. In his capacity as War Commissar and as Chairman of the Military-Revolutionary Council, Comrade Trotsky is fully able to act as a member of the Military-Revolutionary Council of the southern front in cooperation with the Commander of the front, whom he himself proposed and whom the Central Committee accordingly appointed. The Organizational and Political Bureau of the Central Committee give Comrade Trotsky full power to use all means for securing whatever he thinks will correct the line from the military point of view, and if he wishes, to expedite the party congress. LENIN, KAMENEV, KRESTINSKY, KALININ, SEREBRYAKOV, STALIN, STASOVA.

This decision carries Stalin's name among the others. Although he was carrying on an intrigue behind the scenes and accusing Lenin of lack of courage and firmness, Stalin did not have spirit enough to go into open opposition to the Central Committee. The southern front, as already mentioned, assumed the principal place in the civil war. The enemy's forces were composed of two independent parts: the Cossacks – particularly in the province of Kuban – and the volunteer White army, recruited from all over the country. The Cossacks were anxious to defend their borders from the onslaught of the workers and peasants. The volunteer army was anxious to capture Moscow. These two interests merged only so long as the volunteers formed a common front with the Kuban Cossacks in the northern Caucasus. But Denikin found it very difficult, and in fact impossible to bring the Cossacks out of their province of Kuban. Our high command approached the problem of the southern front as one of abstract strategy, ignoring its social basis. The Kuban province was the chief base of the volunteers. The high command, therefore, decided to deliver the decisive blow at that base from the Volga. It reasoned: Let Denikin rush on and try to reach Moscow at the head of his armies; in the meantime we will sweep away his Kuban base behind his back; then Denikin will be suspended in the air and we will catch him barehanded. That was the general strategic scheme. Had this not been a civil war, the plan would have been correct. But in its application to the real southern front, the plan proved to be merely a theoretical one, and greatly helped the enemy. Whereas Denikin had failed to persuade the Cossacks to a long marching campaign against the north, he now was helped by our striking at the Cossack nests from the south. After this the Cossacks could no longer defend themselves on their own land; we had ourselves bound up their fate with that of the volunteer army.

In spite of the careful preparation for our operations and the concentration of forces and technical means, we had no success. The Cossacks formed a formidable bulwark in Denikin's rear. They seemed to be rooted to their land, and held on with their claws and teeth. Our offensive put the whole Cossack population on their feet. We were expending our time and energy and managing only to drive all those capable of bearing arms directly into the White army. In the meantime Denikin swept the Ukraine, filled his ranks, advanced towards the north, took Kursk and Oryol, and was threatening Tula. The surrender of Tula would have been a catastrophe, because it would have involved the loss of the rifle- and cartridge-manufacturing plants.

The plan that I advocated from the outset was exactly the opposite. I demanded that with our first blow we cut the volunteers off from the Cossacks and, leaving the Cossacks to themselves, concentrate all our strength against the volunteers. The main direction of the blow, according to this plan, would be not from the Volga towards Kuban, but from Voronezh towards Kharkoff and the Donyetsk region. In this section of the country which divides the northern Caucasus from the Ukraine the peasants and workers were wholly on the side of the Red army. Advancing in this direction, the Red army would have been moving like a knife through butter. The Cossacks would have remained in their places to guard their borders from strangers, but we would not have touched them. The question of the Cossacks would have been an independent one, more political than military in nature. But it was necessary in the first place to separate this as strategy from the routing of the volunteer army of Denikin. In the end it was this plan that was eventually adopted, but not before Denikin had begun to threaten Tula, whose loss would have been more dangerous than that of Moscow. We wasted several months, suffered many needless losses and lived through some very menacing weeks.

In passing, I should like to point out that the strategic disagreements about the southern front were most closely related to the question of the appreciation or 'under-appreciation' of the peasantry. I built my plan on the relations of the peasants and workers on the one side and the Cossacks on the other, and on this line of argument I opposed my own plan to the academic scheme of the high command, which met with support from the majority of the Central Committee. If I had spent a thousandth part of the effort used to prove my 'under-appreciation' of the peasantry, I could have built up just as absurd an accusation, not only against Zinoviev, Stalin and the rest, but against Lenin as well, on the basis of our disagreement over the southern front.

The third conflict of a strategic nature arose in connection with Yudenich's offensive against Petrograd. This incident was described in an earlier chapter and need not be gone over again. I will add only that, influenced by the very serious situation in the South, from which the chief menace was directed, and influenced also by the reports from Petrograd of the extraordinary technical equipment of Yudenich's army, Lenin began to believe that it was necessary to shorten the front line by surrendering Petrograd. This was probably the only occasion when Zinoviev and Stalin supported me against Lenin; and he himself abandoned his obviously mistaken plan a few days later.

The last disagreement, and undoubtedly the most violent of all, had to do with the fate of the Polish front in the summer of 1920. Bonar Law, then the British Premier, in the House of Commons quoted my letter to the French communists as proof of our intention of crushing Poland in the fall of 1920. A similar assertion is to be found in a book by the late Polish war minister, Sikorsky, but this time it is supported by a reference to my speech at the International congress in January 1920. All this is sheer drivel from beginning to end. Of course I never had an occasion to express my sympathy with the Poland of Pilsudski; that is, a Poland of oppression and repression under a cloak of patriotic phraseology and heroic braggadocio. It would be easy to pick out a number of my statements to the effect that, in the event that war was forced on us by Pilsudski, we would try not to stop half-way. Such statements were the result of the entire setting. But to draw the conclusion from this that we wanted a war with Poland, or were even preparing it, is to lie in the face of facts and common sense. *We strained every effort to avoid that war.* We spared no measure to achieve this end. Sikorsky admits that we conducted peace propaganda with extraordinary 'cleverness'. He does not understand, or pretends that he does not, that the secret of that cleverness was very simple: it was merely that we were trying with all our might to secure peace, even at the price of the greatest concessions. Even more perhaps than anyone else, I did not want this war, because I realized only too clearly how difficult it would be to prosecute it after three years of continuous civil war. The Polish government, as Sikorsky's book makes clear, consciously and determinedly began the war in spite of our indefatigable efforts to preserve peace, efforts that made of our foreign policy a combination of patience and pedagogical persistence. We sincerely wanted peace. Pilsudski imposed war on us. We could wage it only because the great mass of the people had been watching our diplomatic duel continuously and were thoroughly convinced that the war had been forced on us; in this they were absolutely right.

The country made one more truly heroic effort. The capture

of Kiev by the Poles, in itself devoid of any military significance, did us a great service; it awakened the country. Again I had to make the rounds of armies and cities, mobilizing men and resources. We recaptured Kiev. Then our successes began. The Poles were rolled back with a celerity I never anticipated, since I could hardly believe the foolhardiness that actually lay at the bottom of Pilsudski's campaign. But on our side, too, after our first major successes, the idea of the possibilities that were opened to us became greatly exaggerated. A point of view that the war which began as one of defence should be turned into an offensive and revolutionary war began to grow and acquire strength. In principle, of course, I could not possibly have any objection to such a course. The question was simply one of the correlation of forces. The unknown quantity was the attitude of the Polish workers and peasants. Some of our Polish comrades, such as the late J. Markhlevsky, a co-worker of Rosa Luxemburg's, weighed the situation very soberly. The former's estimation was an important factor in my desire to get out of the war as quickly as possible. But there were other voices, too. There were high hopes of an uprising of the Polish workers. At any rate Lenin fixed his mind on carrying the war to an end, up to the entry into Warsaw to help the Polish workers overthrow Pilsudski's government and seize the power. The apparent decision by the government easily captured the imagination of the high command and of the command of the western front. By the time I paid my regular visit to Moscow, I found opinion strongly in favour of carrying on the war 'until the end'. To this I was resolutely opposed. The Poles were already asking for peace. I thought that we had reached the peak of our successes, and if we went farther, misjudging our strength, we would run the risk of passing beyond the victory already won to a defeat. After the terrific effort that enabled the Fourth army to cover 650 kilometres in five weeks it could move forward only through inertia. Everything hung on the nerves, and these were but thin threads. One strong blow would have been enough to shake our front and turn our unprecedented and unexampled offensive thrust – even Foch was obliged to admit this – into a defeat that would be a catastrophe. I demanded an immediate conclusion of peace before the army should grow too exhausted. I was supported, as far as I can remember now, only by Rykov. All the rest were won over by Lenin during my absence. Thus it was decided to continue the offensive.

In contrast with the Brest-Litovsk period the roles had been completely reversed. *Then* it was I who demanded that the signing of the peace be delayed; that even at the price of losing some territory we **giv**e the German proletariat time to understand the situation and get in its word. *Now* it was Lenin who demanded that our army continue its advance and give the Polish proletariat time to appraise the situation and rise up in arms. The Polish war confirmed from the opposite side what was demonstrated by the Brest-Litovsk war: that the events of war and those of the revolutionary mass movement are measured by different yardsticks. Where the action of armies is measured by days and weeks, the movement of the masses of people is usually reckoned in months and years. If this difference in tempo is not taken fully into account, the gears of war will only break the teeth of the revolutionary gears instead of setting them in motion. At any rate, that is what happened in the short Brest-Litovsk war, and in the great Polish war. We passed over and beyond our own victory to a heavy defeat.

One must note that one of the reasons for the extraordinary proportions which the catastrophe before Warsaw assumed was the conduct of the command of the southern group of the Soviet armies, operating in the direction of Lvov (Lemberg). The chief political figure in the Military-Revolutionary Council of this group was Stalin. Stalin wanted, at whatever cost, to enter Lvov at the same time that Smilga and Tukhachevsky entered Warsaw. Some people are capable of having even such ambitions! When the danger to the armies under Tukhachevsky was fully revealed, and the high command ordered the south-western armies to change the direction of their advance so as to strike at the flank of the Polish armies before Warsaw, the south-western command, encouraged by Stalin, continued advancing due west; for was it not more important that they should themselves capture Lvov than that they should help 'others' to take Warsaw? Only after repeated orders and threats did the south-western command change the direction of its advance. But the few days of delay had already had their fatal effect.

Our armies were rolled back four hundred or more kilometres. After the brilliant victories of the day before no one would be reconciled to the situation. On my return from the Wrangel front I found Moscow favouring a second Polish war. Now, even Rykov went over to the other camp. 'Once started', he was saying, 'we must carry it through to the end.' The command of the western front was encouraging hopes; sufficient reserves had come up, the artillery had been replenished, and so on and so forth. The wish was father to the thought. 'What have we on the western front?' I rejoined.

Only morally defeated units into which we have now poured raw human dough. One can't fight with such an army. Or, to be more exact, with an army like this one might be able to engage in defensive operations while retreating and preparing a new army in the rear; but it would be senseless to think that such an army is capable of raising itself to a victorious advance along a road strewn with its own fragments.

I declared that a repetition of the error already committed would cost us ten times as much, and that I would not submit to the decision that was being proposed, but would carry an appeal to the party. Though Lenin formally defended the continuation of the war, this time he did it without his former conviction and insistence. My firm belief in the necessity of concluding peace, even if it were a harsh one, made its impression on Lenin. He proposed that we put off deciding the question until I could visit the western front and get a direct impression of the condition of our armies after the retreat. To me, this meant that Lenin was already with me.

I found the headquarters at the front in favour of another war. But there was no conviction there; it was simply a reflection of the attitude in Moscow. The lower I went on the military ladder – from an army to a division, a regiment, a company – the more I realized the impossibility of an offensive war. I sent Lenin a letter about it, writing it in longhand, without even keeping a copy of it, while I went on with my round of inspection. The two or three days that I spent at the front were enough to confirm the conclusion I had brought with me from Moscow. I returned there, and the Politbureau almost unanimously resolved in favour of an immediate peace.

The error in the strategic calculations in the Polish war had great historical consequences. The Poland of Pilsudski came out of the war unexpectedly strengthened. On the contrary, the development of the Polish revolution received a crushing blow. The frontier established by the Riga treaty cut off the Soviet Republic from Germany, a fact that later was of great importance in the lives of both countries. Lenin, of course, understood better than anyone else the significance of the 'Warsaw' mistake, and returned to it more than once in thought and word.

In the literature of the epigones Lenin is now pictured in somewhat the same light that the ikon painters of Suzdal represent Christ and the saints: instead of an ideal image, you get a caricature. Much as the ikon painters try to rise above themselves, in the end they reflect only their own tastes, and as a result they must paint their own idealized portraits. As the authority of the epigone leadership is maintained by forbidding people to doubt its infallibility, so Lenin is represented in the epigone literature not as a revolutionary strategist who showed genius in his appreciation of the situation, but as a mechanical automaton of faultless decisions. The word *genius* in relation to Lenin was first applied by me at a time when others did not have the courage to pronounce it. Yes, Lenin was as much of a genius as a man can be. But he was not an automatic reckoning machine that makes no mistakes. He made them less often than anyone else in his position would; but he made them all the same, and grave ones, at that, in accord with the titanic scope of all of his work.

38

The Transition to the New Economic Policy, and My Relations with Lenin

Now I am approaching the last period of my collaboration with Lenin, a period deriving further importance from the fact that it contained the foundations of the subsequent victory of the epigones. After the death of Lenin a complicated and many-branched organization of an historical and literary nature was established for the sole purpose of distorting the history of our mutual relations. It has been done chiefly by painting a picture of a constant struggle between two 'principles', by isolating from the past the moments when we disagreed, by making a great deal out of individual polemical expressions and, most of all, by sheer invention. The history of the church as written down by the medieval apologists ia a model of scientific treatment compared with the historical investigations of the epigones. Their work was somewhat facilitated by the fact that when I disagreed with Lenin I mentioned it aloud, and, when I thought it necessary even appealed to the party. Whereas the epigones, when they disagreed with Lenin, which happened much more often than in my case, usually either kept silent about it, or, like Stalin, sulked and hid away for a few days in the country somewhere near Moscow.

In most cases the decisions that Lenin and I arrived at independently of each other were identical in all essentials. A few words would bring about a mutual understanding. When I thought the decision of the Politbureau or of the Soviet of People's Commissaries might turn out wrong, I would send Lenin a brief note on a slip of paper. He would answer: 'Absolutely right. Submit your proposal.' Sometimes he would send me an inquiry whether I agreed with his proposal, and a demand that I speak in his support. Time and again he would arrange with me by telephone the manner in which some matter was to be handled, and if it was important he would insist: 'Please come without fail.' In cases where we worked hand in hand – the usual thing with us on questions of principle – those who were dissatisfied with the decision, among them the present epigones, remained silent. Many a time Stalin, Zinoviev, or Kamenev disagreed with me on some question of great importance, but as soon as they learned that Lenin shared my opinion they lapsed into silence. We may regard the readiness of the 'disciples' to renounce their own ideas in favour of Lenin's in any way we choose, but this readiness clearly contained no guarantee that without Lenin they were capable of arriving at the same conclusions. In this book my disagreements with Lenin assume an importance that they never actually had. There are two reasons for this: our disagreements were the exception and as such attracted attention; after Lenin's death they were magnified by the epigones to astronomic proportions and became an independent political factor in no way connected with either of us.

In a separate chapter I gave a detailed account of my disagreements with Lenin in regard to the Brest-Litovsk peace. Now I will mention another disagreement that set us against each other for a couple of months at the close of 1920 on the very eve of the transition to the New Economic Policy.

One cannot deny that the so-called discussion of trade-unions clouded our relationship for some time. Each of us was too much the revolutionary and too much the politician to be able or even to want to separate the personal from the general. It was during that discussion that Stalin and Zinoviev were given what one might call their legal opportunity to bring their struggle against me out into the open. They strained every effort to take full advantage of the situation. It was for them a rehearsal of their future campaign against 'Trotskyism'. But it was just this aspect of the thing that disturbed Lenin most, and he tried in every way to paralyse it.

The political content of the discussion has had so much refuse heaped upon it that I do not envy the historian of the future who tries to get the truth of the matter. Long after the event, that is, after Lenin died, the epigones discovered that my stand at that time was one of 'under-appreciation of the peasantry', and one almost hostile towards the New Economic Policy. This was really the basis of all the subsequent attacks on me. In point of fact, of course, the roots of the discussion were quite the opposite, and to unmask this fact I must go back a little way.

In the fall of 1919, when 60 per cent of our locomotives were 'in eased', it was thought that by the spring of 1920 the figure would inevitably rise to 75 per cent. That was the expressed opinion of our best experts. Under such conditions the railway traffic was becoming a senseless affair, because the 25 per cent of locomotives in half-health was only enough for the transport needs of the railways, since they depended on bulky wood for fuel. Engineer Lomonosov, who was actually in charge of the transport system during those months, made a diagram of the locomotive epidemic for the government. Indicating a mathematical point in the year 1920, he declared: 'Here comes death.'

'What is to be done then?' asked Lenin.

'There are no such things as miracles,' Lomonosov replied. 'Even the Bolsheviks cannot perform miracles.' We looked at each other, all the more depressed because none of us knew the technical workings of the transport system, nor the technical workings of such gloomy calculations. 'Still, we'll try to perform the miracle,' Lenin muttered dryly through his teeth.

But during the following months the situation grew steadily worse. There was cause enough in actual conditions, but it is also very probable that certain engineers were making the transport situation fit into their diagrams. I spent the winter months of 1919 to 1920 in the Urals directing the economic work. Lenin telegraphed me a proposal that I take charge of transport and try to lift it by emergency measures. I replied stating my acceptance.

From the Urals I brought with me a store of economic observations that could be summed up in one general conclusion: war communism must be abandoned. My practical work had satisfied me that the methods of war communism forced on us by the conditions of civil war were completely exhausted, and that to revive our economic life the element of personal interest must be introduced at all costs; in other words we had to restore the home market in some degree. I submitted to the Central

Committee the project of replacing the food levy by a grain-tax and of restoring the exchange of commodities.

'The present policy of equalized requisition according to the food scale, of mutual responsibility for deliveries, and of equalized distribution of manufactured products, tends to lower the status of agriculture and to disperse the industrial proletariat, and threatens to bring about a complete breakdown in the economic life of the country.' In these words I formulated my view in the statement submitted to the Central Committee in February 1920.

'The food resources,' the statement continued,

are threatened with exhaustion, a contingency that no amount of improvement in the methods of requisition can prevent. These tendencies towards economic decline can be counteracted as follows: (1) The requisition of surpluses should give way to payment on a percentage basis (a sort of progressive income tax in kind), the scale of payment being fixed in such a way as to make an increase of the ploughed area, or a more thorough cultivation, still yield some profit; (2) a closer correspondence should be established between the industrial products supplied to the peasants and the quantities of grain they deliver; this applies not only to rural districts (volosts) and villages, but to the individual peasant households, as well.

These proposals are very guarded. But the basic propositions of the New Economic Policy adopted a year later did not at first go any farther. Early in 1920 Lenin came out firmly against my proposal. It was rejected in the Central Committee by a vote of eleven to four. The subsequent course of events proved the decision of the Committee to be a mistake. I did not carry it to the party congress, which was conducted throughout under the slogan of war communism. For the entire year following the economic life of the country struggled along in a blind alley. My quarrel with Lenin grew out of this blind alley. When the change to the market system was rejected, I demanded that the 'war' methods be applied properly and with system, so that real economic improvements could be obtained. In the system of war communism in which all the resources are, at least in principle, nationalized and distributed by government order I saw no independent rôle for trade-unions. If industry rests on the state's ensuring the supply of all the necessary products to the workers, the trade-unions must be included in the system of the state's administration of industry and distribution of products. This was the real substance of the question of making the trade-unions part of the state organizations, a measure which flowed inexorably from the system of war communism, and it was in this sense that I defended it.

The principles of war communism approved by the Ninth Congress were the basis of my work in the organization of transport. The trade-union of railway men was closely bound to the administrative machinery of the department. The methods of military discipline were extended to the entire transport system. I brought the military administration, the strongest and best disciplined at that time, into close connection with the transport administration. This yielded certain important advantages, especially since military transport again assumed first importance with the beginning of war with Poland. Every day I went from the war commissariat, whose operations destroyed the railways, to the commissariat of transport, where I tried not only to save the railways from final collapse, but to raise them to a higher level of efficiency.

The year of work in transport was a year in school for me. All the fundamental questions of socialist organization of economic life found their most concentrated expression in the sphere of transport. The great variety in the types of locomotives and cars complicated the work of the railways and the repair shops. Extensive preparatory work was set on foot to standardize the transport system, which, before the revolution, had been controlled equally by the state and by private companies. Locomotives were grouped according to class, their repair was more systematically organized, and the repair-shops began to receive precise orders based on their technical equipment. The programme for bringing the transport up to the pre-war standard was to be carried out in four and a half years. The measures adopted were a pronounced success. In the spring and summer of 1920 the transport system began to recover from its paralysis. Lenin never missed an occasion to remark the restoration of the railways. If the war started by Pilsudski in the hope that our transport system would collapse failed to yield Poland the expected result, it was because the curve of railway transport had begun to rise steadily upwards. Those results were obtained by extraordinary administrative measures proceeding inevitably from the serious position of the transport system as well as from the system of war communism itself.

But the working masses, who had gone through three years of civil war, were more and more disinclined to submit to the ways of military rule. With his unerring political instinct, Lenin sensed that the critical moment had arrived. Whereas I was trying to get an ever more intensive effort from the trade-unions, taking my stand on purely economic considerations on the basis of war communism, Lenin, guided by political considerations, was moving towards an easing of the military pressure. On the eve of the Tenth Congress our lines crossed antagonistically. A discussion flared up in the party; it was actually beside the point. The party was considering the rate at which the trade-unions were to be converted into a part of the state mechanism, whereas the question at issue was really one of daily bread, of fuel, of raw material for the industries. The party was arguing feverishly about 'the school of communism', whereas the thing that really mattered was the economic catastrophe hanging over the country. The uprisings at Kronstadt and in the province of Tambov broke into the discussion as the last warning. Lenin shaped the first and very guarded theses on the change to the New Economic Policy. I subscribed to them at once. For me, they were merely a renewal of the proposals which I had introduced a year before. The dispute about the trade-unions instantly lost all significance. At the congress Lenin took no part in that dispute, and left Zinoviev to amuse himself with the shell of an exploded cartridge. During the debate at the congress I gave warning that the resolution on trade-unions adopted by the majority would not live until the next congress, because the new economic orientation would demand a complete revision of the trade-union strategy. And it was only a few months later that Lenin formulated entirely new principles on the role and purpose of trade-unions, based on the new economic policy. I expressed my unreserved approval of his resolution. Our solid front was restored.

Lenin was afraid that as a result of the discussion, which had lasted two months, permanent factions would be established in the party, embittering relationships and making the work much more difficult.

But I wound up all conferences with those who shared my view on the question of trade-unions while the congress was still in session. A few weeks after the congress Lenin was assured that I was as anxious as he to do away with the temporary factions, which no longer had any basis in principle. Lenin felt as if a weight had been lifted from his chest. He took advantage of some impudent remark that Molotov, who had just been elected to the Central Committee, aimed at me, to charge him with more zeal than reason, and to add then and there: 'Comrade Trotsky's loyalty in the inter-party relations is absolutely irreproachable.' He repeated it several times. It was obvious that in this way he was thrusting back not only at Molotov but at someone else, for Stalin and Zinoviev were trying artificially to prolong the atmosphere of the dispute.

At this Tenth Congress, on Zinoviev's initiative and quite against Lenin's will, Stalin was put forward as a candidate for the post of the general secretary of the party. The Congress believed that he had the backing of the entire Central Committee. But no one attached much importance to this appointment. Under Lenin the post of general secretary, established by the Tenth Congress, could have only a technical character, never political. Yet Lenin had his fears. 'This cook will make only peppery dishes,' he would say of Stalin. That was why Lenin, at one of the first meetings of the Central Committee after the congress, insisted on emphasizing 'Trotsky's loyalty'; it was a thrust at a subterranean intrigue.

Lenin's remark was no casual one. During the civil war, Lenin had once expressed his moral confidence in me, not by word but by action, so completely that no man could either have asked or received more. The occasion was provided by that same military opposition directed behind the scenes by Stalin. During the war I had practically unlimited power. The revolutionary tribunal held its sessions in my train, the fronts were subordinate to me, and the bases auxiliary to the fronts – and at times nearly the entire territory belonging to the republic, not occupied by Whites, consisted of bases and fortified regions. Those who happened to get run over by the wheels of the military had relatives and friends who did whatever they could to get relief for them. Petitions, complaints and protests concentrated in Moscow by various channels, and especially at the presidium of the Central Executive Committee.

The first episodes of this sort were connected with events that had taken place as long before as the month at Sviyazhsk. I have already told about the incident of the commander of the fourth Latvian regiment who was put on trial by me for threatening to withdraw it from its position. The tribunal sentenced the commander to five years' imprisonment. Several months later, petitions began to come in, pleading for his release. The pressure on Svyerdlov was especially great. He put the question to the Politbureau. I briefly described the military situation of that time, when the regiment commander had threatened me with 'consequences that would be dangerous for the revolution'. During my narrative, Lenin's face grew greyer and greyer. I had hardly finished my story when he exclaimed in that stifled, hoarse voice that with him always indicated excitement: 'Let him stay in. Let him stay there!' Svyerdlov looked at both of us and said, 'I think so, too.'

The second episode, a much more significant one, was that connected with the shooting of the commander and the commissary who withdrew their regiment from its post, seized a steamer by threat of arms, and prepared to steam to Nijni-Novgorod. The regiment had been formed at Smolyensk under the direction of those opponents of my military policy who later became its ardent supporters. But at that time they were loud in protest. The commission of the Central Committee, appointed at my request, was unanimous in stating that the action of the military authorities was absolutely right; that the situation had warranted it. But the ambiguous rumours continued. Several times I felt that their source was not far from the Politbureau, but I was too busy to conduct an investigation or to disentangle intrigues. Only once did I remark at the meeting of the Politbureau that if it had not been for the ruthless measures at

Sviyazhsk, we would not have been holding our meeting. 'Absolutely', Lenin picked it up, and then and there began to write very fast, as he always did, in red ink at the bottom of a blank sheet that bore the seal of the Soviet of People's Commissaries. Lenin was in the chair and so the meeting stopped. Two minutes later, he handed me the sheet of paper. [Reproduced below].

R. S. F. S. R.
Chairman of the Soviet of
People's Commissaries,
Moscow, the Kremlin.
July........1919.

COMRADES:

Knowing the strict character of Comrade Trotsky's orders, I am so convinced, so absolutely convinced, of the correctness, expediency, and necessity for the success of the cause of the order given by Comrade Trotsky, that I unreservedly endorse this order.

V. ULYANOV/LENIN.

'I will give you', said Lenin, 'as many forms like this as you want.' In circumstances as serious as those of civil war, with its necessity of making hasty and irrevocable decisions, some of which might have been mistaken, Lenin gave his signature in advance to any decision that I might consider necessary in the future. And these were decisions that carried life or death with them. Could there be a greater confidence of one man in another? The very idea of this extraordinary document could have come to Lenin only because he knew better than I did, or else suspected the source of the intrigue and thought it necessary to strike back at it with the utmost vigour. But he could risk such a step only because he was so firmly convinced that I could not be disloyal or abuse the power. This confidence in me he expressed to the full in a few lines. The epigones may look in vain for such a document among their possessions. If Stalin finds anything in his archives, it could only be Lenin's 'Will', which Stalin concealed from the party – the 'Will' in which Stalin himself is referred to as a disloyal man, capable of abuse of power. It is enough simply to juxtapose these two texts – the unlimited moral power of attorney which Lenin conferred on me, and the moral 'wolf's passport'* issued to Stalin – to realize to the full his attitude towards each of us.

*The name of 'wolf's passport' was applied colloquially in Tsarist Russia to a document, also known as 'the transit certificate', issued to criminals in lieu of a passport; it usually made them outcasts not allowed to stay long in any one place. – *Translator*.

I took my first leave in the spring of 1920 before the second congress of the Communist International, and spent about two months near Moscow. My time was given over to a course of medical treatment (I was just beginning to take my health seriously), working on the manifesto that during the following years served as a substitute for the programme of the Communist International, and hunting for game. After the years of strain I felt the need of rest. But I didn't have the habit, and walks did not rest me any more then than they do today. The attraction in hunting is that it acts on the mind as a poultice does on a sore.

One Sunday early in May 1922 I went fishing with a net in the old channel of the Moscow river. It was raining, the grass was wet, and I slipped and broke the ligaments of my foot. It was nothing serious and I had merely to spend a few days in bed. On the third day Bukharin came to see me.

'You, too, are in bed?' he exclaimed in horror.

'And who besides?' I asked him.

'Lenin is very ill. He has had a stroke, and he cannot walk or talk. The doctors are utterly at a loss.'

Lenin always showed great interest in the health of his colleagues, and often quoted the words of some émigré: 'The old men will die and the young ones will surrender.'

'How many of us know what Europe is, what the world labour movement is? As long as we are the only ones with a revolution,' he said frequently, 'the international experience of the upper group of our party cannot be replaced.' Lenin himself was considered a man of robust health, and this health seemed to be one of the indestructible pillars of the revolution. He was always active, alert, even-tempered and gay. Only occasionally did I notice alarming symptoms. During the First Congress of the Communist International, he surprised me with his tired look, the unevenness of his voice, and his sick man's smile. More than once I told him that he was spending himself on matters of secondary importance. He agreed, but said that he couldn't do otherwise. Sometimes he complained of headaches, always casually and with a little embarrassment. But two or three weeks of rest sufficed to restore him. It seemed as if Lenin would never wear out.

At the close of 1921 his condition grew worse. On 7 December he sent a note to the members of the Politbureau: 'I am going away today. Despite my working less and resting more during recent days, the insomnia has grown hellishly worse. I am afraid that I shall not be able to make any reports either at the party conference or at the Congress of the Soviets.' Lenin began to spend a great deal of his time in a village near Moscow. But he watched the progress of the work most carefully from there. At that time, preparations for the Geneva conference were under way. On 23 January 1922 Lenin wrote to the members of the Politbureau:

I have just received two letters from Chicherin (dated the twentieth and the twenty-second). He asks whether it wouldn't be desirable to agree, for a proper compensation, to some small changes in the constitution, namely to the representation of the parasitic elements in the Soviets. This to please the Americans. This proposal of Chicherin's shows in my opinion that he must be sent to a sanatorium at once; every concession in this respect, agreement to a delay, etc., will, in my opinion, be the greatest menace to all the negotiations.

In every word of this note, in which political ruthlessness is tinged with sly good-nature, is the living, breathing Lenin.

His health continued to grow worse. In March his headaches grew more frequent. The doctors found no organic disorders, however, and prescribed a prolonged rest. Lenin settled down permanently in a Moscow village. And it was there that he had his first stroke, early in May. It seems that Lenin had been taken ill two days before Bukharin's visit. Why had I been told nothing about it? At the time I never thought of being suspicious.

'We did not want to disturb you', Bukharin told me, 'and were waiting to see how his illness would develop.' Bukharin spoke quite sincerely, merely repeating what the 'grown-ups' had persuaded him into believing. At that time Bukharin was attached to me in his characteristic 'Bukharin' way, half hysterically, half childishly. He finished his account of Lenin's illness by dropping down on my bed and muttering, as he pressed his arms about me over the blanket: 'Don't you get sick, I implore you, don't get sick... There are two men of whose death I always think with horror – Lenin and you.' I rallied him in a friendly way to restore his poise. He was preventing me from concentrating on the alarm that his news had caused. The blow was overwhelming. It seemed as if the revolution itself were holding its breath.

'The first rumours of Lenin's illness', writes N. I. Sedova in her notes,

were only whispered. It seemed that no one thought that Lenin could ever be taken ill. Many knew that he watched intently over the health of others, but it seemed that he himself was immune to disease. Nearly all the revolutionaries of the older generation had some affection of the heart, weakened by the excessive strain put on it. The doctors would complain: 'Nearly all of them have their motors misfiring.'

'There are only two hearts in proper order,' Professor Guetier said to Lev Davydovich, 'Lenin's and yours. With such a heart, one can live to be a hundred.' The examinations by foreign specialists confirmed this – that out of all the hearts examined by them in Moscow, only those of Lenin and Trotsky worked exceptionally well. When Lenin's sudden turn of health became known more widely, it was like a shift in the revolution itself. Was it possible that Lenin could fall ill and die, like anyone else? It was terrible to hear that Lenin had lost his ability to move about and speak. I could not help firmly believing that he would overcome it all, would rise and recover.

This was the sentiment of the entire party.

Looking back considerably later, I remembered with fresh surprise that I had not got news of Lenin's illness until the third day. At that time I did not stop to think about it. But this could have been no accident. Those who for a long time had been preparing to become my opponents – Stalin above all – were anxious to gain time. Lenin's illness was of the sort that might come to a tragic end at any moment. Tomorrow, or even today, all questions of leadership might become crucial ones. My opponents thought it important to gain time for preparation, even if it were only a day. They conferred secretly and sounded out ways and means. It must be assumed that the idea of the trio (Stalin – Zinoviev – Kamenev) to oppose me was already decided on. But Lenin recovered. Driven by his unyielding will, his entire organism made a gigantic effort; the brain that was failing from lack of blood, that had lost the power to join together sounds or letters, suddenly revived.

Towards the end of May I went on a fishing trip to a place about eighty versts away from Moscow. The place happened to have a sanatorium named after Lenin. The children walked along the lake with me, asked me questions about Lenin's health, and gave me field flowers and a letter for him. Lenin as yet could not write. He dictated a few lines through his secretary:

Vladimir Ilyich has asked me to write you that he welcomes your suggestion to take a present from him to the children of the sanatorium at the station of Podsolnechnaya. Vladimir Ilyich also requests you to tell the little ones that he thanks them very much for their kind letter and flowers, and is sorry that he is unable to take advantage of their invitation; he has no doubt that he would soon recover in their company.

In July Lenin was on his feet again and, although he did not officially return to work until October, he kept his eye on everything and studied everything. During those months of convalescence, among the things that engaged his attention was the trial of the Socialist-Revolutionists. The Socialist-Revolutionists had killed Volodarsky and Uritzky, had wounded Lenin seriously, and had made two attempts to blow up my train. We could not treat all this lightly. Although we did not regard it from the idealistic point of view of our enemies, we appreciated 'the rôle of the individual in history'. We could not close our eyes to the danger that threatened the revolution if we were to allow our enemies to shoot down, one by one, the whole leading group of our party.

Our humanitarian friends of the neither-hot-nor-cold species have explained to us more than once that they could see the necessity of reprisals in general, but that to shoot a captured enemy means to overstep the limits of necessary self-defence. They demanded that we show 'magnanimity'. Clara Zetkin and other European communists who still dared at that time to say what they thought, in opposition to Lenin and me, insisted that we spare the lives of the men on trial. They suggested that we limit their punishment to confinement in prison. This seemed the simplest solution. But the question of reprisals on individuals in times of revolution assumes a quite specific character from which humanitarian generalities rebound in impotence. The struggle then is for actual power, a struggle for life or death – since that is what revolution is. What meaning, under such conditions, can imprisonment have for people who hope to seize the power in a few weeks and imprison or destroy the men at the helm? From the point of view of the absolute value of the human personality revolution must be 'condemned', as well as war – as must also the entire history of mankind taken in the large. Yet the very idea of personality has been developed only as a result of revolutions, a process that is still far from complete. In order that the idea of personality may become a reality and the half-contemptuous idea of the 'masses' may cease to be the antithesis of the philosophically privileged idea of 'personality', the masses must lift themselves to a new historical rung by the revolutionary crane, or, to be more exact, by a series of revolutions. Whether this method is good or bad from the point of view of normative philosophy I do not know, and I must confess I am not interested in knowing. But I do know definitely that this is the only way that humanity has found thus far.

These considerations are in no sense an attempt to 'justify' the revolutionary terror. To attempt to justify it would mean to take notice of the accusers. And who are they? The organizers and exploiters of the great world slaughter? The *nouveaux riches* who offer up to the 'unknown soldier' the aroma of their after-dinner cigars? The pacifists who fought war only when there was none, and who are ready to repeat their repulsive masquerade? Lloyd George, Wilson, and Poincaré, who considered themselves entitled to starve German children for the crimes of the Hohenzollerns – and for their own crimes? The English conservatives or French Republicans who fanned the flames of civil war in Russia from a safe distance while they were trying to coin their profits out of its blood? This roll-call could be continued without end. For me, the question is not one of philosophical justification but rather of political explanation. Revolution is revolution only because it reduces all contradictions to the alternative of life or death. Is it conceivable that men who solve the question of sovereignty over Alsace-Lorraine every half-century by means of mountains of human corpses are capable of rebuilding their social relations by nothing more than parliamentary ventriloquism? At any rate, no one has shown us as yet how it can be done. We were breaking up the resistance of the old rocks with the help of steel and dynamite. And when our enemies shot at us, in most cases with rifles from the most civilized and democratic nations, we replied in the same vernacular. Bernard Shaw shook his beard reproachfully over this in the direction of both parties, but no one took any notice of his sacramental argument.

In the summer of 1922 the question of reprisals took on special urgency, because it was concerned with the leaders of a party that had once waged the revolutionary fight against Tsarism side by side with us, but had turned the weapon of terror against us after the October revolution. Deserters from the camp of the Socialist-Revolutionists disclosed to us the fact that the worst acts of terrorism were not instigated by individuals, as we had at first been inclined to believe, but by the party, although it did not risk a formal acknowledgement of its responsibility for the assassinations it was committing. The death-sentence by the tribunal was inevitable, but carrying it out meant just as inevitably a retaliating wave of terrorism. To limit the method of punishment to imprisonment, even for a long period of time, was tantamount to encouraging the terrorists, since they were the least likely to believe in the longevity of the Soviet. There was no alternative but to make the execution of the sentence dependent on whether or not the party continued the terrorist struggle. In other words the leaders of the party must be held as hostages.

My first meeting with Lenin after his recovery was during the trial of the Socialist-Revolutionists. It was instantly and with relief that he agreed to the proposition that I made: 'Quite right, there is no alternative.' His recovery was apparently inspiriting to him. But he still had some inner fear. 'You understand,' he said, quite bewildered, 'I could not even speak or write, and I had to learn everything all over again.' And he lifted his eyes questingly to me.

In October Lenin officially returned to work; he presided at the Politbureau and at the Soviet of People's Commissaries, and in November made programme speeches, to all appearances at heavy cost to his arteries. He seemed to sense the almost imperceptible threads of a conspiracy being woven behind our backs in connection with his illness. The epigones were not yet burning their bridges behind them, but here and there they were sawing through the beams and hiding away sticks of dynamite. Whenever opportunity offered they opposed me, as if they were taking exercises in being independent, and were carefully preparing such demonstrations. As Lenin got deeper into the work he began to observe with anxiety the changes that had been taking place during the months preceding, but he said nothing about them for fear of aggravating the situation. He was preparing to rebuff the 'trio', and began by doing it in individual matters.

Among the some odd-dozen jobs that I was directing as part of the party work – that is, privately and unofficially – was the anti-religious propaganda, in which Lenin was very much interested. He asked me insistently not to let this work out of my sight. While convalescent, he had somehow learned that Stalin was manoeuvring against me there by renewing the apparatus of the anti-religious propaganda and moving it away from me. From the country Lenin sent the Politbureau a letter in which, without apparent necessity, he quoted my book on Kautsky and praised the author, without mentioning either him or the book by name. I must confess that I did not at the time guess that this was a roundabout way of saying that Lenin condemned Stalin's manoeuvres against me. In the meantime Yaroslavsky, I think in the guise of my deputy, was pushed forward to take charge of the anti-religious propaganda. When Lenin got back to work and heard about it, he ferociously attacked Molotov – and through him Stalin – at one of the meetings of the Politbureau: 'Yar-os-lavsky? Don't you know what Yar-os-lavsky is? Why, it would make a hen chuckle. He will never be able to manage this work,' and so on. Lenin's vehemence may seem excessive to the uninitiated. But it was not a question of Lenin's being unable to bear Yaroslavsky, but rather the party direction. Incidents like this were frequent enough.

If one looks into it more deeply, one sees that Stalin, from the very moment that he came into close contact with Lenin, and especially since the October revolution, had always been suppressed and impotent in his opposition to him, and was all the more irritable because of it. Because of his enormous envy and ambition, Stalin could not help feeling at every step his intellectual and moral inferiority. It seems that he tried to get closer to me. Not until much later did I realize the meaning of attempts to establish something approaching familiarity between us. But I was repelled by those very qualities that were his strength on the wave of decline – the narrowness of his interests, his empiricism, the coarseness of his psychological make-up, his peculiar cynicism of a provincial whom Marxism has freed from many prejudices without, however, replacing them with a philosophical outlook thoroughly thought out and mentally assimilated. Judged by some of his casual remarks, which at the time seemed accidental but actually were not, Stalin was trying to find in me support against Lenin, whose control he found so irksome. At every attempt of this sort I instinctively drew away from him and walked on. I believe that the sources of his cold and at first cowardly but thoroughly treacherous hatred of me are to be found in this. He systematically gathered about him either men who were like him, or simple fellows who wanted to live without being bothered by subtle problems, or those whose feelings had been hurt. The first, the second, and the third groups – all were numerous.

There is no doubt that in routine work it was more convenient for Lenin to depend on Stalin, Zinoviev or Kamenev rather than on me. Lenin was always trying to save his time as well as every one else's. He tried to reduce to a minimum the energy spent in overcoming friction. I had my own views, my own ways of working, and my own methods of carrying out a decision once it had been adopted. Lenin knew this well enough and respected it. That was why he understood only too well that I was not suited for executing commissions. When he needed men to carry out his instructions, he turned to someone else. In certain periods, especially when Lenin and I had had a disagreement, this probably made his assistants believe that they were particularly close to him. For example, he invited Rykov and Tzyurupa to be his deputies as Chairman of the Soviet of People's Commissaries and later on added Kamenev to them. I thought this was a good choice. Lenin needed practical, obedient assistants. I was unsuited to the rôle and I could only be grateful to Lenin for not offering me the deputyship. Far from considering this a lack of confidence in me, I saw in it on the contrary a definite and not unflattering appreciation of me and of our mutual relations. Later on I had occasion to be completely convinced of this. In the interval between his first and second strokes Lenin could work only half as much as before. Slight but none the less ominous warnings from his blood-vessels reached him off and on throughout this period. At one of the meetings of the Politbureau, as he got up to hand someone a note – Lenin always exchanged notes this way to speed up the work – he reeled a little. I noticed it only because his face changed expression instantly. This was one of many warnings from his vital centres. Lenin had no illusions on this score. He kept pondering from all points of view how the work would go on without him, and after him. It must have been then that he formulated mentally the document that later became known as his 'Will'. And it was at this time – during the last weeks before his second stroke – that Lenin and I had a long conversation about my work in the future. Because of its political importance, I immediately repeated this conversation to a number of people (Rakovsky, I. N. Smirnov, Sosnovsky, Pryeobrazhensky, and others). If only because of this repetition, the conversation has been very clearly recorded in my memory.

It came about in this way. The central committee of the union of educational workers sent a delegation to Lenin and me with the request that I take over the commissariat of education in addition to my other duties, in the same way that I had taken charge of the commissariat of transport for a year past. Lenin wanted to know what I thought about it. I told him that in the educational field, as in every other, the difficulty would come from the administrative apparatus. 'Yes, our bureaucratism is something monstrous,' Lenin replied, picking up my train of thought. 'I was appalled when I came back to work. . . It is just because of this that you should not – or at least I think so – get drawn into any departmental work besides the military.' Lenin proceeded to state his plan with passionate conviction. He had a limited amount of strength to give to the work of direction. He had three deputies. 'You know them. Kamenev is of course a clever politician, but what sort of an administrator is he? Tzyurupa is ill. Rykov is perhaps an administrator, but he will have to go back to the Supreme Economic Council. You must become a deputy. The situation is such that we must have a radical realignment of personnel.' Again I pointed out the 'apparatus' that made even my work in the war department increasingly difficult. 'Well, that will be your chance to shake up the apparatus,' Lenin retorted quickly, hinting at an expression I had once used. I replied that I referred to the bureaucracy not only in the state institutions, but in the party as well; that the cause of all the trouble lay in the combination of the two apparatuses and in the mutual shielding among the influential groups that gathered round the hierarchy of party secretaries. Lenin listened intently, and confirmed my suggestions in that deep tone which came straight from the chest, a tone that would break through in him only when, sure that the person he was talking to understood him completely, he would dispense with the conventionalities of conversation, and touch openly on what was the most important and disturbing. After thinking it over for a moment Lenin put the question point blank: 'You propose then to open fire not only against the state bureaucracy, but against the Organizational Bureau of the Central Committee as well?' I couldn't help laughing, this came so unexpectedly.

'That seems to be it.' The Organizational Bureau meant the very heart of Stalin's apparatus.

'Oh, well,' Lenin went on, obviously pleased that we had called the thing by its right name, 'if that's the case, then I offer you a bloc against bureaucracy in general and against the Organizational Bureau in particular.'

'With a good man it is an honour to form a good bloc,' I replied.

We agreed to meet again some time later. Lenin suggested that I think over the organization end of the question. He planned to create a commission attached to the Central Committee for fighting bureaucracy. We were both to be members. This commission was essentially to be the lever for breaking up the Stalin faction as the backbone of the bureaucracy, and for creating such conditions in the party as would allow me to become Lenin's deputy, and, as he intended, his successor to the post of Chairman of the Soviet of People's Commissaries.

Only in this connection does the full meaning of the so-called 'Will' become clear. Lenin names only six people there, and sums them up briefly, weighing each word. Unquestionably, his object in making the Will was to facilitate the work of direction for me. He naturally wanted to do it with the least possible amount of friction. He talks about everyone most guardedly, softening the most devastating judgements. At the same time he qualifies with reservations the too definite indication of the one whom he thinks entitled to first place. Only in his analysis of Stalin does one feel a different tone, a tone which in the later postscript to the will is nothing short of annihilating.

Of Zinoviev and Kamenev Lenin writes, with an effect of casualness, that their capitulation in 1917 was 'not an accident'; in other words, it is in their blood. Obviously such men cannot direct the revolution, but they should not be reproached for their pasts. Bukharin is not a Marxist but a scholastic; he is, however, a sympathetic person. Pyatakov is an able administrator, but a very bad politician. It is quite possible, however, that these two, Bukharin and Pyatakov, will still learn. The ablest is Trotsky; his defect is his excess of self-confidence. Stalin is rude, disloyal, and capable of abuse of the power that he derives from the party apparatus. Stalin should be removed to avoid a split. This is the substance of the 'Will'. It rounds out and clarifies the proposal that Lenin made me in our last conversation.

Lenin came to know Stalin really only after the October revolution. He valued his firmness and his practical mind, which is three-quarters cunning. And yet at every step Lenin struck at Stalin's ignorance, at his very narrow political horizon, and his exceptional moral coarseness and unscrupulousness. Stalin was elected to the post of general secretary of the party against the will of Lenin, who acquiesced only so long as he himself headed the party. But after his first stroke, when he returned to work with his health undermined, Lenin applied himself to the entire problem of leadership. This accounts for the conversation with me. Hence, too, the Will. Its last lines were written on 4 January. After that two more months passed, during which the situation took definite shape. Lenin was now preparing not only to remove Stalin from his post of general secretary but to disqualify him before the party as well. On the question of monopoly of foreign trade, on the national question, on questions of the régime in the party, of the worker-peasant inspection, and of the commission of control, he was systematically preparing to deliver at the Twelfth Congress a crushing blow at Stalin as personifying bureaucracy, the mutual shielding among officials, arbitrary rule and general rudeness.

Would Lenin have been able to carry out the regrouping in the party direction that he planned? At that moment he undoubtedly would. There had been several precedents for it, and one of them was quite fresh in mind and significant. In November 1922, while Lenin was still convalescent and living in the country, and while I was absent from Moscow, the Central Committee unanimously adopted a decision that dealt an irreparable blow at the monopoly of foreign trade. Both Lenin and I sounded the alarm, independently of each other, and then wrote to each other and coordinated our action. A few weeks later the Central Committee revoked its decision as unanimously as it had adopted it. On 21 December Lenin wrote triumphantly to me: 'Comrade Trotsky, it seems that we have managed to capture the position without a single shot, by a mere manoeuvre.

I suggest that we do not stop but press the attack.' Our joint action against the Central Committee at the beginning of 1923 would without a shadow of a doubt have brought us victory. And, what is more, I have no doubt that, if I had come forward on the eve of the Twelfth Congress in the spirit of a 'bloc of Lenin and Trotsky' against the Stalin bureaucracy, I should have been victorious even if Lenin had taken no direct part in the struggle. How solid the victory would have been is, of course, another question. To decide that, one must take into account a number of objective processes in the country, in the working class, and in the party itself. That is a separate and large theme. Lenin's wife said in 1927 that if he had been alive he would probably have been doing time in a Stalin prison. I think she was right. For the thing that matters is not Stalin, but the forces that he expresses without even realizing it. In 1922 to 1923, however, it was still possible to capture the commanding position by an open attack on the faction then rapidly being formed of national socialist officials, of usurpers of the apparatus, of the unlawful heirs of October, of the epigones of Bolshevism. The chief obstacle was Lenin's condition. He was expected to rise again as he had after his first stroke and to take part in the Twelfth Congress as he had in the Eleventh. He himself hoped for this. The doctors spoke encouragingly, though with dwindling assurance. The idea of a 'bloc of Lenin and Trotsky' against the apparatus-men and bureaucrats was at that time fully known only to Lenin and me, although the other members of the Politbureau dimly suspected it. Lenin's letters on the national question and his Will remained unknown. Independent action on my part would have been interpreted, or, to be more exact, represented as my personal fight for Lenin's place in the party and the state. The very thought of this made me shudder. I considered that it would have brought such a demoralization in our ranks that we would have had to pay too painful a price for it even in case of victory. In all plans and calculations there remained the positive element of uncertainty – Lenin and his physical condition. Would be he able to state his own views? Would he still have time? Would the party understand that it was a case of a fight by Lenin and Trotsky for the future of the revolution and not a fight by Trotsky for the place held by Lenin, who was ill? Because of Lenin's exceptional position in the party, the uncertainty of his personal condition became the uncertainty of the condition of the entire party. The indefinite situation was being prolonged. And the delay simply played into the hands of the epigones, since Stalin, as general secretary, became the majordomo of the apparatus for the entire period of the interregnum.

It was the beginning of March 1923. Lenin was lying in his room in the huge building of the courts of justice. The second stroke was near; it was preceded by a series of lesser shocks. I spent several weeks in bed with lumbago in the former Kavalersky building, where we had our apartment, and was separated from Lenin by the enormous courtyard of the Kremlin. Neither Lenin nor I could reach the telephone; furthermore, the doctors strictly forbade Lenin to hold any telephone conversations. Lenin's two secretaries, Fotiyeva and Glasser, did service as liaison officers. This is what they came to tell me: Vladmir Ilyich was very much disturbed by Stalin's preparations for the coming party congress, especially in connection with his factional machinations in Georgia. 'Vladimir Ilyich is preparing a bomb for Stalin at the congress' – that was Fotiyeva's phrase, verbatim. The word 'bomb' was Lenin's, not hers. 'Vladimir Ilyich asks you to take the Georgian case in your hands: he will then feel confident.' On 5 March Lenin dictated this note to me:

Dear Comrade Trotsky: I wish very much to ask you to take upon yourself the defence of the Georgian case in the Central Committee of the party. At present the case is under the 'persecution' of Stalin and Dzerzhinsky, and I cannot trust their impartiality. Quite the opposite. If you were to agree to undertake the defence, my mind would be at rest. If for some reason you cannot agree to do so, please return the entire *dossier* to me; I shall consider that a sign of refusal from you. With best comradely greetings, LENIN.

What had brought the question to such an acute stage? – I inquired. It turned out that Stalin had betrayed Lenin's confidence; in order to ensure himself support in Georgia, acting behind Lenin's back and without the knowledge of the entire Central Committee, he had carried out, with the help of Ordzhonikidze and not without support from Dzerzhinsky, an organized *coup d'état* there against the best section of the party, shielding himself falsely behind the authority of the Central Committee. As Lenin's illness made it impossible for him to meet other comrades, Stalin had taken advantage of this and had surrounded him with misinformation. Lenin instructed his secretaries to gather all the material they could on the Georgian matter and decided to come out openly with a statement. It is hard to say what shocked Lenin most — Stalin's personal disloyalty or his rough and bureaucratic policy on the national question. Probably it was a combination of both. Lenin was getting ready for the struggle, but he was afraid that he would not be able to speak at the congress, and this worried him. Why not talk the matter over with Zinoviev or Kamenev? – his secretaries kept prompting him. But Lenin waved them aside impatiently. He foresaw that if he withdrew from activity Zinoviev and Kamenev would join Stalin to make up a trio against me, and thus would betray him. 'Do you happen to know Trotsky's attitude on the Georgian question?' Lenin asks. 'At the plenary meeting Trotsky spoke in agreement with your views,' answers Glasser, who acted as the secretary at the meeting.

'Are you sure?'

'Quite. Trotsky accused Ordzhonikidze, Voroshilov and Kalinin of failing to understand the national question.'

'Verify it again,' Lenin demands.

The next day at the meeting of the Central Committee at my house Glasser handed me a note with a brief summary of my speech of the day before, concluding with the question: 'Did I understand you correctly?'

'What do you want it for?' I asked. 'For Vladimir Ilyich,' Glasser answered. 'Yes, this is correct,' I replied. In the meantime Stalin watched our correspondence with alarm, but at that moment I was still unaware of what it was all about. 'After he read my correspondence with you,' Glasser told me afterwards, 'Vladimir Ilyich fairly shone . . . "Now, it is a different matter."' And he instructed me to hand over to you all the manuscripts

that were to make part of his *bomb* for the Twelfth Congress.'
Lenin's intentions now were quite clear to me; by taking the
example of Stalin's policy he wanted to expose to the party, and
ruthlessly, the danger of the bureaucratic transformation of the
dictatorship.

'Tomorrow Kamenev is going to Georgia for the party conference,' I said to Fotiyeva. 'I can acquaint him with Lenin's
manuscripts so as to induce him to act properly in Georgia. Ask
Vladimir Ilyich about it.' A quarter of an hour later Fotiyeva
returned out of breath:

'Under no circumstances.'

'Why?'

'Vladimir Ilyich says: "Kamenev will immediately show
everything to Stalin, and Stalin will make a rotten compromise
and then deceive us.' "

'Then the thing has gone so far that Vladimir Ilyich no longer
thinks that we can compromise with Stalin even on the right
line?'

'Yes, he does not trust Stalin, and wants to come out against
him openly, before the entire party. He is preparing a bomb.'

About an hour after this conversation Fotiyeva came to me
again with a note from Lenin addressed to an old revolutionary,
Mdivani, and to other opponents of Stalin's policy in Georgia.
Lenin wrote to them: 'I am watching your case with all my heart
and soul. Ordzhonikidze's rough methods and Stalin's and
Dzerzhinsky's encouragement fill me with indignation. I am
preparing notes and a speech for you.' The copy of the note was
addressed not only to me, but to Kamenev as well. This surprised me.

'Then Vladimir Ilyich has changed his mind?' I asked.

Yes, his condition is getting worse every hour. You must not
believe the reassuring statements of the doctors. He can speak
now only with difficulty ... The Georgian question worries him
terribly. He is afraid he will collapse before he can undertake
anything. When handing me this note he said: 'Before it is too
late ... I am obliged to come out openly before the proper
time!'

'But this means that now I can talk to Kamenev?'

'Obviously.'

'Ask him to come to see me.'

Kamenev came an hour later. He was completely at sea. The idea of a trio – Stalin, Zinoviev, Kamenev – had long been established. Their spear-point was directed at me. The whole plan of the conspirators was that after they had mustered enough support in the organizations they would be crowned legitimate successors to Lenin. The little note cut into their plan like a sharp wedge. Kamenev did not know what to do and admitted it to me quite frankly. I gave him Lenin's manuscript to read over. Kamenev was an experienced enough politician to understand at once that for Lenin the question was not only one of Georgia but of Stalin's entire role in the party. Kamenev gave me some additional facts. He had just been to see Nadyezhda Konstantinovna Krupskaya at her request. She told him in great alarm: 'Vladimir has just dictated to his stenographer a letter to Stalin saying that he breaks off all relations with him.' The immediate cause of this was of a semi-personal character. Stalin had been trying to isolate Lenin from all sources of information, and in this connection had been very rude to Nadyezhda Konstantinovna. 'But you know Vladimir,' Krupskaya added. 'He would never have decided to break off personal relations if he had not thought it necessary to crush Stalin politically.' Kamenev was quite pale and agitated. The ground was slipping away under his feet. He did not know what to do next, or which way to turn. It is quite likely that he was simply afraid of my acting in an unfriendly way towards him.

I gave him my opinion of the situation. 'Sometimes', I said, 'out of fear of an imaginary danger people are capable of bringing real danger down upon themselves. Remember, and tell others, that the last thing I want is to start a fight at the congress for any changes in organization. I am for preserving the *status quo*. If Lenin gets on his feet before the congress, of which there is unfortunately little chance, he and I will discuss the matter together anew. I am against removing Stalin, and expelling Ordzhonikidze, and displacing Dzerzhinsky from the commissariat of transport. But I do agree with Lenin in substance. I want a radical change in the policy on the national question, a discontinuance of persecutions of the Georgian opponents of Stalin, a discontinuance of the administrative oppression of the party, a firmer policy in matters of industrialization, and an honest cooperation in the higher centres. On the national question the Stalin resolution is good for nothing. It places the high-handed and insolent oppression by the dominant nation on the same level with the protest and resistance of small, weak and backward nationalities. I gave my resolution the form of amendments to Stalin's to make it easier for him to alter his line of policy. But there must be an immediate and radical change. In addition it is necessary that Stalin should writ eto Krupskaya at once to apologize for his rudeness and that he revise his behaviour. Let him not overreach himself. There should be no more intrigues but honest cooperation. And you,' and here I turned to Kamenev, 'when you are at the conference at Tiflis, must arrange a complete reversal of the policy towards Lenin's Georgian supporters on the national question.'

Kamenev gave a sigh of relief. He accepted all my proposals. His only fear was that Stalin would be obstinate: 'He's rude and capricious.'

'I don't think', I answered, 'that Stalin has any alternative now.' Late that night Kamenev informed me that he had been to see Stalin in the country and that Stalin had accepted all the terms. Krupskaya had already received his letter of apology, but she could not show it to Lenin, for his condition had grown worse. I gained the impression, however, that Kamenev's tone was different from that at our parting a few hours earlier. It was not until later that I realized that the changes was the result of Lenin's more serious condition. On his way to Tiflis or immediately after his arrival, Kamenev received from Stalin a telegram in code telling him that Lenin was paralysed again, and unable to speak or write. At the Georgian conference Kamenev carried out Stalin's policy against Lenin's. Cemented by personal treachery, the trio had become a fact.

Lenin's offensive was directed not only against Stalin personally, but against his entire staff, and first of all his assistants, Dzerzhinsky and Ordzhonikidze. Both of them are mentioned constantly in Lenin's correspondence on the Georgian question.

Dzerzhinsky was a man of great and explosive passion. His energy was held at a high pitch by constant electric discharges. In every discussion, even of things of minor importance, he would fire up, his nostrils would quiver, his eyes would sparkle, and his voice would be so strained that often it would break. Yet in spite of this high nervous tension Dzerzhinsky had no apathetic intervals. He was always in that same state of tense mobilization. Lenin once compared him to a spirited thoroughbred. Dzerzhinsky fell in love in a mad infatuation with everything he did, and guarded his associates from criticism and interference with a passionate fanaticism that had no element of the personal in it, for he was completely dissolved in his work.

Dzerzhinsky had no opinions of his own. He never thought of himself as a politician, at least while Lenin was alive. On various occasions he said to me: 'I am not a bad revolutionary, perhaps, but I am no leader, statesman or politician.' This was not mere modesty; his self-appraisal was essentially right. In political matters Dzerzhinsky always needed someone's immediate guidance. For many years he had followed Rosa Luxemburg and with her had gone through not only the struggle against Polish patriotism, but that against Bolshevism as well. In 1917 he joined the Bolsheviks. Lenin said to me with great joy, 'No traces of the old fight are left.' During the first two or three years Dzerzhinsky was especially drawn to me. In his last years he supported Stalin. In his economic work he accomplished things through sheer temperament – appealing, urging, and lifting people off their feet by his own enthusiasm. He had no considered ideas about economic development. He shared all Stalin's errors and defended them with all the passion of which he was capable. He died practically on his feet, just after he had left the platform from which he had so passionately been denouncing the opposition.

Stalin's other ally, Ordzhonikidze, Lenin thought it necessary to expel from the party because of his bureaucratic high-handedness in the Caucasus. I argued against it. Lenin answered me through his secretary: 'At least for two years.' How little could he imagine at that time that Ordzhonikidze would become head of the Control Commission that Lenin was planning to create to fight Stalin's bureaucracy, and which was to embody the conscience of the party!

Aside from its general political aims, the campaign that Lenin opened had as its immediate object the creation of the best conditions for my work of direction, either side by side with him if he regained his health, or in his place if he succumbed to his illness. But the struggle, which was never carried out to its end, or even part way, had exactly an opposite result. Lenin managed only to *declare* war against Stalin and his allies, and even this was known only to those who were directly involved in it, and not to the party as a whole. Stalin's faction – at that time it was still the faction of the trio – closed its ranks more tightly after the first warning. The indefinite situation continued. Stalin stood at the helm of the apparatus. Artificial selection was carried on there at a mad pace. The weaker the trio felt in matters of principle the more they feared me – because they wanted to get rid of me – and the tighter they had to bolt all the screws and nuts in the state and party system. Much later, in 1925, Bukharin said to me in answer to my criticism of the party oppression: 'We have no democracy because we are afraid of you.'

'Just you try to stop being afraid', I proffered by way of advice, 'and let us work properly.' But my advice was vain.

The year 1923 was the first year of the intense but still silent stifling and routing of the Bolshevist party. Lenin was struggling with his terrible illness. The trio were struggling with the party. The atmosphere was charged, and towards autumn the tension resolved itself into a 'discussion' of the opposition. The second chapter of the revolution had begun – the fight against Trotskyism. In reality it was a fight against the ideological legacy of Lenin.

40

The Conspiracy of the Epigones

t was the early weeks of 1923 and the Twelfth Congress was drawing near. There remained little hope that Lenin could take part in it. The question of who was to make the principal political report arose. At the meeting of the Politbureau Stalin said, 'Trotsky, of course.' He was instantly supported by Kalinin, Rykov, and, obviously against his will, by Kamenev. I objected.

'The party will be ill at ease if any one of us should attempt, as it were personally, to take the place of the sick Lenin. This time let us manage without an introductory political report, and say what we have to say in connection with the separate items of the agenda. Besides', I added, 'there are differences between us on economic questions.'

'I don't see any differences,' Stalin replied, while Kalinin added: 'On almost all questions the Politbureau adopts your proposals.' Zinoviev was on leave in the Caucasus. The question remained undecided. At any rate I agreed to report on industry.

Stalin knew that a storm was menacing him from Lenin's direction and tried in every way to ingratiate himself with me. He kept repeating that the political report should be made by the most influential and popular member of the Central Committee after Lenin: *i. e.*, Trotsky, and that the party expected it and would not understand anything else. In his feigned attempts at friendliness he seemed even more alien than in his frank exhibitions of enmity, the more so because his motives were so obvious.

Zinoviev soon returned from the Caucasus. At that time very close factional conferences were continually being held behind my back. Zinoviev demanded that he be allowed to make the political report. Kamenev was asking the 'old Bolsheviks', the majority of whom had at some time left the party for ten or fifteen years: 'Are we to allow Trotsky to become the one person empowered to direct the party and the state?' They began more frequently to rake up my past and my old disagreements with Lenin; it became Zinoviev's specialty. In the meantime Lenin's condition took a sharp turn for the worse, so that danger no longer threatened there. The trio decided that the political report should be made by Zinoviev. I raised no objection when, after due preparation behind the scenes, the question was put before the Politbureau. Everything bore the stamp of a temporary arrangement. No disagreements were manifest, just as no independent line could be found anywhere in the policy of the trio. My theses on industry were at first accepted without discussion. But when it seemed certain that there was no prospect of Lenin's returning to work, the trio made a sharp about-face, frightened by the too peaceful preparations for the congress. It was looking now for a chance to line itself up against me in the upper circle of the party. At the last moment before the congress Kamenev proposed the addition of a clause about the peasantry to my resolution, which had already been approved. There would be no sense in dwelling on the subject-matter of this amendment, which had no theoretical or political importance, but was designed as an act of 'provocation', to provide the basis for accusations – so far, only behind the scenes – of my 'under-appreciation' of the peasantry. Three years after his break with Stalin, Kamenev, with his characteristic good-humoured cynicism, told me how they had cooked up this accusation, which of course none of its authors took seriously.

To operate with abstract moral criteria in politics is notoriously hopeless. Political morals proceed from politics itself and are one of its functions. Only a politics that serves a great historical task can insure itself morally irreproachable methods. On the contrary the lowering of the level of political aims inevitably leads to moral decline. Figaro, as everyone knows, refused to differentiate at all between politics and intrigue. And he lived before the advent of the era of parliamentarism! When the moralists of the bourgeois democracy attempt to perceive the source of bad political morals in revolutionary dictatorship as such, one can

nly shrug one's shoulders compassionately. It would be very
nstructive to make a cinematic record of modern parliamen-
arism, if but for a single year. But the camera should be placed
ot alongside the president of the chamber of deputies at the
noment when a patriotic resolution is being adopted, but in
quite other places: in the offices of bankers and industrialists, in
he private rooms of editorial offices, in the palaces of the princes
f the church, in the salons of political ladies, in the ministries –
nd, with it, let the eye of the camera record also the secret corre-
pondence of the party leaders. On the other hand it would be
erfectly right to say that very different demands should be im-
osed on the political morals of a revolutionary dictatorship and
n those of parliamentarism. The sharpness of the weapons and
nethods of dictatorship demand watchful antiseptics. A dirty
lipper is nothing to fear, but an unclean razor is very dangerous.
The very methods of the 'trio' were, in my eyes, a sign of
olitical backsliding.

The chief difficulty that the conspirators faced was that of
oming out openly against me before the masses of the people.
The workers knew Zinoviev and Kamenev, and listened to them
eadily. But their behaviour during 1917 was still too fresh in
veryone's memory. They had no moral authority in the party.
Stalin, beyond the narrow circle of the old Bolsheviks, was al-
nost unknown. Some of my friends used to say to me: 'They
vill never dare to come out against you in the open. In the minds
f the people you are too inseparably bound to Lenin's name. It
s impossible to erase the October revolution, or the Red army,
r the civil war.' I did not agree with this. In politics, and
specially in revolutionary politics, popular names of acknow-
edged authority play a very important, sometimes gigantic, but
et not decisive part. In the final analysis the fate of personal
uthority is determined by the deeper processes going on in the
nasses. During the rising tide of the revolution the slanders
gainst the Bolshevist leaders only strengthened the Bolshevists.
During the ebb tide of the revolution the slanders against the
ame men were able to provide the weapons of victory for the
Thermidorian reaction.

The objective processes in the country and in the world arena were helping my opponents. But their task nevertheless was no easy one. The literature, press and agitators of the party were still living on the memories of the preceding days passed under the sign of Lenin and Trotsky. It was necessary to turn all this around 180 degrees, not at once, of course, but by several stages. To show the extent of the turn one must give at least a few illustrations of the prevailing tone of the party press towards the leading figures of the revolution.

On 14 October 1922, at the time when Lenin had already returned to work after his first stroke, Radek wrote in the *Pravda:*

> If Comrade Lenin may be called the reason of the revolution, dominating through his transmission of will, Comrade Trotsky may be characterized as the iron will bridled by reason. Trotsky's speech sounded like a bell summoning to work. All its importance, all its meaning, as well as the meaning of our work during the last few years, appears very clearly.

And so forth. It is true that Radek's personal exuberance became a byword; he was capable of saying one thing and just as capable of following it with another. Much more important is the fact that these lines were printed in the central organ of the party while Lenin was still alive without jarring on anyone's ears.

In 1923, with the conspiracy of the trio already a fact, Lunacharsky was one of the first to try to raise Zinoviev's prestige. But how did he set about his work? 'Of course,' he wrote in his character sketch of Zinoviev, 'Lenin and Trotsky have become the most popular (whether loved or hated) personalities of our epoch, perhaps of the whole world. Zinoviev somewhat recedes before them, but then Lenin and Trotsky had for so long been regarded in our ranks as men of such great gifts, as such undisputed leaders, that no one was much surprised at their amazing growth during the revolution.'

If I quote these pompous panegyrics in somewhat doubtful taste, I do it only because I need them as elements in the general picture, or, if you like, as evidence for a court trial. It repels me to have to quote yet a third witness, Yaroslavsky, whose panegyrics are perhaps even more insufferable than his calumnies.

This man now plays a most important role in the party, measuring by his insignificant stature the depth of the downfall of its leadership. Yaroslavsky rose to his present position entirely by his slandering of me. As the official corrupter of the history of the party, he represents the past as an unbroken struggle of Trotsky against Lenin. It goes without saying that Trotsky 'under-appreciated' the peasantry, 'ignored' the peasantry, 'did not notice' the peasantry. But in February of 1923 – that is, at a time when Yaroslavsky must already have been familiar with my relations to Lenin and my views on the peasantry, in a long article dealing with the first steps of my literary activity (the years 1900 to 1902) he characterized my past in the following way:

'The brilliant work of Comrade Trotsky as a writer and publicist has earned him the world-name of "prince of pamphleteers", as he was called by the English author, George Bernard Shaw. Those who have watched his activity for a quarter of a century, will find that his talent shone with particular brightness . . .' and so on and so forth.

Many readers must have seen the much-reproduced photograph of the youthful Trotsky . . . [etc.] Under this high forehead there was already seething even then a stormy flow of images, thoughts, and impressions which sometimes carried Comrade Trotsky a bit away from the highroad of history, at times either forcing him to choose paths too roundabout or, on the contrary, to attempt fearlessly to break through where no path was possible. But in all these efforts to find the right way we had before us a man profoundly devoted to the revolution, matured for the role of a tribune, with a tongue as sharp and flexible as steel, that cuts down the opponent . . .

And so forth.

'The Siberians were carried away with enthusiasm', Yaroslavsky gushes with an excess of zeal, 'after reading these brilliant articles, and waited impatiently for their appearance. Only a few knew their author, and those who knew Trotsky were the last to imagine at that time that he would be one of the recognized leaders of the most revolutionary army and the greatest revolution in the world.' The case of my ignoring the peasantry fares, if possible, even worse at the hands of Yaroslavsky. The first of my literary works was dedicated to the peasants. Here is what Yaroslavsky says about it:

'Trotsky could not stay in a Siberian village without exploring all the petty details of its life. First of all he turns his attention to the administrative machinery of the Siberian village. In a series of articles he gives a brilliant characterization of this machinery . . .' And further on: 'Around himself Trotsky saw only the village. He suffered over its needs. He was oppressed by its benighted condition, its outlawry.' Yaroslavsky demands that my articles on country life be included in the text-books. All this in February 1923, the same month when the version of my inattention to the country was being created for the first time. But Yaroslavsky was then in Siberia, and therefore not yet well informed about the new 'Leninism'.

The last example that I want to quote concerns Stalin himself. As early as the occasion of the first anniversary of the revolution, he wrote an article which, though disguised, was directed straight at me. In explanation one must remember that during the preparation for the October insurrection Lenin was hiding in Finland; Kamenev, Zinoviev, Rykov, and Kalinin were opposed to an uprising, and no one knew anything about Stalin. As a result the party connected the October revolution chiefly with my name. During the first anniversary of the October revolution, Stalin made an attempt to weaken this impression by setting up against me the general leadership by the Central Committee. But to make his account at all acceptable he was obliged to write:

'The entire work of the practical organization of the uprising was carried on under the immediate direction of the chairman of the Petrograd Soviet, Trotsky. One may state without hesitation that the party was indebted first and foremost to Comrade Trotsky for the garrison's prompt going over to the Soviet and for the able organization of the work of the Military-Revolutionary Committee.'

If Stalin wrote in this vein, it was because at that time ever he could not write in any other way. It needed years of unbridled baiting before Stalin could venture to state in public: 'Comrade

Trotsky did not and could not play any special role either in the party or in the October revolution.' When the contradiction was pointed out to him, he replied by merely redoubling his rudeness.

The 'trio' could under no circumstances pit itself against me. It could pit against me only Lenin. But for this it was necessary that Lenin himself no longer be able to oppose the trio. In other words the success of their campaign required either a Lenin who was fatally ill, or his embalmed corpse in a mausoleum. But even this was not enough. It was necessary that I too be out of the fighting ranks during the campaign. This happened in the fall of 1923.

I am not dealing here with the philosophy of history, but recounting my life against the background of the events with which it was bound up. But I cannot help noting how obligingly the accidental helps the historical law. Broadly speaking the entire historical process is a refraction of the historical law through the accidental. In the language of biology one might say that the historical law is realized through the natural selection of accidents. On this foundation there develops that conscious human activity which subjects accidents to a process of artificial selection.

But at this point I must interrupt my account to tell something about my friend Ivan Vasilyevich Zaytzev, from the village of Kaloshino on the river Dubna. This locality is known as Zabolotye (Beyond the Swamps), and, as its name suggests, is rich in wild game. Here the river Dubna floods the country over wide areas. Swamps, lakes, and shallow marshes, framed by reeds, stretch along in a wide ribbon for almost forty kilometres. In the spring the place is visited by geese, storks, ducks of all kinds, curlew, snipe, and all the rest of the swamp brotherhood. Two kilometres away in the small woods, between hummocks of moss, woodcocks are clucking over the red bilberry shrubs. With a single short oar Ivan Vasilyevich drives his hollow canoe along the narrow furrow between the banks of swamp. The furrow had been dug no one knows when, perhaps two or three hundred years or even longer ago, and it must be dredged out every year to prevent its being sucked in. We are obliged to leave Kaloshino at midnight to get to the tent before dawn. With every step the peat bog lifts its wobbling belly. Once this used to frighten me. But Ivan Vasilyevich said to me on my very first visit: step without fear; people do get drowned in the lake, but nobody has ever lost his life on the swamp.

The canoe is so light and shaky that it is safer to lie on one's back motionless, especially if there is a wind blowing. Boatmen usually stand on their knees for safety. Only Ivan Vasilyevich, though lame in one leg, stands upright. Ivan Vasilyevich is the duck-lord of these lands. His father, his grandfather, and his great-grandfather were all duck-men. Probably some ancestor of his supplied ducks, geese, and swans to the table of Ivan the Terrible. Zaytzev has no interest in moorcocks, woodcocks, or curlews. 'Not of my guild,' he will say cursorily. But he knows the duck through and through, its feathers, its voice, its soul. Standing in his moving boat, Ivan Vasilyevich picks up from the water a feather, then a second and a third and, after looking at them, declares:

'We shall go to Gushchino; the duck rested there in the evening.'

'How do you know?'

'The feather, you see, floats on the water, it is not soaked yet; a fresh feather: the duck was flying in the evening and there is no other place she could fly to but Gushchino.'

And so, whereas other sportsmen bring back a brace or two, Ivan and I bring five or even eight braces. His the merit, mine the credit. It often happens so in life. In the reed tent Ivan Vasilyevich would put his rough palm to his lips and begin quacking like a duck, so tenderly that the most cautious drake, shot at many a time, would succumb to the spell and come swinging around the tent or alight plop on the water a few paces off, so that one actually felt ashamed to shoot it. Zaytzev notices everything, knows everything, senses everything. 'Get ready,' he whispers to me, 'the drake is heading right towards you.' I see the two commas of his wings far off over the woods, but cannot figure out that this is a drake — such mysteries are open only to Ivan Vasilyevich, the great master of the duck-guild. But the drake is really heading towards me. If you miss, Ivan Vasilyevich will emit a low, polite groan – but it is better never to have been born than to hear this groan behind you.

Before the war Zaytzev worked in a textile factory. In the winter he now goes to Moscow to work as a fireman or in a power station. During the first years after the revolution battles were going on all over the country, woods and peat-bogs were burning, the fields were bare, and the ducks stopped flying. Zaytzev had his doubts then about the new régime. But after 1920 the ducks came again, this time in hordes, and Ivan Vasilyevich fully recognized the Soviet power.

About two kilometres from here a small Soviet wick factory ran for a year. Its director was the former chauffeur of my military train. Zaytzev's wife and daughter used to bring home about thirty roubles a month apiece. This was untold wealth. But the factory soon supplied the whole district with wicks and then closed down, and the duck again became the basis of the family's well-being.

One May Day Ivan Vasilyevich found himself in a large Moscow theatre, among the guests of honour on the stage. Ivan Vasilyevich sat in the first row, with his lame leg under him, showing a little embarrassment but, as always, a marked dignity, and listened to my report. He had been brought there by Muralov, with whom I usually shared the joys and sorrows of game-shooting. Ivan Vasilyevich was pleased with the report, understood absolutely everything, and recounted it all back at Kaloshino. This cemented the friendship of the three of us even more solidly. It should be noted that the old hunters, especially from the parts near Moscow, are all spoiled; they rubbed shoulders with the great of the earth and are masters of flattery, lying, and braggadocio. But Ivan Vasilyevich is different. He has a great deal of simplicity, a power of observation, and personal dignity. It is because he is not at heart a trader, but an artist.

Lenin also went hunting with Zaytzev, and Ivan Vasilyevich would always point out the place in a wooden shed where Lenin had lain on the hay. Lenin was passionately fond of game hunting, but he rarely went for a hunt. When he did, he usually got excited, in spite of his great self-control in important things. Just as great strategists usually are bad chess-players, so men with a genius for political marksmanship can be mediocre shots. I remember how Lenin, almost in despair, as if conscious of something that could never be repaired, complained to me of missing a fox at twenty-five paces in a drive-hunt. I understood him and my heart swelled with sympathy.

Lenin and I never had a chance to go hunting together, though we agreed to do so and made firm plans for it many times. In the first years after the revolution there was generally no time for this sort of thing. Lenin occasionally managed to leave Moscow for the open spaces, but I was hardly ever free of the railway carriage, the staffs, or the automobile, and I did not once have a shotgun in my hands. And in the later years after the end of the civil war, something unforeseen was always cropping up to prevent one or the other of us from keeping our agreement. Later on Lenin's health began to give way. A short time before he was laid low we arranged to meet on the river Shosha in Tver province. But Lenin's automobile got stuck on the country road, and I waited for him in vain. When he recovered from his first stroke, he fought insistently to go shooting game. Finally the doctors yielded, on the condition that he not over-exert himself. At some agronomic conference Lenin sidled up to Muralov. 'You and Trotsky often go game shooting together, don't you?'

'Sometimes.'

'And do you fare well?'

'Sometimes.'

'Take me with you, will you?'

'But are you allowed to go?' Muralov asks cautiously.

'Of course I am allowed. . . So you will take me?'

'How can I refuse to take you, Vladimir Ilyich?'

'I'll give you a ring, shall I?'

'We'll be looking forward to it.'

But Lenin did not ring. His illness rang a second time instead. Then death.

All this digression has been necessary to explain how and why one of the Sundays in October 1923 found me in Zabolotye on the bog among the reeds. There was a slight frost that night and I sat in the tent in felt boots. But in the morning the sun was warm and the bog thawed. The automobile was waiting for me on the rise of land. The chauffeur, Davydov, with whom I had gone shoulder-to-shoulder throughout the entire civil war, was as usual consumed with impatience to learn what game I had. From the canoe to the automobile I had to walk about a hundred steps, not more. But the moment I stepped onto the bog in my felt boots my feet were in cold water. By the time I leaped up to the automobile my feet were quite cold. Sitting beside Davydov, I took off my boots and tried to warm my feet by the heat of the motor. But the cold got the better of me. I had to stay in bed. After the influenza some cryptogenic temperature set in. The doctors ordered me to stay in bed, and thus I spent the rest of the autumn and winter. This means that all through the discussion of 'Trotskyism' in 1923 I was ill. One can foresee a revolution or a war, but it is impossible to foresee the consequences of an autumn shooting-trip for wild ducks.

Lenin was laid up at Gorki; I was in the Kremlin. The epigones were widening the circle of the conspiracy. At first they proceeded cautiously and insinuatingly, adding to their praise ever larger doses of poison. Even Zinoviev, the most impatient of them, surrounded his slander with reservations. 'The authority of Comrade Trotsky is known to everyone', Zinoviev was saying at the party conference in Petrograd on 15 December 1923, 'as well as his services. In our midst there is no need of dwelling on it. But errors remain errors. When I erred, the party pulled me up sharply enough.' And so on, in that cowardly yet aggressive tone that was for so long the one characteristic of the conspirators. Only after a deeper sounding of their ground, and a further occupying of position, did they grow bolder.

A whole science was created for fabricating artificial reputations, composing fantastic biographies, and boosting the appointed leaders. A special small science was devoted to the question of the honorary presidium. Since October it had been the custom at the meetings to elect Lenin and Trotsky to the honorary presidium. The combination of these two names was included in everyday speech, in articles, poems, and folk-ditties. It now became necessary to separate the two names, at least mechanically, so that later on it might be possible to pit one against the other politically. Now the presidium began to include all the members of the Politbureau. Then they began to be placed on the list in alphabetical order. Later on the alphabetical order was abandoned in favour of the new hierarchy of leaders. The first place came to be accorded to Zinoviev – in that Petrograd set the example. Some time later the honorary presidiums would appear here and there without Trotsky at all. Stormy protests from the body of the gathering always greeted this, and on occasion the chairman was obliged to explain the omission of my name as a mistake. But the newspaper report was of course silent on this point. Then the first place began to be given to Stalin. If the chairman was not clever enough to guess what was required of him, he was invariably corrected in the newspapers. Careers were made and unmade in accordance with the arrangement of names in the honorary presidium. This work, the most persistent and systematic of all, was justified by the necessity of fighting against the 'cult of the leaders'. At the Moscow conference of January 1924 Pryeobrazhensky said to the epigones: 'Yes, we are against the cult of the leaders, but we are also against practising, instead of the cult of one leader, the cult of others merely of smaller stature.'

'Those were hard days,' my wife writes in her memoirs,

days of tense fighting for Lev Davydovich at the Politbureau against the rest of the members. He was alone and ill, and had to fight them all. Owing to his illness, the meetings were held in our apartment; I sat in the adjoining bedroom and heard his speeches. He spoke with his whole being; it seemed as if with every such speech he lost some of his strength – he spoke with so much 'blood'. And in reply, I heard cold, indifferent answers. Everything of course had been decided in advance, so what was the need of getting excited? After each of these meetings, L. D.'s temperature mounted; he came out of his study soaked through, and undressed and went to bed. His linen and clothes had to be dried as if he had been drenched in a rain-storm. At that time the meetings were frequent and were held in L. D.'s room, whose faded, old carpet appeared in my dreams every night in the shape of a live panther; the meetings during the day became nightmares. Such was the first stage of the struggle before it came out into the open.

In the later struggle by Zinoviev and Kamenev against Stalin the secrets of this period were disclosed by the members of the conspiracy themselves. For it was a real conspiracy. A secret political bureau of seven was formed; it comprised all the members of the official Politbureau except me, and included also Kuybyshev, the present chairman of the Supreme Economic Council. All questions were decided in advance at that secret centre, where the members were bound by mutual vows. They undertook not to engage in polemics against one another and at the same time to seek opportunities to attack me. There were similar centres in the local organizations and they were connected with the Moscow 'seven' by strict discipline. For communication special codes were used. This was a well-organized illegal group within the party, directed orginally against one man. Responsible workers in the party and state were systematically selected by the single criterion: Against Trotsky. During the prolonged 'interregnum' created by Lenin's illness this work was carried on tirelessly but still under cover, so that in the event of Lenin's recovery the mined bridges could be preserved intact. The conspirators acted by hints. Candidates for posts were required to guess what was wanted of them. Those who 'guessed' went up the ladder. In this war a special 'careerism' was developed, which later on received unashamed the name of 'anti-Trotskyism'. Lenin's death freed the conspirators and allowed them to come out into the open. The process of personal selection descended a rung lower. It now became impossible to obtain a post as director of a plant, as secretary of a party local, as chairman of a rural executive committee, as bookkeeper or typist, unless one had proved one's anti-Trotskyism.

The members of the party who raised their voices in protest against this conspiracy became the victims of treacherous attacks, made for reasons entirely remote and frequently invented. On the other hand the morally unstable elements, who were being mercilessly driven out of the party during the first five years, now squared themselves by a single hostile remark against Trotsky. From the end of 1923 the same work was carried on in all the parties of the Communist International; certain leaders were dethroned and others appointed in their stead solely on the basis of their attitude towards Trotsky. A strenuous artificial selection was being effected, a selection not of the best but of the most suitable. The general policy became one of a replacement of independent and gifted men by mediocrities who owed their posts entirely to the apparatus. It was as the supreme expression of the mediocrity of the apparatus that Stalin himself rose to his position.

41

Lenin's Death and the Shift of Power

I was often asked, and even now I still am asked: 'How could you lose power?' In most instances the question covers a naïve conception of letting some material object slip from one's hands, as if losing power were the same thing as losing a watch or a note-book. But as a matter of fact, when the revolutionaries who directed the seizure of power begin at a certain stage to lose it, whether peacefully or through catastrophe, the fact in itself signifies either a decline in the influence of certain ideas and moods in the governing revolutionary circles or the decline of revolutionary mood in the masses themselves. Or it may be both at the same time. The leading groups of the party that emerged from underground were inspired by the revolutionary tendencies which the leaders of the first period of the revolution were able to formulate clearly and to carry out completely and successfully in practice. It was exactly this that made them the leaders of the party, and, through the party, leaders of the working class, and, through the working class, leaders of the country. It was thus that certain individuals had concentrated power in their hands. But the ideas of the first period of the revolution were imperceptibly losing their influence in the consciousness of the party stratum that held the direct power over the country.

In the country itself processes were shaping themselves that one may sum up under the general name of reaction. These extended in varying degree to the working class as well, including even its party. The stratum that made up the apparatus of power developed its own independent aims and tried to subordinate the revolution to them. A division began to reveal itself between the leaders who expressed the historical line of the class and could see beyond the apparatus, and the apparatus itself – a huge, cumbrous, heterogeneous thing that easily sucked in the average communist. At first this division was more psychological than political in character. Yesterday was still too fresh in mind; the slogans of October had not had time to vanish from the memory, and the authority of the leaders of the first period was still strong. But under cover of the traditional forms a different psychology was developing. The international prospects were growing dim. The everyday routine was completely absorbing the people. New methods, instead of serving the old aims, were creating new ones and most of all a new psychology. In the eyes of many the temporary situation began to seem the ultimate goal. A new type was being evolved.

In the final analysis revolutionaries are made of the same social stuff as other people. But they must have had certain very different personal qualities to enable the historical process to separate them from the rest into a distinct group. Association with one another, theoretical work, the struggle under a definite banner, collective discipline, the hardening under the fire of danger, these things gradually shape the revolutionary type. It would be perfectly legitimate to speak of the psychological type of the Bolshevik in contrast, for example, to that of the Menshevik. An eye sufficiently experienced could tell a Bolshevik from a Menshevik even by his outward appearance, with only a slight percentage of error.

This doesn't mean, however, that a Bolshevik was always and in everything a Bolshevik. To absorb a certain philosophic outlook into one's flesh and blood, to make it dominate one's consciousness and to coordinate with it one's sensory world is given not to everyone but to only a few. In the working masses a substitute is found in the class instinct, which in critical periods attains a high degree of sensitiveness. But there are many revolutionaries in the party and the state who come from the masses but have long since broken away from them and who, because of their position, are placed in a separate and distinct class. Their class instinct has evaporated. On the other hand they lack the theoretical stability and outlook to envisage the process in its entirety. Their psychology retains many unprotected surfaces, which, with the change of circumstances, expose them to the easy penetration of foreign and hostile ideological influences.

In the days of the underground struggle, of the uprisings and the civil war, people of this type were merely soldiers of the party. Their minds had only one string, and that sounded in harmony with the party tuning-fork. But when the tension relaxed and the nomads of the revolutions passed on to settled living, the traits of the man in the street, the sympathies and tastes of self-satisfied officials, revived in them.

Quite frequently I heard isolated remarks of Kalinin, Voroshilov, Stalin or Rykov with alarm. Where does this come from? – I asked myself – from what well does it gush? When I came to a meeting and found groups engaged in conversation, often they would stop when they saw me. There was nothing directed against me in those conversations, nothing opposed to the principles of the party. But they showed an attitude of moral relaxation, of self-content and triviality. People began to feel an urge to pour out these new moods upon each other – moods in which the element of philistine gossip came to have a very prominent place. Heretofore they had realized the impropriety of this sort of thing not only in Lenin's or my presence but even with one another. On occasions when vulgarity showed itself – for example on the part of Stalin – Lenin, without even lifting his head from his papers, would look around as if trying to find someone else who was repelled by the remark. In such cases a swift glance, or an intonation in the voice, was enough to reveal indisputably to both of us our solidarity in these psychological appraisals.

If I took no part in the amusements that were becoming more and more common in the lives of the new governing stratum, it was not for moral reasons, but because I hated to inflict such boredom on myself. The visiting at each other's homes, the assiduous attendance at the ballet, the drinking-parties at which people who were absent were pulled to pieces had no attraction for me. The new ruling group felt that I did not fit in with this way of living and they did not even try to win me over. It was for this very reason that many group conversations would stop the moment I appeared, and those engaged in them would cut them short with a certain shamefacedness and a slight bitterness towards me. This was, if you like, a definite indication that I had begun to lose power.

I am here limiting myself to the psychological aspect of the matter and disregarding its social basis, that is, the changes in the anatomy of the revolutionary society. In the final reckoning it is, of course, these latter changes that decide. But in actual life it is their psychological reflection that one encounters directly. The inner events were developing rather slowly, facilitating the molecular processes of the transformation of the upper stratum and leaving no opening for contrasting the two irreconcilable positions before the masses. One must add that the new moods were for a long time, and still are, disguised by traditional formulas. This made it all the more difficult to determine how far the process of metabolism had gone. The Thermidor conspiracy at the end of the eighteenth century, prepared for by the preceding course of the revolution, broke out with a single blow and assumed the shape of a sanguinary finale. Our Thermidor was long drawn out. The guillotine found its substitute – at least for a while – in intrigue. The falsifying of the past, systematized on the conveyer plan, became a weapon for the ideological re-arming of the official party. Lenin's illness and the expectation of his return to the leadership made the temporary situation indefinite, and it lasted, with an interval, for over two years. If the revolution had been in the ascendancy, the delay would have played into the hands of the opposition. But the revolution on the international scale was suffering one defeat after another, and the delay accordingly played into the hands of the national reformism by automatically strengthening the Stalin bureaucracy against me and my political friends.

The out-and-out philistine, ignorant, and simply stupid baiting of the theory of permanent revolution grew from just these psychological sources. Gossiping over a bottle of wine or returning from the ballet, one smug official would say to another: 'He can think of nothing but permanent revolution.' The accusations of unsociability, of individualism, of aristocratism, were closely connected with this particular mood. The sentiment of 'Not all and always for the revolution, but something for oneself as well', was translated as 'Down with permanent revolution.' The revolt against the exacting theoretical demands of Marxism and the exacting political demands of the revolution gradually assumed, in the eyes of these people, the form of a struggle against 'Trotskyism'. Under this banner the liberation of the philistine in the Bolshevik was proceeding. It was because of this that I lost power, and it was this that determined the form which this loss took.

I have said before that Lenin, from his death-bed, was preparing a blow at Stalin and his allies, Dzerzhinsky and Ordzhonikidze. Lenin valued Dzerzhinsky highly. The estrangement began when Dzerzhinsky realized that Lenin did not think him capable of directing economic work. It was this that threw Dzerzhinsky into Stalin's arms, and then Lenin decided to strike at him as one of Stalin's supports. As for Ordzhonikidze, Lenin wanted to expel him from the party for his ways of a governor-general. Lenin's note promising the Georgian Bolsheviks his full support against Stalin, Dzerzhinsky, and Ordzhonikidze was addressed to Mdivani. The fates of the four reveal most vividly the sweeping change in the party engineered by the Stalin faction. After Lenin's death Dzerzhinsky was put at the head of the Supreme Economic Council, that is, in charge of all state industries. Ordzhonikidze, who had been slated for expulsion, has been made the head of the Central Control Commission. Stalin not only has remained the general secretary contrary to Lenin's wish, but has been given unheard-of powers by the apparatus. Finally, Budu Mdivani, whom Lenin supported against Stalin, is now in the Tobolsk prison. A similar 'regrouping' has been effected in the entire directing personnel of the party and in all the parties of the International without exception. The epoch of the epigones is separated from that of Lenin not only by a gulf of ideas, but also by a sweeping overturn in the organization of the party.

Stalin has been the chief instrument in carrying out this overturn. He is gifted with practicability, a strong will, and persistence in carrying out his aims. His political horizon is restricted, his theoretical equipment primitive. His work of compilation, *The Foundations of Leninism*, in which he made an attempt to pay tribute to the theoretical traditions of the party, is full of sophomoric errors. His ignorance of foreign languages compels him to follow the political life of other countries at second-hand.

His mind is stubbornly empirical and devoid of creative imagination. To the leading group of the party (in the wider circles he was not known at all) he always seemed a man destined to play second and third fiddle. And the fact that today he is playing first is not so much a summing-up of the man as it is of this transitional period of political backsliding in the country. Helvetius said it long ago: 'Every period has its great men, and if these are lacking, it invents them.' Stalinism is above all else the automatic work of the impersonal apparatus on the decline of the revolution.

Lenin died on 21 January 1924. Death was for him merely a deliverance from physical and moral suffering. He must have felt it intolerably humiliating to be so utterly helpless, and especially to lose his power of speech while he was still fully conscious. He grew unable to endure the patronizing tone of the doctors, their banal jokes and their false encouragements. While he was still able to speak he casually put test questions to the doctors, caught them unawares in contradictions, insisted on additional explanations, and dipped into the medical books himself. In this case as in everything else he was striving most of all for clarity. The only medical man he could endure was Fyodor Alexandrovich Guetier. A good physician and a good man, unsullied by the traits of a courtier, Guetier was attached to Lenin and Krupskaya by a genuine affection. During the period when Lenin would not allow any other doctor to come near him Guetier continued to visit him. Guetier was also a close friend and house-physician to my family during all the years of the revolution. Thanks to him, we always had most trustworthy and intelligent reports on the condition of Vladimir Ilyich, to supplement and correct the impersonal official bulletins.

More than once I asked Guetier whether Lenin's intellect would retain its power in case of recovery. Guetier answered me in this strain: the tendency to fatigue would increase, there would not be the former clarity in work, but a virtuoso would remain a virtuoso. In the interval between the first and second strokes this prediction was confirmed to the letter. Towards the end of the meetings of the Politbureau Lenin gave one the impression of being a hopelessly tired man. All the muscles of his face sagged, the gleam went out of his eyes, and even his formidable forehead seemed to shrink, while his shoulders drooped heavily. The expression of his face and of his entire figure might have been summed up in a word: tired. At such ghastly moments Lenin seemed to me a doomed man. But with a good night's sleep he would recover his power of thought. The articles written in the interval between his two strokes hold their own with his best work. The fluid of the source was the same, but the flow was growing less. Even after the second stroke Guetier did not take away all hope. But his reports continued to grow more pessimistic. The illness dragged on. Without malice or mercy, the blind forces of nature were sinking the great sick man into a state of impotence from which there was no way out. Lenin could not and should not have lived on as an invalid. But still we did not abandon hope for his recovery.

In the meantime my own indisposition lingered on. 'At the insistence of the doctors', writes N. I. Sedova, 'L. D. was moved to the country. There Guetier visited the sick man for whom he had a tender regard. Politics did not interest him, but he suffered deeply for us without knowing how to express his sympathy. The persecution of L. D. caught him unprepared. He did not understand it and was waiting and worrying. At Archangelskoye he spoke to me excitedly about the necessity of taking L. D. to Sukhum. In the end we decided to take the step. The journey, which was long in itself – via Baku, Tiflis, and Batum – was made still longer by the snow-drifts that covered the tracks. But the travelling had a soothing effect. The farther we went from Moscow the more we broke away from the depression that we had found there of late. But in spite of it all I still had the feeling that I was accompanying a very sick man. The uncertainty tried one's patience: what sort of life would there be at Sukhum? Would we have enemies or friends about us there?'

21 January found us at the station in Tiflis on our way to Sukhum. I was sitting with my wife in the working half of my car, with the high temperature that was the usual thing at that time. There was a knock on the door and my faithful assistant, Syermuks, who was accompanying me to Sukhum, entered. From

his manner as he walked in, from his livid-grey face as he handed me a sheet of paper, looking past me with glassy eyes, I sensed a catastrophe. It was the decoded telegram from Stalin telling me that Lenin had died. I passed it to my wife; she had already guessed it.

The Tiflis authorities soon received a similar telegram. The news of Lenin's death was spreading in ever-widening rings. I got the Kremlin on the direct wire. In answer to my inquiry I was told: 'The funeral will be on Saturday, you can't get back in time, and so we advise you to continue your treatment.' Accordingly, I had no choice. As a matter of fact the funeral did not take place until Sunday, and I could easily have reached Moscow by then. Incredible as it may appear, I was even deceived about the date of the funeral. The conspirators surmised correctly that I would never think of verifying it, and later on they could always find an explanation. I must recall the fact that the news of Lenin's first illness was not communicated to me until the third day. This was a system. The object was to 'gain time'.

The Tiflis comrades came to demand that I write on Lenin's death at once. But I knew only one urgent desire – and that was to be alone. I could not stretch my hand to lift my pen. The brief text of the Moscow telegram was still resounding in my head. Those who gathered at the train waited for a response. They were right. The train was held up for half an hour, and I wrote the farewell lines: 'Lenin has gone. Lenin is no more.' The few handwritten pages were transmitted to the direct wire.

'We arrived quite broken down,' writes my wife. 'It was the first time we had seen Sukhum. The mimosa were in full bloom – they were plentiful there. Magnificent palms. Camellias. It was January; in Moscow the cold was bitter. The Abhazians greeted us on our arrival in a friendly manner. In the dining-room of the rest-house there were two portraits on the wall, one – draped in black – of Vladimir Ilyich, the other of L. D. We felt like taking the latter one down, but thought it would look too demonstrative.'

At Sukhum I spent long days lying on the balcony facing the sea. Although it was January, the sun was warm and bright.

Between the balcony and the glittering sea there were huge palms. With the constant sensation of running a temperature were mingled thoughts of Lenin's death. In my mind I went through all the stages of my life: my meetings with Lenin, our disagreements, polemics, our renewed friendliness, our fellowship of work. Individual episodes emerged with the vividness of a dream. Gradually all of it began to assume increasingly sharp outlines. With amazing clarity I saw those 'disciples' who were true to their master in the little things and not in the big. As I breathed the sea air in I assimilated with my whole being the assurance of my historical rightness in opposition to the epigones.

27 January 1924. Over the palms and the sea reigned silence, sparkling under the blue canopy. Suddenly it was pierced by salvos of artillery. The cannonading was going on somewhere below on the seashore. It was Sukhum's salute to the leader who at that hour was being buried in Moscow. I thought of him and of the woman who had been his life-companion for so many years, receiving through him her impressions of the world. Now she was burying him, and must inevitably feel lonely among the grieving millions around her – grieving, but not as she was grieving. I thought of Nadyezhda Konstantinovna Krupskaya. I wanted to speak a word of greeting, of sympathy, of endearment to her from where I was. But I could not bring myself to do it. Words seemed much too light in the face of what had happened. I was afraid that they would only sound conventional. And so I was shaken with gratitude when I received a letter a few days later from Nadyezhda Konstantinovna. This is how it read:

DEAR LEV DAVYDOVICH,

I write to tell you that about a month before his death, as he was looking through your book, Vladimir Ilyich stopped at the place where you sum up Marx and Lenin, and asked me to read it over again to him; he listened very attentively, and then looked it over again himself. And here is another thing I want to tell you. The attitude of V. I. towards you at the time when you came to us in London from Siberia has not changed until his death. I wish you, Lev Davydovich, strength and health, and I embrace you warmly.

N. KRUPSKAYA.

In the book which Vladimir Ilyich was looking over before his death I compared him with Marx. I knew only too well Lenin's attitude towards Marx, an attitude made up of a disciple's grateful love and of the pathos of distance. The r elationship between master and disciple became, in the course of history, the relationship of the theoretical precursor and the first realizer. In my article I did away with the traditional pathos of distance. Marx and Lenin, so closely linked historically and yet so different, were to me the two unsurpassable summits of man's spiritual power. And I rejoiced at the thought that Lenin had read my lines about him attentively a short time before he died, and probably with emotion, since for him, as for me, the Marx scale was the most titanic for measuring human personality.

And with emotion I now read Krupskaya's letter. She took two extreme points in my connection with Lenin – the October day in 1902 when, after escaping from Siberia, I had raised Lenin from his hard London bed early in the morning, and the end of December 1923, when Lenin had twice read my appreciation of his life-work. Between these two points there had passed two decades – at first joint work, then bitter factional struggle, then joint work again on a higher historical foundation. In Hegel's phrase: thesis, antithesis, synthesis. And now Krupskaya bore witness that Lenin's attitude towards me, despite the protracted period of antithesis, remained the 'London' one; that is, one of warm support and friendly sympathy, but now on a higher historical plane. Even if there were nothing else, all the folios of the dissemblers could not outweigh in the judgement of history this little note written by Krupskaya a few days after Lenin's death.

Considerably delayed by the snow, the newspapers began to bring us the memorial speeches, obituaries, and articles. Our friends were expecting L. D. to come to Moscow, and thought that he would cut short his trip in order to return, since no one imagined that Stalin's telegram had cut off his return. I remember my son's letter, received at Sukhum. He was terribly shocked by Lenin's death, and though suffering from a cold, with a temperature of 104, he went in his not very warm coat to the Hall of Columns to pay his last respects, and waited, waited, and waited with impatience for our arrival. One could feel in his letter his bitter bewilderment and diffident reproach.

This again is quoted from my wife's notes.

A delegation of the Central Committee composed of Tomsky, Frunze, Pyatakov, and Gusyev came to me at Sukhum to coordinate with me in making changes in the personnel of the war department. This was sheer farce. The renewal of the personnel in the war department had for some time been going on at full speed behind my back, and now it was simply a matter of observing the proprieties.

The first blow in the war department fell on Sklyansky. He was the first to bear Stalin's revenge for the latter's reverses before Tsaritsin, his failure on the southern front, and his adventure before Lvov. Intrigue reared high its serpentine head. To uproot Sklyansky – and me in the future – an ambitious but relentless intriguer named Unschlicht had been installed in the war department a few months before. Sklyansky was dismissed and Frunze, who was in command of the armies in the Ukraine, was appointed in his place. Frunze was a serious person. His authority in the party, due to his sentence of hard-labour in Siberia in the past, was higher than the more recent authority of Sklyansky. Furthermore he had revealed an indisputable talent for military leadership during the war. But as a military administrator he was far inferior to Sklyansky. He was too apt to be carried away by abstract schemes; he was a poor judge of character; and he succumbed easily to the influence of experts, especially those of the second order.

But I must finish Sklyansky's story. With that rudeness characteristic of Stalin, without even being consulted about it, he was transferred to economic work. Dzerzinsky, who was glad to get rid of Unschlicht, his deputy at the GPU, and secure for industry such a first-class administrator as Sklyansky, put him in charge of the cloth trust. With a shrug of his shoulders Sklyansky plunged into his new work. A few months later he decided to visit the United States, to look about, study, and buy machinery. Before he left he called on me to say good-bye and to ask my advice. We had worked hand in hand during the years of civil war. But our talk had usually been about troop units, military rules, speeding up the graduation of officers, supplies of copper and aluminium for military plants, uniforms and food, rather than about the party. We were both too busy for that. After Lenin was taken ill, when the plots of the epigones began to

force their way into the war department, I refrained from dis
cussing party matters, particularly with the military staff. The
situation was very indefinite, the differences were then only be
ginning to crop up, and the forming of factions in the army con
cealed many dangers. Later on I was ill myself. At that meeting
with Sklyansky in the summer of 1925, when I was no longer in
charge of the war department, we talked over almost everything.

'Tell me,' Sklyansky asked, 'what is Stalin?'

Sklyansky knew Stalin well enough himself. He wanted my
definition of Stalin and my explanation of his success. I thought
for a minute.

'Stalin', I said, 'is the outstanding mediocrity in the party.'
This definition then shaped itself for me for the first time in its
full import, psychological as well as social. By the expression on
Sklyansky's face I saw at once that I had helped my questioner
to touch on something significant.

'You know,' he said, 'it is amazing how, during this last period,
the mean, the self-satisfied mediocrity is pushing itself into every
sphere. And all of it finds in Stalin its leader. Where does it all
come from?'

'This is the reaction after the great social and psychological
strain of the first years of revolution. A victorious counter-re
volution may develop its great men. But its first stage, the
Thermidor, demands mediocrities who can't see farther than
their noses. Their strength lies in their political blindness,
like the mill-horse that thinks that he is moving up when
really he is only pushing down the belt-wheel. A horse that sees
is incapable of doing the work.'

In that conversation I realized for the first time with absolute
clarity the problem of the Thermidor – with, I might even say,
a sort of physical conviction. I agreed with Sklyansky to return
to the subject after he got back from America. Not many weeks
later a cable informed us that Sklyansky had been drowned in
some American lake while boating. Life is inexhaustible in its
cruel inventions.

The urn with Sklyansky's ashes was brought back to Moscow.
Everyone was sure that it would be immured in the Kremlin
wall in the Red Square, which had become the Pantheon of the

evolution. But the secretariat of the Central Committee decided
o bury Sklyansky outside of the city. Sklyansky's farewell visit
o me had apparently been noted and taken into account. The
atred extended to the burial-urn. The belittling of Sklyansky
vas part of the general fight against the leadership that had inured victory in the civil war. I do not think that Sklyansky
live was interested in the matter of where he was to be buried.
But the decision of the Central Committee took on a character
f personal and political meanness. Throwing aside my sense of
epulsion, I called Molotov. But the decision could not be
ltered. History has yet to pass its verdict on it.

In the autumn of 1924 my temperature again began to mount.
By that time another discussion had blazed up, brought about
his time from above in accordance with some prearranged plan.
n Leningrad, in Moscow, and in the provinces hundreds and
housands of preliminary secret conferences had been held to
prepare the so-called 'discussion', to prepare, that is, a syste-
natic and well-organized baiting, now directed not at the oppo-
ition but at me personally. When the secret preparations were
ver, at a signal from the *Pravda* a campaign against Trotskyism
urst forth simultaneously on all platforms, in all pages and
olumns, in every crack and corner. It was a majestic spectacle
f its kind. The slander was like a volcanic eruption. It was a
reat shock to the large mass of the party. I lay in bed with a
emperature and remained silent. Press and orators did nothing
ut expose Trotskyism, although no one knew exactly what it
neant. Day after day they served up incidents from the past,
olemical excerpts from Lenin's articles of twenty years' stand-
ng, confusing, falsifying and mutilating them, and in general
resenting them as if everything had happened just the day be-
ore. No one could understand anything of all this. If it had
eally been true, then Lenin must have been aware of it. But was
here not the October revolution after all that? Was there not the
ivil war after the revolution? Had not Trotsky worked together
vith Lenin in creating the Communist International? Were not
rotsky's portraits hanging everywhere next to those of Lenin?
But slander poured forth in a cold lava stream. It pressed down

automatically on the consciousness, and was even more deva
stating to the will.

The attitude towards Lenin as a revolutionary leader gave way
to an attitude like that towards the head of an ecclesiastical hierarchy. Against my protests a mausoleum was built on the Red
Square, a monument unbecoming and offensive to the revolutionary consciousness. The official books about Lenin evolved
into similar mausoleums. His ideas were cut up into quotations
for hypocritical sermons. His embalmed corpse was used as a
weapon against the living Lenin – and against Trotsky. The
masses were stunned, puzzled, and overawed. Thanks to its
sheer bulk, the campaign of ignorant lies took on political
potency. It overwhelmed, oppressed, and demoralized the
masses. The party found itself condemned to silence. A régime
was established that was nothing less than a dictatorship of the
apparatus over the party. In other words the party was ceasing
to be a party.

In the morning papers were brought to me in bed. I looked
over the cable reports and the titles and signatures of the articles.
I knew those men well enough; I knew their inner thoughts,
what they were capable of saying and what they had been ordered
to say. In the majority of cases they were men already exhausted
by the revolution. Some were simply narrow-minded fanatics
who had let themselves be deceived. Others were young 'career-
ists' in a hurry to prove how invaluable they were. All of them
contradicted each other and themselves. But the slander kept up
incessantly in the newspapers: it howled and shrieked, drowning
its contradictions and superficiality in its own noise. It succeeded
by sheer volume alone.

'The second attack of L. D.'s illness,' writes N. I. Sedova,

coincided with a monstrous campaign of persecution against him
which we felt as keenly as if we had been suffering from the most
malignant disease. The pages of the *Pravda* seemed endless, and every
line of the paper, even every word, a lie. L. D. kept silent. But what
it cost him to maintain that silence! Friends called to see him during
the day and often at night. I remember that someone once asked him
if he had read that day's paper. He replied that he no longer read the
newspapers. And it is true that he only took them up in his hands, ra-

s eyes over them, and then threw them aside. It seemed as if it were
ough for him merely to look at them to know all that they contained.
e knew only too well the cooks who had made the dish, and the same
sh every day, to boot. To read the papers at that time was exactly,
e would say, like pushing a funnel brush into one's own throat. It
ight have been possible to force himself to read them if L. D. had
ecided to reply. But he remained silent. His cold lingered on, thanks
 his critical nervous condition. He looked pale and thin. In the
mily we avoided talking about the persecution and yet we could talk
 nothing else. I remember how I felt when I went to my work every
ay at the Commissariat of Education; it was like running a gauntlet.
ut never once did anyone permit himself an unpleasant insinuation.
de by side with the inimical silence of the small ruling group there
as unquestionable sympathy from most of my colleagues. The life of
e party seemed to be split in half; the inner, hidden life and the
atward life for show only, and the two lives were in absolute contra-
ction to each other. Only a few brave souls ventured to reveal what
as latent in the minds and hearts of most of those who concealed
eir sympathies under a 'monolithic' vote.

My letter to Chiedze against Lenin was published during this
eriod. This episode, dating back to April 1913, grew out of the
ct that the official Bolshevik newspaper then published in St
etersburg had appropriated the title of my Viennese publi-
ation, 'The Pravda – a Labour Paper'. This led to one of those
aarp conflicts so frequent in the lives of the foreign exiles. In a
tter written to Chiedze, who at one time stood between the
olsheviks and the Mensheviks, I gave vent to my indignation
 the Bolshevik centre and at Lenin. Two or three weeks later
would undoubtedly have subjected my letter to a strict censor's
evision; a year or two later still it would have seemed a curiosity
 my own eyes. But that letter was to have a peculiar destiny.
 was intercepted on its way by the Police Department. It
sted in the police archives until the October revolution, when
 went to the Institute of History of the Communist party.
enin was well aware of this letter; in his eyes, as in mine, it
as simply 'the snows of yesteryear' and nothing more. A good
any letters of various kinds had been written during the years
 foreign exile! In 1924 the epigones disinterred the letter from
e archives and flung it at the party, three quarters of which at

that time consisted of new members. It was no accident that th
time chosen for this was the months immediately followin
Lenin's death. This condition was doubly essential. In the firs
place Lenin could no longer rise to call these gentlemen by thei
right names and in the second place the masses of the peopl
were torn with grief over the death of their leader. With no ide
of the yesterdays of the party the people read Trotsky's hostil
remarks about Lenin and were stunned. It is true that the re
marks had been made twelve years before, but chronology wa
disregarded in the face of the naked quotations. The use tha
the epigones made of my letter to Chiedze is one of the greates
frauds in the world's history. The forged documents c
the French reactionaries in the Dreyfus case are as nothin
compared to the political forgery perpetrated by Stalin and hi
associates.

Slander becomes a force only when it meets some historic
demand. There must have been some shift, I reasoned, in soci
relations or in the political mood, if slander could find such a
endless market. It is necessary to analyse the content of thi
slander. As I lay in bed I had plenty of time to do so. Fro
what does this accusation of Trotsky's wishing 'to rob the peas
ant' derive – that formula which the reactionary agrarians, th
Christian socialists, and the Fascists always direct against soci
lists and against communists in particular? Whence this bitte
baiting of the Marxist idea of permanent revolution, this nation
bragging which promises to build its own socialism? What se
tions of the people make demands for such reactionary vulgarity
And lastly, how and why this lowering of the theoretical leve
this retrogression to political stupidity? Lying in bed, I wei
over my old articles, and my eyes fell on these lines written i
1909, at the peak of the reactionary régime under Stolypin:

When the curve of historical development rises, public thinkir
becomes more penetrating, braver and more ingenious. It grasps fac
on the wing, and on the wing links them with the thread of genera
ization . . . But when the political curve indicates a drop, public thin
ing succumbs to stupidity. The priceless gift of political generalizatic
vanishes somewhere without leaving even a trace. Stupidity grows i
insolence, and, baring its teeth, heaps insulting mockery on ever

attempt at a serious generalization. Feeling that it is in command of the field, it begins to resort to its own means.

One of its most important means is slander.

I say to myself that we are passing through a period of reaction. A political shifting of the classes is going on as well as a change in class-consciousness. After the great effort there is the recoil. How far will it go? Certainly not back to its starting-point. But no one can indicate the line in advance. The struggle of the inner forces will determine that. First, one must understand what is happening. The deep molecular processes of reaction are emerging to the surface. They have as their object the eradicating, or at least the weakening, of the dependence of the public consciousness on the ideas, slogans and living figures of October. That is the meaning of what is now taking place. So let us not become too subjective, or quarrel or feel put out with history for conducting its affairs in such involved and tangled ways. To understand what is happening is already to half ensure the victory.

42

The Last Period of Struggle within the Party

In January 1925 I was relieved of my duties as the People'
Commissary of War. This decision had been carefully prepare(
for by the preceding struggle. Next to the traditions of th
October revolution the epigones feared most the traditions o
the civil war and my connection with the army. I yielded u)
the military post without a fight, with even a sense of relie1
since I was thereby wresting from my opponents' hands thei
weapon of insinuation concerning my military intention:
The epigones had first invented these fantasies to justify thei
acts and then began almost to believe them. Ever sinc
1921 my personal interests had shifted to another field. Th
war was over; the army had been reduced from 5,300,00
men to 600,000. The military work was entering bureau
cratic channels. Economic problems were of first importanc
in the country; from the moment the war ended they had absorbe
my time and attention to a far greater extent than militar
matters.

I was made chairman of the Concessions Committee in Ma
1925, head of the electro-technical board, and chairman of th
scientific-technical board of industry. These three posts were i
no way connected. Their selection was made behind my back an(
determined by certain specific considerations: to isolate me fror
the party, to submerge me in routine, to put me under specia
control, and so on. Nevertheless I made an honest attempt t
work in harmony with the new arrangements. When I began m
work in three institutions utterly unfamiliar to me, I naturall
plunged in up to my ears. I was specially interested in the insti
tutes of technical science which had developed in Soviet Russi
on quite a large scale, because of the centralized character c
industry. I assiduously visited many laboratories, watched ex

periments with great interest, listened to explanations given by
the foremost scientists, in my spare time studied text-books on
chemistry and hydro-dynamics, and felt that I was half-admini-
strator and half-student. Not for nothing had I planned in my
youth to take university courses in physics and mathematics. I
was taking a rest from politics and concentrating on questions of
natural science and technology. As head of the electro-technical
board, I visited power stations in the process of construction and
made a trip to the Dnieper, where preparatory work on a large
scale was under way in the construction of a hydro-electric power
station. Two boatmen took me down the rapids in a fishing-
boat, along the ancient route of the Zaporozhtzi-Cossacks. This
adventure of course had merely a sporting interest. But I became
deeply interested in the Dnieper enterprise, both from an economic and a technical point of view. I organized a body of American experts, later augmented by German experts, to safeguard
the power station from defective estimates, and tried to relate
my new work not only to current economic requirements but also
to the fundamental problems of socialism. In my struggle against
the stolid national approach to economic questions ('independence' through self-contained isolation) I advanced the project
of developing a system of comparative indices of the Soviet and
the world economy. This was the result of our need for correct
orientation in the world market, being intended on its part to
serve the needs of the import and export trade and of the policy
of concessions. In essence, the project of comparative indices
which grew inevitably from a recognition of the productive forces
of the world as dominating those of a single nation implied an
attack on the reactionary theory of 'socialism in a single country'.

I made public reports on matters connected with my new
activity and published books and pamphlets. My opponents
neither could nor cared to accept battle on this ground. They
summed up the situation in the formula: Trotsky has created a
new battlefield for himself. The electro-technical board and the
scientific institutions began now to worry them almost as much
as the war department and the Red army previously had. The
Stalin apparatus followed on my heels. Every practical step that

I took gave rise to a complicated intrigue behind the scenes
every theoretical conclusion fed the ignorant myth of 'Trotsky
ism'. My practical work was performed under impossible con
ditions. It is no exaggeration to say that much of the creativ
activity of Stalin and of his assistant Molotov was devoted t
organizing direct sabotage around me. It became practically im
possible for the institutions under my direction to obtain th
necessary wherewithal. People working there began to fear fo
their futures or at least for their careers.

My attempt to win a political holiday for myself was patentl
a failure. The epigones could not stop half-way. They were to
afraid of what they had already done. Yesterday's slande
weighed heavily on them, demanding double treachery today.
ended by insisting on being relieved of the electro-technica
board and the institutions of technical science. The chie
concessions committee did not provide the same scope fo
intrigue, since the fate of each concession was decided in th
Politbureau.

Meanwhile party affairs had reached a new crisis. In the firs
period of the struggle a trio had been formed to oppose me, bu
it was far from being a unit. In theoretical and political respec
both Zinoviev and Kamenev were probably superior to Stali
But they both lacked that little thing called character. The
international outlook, wider than Stalin's, which they acquire
under Lenin in foreign exile, did not make their position an
stronger; on the contrary it weakened it. The political tendenc
was towards a self-contained national development, and the ol
formula of Russian patriotism. 'We'll bury the enemy under
shower of our caps,' was now assiduously being translated int
the new socialist language. Zinoviev's and Kamenev's attempt
uphold the international viewpoint, if only to a limited degre
turned them into 'Trotskyists' of the second order in the ey
of the bureaucracy. This led them to wage their campaig
against me with even more fury, so that they might win great
confidence from the apparatus. But these efforts were also vai
The apparatus was rapidly discovering that Stalin was flesh
its flesh. Zinoviev and Kamenev soon found themselves in ho
tile opposition to Stalin; when they tried to transfer the dispu

from the trio to the Central Committee, they discovered that Stalin had a solid majority there.

Kamenev was considered the official leader of Moscow. But after the routing with Kamenev's participation of the Moscow party organization in 1923, when the party came out in its majority to support the opposition, the rank-and-file of the Moscow communists maintained a grim silence. With the first attempts to resist Stalin, Kamenev found himself suspended in air. The situation in Leningrad* was different. The Leningrad communists were protected from the opposition of 1923 by the heavy lid of Zinoviev's apparatus. But now their turn came. The Leningrad workers were aroused by the political trend in favour of the rich peasants – the so-called kulaks – and a policy aimed at one-country socialism. The class protest of the workers coincided with the high-official opposition of Zinoviev. Thus a new opposition came into existence, and one of its members in the first stages was Nadyezhda Konstantinovna Krupskaya. To everyone's utter surprise, their own most of all, Zinoviev and Kamenev found themselves obliged to repeat word for word the criticisms by the opposition, and soon they were listed as being in the camp of the 'Trotskyists'. It is little wonder that in our circle closer relations with Zinoviev and Kamenev seemed, to say the least, paradoxical. There were among the oppositionists many who opposed such a bloc. There were even some, though only a few, who thought it possible to form a bloc with Stalin against Zinoviev and Kamenev. One of my closest friends, Mrachkovsky, an old revolutionary and one of the finest commanders in the civil war, expressed himself as opposed to a bloc with anyone and gave a classic explanation of his stand: 'Stalin will deceive and Zinoviev will sneak away.' But such questions are finally decided not by psychological but by political considerations. Zinoviev and Kamenev openly avowed that the 'Trotskyists' had been right in the struggle against them ever since 1923. They accepted the basic principles of our platform. In such circumstances it was impossible not to form a bloc with

---

* St Petersburg, renamed Petrograd during the war, had been rechristened again as Leningrad. – *Translator.*

them, especially since thousands of revolutionary Leningra
workers were behind them.

I had not met Kamenev outside the official meetings for thre
years, that is, since the night on the eve of his trip to Georgi
when he promised to uphold the stand taken by Lenin and m
but, having learned of Lenin's grave condition, went over 1
Stalin. At our very first meeting Kamenev declared: 'It
enough for you and Zinoviev to appear on the same platform
and the party will find its true Central Committee.' I could n
help laughing at such bureaucratic optimism. Kamenev ob
viously underestimated the disintegrating effect on the party (
the three years' activity of the trio. I pointed it out to him, with
out the slightest concession to his feelings. The revolutiona
ebb-tide that had begun at the end of 1923, that is, after the de
feat of the revolutionary movement in Germany, had assume
international proportions. In Russia the reaction against Octob
was proceeding at full speed. The party apparatus more an
more was lining itself up with the right wing. Under such co
ditions it would have been childish to think that all we need (
was join hands and victory would drop at our feet like a ri
fruit. 'We must aim far ahead,' I repeated dozens of times 1
Kamenev and Zinoviev. 'We must prepare for a long and seriou
struggle.' On the spur of the moment my new allies accepte
this formula bravely. But they didn't last long; they were fadir
daily and hourly. Mrachkovsky proved right in his appraisal
their personalities. Zinoviev did sneak away after all, but he w
far from being followed by all of his supporters. At any rate h
double about-face inflicted an incurable wound on the legend (
'Trotskyism'.

In the spring of 1926 my wife and I made a trip to Berlin. T
Moscow physicians, at a loss to explain the continuance of n
high temperature, and unwilling to shoulder the entire respons
bility, had been urging me for some time to take a trip abroa
I was equally anxious to find a way out of the impasse, for n
high temperature paralysed me at the most critical moment
and acted as my opponents' most steadfast ally. The matter
my visit abroad was taken up at the Politbureau, which stat

hat it regarded my trip as extremely dangerous in view of the nformation it had and the general political situation, but that it eft the final decision to me. The statement was accompanied by a note of reference from the GPU indicating the inadmissibility of my trip. The Politbureau undoubtedly feared that in he event of any unpleasant accident to me while abroad the party would hold it responsible. The idea of my enforced exile abroad, and in Constantinople at that, had not yet dawned within he policeman's skull of Stalin. It is possible that the Politbureau was also apprehensive of my taking action abroad to consolidate the foreign opposition. Nevertheless, after consulting ny friends, I decided to go.

Arrangements with the German embassy were completed without difficulty, and about the middle of April my wife and I left with a diplomatic passport in the name of Kuzmyenko, a member of the Ukrainian *collegium* of the commissariat of education. We were accompanied by my secretary, Syermuks, by the former commander of my train, and by a representative of the GPU. Zinoviev and Kamenev parted from me with a show of real feeling; they did not like the prospect of remaining eye-to-eye with Stalin.

In the years before the war I had known Hohenzollern Berlin very well. It had then its own peculiar physiognomy, which no one could call pleasant but which many thought imposing. Berlin has changed. It has now no physiognomy at all, at least none hat I could discover. The city was slowly recovering from a ong and serious disease whose course had been accompanied by many surgical operations. The inflation was already over, but he stabilized mark served only as a means of measuring the general anaemia. In the streets, in the shops, on the faces of the pedestrians, one sensed the impoverishment and also that impatient, often avid, desire to rise again. The German thoroughness and cleanliness during the hard years of war, of the defeat and the Versailles brigandage, had been swallowed up by dire poverty. The human ant-hill was stubbornly but joylessly restoring the passages, corridors, and store-rooms crushed by the boot of war. In the rhythm of the streets, in the movements and gestures of the passers-by, one felt a tragic undercurrent of fatalism: 'Can't be helped; life is an indefinite term at hard labour; we must begin again at the beginning.'

For a few weeks I was under medical observation in a private clinic in Berlin. In search of the roots of the mysterious temperature the doctors shunted me from one to another. Finally, throat specialist advanced the hypothesis that the source was my tonsils, and advised having them removed in any case. The diagnosticians and therapeutists hesitated, being middle-aged medical base men. But the surgeon, with the experience of the war behind him, treated them with a devastating contempt. He implied that tonsils were now removed as easily as shaving off moustache. I was obliged to consent.

The assistants were getting ready to tie my hands, but the surgeon decided to accept moral guarantees. Behind his encouraging jocosity I could feel the tension and controlled excitement. It was a most unpleasant sensation to lie on the table and choke in one's own blood. The proceeding lasted from forty fifty minutes. Everything went off well – if one overlooks the fact that the operation was apparently useless, as the temperature set in again some time later.

But my time in Berlin, at least that spent in the clinic, was not wasted. I immersed myself in the German press, from which had been almost completely cut off ever since August 1917 Every day I was provided with a score of German and a few foreign publications, and after reading them I would throw them on the floor. The specialists who visited me had to walk on carpet of newspapers of all shades of political opinion. It was really my first opportunity to listen to the entire range of German republican politics. I must confess that I did not find anything unexpected there. The republic as the foundling of the military *debâcle*, the republicans as creatures of the Versailles compulsion, the Social Democrats as the executors of the November revolution which they themselves had smothered, Hindenburg as a democratic president – in general, it was just as I had imagined it. And yet it was very instructive to be able to view at close range.

On 1 May my wife and I went out for a drive around the city in an automobile. We visited the principal districts, watched processions, read placards, listened to speeches, drove to the Alexanderplatz, and mingled with the crowd. I had seen many May Day processions that were more imposing and more decorative, but it was long since I had been able to move about in a crowd without attracting anyone's attention, feeling myself a part of the nameless whole, listening and observing. Only once did our companion say to me cautiously: 'There they are selling your photographs.' But from those photographs no one would have recognized the member of the *collegium* of the commissariat of education, Kuzmyenko. In case these lines should meet the eyes of Count Westarp, or Hermann Müller, Stresemann,* Count Reventlow, Hilferding, or of any others who opposed my admission into Germany, I think it necessary to inform them that I did not proclaim any reprehensible slogans, stick up any outrageous posters, that in general I was merely an observer waiting to undergo an operation a few days later.

We also attended the 'wine festival' outside the city. Here were hordes of people, but in spite of the spring mood, enhanced by sun and wine, the grey shadow of past years lay over the merry-making, as well as over those who were trying to make merry. You had only to look closer and they all seemed like slowly recovering convalescents; their gaiety still cost them a great effort. We spent a few hours in the thick of the crowd, observed, talked, ate frankfurters from paper plates, and even drank beer, the very taste of which we had forgotten since 1917.

I was recovering from the operation quickly, and was considering the date of our departure. At this point an unexpected thing happened, which even today is still something of a puzzle to me. About a week before my intended departure there appeared in the corridor of the clinic two gentlemen of that indefinite appearance which so definitely proclaims the police profession. Looking into the courtyard from the window, I discovered below me about half a dozen men like them, who, though differing somewhat among themselves, still resembled each other remarkably. I drew Krestinsky's attention to it. A few minutes later one of the assistant doctors knocked on the door

*Written before the recent death of Stresemann. – *Translator.*

and excitedly announced – at the request of his chief – that I was in danger of an attempt on my life. 'Not by the police, I hope?' I asked, pointing to the many agents. The doctor hazarded a suggestion that the police were there to prevent the attempt. Two or three minutes later a police-inspector (*polizeirat*) arrived and told Krestinsky that the police had actually received information about an attempt on my life and had taken extraordinary protective measures. The entire clinic was agog. The nurses told each other and the patients that the clinic was harbouring Trotsky, and because of that several bombs were going to be thrown at the building. The atmosphere created was little suited to a curative institution. I arranged with Krestinsky to go at once to the Soviet embassy. The street in front of the clinic was barricaded by the police. I was escorted by police motor-cars.

The official version of the episode was something like this: One of the German monarchists arrested in connection with a newly discovered conspiracy made a statement to the court examiner – or so it was alleged – that the Russian White Guards were arranging for an early attempt on the life of Trotsky, who was stated to be in Berlin. The German diplomacy, through which my trip had been arranged, had deliberately refrained from informing its police because of the considerable number of monarchists among the ranks. The police did not give much credence to the report of the arrested monarchist, but nevertheless checked up on his statement about my staying at the clinic. To their great amazement the information proved correct. As inquiries had been made of the physicians as well, I received two simultaneous warnings – one from the assistant doctor, the other from the police inspector. Whether an attempt had really been planned, and whether the police really learned of my arrival through the arrested monarchist, are questions that even today I cannot answer.

But I suspect that the case was much simpler. One may assume that the diplomatic circles failed to keep the 'secret', and the police, hurt by the lack of confidence in them, decided to demonstrate, either to Stresemann or to me, that tonsils could not be removed without their aid. Whatever the explanation, the clinic was turned upside down, while under this mighty protection against my hypothetical enemies I moved over to the embassy. Vague and feeble echoes of this story later found their way into the German press, but it seems that no one was inclined to believe them.

The days of my stay in Berlin coincided with certain important events in Europe: the general strike in England, and Pilsudski's *coup d'état* in Poland. Both these occurrences greatly accentuated my disagreements with the epigones, and determined in advance the stormier development of our later struggle. A few words on the subject should be included here.

Stalin, Bukharin, and – in the first period – Zinoviev as well, saw the crowning achievement of their policy in the diplomatic bloc between the higher groups of the Soviet trade-unions and the Greater Council of the British trade-unions. In his provincial narrowness Stalin imagined that Purcell and other trade-union leaders were ready or able, in a difficult moment, to lend support to the Soviet republic against the British bourgeoisie. As for the British union leaders, they believed, with some justification, that in view of the crisis in British capitalism and the increasing discontent of the masses, it would be politic for them to be covered on their left by means of an official but actually non-committal friendship with the leaders of the Soviet trade-unions. Both sides did a great deal of beating about the bush, for the most part avoiding calling things by their real names. A rotten policy has more than once been wrecked on great events. The general strike in England in May 1926 proved to be a great event not only in English life but also in the inner life of our party.

England's fate after the war was a subject of absorbing interest. The radical change in her world position could not fail to bring about changes just as radical in the inner correlation of her forces. It was clear that even if Europe, including England, were to restore a certain social equilibrium for a more or less extended period England herself could reach such an equilibrium only by means of a series of serious conflicts and shake-ups. I thought it probable that in England, of all places, the fight in the coal industry would lead to a general strike. From this I assumed that the essential contradiction between the old organizations of the working class and its new historical tasks would of course be revealed in the near future. During the winter and spring of 1925, while I was in the Caucasus, I wrote a book on this – *Whither England?* The book was aimed essentially at the official conception of the Politbureau, with its hope of an evolution to the left by the British General Council, and of a gradual and painless penetration of communism into the ranks of the British Labour Party and trade-unions. In part to avoid unnecessary complications, in part to check up on my opponents, I submitted the manuscript of the book to the Politbureau. Since it was a question of forecast, rather than of criticism after the fact, none of the members of the Politbureau ventured to express himself. The book passed safely by the censors and was published exactly as it had been written. A little later it also appeared in English. The official leaders of British Socialism treated it as the fantasy of a foreigner who did not know British conditions, who could dream of transferring the 'Russian' general strike to the soil of the British Isles. Such estimates could have been counted by the dozens, even by the hundreds, beginning with MacDonald himself, who in the political-banalities contest indisputably carried off first prize. But within a few months the strike of the coal miners became a general strike. I had not expected such an early confirmation of my forecast. If the general strike proved the rightness of the Marxist forecast against the home-made estimates of the British reformists, the behaviour of the General Council during the general strike signified the collapse of Stalin's hopes of Purcell. I eagerly gathered and collated in the clinic all the information about the course of the general strike and especially about the relations between the masses and their leaders. The thing that made my gorge rise was the nature of the articles in the Moscow *Pravda*. Its chief concern was to screen bankruptcy and save its face. This could be achieved only by a cynical distortion of the facts. There can be no greater proof of the intellectual downfall of a revolutionary politician than deception of the masses.

Upon my return to Moscow I demanded an immediate breaking up of the bloc with the British General Council. Zinoviev, after the inevitable vacillation, sided with me. Radek was opposed. Stalin clung to the bloc, even to the semblance of one, for all he was worth. The British trade-unionists waited until their acute inner crisis was at an end and then uncivilly kicked their generous but muddle-headed ally away.

Events just as significant were taking place in Poland at the same time. In frantic search for a way out the petty bourgeoisie entered on a rebellion and raised Pilsudski on its shield. The leader of the communist party, Varski, decided that 'a democratic dictatorship of the proletariat and peasantry' was developing there before his very eyes, and called on the Communist party to support Pilsudski. I had known Varski for a long time. When Rosa Luxemburg was still alive, he was perhaps able to hold his place in the revolutionary ranks. Left alone he was always a vacancy. In 1924, after great hesitation, he announced that at last he realized the evil of 'Trotskyism', that is, of the under-appreciation of the peasantry for the success of the democratic dictatorship. As a reward for his obedience he was given the post of leader, and watched impatiently for an occasion for using the spurs that it had taken him so long to win. In May 1926 he seized his opportunity, only to disgrace himself and spatter the flag of the party. He went unpunished of course; the Stalin apparatus shielded him from the wrath of the Polish workers.

During 1926 the party struggle developed with increasing intensity. In the autumn the opposition even made an open sortie at the meetings of the party locals. The apparatus counter-attacked with fury. The struggle of ideas gave place to administrative mechanics: telephone summons of the party bureaucrats to attend the meetings of the workers' locals, an accumulation of automobiles with hooting sirens in front of all the meetings, and a well-organized whistling and booing at the appearance of the oppositionists on the platform. The ruling faction exerted its pressure by a mechanical concentration of its forces, by threats and reprisals. Before the mass of the party had time to hear, grasp or say anything they were afraid of the possibility of a split and a catastrophe. The opposition was obliged to beat a retreat. On 16 October we made a declaration announcing that although we considered our views just and reserved the right of

fighting for them within the framework of the party, we renounced the use of activities that might engender the danger of
a split. The declaration of 16 October was intended not for the
apparatus but for the mass of the party. It was an expression of
our desire to remain in the party and serve it further. Although
the Stalinites began to break the truce the day after it was concluded, still we gained time. The winter of 1926 to 1927 gave us
a certain breathing-spell which allowed us to carry out a more
thorough theoretical examination of many questions.

As early as the beginning of 1927 Zinoviev was ready to capitulate, if not all at once, at least gradually. But then came the
staggering events in China. The criminal character of Stalin's
policy hit one in the eye. It postponed for a time the capitulation
of Zinoviev and of all who followed him later.

The epigones' leadership in China trampled on all the traditions of Bolshevism. The Chinese Communist party was forced
against its will to join the bourgeois Kuomintang party and submit to its military discipline. The creating of Soviets was forbidden. The Communists were advised to hold the agrarian
revolution in check, and to abstain from arming the workers
without the permission of the bourgeoisie. Long before Chiang
Kai-shek crushed the Shanghai workers and concentrated the
power in the hands of a military clique we issued warnings that
such a consequence was inevitable. Since 1925 I had demanded
the withdrawal of the communists from the Kuomintang. The
policy of Stalin and Bukharin not only prepared for and facilitated the crushing of the revolution but, with the help of reprisals by the state apparatus, shielded the counter-revolutionary
work of Chiang Kai-shek from our criticism. In April 1927, at
the party meeting in the Hall of Columns, Stalin still defended
the policy of coalition with Chiang Kai-shek and called for confidence in him. Five or six days later Chiang Kai-shek drowned
the Shanghai workers and the Communist party in blood.

A wave of excitement swept over the party. The opposition
raised its head. And disregarding all rules of *conspiratzia* – and
at that time, in Moscow, we were already obliged to defend the
Chinese workers against Chiang Kai-shek by using the methods
of *conspiratzia* – the oppositionists came to me by scores in the

offices of the Chief Concessions Committee. Many younger comrades thought the patent bankruptcy of Stalin's policy was bound to bring the triumph of the opposition nearer. During the first days after the *coup d'état* by Chiang Kai-shek I was obliged to pour many a bucket of cold water over the hot heads of my young friends – and over some not so young. I tried to show them that the opposition could not rise on the *defeat* of the Chinese revolution. The fact that our forecast had proved correct might attract one thousand, five thousand, or even ten thousand new supporters to us. But for the millions the significant thing was not our forecast, but the fact of the crushing of the Chinese proletariat. After the defeat of the German revolution in 1923, after the break-down of the English general strike in 1925, the new disaster in China would only intensify the disappointment of the masses in the international revolution. And it was this same disappointment that served as the chief psychological source for Stalin's policy of national-reformism.

In a very short time it was apparent that as a faction we had undoubtedly gained in strength – that is to say, we had grown more united intellectually, and stronger in numbers. But the umbilical cord that connected us with power was cut by the sword of Chiang Kai-shek. His finally discredited Russian ally, Stalin, now had only to complete the crushing of the Shanghai workers by routing the opposition within the party. The backbone of the opposition was a group of old revolutionaries. But we were no longer alone. Hundreds and thousands of revolutionaries of the new generation were grouped about us. This new generation had been awakened by the October revolution; it had taken part in the civil war; it stood at attention before the great authority of Lenin's Central Committee. Only since 1923 had it begun to think independently, to criticize, to apply Marxist methods to new turns in the development, and, what is still more difficult, to learn to shoulder the responsibility of revolutionary initiative. At present there are thousands of such young revolutionaries who are augmenting their political experience by studying theory in the prisons and the exile of the Stalin régime.

The leading group of the opposition faced this finale with its eyes wide open. We realized only too clearly that we could make our ideas the common property of the new generation not by diplomacy and evasions but only by an open struggle which shirked none of the practical consequences. We went to meet the inevitable *débâcle*, confident, however, that we were paving the way for the triumph of our ideas in a more distant future.

The pressure of material force has always played, and still plays, a great rôle in humanity's history; sometimes it is a progressive rôle, more often a reactionary one; its character depends on what class applies the force and to what end. But it is a far cry from this to the belief that force can solve *all* problems and overcome *all* obstacles. It is possible by force of arms to check the development of progressive historical tendencies; it is not possible to block the road of the advance of progressive ideas forever. That is why, when the struggle is one for great principles, the revolutionary can only follow one rule: *Fais ce que dois advienne que pourra.*

The nearer drew the time of the Fifteenth Congress, set for the end of 1927, the more the party felt that it had reached a cross-roads in history. Alarm was rife in the ranks. In spite of a monstrous terror, the desire to hear the opposition awoke in the party. This could be achieved only by illegal means. Secret meetings were held in various parts of Moscow and Leningrad, attended by workers and students of both sexes, who gathered in groups of from twenty to one hundred and two hundred to hear some representative of the opposition. In one day I would visit two, three, and sometimes four of such meetings. They were usually held in some worker's apartment. Two small rooms would be packed with people, and the speaker would stand at the door between the two rooms. Sometimes everyone would sit on the floor; more often the discussion had to be carried on standing, for lack of space. Occasionally representatives of the Control Commission would appear at such meetings and demand that everyone leave. They were invited to take part in the discussion. If they caused any disturbance they were put out. In all, about 20,000 people attended such meetings in Moscow and Leningrad. The number was growing. The opposition cleverly prepared a huge meeting in the hall of the High Technical School, which had been occupied from within. The hall was crammed with 2,000 people, while a huge crowd remained outside in the street. The attempts of the administration to stop the meeting proved ineffectual. Kamenev and I spoke for about two hours. Finally the Central Committee issued an appeal to the workers to break up the meetings of the opposition by force. This appeal was merely a screen for carefully prepared attacks on the opposition by military units under the guidance of the GPU. Stalin wanted a bloody settlement of the conflict. We gave the signal for a temporary discontinuance of the large meetings. But this was not until after the demonstrations of 7 November.

In October of 1927 the Central Executive Committee held its session in Leningrad. In honour of the occasion the authorities staged a mass demonstration. But through an unforeseen circumstance the demonstration took an entirely unexpected turn. Zinoviev and I and a few others of the opposition were making the rounds of the city by automobile, to see the size and temper of the demonstration. Towards the end of our drive we approached the Taurid Palace where motor-trucks were drawn up as platforms for the members of the Central Executive Committee. Our automobile stopped short before a line of police; there was no further passage. Before we could make up our minds how to get out of the impasse, the commander hurried to our car and quite guilelessly offered to escort us to the platform. Before we could overcome our hesitation two lines of police opened a way for us to the last motor-truck, which was still unoccupied. When the masses learned that we were on the last platform, the character of the demonstration changed instantly. The people began to pass by the first trucks indifferently, without even answering the greetings from them, and hurried on to our platform. Soon a bank of thousands of people had been formed around our truck. Workers and soldiers halted, looked up, shouted their greetings, and then were obliged to move on because of the impatient pressure of those behind them. A platoon of police which was sent to our truck to restore order was itself caught up by the general mood and took no action. Hundreds of trusted agents of the apparatus were dispatched into the thick of the crowd. They tried to whistle us down, but their isolated whistles were quite drowned by the shouts of sympathy. The longer this continued the more intolerable the situation became for the official leaders of the demonstration. In the end the chairman of the Central Executive Committee and a few of its most prominent members came down from the first platform around which there was nothing but a vast gulf of emptiness and climbed onto ours, which stood at the very end and was intended for the least important guests. But even this bold step failed to save the situation, for the people kept shouting names – and the names were not those of the official masters of the situation.

Zinoviev was instantly optimistic, and expected momentous consequences from this manifestation of sentiment. I did not share his impulsive estimate. The working masses of Leningrad demonstrated their dissatisfaction, in the form of platonic sympathy for the leaders of the opposition, but they were still unable to prevent the apparatus from making short work of us. On this score I had no illusions. On the other hand the demonstration was bound to suggest to the ruling faction the necessity of speeding up the destruction of the opposition, so that the masses might be confronted with an accomplished fact.

The next landmark was the Moscow demonstration in honour of the tenth anniversary of the October revolution. The organizers of the demonstration, the authors of the jubilee articles and the speakers were, in most cases, people who either had been on the other side of the barricade during the events of October or had simply sought shelter under the family roof until they could see what had happened and had joined the revolution only after it had won a secure victory. It was with amusement rather than bitterness that I read articles and listened to radio speeches in which these hangers-on accused me of treason to the October revolution. When you understand the dynamics of the historical process and see how your opponent is being pulled by strings controlled by a hand unknown to him, then the most disgusting acts of turpitude and perfidy lose their power over you.

The oppositionists decided to take part in the general procession, carrying their own placards, with their slogans. These were in no sense directed against the party; they read, for example: 'Let us turn our fire to the right – against the kulak, the nepman and the bureaucrat' ... 'Let us carry out Lenin's Will' ... 'Against opportunism, against a split, and for the unity of Lenin's party.' Today these slogans form the official credo of the Stalin faction in its fight against the right wing. On 7 November the placards of the opposition were snatched from their hands and torn to pieces, while their bearers were mauled by specially organized units. The official leaders had learned their lesson in the Leningrad demonstration, and this time their preparations were much more efficient. The masses were showing signs of uneasiness. They joined in the demonstration with minds that were profoundly disquieted. And above the alarmed and bewildered people two active groups were rising – the opposition and the apparatus. As volunteers in the fight against the 'Trotskyists', notoriously non-revolutionary and sometimes sheer Fascist elements in the streets of Moscow were now coming to the aid of the apparatus. A policeman, pretending to be giving a warning, shot openly at my automobile. Someone was guiding his hand. A drunken official of the fire-brigade, shouting imprecations, jumped on the running-board of my automobile and smashed the glass. To one who could see, the incidents in the Moscow streets on 7 November 1927 were obviously a rehearsal of the Thermidor.

A similar demonstration took place in Leningrad. Zinoviev and Radek, who had gone there, were laid hold of by a special detachment, and under the pretence of protection from the crowd, were shut up in one of the buildings for the duration of the demonstration. On the same day Zinoviev wrote us in Moscow: 'All the information at hand indicates that this outrage will greatly benefit our cause. We are worried to know what happened with you. Contacts [that is, secret discussions with the workers] are proceeding very well here. The change in our favour is great. For the time being we do not propose to leave.' This was the last flash of energy from the opposition of Zinoviev. A day later he was in Moscow, insisting on the necessity of surrender.

On 16 November Joffe committed suicide; his death was
wedge in the growing struggle.

Joffe was a very sick man. He had been brought back fro:
Japan, where he was Soviet ambassador, in a serious conditio:
Many obstacles were placed in the way of his being sent abroa
but his stay there was too brief and, although it had its benefici
results, they were not sufficient compensation. Joffe became m
deputy in the Chief Concessions Committee, and all the heav
routine fell on him. The crisis in the party disturbed him great!
The thing that worried him most was the treachery. Sever
times he was ready to throw himself into the thick of the struggl
Concerned for his health, I tried to hold him back. Joffe w
especially furious at the campaign in connection with the theo:
of permanent revolution. He couldn't stomach the vile baiting
those who had foreseen, long in advance of the rest, the cour
and character of the revolution, by those who were merely e:
joying its fruits. Joffe told me of his conversation with Lenin –
took place in 1919, if I am not mistaken – on the subject of pe:
manent revolution. Lenin said to him: 'Yes, Trotsky proved
be right.' Joffe wanted to publish that conversation, but I tri
my best to dissuade him. I could visualize the avalanche
baiting that would crash down upon him. Joffe was peculiar
persistent, and under a soft exterior he concealed an inalterat
will. At each new outburst of aggressive ignorance and politic
treachery he would come to me again, with a drawn and indi
nant face, and repeat: 'I must make it public.' I would arg
with him again that such 'evidence of a witness' could chan
nothing; that it was necessary to re-educate the new generati
of the party, and to aim far ahead.

Joffe had been unable to complete his cure abroad, and h
physical condition was growing worse every day. Towar
autumn he was compelled to stop work, and then he was la
low altogether. His friends again raised the question of sendi:
him abroad, but this time the Central Committee refused poi:
blank. The Stalinites were now preparing to send the opp:
sitionists in quite a different direction. My expulsion from t
Central Committee and then from the party startled Joffe mc
than anyone else. To his personal and political wrath was add

ie bitter realization of his own physical helplessness. Joffe felt
inerringly that the future of the revolution was at stake. It was
io longer in his power to fight, and life apart from struggle
ieant nothing for him. So he drew his final conclusion.

At the time I had already moved from the Kremlin to the
iome of my friend Byeloborodov, who formally was still people's
ommissary of the interior, although the agents of the GPU
vere on his heels wherever he went. Byeloborodov was then
iway in his native Urals, where he was trying to reach the workers
i the struggle against the apparatus. I telephoned Joffe's apart-
ient to ask the state of his health. He himself answered; the
ielephone was beside his bed. In the tone of his voice – but
realized this only later – there was something strange and alarm-
ig. He asked me to come to him. Some chance prevented me
rom doing so immediately. In those stormy days comrades called
ontinuously at Byeloborodov's house to confer with me on
nportant matters. An hour or two later an unfamiliar voice in-
ormed me over the telephone: 'Adolph Abramovich has shot
imself. There is a packet for you on his bedside table.' In
iyeloborodov's house there were always a few military opposi-
ionists on duty to accompany me in my movements about town.
Ve set off in haste for Joffe's. In answer to our ringing and knock-
ig someone demanded our names from behind the door and
ien opened it after some delay; something mysterious was going
in inside. As we entered I saw the calm and infinitely tender face
f Adolph Abramovich against a blood-stained pillow. B., a
iember of the board of the GPU, was at Joffe's desk. The
acket was gone from the bedside table. I demanded its return
t once. B. muttered that there was no letter at all. His manner
nd voice left me in no doubt that he was lying. A few minutes
iter friends from all parts of the city began to pour into the
partment. The official representatives of the commissariat of
ireign affairs and of the party institutions felt lost in the midst
f the crowd of oppositionists. During the night several thousand
eople visited the house. The news of the theft of the letter
pread through the city. Foreign journalists were sending dis-
atches, and it became quite impossible to conceal the letter any
inger. In the end a photostatic copy of it was handed to Rakov-

sky. Why a letter written by Joffe to me and sealed in an envelop
that bore my name should have been given to Rakovsky, and a
that in a photostatic copy instead of the original, is somethin
that I cannot even attempt to explain. Joffe's letter reflects hi
to the end, but as he was half an hour before his death. Jof
knew my attitude towards him; he was bound to me by a dee
moral confidence and gave me the right to delete anythin
I thought superfluous or unsuitable for publication. Failing t
conceal the letter from the whole world, the cynical enemy trie
to exploit for its own purposes those very lines not written fo
the public eye.

Joffe tried to make his death a service to the same cause t
which he had dedicated his life. With the same hand that wa
to pull the trigger against his own temple half an hour later, h
wrote the last evidence of a witness and the last counsel of
friend. This is what he addressed directly to me in his last letter

You and I, dear Lev Davydovich, are bound to each other b
decades of joint work, and, I make bold to hope, of personal friend
ship. This gives me the right to tell you in parting what I think yo
are mistaken in. I have never doubted the rightness of the road yo
pointed out, and as you know I have gone with you for more tha
twenty years, since the days of 'permanent revolution'. But I hav
always believed that you lacked Lenin's *unbending will*, his *unwilling
ness to yield*, his readiness even to remain alone on the path that h
thought right in the anticipation of a future majority, of a futur
recognition by everyone of the rightness of his path. *Politically*, yo
were always right, beginning with 1905, and I told you repeatedly tha
with my own ears I had heard Lenin admit that even in 1905, *you, an
not he*, were right. One does not lie before his death, and now I repea
this again to you . . . But you have often *abandoned your rightness* fo
the sake of an overvalued agreement or compromise. This is a mistake
I repeat: politically you have always been right, and now *more righ
than ever*. Some day the party will realize it, and history will not fai
to accord recognition. Then don't lose your courage if someone leave
you now, or if not as many come to you, and not as soon, as we al
would like. You are right, but the guarantee of the victory of you
rightness lies in nothing but the extreme unwillingness to yield, th
strictest straightforwardness, the absolute rejection of all compro
mise; in this very thing lay the secret of Lenin's victories. Many .

ime I have wanted to tell you this, but only now have I brought my-
elf to do so, as a last farewell.

Joffe's funeral was set for a working-day, at an hour that
vould prevent the Moscow workers from taking part in it. But
1 spite of this, it attracted no less than 10,000 people and
urned into an imposing oppositionist demonstration. Mean-
vhile Stalin's faction was preparing for the congress, hastening
ɔ place a split before it as an accomplished fact. The so-called
lections to local conferences which sent delegates to the con-
ress were carried out *before* the official opening of the sham
liscussion', during which groups of whistlers, organized in
nilitary fashion, broke up meetings in the regular Fascist way.
t is difficult even to imagine anything more disgraceful than the
reparations for the Fifteenth Congress. Zinoviev and his group
ad no difficulty in perceiving that the congress would put the
olitical capsheaf on the physical rout that had begun in the
treets of Moscow and Leningrad on the tenth anniversary of
he October revolution. The only concern of Zinoviev and his
riends was to capitulate while there was yet time. They could
ot fail to understand that the Stalin bureaucrats saw their real
nemy not in them, the oppositionists of the second draft, but in
he main group of the opposition, linked to me. They hoped to
uy forgiveness, if not to win favour, by a demonstrative break
vith me at the time of the Fifteenth Congress. They did not fore-
ee that by a double betrayal they would achieve their own
olitical elimination. Although they weakened our group tempor-
rily by stabbing it in the back, they condemned themselves to
olitical death.

The Fifteenth Congress resolved to expel the opposition *en
loc*. The expelled were placed at the disposal of the GPU.

43
The Exile

I will quote in full my wife's account of the exile to Central Asi

16 January 1928: packing all morning. I have a temperature; r
head is going round with fever and weakness in the midst of the thin
that have just been brought over from the Kremlin, and the thin
that are being packed to go with us. A medley of furniture, box
linen, books and endless visitors – friends coming to say good-by
F. A. Guetier, our doctor and friend, was naïvely advising us to p
off the departure because of my cold. He did not realize what o
journey meant, and what it would mean to postpone it now. We hop
that I would improve more readily on the train, because at hom
under the conditions of the 'last days' before we left, there was litt
chance of an early recovery. New faces kept flashing before our ey
many of whom I was seeing for the first time. Embraces, han
shaking, expressions of sympathy and good wishes.

The chaos is being increased by people bringing flowers, bool
candy, warm clothing, etc. The last day of bustle, strain, and excit
ment is nearing its end. The things have been taken to the static
Our friends have gone there too. We are sitting – the entire family –
the dining-room, ready to leave, waiting for the agents of the GP
We watch the time; nine o'clock, half past nine . . . No one com
Ten o'clock – the hour of the train's departure. What has happene
Rescinded? The telephone rings. The GPU informs us that our d
parture has been put off, for reasons not stated. For how long? as
L. D. For two days, comes the answer – you will have to leave t
day after tomorrow.

Half an hour later friends from the station rushed in – first you
people, than Rakovsky and others. There had been a tremendo
demonstration at the station. People waited, shouting 'Long li
Trotsky'. But Trotsky was nowhere to be seen. Where was h
Around the car reserved for us, there was a stormy crowd. You
friends set up a large portrait of L. D. on the roof of the car. It w
greeted with jubilant 'hurrahs'. The train started, first one jerk, th

nother; it moved forward a little and then stopped suddenly. The demonstrants had run in front of the engine; they clung to the cars nd stopped the train, demanding Trotsky. A rumour had run through he crowd that the GPU agents had conducted L. D. secretly into the ar and were preventing him from showing himself to those who had ome to see him off. The excitement at the station was indescribable. There were clashes with the police and the agents of the GPU, with asualties on both sides. Arrests were made. The train was detained or about an hour and a half. Some time later our baggage came back rom the station. For a long time afterwards friends kept telephoning o find out if we were at home and to tell us what had happened at he station. It was long after midnight when we went to bed.

After the worries of the last few days, we slept until eleven the next day. There were no telephone calls. Everything was quiet. The wife f our older boy went to her work – there were still two days ahead of s. But we had hardly finished breakfast when the bell rang; it was Byeloborodov's wife; next came Joffe's wife. Another ring – and the vhole apartment filled with agents of the GPU in civilian clothes and uniforms. An order was handed to L. D. declaring him under arrest or immediate conveyance under escort to Alma-Ata. And the two days of which the GPU had spoken the day before? Another deception · a ruse to avoid a new demonstration at the send-off. The telephone ang continually, but an agent stood beside it and good-humouredly revented us from answering. It was only by chance that we managed o let Byeloborodov know that our house had been occupied and that ve were being carried away by force. Later on we were informed that he 'political direction' of the send-off had been Bukharin's. This was quite in the spirit of the Stalin machinations.

The agents were noticeably excited. L. D. refused to leave of his own accord. He took advantage of the occasion to make the situation perfectly clear. The Politbureau was trying to make his exile, as well s that of at least the most prominent oppositionists, seem like a oluntary affair. It was in this light that the exile was being represented to the workers. Now it was necessary to explode this legend, nd to show the reality in such a way that the facts could be neither suppressed nor distorted. Hence L. D.'s decision to compel his opponents to an open use of force. We locked ourselves in one of the rooms vith our two guests. Parleys with the agents of the GPU were carried n through locked doors. The agents did not know what to do; they hesitated, consulted with their chiefs by telephone, and when they ad received instructions, announced that they were going to force the oor, since they must carry out their orders. Meantime, L. D. was

dictating instructions for the future conduct of the opposition. Th
door remained locked. We heard a hammer-blow, the glass crashe
and a uniformed arm was thrust inside. 'Shoot me, Comrade Trotsky
shoot me,' Kishkin, a former officer who had often accompanied L. D
on his trips to the front, kept saying excitedly. 'Don't talk nonsense
Kishkin,' L. D. replied calmly. 'No one is going to shoot you. G
ahead with your job.' The agents opened the door and entered th
room confused and agitated. Seeing L. D. in his slippers, they foun
his shoes and put them on him. Then they found his fur coat and ca
and put them on him. L. D. refused to go. They lifted him in thei
arms and started away. We hurried after. I slipped on my snow-boot
and my fur coat . . . The door slammed behind me. On the other sid
of it I heard a commotion. I shouted to the men who were carryin
L. D. down the stairs and demanded that they let out my sons, th
elder of whom was to accompany us into exile. The door was flun
open, and my sons burst out, followed by our women guests, Byelo
borodova and Joffe. They all forced their way through with the ai
of athletic measures on Seryozha's part. On the way down the stair
Lyova rang all the door-bells, shouting: 'They're carrying Comrad
Trotsky away!' Frightened faces flashed by us at the doors and on th
staircase; in this house, only prominent Soviet workers were living
We were all crammed into one automobile; Seryozha could hardl
get his legs in. Byeloborodova was also with us.

We drove along the streets of Moscow. It was freezing cold. Sery
ozha had no cap; he had not had time to take it; everybody was with
out galoshes and gloves; there was not a travelling-bag among us, no
even a hand-bag, and we were all empty-handed. We were not bein
taken to the Kazan station, but in another direction – as it developed
to the Yaroslav station. Seryozha made an attempt to jump out of th
automobile, intending to run into the place where his brother's wif
was working and tell her that we were being taken away. The agent
seized his arms and appealed to L. D. to persuade him not to jum
out of the automobile. We arrived at the empty station. The agent
bore L. D. in their arms, as they had from the house. Lyova shoute
to various railway-workers: 'Comrades, see how they are carryin
Comrade Trotsky away!' An agent of the GPU who had at one tim
accompanied L. D. on hunting trips caught him by the collar. 'Yo
wriggler!' he exclaimed insolently. Seryozha answered him with
trained athlete's blow in the face. We were in the car. The men of th
escort were at the windows and doors of our compartment. The othe
compartments were occupied by the agents of the GPU. Where wer
we going? We didn't know. Our baggage had not been brought i

when the locomotive started off with our solitary car. It was two o'clock in the afternoon. We found that we were going by a circuitous route to a small station where our car was to be attached to the mail-train that had left Moscow from the Kazan station for Tashkent. At five o'clock we said good-bye to Seryozha and Byeloborodova, who had to return to Moscow.

We continued on our way. I had a fever. L. D. was brisk and almost gay. The situation had taken definite shape; the general atmosphere had cleared. The escort was considerate and civil. We were told that our baggage was coming by the next train, and that it would overtake us at Frunze (the end of our journey by rail) – that is, on the ninth day. We had no change of linen, and no books. And with what love and care Syermuks and Poznansky had packed those books, sorting them so carefully – these for the journey, and those for early studies! And with what solicitude Syermuks, who knew L. D.'s tastes and habits so well, had packed his writing materials. He had made so many trips with L. D. during the revolution in the capacity of steno-grapher and secretary. L. D. always worked with triple energy while he was travelling, taking advantage of the absence of telephone and visitors, and the chief burden of this work fell first on Glazman and later on Syermuks. And now we found ourselves launched on a long journey without a single book, pencil, or sheet of paper. Before we left Moscow Seryozha had got us Semyonov-Tyanshansky's book on Turkestan, a scientific work, and we were planning to acquaint our-selves while on the train with our future place of residence, of which we had but a vague conception. But Semyonov-Tyanshansky re-mained in the travelling-bag along with the rest of the luggage in Moscow. We sat in the car empty-handed, as if we were driving from one part of the city to another. In the evening we stretched out on the benches and leaned our heads against the elbow rests. A sentry stood on duty at the half-opened door of the compartment.

What was in store for us? What would our journey be like? And the exile? What would our condition be there? The start had not been very promising. Nevertheless we were calm. The car rolled along smoothly. We lay stretched on the benches. The half-opened door re-minded us that we were prisoners. We were tired out by the surprises, uncertainties and the tension of those last days, and now we were resting. Everything was quiet; the guard was silent. I was a little in-disposed. L. D. tried everything he could think of to make things easier for me, but he had nothing but his gay and tender mood to transmit to me. We had stopped being aware of our surroundings and were enjoying the rest. Lyova was in the adjoining compartment. In

Moscow he had been completely absorbed in the work of the oppo sition; now he was accompanying us into exile to lighten our lot – h had not even had time to say good-bye to his wife. From that moment he became our only means of contact with the outside world. It wa almost dark in the car; the candles were burning dimly over the door We were moving steadily eastwards.

The farther we left Moscow behind the more considerate the escor became. At Samara they bought us a change of underwear, soap, tooth powder, brushes, etc. Our meals and the escort's came from th station-restaurants. L. D., who was always obliged to follow a stric diet, now gaily ate everything that was served and kept cheerin Lyova and me. I watched him with astonishment and apprehension The things they bought for us in Samara were given special names the towel was named 'Menzhinsky',* the socks, 'Yagoda' (Menzhin sky's deputy) and so forth. Articles by such names were much gaye The progress of the train was considerably delayed by snowdrift But every day we went deeper into Asia.

Before he left Moscow, L. D. had asked for his two old assistants but his request was refused. And so Syermuks and Poznansky de cided to make the trip independently, travelling in the same trai with us. At the false start they took seats in another car, saw th demonstration, but did not leave their seats, thinking that we were o the same train. A little later they discovered our absence, left the trai at Arys, and waited for us to come on the next train. It was there w found them. Lyova, who was allowed a certain freedom, was the onl one who saw them, but it made us all very happy. Here is my son' account, written at the time:

'In the morning I set out for the station on the chance that I migh find the comrades whose fate we had constantly been talking an worrying about. And I did; there the two of them were, sitting at table in the buffet and playing chess. It would be hard to describe m joy. I made signs to them not to come near me; my appearance in th buffet, as usual, had increased the activity of the agents. I hastened the car to tell of my discovery. There was general rejoicing. Even L. D found it hard to be cross with them, although they had disobeyed in structions, and instead of continuing their journey were waiting ther in the face of everyone – an unnecessary risk. After talking the matte over with L. D. I wrote a note which I intended to hand to them aft dark. The instructions were as follows: Poznansky was to separat from us and proceed immediately to Tashkent and wait there for summons. Syermuks was to go to Alma-Ata without meeting us.

*Then head of the GPU. – *Translator*.

managed in passing to tell Syermuks to meet me behind the station in an inconspicuous corner where there were no lamps. Poznansky came there; at first we couldn't find each other, and began to get disturbed; when we did meet we talked rapidly, continually interrupting each other. I said to him: "Smashed the doors, carried out in arms!" He did not understand who did the smashing or the reason for the carrying. There was no time to explain; we were fearful of discovery. The meeting yielded no results.'

After my son's discovery at Arys we went on our way feeling that we had a trusted friend on the train with us. It made us very happy. On the tenth day we received our baggage and rushed to get at Semyonov-Tyanshansky. We read about the natural features, the population, the apple orchards; best of all, we found that the hunting was good. L. D. opened with delight the writing materials that Syermuks had packed. We arrived at Frunze (Pishpek) early in the morning. It was the last railway station. There was a biting frost. The sun's rays pouring on the clean white snow blinded us. We were given felt boots and sheepskins. I could hardly breathe for the weight of my clothes, and yet it was cold on the road. The autobus moved slowly over the creaking snow packed down by vehicles; the wind lashed our faces. After making thirty kilometres, we stopped. It was dark; we seemed to be in the midst of a snow-covered desert. Two of the guards (the escort comprised from twelve to fifteen men) came up and told us with some embarrassment that the sleeping quarters were not very good. We got out of the bus with a little difficulty and, after groping about in the dark for the doorstep and the low door of the mail-station, walked inside and shed our sheepskins with relief. But the hut was cold, not having been heated. The tiny windows were frosted right through. In the corner there was a huge Russian stove, but alas! as cold as ice. We warmed ourselves with tea and ate something. We got into conversation with the hostess at the post, a Cossack woman. L. D. asked her many questions about her life and also about the hunting. Everything stirred our curiosity; the outstanding thing was that we didn't know how it all would end. We began to get ready for the night. The guards had found shelter in the neighbourhood. Lyova lay on a bench, L. D. and I on a big table on top of the sheepskins. When finally we all were lying quietly in a cold room with a low ceiling, I burst out laughing. 'Quite unlike the apartment in the Kremlin!' I said. L. D. and Lyova laughed with me.

At dawn we set off again. Before us lay the most difficult part of the journey. We crossed the Kurday mountain range. Bitter cold. The weight of the clothes was unbearable – it was as if a wall had fallen down on one. At the next stop, for tea, we talked with the chauffeur and with the agent of the GPU who had come from Alma-Ata to meet us. Gradually the strange, unknown life ahead was being disclosed to us. The road was difficult for the automobile; snow had drifted over the glassy surface. The chauffeur handled the machine expertly; he knew the peculiarities of the road well, and kept himself warm with vodka. Towards night the frost grew sharper and sharper. Well aware that in this desert of snow everything depended on him, the chauffeur relieved his feelings by a most unceremonious criticism of the authorities and their general methods. The Alma-Ata representative, who was sitting beside him, spoke to him appeasingly – anything to get home safely! In the third hour after midnight the car stopped in utter darkness. We had arrived. But where? We learned that it was Gogol Street, in front of the 'Hotel Dzhetysa' – a hostelry unquestionably dating from Gogol's time. We were given two little rooms. The adjoining rooms were taken by the escort and the local agents of the GPU. Lyova checked up on our baggage – two cases of underwear and books were missing, lost somewhere in the snow. Alas, we were again without Semyonov-Tyanshansky, gone were L. D.'s maps and books about China and India; gone were the writing materials. Fifteen pairs of eyes – and yet they failed to look after the luggage properly!

In the morning, Lyova went out to reconnoitre. He became acquainted with the town, first of all with the post-and-telegraph office which was to be the centre of our life. He found a chemist's shop too, and searched tirelessly for all the needed articles – pens, pencils, bread, butter, and candles ... For the first few days, L. D. and I never left our room. Later on we began to go out for short walks in the evening. All our connections with the outside world were through our son.

Dinner was brought in from an eating-place near by. Lyova was busy all day long. We waited impatiently for him. He brought us papers and various bits of information about the people and the life of the town. We were anxious to know if Syermuks had reached Alma-Ata. Suddenly, on the morning of our fourth day there, we heard the familiar voice in the corridor. How dear it was to us! We listened tensely from behind the door to Syermuks's words and footsteps. His coming opened new prospects before us. Syermuks was given a room just opposite ours. I stepped out into the corridor; he bowed to me from a distance. We still could not risk entering into conversation with him, but we rejoiced silently in his nearness. The next day we stealthily let him into our room, told him hastily what had happened and planned for our joint future. But that future proved to be very brief. That very night, at ten o'clock, came the finish. The hotel was quiet. L. D. and I were sitting in our room, with the door half open on the cold corridor because the iron stove made the room unbearably hot. Lyova was in his room. We heard the soft, cautious padding of felt boots in the hall and listened intently. (Lyova, as we learned later, was also listening; he had guessed what was happening). They have come, flashed through our minds. We could hear someone enter Syermuks's room without knocking, and say, 'Hurry up, now!' and then Syermuks's reply: 'May I at least put the felt boots on?' – evidently he was in his slippers. Again the soft, almost noiseless steps and then deep silence. Later the doorman came and locked Syermuks's room. We never saw him again. He was kept on starvation rations for a few weeks in the basement of the GPU in Alma-Ata together with the criminals, and then was sent to Moscow with a daily allowance of 25 kopecks, which was not even enough to buy bread. Poznansky, as we learned later, was arrested at the same time in Tashkent and taken to Moscow. About three months later we got news from them from their places of exile. By some happy chance, when they were being taken to the East, they were put in the same railway carriage in seats facing each other. Separated for a time, they met thus only to be separated again; they were exiled to different places.

And so L. D. found himself without his assistants. His opponents revenged themselves on them for their faithful service with L. D. to the revolution. The gentle, modest Glazman had been driven to suicide as early as 1924. Syermuks and Poznansky wert sent into exile. Butov, the quiet industrious Butov, was arrested, pressed for false evidence, and driven to a hunger-strike that ended in his death in the prison hospital. Thus was the 'secretariat' which L. D.'s enemies regarded with mystic hatred as the source of all evil finally wiped out. The enemies now considered L. D. completely disarmed in the far-away Alma-Ata. Voroshilov openly gloated: 'Even if he dies there, we won't hear of it soon.' But L. D. was not disarmed. We formed a cooperative of three. The work of establishing contact with the outside world fell on our son's shoulders. He was in charge of the correspondence. L. D. sometimes called him minister of foreign affairs, and sometimes minister of post and telegraph. Our correspondence soon grew to a huge volume, and the burden of it was Lyova's. He was bodyguard as well. He also found for L. D. the material for his literary work, searched the bookshelves of the library, secured back numbers of newspapers, and copied excerpts. He conducted all negotiations with the local authorities, organized the hunting trips, took care of the dog and the guns. And on top of all that he studied economic geography and languages assiduously.

A few weeks after our arrival L. D.'s scientific and political work was already in full swing. Later on Lyova found a girl typist. The GPU did not molest her, but they evidently compelled her to report everything that she typed for us. It would have been amusing to hear the report of this young girl, so little experienced in the struggle against Trotskyism.

A fine thing in Alma-Ata was the snow, white, clean, and dry. As there was very little walking or driving it kept its freshness all winter long. In the spring it yielded to red poppies. Such a lot of them – like gigantic carpets! The steppes glowed red for miles around. In the summer there were apples – the famous Alma-Ata variety, huge and also red. The town had no central waterworks, no lights, and no paved roads. In the bazaar in the centre of the town, the Kirghizes sat in the mud at the doorsteps of their shops, warming themselves in the sun and searching their bodies for vermin. Malaria was rampant. There was also pestilence, and during the summer months an extraordinary number of mad dogs. The newspapers reported many cases of leprosy in this region.

In spite of all this we spent a good summer. We rented a peasant house from a fruit-grower up on the hills with an open view of the snow-capped mountains, a spur of the Tyan-Shan range. With the owner and his family, we watched the fruit ripen and took an active part in gathering it. The orchard was a picture of change. First the white bloom; then the trees grew heavy, with bending branches held up by props. Then the fruit lay in a motley carpet under the trees on straw mats, and the trees, rid of their burden, straightened their branches again. The orchard was fragrant with the ripe apples and pears; bees and wasps were buzzing. We were making preserves.

In June and July work was in full swing in the little reed-thatched house in the apple orchard, with a typewriter clicking incessantly, a thing unknown in those parts. L. D. was dictating a criticism of the programme of the Communist International, making corrections and handing it back for retyping. The mail was large – from ten to fifteen letters every day, with all sorts of theses, criticisms, internal polemics, news from Moscow, as well as many telegrams about political matters and inquiries about L. D.'s health. Great world problems were mingled with minor local matters that here seemed also important. Sosnovsky's letters were always topical, with his usual enthusiasm and pungency. Rakovsky's remarkable letters we copied and sent out to others. The little low-ceilinged room was crammed with tables spread with manuscripts, files, newspapers, books, copied excerpts, and clippings. Lyova stayed in his little room next to the stables for whole days, typing, correcting the typist's copy, sealing packages, sending and receiving the mail, and searching for the necessary quotations. The mail was brought to us from the town by an invalid who came by horse. Towards evening, with a dog and a gun, L. D. would often go up into the mountains, sometimes with me, sometimes with Lyova. We would come back with quails, pigeons, mountain-fowl, or pheasants. Everything went well until the regularly recurring attacks of malaria.

Thus we spent a year in Alma-Ata, a town of earthquakes and floods, at the foot of the Tyan-Shan range on the borders of China, 250 kilometres from the railway and 4,000 from Moscow, a year spent with letters, books, and nature. Although we came across secret friends at every step (it is still too early to say more of this), we were outwardly completely isolated from the surrounding population, for everyone who tried to get in touch with us was punished, sometimes very severely.

To my wife's account I will add a few excerpts from the correspondence of that period. On 28 February, soon after our arrival, I wrote to a few exiled friends:

In view of the forthcoming transfer of the Kazakstan government to this place all the houses here are on the register. Only as a result of the telegrams that I sent the most exalted personages in Moscow were we at last given a house after a three weeks' stay in the hotel. We had to buy some furniture, restore the ruined stove, and in general build up a home – though not on the state-planning system. This work fell to Natalia Ivanovna and to Lyova. The home-building is not completed to this day, for the stove will not get hot . . .

I give much time to the study of Asia, its geography, economics, history, and so forth. I miss foreign papers terribly. I have already written to the necessary places, asking to have papers sent me, even if they are not recent. Mail reaches here with difficulty, and is often lost.

The rôle of the communist party of India is difficult to understand. The newspapers have printed reports of the activities in various provinces of 'workers and peasants' parties'. The very name arouses a just alarm. The Kuomintang, too, was at one time declared to be a workers and peasants' party. Will not this prove to be a repetition of the past?

The Anglo-American antagonism has at last come seriously to the surface. Now, even Stalin and Bukharin seem to be beginning to understand what the trouble is. Our newspapers, however, simplify the question when they represent the situation as if the Anglo-American antagonism, which is growing in intensity, would lead directly to war. One cannot doubt that there will be several turning-points in this process. For war would be too dangerous a thing for both sides. They will still make more than one effort to achieve agreement and peace. But, taken in general, the process is developing by giant strides towards a bloody finale.

On the way here I read for the first time Marx's pamphlet, 'Herr Vogt'. To refute some dozen slanders by Karl Vogt, Marx wrote a two-hundred-page book, in small type, marshalling documents and the evidence of witnesses and analysing direct and circumstantial evidence ... If we had begun to refute the Stalin slanders on the same scale, we should probably have to publish an encyclopedia of a thousand volumes.

In April I shared with the 'initiated' my joys and sorrows in the business of hunting:

My son and I made a trip to the river Ili with the intention of making the fullest possible use of the spring season. This time we took with us tents, skins, fur coats, etc., so that we shouldn't have to sleep in the native 'yurtas'. But snow fell again and the weather turned bitter cold. Those were trying days. At night the temperature dropped to fourteen degrees above zero. Nevertheless for nine days we didn't go inside a house. Thanks to our warm underwear and plenty of warm clothes, we scarcely suffered from the cold. But our boots froze at night and we had to thaw them out over the fire to get them on our feet. The first few days we hunted in the swamp and after that on the open lake. I had a small tent set up on a little hill where I spent from twelve to fourteen hours a day ... But Lyova stood right in the reeds under the trees.

But because of the bad weather and the irregular flights of the game, the trip as a hunt was not a success. We brought back only some forty ducks and a brace of geese. But it gave me an immense amount of pleasure, especially this temporary lapse into barbarism, this sleeping in the open air, eating mutton cooked in a pail under the sky, not washing or undressing and consequently not dressing, falling from horseback into the river (the only time that I had to undress, under the hot rays of the noon sun), spending almost all day and night on a small log-perch in the midst of the water and reeds – such experiences do not often come one's way. I returned home without even the suggestion of a cold. But after I got home I caught one on the second day and was laid low for a week.

Foreign papers have now begun to reach us from Moscow and Astrakhan, through Rakovsky. Today I received a letter from him. He is preparing a work on Saint Simonism for the Marx-Engels Institute. Besides this, he is working on his memoirs. Anyone who knows anything about Rakovsky's life can easily imagine what a tremendous interest his memoirs will have.

On 24 May I wrote to Pryeobrazhensky, who was already vacillating in his views:

After receiving your theses, I did not write a word about them to anyone. Day before yesterday I received the following telegram from Kalpashovo: 'Absolutely reject Pryeobrazhensky's proposals and estimate. Reply immediately. Smilga, Alsky, Nyechayev.' Yesterday I received a telegram from Ust-Kulom: 'Consider Pryeobrazhensky's proposals wrong. Byeloborodov, Valyentinov.' From Rakovsky, I received a letter yesterday in which he does not praise you, and expresses his attitude to Stalin's 'left policy' in an English formula, 'Wait and see.' Yesterday I received also a letter from Byeloborodov and Valyentinov. They are much disturbed by some epistle from Radek to Moscow which expresses a sour mood. They are raving. If their version of Radek's letter is right, I am completely at one with them. Leniency towards impressionables is not to be recommended.

Since my return from the hunting trip – that is, since the last of March – I have not left the house; I have simply been sitting over a book or working with my pen from about seven or eight o'clock in the morning until ten at night. I am going to have a break of a few days; there being no hunting now, Natalia Ivanovna, Seryozha – he is here now – and I will go on a fishing trip to the river Ili. You will receive an account of this in due time.

Have you been able to understand what happened in the French elections? I have not. The *Pravda* did not even give the figures of the total number of elected candidates as compared with those at the last election, so that one cannot tell whether the ratio of communists has changed. But I intend to investigate this through foreign papers, and I will write then.

On 26 May I wrote to Mikhail Okudzhava, one of the oldest of the Georgian Bolsheviks:

In so far as Stalin's new policy sets aims for itself it undoubtedly represents an attempt to approach our point of view. In politics, however, it is not merely *what*, but *how* and *who* that decides. The principal battles to decide the fate of the revolution are still ahead . . .

We always considered, and more than once stated, that the progress of the political back-sliding on the part of the ruling faction should not be represented as an absolutely unbroken falling curve. After all, back-sliding takes place not in empty space but in a class society, amid deep, inner frictions. The chief mass of the party is far from being a solid homogeneous block; to an overwhelming degree it represents simply political raw material. It is inevitably subject to processes of differentiation – under pressure of class impacts, both from the right and left. The significant events during the last period of party affairs, of which you and I are bearing the consequences, are only an overture to the further progress of events. Just as the overture to an opera anticipates the musical themes of the entire opera and states them in compressed form, so does our political 'overture' merely anticipate the melodies that will be developed in full in the future, swelled by trumpets, contra-basses, drums, and all the other instruments of a serious class music. The way things have progressed has convinced me beyond any doubt that we were and are right, not only against the weathercocks and turncoats (the Zinovievs, Kamenevs, Pyatakovs etc.) but also against our dear friends on the left – the ultra-lefts, muddle-headed in so far as they are apt to accept the overture for the opera; that is, to think that all the fundamental processes in the party and the state have already reached completion, and that the Thermidor of which they first heard from us, is already an accomplished fact. Not to give way to one's nerve, not to worry oneself and others unnecessarily; to study, to wait, to look sharply ahead and not allow our political line to be corroded by the rust of personal irritation – that should be our attitude.

On 9 June my daughter Nina, my ardent supporter, died in Moscow. She was twenty-six. Her husband had been arrested shortly before my exile. She continued the oppositionist work until she was laid low by illness – a quick consumption that carried her off in a few weeks. The letter she wrote to me from the hospital was seventy-three days reaching me, and came after she died.

Rakovsky wired me on 16 June:

Yesterday received your letter about Nina's grave illness. Wired

Alexandra Georgiyevna [Rakovsky's wife] in Moscow. Learned today from the papers that Nina's brief but revolutionary life came to an end. I am wholly with you, dear friend. It pains me to be separated from you by such an unsurmountable distance. I embrace you many times from my heart. CHRISTIAN.

A fortnight later came Rakovsky's letter:

Dear friend,

I am greatly pained about Ninochka,* for you and yours. You have long been bearing the heavy cross of a revolutionary Marxist, but now for the first time you are experiencing the boundless sorrow of a father. I am with you, with all my heart. I grieve that I am so far from you ... You must have heard from Seryozha of the absurd measures dealt out to your friends after the senseless treatment of you in Moscow. I came to your house half an hour after your departure. A group of comrades, mostly women, and with them Muralov, were in the sitting-room.

'Who is citizen Rakovsky?' I heard a voice say.

'I am. What do you want?'

'Follow me.'

I was led through the hall into a little room. Before the door of the room I was commanded: 'Hands up.' Then my pockets were searched and I was put under arrest. I was freed at five o'clock. Muralov, who was afterwards subjected to the same thing, was detained until late that night ... 'Lost their heads,' I said to myself, feeling not so much angered as ashamed for my own comrades.

I wrote to Rakovsky on 14 July:

Dear Christian Georgiyevich, I have not written to you, or other friends, for an eternity; I have confined myself to sending out various material. After my return from the Ili, where I first got news of Nina's grave condition, we moved at once to a country house. There, a few days later, came the news of her death. You understand what that meant ... But it was necessary, without any loss of time, to get documents ready for the Sixth Congress of the Communist International. It was difficult. On the other hand the need of carrying out this work at any cost acted like a mustard-plaster and helped us to bear up through the first, most difficult weeks.

We were waiting here all July for Zinushka [the elder daughter].

*Ninochka and Ninushka, Zinochka and Zinushka, are endearing diminutives of Nina and Zina respectively. – *Translator.*

Alas! we were to be denied this visit. Guetier demanded that she b placed immediately in a sanatorium for consumptives. She had had the germ for a long time and nursing Ninushka during the three month after the doctors had already given her up greatly undermined he health . . .

Now about the work for the congress. I have decided to start with a criticism of the draft of the programme in connection with all the questions on which we are opposed to the official leaders. I have ended by producing a book of about 175 pages. Generally speaking I have summed up the result of our collective work during the last five years, when Lenin retired from the party leadership and the reckless epigonism came in, at first living on the interest from the old capital but soon beginning to spend the capital itself.

Concerning the appeal to the congress, I have received several dozen letters and telegrams. Complication of the votes has not yet been made. At any rate, out of over a hundred votes, only three are in favour of Pryeobrazhensky's theses.

It is very probable that Stalin's bloc with Bukharin and Rykov will keep the appearance of unity at this congress in order to make a last hopeless attempt to cover us with a very final tombstone. But just this new effort and its inevitable failure may greatly expedite the progress of divergence within the bloc, for on the day after the congress the question 'What next?' will rise in even greater nakedness. What answer will be given? After letting the revolutionary situation in Germany in 1923 slip by, we were compensated by the ultra-Left zigzag of 1924 to 1925. The ultra-Left policy of Zinoviev rose from the Right yeast – the struggle against the industrializers, the romance with Raditsch, La Follette, the Krestintern, the Kuomintang, etc. When the policy of the ultra-Lefts smashed its head, the Right policy rose from the same Right yeast. The chance of a broader repetition of this at some new stage is not barred, that is, *a new ultra-Left phase based on the same opportunist premises*. But the latent economic forces may break off this ultra-Left trend and twist the policy definitely to the Right.

In August I wrote to several of the comrades:

Of course you have noticed that our newspapers reprint absolutely no comments by the American and European press on the events taking place in our party. This alone made one suspect that such comments do not quite suit the requirements of the 'new policy'. Now I have something that is no mere guess, but a very striking bit of evilence from the press. Comrade Andreychin has sent me a page torn from a February number of the American paper, *The Nation*. After giving a brief summary of our latest events, this important left-democratic journal says:

'This action brings to the front the question: Who represents the continuation of the Bolshevik programme in Russia and who the inevitable reaction from it? To the American readers it has seemed as if Lenin and Trotsky represented the same thing and the conservative press and statesmen have arrived at the same conclusion. Thus, the *New York Times* found a chief cause for rejoicing on New Year's Day in the successful elimination of Trotsky from the Communist Party, declaring flatly that "the ousted opposition stood for the perpetuation of the ideas and conditions that have cut off Russia from Western civilization". Most of the great European newspapers wrote similarly. Sir Austen Chamberlain during the Geneva Conference was quoted as saying that England could not enter into conversations with Russia for the simple reason that "Trotsky had not yet been shot against a wall" – he must be pleased by Trotsky's banishment ... At any rate the mouthpieces of reaction in Europe are one in their conclusion that Trotsky, and not Stalin, is their chief Communist enemy.'*
This is eloquent enough, isn't it?

Here are a few bits of statistical data from my son's notes: For the period of April to October 1928 we sent out from Alma-Ata about 800 political letters, among them quite a few large works. The telegrams sent amounted to about 550. We received about 1,000 political letters, both long and short, and about 700 telegrams, in most cases from groups of people. All this refers chiefly to the correspondence within the region of exile, but letters from exile filtered out into the country as well. Of the correspondence sent us, we received, in the best months, not more than half. In addition we received about eight or nine secret mails from Moscow, that is, secret material and letters forwarded by special courier. About the same number were sent by us in similar fashion to Moscow. The secret mail kept us informed of everything that was going on there and enabled us, though only after much delay, to respond with our comments on the most important events.

Towards autumn the state of my health grew much worse.

* *The Nation*, 1 February 1928.

Rumours of this reached Moscow. Workers began to raise questions about it at the meetings. The official reporters found that
their best course was to picture my health in the brightest colours.
On 20 September, my wife sent the following telegram to
Uglanov, then secretary of the Moscow party organization:

In your speech at the plenary meeting of the Moscow committee
you speak of the *fictitious* illness of my husband, L. D. Trotsky. Referring to the anxiety and protests of many comrades you exclaim
indignantly: 'These are the measures they resort to!' You make it
appear that unbecoming measures are resorted to not by the men who
banish Lenin's collaborators and condemn them to illness, but by
those who protest against this. On what grounds and by what right do
you inform the party, the workers and the whole world that the reports
of L. D.'s illness are false? You are actually deceiving the party. The
archives of the Central Committee contain reports by our best physicians on the state of L. D.'s health. Consultations of these physicians
were held more than once at the instigation of Vladimir Ilyich, who
showed the greatest concern for L. D.'s health. Those consultations
called also after V. I.'s death have established the fact that L. D. is
suffering from colitis and gout caused by faulty assimilation of matter.
You probably know that in May 1926 L. D. underwent an operation
in Berlin to rid himself of the high temperature that had tormented
him for several years; but he found no relief. Colitis and gout are not
the sort of diseases that can be cured, especially at Alma-Ata. As the
years go by they get worse. Health can be maintained at a certain level
only through a proper regimen and the right sort of treatment.
Neither one nor the other is procurable at Alma-Ata. As to what regimen and treatment are necessary, you may ask the People's Commissary of Health, Syemashko, who participated several times in the
consultations ordered by Vladimir Ilyich. In addition to this L. D.
has here fallen a victim to malaria, which also affects both the colitis
and the gout and often causes vicious headaches. The weeks and
months when his condition is better are followed by more weeks and
months of severe illness. That is the actual state of affairs. You have
exiled L. D. by virtue of article 58 as a 'counter-revolutionary'. It
would be understandable if you had said that L. D.'s health did not
interest you at all. In that case you would be consistent, with that
dangerous consistency which, if it is not stopped, will lead to the grave
not only the best revolutionaries but possibly the party and the revolution itself. But now, apparently under pressure of public opinion
of the workers, you lack the courage to be consistent. Instead of saying

that Trotsky's illness is to your advantage, because it can prevent his thinking and writing, you simply deny the illness. Kalinin, Molotov and others act the same way in their public statements. The fact that you are now *obliged* to answer inquiries from the masses and to try to wriggle out in such an unseemly manner, proves that the working class does not believe the political slander of Trotsky. Neither will it believe your lies about L. D.'s state of health.

N. I. SEDOVA-TROTSKAYA.

44
The Deportation

In October a rigorous change in our situation took place
Communication with our personal and political friends, ever
with our relatives in Moscow, ceased abruptly; letters and
telegrams no longer reached us. The Moscow telegraph office
as we learned through special channels, accumulated several
hundred telegrams for me, especially telegrams on the anniver
sary of the October revolution. The ring around us was closing
in tighter and tighter.

During 1928 the opposition, in spite of the unbridled persecu
tion, obviously was growing, especially in the large industria
plants. This was responsible for the increase of reprisals, includ
ing even the complete suppression of correspondence among the
exiles themselves. We expected other measures of the same sort
to follow and we were not mistaken.

On 16 December a special representative of the GPU, coming
from Moscow, in the name of that institution handed me an
ultimatum: I must stop directing the opposition; if I did not
measures would be taken 'to isolate me from political life'. The
question of deporting me abroad, however, was not raised then
the measures under consideration, as far as I understood, wer
simply of a domestic character. I replied to this ultimatum with
a letter addressed to the Central Committee of the party and the
presidium of the Communist International. I think it necessary
to quote the main points of this letter here:

Today, 16 December, the representative of the *collegium* of th
GPU, Volynsky, acting in the name of the *collegium*, delivered th
following verbal ultimatum to me:
'The work of your political sympathizers throughout the country
(almost word for word) 'has lately assumed a definitely counter-revo
lutionary character; the conditions in which you are placed at Alma

ta give you full opportunity to direct this work; in view of this, the *llegium* of the GPU has decided to demand from you a categorical omise to discontinue your activity; failing this, the *collegium* will be bliged to alter the conditions of your existence to the extent of competely isolating you from political life. In this connection, the question changing your place of residence will arise.'

I informed the representative of the GPU that I can only give him written reply provided I receive from him a written statement of the PU's ultimatum. My refusal to give any oral reply was based on my lief, derived from all my past experience, that my words would gain be viciously distorted to mislead the working masses of the SSR and of the rest of the world.

But regardless of further action by the *collegium* of the GPU – hich in this case is playing no independent role but is only mechanilly executing the old decision, long familiar to me, of Stalin's narrow ction – I think it necessary to bring the following to the notice of e Central Committee of the All-Union Communist Party and of the xecutive Committee of the Communist International:

The demand that I abstain from political activity is a demand that renounce the struggle for the interests of the international proletariat, struggle which I have been waging continually for thirty-two years, roughout all of my conscious life. The attempt to represent this tivity as 'counter-revolutionary' comes from those whom I charge, fore the international proletariat, with violating the fundamental inciples of the teachings of Marx and Lenin, with infringing on the storical interests of the world revolution, with renouncing the aditions and precepts of October, and with unconsciously, but all e more menacingly, preparing the Thermidor.

To sustain from political activity would be tantamount to ending e struggle against the blindness of the present direction of the Comunist party, which adds to the objective difficulties of the construce Socialist work an ever-increasing number of political difficulties used by its opportunist inability to conduct the proletarian policy a large, historical scale.

It would be tantamount to renouncing the struggle against a straning party régime that reflects the growing pressure of the enemy asses on the proletarian vanguard; it would be tantamount to passvely acquiescing in that economic policy of opportunism which is dermining and shaking the foundations of the dictatorship of the oletariat, retarding the latter's material and cultural progress, and the same time dealing severe blows at the union of the workers and e toiling peasants – the foundation of the Soviet power.

The Lenin wing of the party has been under a hail of blows ev[er] since 1923, that is, ever since the unexampled collapse of the Germa[n] revolution. The increasing force of these blows keeps pace with th[e] further defeats of the international and Soviet proletariat as a con[n]sequence of opportunist leadership.

Theoretical reasoning and political experience attest that a peri[od] of historical recoil or reaction can follow not only a bourgeois, but [a] proletarian revolution as well. For six years we have been living [in] the USSR under the conditions of a growing reaction against Octobe[r] and, consequently, of a clearing of the way for the Thermidor. Th[e] most obvious and complete expression of this reaction within th[e] party is the savage persecution and routing of the Left wing in th[e] party organization.

In its latest attempts at resistance to the out-and-out Thermidorian[s] the Stalin faction is living on the chips and fragments of the ideas [of] the opposition. Creatively, it is impotent. The struggle against th[e] Left deprives it of stability. Its practical policy has no backbone, bei[ng] false, contradictory and unreliable. The noisy campaign against th[e] danger from the Right is three-quarters sham, and serves first of [all] as a screen before the masses for the war of real extermination again[st] the Bolshevik-Leninists. The world bourgeoisie and the world Me[n]shevism have equally blessed this war; these judges have long sin[ce] recognized 'historical rightness' as being on Stalin's side.

But for this blind, cowardly and utterly inept policy of adaptati[on] to bureaucracy and philistinism, the position of the working mass[es] in the twelfth year of the dictatorship would be infinitely more favou[r]able, the military defence much stronger and more reliable, and t[he] Communist International would be standing upon a higher level, i[n]stead of retreating step by step before the treacherous and ver[y] Social Democracy.

The incurable weakness of the reaction headed by the apparat[us] in spite of its apparent power, lies in the fact that 'they know n[ot] what they do'. They are executing the orders of the enemy class[es] There can be no greater historical curse on a faction, which came o[ut] of the revolution and is now undermining it.

The greatest historical strength of the opposition, in spite of [its] apparent weakness, lies in the fact that it keeps its fingers on t[he] pulse of the world historical process, that it sees the dynamics of t[he] class forces clearly, foresees the coming day and consciously prepa[res] for it. To abstain from political activity would mean to abstain fr[om] getting ready for tomorrow.

The threat to change the conditions of my life and isolate me fr[om]

●litical activity sounds as if I had not already been banished to a
●ace 4,000 kilometres distant from Moscow, 250 kilometres distant
●m the railway, and about as far from the borders of the western
●sert provinces of China – a region where malignant malaria, leprosy,
●d plague hold dominion. It sounds as if the Stalin faction, whose
●rect organ is the GPU, had not already done everything it could to
●olate me from political as well as from any other life. The Moscow
●wspapers take from ten days to a month or more to reach here. Let-
●rs come to me, with few exceptions, only after resting for one, two
●three months in the files of the GPU and the secretariat of the
●ntral Committee.

Two of my closest co-workers from the time of the civil war, Com-
●des Syermuks and Poznansky, who ventured of their own accord
●accompany me to my place of exile, were arrested immediately on
●eir arrival, incarcerated in a cellar with criminals, and then exiled
●distant parts of the north country. A letter from my daughter,
●tally ill, whom you expelled from the party and removed from her
●ork, took seventy-three days to reach me from the Moscow hospital,
●that my reply found her no longer living. A letter about the serious
●ness of my other daughter, who was also expelled from the party by
●u and removed from work, was delivered to me a month ago,
●rty-three days after leaving Moscow. Telegraph inquiries about my
●alth in most cases never even reach their destination.

Thousands of irreproachable Bolshevik-Leninists, whose services to
●e October revolution and the international proletariat far surpass
●e services of those who have imprisoned and banished them, are in
●e same situation or worse.

In planning increasingly severe reprisals against the opposition, the
●rrow faction of Stalin – whom Lenin in his 'Will' called 'rude and
●sloyal' at a time when those characteristics had not been revealed
●even one hundredth part of their present degree – is constantly
●deavouring, with the aid of the GPU, to plant upon the opposition
●me 'connection' with the enemies of the proletarian dictatorship.
●ithin their small circle the present leaders say: 'This is necessary
● the masses'; sometimes, even more cynically: 'This is for the
●ols.' My closest co-worker, Geórgy Vasilyevich Butov, who had
●en in charge of the secretariat of the Military-Revolutionary Council
● the Republic during all the years of civil war, was arrested and held
●der intolerable conditions. From this pure and modest man, this
●eproachable party worker, they tried by force to extort a confir-
●ation of charges in the spirit of the Thermidorian fabrications,
●arges known in advance to be false and counterfeit. Butov's answer

was a heroic hunger strike that lasted about fifty days; in Septemb
of this year he died in prison. Violence, beatings, torture – bo
physical and moral – are inflicted on the best Bolshevik workers f
their adherence to the precepts of October. Such are the general co
ditions which, in the words of the *collegium* of the GPU, 'present 1
obstacle' at present to the political activity of the opposition in gener
and to mine in particular.

The sorry threat to change these conditions for me in the directic
of further isolation is nothing but the decision of the Stalin faction
substitute prison for exile. This decision, as I have already said abov
is nothing astounding. As early as 1924 it was formed in prospec
and has been carried out gradually step by step, so that the oppresse
and deceived party might imperceptibly grow accustomed to the Stali
methods, whose rudeness and disloyalty have now ripened into po
soned bureaucratic dishonesty.

In the 'Declaration' submitted to the Sixth Congress – as if fore
seeing the ultimatum presented to me today – we wrote verbatim: 'T
demand from a revolutionary such a renunciation (of political activit
i.e., in the service of the party and the international revolution) woul
be possible only for a completely depraved officialdom. Only co
temptible renegades would be capable of giving such a promise.

I cannot alter anything in these words . . . To everyone his du
You wish to continue carrying out policies inspired by class forc
hostile to the proletariat. We know our duty and we will do it to th
end.   L. TROTSKY.
16 December 1928. Alma-Ata.

After this reply a month passed without change. Our co
nections with the outside world had been completely broken of
including the secret ones with Moscow. During January w
received only the Moscow newspapers. The more they wro
about the struggle against the Right, the more confidently w
waited for a blow against the Left. That is the Stalin metho
The Moscow emissary of the GPU, Volynsky, remained
Alma-Ata awaiting instructions. On 20 January he appeared
my house, accompanied by many armed agents of the GP
who occupied the entrance and exits, and handed me the follow
ing extract from the minutes of the GPU for 18 January 192

'*Considered:* the case of citizen Trotsky, Lev Davydovic
under article 58/10 of the Criminal Code, on a charge of counte
revolutionary activity expressing itself in the organization of a

egal anti-Soviet party, whose activity has lately been directed
wards provoking anti-Soviet actions and preparing for an
med struggle against the Soviet power. *Resolved:* Citizen
rotsky, Lev Davydovich, to be deported from the territory of
e USSR.'

When later I was asked to sign a slip to the effect that I had
quainted myself with this decision, I wrote: 'The decision of
e GPU, criminal in substance and illegal in form, has been
nounced to me, 20 January 1929. Trotsky.'

I called the decision criminal because it tells a deliberate lie
charging me with preparing for an armed struggle against the
viet power. This formula, necessary for Stalin to justify the
portation, is in itself a most vicious attempt to undermine the
viet power. If it were true that the opposition directed by the
ganizers of the October revolution, the builders of the Soviet
public and the Red Army was preparing for an overthrow
the Soviet power by force of arms, this in itself would have
elled catastrophe for the country. Fortunately the GPU
rmula is an insolent lie. The policy of the opposition has noth-
g to do with preparation for an armed struggle. We are guided
olly by a conviction of the profound vitality and elasticity of
e Soviet régime. Our course is one of inner reform.

When I asked how and to where I was to be deported, I
ceived the answer that I would be informed of this in European
ussia by the representative of the GPU who was to meet me
ere. The whole next day was taken up with a feverish packing,
most exclusively of manuscripts and books. In passing I may
te that there was no suggestion of hostility on the part of the
ents of the GPU. Quite the contrary.

At dawn on the twenty-second my wife, my son, and I, with
e escort, set off in an autobus which drove us along a smooth,
m road of snow to the top of the Kurday mountain range.
t the summit there were heavy snowdrifts and a strong wind.
e powerful tractor that was to tow us over the Kurday pass
t lodged in the snow up to its neck, together with the seven
tomobiles it was towing. During the snowstorms seven men
d a good many horses were frozen to death on the pass. We
re obliged to transfer to sleighs. It took us more than seven

hours to advance about thirty kilometres. Along the drifted ro
we encountered many sleighs with their shafts sticking up, mu
material for the Turkestan–Siberian railway, in the process
construction, many kerosene-tanks – all deep in snow. Men a
horses had found shelter from the snowstorms in the near-
winter camps of the Kirghizes.

On the other side of the ridge, an automobile again, and
Pishpek, a railway car. The Moscow papers which we get on t
way reveal a preparing of public opinion for the deportation
foreign countries of the leaders of the opposition. In the A
tyubinsk district we are met with a communication, transmitt
over a direct wire, that the place of deportation is to be Co
stantinople. I demand to see two members of my family
Moscow, my second son and my daughter-in-law. They a
brought to the station Ryazhsk, and placed under the sa
régime as we. The new representative of the GPU, Bulan
tried to convince me of the advantages of Constantinople. I refu
categorically to avail myself of them. Bulanov engages
negotiations over a direct wire with Moscow. There everythi
has been foreseen except the obstacle of my refusal to go abro
voluntarily.

Our train, turned aside from the direction in which it has be
going, moves along slowly, stops on a side-line near a dead lit
station and there sinks into a coma between two stretches
thin woods. Day after day goes by. The number of empty ca
about the train grows steadily. Crows and magpies gather
the feast in ever-increasing flocks. Waste... Solitude... The
are no hares here; they were wiped out in the autumn by a cr
epidemic, and so the fox has laid his stealthy tracks to the ve
train. The engine makes daily trips with one car to a larg
station for our midday meal and our newspapers. Grippe rag
in our car. We re-read Anatole France and Klyuchevsk
Russian history. I make my first acquaintance with Istrati. T
cold reaches 53 degrees below zero (Fahrenheit). Our engi
keeps rolling back and forth over the rails to keep from freezi
In the ether radio stations call to one another, asking our whe
abouts. We don't hear these inquiries; we are playing chess. B

en if we heard them we could not answer; we were brought
re at night, and we ourselves don't know where we are.

Thus we spent twelve days and twelve nights. We learned
om the newspapers of new arrests of several hundred people,
cluding 150 of the so-called 'Trotskyist centre'. The pub-
hed names included Kavtaradze, the former chairman of the
viet of People's Commissaries of Georgia, Mdivani, the former
ade representative of the USSR in Paris, and Voronsky, our
st literary critic, and others – all old party members, leaders
the October revolution.

On 8 February Bulanov announced: 'In spite of all the efforts
om Moscow, the German government has categorically refused
admit you to Germany. I have been given final instructions
conduct you to Constantinople.'

'But I will not go voluntarily, and I will say so at the Turkish
ontier.'

'That will not change matters; you will be conducted into
urkey in any case.'

'Then you have made a deal with the Turkish police for my
rcible deportation into Turkey?'

An evasive gesture: 'We only carry out our orders.'

After a twelve-day halt, the train began to move. Our small
ain grew with the increase in our escort. Throughout the trip,
er since we had boarded the train at Pishpek, we were not
lowed to leave our car. Now we were going at full speed towards
e south, stopping only at small stations to take on water and
el. These extreme precautions were due to the memories of the
oscow demonstration in connection with my exile in January
28. The newspapers received en route brought to us echoes
' the great new campaign against the Trotskyists. Between
e lines was visible a struggle in the upper groups over the
estion of my deportation. The Stalin faction was in a hurry
d for this there was reason enough: it had to overcome not
ly political but physical obstacles as well. The steamer
alinin had been appointed to take us from Odessa, but it
came ice-bound and all the efforts of the ice-breakers were in
in. Moscow was standing at the telegraph-line and urging

haste. The steamer *Ilyich* put on steam by urgent order. Ou
train arrived in Odessa on the night of 10 February. I looke
through the car-window at familiar places; I had spent seve
years of my school life in this city. Our car was brought rig
up to the steamer. It was bitterly cold. Despite the lateness
the hour, the pier was surrounded by troops and agents of th
GPU. Here I had to say good-bye to my younger son and m
daughter-in-law, who had shared our imprisonment with us f
the past two weeks. Peering through the car-window at th
steamer awaiting us, we remembered that other boat that likewi
had not been taking us to our proper destination. That was
March 1917, off Halifax, when British marines, before the ey
of a crowd of passengers, had carried me on their shoulde
from the Norwegian steamer *Christianiafjord*. Our family ha
been the same then, but we were twelve years younger.

The *Ilyich*, which carried no cargo or passengers, cleare
about one o'clock in the morning. For a distance of sixty mil
an ice-breaker made passage for us. The gale that had bee
raging caught us here on the last strokes of its wings. O
12 February we entered the Bosphorus. To the Turkish poli
who boarded the steamer at Buyukdere to check off the passenge
– besides my family and the agents of the GPU there we
no passengers on the boat – I handed the following statemer
for transmission to the President of the Turkish Republic, Kem
Pasha:

Dear Sir,
   At the gate of Constantinople I have the honour to inform you th
I have arrived at the Turkish frontier not of my own choice, and th
I will cross this frontier only by submitting to force. I request yo
Mr President, to accept my appropriate sentiments. L. Trotsky.
February 1929.

This declaration had no consequences. The steamer proceede
into the harbour. After a journey of twenty-two days, durir
which we had covered a distance of 6,000 kilometres, we four
ourselves in Constantinople.

The Planet without a Visa

We found ourselves in Constantinople, first in the consulate building and then in a private apartment. Here are a few lines from my wife's notes dealing with the first period:

It is probably not worth while to dwell on the petty adventures connected with our settling down in Constantinople – the little deceptions and coercions. I will record only one episode. We were still in the train on our way to Odessa. The representative of the GPU, Bulanov, was setting forth all sorts of absolutely valueless considerations touching our security abroad, when L. D. interrupted him with the words: 'You had better let my co-workers Syermuks and Poznansky go with me – that would be the only really effective thing to do.' Bulanov immediately transmitted these words to Moscow. At one of the next stations he triumphantly brought us a reply received by direct wire: the GPU, that is, the Politbureau, had agreed. L. D. laughed. 'You will deceive us anyway.' Apparently genuinely hurt, Bulanov exclaimed: 'Then you can call me a blackguard.' 'Why should I insult you?' L. D. answered. 'It won't be you but Stalin who will do the deceiving.' On our arrival at Constantinople L. D. inquired about Syermuks and Poznansky. A few days later a representative of the consulate brought us a cabled reply from Moscow: they would not be released. The rest of our experiences were of much the same sort.

An endless stream of rumours, suppositions and plain inventions about our destiny poured over us through the newspapers as soon as we arrived in Constantinople. The press tolerates no gaps in its information and works prodigiously. To make one seed grow nature must cast a multitude of seeds to the wind. The press acts in the same way. It picks up rumours and disseminates them, multiplying them endlessly. Hundreds and thousands of reports die before the correct version even takes root.

Sometimes that doesn't happen until several years later. Sometimes, too, it happens that the time for truth never comes.

The thing that amazes one on occasions when public opinion is touched to the quick is man's capacity for lying. I speak of this with no moral indignation but rather in the tone of naturalist who is simply stating a fact. The urge to lie, and the habit of it, reflect the contradictions in our lives. One may say that the newspapers tell the truth only as the exception. In saying this I have no desire to offend the journalists; they are not very different from other people, being merely their megaphones.

Zola wrote of the French financial press that it could be divided into two groups: the venal and the so-called 'incorruptible' that sells itself only in exceptional cases and at a very high price. Something of the sort may be said of the mendacity of newspapers in general. The yellow press lies as a matter of course without hesitating or looking back. Newspapers like *The Times* or *Le Temps* speak the truth on all unimportant and inconsequential occasions, so that they can deceive the public with all the requisite authority when necessary.

The Times later published reports that I had come to Constantinople by arrangement with Stalin, to prepare for a military conquest of the countries of the Near East. The six years of struggle between me and the epigones were represented as comedy with the parts distributed in advance. 'Who will believe that?' some optimist may ask. He is wrong – many will believe it. Churchill probably will not believe his newspaper, but Clynes is sure to believe it, or at least half of it. It is this that constitutes the mechanics of the capitalist democracy or, to be more exact, one of its most essential springs. But all this is merely in passing. Clynes will be discussed further along.

Soon after my arrival in Constantinople I read in one of the Berlin papers the speech of the president of the Reichstag delivered on the occasion of the tenth anniversary of the Weimar National Assembly. It closed with these words: '*Vielleicht kommen wir sogar dazu, Herrn Trotzki das freiheitliche Asyl zu geben*' (*Lebhafter Beifall bei der Mehrheit*).*

*Perhaps we shall even arrive at the point of granting Mr Trotsky the democratic right of asylum (Vigorous applause from the majority).

Löbe's words were a great surprise to me, since everything that had gone before had given me reason to believe that the German government had decided against my admission to Germany. Such, at any rate, had been the categorical statement of the agents of the Soviet government. On 15 February I called on the representative of the GPU who had accompanied me to Constantinople and said to him: 'I must draw the conclusion that the information given me was false. Löbe's speech was made on 6 February. We sailed from Odessa for Turkey on the night of 10 February. Löbe's speech was known to Moscow at that time. I recommend that you send at once to Moscow a telegram suggesting that on the strength of Löbe's speech they make an *actual* request to Berlin to grant me a visa. That will be the least discreditable way of winding up the intrigue that Stalin has apparently built up around the question of my admission to Germany.' Two days later the representative of the GPU brought me the following reply:

In answer to my telegram to Moscow I have received the confirmation that the German government had categorically refused to issue the visa as early as the beginning of February; a new application would be useless; Löbe's speech was irresponsible. If you wish to verify this, you can apply for the visa yourself.

This version did not seem to me credible. I considered that the president of the Reichstag was in a better position to know the intentions of his party and his government than the agents of the GPU. The same day I wired Löbe informing him that on the strength of his statement I had applied to the German Consulate with a request for a visa. The democratic and Social-Democratic press derived malicious satisfaction from pointing out the fact that a believer in the revolutionary dictatorship was obliged to seek asylum in a democratic country. Some even expressed the hope that this lesson would teach me better to appreciate the institutions of democracy. Nothing was left me but to wait and see how the lesson would realize itself.

The democratic right of asylum obviously does not consist in a government's showing hospitality to people who hold views similar to its own – even Abdul Hamid did that. Nor does it consist in a democracy's admitting exiles only with the permission

of the government that exiled them. The right of asylum consist
(on paper) in a government's giving refuge even to its opponents
provided they undertake to observe the country's laws. I o
course could enter Germany only as an irreconcilable opponer
of the Social-Democratic government. In giving an intervie
to the Constantinople representatives of the German Social
Democratic press who called on me for that purpose, I supplie
the necessary explanations, which I will quote here just as
wrote them down immediately after the conversation:

As I am now applying for admission to Germany, where th
majority of the government consists of Social Democrats, I am chief
interested in clarifying my attitude towards the Social Democracy. I
this respect there has been no change. My attitude towards the Soci
Democracy is just what it was. Moreover my struggle against th
centrist faction of Stalin is only a reflection of my general strugg
against the Social Democracy. Neither you nor I stand in any need
vagueness or ambiguity.

Some Social-Democratic publications are trying to see a contr
diction between my stand on the question of democracy and m
request for admission to Germany. There is no contradiction. We c
not at all 'deny' democracy as the anarchists 'deny' it, verbally. Th
bourgeois democracy has advantages in comparison with the sta
forms that preceded it. But it is not eternal. It must yield to Sociali
society. The dictatorship of the proletariat is the bridge to Sociali
society.

In all the capitalist countries Communists take part in the parli
mentary struggle. There is no difference in principle in the usage
the right of asylum and the usage of suffrage, of the freedom of th
press and assembly, and so forth.

So far as I am aware this interview was never publishe
There is nothing surprising in that. In the meantime voices we
raised in the Social-Democratic press insisting on the necessit
of granting me the right of asylum. One of the Social-Democrat
lawyers, Dr K. Rosenfeld, acting on his own initiative, took
upon himself to intercede on my behalf with a view to securi
my admission to Germany. But at the outset he encountere
difficulties, for a few days later I received a telegram from hi
asking to what restrictions I would be willing to submit durir

ıy stay in Germany. I replied: 'I intend to live in complete
ısolation outside of Berlin; not to speak at public meetings under
ıny circumstances; and to confine myself to literary work within
ıe bounds of the German laws.'

So the matter under discussion was no longer the *democratic
ight of asylum*, but the right of residence in Germany *on an
xceptional basis*. The lesson in democracy that my opponents
ere going to accord me was given a restrictive interpretation
t the very outset. But this was not the end of it. A few days
ıter I received a new telegraphic inquiry: would I agree to come
ı Germany only for purposes of medical treatment? I wired in
ıply: 'I request that I be given at least the possibility of staying
ı Germany for a course of treatment absolutely necessary for
ıy health.'

Thus the *right of asylum* at this stage shrank to the *right of
ıeatment*. I named several well-known German physicians who
ıad treated me during the past ten years, whose aid I needed
ıow more than ever before.

Towards Easter, the German press sounded a new note: in
ıovernment circles, it was stated, the opinion was held that
ırotsky was not really so ill as to be absolutely in need of the
ıelp of German doctors and of German health resorts. On
ı March I telegraphed Dr Rosenfeld:

According to the newspaper reports my illness is not sufficiently
ıopeless to obtain my admission to Germany. I ask, did Löbe offer
ıe the *right of asylum* or the *right of interment* ? I am willing to submit
ı any examination by any medical commission. I undertake to leave
ıermany at the close of the health-resort season.

In this way, in the course of a few weeks the democratic prin-
ıiple was three times truncated. The right of asylum was at first
ıeduced to the right of residence on a specially restricted basis,
ıen to the right of treatment and, finally, to the right of inter-
ıent. But this meant that I could appreciate the full advantages
f democracy only as a corpse.

There was no reply to my telegram. After waiting a few days
ı telegraphed Berlin again: 'Regard the absence of reply as a
ıisloyal form of refusal.' Only after this, on 12 April, that is,

after two months, did I receive a communication that the German government had refused my application for admission. There was nothing left but to telegraph the president of the Reichstag, Löbe: 'Regret have not received the possibility for practical education in the advantages of the democratic right of asylum. Trotsky.' Such is the brief and instructive history of my first attempt to find a 'democratic' visa in Europe.

Of course it is understood that if the right of asylum had been accorded me, that in itself would not in the least mean a refutation of the Marxist theory of a class state. The régime of democracy, which derives not from self-sufficient principles but from the real requirements of the dominant class, by the force of its inner logic also includes within itself the right of asylum. The granting of refuge to a proletarian revolutionary in no way contradicts the bourgeois character of democracy. But there is no need of such arguments now, for in Germany, as directed by the Social Democrats, no right of asylum has been found to exist.

Through the GPU, Stalin proposed on 16 December that I renounce my political activity. During the discussion of the question of the right of asylum in the press the same condition was advanced by the Germans as something taken for granted. This means that the government of Mueller and Streseman likewise regards those ideas that are being fought by Stalin and his Thälmanns as dangerous and harmful. Stalin, by diplomatic means, and the Thälmanns, by means of agitation, demanded that the Social-Democratic government refuse me admission to Germany – presumably in the name of the interests of the proletarian revolution. On the other flank Chamberlain, Count Westarp and their like demanded that I be refused the visa – in the interests of the capitalist order. Hermann Mueller was able in this way to satisfy both his partners on the right and his allies on the left. The Social-Democratic government became the connecting link in the united international front against revolutionary Marxism. For an image for this united front one need only turn to the first lines of the Communist Manifesto by Marx and Engels: 'For a holy war against this ghost [communism], all the forces of old Europe joined hands – the Pope and the Tsar, Metternich and Guizot, the French radicals and the

German policemen.' The names are different, but the substance
is the same. The fact that today the rôle of the German policemen is played by the Social Democrats alters the situation but
little. Essentially they are protecting the same thing as the
Hohenzollern policemen.

The variety of reasons that induce democracies to refuse a
visa is great. The Norwegian government, if you please, pro-
ceeds solely from consideration for my safety. I had never
imagined that I had so many considerate friends in high places
in Oslo. The Norwegian government is of course unreservedly
in favour of the right of asylum, just as are the German, French,
English, and all the other governments. The right of asylum, as
everyone knows, is a sacred and impregnable principle. But an
exile must first of all submit to Oslo a certificate guaranteeing
that he is not going to be killed by anyone. Then they will extend hospitality to him – provided, of course, that no other obstacles arise.

The two debates in the Storthing about my visa constitute an
inimitable political document. Reading it has given me at least a
partial compensation for the refusal of the visa which my friends
in Norway were trying to get for me. First the Norwegian
premier had of course a conversation in regard to my visa with
the chief of the secret police, whose competence in democratic
principles – I hasten to admit – is unquestioned. The chief of
the secret police, according to Mr Mohwinkel, put forward the
consideration that the wisest thing to do was to let Trotsky's
enemies finish him off outside of Norwegian territory. It was
expressed not quite so precisely, but that was what was meant.
The minister of justice on his part explained to the Norwegian
parliament that the cost of protecting Trotsky would be too
great for the Norwegian budget. The principle of state economy
– also one of the indisputable democratic principles – proved
this time to be in irreconcilable opposition to the right of asylum.
At all events the conclusion was that the person who most needs
an asylum has the least chance of obtaining it.

Much wittier was the French government, which simply
pointed to the fact that the order for my expulsion from France,
as issued by Malvy, had never been rescinded. An utterly unsur-

mountable obstacle in the way of democracy! I have related
earlier in this book how after that expulsion, and in spite of the
unrescinded order by Malvy, the French government was ready
to place its officers at my disposal; how I was visited by French
deputies, ambassadors, and one of the premiers. But these phe-
nomena apparently were proceeding along two different planes
that did not meet. And at present the position is this: asylum in
France would doubtless be accorded me if the archives of the
French police did not contain an order for my expulsion from
France issued at the demand of Tsarist diplomacy. It is known
that a police order is something like the Pole-Star; it is as impossible to annul it as is to remove it.

Be that as it may, the right of asylum has been banished from
France as well. Where then is the country in which this right
has found its – asylum? Perhaps England?

On 5 June 1929 the Independent Labour Party, of which
Ramsay MacDonald is a member, sent me an official invitation,
on its own initiative, to come to England and deliver a lecture at
the party school. The invitation, signed by the general secretary
of the party, read: 'With the formation of the Labour government here, we cannot believe that any difficulties are likely to
arise in connection with your visit to England for the purpose.'
Nevertheless difficulties did arise. I was neither allowed to deliver a lecture before the supporters of MacDonald, nor was I
allowed to avail myself of the aid of English physicians. My
application for a visa was flatly refused. Clynes, the Labour
Home Secretary, defended this refusal in the House of Commons. He explained the philosophical meaning of democracy
with a directness that would have done credit to any minister of
Charles II. According to Clynes, the right of asylum does not
mean the right of an exile to demand asylum, but the right of
the state to refuse it. Clynes's definition is remarkable in one
respect: by a single blow it destroys the very foundations of so-
called democracy. The right of asylum, in the style of Clynes,
always existed in Tsarist Russia. When the Shah of Persia failed
to hang all the revolutionaries and was obliged to leave his beloved country, Nicholas II not only extended to him the right
of asylum, but supplied him with sufficient comforts to live in

dessa. But it never occurred to any of the Irish revolutionaries to seek asylum in Tsarist Russia, where the constitution consisted entirely of the one principle expounded by Clynes, namely, that the citizens must be content with what the state authorities give them or take from them. Mussolini accorded the right of asylum to the King of Afghanistan in exact agreement with this very principle.

The pious Mr Clynes ought at least to have known that democracy, in a sense, inherited the right of asylum from the Christian church, which, in turn, inherited it, with much besides, from paganism. It was enough for a pursued criminal to make his way into a temple, sometimes enough even to touch only the ring of the door, to be safe from persecution. Thus the church understood the right of asylum as the right of the persecuted to an asylum, and not as an arbitrary exercise of will on the part of pagan or Christian priests. Until now I had thought the pious Labourites, though little informed in matters of socialism, certainly well versed in the tradition of the church. Now I find that they are not even that.

But why does Clynes stop at the first lines of his theory of the state law? It is a pity. The right of asylum is only one component part of the system of democracy. Neither in its historical origin nor in its legal nature does it differ from the right of freedom of speech, of assembly, etc. Mr Clynes, it is to be hoped, will soon arrive at the conclusion that the right of freedom of speech stands not for the right of citizens to express their thoughts, whatever they may be, but for the right of the state to forbid its subjects to entertain such thoughts. As to the freedom of strikes, the conclusion has already been drawn by British law.

Clynes's misfortune is that he had to explain his actions aloud, for there were members of the Labour faction in Parliament who put respectful but inconvenient questions to him. The Norwegian premier found himself in the same unpleasant situation. The German cabinet was spared this discomfiture because in the whole Reichstag there was not a single deputy who took any interest in the question of the right of asylum. This fact assumes special significance when one remembers that the president of the Reichstag, in a statement that was applauded by the majority of the deputies, promised to accord me the right of aslyum at a time when I had not even asked for it.

The October revolution did not proclaim the abstract prin ciples of democracy not that of the right of asylum. The Sovie state was founded openly on the right of revolutionary dictator ship. But this did not prevent Vandervelde or other Socia Democrats from coming to the Soviet republic and even appear ing in Moscow as public defenders of persons guilty of terroris attempts on the lives of the leaders of the October revolution.

The present British ministers were also among our visitors. cannot remember all of those who came to us – I haven't th necessary data at hand – but I remember that among them wer Mr and Mrs Snowden. This must have been as far back a 1920. They were received not simply as tourists but as guests which was probably carrying it a little too far. A box in th Grand theatre was placed at their disposal. I remember this i connection with a little episode that it may be worth recountin at this point. I had arrived in Moscow from the front, and m thoughts were far away from the British guests; in fact I did n even know who those guests were, because in my absorption i other things I had hardly read any newspapers. The commissio that was receiving Snowden, Mrs Snowden and, if I am not mis taken, Bertrand Russell and Williams, as well as a number c others, was headed by Lozovsky, who told me by telephone tha the commission demanded my presence in the theatre where th English guests were. I tried to excuse myself, but Lozovsky in sisted that his commission had been given full power by th Politbureau and that it was my duty to set others an example c discipline. I went unwillingly. There were about a dozen Britis guests in the box. The theatre was crammed to over-flowing We were gaining victories at the front and the theatre applaude them violently. The British guests surrounded me and applaude too. One of them was Snowden. Today of course he is a littl ashamed of this adventure. But it is impossible to erase it. An yet I too should be glad to do so, for my 'fraternizing' with th Labourites was not only a mistake, but a political error as wel As soon as I could get away from the guests I went to see Lenir He was much disturbed. 'Is it true that you appeared in the bo with those people?' (Lenin used a different word for 'people'.) An excuse I referred to Lozovsky, to the commission of the Central Committee, to discipline, and especially to the fact that I had not the remotest idea who the guests were. Lenin was furious with Lozovsky and the whole commission in general, and for a long time I too couldn't forgive myself for my imprudence.

One of the present British ministers visited Moscow several times, I believe; at any rate he rested in the Soviet republic, stayed in the Caucasus and called on me. It was Mr Lansbury. The last time I met him was at Kislovodsk. I was urged to drop in, if only for a quarter of an hour, at the House of Rest where some members of our party and a few foreign visitors were staying. A goodly number of people were sitting around a large table. It was in the nature of a modest banquet. The place of honour was held by the guest, Lansbury. On my arrival he offered a toast and then sang: 'For he's a jolly good fellow.' Those were Lansbury's feelings towards me in the Caucasus. Today he too would probably like to forget about it.

When I applied for the visa, I sent special telegrams to Snowden and Lansbury, reminding them of the hospitality that had been accorded them by the Soviets and in part by myself. My telegrams had little effect. In politics recollections carry as little weight as democratic principles.

Mr and Mrs Sidney Webb most courteously paid me a visit quite recently, early in May of 1929, when I was already on Prinkipo. We talked about the possible advent of the Labour party to power. I remarked in passing that immediately after the formation of MacDonald's government I intended to demand a visa. Mr Webb expressed the view that the government might find itself not strong enough and, because of their dependence on the Liberals, not free enough, either. I replied that a party that isn't strong enough to be able to answer for its actions had no right to power. Our irreconcilable differences needed no new test. Webb came into power. I demanded a visa. MacDonald's government refused my application, but not because the Liberals prevented it from following its democratic convictions. Quite the contrary. The Labour government refused the visa, despite the protests of the Liberals. This was a variant that Mr Webb did not foresee. It must be pointed out, however, that at that time he was not yet Lord Passfield.

Some of these men I know personally. Others I can judge only by analogy. I think that I measure them correctly. They have been raised up by the automatic growth of labour organizations, especially since the war, and by the sheer political exhaustion of liberalism. They have completely shed the naïve idealism that some of them had twenty-five or thirty years ago. In its stead they have acquired political routine and unscrupulousness in the choice of means. But in their general outlook they have remained what they were – timid, petty bourgeois whose methods of thought are far more backward than the methods of production in the British coal-mining industry. Today their chief concern is that the court nobility and the big capitalists may refuse to take them seriously. And no wonder. Now that they are in power they are only too sharply aware of their weakness. They have not and cannot have the qualities possessed by the old governing cliques in which traditions and habits of rulership have been handed down from generation to generation and often take the place of talent and intellect. But neither do they have what might have constituted their real strength – faith in the masses and the ability to stand on their own feet. They are afraid of the masses who put them there, just as they are afraid of the conservative clubs whose grandeur staggers their feeble imaginations. To justify their coming to power, they must needs show the old ruling classes that they are not simply revolutionary upstarts. God forbid! No, they really deserve every confidence because they are loyally devoted to the church, to the King, to the House of Lords, to the system of titles; that is to say, not simply to the sacrosanct principle of private property, but to all the rubbish of the Middle Ages. For them to refuse a visa to a revolutionary is really a happy opportunity to demonstrate their respectability once again. I am very glad that I gave them such an opportunity. In due time this will be taken into account, since in politics as in nature there is no waste.

One needs no great imagination to picture Mr Clynes's interview with his subordinate, the chief of the political police. During he interview Mr Clynes feels as if he were undergoing an examination and is afraid that he will not seem firm enough to the examiner, or statesmanlike or conservative enough. Thus it needs little ingenuity on the part of the chief of the political police to prompt Mr Clynes to a decision that will be greeted with full approval in the conservative papers next day. But the conservative press does not merely praise – it kills with praise. It mocks. It does not take the trouble to conceal its disdain for the people who so humbly seek its approval. No one will say for instance that the *Daily Express* belongs to the most intelligent institutions in the world. And yet this paper finds very caustic words to express its approval of the Labour government for so carefully protecting the 'sensitive MacDonald' from the presence of a revolutionary observer behind his back.

And are these the people who are called upon to lay the foundations of a new human society? No, they are only the penultimate resource of the old society. I say 'penultimate' because the ultimate resource is physical repression. I must admit that the roll-call of the western European democracies on the question of the right of asylum has given me, aside from other things, more than a few merry minutes. At times it seemed as if I were attending a 'pan-European' performance of an one-act comedy on the theme of principles of democracy. Its text might have been written by Bernard Shaw if the Fabian fluid that runs in his veins had been strengthened by even so much as five per cent of Jonathan Swift's blood. But whoever may have written the text, the play remains very instructive: *Europe without a Visa*. There is no need to mention America. The United States is not only the strongest, but also the most terrified country. Hoover recently explained his passion for fishing by pointing out the democratic nature of this pastime. If this be so – although I doubt it – it is at all events one of the few survivals of democracy still existing in the United States. There the right of asylum has been absent for a long time. *Europe and America without a Visa*. But these two continents own the other three. This means – *The Planet without a Visa*.

On many sides it has been explained to me that my disbelief in democracy is my greatest sin. How many articles and even books have been written about this! But when I ask to be given a brief object-lesson in democracy, there are no volunteers. Th planet proves to be without a visa. Why should I believe tha the much more important question – the trial between the ric and poor – will be decided with strict observance of the form and rituals of democracy?

And has the revolutionary dictatorship produced the result expected of it? – I hear a question. It would be possible to answe it only by taking a reckoning of the experience of the Octobe revolution and trying to indicate its future prospects. An auto-biography is no place for this, and I will try to answer the ques-tion in a special book on which I had already begun to work during my stay in Central Asia. But I cannot end the story of my life without explaining, if only in a few lines, why I adhere so completely to my old path.

That which has happened in the memory of my generation, already mature or approaching old age, can be described sche-matically as follows: During several decades – the end of the last century and the beginning of the present – the European popu-lation was being severely disciplined by industry. All phases of social education were dominated by the principle of the productivity of labour. This yielded stupendous results and seemed to open up new possibilities to people. But actually it only led to war. It is true that through the war humanity has been able to convince itself, in the face of the crowings of anaemic philosophy, that it is not degenerating after all; on the contrary it is full of life, strength, bravery, enterprise. Through the same war it realized its technical power with unprecedented force. It was as if a man, to prove that his pipes for breathing and swallowing were in order, had begun to cut his throat with a razor in front of a mirror.

After the end of the operations of 1914 to 1919 it was declared that from now on the highest moral duty was to care for the wounds which it had been the highest moral duty to inflict dur-ing the preceding four years. Industry and thrift were not only restored to their rights but were put into the steel corsets of rationalization. The so-called 'reconstruction' is directed by

...ose same classes, parties, and even individuals who guided the ...estruction. Where a change of political régime has taken place, ...s in Germany, the men who play the leading rôles in the direc-...on of reconstruction are those who played second and third ...les in guiding the destruction. That, strictly speaking, is the ...nly change.

The war has swept away an entire generation, as if to create a ...reak in the memory of peoples and to prevent the new genera-...on from noticing too closely that it is actually engaged in re-...eating what has been done before, only on a higher historical ...ing, which implies more menacing consequences.

The working class of Russia, under the leadership of the Bol-...neviks, made an attempt to effect a reconstruction of life that ...ould exclude the possibility of humanity's going through these ...eriodical fits of sheer insanity and would lay the foundations ...f a higher culture. That was the sense of the October revo-...ition. To be sure, the problem it has set itself has not yet been ...olved. But in its very essence this problem demands many ...ecades. Moreover, the October revolution should be considered ...s the starting-point of the newest history of humanity as a ...hole.

Towards the end of the Thirty Years' War the German Refor-...nation must have appeared the work of men who had broken out ...f a lunatic asylum. To a certain extent it really was: European ...umanity broken out of the medieval monastery. Modern Ger-...any, England, the United States and the modern world in ...eneral would never have been possible without the Reformation ...ith its countless victims. If victims are generally to be per-...itted – but whose permission could one ask? – it is certainly ...ctims that move humanity forward.

The same can be said of the French Revolution. That narrow-...inded, reactionary pedant, Taine, imagined that he was making ... most profound discovery when he established the fact that a ...w years after the execution of Louis XVI the French people ...ere poorer and more unhappy than under the old régime. But ...e whole point of the matter is that such events as the great ...rench Revolution cannot be viewed on the scale of 'a few years'. ...ithout the great revolution the entire new France would never

have been possible, and Taine himself would still have been
clerk in the service of some contractor of the old régime instea
of being able to blacken the revolution that opened a new caree
to him.

A still greater historical perspective is necessary to view th
October revolution. Only hopeless dullards can quote as evidenc
against it the fact that in twelve years it has not yet create
general peace and prosperity. If one adopts the scale of the Ger
man Reformation and the French Revolution, representing tw
different stages in the evolution of bourgeois society, separate
from each other by almost three centuries, one must expres
amazement at the fact that a backward and isolated Russi
twelve years after the revolution has been able to ensure for th
masses of the people a standard of living that is not lower tha
that existing on the eve of the war. That alone is a miracle of it
kind. But of course the significance of the October revolutio
does not lie in that. The revolution is an experiment in a ne
social régime, an experiment that will undergo many change
and will probably be remade anew from its very foundation
It will assume an entirely different character on the basis of th
newest technical achievements. But after a few decades an
centuries the new social order will look back on the Octobe
revolution as the bourgeois does on the German Refor
mation or the French Revolution. This is so clear, so incontes
ably clear, that even the professors of history will understand i
though only after many years.

And what of your personal fate? – I hear a question, in whic
curiosity is mixed with irony. Here I can add but little to wha
I have said in this book. I do not measure the historical proce
by the yardstick of one's personal fate. On the contrary,
appraise my fate objectively and live it subjectively, only as it
inextricably bound up with the course of social development.

Since my exile I have more than once read musings in th
newspapers on the subject of the 'tragedy' that has befallen m
I know no *personal* tragedy. I know the change of two chapte
of the revolution. One American paper which published a
article of mine accompanied it with a profound note to the effe
that in spite of the blows the author had suffered, he had, as ev

enced by his article, preserved his clarity of reason. I can only express my astonishment at the philistine attempt to establish a connection between the power of reasoning and a government post, between mental balance and the present situation. I do not know, and I never have, of any such connection. In prison, with book or a pen in my hand, I experienced the same sense of deep satisfaction that I did at the mass meetings of the revolution. I felt the mechanics of power as an inescapable burden, rather than as a spiritual satisfaction. But it would perhaps be briefer to quote the good words of someone else.

On 26 January 1917 Rosa Luxemburg wrote to a woman friend from prison:

This losing oneself completely in the banalities of daily life is something that I generally cannot understand or endure. See, for example, how Goethe rose above material things with a calm superiority. Just think of what he had to live through: the great French Revolution, which at near range must have seemed a bloody and utterly aimless farce, and then from 1793 to 1815 a continuous sequence of wars. I do not demand that you write poetry as Goethe did, but his view of life, the universality of his interests, the inner harmony of the man, everyone can create for himself or at least strive for. And should you say that Goethe was not a political fighter, I maintain that it is precisely the fighter who must try to be above things, or else he will get his nose stuck in all sorts of rubbish – of course, in this case, I am thinking of a fighter in the grand style . . .

Brave words. I read them for the first time the other day, and they immediately brought the figure of Rosa Luxemburg closer and made her dearer to me than ever before.

In his views, his character, his world outlook, Proudhon, that Robinson Crusoe of socialism, is alien to me. But Proudhon had the nature of a fighter, a spiritual disinterestedness, a capacity for despising official public opinion, and, finally, the fire of a many-sided curiosity never extinguished. This enabled him to rise above his own life, with its ups and downs, as he did above all contemporaneous reality.

On 26 April 1852 Proudhon wrote to a friend from prison:

The movement is no doubt irregular and crooked, but the tendency constant. What every government does in turn in favour of revo-

lution becomes inviolable; what is attempted against it passes ov
like a cloud: I enjoy watching this spectacle, in which I understar
every single picture; I observe these changes in the life of the wor
as if I had received their explanation from above; what oppress
others, elevates me more and more, inspires and fortifies me; ho
can you want me then to accuse destiny, to complain about peop
and curse them? Destiny – I laugh at it; and as for men, they are to
ignorant, too enslaved for me to feel annoyed at them.

Despite their slight savour of ecclesiastical eloquence tho
are fine words. I subscribe to them.

rincipal Events and Writings of Leon Trotsky
om My Life in 1929 to his assassination in 1940)

he Turkish Years

29

ly: Issues first number of Russian *Bulletin of the Opposition* (published first in Paris, then Berlin, Paris and the US), which serves to rally forces of International Left Opposition (Bolshevik-Leninists), which proclaims itself a faction of Communist International, dedicated to returning it to Leninist principles and practice.

ovember: Completes *The Permanent Revolution*.

30

pril: First international conference of International Left Opposition.

ay: Almost a year before downfall of Spanish monarchy and establishment of Spanish Republic, Trotsky begins writing series of articles, pamphlets and letters on problems of Spanish revolution that he is to continue until his death (*The Spanish Revolution, 1931–1939*).

ptember: More than two years before Hitler comes to power, Trotsky begins series of pamphlets and articles warning that Stalinists and Social Democrats in Germany are paving the way for Nazi victory (*The Struggle Against Fascism in Germany*).

31

iblishes first volume of three-volume *History of the Russian Revolution*.

32

iblishes *The Stalin School of Falsification*.

February: Is deprived of Soviet nationality by Stalin government.

ovember: Is permitted to visit Copenhagen to give a lecture to students, published as *In Defence of the Russian Revolution*.

ine: Publishes *Problems of the Chinese Revolution*.

33

nuary: Daughter Zina commits suicide in Berlin. Hitler is appointed chancellor of Germany.

arch: After German Communist Party capitulates to Hitler without firing one shot, and Communist International approves its policy,

Trotsky says Stalinist party in Germany can no longer be refor■ and must be replaced by a new Leninist party.

July: Trotsky decides Communist International also cannot be formed, and that a new international is necessary. Internati◖ Communist League (Bolshevik-Leninists) formed.

17 July: Trotsky and Natalia Sedova get visa for France and le■ Turkey.

The French Years

1933

24 July: Arrives in France, where he is harassed by governm◖ Stalinists, Fascists and sickness.

1 October: Proclaims need for political revolution to restore work■ democracy in Soviet Union.

1934

February: His former friend, Christian Rakovsky, becomes las▮ Opposition leaders in Russia to capitulate to Stalin.

February: French Fascist attempt to overthrow government is■ feated, but results in pushing government to the right.

April: French government issues a decree ordering Trotsky's portation but cannot enforce it for more than a year because other government will accept him.

November: Writes first part of the collection entitled *Whither Fran■*

December: Soviet leader Sergei Kirov is assassinated, and Stalin ◗ occasion to launch new purge and charge opponents, includ▮ Trotsky, with terrorism. Trotsky answers in pamphlet entitled *Kirov Assassination.*

1935

Writes first part of his biography of Lenin, *The Young Lenin.*

June: Gets visa from Norway and with Natalia Sedova leaves Fra■ for last time.

The Norwegian Years

1935

18 June: Disembarks in Norway, where he has been granted asyl▮ by Labour Party government.

1936

Spring: Huge strike wave in France, now governed by Leon Bl■ and People's Front. Civil War begins in Spain.

y: At initiative of International Communist League, first conference for Fourth International is held in Europe.

gust: Completes *The Revolution Betrayed*. Members of Fascist party headed by Major Quisling break into Trotsky's home while he is out to seize documents they want to use to get him ejected from Norway. First Moscow trial (of sixteen defendants headed by Zinoviev and Kamenev) where Trotsky and son Leon Sedov are charged with conspiracy to overthrow Soviet régime. Trotsky begins to expose trial as frame-up when Norwegian government, responding to pressure from Moscow, tries to shut him up and, failing, places him under house arrest. Minister of Justice Trygve Lie cuts Trotsky off from rest of world.

December: Trotsky at last has chance to defend himself in court, but Trygve Lie has arranged it so that neither press nor public can be present to hear him.

December: Norwegian government puts Trotsky and Natalia Sedova on a tanker bound for Mexico.

he Mexican Years

37

anuary: Disembarks in Mexico, where he has been granted asylum by the government of Lázaro Cárdenas.

nuary: Second Moscow trial (of seventeen defendants headed by Radek and Pyatakov) begins; now Trotsky and Leon Sedov are charged with being agents of Fascism. Trotsky is able to refute charges in world press; son Sergei is arrested in Soviet Union, later to die in concentration camp.

February: Prepares talk by phone to New York meeting, offering to turn himself over to Moscow if an international commission of inquiry finds him guilty of any charges in Moscow trials. Talk cannot be heard, but appears as pamphlet, *I Stake My Life*.

–17 April: Testifies before commission of inquiry headed by John Dewey. Transcript of hearings is published under title *The Case of Leon Trotsky*.

ptember: Dewey Commission finds Trotsky and son not guilty of charges in first two Moscow trials and pronounces them frame-ups.

38

February: Leon Sedov dies under mysterious circumstances in Paris hospital; evidence accumulates that it was a GPU killing.

Trotsky writes *Leon Sedov – Son, Friend, Fighter* and dedic
Their Morals and Ours to his son.

March: Third Moscow trial (of twenty-one defendants headed
Bukharin, Rykov, and Rakovsky) is staged; Trotsky exposes tr.
falsifications and contradictions.

April–May: Defends Mexican government's expropriation of
perialist oil holdings. Holds discussions with Americans on
gramme for the Fourth International, leading to his writing of
Death Agony of Capitalism and the Tasks of the Fourth Internati
(*The Transitional Program for Socialist Revolution*).

June–July: In collaboration with André Breton and Diego Ri
Trotsky writes manifesto on revolutionary art (in *Leon Trotsk*
Literature and Art.

July: Rudolf Klement, former secretary of Trotsky, helping
organize the founding conference of Fourth International, is
napped in Paris by GPU and murdered.

September: Fourth International holds founding conference
Europe. Munich crisis leads to Hitler's dismemberment of Czec
slovakia with agreement of England and France; Trotsky anal
crisis and nature of coming war in 'A Fresh Lesson' (*Writing*
Leon Trotsky, 1938–39.

1939

March: Writes *Marxism in Our Time*, printed as introduction to
Living Thoughts of Karl Marx. (Pathfinder Press, New York, 19

April: Engages in three discussions on the nature of the Afro-Ameri
struggle (later collected in *Leon Trotsky on Black Nationalism*
Self-Determination).

22 August: Stalin and Hitler sign a pact, as Trotsky had predicte

September: Second World War begins. A struggle breaks ou
Socialist Workers Party over whether Fourth International sh
continue to defend Soviet Union against imperialism; Trots
writings on this and related disputes are collected in *In Defens*
Marxism.

1940

24 May: GPU forces led by painter David Alfaro Siqueiros break
Trotsky home at night, attempting to machine-gun Trotsky
family but failing; they kidnap and kill an American gu
Robert Sheldon Harte.

May: Emergency Conference of Fourth International meets in N
York and adopts manifesto, written by Trotsky, opposing imperi
war and reaffirming Fourth International position on Soviet Ur
(in *Writings of Leon Trotsky, 1939–40*).

20 August: An agent of GPU drives pickaxe into Trotsky's brain.

21 August: Trotsky dies. Important unfinished work: *Stalin – An Appraisal of the Man and His Influence.*

Books by Trotsky in Print in English

The Challenge of the Left Opposition (1923–29) (a series including *The New Course, Lessons of October, Toward Socialism or Capitalism?* and *Platform of the Opposition*), Pathfinder Press, New York.

The First Five Years of the Communist International (2 volumes), Monad Press, New York, 1973.

History of the Russian Revolution, Gollancz, 1965.

In Defense of Marxism, Pathfinder Press, New York, 1973.

Lenin's Fight Against Stalinism (with V. I. Lenin), Pathfinder Press, New York, 1974.

Leon Trotsky on Black Nationalism and Self Determination, Pathfinder Press, New York, 1970.

Leon Trotsky Speaks, Pathfinder Press, New York, 1972.

Literature and Revolution, University of Michigan Press, Ann Arbor, 1960.

Military Writings, Pathfinder Press, New York, 1969.

1905, Allen Lane, 1972; Penguin Books, 1974.

On Britain, Monad Press, New York, 1973.

On France (includes *Whither France?*), Pathfinder Press, New York, 1968.

On Lenin: Notes Towards a Biography, Harrap, 1971.

On Literature and Art, Lawrence & Wishart, 1967.

Our Revolution, Hyperion Press, Connecticut, 1973.

The Permanent Revolution and *Results and Prospects*, Pathfinder Press, New York, 1969.

Political Profiles, New Park, 1973.

Problems of the Chinese Revolution, New Park, 1969.

Problems of Everyday Life, Monad Press, New York, 1973.

The Revolution Betrayed, Pathfinder Press, New York, 1972.

The Spanish Revolution (1931–39), Pathfinder Press, New York, 1972.

Stalin, Panther, 1969.

The Stalin School of Falsification, Pathfinder Press, New York, 19'

The Struggle against Fascism in Germany, Penguin Books, 1975.

Terrorism and Communism, University of Michigan Press, Ann Arb
1961.

Their Morals and Ours (with essays by John Dewey and Geor
Novack), New Park, 1974.

The Third International after Lenin, Pathfinder Press, New York, 19'

The Transitional Program for Socialist Revolution, Pathfinder Pre
New York, 1973.

The Trotsky Papers: 1917–1922 (2 volumes, facing pages in Russi
and English), Humanities Press, New York, 1971.

Trotsky's Diary in Exile: 1935, Atheneum Publishers, New Yo
1964.

War and the International, Young Socialist Publication, 1971.

Women and the Family, Pathfinder Press, New York, 1973.

Writings of Leon Trotsky (1929–40) (in 12 volumes), Pathfinder Pre
New York, 1973.

The Young Lenin, David & Charles, 1972; Penguin Books, 1974.

The Age of Permanent Revolution (anthology, edited by Isaac Deu
cher), Dell Publishing Company, New York.

The Basic Writings of Trotsky (anthology, edited by Irving How
Heinemann, 1964.

The Essential Trotsky (anthology), Allen & Unwin, 1963.

The Case of Leon Trotsky (report and verbatim transcript of Dew
Commission Hearings at which Trotsky was chief witness), Pathfind
Press, New York, 1968.

* Contains writings of years specified not otherwise permanently availab
in book or pamphlet form; available through Pathfinder Press, 47, The C
London SE1 8LL.

ndex

More about Penguins and Pelicans